The Science of Mental Health

Volume 10
Fear and Anxiety

Series Content

The Science
of Mental Health

Volume 10
Fear and Anxiety

Edited with introductions by

Steven Hyman
National Institute of Mental Health

ROUTLEDGE
New York/London

Published in 2001 by

Routledge
29 West 35th Street
New York, NY 10001

Published in Great Britain by
Routledge
11 New Fetter Lane
London EC4P 4EE

Routledge is an Imprint of Taylor & Francis Books, Inc.
Copyright © 2001 by Routledge

Printed in the United States of America on acid-free paper.

10 9 8 7 6 5 4 3 2 1

Library of Congress Cataloging-in-Publication Data

The science of mental health / edited with introductions by Steven Hyman.
        p. cm.
Includes bibliographical references.
  ISBN 0-8153-3743-4 (set)
 1. Mental health. I. Hyman, Steven E.
RA790 .S435 2002
616.89--dc21

                                2001048491

ISBN 0-8153-3743-4 (set)
ISBN 0-8153-3744-2 (v.1)
ISBN 0-8153-3745-0 (v.2)
ISBN 0-8153-3746-9 (v.3)
ISBN 0-8153-3747-7 (v.4)
ISBN 0-8153-3748-5 (v.5)
ISBN 0-8153-3749-3 (v.6)
ISBN 0-8153-3750-7 (v.7)
ISBN 0-8153-3751-5 (v.8)
ISBN 0-8153-3752-3 (v.9)
ISBN 0-8153-3753-1 (v.10)

Contents

Treatment

Introduction

The word "emotion" is used in ordinary parlance to refer to subjective feelings, but at the level of brain and behavior emotions are critical survival mechanisms. In response to salient environmental or internal stimuli, "emotion circuitry" in the brain must rapidly appraise the significance of what is happening, and then activate output systems that prepare a person (or animal) to respond adaptively. These output systems produce changes in physiology and automatic patterns of behavior. They also produce changes in cognition and, indeed, accompanying subjective feelings that are congruent with the situation (LeDoux, 2000).

In addition to its immediate effects, emotion facilitates the formation of memories (Fendt and Fanselow, 1999). An important aspect of survival is the ability to learn environmental cues that predict danger as well as the necessities of life. Although humans exhibit many subtle forms of emotion, at a crude level emotions can be divided into two broad classes: "negative" emotions (such as fear), which under normal circumstances are elicited by aversive stimuli and which generally lead to avoidance, escape, or protective responses; and "positive" or "appetitive" emotions, which are elicited by rewarding stimuli and which lead to approach behaviors.

During the past decade there has been substantial progress in the understanding of one emotion in particular: fear (LeDoux, 2000). This progress has been possible, in part, because fear can readily be elicited and studied in the laboratory. This research is an important step toward a deeper understanding of one of our basic emotions. But it also has important implications for health. Fear and the closely related state of anxiety are core symptoms in common and debilitating mental disorders, including panic disorder, post-traumatic stress disorder (PTSD), generalized anxiety disorder (GAD), social anxiety disorder (also called social phobia), and simple phobias (for example, phobias elicited by specific stimuli such as heights or spiders). Anxiety also commonly occurs in the course of major depression and may be severe. Panic disorder, PTSD, GAD, social anxiety disorder, and simple phobias are often grouped together as the so-called anxiety disorders. In some classifications, including that of the American Psychiatric Association's *Diagnostic and Statistical Manual of Mental Disorders*, 4th edition, obsessive-compulsive disorder (OCD) is grouped with the anxiety disorders because, in addition to its core features of obsessions (intrusive, unwanted thoughts) and compulsions, intense anxiety may be a characteristic response to these obsessions and may be discharged by the performance of compulsive rituals. However, increasing evidence of the differences in the pathogenesis between the other anxiety disorders and obsessive-compulsive disorder has led many scientists to group the latter with Tourette's syndrome, a grouping reflected in these volumes.

As in other volumes in this series, there are descriptions of some of the clinical syndromes followed by sections on epidemiology, genetic and environmental risk factors, and natural history (course of illness). Because anxiety disorders so often co-occur with other mental disorders, there is a section devoted to this issue. The volume also includes an article on the evolutionary psychology of anxiety disorders (Marks and Nesse, 1994) and a long section on brain and behavior that, among other issues, illustrates current attempts to use new insights into fear circuitry in the brain to help investigate the pathogenesis of anxiety disorders. The volume ends with a section on treatment. In some sections there are articles on panic disorder, PTSD, GAD, social anxiety disorder, and, where appropriate, childhood anxiety disorders (which are not always readily separated into their adult forms). Because simple phobias cause relatively little harm or impairment compared with the other anxiety disorders, they are little discussed.

Fear generally represents a transient response to a specific stimulus that connotes danger. Anxiety differs from fear in that a stimulus is either not present or not immediately threatening. Nevertheless, negative effects and cognitions occur that are associated with danger or lack of control over events and that are accompanied by the types of arousal induced by fear. Because it is not stimulus-bound, anxiety may be prolonged. Although anxiety occurs as a core symptom in all of the anxiety disorders, the precise forms it takes differ across these disorders, as do prevalence (Kessler et al., 1999; Kessler et al., 1998), genetic and environmental risk factors, life course, pathophysiology, and treatment.

The central feature of panic disorder is the unexpected panic attack, a discrete period of intense fear accompanied by bodily symptoms that may include a pounding heart, sweating, trembling, perceived shortness of breath, chest pain, nausea, dizziness, and tingling of limbs. There may also be feelings of unreality or detachment, fear of losing control, and fear of dying. The diagnosis of panic disorder is made when panic attacks are recurrent and are accompanied by persistent fear of having additional attacks. People with panic disorder may progressively restrict their lives to avoid situations in which panic attacks have occurred or are feared. For example, people may avoid being in crowds, traveling, or being on a bridge or in an elevator and may ultimately avoid leaving the home altogether. When avoidance becomes pervasive, the diagnosis of agoraphobia is made. While this synopsis relates the two, panic disorder may occur without agoraphobia, and agoraphobia may occur without panic disorder (Katsching and Amering, 1998; Bouton et al., 2001).

Post-traumatic stress disorder follows serious trauma. It is characterized by a sense of numbness, by intrusive reliving of the traumatic experience that is often initiated by otherwise harmless cues that serve as reminders of the trauma, by hyperarousal (for example, increased startle), and by disturbed sleep that may include nightmares. Generalized anxiety disorder (Yonkers et al., 1996) is characterized by unrealistic and excessive worry for more than six months, accompanied by specific anxiety-related symptoms such as motor tension, sympathetic hyperactivity, and excessive vigilance. Social anxiety disorder

(Liebowitz et al., 1985) is characterized by serious persistent fear of social situations or performance situations (examples of the latter include stage fright) that expose a person to potential scrutiny by others. The affected person has intense fear that he or she will act in a way that will be humiliating. Attempts to separate social anxiety disorder (or social phobia) from more extreme temperamental shyness have led to the requirement in the American Psychiatric Association's *Diagnostic and Statistical Manual of Mental Disorders*, 4th edition,[1] that the symptoms cause distress and interfere significantly with an individual's occupational or social role functioning. Despite such a requirement, the boundaries separating social phobia, avoidant personality disorder, and shyness are difficult to delineate.

There is less genetic data on anxiety disorders than on schizophrenia, bipolar disorder, or autism. Nonetheless, some family studies have been done on the genetic risks of anxiety disorders, with the most substantial investigations focusing on panic disorder, in part because the phenotype may be easier to define than that in other anxiety disorders (Biederman et al., 2001). Genetic linkage studies have been performed on panic disorder, but given the lack of convincing replication, none is included here. As in the case of all mental disorders, the data on panic disorder and other anxiety disorders suggest genetic complexity. This means that anxiety disorders do not appear to be "caused" by a single gene. Rather, multiple genes work as susceptibility factors, acting together with developmental and environmental factors to produce illness. Studies of children at risk for anxiety disorders have identified early markers of vulnerability (Merikangas et al., 1999; Kagan and Snidman, 1999); the search for specific risk factors is in its early stages. One interesting possibility is that early-onset anxiety disorders may create risk of subsequent alcoholism (Merikangas et al., 1998), as alcohol may serve as a misguided attempt at self-medication. Overall, the interaction among anxiety disorders, addictive disorders, and mood disorders is clinically significant and may provide opportunities for prevention of secondary disorders (Merikangas et al., 1998; Mineka et al., 1998; Regier et al., 1998).

Studies of brain and behavior have led to greater understandings of the neural substrates of both fear and anxiety (LeDoux, 2000; Kalin et al., 2001). There is a long way to go in relating these basic advances to the understanding of anxiety disorders, but research from several scientific traditions is already building bridges between neuroscience and clinical investigation (Gorman et al., 2000; Stein, 1998). One important strand of clinical investigation has been the careful analysis of individuals with informative brain lesions resulting from illness or injury. Studies have examined such individuals and can demonstrate in humans that different neural structures underlie the cognitive and conscious aspects of memory (hippocampus) versus the emotional and unconscious aspects that regulate physiologic responses (the amygdala). Such human studies extend the findings from animal studies in which invasive techniques such as placing of brain lesions permit a more detailed tracing of fear pathways (Fendt and Fanselow, 1999). A second approach that extends basic findings to the human situation is the use of noninvasive imaging. Studies are included here that investigate the neural circuits activated by fear in healthy volunteers (Phelps et al., 2001) and in individuals with anxiety disorders such as PTSD. Other studies in normal volunteers examine different aspects of the encoding of fear-related memories (Buchel et al., 1998).

Many of the initial studies in humans have focused on the amygdala, a small but complex structure in the temporal lobes that plays a key role in fear and other emotions. It is already clear from basic investigation, however, that other brain regions, such as the prefrontal cerebral cortex, also play important roles in fear (Garcia et al., 1999). Ultimately, the brain works not as a phrenologist might have imagined (brain regions functioning in isolation) but as distributed circuits across which specialized regions interact.

Another important aspect of research is the role of development in creating risk for anxiety disorders. There have been recent investigations of both temperamental factors (Kagan and Snidman, 1999) and environmental factors, especially the role of trauma.

Treatment of anxiety disorders involves both medication and cognitive-behavioral psychotherapies, or some combination of the two. In the Brain and Behavior section there is a review by Bouton et al. (2001) bringing a learning-theory perspective to the pathogenesis of panic disorder. This understanding has direct implications for understanding the use of cognitive-behavioral therapies (Barlow et al., 2000), which are highly efficacious in panic disorder and also in PTSD (Foa and Meadows, 1997) and simple phobias. The recognition that antidepressant drugs, initially the tricyclics, were efficacious for panic disorder was an important watershed for psychopharmacology (Klein, Klein, and Fink, 1962). These findings also had important implications for the classification of anxiety disorders. More recently, selective serotonin reuptake inhibitors (SSRIs) have proven efficacious in panic disorder, GAD, PTSD (Davidson et al., 2001), social anxiety disorder (Stein et al., 1998), and pediatric anxiety disorders (The Research Unit on Pediatric Psychopharmacology Anxiety Study Group, 2001). While benzodiazepines and anxiolytics can also be used effectively for a variety of anxiety disorders, the move to SSRIs reflects the fact that, unlike benzodiazepines, they do not produce dependence. This broad use of SSRIs is a reminder that the term "antidepressant" is a misnomer.

In summary, anxiety disorders are common and cause both distress and impairment. As will be seen from the articles in this collection, existing treatments are extremely useful but far from perfect. Thus the research progress in understanding fear and anxiety has created real excitement about the possibility of more effective interventions in the coming years.

References
1. American Psychiatric Association. *Diagnostic and Statistical Manual of Mental Disorders*, 4th ed. Washington, D.C.: American Psychiatric Press, 1994.

The Science
of Mental Health

British Journal of Psychiatry (1996), **168**, 308–313

Phenomenology and Course of Generalised Anxiety Disorder

KIMBERLY A. YONKERS, MEREDITH G. WARSHAW, ANN O. MASSION and MARTIN B. KELLER

Background. The diagnostic category of generalised anxiety disorder (GAD) was originally intended to describe residual anxiety states. Over the years clinical criteria have been refined in an attempt to describe a unique diagnostic entity. Given these changes, little is known about the clinical course of this newly defined disorder. This study investigates the longitudinal course, including remission and relapse rates, for patients with DSM–III–R defined GAD.

Method. Analysis of the 164 patients with GAD participating in the Harvard Anxiety Research Program. Patients were assessed with a structured clinical interview at intake and re-examined at six month intervals for two years and then annually for one to two years. Psychiatric Status Ratings were assigned at each interview point. Kaplan–Meier curves were constructed to assess likelihood of remission.

Results. Comorbidity was high, with panic disorder and social phobia as the most frequently found comorbid disorders. The likelihood of remission was 0.15 after one year and 0.25 after two years. The probability of becoming asymptomatic from all psychiatric symptoms was only 0.08.

Conclusions. This prospective study confirms the chronicity associated with GAD and extends this finding to define the one and two year remission rates for the disorder. Likelihood of remission for GAD and any other comorbid condition after one year was half the annual remission rate for GAD alone.

Generalised anxiety disorder (GAD), a disorder characterised by extreme anxiety and worry, was introduced as a category in DSM–III–R (American Psychiatric Association, 1980). It develops insidiously between the late teens and early twenties and some investigators (Anderson *et al*, 1984; Barlow *et al*, 1986), but not all (von Korff *et al*, 1985), find it develops before other anxiety disorders such as panic disorder. Stress plays a role in the genesis of GAD (Barlow *et al*, 1986) but genetic factors cannot be ruled out (Kendler *et al*, 1992). Retrospectively collected data show that the course of generalised anxiety is protracted and average illness duration may be as long as 20 years (Barlow *et al*, 1986). Few remissions occur after illness onset (Anderson *et al*, 1984). The remission rate for patients with anxiety neurosis, an older diagnostic category that includes patients with panic disorder and GAD, was only 12% after six years (Noyes *et al*, 1980).

A notable feature of GAD is the high degree of comorbidity with other psychiatric disorders (Massion *et al*, 1993). Community studies (Blazer *et al*, 1991; Wittchen *et al*, 1994) show frequent co-occurrence with major depression and panic. Studies using clinical cohorts also document extensive comorbidity (Barlow *et al*, 1986; Breier *et al*, 1986;

Fava *et al*, 1988; Garvey *et al*, 1988; Brawman-Mintzer *et al*, 1993) which generates questions regarding the diagnostic integrity of the category (Massion *et al*, 1993). Because most data on GAD utilise older diagnostic systems and are retrospective in nature, it is unclear how accurate this information is for patients meeting the newer DSM–III–R definition. Prospectively collected information regarding comorbidity and longitudinal course of patients with DSM–III–R defined GAD would be useful in distinguishing it from other anxiety disorders and establishing its diagnostic integrity.

Methods

The Harvard/Brown Anxiety Research Program (HARP) is a prospective, naturalistic, longitudinal study of patients with DSM–III–R defined anxiety disorders. The design of the study has been described in detail elsewhere (Keller *et al*, 1994). Patients were recruited voluntarily from eleven Boston area hospitals with current or past diagnoses of: panic disorder (with or without agoraphobia); agoraphobia without a history of panic disorder; generalised anxiety disorder, or social phobia. Patients were at least 18-years-old and free of any organic mental disorder, schizophrenia, or psychosis for the six months prior to intake. The intake diagnostic evaluation included a structured interview with the SCAL-UP (Keller *et al*, 1987*a*), which combines the Structured Clinical Interview for the DSM–III–R Patient Version (Spitzer *et al*, 1988) and the Schedule for Affective Disorders and Schizophrenia-Lifetime Version (Endicott & Spitzer 1978). Follow-up was conducted at six month intervals for the first two years and annually thereafter, using the Longitudinal Interval Follow-Up Evaluation (LIFE; Keller *et al*, 1987*b*). Information on psychosocial treatment was collected using the Psychosocial Treatment Inventory (Perry *et al*, 1993). The majority of interviews were conducted in person by experienced clinical interviewers, who were closely supervised by the site project director. Clerical errors were corrected before inclusion in the computer master file. This paper includes an analysis of 164 patients with an active diagnosis of GAD at intake. Of these, 153 (93%) were interviewed at one year, 141 (86%) at two years and 112 (68%) at three years.

Psychiatric status ratings

The LIFE was used to collect information on the severity of symptoms during the study. Psychopathology is rated on a six-point Psychiatric Status Rating (PSR) scale which is scored on a week by week basis at each interview. The greatest severity of illness for GAD, a PSR of six, requires full DSM–III–R criteria as does a PSR of five, although functioning is not disrupted. A PSR of four is assigned when worry is present most days with three to five symptoms or worry less than 50% of the time and six symptoms. A PSR of three includes three symptoms and worry less than 50% of the time. Occasional worry is designated by a PSR of two and lack of symptoms, a PSR of one.

Definition of remission

Remission is defined as symptom improvement for eight consecutive weeks. This time period detects noticeable changes in morbidity and minimises transient changes in psychopathological state. Full remission requires improvement to a PSR of two or less. A partial remission is defined as a decrease in symptoms to a PSR of three. Also examined was improvement marked by loss of full criteria, i.e. decrease to a PSR of four during an eight week interval. Relapse was defined as a return to PSR of five or six for any length of time.

Patients were considered to be in an episode at intake if they met full criteria (PSR = 5 or 6) for GAD at any point during the previous six months and had not been well for eight consecutive weeks or longer at the time of intake. Because of this definition, some patients who were considered 'in episode' at intake did not meet full criteria at that time.

Psychosocial treatment

The Psychosocial Treatment Inventory (Perry *et al*, 1993) was administered at the first six month follow-up. Patients were scored as receiving treatment if they reported undergoing at least one of its constituent modalities at the 'frequent' level (0 = never, 1 = sometimes and 2 = frequent).

Statistical analysis

All statistical analyses were conducted using SAS Version 6.07 (SAS Institute, 1990) using PROC freq, PROC NPAR1WAY, PROC *t*-test and PROC LIFE test. Longitudinal data were analysed using standard survival analysis techniques (Kalbfleish & Prentice, 1980). Kaplan–Meier life tables were constructed for times to remission and relapse for varying definitions of remission.

Results

Subject characteristics

Seventy-two per cent of patients with GAD were female and the average intake age was 41 (range 19–75). The age of onset for GAD varied between 2 and 61 years, with a mean of 21 years. The average length of illness by retrospective report was 20 years.

Comorbidity with other anxiety disorders and depression

Sixty per cent of the patients gave a history of only one episode of GAD during their lifetime while remaining patients had multiple episodes. Thirty-five per cent had experienced psychiatric hospitalisation, but not necessarily for GAD. Eighty-seven per cent had a lifetime history of another anxiety disorder and 83% had another anxiety disorder active at intake. Nearly one-quarter (23%) had two additional anxiety disorders active at intake and another 16% had three or four other active anxiety disorders. The most frequently seen coexisting anxiety disorders were panic disorder with agoraphobia (PDA) and social phobia (Table 1). Both were target diagnoses; simple phobia was the most frequently found non-target anxiety disorder. Over one-third of patients with GAD also had major depression.

One hundred and forty-nine patients had a concurrent anxiety disorder diagnosis. Of those, 47% (70/149) reported the first onset of GAD before the comorbid disorders, 13% (20/149) reported the first onsets occurring within four weeks of each other, with the remaining 40% (59/149) reporting first onset of GAD after the other anxiety disorders.

Gender

Women with GAD were more likely than men to have a lifetime history of an additional anxiety disorder (95% v. 80%, $\chi^2 = 7.93$, $P = 0.005$). In particular, they were more likely to have histories of PDA (56% v. 28%, $\chi^2 = 10.46$, $P = 0.001$). There was no gender difference for history of major depressive disorder. The (in episode) comorbidity rates at intake were equivalent for men and women.

Course

Remission

At study intake, 135 of 164 patients met full criteria for GAD. As shown in Table 2 the remission rate at one year was 0.15 and increased to 0.25 by two years. Less rigorous definitions of remission were associated with higher rates of remission.

At intake, a subset of GAD patients, 18% (29/164), only met partial criteria for GAD even though they had been at full criteria sometime during the preceding six months. Patients meeting partial criteria at intake had essentially the same probabilities of remission at one year (0.14 for full criteria and 0.17 for partial criteria). At two years, the probability of remitting for both groups was 0.25.

We also investigated remission from GAD plus concurrent psychiatric disorders for patients who entered the study meeting either full or partial criteria. At 26 weeks, the likelihood of full remission

Table 1
Co-occurring anxiety and depressive disorders present at intake ($n = 164$)

	n (%)
Panic disorder	18 (11)
Panic disorder with agoraphobia	67 (41)
Agoraphobia without panic	6 (41)
Social phobia	52 (32)
Simple phobia	30 (18)
Obsessive–compulsive disorder	30 (18)
Post-traumatic stress disorder	13 (5)
Anxiety disorder	9 (6)
Dysthymia	28 (17)
Major depression	61 (37)

Table 2
Probability for varying degrees of GAD symptom improvement in patients with full criteria at intake ($n = 135$)

Week	Full remission (PSR < 3 for 8 wks)	Partial remission (PSR < 4 for 8 wks)	Loss of criteria (PSR < 5 for 8 wks)
0	0.04	0.07	0.15
26	0.11	0.16	0.29
52	0.15	0.23	0.41
78	0.18	0.29	0.48
104	0.25	0.33	0.51
130	0.27	0.33	0.53

from GAD was 0.11 but the probability for remission from both GAD and coexisting anxiety disorders diminished to 0.03 during this same interval. The chances of becoming asymptomatic from GAD and other anxiety disorders increased slightly by one year and was flat after that (Table 3). Adding the requirement of concurrent remission from MDD does not further effect the remission rate.

Given the low probability for remission, we examined the general symptom status for the group over this initial six month period. In any given week, the majority of patients had anxiety more days than not and at least six DSM–III–R symptoms without a major disruption in functioning (PSR = 5). Figure 1 shows the distribution of PSRs among patients in episode of GAD at three time points. Although there was a trend toward some amelioration of symptoms over the 26 weeks, most patients remained stably symptomatic: 88% stayed at the same PSR during the first six months of follow-up, 9% changed by one level and only 3% changed by two or three levels (Fig. 1).

Relapse

Relapse was examined in the 42 patients who achieved a full remission (PSR < 3 for eight weeks). The risk of relapse was 0.07 after six months and 0.15 after one year. The risk of relapse was higher for the 43

Table 3
Probability of remission from GAD and comorbid disorders

Week	GAD (only) ($n = 164$)	GAD & other anxiety disorder(s) ($n = 164$)	GAD, MDD and other anxiety disorders ($n = 164$)
26	0.11	0.03	0.03
52	0.15	0.07	0.08
78	0.18	0.09	0.10
104	0.25	0.17	0.26
130	0.27	0.17	0.17

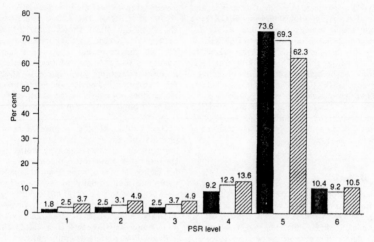

Fig. 1 PSR levels at three time points. ■, week one; ▨, week 13; ▧, week 26.

patients who had a partial remission (PSR of 3 or 4 = 0.34 at one year) and for patients who had comorbid anxiety (0.23 at one year) or depressive disorders (0.28 at one year).

Treatment

Psychotherapy treatment data are available for 131 patients, and 88% of this group described involvement with some psychosocial treatment. Techniques consistent with psychodynamic psychotherapy were reported by 50%, 24% reported cognitive therapy, 15% reported behavioural therapy and 14% indicated treatment consistent with relaxation or meditation techniques.

Somatic treatment data were available for 163 of 164 patients. Eighty-four per cent of the group received pharmacological treatment during the first six months of the study. Thirty-five per cent of patients took one medication, 31% took two and 18% took more than two psychoactive agents during this six month interval. The majority (69%) received a benzodiazepine anxiolytic while 31% received tricyclic antidepressants. The most frequently reported drugs were alprazolam (51/163 = 31%), clonazepam (37/163 = 23%) and fluoxetine (30/163 = 18%). Sixteen per cent (8/51) of patients taking alprazolam, 14% (5/37) of those taking clonazepam and none of those taking fluoxetine reported PRN usage.

Discussion

Comorbidity

In prior reports, we note that solo anxiety disorder diagnoses are rare (White *et al*, 1992; Massion *et al*, 1993). For patients with GAD, 90% had a lifetime history of another anxiety disorder and 83% had at least one other anxiety disorder diagnosis active at intake. A recent study (Brawman-Mintzer *et al*, 1993) finds slightly lower rates (74%) of comorbidity in a clinical sample of patients with GAD. One would wonder whether these high comorbidity rates occur because clinical cohorts versus community samples, are likely to be more ill and to suffer from multiple conditions. However, data from the National Comorbidity Study (NCS) finds lifetime comorbidity rates of 90% and one month comorbidity rates of 66% (Wittchen *et al*, 1994). In that study, the most likely comorbid diagnoses are dysthymia, panic disorder, mania and major depression. Comorbidity rates in our study were influenced by intake criteria and thus high rates for mania were not seen. These reports suggest that patients requesting treatment for generalised anxiety should be carefully screened for comorbid psychiatric disorders.

The comorbidity between the various anxiety disorders suggests shared predisposing biological and developmental factors, as previously proposed (Massion *et al*, 1993; Brown *et al*, 1994).

GAD was constructed to encapsulate residual and prodromal anxiety and the symptoms of GAD are commonly found among the other anxiety disorders (Barlow *et al*, 1986). Modifications in DSM–III–R appear not to have changed this characteristic. In fact, eliminating the DSM–III–R hierarchical exclusions with agoraphobia and obsessive–compulsive disorder (OCD), or lessening exclusions when GAD co-occurs with simple phobia, panic disorders and social phobia, have increased the apparent comorbidity in a clinical study (Boyd *et al*, 1984) but did not appreciably change rates in the NCS (Wittchen *et al*, 1994).

Course of illness

Retrospective report of average illness length was 20 years, similar to other reports (Barlow *et al*, 1986). The average age of illness onset is also consistent (Garvey *et al*, 1988; Kendler *et al*, 1992). After one year, the chance of experiencing complete remission was only 0.15, a rate reported by a number of groups (Schapira *et al*, 1972; Noyes *et al*, 1980; Wittchen, 1988). The full remission rate at two years, 0.25, is considerably higher than that found in other studies. Perhaps the rate found by others reflects remission rates from both GAD and other psychiatric disorders which is only 0.17 in HARP. Studies which assess anxious symptomatology rather than symptom clusters, might well find that few patients become asymptomatic. Partial remissions and loss of full criteria were far more likely (0.23–0.41 at one year). Huxley (1979) found rates of 0.30 in patients using 50% improvement criteria and Kedward & Cooper (1966) found improvement in 24% of their group. These rates are remarkably similar to our remission rates despite differences in diagnostic criteria between studies.

Despite improvement in GAD, many of our patients continued to have other psychiatric symptoms as evidenced by a lower remission rate from GAD together with other anxiety disorders. In a separate paper, we report that one-third of patients with GAD (and no comorbid panic) were never married and 17% were separated, widowed or divorced (Massion *et al*, 1993). Patients were also under-employed and 37% had received public assistance. Thus, GAD may be a marker for chronicity and functional impairment.

Brown *et al* (1994) note problems with diagnostic reliability but also describe features of GAD which differ from other anxiety disorders. Data on course of illness can contribute to this discussion of diagnostic reliability and validity. Our group finds

a one year remission rate from panic disorder of 0.37 (Keller *et al*, 1994). The unique course for GAD as shown in this study shows some differentiation between this diagnostic category and other anxiety disorder diagnoses but it does not rule out the possibility that GAD, which begins earlier and has a lower remission rate, shares psychobiological features with other anxiety disorders such as panic. It also does not eliminate the possibility that GAD is a prodromal substrate or residua of other anxiety disorders.

Over 80% of the group received either pharmacotherapy or psychotherapy with the majority of patients receiving both treatments. Despite this, patients infrequently remitted. Inspecting data for somatic treatment suggests under treatment (median daily doses for alprazolam and clorazepam were 1.4 and 1.0 mg respectively). Future research should more thoroughly investigate the intensity and types of treatment received to understand whether this is a factor in so few individuals becoming asymptomatic.

Clinical Implications

- Generalised anxiety disorder is associated with extensive comorbidity.
- Remission from generalised anxiety is rare (0.15 at one year) and the majority of patients remain stably symptomatic.
- Even if patients remit from generalised anxiety disorder, approximately one-half will continue to have symptoms associated with a comorbid anxiety disorder.

Limitations

- Data from clinical samples may be representative of patients with more severe, comorbid, chronic illnesses.
- Observational data which does not control treatment may underestimate the likelihood of remission compared to controlled, adequately treated cohorts.
- The existence of comorbid illness in patients with generalised anxiety disorder may have affected the likelihood of remission from generalised anxiety disorder.

Acknowledgements

Supported by the Upjohn Company, the Harvard/Brown Anxiety Disorders Research Program is conducted with the participation of the following investigators: M. B. Keller, Chairperson; S. Rasmussen, Co-Chairperson; R. Stout, M. Warshaw, P. Alexander, A. Gordon, Butler Hospital, Brown University School of Medicine; J. Reich, Brown University School of Medicine; K. White, J. Curran, Veterans Administration Hospital, Providence, Brown University School of Medicine; P. Lavori, Stanford University;

H. Samuelson, Brigham and Women's Hospital; G. Mallya, McLean Hospital, Harvard School of Medicine; E. Fierman, F. Rodriquez-Villa, Beth Israel Hospital, Harvard Medical School; M. P. Rogers, N. Weinschenker, Massachusetts Mental Health Center, Harvard Medical School; J. Ellison, New England Medical Center and Cambridge Hospital; A. Massion, University of Massachusetts Medical School; J. C. Perry, Jewish General Hospital, McGill School of Medicine, Montreal; L. G. Peterson Veterans Administration Hospital, Togus, Maine; J. Rice, Renard Hospital, Washington University School of Medicine, St. Louis; G. S. Stekett, Boston University School of Social Work; K. A. Yonkers, University of Texas, Dallas. Additional contributions from R. M. A. Hirschfeld, University of Texas, Galveston; J. Hooley, Harvard University; M. Weissman, Columbia University.

The Quintiles Corporation provided valuable consultation services to this project.

References

AMERICAN PSYCHIATRIC ASSOCIATION (1980) *Diagnostic and Statistical Manual of Mental Disorders* (3rd edn revised) (DSM–III–R). Washington, DC: APA.

ANDERSON, D. J., NOYES, R. & CROWE, R. R. (1984) A comparison of panic disorder and generalized anxiety disorder. *American Journal of Psychiatry*, 141, 572–575.

BARLOW, D. H., BLANCHARD, E. B., VERMILYEA, J. A., *et al* (1986) Generalized anxiety and generalized anxiety disorder: Description and reconceptualization. *American Journal of Psychiatry*, 143, 40–44.

BLAZER, D. G., HUGHES, D., GEORGE, L. K., *et al* (1991) In *Psychiatric Disorders in America* (1st edn) (eds L. N. Robins & D. A. Regier), pp. 181–203. New York: Free Press.

BOYD, J. H., BURKE, J. D., GRUENBERG, E., *et al* (1984) Exclusion criteria of DSM–III. A study of co-occurrence of hierarchy-free syndromes. *Archives of General Psychiatry*, 41, 983–989.

BRAWMAN-MINTZER, O., LYDIARD, R. B., EMMANUEL, N., *et al* (1993) Psychiatric comorbidity in patients with generalized anxiety disorder. *American Journal of Psychiatry*, 150, 1216–1218.

BREIR, A., CHARNEY, D. S. & HENINGER, G. R. (1986) Agoraphobia with panic attacks. *Archives of General Psychiatry*, 43, 1029–1036.

BROWN, T. A., BARLOW, D. H. & LIEBOWITZ, M. R. (1994) The empirical basis of generalized anxiety disorder. *American Journal of Psychiatry*, 151, 1272–1280.

ENDICOTT, J. & SPITZER, R. L. (1978) A diagnostic interview: The schedule for affective disorders and schizophrenia (SADS-L). *Archives of General Psychiatry*, 35, 837–844.

FAVA, A., GRANDI, S. & CANESTRATI, R. (1988) Prodomal symptoms in panic disorder with agoraphobia. *American Journal of Psychiatry*, 145, 1564–1567.

GARVEY, M. J., COOK, B. & NOYES, Jr., R. (1988) The occurrence of a prodrome of generalized anxiety in panic disorder. *Comprehensive Psychiatry*, 29, 445–449.

HUXLEY, P. J., GOLDBERG, D. P., MAGUIRE, G. P., *et al* (1979) The prediction of the course of minor psychiatric disorders. *British Journal of Psychiatry*, 135, 535–543.

KALBFLEISH, J. G. & PRENTICE, R. L. (1980) *The Statistical Analysis of Failure Time Data*. New York: John Wiley and Sons.

KEDWARD, H. B. & COOPER, B. (1966) Neurotic disorders in urban practice. A three-year follow-up. *Journal of the Royal College of Physicians of London*, 12, 148–163.

KELLER, M. B., LAVORI, P. W. & NIELSON, E. (1987a) SCALUP (SCID-P plus SADS-L). Available from authors (Dr Keller).

——, ——, FRIEDMAN, E., *et al* (1987b) The longitudinal interval follow-up evaluation: A comprehensive method for assessing outcome in prospective longitudinal studies. *Archives of General Psychiatry*, 540–548.

——, YONKERS, K. A., WARSAW, M. G., *et al* (1994) Remission and relapse in subjects with panic disorder and panic with agoraphobia: A prospective short-interval naturalistic follow-up. *Journal of Nervous and Mental Disorders*, 182, 290–296.

KENDLER, K. S., NEAGLE, M. C., KESSLER, R. C., *et al* (1992) Generalized anxiety disorder in women. A population-based twin study. *Archives of General Psychiatry*, 49, 267–272.

MASSION, A., WARSHAW, M. & KELLER, M. (1993) Quality of life and psychiatric morbidity in panic disorder versus generalized anxiety disorder. *American Journal of Psychiatry*, 150, 600–607.

NOYES, R., CLANCEY, J., HOENK, P. R., *et al* (1980) The prognosis of anxiety neurosis. *Archives of General Psychiatry*, 37, 173–178.

PERRY, J. C., STEKETEE, G., MASSION, A., *et al* (1993) The Psychosocial Treatment Interview: A method format for follow-along studies. Available from Dr Perry, Jewish General Hospital 3755 Cote St. Catherine Road, Montreal, Quebec H3T1E2.

RASKIN, M., PEEKE, H. V. S., DICKMAN, W., *et al* (1982) Panic and generalized disorders. *Archives of General Psychiatry*, 39, 687–689.

SAS INSTITUTE, Inc. (1990) *Statistical Analysis Software*. Available from SAS Circle, Box 8000, Cary, NC, 27512–8000.

SCHAPIRA, K., ROTH, M., KERR, T. A., *et al* (1972) The prognosis of affective disorders: the differentiation of anxiety states from depressive illness. *British Journal of Psychiatry*, 121, 175–181.

SPITZER, R. L., WILLIAMS, J. B., GIBBON, M., *et al* (1988) *Structured Clinical Interview for DSM-III-R-Patient Version (SCID-P)*. New York: New York State Psychiatric Institute.

VON KORFF, M., EATON, W. & KEYL, P. (1985) The epidemiology of panic attacks and panic disorder: Results from three community surveys. *American Journal of Epidemiology*, 122, 970–981.

WHITE, K., GOLDENBERG, I., YONKERS, K. A., *et al* (1992) The infrequency of "pure culture" diagnoses among anxiety disorders. *Clinical Neuropharmacology*, 15 (Suppl. 1), 56B.

WITTCHEN, H.-U. (ed.) (1988) Natural course and spontaneous remissions of untreated anxiety disorder: Results of the Munich follow-up study (MFS). In *Panic and Phobias 2: Treatments and Variables Affecting Course and Outcome*. New York: Springer-Verlag.

——, ZHAO, S., KESSLER, R. C., *et al* (1994) DSM-III-R Generalised anxiety disorder in the National Comorbidity Survey. *Archives of General Psychiatry*, 51, 355–364.

Kimberly A. Yonkers, MD, Departments of Psychiatry and Obstetrics & Gynecology, The University of Texas, Southwestern Medical Center at Dallas; Ann O. Massion, MD, Department of Psychiatry, University of Massachusetts Medical School, Worcester, MA; Meredith G. Warshaw, MSS, Brown University, Providence, RI; Martin B. Keller, MD, Butler Hospital, 345 Blackstone Blvd., Providence, RI 02906

Correspondence: Professor Yonkers, 5959 Harry Hines Blvd., Dallas, TX 75235-9101

(*First received 27 March 1995, final revision 31 July 1995, accepted 18 August 1995*)

Social Phobia

Review of a Neglected Anxiety Disorder

Michael R. Liebowitz, MD; Jack M. Gorman, MD; Abby J. Fyer, MD; Donald F. Klein, MD

• While other anxiety disorders have recently become the subjects of increasing investigation, social phobia remains, except among behavior therapists, relatively unstudied. As a result, major uncertainties exist concerning classification, prevalence, severity, etiology, assessment, and treatment of social phobia. Existing findings do suggest that in its own right and as a comparison for other anxiety disorders, social phobia should prove a fertile area for psychobiological and clinical investigation.

(Arch Gen Psychiatry 1985;42:729-736)

From both research and clinical perspectives, social phobia is among the most neglected of the major anxiety disorders classified in *DSM-III*. While panic disorder, agoraphobia, generalized anxiety disorder, and obsessive compulsive disorder have become the subjects of increasing investigation, social phobia remains, except among behavior therapists, relatively unstudied. Thus, despite the suggestion made more than 15 years ago by Marks and Gelder[1] that social phobia differed from other phobic disorders, to our knowledge, there have been no published family or biological challenge studies of social phobics. The few available psychopharmacology studies are limited by major problems in design and analysis. Also, no general agreement exists as to diagnostic criteria or prevalence. The review that follows was undertaken to focus attention on what is known as well as the uncertainties concerning the classification, prevalence, severity, etiology, pathophysiology, assessment, and treatment of social phobia.

DEFINITION

Marks and Gelder[1] initially defined *social phobia* to include "fears of eating, drinking, shaking, blushing, speaking, writing or vomiting in the presence of other people," the core feature being fear of seeming ridiculous to others. Defined this way, social phobics were found to become symptomatic and seek treatment earlier, to have a greater male-female ratio, and to have different anxiety symptoms than agoraphobics.[2,3] Marks and Gelder's original concept included patients with

---

Accepted for publication Oct 9, 1984.

From the Anxiety Disorders Clinic (Drs Liebowitz, Fyer, and Gorman) and Department of Therapeutics (Dr Klein), New York State Psychiatric Institute, and the Department of Psychiatry, College of Physicians and Surgeons, Columbia University (Drs Liebowitz, Gorman, Fyer, and Klein), New York.

Reprint requests to New York State Psychiatric Institute, 722 W 168th St, New York, NY 10032 (Dr Liebowitz).

specific social fears (fear of speaking, signing a check, or eating in public) *and* those with more generalized forms of social anxiety (fears of initiating conversations or dating). This "broad" definition has been challenged in several ways.

Some investigators believe that patients with more generalized social anxiety should be classified as having avoidant personality disorder,[4] and restrict social phobia to patients with discrete or specific forms of performance or social anxiety. However, no empirical basis exists for this distinction. In the absence of data, arbitrarily viewing socially fearful patients as personality disordered carries the risk that pharmacological interventions will not even be tried.

The original *DSM-III* description of social phobia suggests a broad definition. However, the examples given in the *DSM-III* description are all limited to specific social fears and involve anxiety about speaking or performing in public, using public lavatories, eating in public, and writing in the presence of others. Moreover, *DSM-III* asserts that social phobics generally have only one fear, implying that patients with multiple fears or more generalized social anxiety are either rare or should be included in some other diagnostic category. Also, without empirical justification, *DSM-III* excludes patients from the social phobia category whose social anxiety symptoms are due to avoidant personality disorder.

Also problematic is how to classify patients who develop spontaneous panic attacks leading to panic disorder or agoraphobia and then, as aspects of a larger syndrome, begin to avoid certain performance or social situations. By *DSM-III* criteria, such social performance avoidance is secondary to panic disorder (or agoraphobia), and thus not social phobia. Yet such patients ("secondary" social phobics as opposed to "primary" social phobics with no history of spontaneous panic attacks) do fear embarrassment or humiliation were they to have a panic attack in front of others, and thus avoid giving speeches, giving parties, etc.

An important difference, in our view, is that primary social phobics fear scrutiny or evaluation by others, and their anxiety is confined to such situations or anticipation of such situations. Patients with panic disorder or agoraphobia with panic attacks, on the other hand, also have panic attacks in a variety of nonsocial situations (subways, supermarkets, tunnels, bridges), and tend to fear or avoid any situation where easy or unobtrusive exit is difficult. We observe that patients with panic disorder are also comforted by the presence of familiar figures when experiencing anxiety, while primary social phobics feel more comfortable if they can be alone. Developmental, biological, treatment, family, and follow-up studies are needed to determine the similarities and differences between primary and secondary social phobics.

DISTINCTION FROM OTHER DISORDERS

Demographic and clinical data lend some support for a distinction between social phobia and agoraphobia. Two studies have found demographic differences between the two phobic subtypes. In Marks'[2] series, the social phobics were 50% male, had an

9

average age of onset of 19 years, and sought treatment at a mean age of 27 years; agoraphobics were 25% male, had a mean age of onset of 24 years, and sought treatment at an average age of 32 years. While these differences were not statistically significant, Aimes et al[1] reported similar differences that were significant. Of 87 social phobics, 60% were male v 14% male among 57 agoraphobics. There were also significant differences in referral age (30.7 years for social phobics v 37.2 years for agoraphobics).

Somatic anxiety symptoms reported by social phobics may also show differences from those of agoraphobics. While further investigations are needed, in one series the social phobics reported more blushing and muscle twitching, and less limb weakness, breathing difficulty, dizziness or faintness, actual fainting, and buzzing or ringing in the ears than did agoraphobics.[2] Social phobics were also found to have lower extraversion scores on the Eysenck Personality Inventory than agoraphobics, whose scores were similar to normal controls.[3]

Findings from biological challenge and treatment studies can also clarify the relationship of social phobia to panic disorder and agoraphobia. Patients with panic disorder and agoraphobia with panic attacks show high rates of panic during sodium lactate infusion.[4,5] The distinction between these two anxiety disorders and social phobia would be supported if social phobics were found to panic less frequently in response to sodium lactate. Our preliminary finding, reported in detail elsewhere,[7] is that social phobics show a lower rate of panic to sodium lactate infusion than agoraphobics. As part of a larger study, nine patients meeting DSM-III criteria for agoraphobia with panic attacks, and 15 patients meeting DSM-III criteria for social phobia, were challenged with 0.5M racemic sodium lactate (10 mL/kg of body weight) administered intravenously over 20 minutes. As judged by a psychiatric evaluator "blind" to patient diagnosis, four (44%) of nine agoraphobics panicked during the lactate challenge, in contrast to one (7%) of 15 social phobics ($\chi^2 = 4.87$, degrees of freedom = 1, $P \le .03$).

Patients with spontaneous panic attacks have also been found to be highly responsive to the tricyclic imipramine[8,9] and the monoamine oxidase inhibitor (MAOI) phenelzine sulfate.[10] However, the responsiveness of social phobics to these medications is as yet unclear. As discussed in the "Treatment" section, preliminary evidence suggests that social phobics may be as responsive to MAOIs as patients with panic disorder or agoraphobia, but more responsive to β-adrenergic blockers. Family and follow-up studies of social phobics, now lacking, may also help to clarify its relation to agoraphobia.

Some evidence also exists to support the distinction between social phobia and the simple phobias, which consist of specific animal (birds, cats, insects) and situational (heights, darkness, thunderstorms) phobias. Marks and Gelder[1] found social phobics to differ in age of onset from simple phobics, while in a later study, Marks[2] found social phobics to have a later age of onset, higher overt anxiety level, and higher Maudsley Neuroticism scores than animal phobics. Lader et al[11] also found social phobics to have more spontaneous fluctuations in galvanic skin response than animal phobics, although in this regard the social phobics did not differ from agoraphobics. Weerts and Lang[12] also found students fearful of spiders to react with greater affect and greater changes in heart rate to fear relevant scenes than did students fearful of public speaking.

We lack the data to definitively compare drug responsiveness of social and simple phobics. Simple phobics have been found unresponsive to tricyclics,[8] and only weakly if at all responsive to β-adrenergic blockers[13,14]; but controlled studies of these agents in social phobia, as well as further studies of simple phobics, remain to be done. Family history and follow-up studies may also help to clarify the degree of distinctness between social phobics and simple phobics.

Social phobics appear distinct from schizoid patients in our view. Although both may avoid social interactions, by definition the social phobics desire social contact but are blocked by anxiety, while schizoid patients lack interest in social interaction. Schizophrenics may at times appear socially phobic, but their social anxieties can logically be attributed to the primary disorder. However, the commonalities of social anxiety in schizophrenic and nonschizophrenic populations remain to be assessed.

MAGNITUDE OF THE PROBLEM

While epidemiological studies have indicated that phobic disorders in general may affect as much as 7% of the general population,[15] the prevalence of social phobia is only now being investigated. Preliminary data from a multisite psychiatric epidemiological investigation reveal that the six-month prevalence of social phobia in two urban populations ranged from 0.9% to 1.7% for men and 1.5% to 2.6% for women.[16] However, these figures are based on responses to screening questionnaires, where patients whose social anxiety was part of another disorder (such as agoraphobia with panic attacks) would be also counted as socially phobic. Therefore, the prevalence of phobic syndromes meeting DSM-III criteria for social phobia would be expected to be lower. Other data available for social phobia, such as a 1971 questionnaire survey by Bryant and Trower,[17] estimated that approximately 3% to 10% of first-year students at a British college manifested typical social phobic symptoms.

Looking at clinical samples, Marks[2] found 8% of a Maudsley Hospital phobic population to have social phobia, while 60% were agoraphobic. Other investigators, however, have found a higher ratio of social phobics to agoraphobics among treatment applicants once the investigator's interest in social phobia became known.[1] Among outpatients applying for treatment to one US anxiety and phobia center, eight (13.3%) of 60 were found to be social phobics, which equaled the proportion with panic disorder and was exceeded only by the 38.3% with agoraphobia.[18] In our Anxiety Disorders Clinic, social phobics represent the third most common anxiety disorder (after panic disorder and agoraphobia). Moreover, some patients with panic disorder or agoraphobia have a history of social phobia that predates the onset and persists after successful treatment of their panic attacks.

In terms of morbidity, social phobia seems to begin early (characteristically between ages 15 and 20 years) and to follow a chronic, unremitting course.[18] The symptom pattern appears rather standard; of 11 patients meeting DSM-III social phobia criteria recently studied by us, all complained of tachycardia, pounding heart, trembling, sweating, and shortness of breath when in performance or a social situation. The attendant disability, in terms of vocational and social impairment, is often significant. In our series, two of 11 patients were unable to work, two dropped out of school, four had abused alcohol, one had abused tranquilizers, six were blocked from work advancement, and five avoided almost all social interaction outside their immediate family.

Significant depressive symptoms are reported to be quite common in social phobics, and were found in half of the patients in one large sample.[3] In a smaller series, one third of the patients were found to have either a past or present history of depression.[2] Among our patients, five of 11 had either past or present secondary major depression. Aimes et al[1] also found that 14% of their social phobics had a history of "parasuicidal acts," which exceeded the 2% rate among agoraphobics.

Social phobic symptoms are also frequently found among alcoholics, usually predating the drinking problem.[20,21] In one sample of 102 alcoholics admitted to an alcoholism treatment unit, 25% of the men and 17% of the women were social phobics, meaning that they experienced disabling anxiety in or could not face social situations when not under the influence of medication or alcohol.[20] A further 35% of the men and 28% of the women were rated as "borderline" social phobics because they experienced social anxiety that was subjectively distressing but not disabling or accompanied by marked avoidance. Surprised by these findings, Smail et al[21] attempted to replicate them, and found that of 60 abstinent alcoholics surveyed, 39% suffered from social phobia during their last typical drinking period. Sixty percent to 70% of the social phobic alcoholics reported alcohol helpful in coping with social anxiety. In another study, 20% of the social phobics were found to consume excessive amounts of alcohol, significantly more than the 7% of agoraphobics who did so.[3]

PATHOPHYSIOLOGY AND ETIOLOGY

It is unclear if normal and pathological social (or performance) anxiety lie on a continuum or are categorically distinct. A certain

10

degree of social or performance anxiety is ubiquitous and may have evolutionary adaptive advantage by motivating preparation and rehearsal of important interpersonal events. Such anxiety in normals, however, lessens with repeated exposure and also usually attenuates over the course of any given performance or social encounter.[22]

In contrast, in our experience social phobics often report their symptoms to be refractory to self-administered rehearsal or exposure. (Few have participated in systematic exposure or desensitization programs.) Moreover, their anxiety does not seem to attenuate during the course of a single social event or performance. Rather, they often report that their symptoms augment, as initial somatic discomfort becomes a further distraction and embarrassment to the already nervous individual, leading to further symptoms, which gives rise to more distraction, etc. Systematic studies are needed to determine if, and if so, why social phobics lack the ability to habituate in social or performance situations.

The symptoms social phobics experience when feeling under evaluation or scrutiny virtually always include tachycardia, sweating, blushing, and trembling, all suggesting heightened autonomic arousal. Since normal individuals have been shown to experience brief twofold to threefold increases in plasma epinephrine levels during stressful public speaking,[23] it is tempting to speculate that social phobics either experience greater or more sustained increases or are more sensitive to normal stress-mediated catecholamine elevations. These two possibilities can be examined experimentally by in vivo biochemical monitoring of social phobics in their feared situations and challenges with epinephrine infusions.

As discussed in detail in the section on "Treatment," the majority of studies in normal volunteer samples (analogue studies)[23-35] suggest that β-adrenergic blockers are quite helpful in reducing performance anxiety, which supports peripheral catecholamine mediation of social phobic symptoms. If this holds for clinical populations, social phobic anxiety may differ from panic attacks, which do not appear to be prevented by β-adrenergic blockers,[34-38] and appear to be mediated by central sympathetic mechanisms.[39]

Should a biological mediator of social phobic symptoms be found, questions will arise as to its inherited or acquired nature. To date, no family studies of social phobia have been conducted, so no genetic hypotheses can be tested. Social anxiety may, however, have an inheritable component. Torgersen[40] compared social fears among 95 monozygotic and dizygotic twin pairs chosen for the most part on an unselected basis from a Norwegian twin registry. The monozygotic twins were significantly more concordant for such social phobic features as discomfort when eating with strangers or when being watched working, writing, or trembling, suggesting a genetic contribution to social anxiety.

Sheehan[41] has postulated that social phobias are one aspect of an "endogenous anxiety disease," a later development of which is agoraphobia. This is based on the observation that following the onset of panic attacks, many individuals begin to avoid performance or social situations as a prelude to more widespread phobic avoidance. However, this conflates primary and secondary social phobia. Also, many individuals with social phobia never develop panic attacks or nonsocial phobias, arguing against a common diathesis for social phobia and panic disorder or agoraphobia.

Among the postulated acquired causes of social phobia are social skills deficits, traumatic early social or performance experiences, and faulty cognitions.[42,43] Other psychological antecedents and correlates of social anxiety were presented by Leary[44] in 1983. As noted by Nichols,[45] many social phobics also appear hypersensitive to rejection or criticism, suggesting an overlap with atypical depression or hysteroid dysphoria, where extreme rejection sensitivity is also a cardinal feature.[46,47]

The traditional psychoanalytic view that phobias represent the transformation of internal anxiety into external fear through displacement, and that the specific content of a phobia has symbolic meaning,[48] is also theoretically applicable to social phobia. This has not as yet, however, been subject to systematic controlled investigation. Nichols[45] has cataloged a variety of other psychological and somatic traits observed in a social phobic sample. These include low self-evaluation, an unrealistic tendency to experience others as critical or disapproving, rigid concepts of appropriate social behavior, negative fantasy-producing anticipatory anxiety, an increased awareness and fear of scrutiny by others, a fear of social situations from which it is difficult to leave unobtrusively, an exaggerated awareness of minimal somatic symptoms such as blushing or feeling faint, a tendency to overreact with greater anxiety to the somatic symptoms of anxiety, and an exaggerated fear of others noticing that one is anxious. It is unclear, however, which among these or other factors are causal, which are consequences of, and which are not even specifically related to social phobia.

Several controlled studies have also compared how adult social phobics, agoraphobics, simple phobics, and normal controls retrospectively rate their parents' child rearing practices and attitudes. As a group, social phobics perceived their parents to have been less caring, more rejecting, and overprotective as compared with normal controls.[49,50] However, no contrasts were carried out among the phobic groups, so the specificity of these findings for social phobics is uncertain. These studies also suffer from the deficiencies inherent in retrospective assessment.

ASSESSMENT

Various investigators have employed subjective (rater and self-assessments), biological, and performance measures to assess social phobics. Several structured interview schedules designed to facilitate diagnostic evaluation of anxiety patients are currently under development or in testing. Using one called the Anxiety Disorders Interview Schedule, DiNardo and colleagues[51] found that pairs of trained clinicians achieved a test-retest reliability κ of 0.771 for diagnosing social phobia, which is considered quite satisfactory.

A review of the literature revealed several self-rating scales with demonstrated reliability that appear relevant to social phobics. These include the Willoughby Personality Schedule, a 25-item scale containing 14 items pertinent to social phobia[51]; the Fear Questionnaire developed by Marks and Mathews,[52] which contains a social phobia subscale; the Social Avoidance and Distress Scale, a 28-item true-false inventory; and the Fear of Negative Evaluation Scale, a 30-item true-false inventory, both developed by Watson and Friend[53]; and the interpersonal sensitivity subscale of the 90-item Hopkins Symptom Check List (SCL).[54]

There are few studies, however, reporting use of these scales with social phobics diagnosed according to DSM-III criteria. Patients meeting DSM-III criteria for social phobia have been found to have higher Willoughby Personality Schedule scores than patients with agoraphobia or simple phobia, suggesting utility for this scale.[55] The Social Avoidance and Distress and Fear of Negative Evaluation scales have been used to study socially inadequate psychiatric patients[56] and socially anxious community residents.[57] At present no one scale has demonstrated superiority, and investigators should use a battery of several self-rating scales.

Biological monitoring of social phobics in resting and performance situations has mainly involved measurement of heart rate, respiration, and skin conductance.[12,58-60] Lande[58] found that heart rate, respiration rate, and subjective anxiety were highly correlated during prolonged imaginal flooding of two social phobics. Johansson and Ost[59] monitored heart rate in 34 social phobics who participated in a short conversation with a person they did not know of the opposite sex, and found significant increases in heart rate that were highly correlated with self-perceived physiological arousal. In contrast, a comparison group of 36 claustrophobics who were placed in a small room experienced less heart rate increase and negative correlations between perceived and actual physiological arousal.

Measures not yet studied in social phobics might also include cardiac rhythm (to detect possible arrhythmias in subjects under stress) and in vivo biochemical monitoring of catecholamine levels, free fatty acid levels, cortisol levels, etc. A major limitation of biological-dependent measures for pharmacological studies is that most classes of psychotropic drugs influence biochemical and physiological factors regardless of therapeutic effects. Biological monitoring as an index of change is thus most suitable for nonsomatic treatment studies.

Performance evaluations can involve observations by profes-

11

Table 1.—Controlled Trials of MAOIs* in Social Phobia

Source	Sample Completers	Design	Daily Dosage	Duration	Final Outcome	Limitation
Tyrer et al[63]	Agoraphobia and social phobia (N = 32)	Phenelzine sulfate v placebo	Up to 90 mg/day	8 wk	Phenelzine superior to placebo on secondary phobias (patient rated) and overall outcome (psychiatrist rated)	Outcome of agoraphobics and social phobics not reported separately; unclear if patients had panic attacks
Solyom et al[64]	Agoraphobia, social phobia, specific phobia (N = 30)	Flooding v phenelzine plus brief psychotherapy v placebo plus brief psychotherapy	Up to 45 mg/day	3 mo	Flooding produced greater decrease on Wolpe Lang Fear Survey than phenelzine; phenelzine had greater antianxiety effects than other treatments; significant phenelzine-placebo difference in reduction of phobia, neurotic symptoms and social maladjustment; six of six patients stopping phenelzine therapy relapsed by 2 yr follow-up	Only phenelzine v placebo contrast assessed blindly; results not presented separately for different types of phobias; presence of panic attacks at baseline not specified or rated
Mountjoy et al[65]	Anxiety neurosis (N = 36), agoraphobia or social phobia (N = 22), depressive, neurosis (not discussed herein)	Phenelzine plus diazepam v placebo plus diazepam	Phenelzine to 75 mg/day; diazepam 5 mg three times a day	4 wk	Phenelzine plus diazepam superior on social phobia scale for all phobic patients; placebo plus diazepam superior on Hamilton Anxiety Scale in anxiety neurotics	Heterogeneous sample; duration short; small Ns for different treatment groups within each diagnosis; panic attacks not rated at baseline or completion
Solyom et al[66]	Agoraphobia or social phobia (N = 40)	2 × 2 phenelzine v placebo; exposure v no exposure	Up to 45 mg/day	6 wk	Phenelzine greater than placebo on anxiety reduction during exposure; exposure superior to nonexposure on several measures; no significant differences between exposure and phenelzine	Data not reported separately for two types of phobias; low phenelzine dose; lack of control for exposure; panic attacks not specified or rated

*MAOI indicates monoamine oxidase inhibitor.

sional or patient peer raters before and after treatment,[60,61] observation during role rehearsal in simulated situations in the clinic,[60] or evaluation of patient responses in staged situations where the patient is unaware of the staging, such as when research assistants call patients and pretend to be intrusive high-pressure salespeople.[62] All require further study in regard to utility, and the last in terms of research ethics. Interestingly, self-rated anxiety of social phobics in performance situations has been found to be higher than simultaneous peer observer ratings,[62] suggesting that exclusive reliance on one or the other source may be misleading.

TREATMENT

Two types of treatment for social phobia have been subject to at least some controlled evaluation. These are pharmacotherapy and behavioral therapy.

Pharmacological Treatment of Social Phobia

Social phobia has not been regarded by pharmacologists as a discrete syndrome in need of independent study. Instead it has been viewed as a more severe form of a normal human trait (social anxiety) whose treatment could be elucidated by analogue rather than clinical studies[22-24]; a manifestation of one or more personality disorders that are a priori unresponsive to drug treatment[4]; or as so related to agoraphobia[25-28] or simple phobia[9] that the groups could

be merged rather than studied independently.

The unfortunate result is that, with the exception of one small propranolol study,[70] no data on the drug responsiveness of a pure social phobic sample have been reported (to our knowledge). The results of analogue studies and clinical studies in mixed diagnostic groups, however, are suggestive of possible MAOI and β-adrenergic blocker efficacy.

MAOIs.—Several types of data suggest possible MAOI efficacy for social phobics. Four controlled studies found positive phenelzine effects in patient samples that consisted of both agoraphobics and social phobics (Table 1).[63-66] However, none reported response among the social phobics separately from the sample as a whole. Since agoraphobic patients have been shown to benefit from MAOIs,[63,71] it is impossible to be sure that the social phobics in the mixed patient studies benefited from MAOI therapy. Also limiting the usefulness of those studies were lack of specified diagnostic criteria, low dosages (45 mg/day or less of phenelzine sulfate in two), small sample sizes, and no specification as to whether patients also suffered spontaneous panic attacks or associated depressive features.

Nevertheless, all four studies did find some superiority of phenelzine over placebo. The earlier Solyom et al[64] study found a significant phenelzine effect on social maladjustment. In the

12

Source	Sample	Design	Dosage, Drug Type	Final Outcome
Liden and Gottfries[23]	15 musician volunteers from among the most symptomatic members of a professional symphony orchestra	Double-blind comparison of single-dose alprenolol and placebo, each taken before 2 concerts	Alprenolol 50 and 100 mg; nonselective β-blockers	Positive: alprenolol effects on palpitations, increased muscle tone, and tremor greater than for placebo
Gottschalk et al[24]	Nonanxious college volunteers	Double-blind comparison of short-term propranolol hydrochloride or placebo on response to stressful interview	Propranolol hydrochloride 60 mg in divided doses over 12-14 hr prior to testing; nonselective β-blockers	Negative: active drug effect in lowering anxiety prior to but not during interview
Krishnan[25]	32 college students; selection criteria not stated	Double-blind comparison of maintenance dose of oxprenolol or diazepam on examination performance	Oxprenolol 40 mg twice a day; diazepam 2 mg twice a day; nonselective β-blockers	Positive: only oxprenolol group showed better than predicted examination performance; only diazepam group expressed subjective sense of performance improvement; no statistical comparisons given
Siitonen and Janne[26]	17 amateur bowlers	Double-blind comparison of single-dose oxprenolol or placebo on bowling competitions	Oxprenolol 40 mg; nonselective β-blockers	Negative: no overall difference between group; oxprenolol helpful to subgroup of bowlers (one-third of sample) with high heart rate; 50% of oxprenolol sample bowled worse with drug than with placebo
James et al[27]	24 volunteer string musician players	Double-blind crossover comparison of single-dose oxprenolol and placebo taken before solo performance	Oxprenolol 40 mg; nonselective β-blockers	Positive: less subjective nervousness and better objective performance with oxprenolol
Brantigan et al[28]	29 volunteer musicians	Double-blind crossover comparison of single-dose propranolol and placebo taken before musical performance	Propranolol hydrochloride 40 mg; nonselective β-blockers	Positive: subjective anxiety, physical symptoms, and performance better with propranolol

Continued on p 734.

Mountjoy et al[66] study, phenelzine was significantly better than placebo in lowering social phobia scale scores for all phobic patients; also, fear of telephoning in public was the only measure to show significant correlation with overall improvement with phenelzine among patients as a whole. Controlled trials of MAOIs in social phobia are indicated.

The MAOI-tricyclic comparisons in outpatient depressives also suggest phenelzine efficacy in reducing social anxiety and social discomfort. Liebowitz et al[46] found phenelzine superior to both imipramine and placebo at six weeks on the interpersonal sensitivity (social discomfort) and paranoia (touchiness, not psychosis) SCL-90 scales in atypical depressives. Nies and co-workers[72] also found phenelzine superior to amitriptyline on the SCL-90 anxiety and interpersonal sensitivity scales in outpatient depressives. In both studies, interpersonal sensitivity was a better measure than depression for distinguishing between MAOI and tricyclic effects, suggesting a primary phenelzine effect on social discomfort.

This is especially interesting in light of Marks et al's[73] assertion that antidepressants have efficacy in anxiety disorders only by relieving associated dysphoric or depressive features. While a number of social phobics meet criteria for past or present major depression, atypical depression, or dysthymia, they appear to remain socially phobic during depression-free periods as well, suggesting that in this population, affective syndromes, when they occur, are secondary. This is in contrast to patients who become socially avoidant only during affective episodes who do not meet DSM-III social phobia criteria. The unremittingly depressed, chronically socially avoidant patient does, however, present a problem in differential diagnosis.

β-Adrenergic Blockers.—The only reported placebo-controlled study of β-blockers in social phobics involved 16 patients, all of whom were concomitantly receiving social skills training.[70] Patients were randomized to propranolol hydrochloride or placebo, and propranolol dose adjusted to lower heart rate to 60 beats per minute. No significant differences were noted between the six patients who received propranolol and the six patients who received placebo who completed the trial. Limitations of this study include small sample size, lack of specific diagnostic criteria, lack of controls and blind ratings for social skills training, and the fact that four patients had panic attacks.

Numerous analogue studies have examined the effect of β-blockers on anxiety during observed performance in nonpatient samples, which shares many features with social anxiety in patient samples, including symptom pattern and evoking situations. Of 11 controlled trials reviewed,[23-28] eight found a β-blocker superior to placebo in reducing some aspect of performance anxiety, while three others found no overall difference (Table 2). Since the majority of these studies involved administration of short-term doses prior to a performance situation, the findings are most relevant for those social phobics who experience only occasional and predictable anxiety episodes, such as those with public speaking or audition anxiety. For those social phobics whose symptoms occur more frequently or in less easily predicted situations, continuous treatment is more appropriate, and controlled studies

13

Source	Sample	Design	Dosage, Drug Type	Final Outcome
Neftel et al[29]	22 volunteer string musicians	Double-blind parallel group comparison of single-dose atenolol and placebo taken before performance with and without an audience	Atenolol 100 mg; cardioselective β-blockers	Positive: atenolol group showed less stress, fright, and performance impairment in front of audience than did placebo; effects statistically weak
Krope et al[30]	104 student volunteers	Double-blind parallel group comparison of single-dose mepindolol or placebo with real examinations	Mepindolol 5 or 10 mg; nonselective β-blockers	Negative: no drug placebo differences found for subjective anxiety or test performance
Hartley et al[31]	Sample 1: 16 student volunteers with high anxiety scores	Double-blind crossover of short-term propranolol and placebo, each taken before public speaking	Propranolol hydrochloride 40 mg; nonselective β-blockers	Positive: propranolol had significantly greater effect on self-report and observed anxiety than placebo
	Sample 2: 17 student volunteers with high anxiety scores and 12 with low scores	Same as above	Same as above	Propranolol more effective than placebo in reducing observed performance anxiety in the high anxiety group
James et al[32]	30 professional musicians	Double-blind crossover of single-dose pindolol and placebo taken before recitals	Pindolol 5 mg; nonselective β-blockers	Positive: pindolol more effective than placebo on anxiety; pindolol caused subjective but not objective improvement in musical performance
Desai et al[33]	44 normal student volunteers structured into high and low anxiety groups	Experiment 1: diazepam or placebo double-blind parallel group dosage; experiment 2: oxprenolol or placebo in double-blind parallel group design; memory task	Diazepam 5 mg; oxprenolol 80 mg; nonselective β-blockers	Negative: diazepam improved performance more than placebo in high anxiety group; no oxprenolol-placebo differences noted

of maintenance regimens of β-blockers are needed.

Ten of the 11 studies outlined in Table 2 involved nonselective β-blockers. However, the study by Neftel et al[29] used atenolol, a cardioselective β-blocker that penetrates the central nervous system far less well than propranolol.[74] In addition to the lower incidence of central nervous system side effects reported for atenolol, demonstration of efficacy in social phobia would support peripheral rather than central autonomic medication.

Response to β-blockers may discriminate social phobics from patients with panic disorder or agoraphobia with panic attacks. While β-blocker therapy in patients with agoraphobia or panic disorder has been only preliminarily assessed, available evidence suggests a lack of efficacy on a single-dosage trial. Noyes et al[36] found diazepam superior to propranolol in a four-week double-blind crossover study involving 21 patients with panic disorder or agoraphobia. Heiser and DeFrancisco[37] found that small doses of propranolol given for up to two weeks did not block panic attacks associated with agoraphobia. Also, short-term propranolol administration, which produced marked peripheral β-adrenergic blockade, did not block either the anxiety or tachycardia of lactate-induced panic attacks.[84]

Other Drugs.—There is a paucity of studies of tricyclics in social phobics. Two open[47,68] and one controlled study[69] have reported clomipramine hydrochloride efficacy in mixed samples containing social phobics but did not report outcome separately for the social phobics. In two recent MAOI-tricyclic studies of nonendogenous depression, tricyclics were less effective than MAOIs in reducing social anxiety.[45,71] Klein (personal communication, 1984) also found no evidence of imipramine efficacy among the social phobics included in his simple phobia group.[9]

To our knowledge, benzodiazepines have not been studied in social phobics. In analogue samples, the evidence for efficacy is conflicting.[33,35]

Controlled drug trials of social phobics (and other psychiatric disorders) should involve short-term response, maintenance, and discontinuation phases. Short-term response trials of six to eight weeks' duration answer the question of short-term efficacy. Maintenance trials, where responders to short-term phase trials continue double-blind to receive their study drug for an additional six weeks to six months, reveal whether further improvement occurs with longer treatment and whether short-term phase responses are durable or transient when therapy with medication is continued. Double-blind placebo-controlled discontinuation of drug responders after three to six months of treatment answers the important question of whether continued drug is needed to maintain therapeutic gains. Drug trials should also involve long-term follow-up to assess incidence of relapse following drug withdrawal.

Behavioral Treatment of Social Phobia

Behavioral treatment of social phobics has been the subject of a number of recent reviews[42,43,60,72-77] and will be only briefly summarized herein. The three principal forms of treatment that have been found useful in controlled studies are desensitization or exposure, social skills training, and cognitive restructuring.

On the basis of an extensive review, Emmelkamp[42] concluded that while systematic desensitization had consistently been found effective in the treatment of social anxiety in analogue populations, it was of limited value in clinical samples of social phobics. In contrast, a study by Shaw[78] comparing desensitization, flooding, and social skills training found "useful therapeutic gains" for all three treatments in a clinical population of social phobics. This study, however, did not include a "placebo" therapy control, so the contribution of nonspecific factors to therapeutic change cannot be assessed.

Several controlled studies have demonstrated the superiority of social skills training over systematic desensitization for socially

14

anxious individuals[46]; others did not find consistent differences.[55,76,79] As noted by Brady,[80,79] controlled studies of social skills training in psychiatric outpatients have usually involved loosely defined samples with "social inadequacy" or deficient social skills rather than rigorously classified social phobics. One exception is the previously mentioned study by Shaw[76] that compared the effects of desensitization, flooding, and social skills training on 30 social phobics and found no differences among treatments. Another is a study by Stravynski et al,[60] that compared social skills training and social skills plus cognitive modification in social phobics and found both helpful, with no differences between treatments. Since neither of these studies had a no-treatment control, the reported therapeutic gains cannot be specifically attributed to the treatments under study.

Cognitive therapies have been found helpful in reducing social anxiety,[81] test anxiety,[82] and speech anxiety[83] in analogue populations. Studies of cognitive therapy in clinical populations of social phobics, however, are for the most part lacking. Cognitive restructuring was found superior to desensitization and to a waiting list central in reducing symptoms in socially anxious community volunteers.[67] Kendrick et al[84] found cognitive therapy and behavioral rehearsal more effective than a waiting list control for severe musical performance anxiety assessed five weeks after treatment, although not at the completion of the treatment program.

It remains to be established whether behavioral techniques result in substantial or only modest therapeutic gains when administered to clinical populations of social phobics. It is also uncertain whether the various behavioral treatments have specific or nonspecific effects. That is, is desensitization specifically effective in patients with histories of prior traumatic social or performance experiences, and social skills training most useful for patients deficient in social skills? Or are the various behavioral therapies equally effective in social phobics regardless of preexisting history or baseline deficit? Ost et al[77] have also suggested that social skills training may be more effective for "behavioral reactors" and applied relaxation more effective for "physiological reactors" among social phobic samples.

In addition, no data exist as to how various behavior therapies compare with or interact with pharmacological treatments. Once the pharmacological and behavior therapy response patterns of social phobia are elucidated, the comparative and interactive effects of drug and behavior therapy will require assessment. Other forms of psychotherapy may also be of use but have not been systematically assessed in the treatment of social phobia.

CONCLUSION

Social phobia appears distinct from other phobic subtypes in terms of demographic and clinical features. The disorder is not uncommon and tends to be chronic and at times disabling. Alcoholism and depression are common associated syndromes. Analogue studies suggest efficacy for β-adrenergic blockers and several forms of behavior therapy, while clinical trials in mixed phobic populations suggest MAOIs may be of benefit.

Major uncertainties exist, however, concerning the definition, classification, prevalence, severity, etiology, pathophysiology, assessment, and treatment of social phobia. While social phobia has received some attention from British investigators, it has been dramatically neglected in the US mental health literature, except by behavior therapists. Interest in social phobia among American clinicians and researchers can be expected to grow, however, as the specialized anxiety clinics now being established continue to proliferate.

We believe that this offers a number of exciting opportunities. For one, while social phobics appear to be quite disabled, they may also be highly responsive to treatment, offering mental health professionals an opportunity for refined diagnostic and decisive therapeutic action. In this regard, social phobia may prove to be similar to certain depressive syndromes, or to panic disorder or agoraphobia with panic attacks.

Second, social phobics represent an important comparison group for developmental, biological, and treatment studies of other anxiety patients, particularly agoraphobics. Studying more than one phobic group provides a needed perspective when differences are found between a particular phobic subtype and normal controls, permitting determination of whether the differences are specific to that patient group or pertain to anxiety patients in general.

Social phobia also offers a fertile field for the study of the interaction of biological and psychological factors, both in terms of pathophysiology and treatment. Preliminary investigations suggest that both intrapsychic factors and biological hyperreactivity contribute to social phobic symptoms.

Finally, further research is needed to determine if patients with one anxiety disorder are at greater than expected risk for developing another anxiety disorder. If so, anxiety patients in general may ultimately be found to possess some core vulnerability from which, given certain additional factors, one or another anxiety disorder develops. However, greater recognition and agreement concerning often overlooked or misconstrued social phobias are necessary if the interrelationships of the various anxiety disorders are to be meaningfully assessed.

This investigation was supported in part by grants MH903-1163C, MHCR903C006, and RSDA MH-00416 from the National Institute of Mental Health (Dr Gorman).

References

1. Marks IM, Gelder MG: Different ages of onset in varieties of phobia. Am J Psychiatry 1966;123:218-221.
2. Marks IM: The classification of phobic disorders. Br J Psychiatry 1970;116:377-386.
3. Aimes PL, Gelder MG, Shaw PM: Social phobia: A comparative clinical study. Br J Psychiatry 1983;142:174-179.
4. Greenberg D, Stravynski A: Social phobia. Br J Psychiatry 1983; 143:526.
5. Pitts FN, McClure JN Jr: Lactate metabolism in anxiety neurosis. N Engl J Med 1967;277:1326-1336.
6. Liebowitz MR, Fyer AJ, Gorman JM, Dillon D, Appleby IL, Levy G, Anderson S, Levitt M, Palij M, Davies SO, Klein DF: Lactate provocation of panic attacks: I. Clinical and behavioral findings. Arch Gen Psychiatry 1984;41:764-770.
7. Liebowitz MR, Fyer AJ, Gorman JM, Dillon D, Davies S, Stein JM, Cohen B, Klein DF: Specificity of lactate infusions in social phobia v panic disorders. Am J Psychiatry, in press.
8. Klein DF: Delineation of two drug-responsive anxiety syndromes. Psychopharmacology 1964;5:397-408.
9. Zitrin CM, Klein DF, Woerner MG, Ross DC: Treatment of phobias: I. Comparison of imipramine and placebo. Arch Gen Psychiatry 1983;40:125-138.

10. Sheehan DV, Ballenger J, Jacobson G: Treatment of endogenous anxiety with phobic hysterical and hypochondriacal symptoms. Arch Gen Psychiatry 1980;37:51-59.
11. Lader MH, Gelder MG, Marks IM: Palmar skin-conductance measures as predictors of response to desensitization. J Psychosom Res 1967;11:283-290.
12. Weerts TC, Lang PJ: Psychophysiology of fear imagery: Differences between focal phobia and social performance anxiety. J Consult Clin Psychol 1978;46:1157-1159.
13. Gaind R, Suri AK, Thompson J: Use of beta blockers as an adjunct in behavioural techniques. Scot Med J 1975;20:284-286.
14. Bernadt MW, Silverstone T, Singleton W: Behavioural and subjective effects of beta-adrenergic blockade in phobia subjects. Br J Psychiatry 1980;137:452-457.
15. Agras S, Sylvester D, Oliveau D: The common fears and phobias. Compr Psychiatry 1969;10:151-156.
16. Myers JK, Weissman MM, Tischler GL, Holzer CE, Leaf PJ, Orvaschel H, Anthony JC, Boyd JH, Burke JD, Kramer M, Stoltzman R: Six-month prevalence of psychiatric disorders in three communities: 1980-1982. Arch Gen Psychiatry 1984;41:959-967.
17. Bryant B, Trower PE: Social difficulty in a student sample. Br J Ed Psychol 1974;44:13-21.

15

18. DiNardo PA, O'Brien GT, Barlow DH, Waddell MT, Blanchard EB: Reliability of *DSM-III* anxiety disorder categories using a new structured interview. *Arch Gen Psychiatry* 1983;40:1070-1074.

19. Munjack DJ, Moss HB: Affective disorder and alcoholism in families of agoraphobics. *Arch Gen Psychiatry* 1981;38:869-871.

20. Mullaney JA, Trippett CJ: Alcohol dependence and phobias: Clinical description and relevance. *Br J Psychiatry* 1979;135:563-573.

21. Smail P, Stockwell T, Canter S, Hodgson R: Alcohol dependence and phobia anxiety states: I. A prevalence study. *Br J Psychiatry* 1984;144: 53-57.

22. Dimsdale JE, Moss J: Short-term catecholamine response to psychological stress. *Psychosom Med* 1980;42:493-497.

23. Liden S, Gottfries CG: Beta-blocking agents in the treatment of catecholamine-induced symptoms in musicians. *Lancet* 1974;2:529.

24. Gottschalk LA, Stone WN, Gleser CG: Peripheral versus central mechanisms accounting for anti-anxiety effects of propranolol. *Psychosom Med* 1974;36:47-56.

25. Krishnan G: Oxprenolol in the treatment of examination nerves. *Scot Med J* 1975;20:288-289.

26. Siitonen L, Janne J: Effect of beta-blockade during bowling competitions. *Ann Clin Res* 1976;8:393-398.

27. James IM, Griffith DNW, Pearson RM, Newby P: Effect of oxprenolol on stage-fright in musicians. *Lancet* 1977;2:952-954.

28. Brantigan CO, Brantigan TA, Joseph N: Effect of beta blockade and beta stimulation on stage fright. *Am J Med* 1982;72:88-94.

29. Neftel KA, Adler RH, Kappell L, Rossi M, Dolder M, Kaser HE, Bruggesser HH, Vorkauf H: Stage fright in musicians: A model illustrating the effect of beta blockers. *Psychom Med* 1982;44:461-469.

30. Krope P, Kohrs A, Ott H, Wagner W, Fichts K: Evaluating mepindolol in a test model of examination anxiety in students. *Pharmacopsychiatria* 1982;15:41-47.

31. Hartley LR, Ungapen S, Davie I, Spencer DJ: The effect of beta adrenergic blocking drugs on speakers' performance and memory. *Br J Psychiatry* 1983;142:512-517.

32. James IM, Burgoyne W, Savage IT: Effect of pindilol on stress-related disturbances of musical performance: Preliminary communication. *J R Soc Med* 1983;76:194-196.

33. Desai N, Taylor-Davies A, Barnett DB: The effects of diazepam and oxprenolol on short term memory in individuals of high and low state anxiety. *Br J Clin Pharmacol* 1983;15:197-202.

34. Gorman JM, Levy GF, Liebowitz MR, McGrath PJ, Appleby IL, Dillon DJ, Davies SO, Klein DF: Effect of acute beta-adrenergic blockade on lactate-induced panic. *Arch Gen Psychiatry* 1983;40:1079-1082.

35. Kathol RG, Noyes RN Jr, Slymen DJ, Crowe RR, Clancy J, Kerber R: Propranolol in chronic anxiety disorders: A controlled study. *Arch Gen Psychiatry* 1980;37:1361-1365.

36. Noyes RN Jr, Anderson DJ, Clancy J, Crowe RR, Slymen D, Ghoneim MM, Hinrichs J: Diazepam and propranolol in panic disorder and agoraphobia. *Arch Gen Psychiatry* 1984;41:287-292.

37. Heiser JF, DeFrancisco D: The treatment of pathological panic states with propranolol. *Am J Psychiatry* 1976;133:1389-1394.

38. Hafner J, Milton F: The influence of propranolol on the exposure in vivo of agoraphobics. *Psychol Med* 1977;7:419-425.

39. Liebowitz MR, Gorman JM, Fyer AJ, Levitt M, Dillon D, Levy G, Appleby IL, Anderson S, Palij M, Davies SO, Klein DF: Lactate provocation of panic attacks: II. Biochemical and physiological findings. *Arch Gen Psychiatry*, in press.

40. Torgersen S: The nature and origin of common phobic fears. *Br J Psychiatry* 1979;134:343-351.

41. Sheehan DV: *The Anxiety Disease.* New York, Charles Scribner's Sons, 1983.

42. Emmelkamp PMG: *Phobic and Obsessive-Compulsive Disorder: Theory Research and Practice.* New York, Plenum Press, 1982.

43. Marks IM: *Cure and Care of Neuroses.* New York, John Wiley & Sons Inc, 1981.

44. Leary MR: *Understanding Social Anxiety: Social, Personality, and Clinical Perspectives.* Beverly Hills, Calif, Sage Publications Inc, 1983.

45. Nichols KA: Severe social anxiety. *Br J Med Psychol* 1974;47:301-306.

46. Liebowitz MR, Quitkin FM, Stewart JW, McGrath PJ, Harrison W, Rabkin J, Tricamo E, Markowitz JS, Klein DF: Phenelzine v imipramine in atypical depression: A preliminary report. *Arch Gen Psychiatry* 1984;41: 669-677.

47. Klein DF, Davis JM: *Diagnosis and Drug Treatment of Psychiatric Disorders.* Baltimore, Williams & Wilkins Co, 1969.

48. Freud S: *New Introductory Lectures to Psychoanalysis.* London, Hogarth Press, 1957, pp 110-113.

49. Parker G: Reported parental characteristics of agoraphobics and social phobics. *Br J Psychiatry* 1979;135:555-560.

50. Aprindell WA, Emmelkamp PMG, Monsma A, Brilman E: The role of perceived parental rearing practices in the aetiology of phobic disorders: A controlled study. *Br J Psychiatry* 1983;143:183-187.

51. Willoughby RR: Some properties of the Thurstone personality schedule and a suggested revision. *J Soc Psychol* 1932;3:401-424.

52. Marks IM, Mathews AM: Brief standard self-rating for phobic patients. *Behav Res Ther* 1982;17:263-267.

53. Watson D, Friend R: Measurement of social-evaluative anxiety. *J Consult Clin Psychol* 1969;33:448-457.

54. Derogatis LR, Lipman RS, Covi L: The SCL-90: An outpatient psychiatric rating scale: Preliminary report. *Psychopharmacol Bull* 1973; 9:13-28.

55. Turner RM, Meles D, DiTomasso R: Assessment of social anxiety: A controlled comparison among social phobics, obsessive-compulsives, agoraphobics, sexual disorders and simple phobics. *Behav Res Ther* 1983;21:181-183.

56. Marzillier JS, Lambert C, Kellett J: A controlled evaluation of systematic desensitization and social skills training for socially inadequate psychiatric patients. *Behav Res Ther* 1976;14:225-238.

57. Kanter NJ, Goldfried MR: Relative effectiveness of rational restructuring and self-control desensitization in the reduction of interpersonal anxiety. *Behav Res Ther* 1979;10:472-490.

58. Lande SD: Physiological and subjective measures of anxiety during flooding. *Behav Res Ther* 1982;20:81-88.

59. Johansson J, Ost LG: Perception of autonomic reactions and actual heart rate in phobic patients. *J Behav Assessment* 1982;4:133-143.

60. Brady JP: Social skills training for psychiatric patients: I. Concepts, methods and clinical results. *Am J Psychiatry* 1984;141:333-340.

61. Falloon IR: Psychiatric patients as raters of social behavior. *J Behav Ther Exp Psychiatry* 1980;11:215-217.

62. McEwan KL, Devins GM: Is increased arousal in social anxiety noticed by others? *J Abnorm Psychol* 1983;92:417-421.

63. Tyrer P, Candy J, Kelly D: A study of the clinical effects of phenelzine and placebo in the treatment of phobic anxiety. *Psychopharmacology* 1973;32:237-254.

64. Solyom L, Heseltine GFD, McClure DJ, Solyom C, Ledwedge B, Steinberg G: Behaviour therapy v drug therapy in the treatment of phobic neurosis. *Can J Psychiatry* 1973;18:25-31.

65. Mountjoy CQ, Roth M, Garside RF, Leitch IM: A clinical trial of phenelzine in anxiety depressive and phobic neuroses. *Br J Psychiatry* 1977;131:486-492.

66. Solyom C, Solyom L, LaPierre Y, Pecknold J, Morton L: Phenelzine and exposure in the treatment of phobias. *Biol Psychiatry* 1981;16:239-247.

67. Beaumont G: A large open multicentre trial of clomipramine (Anafranil) in the management of phobic disorders. *J Int Med Res* 1977;5:116-123.

68. Pecknold JC, McClure DJ, Appeltauer L, Allan T, Wrzesinski L: Does tryptophan potentiate clomipramine in the treatment of agoraphobic and social phobic patients? *Br J Psychiatry* 1982;140:484-490.

69. Allsopp LF, Cooper GL, Poole PH: Clomipramine and diazepam in the treatment of agoraphobia and social phobia in general practice. *Curr Med Res Opin* 1984;9:64-70.

70. Falloon IRH, Lloyd GG, Harpin RE: Real-life rehearsal with nonprofessional therapists. *J Nerv Ment Dis* 1981;169:180-184.

71. Kelly D, Guirguis W, Frommer E, Mitchell-Heggs N, Sargant W: Treatment of phobic states with antidepressants: A retrospective study of 246 patients. *Br J Psychiatry* 1970;116:387-398.

72. Nies A, Howard D, Robinson DS: Antianxiety effects of MAO inhibitors, in Mathew RJ (ed): *The Biology of Anxiety.* New York, Brunner/Mazel Inc, 1982, pp 123-133.

73. Marks IM, Gray S, Cohen SD: Imipramine and brief therapist-aided exposure in agoraphobics having self-exposure homework: A controlled trial. *Arch Gen Psychiatry* 1983;40:153-162.

74. Weiner N: Drugs that inhibit adrenergic nerves and block adrenergic receptors, in Gilman AG, Goodman LS, Gilman A (eds): *The Pharmacological Basis of Therapeutics.* New York, Macmillan Publishing Co Inc, 1980, pp 176-210.

75. Stravynski A, Shahar A: The treatment of social dysfunction in nonpsychotic outpatients: A review. *J Nerv Ment Dis* 1983;171:721-728.

76. Brady JP: Social skills training for psychiatric patients: II. Clinical outcome studies. *Am J Psychiatry* 1984;141:491-498.

77. Ost LG, Jerremalm A, Johansson J: Individual response patterns and the effects of different behavioral methods in the treatment of social phobia. *Behav Res Ther* 1980;19:1-16.

78. Shaw P: A comparison of three behaviour therapies in the treatment of social phobia. *Br J Psychiatry* 1979;134:620-623.

79. Hall R, Goldberg D: The role of social anxiety in social interaction difficulties. *Br J Psychiatry* 1977;131:610-615.

80. Stravynski A, Marks I, Yule W: Social skills problems in neurotic outpatients. *Arch Gen Psychiatry* 1982;39:1378-1385.

81. Schelver SR, Gutsch KU: The effects of self-administered cognitive therapy on social-evaluative anxiety. *J Clin Psychol* 1983;39:658-666.

82. Morris LW, Engle WB: Assessing various coping strategies and their effects on test performance and anxiety. *J Clin Psychol* 1981;37:165-171.

83. Weissberg M: A comparison of direct and vicarious treatments of speech anxiety: Desensitization with coping imagery and cognitive modification. *Behav Ther* 1977;8:606-620.

84. Kendrick MJ, Craig KD, Lawson DM, Davidson PO: Cognitive and behavioral therapy for musical-performance anxiety. *J Consult Clin Psychol* 1982;50:353-362.

The Cross-national Epidemiology of Panic Disorder

Myrna M. Weissman, PhD; Roger C. Bland, MB; Glorisa J. Canino, PhD; Carlo Faravelli, MD; Steven Greenwald, MA; Hai-Gwo Hwu, MD; Peter R. Joyce, PhD; Elie G. Karam, MD; Chung-Kyoon Lee, MD; Joseph Lellouch, PhD; Jean-Pierre Lépine, MD; Stephen C. Newman, MD; Mark A. Oakley-Browne, PhD; Maritza Rubio-Stipec, MA; J. Elisabeth Wells, PhD; Priya J. Wickramaratne, PhD; Hans-Ulrich Wittchen, PhD; Eng-Kung Yeh, MD

Background: Epidemiological data on panic disorder from community studies from 10 countries around the world are presented to determine the consistency of findings across diverse cultures.

Method: Data from independently conducted community surveys from 10 countries (the United States, Canada, Puerto Rico, France, West Germany, Italy, Lebanon, Taiwan, Korea, and New Zealand), using the Diagnostic Interview Schedule and *DSM-III* criteria and including over 40 000 subjects, were analyzed with appropriate standardization for age and sex differences among subjects from different countries.

Results: The lifetime prevalence rates for panic disorder ranged from 1.4 per 100 in Edmonton, Alberta, to 2.9 per 100 in Florence, Italy, with the exception of that in Taiwan, 0.4 per 100, where rates for most psychiatric disorders are low. Mean age at first onset was usually in early to middle adulthood. The rates were higher in female than male subjects in all countries. Panic disorder was associated with an increased risk of agoraphobia and major depression in all countries.

Conclusions: Panic disorder is relatively consistent, with a few exceptions, in rates and patterns across different countries. It is unclear why the rates of panic and other psychiatric disorders are lower in Taiwan.

Arch Gen Psychiatry. 1997;54:305-309

The affiliations of the authors appear in the "Acknowledgment" section at the end of the article.

WHILE THE symptoms of panic disorder have been well described for centuries, diagnostic criteria for panic disorder as a separate entity, distinct from other anxiety disorders, first appeared in the official American Psychiatric Association's *Diagnostic and Statistical Manual of Mental Disorders, Third Edition* in 1980.[1] Since then, a considerable amount of information has appeared on familial risk, pathogenesis, morbidity, and treatment of panic disorder.[2-5]

The epidemiology of panic disorder, its prevalence, demographic variations, and comorbidity with other psychiatric disorders have been well described in the United States based on a community survey of 18 571 adults living in 5 US communities in the 1980s and a more recent US national survey of 8098 adults.[6-9]

In this article, we present epidemiological data on panic disorder from community surveys conducted in 10 countries around the world using similar diagnostic methods to determine the consistency of findings across diverse cultures.

RESULTS

PREVALENCE, AGE AT ONSET, AND SEX DIFFERENCES

The annual rate of panic disorder ranged from 1.7 per 100 in West Germany to 0.2 per 100 in Taiwan (**Table 2**), a country that has low rates of all psychiatric disorders.[21] The lifetime rate ranged from 2.9 per 100 in Florence to 0.4 per 100 in Taiwan. The rates are consistently higher in female compared with male individuals in every country. The age at onset of panic disorder is usually the early to middle 20s, with later onset in West Germany (age at onset, 35.5 years) and Korea (age at onset, 32.1 years). In the Beirut study, there were 5 persons with panic disorder, all within the past 6

METHODS

DESCRIPTION OF CROSS-NATIONAL SITES

A detailed description of the cross-national sites has been previously published.[10] This cross-national collaboration included investigators from 10 countries who had conducted epidemiological community surveys based on the Diagnostic Interview Schedule, Version III,[11,12] and the *DSM-III* criteria.[1] The sites span diverse geographical, political, and cultural areas in North America, the Caribbean, Europe, the Middle East, the Orient, and the Pacific Rim. The translation, modification, and piloting of the Diagnostic Interview Schedule were made by the investigators in each country as appropriate, and details on the translations plus the methods used are included in the references.

The data from the National Institute of Mental Health Epidemiological Catchment Area Study (ECA)[13] were derived from 5 US communities (New Haven, Conn; Baltimore, Md; St Louis, Mo; the Piedmont County region of North Carolina; and Los Angeles, Calif). The Edmonton Survey of Psychiatric Disorders[14,15] was conducted in the city of Edmonton, Alberta. The Puerto Rico Study of Psychiatric Disorders[16] included persons living in a household throughout Puerto Rico, in addition to those household members temporarily away and those in institutions. The French Study of Psychiatric Disorders[17] was conducted in Savigny, a newly built city located near Paris. The Munich Follow-up Study from West Germany[18] was a 7-year follow-up investigation of a stratified random general population sample drawn from the adult population of the former Federal Republic of Germany (West Germany) in 1974. The Florence Community Survey of Anxiety Disorders from Italy[19] included 1100 persons who were randomly selected from the lists of persons registered with 6 general medical practitioners living in 3 districts of Florence. The Beirut War Events and Depression Study[20] was conducted in Lebanon and included the assessment of panic disorder in the second wave of interviews. Four communities with differential exposure to acts of war were studied: 2 communities within the city of Beirut (Ashrafieh and Ain Remmaneh), and 2 communities outside Beirut proper (Kornet Shehwan and Bejjeh). The Taiwan psychiatric epidemiology project[21] sampled 3 population areas representing metropolitan Taipei and township and rural areas throughout Taiwan. The Korean Epidemiologic Study of Mental Disorders[22,23] sampled persons in urban Seoul and scattered rural regions across the Republic of Korea. The Christchurch Psychiatric Epidemiology Study[24,25] included adults living in Christchurch in the South Island of New Zealand, oversampling young female individuals.

For comparison purposes, data from the National Comorbidity Survey (NCS),[8] a representative sample of 8098 persons aged 15 to 54 years living in the 48 coterminous US states and conducted during 1990-1992, were included. These data are considered separately because different diagnostic assessment was done using the Composite International Diagnostic Interview,[26] on whose basis *DSM-III-R* criteria–based diagnoses were made.[27]

Table 1 gives sample size, response rate, age, and sex distribution of each study.

SAMPLING DESIGN

The ECA, Edmonton, Puerto Rico, and Christchurch sites were household probability samples; the remaining sites, except for West Germany, were drawn as simple random samples constructed so that each household member had the same probability of selection. Because of unequal selection probability of a respondent in the United States, Edmonton, Puerto Rico, and Christchurch, a design weight was computed. For those sites drawn as random samples, the design weight was set at 1.0 for each respondent.

The stratification method used for the phase II 1981 follow-up in West Germany included all subjects who had high scores on the clinical self-rating scales at the phase I investigation in 1974, plus 40% of the sample who were randomly drawn from among the subjects successfully interviewed in phase I. The design weight for West Germany was computed by weighting back to the original 1974 sample by correcting for the proportion of high and low scorers in that sample.[18]

STATISTICAL ANALYSIS

To make valid comparisons of rates across sites, the rates of panic disorder at each site were standardized to the age and sex distribution of the 1980 US census. Analyses are reported only for the 18- to 64-year-old group, with values for West Germany based on ages 26 to 64 years. Data in the NCS included ages 18 to 54 years as no one older than 54 years was sampled.

The design-weighted rates for the ECA, Edmonton, Puerto Rico, West Germany, and Christchurch, and the raw rates for the other sites have been standardized to the 1980 US census. The standardization was done according to methods described by Breslow and Day.[28(pp52-57)] Prevalence rates weighted in this manner give estimates as if each site has the same age and sex distribution of the 1980 US census. Comparisons of the age at onset across sites were standardized in a similar manner. Because the focus of the comorbidity analysis was the association of panic disorder with agoraphobia and major depression within each site (rather than between sites), the proportions computed for comorbidity were weighted to the design characteristics of each sample.

The data for the NCS were weighted to the national population characteristics defined by the 1989 US National Health Interview Survey[29] and not standardized to the ECA.

All analyses were done with Statistical Analysis System software.[30] The FREQ procedure[30] was used when determining rates and proportions. The UNIVARIATE procedure[30] was used to determine the age at onset. To determine statistical association between panic disorder and another psychiatric disorder, logistic regression was used (PROC LOGIST),[30] weighted to the design characteristics of each sample and adjusted by age and sex, and an odds ratio with its 95% confidence interval was derived from logit procedures.[31]

months, which explains why the annual and lifetime rates are the same. The prevalence rates of panic disorder are higher in the NCS than in the other countries or the ECA; however, the sex ratio and age at onset are comparable to those in the other sites.

COMORBIDITY

As reported in numerous clinical studies,[2] panic disorder is significantly associated with increased risk of both major depression and agoraphobia at every cross-

Table 1. Demographic Characteristics Across Sites

Characteristics	ECA*	Edmonton, Alberta	Puerto Rico	Savigny,† France	West Germany	Florence, Italy	Beirut, Lebanon	Taiwan	Korea	Christchurch, New Zealand	NCS‡
No. of study participants	18571	3258	1513	1746	481§	1100	234	11004	5100	1498	8098
Study period	1980-1984	1983-1986	1984	1987-1988	1981	1984	1987-1989	1982-1985	1984	1986	1990-1992
Response rate, %	76	72	91	63	76	100	77	90	83	70	84
Female, %	59	59	57	62	52	54	58	48	52	66	52
Age, y, at interview, %‖											
18-25	14	22	22	13	...¶	9	17	25	20	20	19
26-45	33	46	50	71	55	36	47	43	49	55	59
46-64	21	21	28	14	45	35	31	24	30	24	16

*Five US sites (New Haven, Conn; Baltimore Md; St Louis, Mo; Piedmont County, North Carolina; Los Angeles, Calif) from the Epidemiologic Catchment Area (ECA) study.
†Suburb of Paris.
‡Forty-eight coterminous US states; participants' ages, 18-54 years, from the National Comorbidity Survey (NCS).
§Drawn, in 1981, from 1366 subjects in 1974.
‖In raw percent, percents may not add to 100 for age because of missing values.
¶No subjects in this category.

Table 2. Prevalence Rates and Age at Onset for Panic Disorder Across Sites: Age 18-64 Years*

	Rate per 100 (SE)					
		Lifetime				
			Sex			
Site	Annual	Total	F	M	F/M Ratio	Mean Age at Onset, y (SD)
ECA†	1.0 (0.11)	1.7 (0.14)	2.3 (0.22)	1.0 (0.15)	2.3 (0.18)	24.8 (9.1)
Edmonton, Alberta	0.9 (0.19)	1.4 (0.24)	1.9 (0.38)	0.9 (0.28)	2.1 (0.37)	23.7 (10.4)
Puerto Rico	1.1 (0.30)	1.7 (0.37)	1.8 (0.54)	1.4 (0.50)	1.3 (0.45)	27.3 (9.6)
Savigny,‡ France	0.9 (0.30)	2.2 (0.46)	3.0 (0.74)	1.3 (0.50)	2.3 (0.47)	25.4 (8.6)
West Germany	1.7 (0.67)	2.6 (0.84)	3.8 (1.38)	1.4 (0.88)	2.7 (0.73)	35.5 (12.5)
Florence, Italy	1.3 (0.45)	2.9 (0.83)	3.9 (0.96)	1.2 (0.70)	3.2 (0.62)	26.1 (9.6)
Beirut, Lebanon	2.1 (0.99)	2.1 (0.99)	3.1 (1.65)	1.1 (1.02)	2.8 (1.09)	27.8 (3.6)
Taiwan	0.2 (0.04)	0.4 (0.06)	0.6 (0.10)	0.2 (0.07)	3.0 (0.37)	24.2 (8.9)
Korea	1.5 (0.17)	1.7 (0.19)	2.9 (0.34)	0.5 (0.15)	5.8 (0.32)	32.1 (10.3)
Christchurch, New Zealand	1.3 (0.34)	2.1 (0.43)	3.3 (0.74)	0.7 (0.37)	4.7 (0.55)	23.2 (7.8)
NCS§	2.2 (0.24)	3.5 (0.30)	5.1 (0.50)	1.9 (0.32)	2.7 (0.19)	25.5 (6.9)

*All values, except for the National Comorbidity Survey (NCS), standardized to the age and sex distribution of the 1980 US census.
†Five US sites (New Haven, Conn; Baltimore, Md; St Louis, Mo; Piedmont County, North Carolina; Los Angeles, Calif) from the Epidemiologic Catchment Area (ECA) study.
‡A suburb of Paris.
§Forty-eight coterminous US states; ages 18-54 from the NCS. Data weighted according to national population characteristics defined by the 1989 US National Health Interview Survey.[29]

national site and in the NCS (**Table 3**). Based on lifetime rates, the odds ratios for comorbidity of panic disorder with agoraphobia range from 7.5 in the ECA to 21.4 in Puerto Rico, and those of panic disorder with major depression range from 3.8 in Savigny to 20.1 in Edmonton. In the NCS, the odds ratio is 10.6 for agoraphobia and 5.7 for major depression.

COMMENT

The major findings from these epidemiological studies
. . . .
patterns (sex ratios, age at onset, and comorbidity) of panic disorder across diverse countries and the consistency with the clinical description of panic disorder.[2]

The limitation of the cross-national data must be acknowledged. While more than 40 000 subjects are included in 11 studies, the samples are very small for some sites (West Germany, Beirut). Moreover, the West German study is a follow-up and has an older sample, so the age at onset should be interpreted with caution in relation to the other sites. Data on comorbidity were not available in Florence. The NCS did not include anyone older than 54 years. Possible medical causes of panic disorder that may vary across sites were not ruled out. The biases introduced by use of a . . . . are unknown. Finally, no data are presented or are available using comparable design and diagnostic methods from most other parts of the world.

Site	Agoraphobia			Major Depression		
	In Persons With Panic, %	In Persons Without Panic, %	OR (95% CI)	In Persons With Panic, %	In Persons Without Panic, %	ORs (95% CI)
ECA†	33.3	5.5	7.5 (5.6-10.1)	32.8	4.7	8.7 (6.4-11.7)
Edmonton, Alberta	31.8	2.7	15.1 (7.6-29.9)	68.2	9.2	20.1 (10.4-38.8)
Puerto Rico	58.2	6.0	21.4 (9.2-50.2)	38.2	3.7	15.3 (6.4-36.6)
Savigny,‡ France	48.9	6.5	12.7 (6.8-24.0)	48.9	17.3	3.8 (2.1-7.1)
Taiwan	22.5	1.4	17.2 (8.0-37.2)	22.5	1.3	19.6 (9.1-42.1)
Korea	34.7	2.1	17.2 (10.6-27.8)	28.4	2.5	13.2 (8.0-21.6)
Christchurch, New Zealand	29.5	3.4	9.4 (4.2-21.2)	40.8	11.2	4.6 (2.2-9.4)
NCS§	38.8	5.1	10.6 (7.3-15.5)	54.5	16.0	5.7 (4.0-8.1)

*Proportions are weighted to the design characteristics of each site, except for the National Comorbidity Survey (NCS). Odds ratios (ORs) with 95% confidence intervals (CIs) are weighted to the design characteristics of the sample and adjusted by age and sex within each site. Data were not available from Florence, Italy. West Germany and Beirut, Lebanon, were excluded because of small sample size.
†Five US sites (New Haven, Conn; Baltimore, Md; St Louis, Mo; Piedmont County, NC; Los Angeles, Calif) from the Epidemiologic Catchment Area (ECA) study.
‡A suburb of Paris.
§Forty-eight coterminous US states; ages 18-54 from the NCS. Data weighted according to national population characteristics defined by the 1989 US National Health Interview Survey.[29]

While the patterns are similar to those in other countries, the rates of panic disorder (as well as most other disorders studied) were lower in Taiwan than in the other countries. The reasons for these differences are unclear and have been examined independently by others.[32] The Taiwanese investigators[32] noted that the DSM-III is widely used in Taiwan, so these were not new criteria. The Taiwan study[32] had a higher proportion of rural settings than the other ECA sites; however, rural-urban comparisons of rates between the ECA and Taiwan still resulted in lower rates in Taiwan. Another analysis[33] showed that the rates of cognitive impairment and generalized anxiety disorders (both of which emphasize somatic symptoms and are less stigmatized disorders in Taiwan) were more comparable to the rates of these disorders in some of the ECA sites. This comparability suggests that social stigma and cultural reluctance to endorse mental symptoms may account for some, but not all, of the differences.[33] This factor is unlikely to explain the lower rates of panic disorder that manifest mainly in somatic symptoms. A study of the rates of psychiatric disorders in Chinese living in the United States and in the Peoples' Republic of China would be useful in determining whether the lower rate of panic and other disorders is uniquely Chinese on a cultural or genetic basis. The older age at onset in West Germany could result from the older age of the sample and possibly less accurate dating of the age at onset, a birth cohort effect, or variability attributable to small sample size. The reason for the close female-male ratio in Puerto Rico is unclear.[16]

The NCS has the highest lifetime rates of panic disorder, which is twice as high as the rate in the ECA (3.5 per 100 and 1.7 per 100, respectively). These differences may be caused by a period effect with increasing rates between the ECA conducted in the early 1980s and the NCS conducted in the early 1990s. It could also be caused by differences in the DSM-III and DSM-III-R criteria for panic disorder; DSM-III requires 3 panic attacks in a 3-week period, while the DSM-III-R criteria

used in the NCS are broader than the DSM-III criteria because they include persistent worry about having another attack rather than having 4 in 4 weeks. This means that some people make criteria for panic disorder in the NCS even if they only had 1 attack in their life as long as they worried about having another one for a month after the attack. The DSM-III-R also includes an additional symptom (nausea or abdominal distress) as one of the criteria. Finally, the difference in rates between the ECA and NCS could be a result of the difference in the diagnostic assessment. The diagnostic interview used in the NCS, the Composite International Diagnostic Interview,[26] included memory probes that could have increased recollection and led to higher rates. The reasons for the higher rates for most disorders in the NCS compared with those in the ECA have been under study by the National Institute of Mental Health in collaboration with Ronald Kessler, PhD. Interestingly, while we also find higher rates of panic disorder in the NCS, there was similarity in age at onset, sex ratios, and comorbidity compared with the other cross-national sites.

Accepted for publication September 16, 1996.

From the Department of Psychiatry, College of Physicians and Surgeons of Columbia University, and Division of Clinical and Genetic Epidemiology, New York State Psychiatric Institute (Drs Weissman and Wickramaratne and Mr Greenwald), New York, NY; the Department of Psychiatry, University of Alberta, Edmonton (Drs Bland and Newman); Behavioral Sciences Research Institute, University of Puerto Rico, San Juan (Dr Canino and Ms Rubio-Stipec); Department of Neurology and Psychiatry, Florence University Medical School, Florence, Italy (Dr Faravelli); Departments of Psychiatry, National Taiwan University Hospital (Drs Hwu and Yeh) and Taipei Medical College (Dr Yeh), Taipei, Taiwan; Departments of Psychological Medicine (Drs Joyce and Oakley-Browne) and Public Health and General Practice (Dr Wells),

Christchurch School of Medicine, Christchurch, New Zealand; Department of Psychiatry and Psychology, St George Hospital and American University of Beirut, and St Joseph University, Beirut, Lebanon (Dr Karam); Keyo Psychiatric Institute, Kyongii-Do, Korea (Dr Lee); Institut National de la Santé et de la Recherche Médicale, Unité 169, Villejuif (Dr Lellouch), and Hôpital Fernand Widal, Paris (Dr Lépine), France; and Max Planck Institute for Psychiatry, Clinical Institute, Munich, Germany (Dr Wittchen).

These analyses were supported by grants MH37592 and MH30906 from the National Institute of Mental Health, Rockville, Md.

Reprints: Myrna M. Weissman, PhD, College of Physicians and Surgeons of Columbia University, Division of Clinical and Genetic Epidemiology, New York State Psychiatric Institute, 722 W 168th St, Unit 14, New York, NY 10032 (E-mail: weissman@child.cpmc.columbia.edu).

REFERENCES

1. American Psychiatric Association, Committee on Nomenclature and Statistics. *Diagnostic and Statistical Manual of Mental Disorders, Third Edition.* Washington, DC: American Psychiatric Association; 1980.
2. Klerman GL, Hirschfeld RMA, Weissman MM, Pellicier Y, Ballenger JC, Costa e Silva JA, Judd LL,Keller, MB. *Panic Anxiety and Its Treatments.* Washington, DC: American Psychiatric Press; 1993.
3. Markowitz JS, Weissman MM, Ouellette R, Lish JD, Klerman GL. Quality of life in panic disorder. *Arch Gen Psychiatry.* 1989;46:984-992.
4. Klerman GL, Weissman MM, Ouellette R, Johnson J, Greenwald S. Panic attacks in the community: social morbidity and health care utilization. *JAMA.* 1991;265:742-746.
5. Weissman MM, Klerman GL, Markowitz JS, Ouellette R. Suicidal ideation and suicide attempts in panic disorder and attacks. *N Engl J Med.* 1989;321:1209-1214.
6. Eaton WW, Dryman A, Weissman MM. Panic and phobias. In: Robins LN, Regier DA, eds. *Psychiatric Disorders in America: The Epidemiologic Catchment Area Study.* New York, NY: The Free Press; 1991:155-179.
7. Horwath E, Johnson J, Hornig CD. Epidemiology of panic disorder in African-Americans. *Am J Psychiatry.* 1993;150:465-469.
8. Kessler RC, McGonable KA, Zhao S, Nelson CB, Hughes M, Eshleman S, Wittchen HU, Kendler KS. Lifetime and 12-month prevalence of *DSM-III-R* psychiatric disorders in the United States: results from the National Comorbidity Survey. *Arch Gen Psychiatry.* 1994;51:8-19.
9. Eaton WW, Kessler RC, Wittchen HU, Magee WJ. Panic and panic disorder in the United States. *Am J Psychiatry.* 1994;151:413-420.
10. Weissman MM, Bland R, Canino G, Faravelli C, Greenwald S, Hwu HG, Joyce PR, Karam EG, Lee CK, Lellouch J, Lépine JP, Newman S, Rubio-Stipec M, Wells JE, Wickramaratne P, Wittchen HU, Yeh EK. Cross-national epidemiology of major depression and bipolar disorder. *JAMA.* 1996;276:293-299.
11. Robins LN, Helzer JE, Croughan JL. The NIMH diagnostic interview schedule: its history, characteristics, and validity. *Arch Gen Psychiatry.* 1981;38:381-389.
12. Robins LN, Orvaschel H, Anthony J, Blazer D, Burnam A, Burke J. The Diagnostic Interview Schedule. In: Eaton WW, Kessler LG, eds. *Epidemiologic Field Methods in Psychiatry: The NIMH Epidemiologic Catchment Area Program.* Orlando, Fla: Academic Press; 1985.
13. Robins LN, Regier DA, eds. *Psychiatric Disorders in America: The Epidemiologic Catchment Area Study.* New York, NY: The Free Press; 1991.
14. Orn H, Newman SC, Bland RC. Design and field methods of the Edmonton survey of psychiatric disorders. *Acta Psychiatr Scand Suppl.* 1988;77:17-23.
15. Bland RC, Orn H, Newman SC. Lifetime prevalence of psychiatric disorders in Edmonton. *Acta Psychiatr Scand.* 1988;77(suppl 338):24-32.
16. Canino GJ, Bird HR, Shrout PE, Rubio-Stipec M, Bravo M, Martinez R, Sesman M, Guevara,LM. The prevalence of specific psychiatric disorders in Puerto Rico. *Arch Gen Psychiatry.* 1987;44:727-735.
17. Lépine JP, Lellouch J, Lovell A, Teherani M, Ha C, Verdier-Taillefer MH, Rambourg N, Lemperiere T. Anxiety and depressive disorders in a French population: methodology and preliminary results. *Psychiatr Psychobiol.* 1989;4:267-274.
18. Wittchen HU, Essau CA, von Zerssen D, Krieg JC, Zaudig M. Lifetime and six-month prevalence of mental disorders in the Munich follow-up study. *Eur Arch Psychiatry Clin Neurosci.* 1992;241:247-258.
19. Faravelli C, Degl'Innocenti BG, Aiazzi L, Incerpi G, Pallanti S. Epidemiology of anxiety disorder in Florence. *J Affect Disord.* 1989;19:1-5.
20. Karam E. Dépression et guerres du Liban: méthodologie d'une recherche. *Ann Psychol SciEduc, Univ St Joseph (Beyrouth).* 1992:99-106.
21. Hwu HG, Yeh EK, Chang LY. Prevalence of psychiatric disorders in Taiwan defined by the Chinese diagnostic interview schedule. *Acta Psychiatr Scand.* 1989;79:136-147.
22. Lee CK, Kwak YS, Yamamoto J, Rhee H, Kim YS, Han JH, Choi J, Lee YH. Psychiatric epidemiology in Korea, I: gender and age differences in Seoul. *J Nerv Ment Dis.* 1990;178:242-246.
23. Lee CK, Kwak YS, Yamamoto J, Rhee H, Kim YS, Han JH, Choi J, Lee YH. Psychiatric epidemiology in Korea, II: urban and rural differences in Seoul. *J Nerv Ment Dis.* 1990;178:247-252.
24. Wells JE, Bushnell JA, Hornblow AR, Joyce PR, Oakley-Browne MA. Christchurch psychiatric epidemiology study, I: methodology and lifetime prevalence for specific psychiatric disorders. *Aust N Z J Psychiatry.* 1989;23:315-326.
25. Oakley-Browne MA, Joyce PR, Wells JE, Bushnell JA, Hornblow AR. Christchurch psychiatric epidemiology study, II: six month and other period prevalences for specific psychiatric disorders. *Aust N Z J Psychiatry.* 1989;23:327-340.
26. World Health Organization. *Composite International Diagnostic Interview (CIDI), Version 1.0.* Geneva, Switzerland: World Health Organization; 1990.
27. American Psychiatric Association, Committee on Nomenclature and Statistics. *Diagnostic and Statistical Manual of Mental Disorders, Third Edition,Revised.* Washington, DC: American Psychiatric Association; 1987.
28. Breslow NE, Day NE. *Statistical Methods in Cancer Research.* Lyon, France: International Agency for Research on Cancer; 1987:2.
29. US Department of Health and Human Services. *National Health Interview Survey: 1989.* Hyattsville, Md: National Center for Health Statistics; 1992.
30. SAS Institute Inc. *SAS Procedures Guide, Version 6.* 3rd ed. Cary, NC: SAS Institute Inc; 1990.
31. Kleinbaum DG, Kupper LL, Morgenstern H. *Epidemiologic Research: Principles and Quantitative Methods.* Belmont, Calif: Wadsworth Inc; 1982.
32. Compton WM, Helzer JE, Hwu, HG, Yeh EK, McEvoy L, Tipp JE, Spitznagel EL. New methods in cross-cultural psychiatry: psychiatric illness in Taiwan and the United States. *Am J Psychiatry.* 1991;148:1697-1704.
33. Yeh EK, Hwu HG, Yeh YL, Chang LY, Yamamoto J, Golding JM. *Life Change Events, Social Support and Mental Disorders: Taiwan-US Cross-cultural Study.* Taipei, Taiwan: Chiang Ching Kuo Foundation for International Scholarly Exchange; June 1994. Research Report Monograph (RG 010-9).

Posttraumatic Stress Disorder in the National Comorbidity Survey

Ronald C. Kessler, PhD; Amanda Sonnega, PhD; Evelyn Bromet, PhD; Michael Hughes, PhD; Christopher B. Nelson, MPH, PhD

Background: Data were obtained on the general population epidemiology of *DSM-III-R* posttraumatic stress disorder (PTSD), including information on estimated lifetime prevalence, the kinds of traumas most often associated with PTSD, sociodemographic correlates, the comorbidity of PTSD with other lifetime psychiatric disorders, and the duration of an index episode.

Methods: Modified versions of the *DSM-III-R* PTSD module from the Diagnostic Interview Schedule and of the Composite International Diagnostic Interview were administered to a representative national sample of 5877 persons aged 15 to 54 years in the part II subsample of the National Comorbidity Survey.

Results: The estimated lifetime prevalence of PTSD is 7.8%. Prevalence is elevated among women and the previously married. The traumas most commonly

associated with PTSD are combat exposure and witnessing among men and rape and sexual molestation among women. Posttraumatic stress disorder is strongly comorbid with other lifetime *DSM-III-R* disorders. Survival analysis shows that more than one third of people with an index episode of PTSD fail to recover even after many years.

Conclusions: Posttraumatic stress disorder is more prevalent than previously believed, and is often persistent. Progress in estimating age-at-onset distributions, cohort effects, and the conditional probabilities of PTSD from different types of trauma will require future epidemiologic studies to assess PTSD for all lifetime traumas rather than for only a small number of retrospectively reported "most serious" traumas.

(Arch Gen Psychiatry. 1995;52:1048-1060)

From the Institute for Social Research (Drs Kessler and Sonnega) and the Department of Sociology (Dr Kessler), University of Michigan, Ann Arbor; Department of Psychiatry and Behavioral Science, State University of New York at Stony Brook (Dr Bromet); Department of Sociology, Virginia Polytechnic Institute and State University, Blacksburg, Va (Dr Hughes); and Max Planck Institute of Psychiatry—Clinical Institute, Munich, Germany (Dr Nelson).

I T HAS LONG been known that pathologic stress response syndromes can result from exposure to war, sexual assault,[2] and other types of trauma.[3-6] The codification of diagnostic criteria for these responses in *DSM-III*[7] under the diagnosis of posttraumatic stress disorder (PTSD) stimulated a considerable amount of research on these responses. A number of traumas have been studied in detail since that time, including criminal victimization,[8,9] sexual assault,[10,11] exposure to natural disaster,[12-14] and combat exposure.[15-18] The empiric information and conceptual refinements[19] generated by this research have importantly advanced our understanding of traumatic stress responses and led to revisions of the diagnostic criteria for PTSD in *DSM-III-R*. These require (A) exposure to a traumatic event that is "outside the range of usual human experience"; (B) reliving the experience in nightmares, flashbacks, or intrusive thoughts; (C) numbing or avoidant symptoms; and (D) hypersensitivity,

either as indicated by general signs and symptoms of autonomic arousal or by hypersensitivity to cues reminiscent of the trauma. These symptoms must persist for at least 1 month.[20] Despite a growing body of work on the extent to which PTSD is associated with specific traumas, limited epidemiologic data are available that describe the population prevalence of PTSD, the kinds of traumas most strongly associated with PTSD, the demographic correlates of PTSD, the comorbidity of PTSD with other disorders, and the typical course of PTSD. The purpose of this article is to present findings of this sort from the National Comorbidity Survey (NCS), the first nationally representative face-to-face general population survey to assess a broad range of *DSM-III-R* disorders that includes PTSD.

See Patients and Methods on next page

PATIENTS AND METHODS

SAMPLE

The data come from the NCS, a survey designed to study the distribution, correlates, and consequences of psychiatric disorders in the United States. The survey is based on a stratified, multistage area probability sample of persons aged 15 to 54 years in the noninstitutionalized civilian population in the 48 contiguous states, including a supplemental sample of students living in campus group housing, selected from a clustered sample of 1205 block-level segments in 176 counties throughout the country. A special nonresponse survey was carried out to ascertain and then statistically adjust for nonresponse bias.[37] Interviews were administered by the staff of the Survey Research Center at the University of Michigan, Ann Arbor, between September 14, 1990, and February 6, 1992. The 158 interviewers who participated in the NCS had an average of 5 years of previous interviewing experience with the Survey Research Center. Interviewers went through a 7-day study-specific training program in the use of the Composite International Diagnostic Interview (CIDI)[38] and were closely monitored throughout the data collection period. The response rate was 82.4%. A total of 8098 respondents participated in the survey.

The NCS was administered in two parts, each of which took somewhat more than 1 hour to complete. Part 1 included the core diagnostic interview, a brief risk factor battery, and an inventory of sociodemographic information. Part 2 included a much more detailed risk factor battery and secondary diagnoses, including PTSD, that were not included in the core diagnostic interview. Part 1 was administered to all 8098 respondents. Budgetary constraints required that we administer part 2 to only a subsample of respondents consisting of all those aged 15 to 24 years (99.4% of whom completed part 2), all others who screened positive for any lifetime diagnosis in part 1 (98.1% of whom completed part 2), and a random subsample of other respondents (99% of whom completed part 2). A total of 5877 respondents completed part 2. More details about the design of the NCS are presented elsewhere.[37]

DIAGNOSTIC ASSESSMENT

The diagnostic interview in the NCS was a modified version of the CIDI.[38,39] The CIDI is a fully structured interview developed collaboratively by the World Health Organization and the US Alcohol, Drug, and Mental Health Administration to foster cross-cultural epidemiologic

research by producing diagnoses according to the definitions and criteria of both *DSM-III-R*[20] and the Diagnostic Criteria for Research of the *International Classification of Diseases, 10th Revision*.[40] The modifications of the CIDI developed at the University of Michigan for the NCS consisted largely of changes in question order to improve flow and the introduction of clarifications to some of the more complex probe questions.[37]

The NCS disorders used to study comorbidity with PTSD included affective disorders (major depressive disorder, dysthymia, bipolar disorder), anxiety disorders (generalized anxiety disorder, panic disorder, phobia), antisocial personality disorder, and substance use disorders (alcohol abuse without dependence, alcohol dependence, drug abuse without dependence, drug dependence). All these diagnoses were based on *DSM-III-R* criteria. Diagnoses were generated by the use of the CIDI diagnostic program[41] for all disorders other than antisocial personality disorder. The latter was assessed with the antisocial personality disorder module from the DIS because this disorder was not part of the CIDI field trials. The field trials documented acceptable reliability and validity for all the CIDI diagnoses used herein.[42]

Posttraumatic stress disorder was assessed with a modified version of the Revised DIS[26] to be consistent with the assessment used in recent US epidemiologic surveys of PTSD.[26,29] In addition to the Revised DIS symptom questions, additional questions were asked about how soon the symptoms began after the trauma and how long the symptoms continued "at least a few times a week." Responses to the latter question were used as the basis for studying speed of recovery.

We also made four modifications to the Revised DIS PTSD section. The first involved the method for inquiring about traumatic stressors. Unlike the Revised DIS, which asks a single question about the lifetime occurrence of a list of traumatic events to oneself and a second question about traumas to others, the NCS asked 12 questions, one for each of 12 types of trauma, in an effort to focus memory search. Eleven questions were about events and experiences that qualify as traumas in *DSM-III-R* (**Figure 1**). A 12th question was an open-ended question about "any other terrible experience that most people never go through." Open-ended responses to this 12th question were subsequently coded as either qualifying under criterion A (eg, discovering a dead body) or not qualifying under criterion A (eg, normal bereavement). Responses that did not refer to specific events, were vague, or were confounded with PTSD (eg, biologic depression) were eliminated. In each case of the 12 events, we asked whether the event had ever occurred. For experiences 1, 9, and 10, that was the only

Continued on next page

PREVALENCE

The two earliest community prevalence studies of PTSD were carried out as part of the Epidemiologic Catchment Area (ECA) Program in St Louis, Mo,[21] and North Carolina.[22] Using *DSM-III* criteria as operationalized in the Diagnostic Interview Schedule (DIS),[23] these studies found lifetime prevalences of 1.0% in St Louis and 1.3%

in North Carolina. A lifetime prevalence of 2.6% was subsequently found in the control sample of a case-control study of the Mount St Helens volcanic eruption[24] with the use of the same diagnostic instrument and criteria as the ECA study. Two recent studies that used *DSM-III-R* criteria reported much higher rates. In a national telephone survey of women, Resnick et al[25] found that 12.3% of respondents (17.9% of those exposed to trauma)

23

question asked. For the others, we also asked the age at which the experience first occurred. Additional probe questions were also asked for some traumas, but are not included in the following analyses.

Second, based on evidence that respondents are sometimes reluctant to admit the occurrence of embarrassing and stigmatizing traumas, such as rape and sexual abuse, the 12 traumatic experiences were presented to respondents in a booklet. Interviewers asked about these experiences by number (eg, "Did you ever experience event number 1 on the list?" "How old were you when event number 1 first happened?") rather than by name.

The third modification is that we evaluated criteria B through D for the "most upsetting" event whether or not that event met the requirement in criterion A that it be outside the range of usual human experience. This allowed us to determine the extent to which the estimated prevalence of PTSD changed when criterion A was relaxed. The standard DIS symptom questions were used to evaluate criteria B through D, and standard DIS coding rules for criteria B through D were used to arrive at a diagnosis of PTSD according to the *DSM-III-R* criteria.

The fourth modification is that we evaluated criteria B through D only for one event per respondent. When a respondent reported the occurrence of more than one type of event, he or she was asked to nominate one of these as "most upsetting" for purposes of this evaluation. The Revised DIS, in comparison, evaluates these symptoms for up to three events. This restriction was imposed because of time and budget constraints in the NCS and with the recognition that only a small number of respondents who fail to meet PTSD diagnostic criteria for their "most upsetting" event are likely to meet these criteria for any other event (Naomi Breslau, PhD, oral communication, 1994).

The failure to obtain a complete trauma history and to assess PTSD for each lifetime trauma, a limitation not only of the NCS but of all previous community epidemiologic surveys of PTSD, means that estimates of lifetime prevalence are lower-bound estimates. It also means that the NCS and other community epidemiologic surveys of PTSD are unable to obtain unbiased data on either age-at-onset distributions or variation across events in the conditional probability of PTSD after trauma exposure. We will return to these limitations in the "Comment" section.

A small validation survey of the NCS PTSD module was conducted in which a probability sample of 29 NCS respondents who reported the occurrence of a lifetime trauma in the NCS were reinterviewed by trained clinical interviewers with a modified version of the PTSD module from an instrument that includes items from both the Structured Clinical Interview for *DSM-III-R*–Patient Version[43] and the Schedule for Affective Disorders and Schizophrenia–Lifetime Version.[44] This combined instrument was developed by researchers at the Harvard-Brown Anxiety Disorders Research Program.[45,46] Respondents who were diagnosed as having PTSD in the NCS (n=18) were oversampled compared with those diagnosed as being noncases (n=11). Interviewers were unaware of the NCS diagnoses. A weighted analysis that took this oversampling into consideration led to an estimated cross-sectional κ of 0.75, with an SE of .11. Positive predictive value was 1.0 and negative predictive value was 0.88, indicating that the NCS procedures somewhat underdiagnose PTSD.

ANALYSIS PROCEDURES

The NCS data were weighted to adjust for variation in within-household and between-household probabilities of selection and differential nonresponse. We also used a weight to adjust for differential nonresponse based on the nonrespondent survey and a comparison of the part 1 data reported by the small number of part 1 respondents who refused to complete part 2 vs those who did complete part 2. Respondents in the part 2 subsample were also weighted by the inverse of their probability of selection into part 2 to make the part 2 sample representative of the total population. Finally, the part 2 data were poststratified by means of an iterative procedure to approximate the national population distributions of the cross-classification of age, sex, race or ethnicity, marital status, education, living arrangements, region, and urbanicity as defined by the 1989 US National Health Interview Survey.[47] As shown in **Table 1**, the part 2 sample is representative of the total US population aged 15 to 54 years on a variety of sociodemographic characteristics. The weighted part 2 sample is used as the basis of the analyses reported in this article, and sample distributions reported reflect the weighted number of respondents (rounded to the nearest whole number).

Most of the results reported below are presented in the form of prevalences and zero-order odds ratios (ORs). The latter were obtained by exponentiating the regression coefficients from logistic models. The speed of recovery curve for the index episode was obtained by means of the Kaplan-Meier method for estimating survival curves. Because of the complex sample design, estimates of SEs of prevalences were obtained by the Taylor series linearization method.[48] The PSRATIO program in the OSIRIS software package[49] was used to make these calculations. Estimates of SEs of logistic regression coefficients were obtained by the method of balanced repeated replication[50,51] in 44 design-based balanced subsamples. The LOGISTIC program in the SAS software package[52] was used to estimate the parameters in each replicate, and an SAS macro was used to calculate the balanced repeated replication estimates of the variances of these parameter estimates across replicates. The speed of recovery curve was estimated by means of the SURVIVAL procedure in the SPSS software package.[53]

had a lifetime history of *DSM-III-R* PTSD. Breslau et al[26] administered the revised version of the DIS for *DSM-III-R* to a sample of young adults enrolled in a health maintenance organization in Detroit, Mich, and found that 11.3% of women (equivalent to 30.7% of those exposed to trauma) and 6% of men (equivalent to 14% of those exposed to trauma) had a lifetime history of PTSD.

Multiple factors might be involved in the much higher prevalences in the *DSM-III-R* vs *DSM-III* studies, including differences in diagnostic criteria, assessment procedures, and other sample characteristics.[27,28] Resnick et al[25] noted that the anonymity of telephone interviews may have contributed to the fact that so many women in their study reported traumatic experiences. Breslau et al[26] noted that recall bias might have been minimized in their study because of the young age of their respon-

Did Any of These Events Ever Happen to You?

1. You had direct combat experience in a war
2. You were involved in a life-threatening accident
3. You were involved in a fire, flood, or natural disaster
4. You witnessed someone being badly injured or killed
5. You were raped (someone had sexual intercourse with you when you did not want to by threatening you or using some degree of force)
6. You were sexually molested (someone touched or felt your genitals when you did not want them to)
7. You were seriously physically attacked or assaulted
8. You were physically abused as a child
9. You were seriously neglected as a child
10. You were threatened with a weapon, held captive, or kidnapped
11. Other ("any other terrible experience that most people never go through")
12. You suffered a great shock because one of the events on this list happened to someone close to you

Figure 1. Questions about events and experiences that qualified as traumas according to DSM-III-R.

dents, and that this could have played an important part in explaining why their prevalence estimate was higher than in previous studies.

TYPES OF TRAUMA

Only limited information is available on the types of traumatic experiences most strongly associated with PTSD. Many of the traumas identified as likely to cause PTSD are common,[9,29] and so the stipulation in criterion A of *DSM-III-R* that the trauma must be outside the range of usual human experience is difficult to defend.[30] Yet, ignoring this stipulation and allowing people with intrusive recollections of any stressful event to be evaluated as potential cases could dilute the meaning of PTSD as a stress-response syndrome.[31] One way of investigating this issue more carefully is to obtain base rates of exposure to specific traumas and to study variation in conditional probabilities of PTSD across different traumas. Data of this sort are presented below.

COMORBIDITY

Another important consideration in understanding PTSD is the high rate of comorbidity. Kulka et al[18] reported that 98.8% of Vietnam theater veterans with PTSD had a history of some other DIS *DSM-III-R* disorder, compared with 40.6% of those without PTSD. Helzer et al[21] and Breslau et al[26] reported that close to 80% of respondents with PTSD had experienced other psychiatric disorders, compared with about 30% and 44.3%, respectively, of those without PTSD. Rates of comorbidity between 62%[22] and 92%[24] have been reported in other population-based surveys of PTSD. Research in both treatment samples[32,33] and population-based samples[29] has used information on age at onset to show that history of other psychiatric disorders is associated with increased risk of subsequent PTSD. It is not clear, however, how large a proportion of all PTSD cases are primary vs secondary. This issue is examined in the present report.

Table 1. National Health Interview Survey (NHIS)*–National Comorbidity Survey (NCS) Part II Demographic Comparisons (n=5877)

	US Population (NHIS), %*	NCS Weighted, %	NCS Unweighted, %
Sex			
Male	49.1	47.8	48.2
Female	50.9	52.2	51.8
Race			
White	75.0	76.3	76.5
Black	11.9	11.4	11.3
Hispanic	8.6	9.0	8.9
Other	4.5	3.3	3.2
Education, y			
0-11	22.5	23.2	20.6
12	36.8	36.7	32.4
13-15	21.2	21.7	26.9
≥16	19.5	18.3	20.1
Marital status			
Married	59.8	62.1	49.3
Separated/widowed/divorced	10.1	9.7	15.3
Never married	30.1	28.2	35.3
Region			
Northeast	20.0	20.2	19.3
Midwest	24.6	25.2	26.3
South	33.7	34.2	33.3
West	21.7	20.4	21.2
Age, y			
15-24	25.5	25.9	29.9
25-34	30.8	30.8	30.4
35-44	25.9	27.4	24.9
≥45	17.8	15.9	14.9
Urbanicity†			
MSAs ≥250 000	71.2	68.1	69.7
MSAs <250 000	8.1	7.3	6.3
Not MSA	20.7	24.6	24.0
Total No.	65 244	5877	5877

*National Health Interview Survey, 1989, US Department of Health and Human Services, National Center for Health Statistics.[47]
†MSA indicates Metropolitan Statistical Area.

CHRONICITY

Finally, we consider the issue of chronicity. The *DSM-III-R* requires a 1-month duration of symptoms as a criterion for PTSD. The sub–work group on PTSD for *DSM-IV* suggested that PTSD that endures for 3 months should be considered chronic based on evidence from several prospective studies of trauma victims that the number of people with PTSD symptoms decreases substantially within 3 months[34] and on evidence that people whose symptoms persist beyond 3 to 6 months have a high probability of becoming chronic cases.[21,24,32,35] Although much of this evidence comes from treatment samples in which chronicity would be expected to be worse, Breslau and Davis[36] found that 57% of PTSD cases in their sample had a duration of more than 1 year. We present data herein on the persistence of an index episode of PTSD in a nationally representative general population sample to investigate whether PTSD does, in fact, become chronic if symptoms last beyond 3 months.

25

Table 2. Lifetime Prevalence of Posttraumatic Stress Disorder by Age, Sex, and Marital Status

	Married		**Previously Married**		**Never Married**		**Total**	
Age, y	**Male**	**Female**	**Male**	**Female**	**Male**	**Female**	**Male**	**Female**
15-24	9.6 (5.0)	16.4 (2.6)	12.6 (9.4)	10.4 (5.3)	1.7 (0.5)	7.9 (1.3)	2.8 (0.7)	10.3 (1.2)
25-34	6.0 (1.7)	9.9 (1.5)	11.1 (5.2)	20.5 (5.9)	2.9 (0.9)	10.0 (2.8)	5.6 (1.0)	11.2 (1.3)
35-44	5.1 (1.7)	8.1 (1.7)	7.0 (2.0)	25.8 (4.9)	1.1 (0.8)	16.3 (6.7)	5.0 (1.4)	10.6 (1.6)
45-54	7.1 (2.1)	8.3 (1.9)	10.2 (5.4)	11.6 (3.8)	4.6 (1.9)	11.8 (7.3)	7.6 (2.0)	8.9 (1.7)
Total	6.1 (0.9)	9.6 (0.8)	9.4 (2.8)	18.9 (3.0)	1.9 (0.4)	8.9 (1.4)	5.0 (0.6)	10.4 (0.8)

RESULTS

PREVALENCE OF PTSD

The estimated lifetime prevalence of *DSM-III-R* PTSD in the total sample was 7.8% (with an SE of 0.5%). This estimate increased only modestly, to 8.4% (SE, 0.5%), when nonqualifying events were included, so the remainder of the analysis was based only on qualifying events. Lifetime prevalence estimates within the cells of the three-way cross-classification of age, sex, and marital status are reported in **Table 2**. As shown there, women were more than twice as likely overall as men to have lifetime PTSD (10.4% vs 5.0%, $z=5.4$, $P<.05$). Gender differences were apparent in all birth cohorts with lifetime prevalence significantly greater among older birth cohorts for men but not women. Lifetime prevalence was higher among the previously married (separated, divorced, or widowed) than the currently married, but this was significant only among women (18.9% vs 9.6%, $z=3.0$, $P=.004$, compared with 9.4% vs 6.1%, $z=1.3$, $P=.17$ among men). Prevalence was also higher among the married than the never married, but this was significant only among men (6.1% vs 1.9%, $z=4.3$, $P=.001$, compared with 9.6% vs 8.9%, $z=0.4$, $P=.37$ among women).

PREVALENCE OF TRAUMA EXPOSURE

Estimates of the lifetime prevalence of trauma exposure are presented in **Table 3** separately for men and women; 60.7% of men and 51.2% of women reported at least one traumatic event ($z=3.8$, $P=.001$). Consistent with previous research,[9] the majority of people with some type of lifetime trauma actually experienced two (14.5%/60.7%=23.9% of men with a lifetime trauma, 13.5%/51.2%=26.4% of women with a lifetime trauma), three (9.5%/60.7%=15.7% of men with a lifetime trauma, 5.0%/51.2=9.8% of women with a lifetime trauma), or more (10.2%/60.7%=16.8% of men with a lifetime trauma, 6.4%/51.2%=12.5% of women with a lifetime trauma) types of trauma. The types of trauma experienced by the largest proportions of people were witnessing someone being badly injured or killed (35.6% of men and 14.5% of women), being involved in a fire, flood, or natural disaster (18.9% of men and 15.2% of women), and being involved in a life-threatening accident (25% of men and 13.8% of women). A significantly higher proportion of men than women reported experiencing each of these

Table 3. Lifetime Prevalence of Trauma Experience

	Lifetime Prevalence of Trauma					
	Men (n=2812)*			**Women (n=3065)***		
Trauma	**%**	**(SE)**	**No.**	**%**	**(SE)**	**No.**
Rape	0.7†	(0.2)	19	9.2	(0.8)	281
Molestation	2.8†	(0.5)	78	12.3	(1.0)	376
Physical attack	11.1†	(1.0)	313	6.9	(0.9)	210
Combat	6.4†	(0.9)	179	0.0	...	0
Shock	11.4	(1.1)	320	12.4	(1.1)	381
Threat with weapon	19.0†	(1.3)	535	6.8	(0.6)	208
Accident	25.0†	(1.2)	703	13.8	(1.1)	422
Natural disaster with fire	18.9†	(1.4)	532	15.2	(1.2)	467
Witness	35.6†	(2.0)	1002	14.5	(0.7)	445
Neglect	2.1†	(0.4)	58	3.4	(0.5)	105
Physical abuse	3.2†	(0.4)	91	4.8	(0.6)	146
Other qualifying trauma	2.2	(0.5)	61	2.7	(0.4)	83
Any trauma	60.7†	(1.9)	1707	51.2	(1.9)	1570
No. of traumas						
1	26.5	(1.5)	745	26.3	(1.7)	806
2	14.5	(0.9)	407	13.5	(0.9)	415
3	9.5†	(0.9)	268	5.0	(0.6)	154
4	10.2†	(0.8)	287	6.4	(0.6)	195

*Sample distributions reflect the weighted number of respondents rounded to the nearest whole number.
†Sex difference significant at the .05 level, two-tailed test.

three as well as physical attacks, combat experience, and being threatened with a weapon, held captive, or kidnapped. A significantly higher proportion of women than men, in comparison, reported rape, sexual molestation, childhood parental neglect, and childhood physical abuse.

DIFFERENCES ACROSS TRAUMAS IN PROBABILITY OF PTSD

As described above, the NCS assessed PTSD either for the respondent's only lifetime trauma or, in the case of respondents who experienced more than one trauma type, for the one lifetime trauma nominated as "most upsetting." As shown in **Table 4**, the probability of a trauma being the basis for the assessment of PTSD (P1 in the table) varied substantially across trauma types. This variation was a complex function of differences in the distribution of the joint occurrences of multiple traumas and the likelihood that some types of trauma are generally more distressing than others. Among men and women alike, rape was the listed trauma with the highest conditional probability of

26

Table 4. Conditional Probabilities of Specific Traumas Being the Basis for the Assessment of Posttraumatic Stress Disorder (PTSD) and, Once Selected for Assessment, for Being Associated With PTSD*

| | Lifetime Prevalence of PTSD | | | | | |
| | Men | | | Women | | |
Trauma	P1 (SE)	P2 (SE)	n_i	P1 (SE)	P2 (SE)	n_i
Rape	62.1 (11.6)	65.0 (15.6)	12	74.4 (4.1)	45.9 (5.9)	209
Molestation	26.9 (6.2)	12.2† (5.3)	21	61.4 (2.8)	26.5 (4.0)	231
Physical attack	35.7 (5.1)	1.8† (0.9)	112	42.0 (7.7)	21.3 (7.3)	88
Combat	57.7 (6.7)	38.8† (9.9)	103	...	...	0
Shock	44.8 (4.7)	4.4† (1.4)	144	55.4 (4.0)	10.4 (2.0)	211
Threat with weapon	32.9 (3.0)	1.9† (0.8)	176	36.4 (4.8)	32.6 (7.8)	76
Accident	44.6 (3.6)	6.3 (1.8)	314	44.5 (4.1)	8.8 (4.3)	188
Natural disaster with fire	35.9 (2.8)	3.7 (1.8)	191	44.4 (4.4)	5.4 (3.8)	207
Witness	52.4 (2.7)	6.4 (1.2)	524	47.1 (4.2)	7.5 (1.7)	209
Neglect	27.8 (5.8)	23.9 (10.3)	16	28.1 (5.8)	19.7 (7.7)	30
Physical abuse	50.4 (4.7)	22.3† (5.2)	46	37.0 (5.0)	48.5 (9.5)	54
Other qualifying trauma	77.6 (7.8)	12.7† (4.8)	48	80.8 (5.0)	33.4 (8.0)	67
Any trauma	...	8.1 (1.0)	1707	...	20.4 (1.5)	1570

*P1 indicates the probability that a respondent who reported the lifetime occurrence of a particular trauma type will have this be the basis for the assessment of PTSD (ie, that this trauma will either be the respondent's only lifetime trauma or the nominated "most upsetting" trauma); P2, the probability that a particular trauma type, once selected as the basis for the assessment of PTSD, will be associated with PTSD; and n_i, the weighted number of respondents (rounded to the nearest whole number) with a particular "only or most upsetting" trauma type who were diagnosed as having lifetime PTSD.
†Sex difference significant at the .05 level, two-tailed test.

being the basis for the assessment of PTSD, while sexual molestation and childhood neglect had the lowest conditional probabilities for men and women, respectively.

Consistent with previous research reviewed by March[31] and by Kilpatrick and Resnick,[9] the columns in Table 4 labeled P2 show that the proportion of respondents with a trauma who met criteria for PTSD varied significantly by type of most upsetting trauma. The trauma of this sort most likely to be associated with PTSD among men and women alike was rape. Sixty-five percent of men and 45.9% of women who reported this as their most upsetting trauma developed PTSD. Other most upsetting listed traumas associated with a high probability of PTSD included combat exposure, childhood neglect, and childhood physical abuse among men (with probabilities of developing PTSD of 38.8%, 23.9%, and 22.3%, respectively) and sexual molestation, physical attack, being threatened with a weapon, and childhood physical abuse among women (with probabilities of developing PTSD of 26.5%, 21.3%, 32.6%, and 48.5%, respectively).

A comparison of the results in Tables 3 and 4 shows that, although men were more likely than women to experience at least one trauma overall, women were more likely than men to experience a trauma associated with a high probability of PTSD. While 44.6% of men with a lifetime trauma reported that their most upsetting trauma was one of those associated with high probability of PTSD among men (ie, rape, combat exposure, childhood neglect, or childhood physical abuse), a significantly higher percentage of women (67.6%; $z=11.5$, $P=.001$) with a lifetime trauma reported that their most distressing trauma was one of those associated with a high probability of PTSD among women (ie, rape, sexual molestation, physical attack, being threatened with a weapon, or childhood physical abuse). Furthermore, for all most upsetting traumas other than rape and childhood neglect, a

higher proportion of women than men met criteria for PTSD. The combination of these influences—greater exposure to high-impact traumas and greater likelihood of developing PTSD once exposed—led to the finding that women exposed to a trauma were more than twice as likely as men to develop PTSD (20.4% of women compared with 8.2% of men, $z=6.7$, $P=.001$).

DISTRIBUTION OF MOST UPSETTING TRAUMAS AMONG PEOPLE WITH PTSD

The probabilities of having each type of most upsetting trauma in the subsample of respondents with lifetime PTSD are presented in **Table 5**. The traumas most commonly associated with PTSD among men were combat exposure, which was the nominated most upsetting trauma for 28.8% of men with PTSD, and witnessing someone being badly injured or killed, which was the nominated trauma for 24.3% of men. Combat exposure was a fairly uncommon event (6.4% lifetime prevalence among men) associated with a high probability of PTSD when it was nominated as most upsetting (38.8%). Witnessing, in comparison, was a much more common event (35.6% lifetime prevalence among men) associated with a low probability of PTSD when it was nominated as most upsetting (6.4%).

Among women, the events most commonly associated with PTSD were rape, which was nominated as most upsetting for 29.9% of women with PTSD, and sexual molestation, which was the nominated event for 19.1% of female cases. Together, rape and molestation were the nominated events for 49% of women with PTSD. These events are both common in the general population of women (9.2% of women in the NCS reported lifetime rape and 12.2% reported molestation) and associated with high probabilities of PTSD when nominated as most upsetting (45.9% for rape and 26.5% for molestation).

27

Table 5. Those With Posttraumatic Stress Disorder (PTSD) Reporting Each Most Upsetting Trauma Type by Sex

Trauma	Men (n=139)[a]		Women (n=320)[a]	
	% (SE)	No.[b]	% (SE)	No.[b]
Rape	5.4† (2.8)	8	29.9 (3.4)	96
Molestation	1.8† (0.7)	3	19.1 (3.1)	61
Physical attack	1.4† (0.6)	2	5.9 (1.6)	19
Combat	28.8 (6.1)	40	...	0
Shock	4.5 (1.4)	6	6.8 (1.2)	22
Threat with weapon	2.5† (1.1)	3	7.7 (2.2)	25
Accident	12.1 (3.4)	20	5.1 (2.4)	16
Natural disaster with fire	5.2 (2.5)	7	3.5 (2.3)	11
Witness	24.3† (4.8)	30	4.9 (1.1)	16
Neglect	2.8 (1.1)	4	1.8 (0.7)	6
Physical abuse	7.4 (2.0)	10	8.2 (2.9)	26
Other qualifying trauma	3.8 (1.6)	6	7.0 (2.1)	22
Any trauma	100.0 (...)	139	100.0 (...)	320

*Sample distributions reflect the weighted number of respondents rounded to the nearest whole number.
†Sex difference significant at the .05 level, two-tailed test.

DEMOGRAPHIC CORRELATES OF PTSD

Multiple logistic regression analyses were carried out to describe the sociodemographic correlates of lifetime PTSD. Sex, age, marital status, and the interactions of age with sex and sex with marital status were all found to be significant predictors of lifetime PTSD. Once these significant predictors were controlled, there were no significant residual associations of PTSD with race, education, urbanicity, or region of the country.

The ORs under model 1 in **Table 6** describe the significant associations of age, sex, and marital status with PTSD. The results in the rest of the table decompose these total associations into components resulting from the relationships of these predictors with exposure to at least one lifetime trauma (model 2), with PTSD in the subsample of respondents exposed to at least one lifetime trauma (model 3), and with PTSD in the subsample of respondents exposed to at least one lifetime trauma after controlling for differences in most upsetting trauma type (model 4). If the association of a particular demographic variable with PTSD results from its being associated with higher-impact traumas, the OR for that variable under model 3 will be larger than the OR under model 4.

Sex

Consistent with our earlier results, Table 6 shows that women had a significantly higher lifetime prevalence of PTSD than men. The coding of the variables in Table 6, however, is such that the OR of 4.87 for women under model 1 is for the comparison between never-married women and never-married men aged 15 to 24 years. A substantial sex difference in PTSD existed in this subsample despite the finding under model 2 that a lower proportion of women than men in this subsample reported ever experiencing a trauma (OR=0.82). As shown under model 3, women in this subsample who had been

exposed to at least one trauma had a much higher odds than comparable men of developing PTSD (OR=6.13). The OR is smaller under model 3 than model 4, which means that this greater vulnerability partly results from the fact that the most upsetting traumas nominated by women were associated with a higher probability of PTSD than those nominated by men (assuming, for purposes of this analysis, that there was no sex difference in the probability of PTSD among men and women who nominated the same most upsetting event). However, the fact that the OR under model 4 remained significant shows that these women were significantly more vulnerable than men even when we controlled for sex differences in the types of most upsetting trauma. This sex difference might be explained by detailed aspects of trauma exposure, such as age at exposure and/or previous trauma history, but we were unable to investigate this possibility because PTSD was not assessed for a random trauma.

Age

Because the relationship between age and lifetime prevalence of PTSD differed by sex, the ORs associated with age were estimated separately for men and women in Table 6. Among men, there was no consistent association between age and PTSD (model 1), controlling for marital status. The results under model 2, however, show that lifetime trauma exposure was significantly and positively associated with age, while the results under models 3 and 4 showed a counterbalancing, but not statistically significant, negative association between age and probability of PTSD given exposure. Among women, in comparison, there was a nonsignificant trend for lifetime PTSD to be negatively associated with age (model 1), controlling for marital status. This is because the increasing prevalence of trauma exposure with age was much less pronounced among women than men, while the same general pattern of a modestly decreasing probability of PTSD among the exposed with increasing age held for women as well as men.

Marital Status

Lifetime PTSD was significantly more prevalent among the previously married (separated, divorced, or widowed) than the currently married for both men and women, controlling for age. Furthermore, among men but not women, PTSD was significantly more prevalent among the currently married than the never married, controlling for age. These associations resulted largely from a combination of significantly elevated probabilities of PTSD among the exposed (models 3 and 4) rather than differential lifetime probabilities of trauma exposure.

LIFETIME COMORBIDITY BETWEEN PTSD AND OTHER DISORDERS

Estimates of the lifetime prevalences of 11 *DSM-III-R* disorders are reported in **Table 7** separately for men and women with and without a lifetime history of PTSD. The ORs show a consistently significant cross-sectional relationship between lifetime PTSD and these other disor-

Table 6. Sociodemographic Correlates of Lifetime Posttraumatic Stress Disorder (PTSD)[c]

	OR (95% Confidence Interval)			
	Model 1: Risk of PTSD	Model 2: Risk of Trauma	Model 3: Risk of PTSD In Trauma Subsample	Model 4: Risk of PTSD In Trauma Subsample Controlling Trauma Type
Sex				
Male	1.00 (...)	1.00 (...)	1.00 (...)	1.00 (...)
Female	4.87† (2.92-8.12)	0.82 (0.65-1.04)	6.13† (3.59-10.46)	4.05† (2.48-6.63)
Age (males), y				
15-24	1.00 (...)	1.00 (...)	1.00 (...)	1.00 (...)
25-34	0.87 (0.36-2.07)	1.25 (0.92-1.70)	0.85 (0.36-1.99)	0.81 (0.32-2.09)
35-44	0.66 (0.21-2.10)	1.46† (1.00-2.13)	0.58 (0.18-1.88)	0.31 (0.09-1.10)
45-54	0.96 (0.34-2.72)	1.76† (1.02-3.05)	0.81 (0.28-2.29)	0.57 (0.17-1.95)
Age (females), y				
15-24	1.00 (...)	1.00 (...)	1.00 (...)	1.00 (...)
25-34	0.89 (0.60-1.31)	1.06 (0.78-1.43)	0.83 (0.52-1.32)	0.82 (0.51-1.33)
35-44	0.81 (0.49-1.35)	1.45† (1.00-2.10)	0.61 (0.36-1.03)	0.58 (0.37-1.05)
45-54	0.64 (0.36-1.30)	1.05 (0.72-1.53)	0.55 (0.31-1.00)	0.59 (0.35-1.01)
Marital status (males)				
Never married	1.00 (...)	1.00 (...)	1.00 (...)	1.00 (...)
Married	3.82† (1.64-8.87)	1.14 (0.79-1.63)	3.56† (1.62-7.82)	3.21† (1.43-7.86)
Previously married	6.00† (1.73-20.79)	1.60 (0.87-2.93)	5.11† (1.39-18.71)	3.47 (0.96-15.04)
Marital status (females)				
Never married	1.00 (...)	1.00 (...)	1.00 (...)	1.00 (...)
Married	1.27 (0.77-2.10)	1.02 (0.73-1.42)	1.33 (0.78-2.26)	1.20 (0.76-1.91)
Previously married	2.86† (1.48-5.53)	1.35 (0.83-2.21)	2.93† (1.14-6.08)	2.59† (1.33-5.06)

*The coefficients are based on multivariate logistic regression models in which age, sex, marital status, age × sex, and marital status × sex are predictors of the outcome. The outcome in the first model is PTSD. The outcome in the second model is trauma. The outcome in the third model is the same as in the first, with the exception that the model is estimated in the subsample of respondents who experienced trauma. The outcome in the fourth model is the same as in the third and in the same subsample, with the exception that the model includes controls for trauma type. The interaction between age and sex (3 dfs) is significant in each of the four models, with Wald χ^2 values (adjusted for design effects) ranging between 10.6 and 16.7. The interaction between marital status and sex (2 dfs) is also significant in all models, with Wald χ^2 (again adjusted for design effects) ranging between 13.1 and 17.5. More detailed modeling failed to find any significant age × sex or age × sex × marital status interactions.

†The odds ratio (OR) is significantly different at the .05 level (two-tailed) from the reference category value of OR=1.0.

ders among both men and women. A lifetime history of at least one other disorder was present in 88.3% of the men with lifetime PTSD and 79% of the women with lifetime PTSD.

The relative magnitudes of the ORs in Table 7 are worth noting in light of observations by previous commentators that comorbidity with PTSD would be expected for some disorders because of overlap in symptom criteria.[54,55] In particular, several of the criteria C and D symptoms of PTSD (eg, diminished interest, restricted range of affect, sleep difficulties, difficulty concentrating) overlap with symptoms of depression, while several criterion C symptoms of PTSD (eg, irritability, hypervigilance, startle) overlap with symptoms of generalized anxiety disorder, and criterion D6 (physiologic reactivity) could create an overlap with social phobia, simple phobia, and panic disorder. The cross-sectional results in Table 7 show that PTSD does, in fact, have substantial comorbidities with all of these disorders.

Absence of a complete PTSD assessment for all lifetime traumas made it impossible to determine unequivocally how often comorbid PTSD was a primary disorder in the sense of having an earlier age at onset than other comorbid conditions. It is possible, however, to place upper and lower bounds on this estimate. The upper bound is the percentage of patients with comorbidity who had

no other NCS/DSM-III-R disorder as of the age at their earliest lifetime trauma. The lower bound is the percentage of patients with comorbidity who had no other NCS/DSM-III-R disorder as of the age at their most upsetting trauma. These upper and lower bound estimates are reported in **Table 8**. The results suggest that PTSD was primary more often than not with respect to comorbid affective disorders and substance use disorders and, among women, with respect to comorbid conduct disorder (range, 52.7% to 84.3%). Posttraumatic stress disorder was less likely to be primary with respect to comorbid anxiety disorders and, among men, comorbid conduct disorder, although even in these cases the percentage of cases in which PTSD was primary was substantial (range, 30.3% to 61.4%). We estimate that PTSD was primary with respect to all other comorbid disorders between 29.3% and 51.3% of the time among men and between 40.8% and 57.6% of the time among women.

PERSISTENCE OF PTSD

As noted earlier, NCS respondents who met criteria for PTSD were asked how many weeks, months, or years after onset of their index episode they continued to have symptoms at least a few times a week. Survival curves based on these retrospective reports are presented in **Figure 2** separately for respondents who ever sought pro-

29

Table 7. Comorbidity of Posttraumatic Stress Disorder (PTSD) With Other Disorders in the Total Sample*

	PTSD		No PTSD		
	% (SE)	No.†	% (SE)	No.†	OR (95% CI)
Men					
Affective disorders					
MDE	47.9 (5.5)	67	11.7 (0.8)	314	6.90‡ (4.36-10.92)
Dysthymia	21.4 (4.5)	30	4.4 (0.4)	117	5.95‡ (3.18-11.13)
Mania	11.7 (3.5)	16	1.3 (0.3)	34	10.41‡ (4.20-25.76)
Anxiety disorders					
GAD	16.8 (4.5)	23	3.3 (0.4)	89	5.89‡ (2.59-13.38)
Panic disorder	7.3 (2.3)	10	1.9 (0.4)	52	4.11‡ (1.60-10.11)
Simple phobia	31.4 (6.0)	44	6.0 (0.5)	161	7.14‡ (4.13-12.35)
Social phobia	27.6 (4.9)	38	11.3 (0.7)	302	2.99‡ (1.77-5.04)
Agoraphobia	16.1 (4.7)	22	4.1 (0.5)	109	4.53‡ (1.88-10.92)
Substance use disorders					
Alcohol abuse/dependence	51.9 (6.7)	72	34.4 (1.2)	919	2.06‡ (1.14-3.70)
Drug abuse/dependence	34.5 (6.9)	48	15.1 (1.0)	403	2.97‡ (1.52-5.79)
Other disorder					
Conduct disorder	43.3 (4.9)	60	19.5 (1.2)	521	3.15‡ (2.12-4.69)
Any disorder§					
No other diagnosis	11.7 (3.0)	67	45.2 (1.9)	1476	0.16‡ (0.07-0.35)
1 diagnoses	14.9 (2.8)	49	24.4 (1.1)	515	2.36 (0.99-5.64)
2 diagnoses	14.4 (3.9)	59	14.7 (1.1)	341	3.80‡ (1.37-10.58)
≥3 diagnoses	59.0 (5.2)	144	15.7 (0.9)	414	14.51‡ (6.65-31.66)
Women					
Affective disorders					
MDE	48.5 (3.4)	155	18.8 (0.9)	516	4.07‡ (3.08-5.39)
Dysthymia	23.3 (3.3)	75	6.8 (0.6)	187	4.14‡ (2.74-6.25)
Mania	5.7 (1.7)	18	1.3 (0.4)	37	4.45‡ (1.74-11.41)
Anxiety disorders					
GAD	15.0 (2.5)	48	5.9 (0.7)	162	2.81‡ (1.60-4.95)
Panic disorder	12.6 (2.3)	40	4.3 (0.5)	119	3.18‡ (1.89-5.37)
Simple phobia	29.0 (2.9)	93	14.5 (1.2)	397	2.42‡ (1.66-3.51)
Social phobia	28.4 (3.1)	91	14.1 (1.2)	387	2.42‡ (1.71-3.43)
Agoraphobia	22.4 (2.8)	72	7.8 (0.7)	214	3.42‡ (2.40-4.88)
Substance use disorders					
Alcohol abuse/dependence	27.9 (3.6)	90	13.5 (1.1)	372	2.48‡ (1.78-3.45)
Drug abuse/dependence	26.9 (3.4)	86	7.6 (0.7)	209	4.46‡ (3.11-6.39)
Other disorder					
Conduct disorder	15.4 (2.0)	49	5.9 (0.7)	163	2.88‡ (1.98-4.18)
Any disorder§					
No other diagnosis	21.0 (3.7)	16	53.8 (2.2)	1209	0.23‡ (0.14-0.37)
1 diagnosis	17.2 (2.2)	20	20.4 (1.4)	522	2.17‡ (1.35-3.48)
2 diagnoses	18.2 (3.1)	9	11.7 (0.8)	398	3.98‡ (2.11-7.50)
≥3 diagnoses	43.6 (3.8)	93	14.1 (1.4)	544	7.91‡ (4.82-12.96)

*OR indicates odds ratio; CI, confidence interval; MDE, major depressive episode; and GAD, generalized affective disorder. n=139 and 2673 for men with and without PTSD, respectively; n=320 and 2745 for women with and without PTSD, respectively.
†Sample distributions reflect the weighted number of respondents rounded to the nearest whole number.
‡Odds ratio significant at the .05 level, two-tailed test.
§Odds ratios for one, two, and three or more disorders from a multivariate model.

fessional treatment for a mental problem and those who did not. The survival curves decreased most steeply in the first 12 months after the onset of symptoms in both subsamples. The curves continued to decline with a more gradual slope for approximately 6 years after symptom onset. The median time to remission was 36 months among the respondents who ever sought professional treatment (n=266) and 64 months among those who did not (n=193). Statistical analysis based on the Lee-Desu χ^2 test[56] showed that these two survival curves were significantly different (χ^2=5.0, df=1, P=.02), although absence of data on the timing of treatment made it impossible to interpret this difference as resulting from the effects

of treatment. Perhaps of more interest than the difference between the two curves was the consistent finding that PTSD failed to remit in somewhat more than one third of persons even after many years not only in the subsample of respondents who did not receive professional treatment but also in the treatment subsample.

COMMENT

PREVALENCE

The results reported herein are based on data that require lifetime recall of traumas and the symptoms associated with them. It is likely that there was some recall failure in respondent reports, leading to underestimation of the lifetime prevalences of both traumatic experiences and PTSD. In addition, PTSD was assessed for only one event per respondent, which could have led to additional underestimation of PTSD. Furthermore, the clinical validation study of the NCS diagnostic assessment showed that PTSD was somewhat underdiagnosed.

Even with these biases toward underreporting, however, the results show that PTSD is a highly prevalent disorder. A full 7.8% of respondents (5% of men and 10.4% of women) were estimated to have a lifetime history of PTSD. Similar prevalence estimates were reported by Breslau et al[26] (6% among men and 11.3% among women) and Resnick et al[25] (12.3% among women) in the two previous epidemiologic surveys of PTSD that used *DSM-III-R* criteria. These are much higher than the 1% to 3% prevalence estimates found in the ECA study[21,22] and in a subsequent study that used the same methods as the ECA.[24]

It is unclear why the results of recent studies differ so dramatically from those of the earlier ECA studies. Differences in diagnostic criteria, sampling frames, years of administration, or administrative procedures could all be involved. There are also differences across studies in the kinds of events that were counted as fulfilling criterion A. For example, Davidson et al,[22] in their analysis of the North Carolina ECA data, included among the qualifying events such things as mother's illness and death and anaphylactic reaction to medication as qualifying events,

while Helzer et al,[21] in their analysis of the St Louis ECA data, included having a miscarriage and Shore et al[24] included husband's illness and death and wife's seizures. Our reading of *DSM-III-R* suggests that none of these is a qualifying event and, as a result, open-ended reports of such events by NCS respondents were not counted in estimating PTSD. At the same time, some of the events that we included might not have been included by previous investigators. Because of these differences, it is difficult to make rigorous comparisons across the different community surveys of PTSD.

The estimated prevalence of PTSD did not increase much when we relaxed criterion A to include nonqualifying events reported in response to an open-ended question about "any other terrible experiences that most people never go through." It is important to recognize, though, that we did not systematically attempt to elicit information about nonqualifying events by asking explicit questions about such things as chronic illness, job loss, or marital difficulties, and we have no way of knowing how often these experiences are associated with PTSD-like symptoms. It would be useful for subsequent research to conduct a more broad-based investigation of this sort to determine which types of nonqualifying life events are most likely to provoke such symptoms and to facilitate research on individual differences in vulnerability aimed at explaining why some people develop PTSD-like symptoms in response to events that are not normally considered traumatic.[9,31] This would be especially useful in light of the substantial changes introduced into *DSM-IV* concerning the definitions of qualifying events.[57]

EXPOSURE TO TRAUMATIC EXPERIENCES

The results concerning the types of traumatic experiences that are associated with PTSD are also relevant to a controversy concerning criterion A in *DSM-III-R*, which stipulates that the trauma must be outside the range of usual human experience and of a type that would be markedly distressing to almost anyone. The NCS results are consistent with recent research in showing that virtually all of the qualifying events for PTSD are quite common[9] and that none is such that virtually everyone exposed to it develops PTSD. There is also enormous

Table 8. Proportions of Comorbid Lifetime Posttraumatic Stress Disorder That Are Primary Disorders

	Men, % (SE)		Women, % (SE)	
	Upper Bound	Lower Bound	Upper Bound	Lower Bound
Any affective disorder	76.8 (6.1)	53.0 (8.1)	78.4 (3.5)	57.9 (4.9)
Any anxiety disorder	50.0 (7.4)	30.3 (6.2)	56.1 (4.9)	37.3 (4.1)
Conduct disorder	61.4 (8.1)	45.9 (7.9)	72.7 (8.8)	56.3 (9.4)
Any alcohol or substance disorder	65.3 (5.9)	52.7 (6.8)	84.3 (2.7)	65.1 (4.2)
Any disorder	51.3 (5.0)	29.3 (4.6)	57.6 (3.6)	40.8 (3.5)

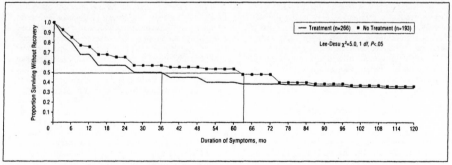

Figure 2. *Survival curves based on duration of symptoms for respondents who did and did not receive treatment for posttraumatic stress disorder.*

variability across nominated most distressing traumatic events in the probability of PTSD. Furthermore, events that are traumatic in one sector of the population may not be traumatic in another. For example, men in the NCS were nearly twice as likely as women to report being seriously physically attacked or assaulted (11.1% vs 6.9%, $z=3.2$, $P=.002$). Yet, this type of event, when nominated as most upsetting, was more than 15 times as likely to be associated with PTSD among women as men (21.3% vs 1.8%, $z=2.6$, $P=.01$). Such subgroup differences make it difficult to categorize stressful events neatly into those that are traumatic and those that are not traumatic.[31]

In evaluating the results concerning the types of traumatic experiences associated with PTSD, it is important to remember that the NCS assessed criteria B through D for only one event per person. As a result, the event-specific analyses focus on the subsample of events that were rated most upsetting by respondents who had two or more lifetime trauma types. This creates the potential for an overestimation of the associations of particular events with PTSD. For example, while 65% of the subsample of men who reported that being raped was either their only or their most upsetting lifetime trauma developed PTSD after that event, a much smaller percentage (46.4%) of the larger group of all men who reported being raped (whether or not it was their only or most upsetting trauma) reported lifetime PTSD associated with their most upsetting trauma. The most plausible way to interpret this discrepancy is to assume that the rapes nominated as most upsetting shared some objective features that made them more traumatizing than the rapes not nominated as most upsetting. If this is the case, it would be a mistake to assume that "typical" traumas are associated with probabilities of PTSD as high as those found herein.

The only way to correct this problem and obtain unbiased estimates of the extent to which traumas of particular types are likely to lead to PTSD is to obtain data on "typical" traumas rather than "most upsetting" traumas. This could be done, in simplest form, by carrying out a survey in which an enumeration of all lifetime traumas was obtained from each respondent and a randomly selected trauma or subset of traumas from this list was assessed for PTSD. A complete assessment of trauma history and whether PTSD occurred after each lifetime trauma would provide much better information. However, this would be a substantial task. The results in Table 3 show that more than 10% of men and 6% of women in the NCS reported four or more types of lifetime traumas, some of which involved multiple occurrences (eg, being in two or more natural disasters at different times in their lives). In some cases, a complete assessment of trauma history would involve an assessment of 20 or more traumas. Nonetheless, our ability to distinguish primary and secondary PTSD, to estimate age-at-onset distributions, to evaluate the significance of intercohort trends in prevalence, and to obtain unbiased estimates of the conditional probabilities of PTSD associated with such things as different types of trauma, different trauma ages, and different trauma histories all require complete assessments of this sort. This should be a goal of future epidemiologic research on PTSD.

The NCS found that PTSD was approximately twice as prevalent among women as men. This is consistent with the findings of Breslau et al[26] in a community survey of young adults, but inconsistent with the results of two reports from the ECA study, neither of which found a sex difference in PTSD.[21,22] Both the NCS and Breslau et al[26] found that women exposed to a trauma are significantly more likely than men exposed to a trauma to develop PTSD and that this is the main reason for the sex difference in PTSD. This evidence of greater vulnerability among women is inconsistent with studies of people exposed to a single trauma that found conflicting results concerning whether men and women exposed to the same trauma differ significantly in the probability of PTSD.[13,58-60]

The NCS findings concerning different patterns of PTSD with age among men and women could reflect sex differences in substantive age effects, in substantive cohort effects, in methodologic artifacts caused by differential recall failure or differential sample attrition, or in some combination of these processes. There is no way to distinguish these possibilities with the data available to us. The situation is especially difficult in that we have no way of establishing age at onset of first PTSD because PTSD was assessed only for a single lifetime trauma.

The NCS found that lifetime PTSD was significantly more prevalent among respondents who were previously married than those who were married at the time of interview and, among men, more prevalent among the currently married than the never married. The only other general population study of PTSD that examined similar associations was that of Davidson et al[22] in the North Carolina ECA, who found an elevated but nonsignificant prevalence of PTSD among married respondents vs others in the sample. Results concerning the effects of marital status in studies of particular traumas are inconsistent.[18,61,62]

COMORBIDITY

The NCS results concerning comorbidity are consistent with previous research[21,22,24,32,33,35] in showing that the relative odds of other lifetime disorders are significantly elevated among people with lifetime PTSD and that the vast majority of these people also have at least one other lifetime DSM-III-R disorder. Absence of age-at-onset data for PTSD in the NCS made it impossible to obtain unbiased estimates of the proportion of cases in which first onset of PTSD (as opposed to onset associated with the most upsetting trauma) occurred at an earlier or later age than comorbid disorders. Estimates of upper and lower bounds, however, showed that while PTSD often occurs before other comorbid conditions, it usually occurs subsequent to at least one previous DSM-III-R disorder. This suggests that a complete assessment of lifetime PTSD would likely show both that it often occurs to people with a history and that it is often associated with the subsequent onset of yet other disorders. Further research is needed to investigate these issues. In the ideal case, this would be done prospectively to avoid the retrospective recall bias that clouds the interpretation of this part of the NCS analysis.

It was noted above that previous commentators have argued that comorbidity with PTSD would be expected for some disorders because of overlap of several criteria C and D symptoms of PTSD with symptoms of depression, of several criterion C symptoms of PTSD with symptoms of generalized anxiety disorder, and of criterion D6 of PTSD with social phobia, simple phobia, and panic disorder.[54,55] It would be useful for future research to determine whether comorbidity of PTSD with these other disorders remains if the definition of PTSD were based on the more distinctive criterion B symptoms concerning flashbacks and reactions to reexposure.

DURATION OF THE INDEX EPISODE

Our analysis of the duration of PTSD symptoms associated with the most upsetting lifetime trauma, finally, yielded several important results. First, we found that the average duration of symptoms was shorter in the subsample of people who ever obtained treatment (36 months) than in the subsample of people who did not obtain treatment (64 months). Although this difference cannot be taken as definitive evidence of the effectiveness of treatment because of differential selection into treatment and the possibility that error in recall of symptom duration is correlated with treatment, it suggests that treatment may be effective in reducing the duration of PTSD. Second, we found that more than one third of persons with PTSD never fully remit even after many years and irrespective of whether they were in treatment. In addition, consistent with the results of several previous prospective and retrospective studies,[21,22,32,36,37] we found that the survival curve decreased most steeply in the first 12 months after the onset of symptoms. We also found that the curve continues to decline with a more gradual slope for approximately 6 years after symptom onset. This part of the pattern is inconsistent with the suggestion of the sub–work group on PTSD for *DSM-IV* that people whose symptoms persist beyond 3 months rarely recover without professional treatment. Indeed, these results suggest that even after 2 years, the average person with PTSD who has not been in treatment still has a 50% chance of eventual remission.

CONCLUSION

The results reported herein show that PTSD is a highly prevalent lifetime disorder that often persists for years. The qualifying events for PTSD are also common, with many respondents reporting the occurrence of quite a few such events during their lifetimes. Although there is great variability in the associations of these different events with PTSD, none is such that virtually everyone exposed to it develops the disorder. Future research should assess PTSD for each respondent's full lifetime trauma history to resolve uncertainties concerning age at onset, cohort effects, the relative risk of PTSD associated with different precipitating events, the impact of previous disorders on subsequent PTSD, and the impact of PTSD on subsequent secondary disorders.

Accepted for publication June 7, 1995.

The NCS is supported by the US Alcohol, Drug Abuse, and Mental Health Administration (grants MH46376 and MH49098) with supplemental support from the W. T. Grant Foundation (grant 90135190). Preparation of this report was also supported by a Research Scientist Development Award to the first author (grant 1 K01 MH00507).

Dr Kessler is the principal investigator in the NCS. Collaborating NCS sites and investigators are as follows: The Addiction Research Foundation, Toronto, Ontario (Robin Room, PhD); Duke University Medical Center, Durham, NC (Dan Blazer, MD, Marvin Swartz, MD); Johns Hopkins University, Baltimore, Md (James Anthony, PhD, William Eaton, PhD, Richard Frank, PhD, Philip Leaf, PhD); the Max Planck Institute of Psychiatry–Clinical Institute, Munich, Germany (Hans-Ulrich Wittchen, PhD); the Medical College of Virginia, Richmond (Kenneth Kendler, MD); the University of Michigan, Ann Arbor (Lloyd Johnston, PhD, Ronald Kessler, PhD); New York (NY) University (Patrick Shrout, PhD); State University of New York at Stony Brook (Evelyn Bromet, PhD); The University of Toronto (Ontario) (R. Jay Turner, PhD); and Washington University School of Medicine, St Louis (Linda Cottler, PhD).

We thank Jonathon Davidson, Mardi Horowitz, and the anonymous reviewers for helpful comments, and Naomi Breslau and Gabrielle Carlson for help in classifying events as either qualifying or nonqualifying according to criterion A of DSM-III-R. Special thanks go to Helena Kraemer, who read multiple drafts and offered sage advice on the special difficulties introduced by the fact that PTSD was not assessed for all lifetime traumas. A complete list of NCS publications can be obtained by writing to the address below. The text of this and other NCS publications, working papers, and instruments can be obtained from the Internet by (1) ftping 141.211.207.206; (2) NAME=anonymous; (3) PASSWORD=(your Internet e-mail address); (4) reading the INSTRUCTIONS to download NCS documents. A public access NCS data file can be obtained from the Internet by (1) ftping ftp.icpsr. umich.edu; (2) NAME=anonymous; (3) PASSWORD= (your Internet e-mail address); (4) reading the INSTRUCTIONS to download NCS data.

Reprint requests to Institute for Social Research, University of Michigan, Box 1248, Ann Arbor, MI 48106-1248 (Dr Kessler).

REFERENCES

1. Freud S. *Introduction to the Psychology of the War Neuroses.* Standard Edition, 18. London, England: Hogarth Press; 1919.
2. Burgess AW, Holstrum L. The rape trauma syndrome. *Am J Psychiatry.* 1974; 131:981-986.
3. Grinker K, Spiegel S. *Men Under Stress.* Philadelphia, Pa: Blakiston; 1945.
4. Horowitz MJ. *Stress Response Syndromes.* New York, NY: Jason Aronson Inc; 1976.
5. Lindemann E. Symptomology and management of acute grief. *Am J Psychiatry.* 1944;101:141-148.
6. Parad H, Resnick H, Parad Z. *Emergency Mental Health Services and Disaster Management.* New York, NY: Prentice Hall; 1976.
7. American Psychiatric Association, Committee on Nomenclature and Statistics. *Diagnostic and Statistical Manual of Mental Disorders, Third Edition.* Washington, DC: American Psychiatric Association; 1980.
8. Kilpatrick DG, Saunders BE, Veronen LJ, Best CL, Von JM. Criminal victim-

ization: lifetime prevalence, reporting to police, and psychological impact. *Crime Delinquency.* 1987;33:479-489.

9. Kilpatrick DG, Resnick HS. Posttraumatic stress disorder associated with exposure to criminal victimization in clinical and community populations. In: Davidson JRT, Foa EB, eds. *Posttraumatic Stress Disorder: DSM-IV and Beyond.* Washington, DC: American Psychiatric Press; 1992.

10. Frank E, Anderson BP. Psychiatric disorders in rape victims: past history and current symptomatology. *Compr Psychiatry.* 1987;28:77-82.

11. Pynoos RS, Nader K. Children who witness the sexual assaults of their mothers. *J Am Acad Child Adolesc Psychiatry.* 1988;27:567-572.

12. Green BL, Grace ML, Gleser CG. Identifying survivors at risk: long-term impairment following the Beverly Hills Supper Club fire. *J Consult Clin Psychol.* 1985;53:672-678.

13. Madakasira S, O'Brien KF. Acute posttraumatic stress disorder in victims of a natural disaster. *J Nerv Ment Dis.* 1987;53:672-678.

14. Wilkinson CB. Aftermath of a disaster: the collapse of the Hyatt Regency Hotel skywalks. *Am J Psychiatry.* 1983;140:1134-1139.

15. Blanchard EB, Kolb LC, Pallmeyer TP, Gerardi RJ. The development of a psychophysiological assessment procedure for posttraumatic stress disorder in Vietnam veterans. *Psychiatr Q.* 1982;54:220-229.

16. Egendorf A, Kashudin C, Laufer RS, Rothbart G, Sloan L. *Legacies of Vietnam: Comparative Adjustment of Veterans and Their Peers.* New York, NY: Center for Policy Research; 1981;5.

17. Keane TM, Malloy PF, Fairbank JA. Empirical development of an MMPI subscale for the assessment of combat-related posttraumatic stress disorder. *J Consult Clin Psychol.* 1984;52:888-891.

18. Kulka RA, Schlenger WE, Fairbank JA, Hough RL, Jordan BK, Marmar CR, Weiss DS. *Trauma and the Vietnam War Generation.* New York, NY: Brunner/Mazel; 1990.

19. Brett EA, Ostroff R. Imagery and posttraumatic stress disorder: an overview. *Am J Psychiatry.* 1985;142:417-424.

20. American Psychiatric Association, Committee on Nomenclature and Statistics. *Diagnostic and Statistical Manual of Mental Disorders, Revised Third Edition.* Washington, DC: American Psychiatric Association; 1987.

21. Helzer JE, Robins LN, McEvoy L. Post-traumatic stress disorder in the general population. *N Engl J Med.* 1987;317:1630-1634.

22. Davidson JRT, Hughes D, Blazer D, George LK. Posttraumatic stress disorder in the community: an epidemiological study. *Psychol Med.* 1991;21:1-19.

23. Robins LN, Helzer JE, Cottier LB, Goldring E. *The Diagnostic Interview Schedule, Version IIIR.* St Louis, Mo: Washington University School of Medicine; 1988.

24. Shore JH, Vollmer WM, Tatum EI. Community patterns of posttraumatic stress disorders. *J Nerv Ment Dis.* 1989;177:681-685.

25. Resnick HS, Kilpatrick DG, Dansky BS, Saunders BE, Best CL. Prevalence of civilian trauma and posttraumatic stress disorder in a representative national sample of women. *J Consult Clin Psychol.* 1993;61:984-991.

26. Breslau N, Davis GC, Andreski P, Peterson E. Traumatic events and posttraumatic stress disorder in an urban population of young adults. *Arch Gen Psychiatry.* 1991;48:216-222.

27. Koss MP. The scope of rape: implications for the clinical treatment of victims. *Clin Psychol.* 1983;36:88-91.

28. Croyle RT, Loftus EF. Improving episode memory performance of survey respondents. In: Tanur JM, ed. *Questions About Questions: Inquiries Into the Cognitive Bases of Surveys.* New York, NY: Russell Sage Foundation; 1992.

29. Resnick HS, Kilpatrick DG, Lipovsky JA. Assessment of rape-related posttraumatic stress disorder: stressor and symptom dimensions. *J Consult Clin Psychol.* 1991;3:561-572.

30. Solomon S, Canino G. Appropriateness of the *DSM-III-R* criteria for posttraumatic stress disorder. *Compr Psychiatry.* 1990;31:227-237.

31. March JS. What constitutes a stressor? The 'criterion A' issue. In: Davidson JRT, Foa EB, ed. *Posttraumatic Stress Disorder: DSM-IV and Beyond.* Washington, DC: American Psychiatric Press; 1992.

32. Mellman TA, Randolph CA, Brawan-Mintzer O, Flores LP, Milanes FJ. Phenomenology and course of psychiatric disorders associated with combat-related posttraumatic stress disorder. *Am J Psychiatry.* 1992;149:1568-1574.

33. Davidson JRT, Kudler HS, Saunders WB, Smith SD. Symptom and morbidity patterns in World War II and Vietnam veterans with posttraumatic stress disorder. *Compr Psychiatry.* 1990;31:162-170.

34. Rothbaum BO, Foa EB. Subtypes of posttraumatic stress disorder and duration of symptoms. In: Davidson JRT, Foa EB, eds. *Posttraumatic Stress Disorder: DSM-IV and Beyond.* Washington, DC: American Psychiatric Press; 1992.

35. McFarlane AC. The longitudinal course of posttraumatic morbidity. *J Nerv Ment Dis.* 1988;1976:30-39.

36. Breslau N, Davis GC. Posttraumatic stress disorder in an urban population of young adults: risk factors for chronicity. *Am J Psychiatry.* 1992;149:671-675.

37. Kessler RC, McGonagle KA, Zhao S, Nelson CB, Hughes M, Eshleman S, Wittchen H-U, Kendler KS. Lifetime and 12-month prevalence of *DSM-III-R* psychiatric disorders in the United States: results from the National Comorbidity Survey. *Arch Gen Psychiatry.* 1994;51:8-19.

38. World Health Organization. *Composite International Diagnostic Interview.* Version 1.0. Geneva, Switzerland: World Health Organization; 1990a.

39. Robins LN, Wing J, Wittchen H-U, Helzer JE. The Composite International Diagnostic Interview: an epidemiologic instrument suitable for use in conjunction with different diagnostic systems and in different cultures. *Arch Gen Psychiatry.* 1988;45:1069-1077.

40. World Health Organization. *The ICD-10 Classification of Mental and Behavioral Disorders: Diagnostic Criteria for Research.* Geneva, Switzerland: World Health Organization; 1993.

41. World Health Organization. *Composite International Diagnostic Interview Computer Programs.* Version 1.1. Geneva, Switzerland: World Health Organization; 1990b.

42. Wittchen H-U. Reliability and validity studies of the WHO-Composite International Diagnostic Interview (CIDI): a critical review. *J Psychiatr Res.* 1994;28: 57-84.

43. Spitzer RL, Williams JBW, Gibbon M, First MD. *Structured Clinical Interview for DSM-III-R—Patient Version (SCID-P).* New York, NY: New York State Psychiatric Institute, Biometrics Research Division; 1989.

44. Endicott J, Spitzer RL. A diagnostic interview: the Schedule for Affective Disorders and Schizophrenia. *Arch Gen Psychiatry.* 1978;35:837-844.

45. Keller MB, Lavori PW, Nelson E. *SCALUP (SCID Plus SADS-L).* Providence, RI: Department of Psychiatry, Butler Hospital; 1987.

46. Warshaw MG, Fierman E, Pratt L, Hunt M, Yonkers KA, Massion AO, Keller MB. Quality of life and dissociation in anxiety disorder patients with histories of trauma or PTSD. *Am J Psychiatry.* 1993;150:1512-1516.

47. US Dept of Health and Human Services. *National Health Interview Survey, 1989.* Hyattsville, Md: National Center for Health Statistics; 1992. Computer file.

48. Woodruff RS, Causey BD. Computerized method for approximating the variance of a complicated estimate. *J Am Stat Assoc.* 1976;71:315-321.

49. *OSIRIS VII.* Ann Arbor, Mich: Institute for Social Research, University of Michigan; 1981.

50. Kish L, Frankel MR. Balanced repeated replications for standard errors. *J Am Stat Assoc.* 1970;65:1071-1094.

51. Koch GG, Leneshow S. An application of multivariate analysis to complex sample survey data. *J Am Stat Assoc.* 1972;67:780-782.

52. SAS Institute. *SAS 6.03.* Cary, NC: SAS Institute Inc; 1988.

53. Norusis MJ. *SPSS Advanced Statistics User's Guide.* Chicago, Ill: SPSS Inc; 1990.

54. Davidson JRT, Foa EB. Diagnostic issues in posttraumatic stress disorder: considerations for the *DSM-IV. J Abnorm Psychol.* 1991;100:346-355.

55. Southwick SM, Krystal JH, Morgan A, Johnson D, Nagy LM, Nicholaou A, Heninger GR, Charney DS. Abnormal noradrenergic function in posttraumatic stress disorder. *Arch Gen Psychiatry.* 1993;50:266-274.

56. Lee E, Desu M. A computer program for comparing k samples with right censored data. *Comput Programs Biomed.* 1972;2:315-321.

57. American Psychiatric Association, Committee on Nomenclature and Statistics. *Diagnostic and Statistical Manual of Mental Disorders, Revised Fourth Edition.* Washington, DC: American Psychiatric Association; 1994.

58. Green BL, Lindy JD, Grace MC, Gleser GC, Leonard AC, Korol M, Winget C. Buffalo Creek survivors in the second decade stability of stress symptoms. *Am J Orthopsychiatry.* 1990:60:45-54.

59. Smith EM, North CS. *Aftermath of a Disaster: Psychological Response to the Indianapolis Ramada Jet Crash.* Boulder, Colo: Natural Hazards Research and Application Information Center; 1988. Quick Response Research Report No. 23.

60. Steinglass P, Gerrity E. Natural disaster and post-traumatic stress disorder: short-term versus long-term recovery in two disaster-affected communities. *J Appl Soc Psychol.* 1990;20:1746-1765.

61. Card JJ. Epidemiology of PTSD in a national cohort of Vietnam veterans. *J Clin Psychol.* 1987;43:6-17.

62. Solomon Z, Mikulincer M, Freid B, Wosner Y. Family characteristics and posttraumatic stress disorder: a follow-up of Israeli combat stress reaction casualties. *Fam Process.* 1987;26:383-394.

34

Impairment in Pure and Comorbid Generalized Anxiety Disorder and Major Depression at 12 Months in Two National Surveys

Ronald C. Kessler, Ph.D., Robert L. DuPont, M.D.,
Patricia Berglund, M.B.A., and Hans-Ulrich Wittchen, Ph.D.

Objective: Generalized anxiety disorder might be better conceptualized as a prodrome, residual, or severity marker of major depression or other comorbid disorders than as an independent diagnosis. The authors questioned whether generalized anxiety disorder itself is associated with role impairment or whether the impairment of patients with generalized anxiety disorder is due to depression or other comorbid disorders. **Method:** The authors assessed data from the National Comorbidity Survey and the Midlife Development in the United States Survey for generalized anxiety disorder and major depression at 12 months by using the DSM-III-R criteria with modified versions of the Composite International Diagnostic Interview. **Results:** The prevalences of generalized anxiety disorder at 12 months were 3.1% and 3.3%, respectively, in the National Comorbidity Survey and the Midlife Development in the United States Survey; the prevalences of major depression at 12 months were 10.3% and 14.1%. The majority of respondents with generalized anxiety disorder at 12 months in the National Comorbidity Survey (58.1%) and the Midlife Development in the United States Survey (69.7%) also met the criteria for major depression at 12 months. Comparisons of respondents with one versus both neither disorder showed that both disorders had statistically significant independent associations with impairment that were roughly equal in magnitude. These associations could not be explained by the other comorbid DSM-III-R disorders or by sociodemographic variables. **Conclusions:** These results show that a substantial amount of generalized anxiety disorder occurs independently of major depression and that the role impairment of generalized anxiety disorder is comparable to that of major depression.

(Am J Psychiatry 1999; 156:1915–1923)

I nterest in comorbidity between generalized anxiety disorder and major depression has grown dramatically

Received Nov. 9, 1998; revision received April 6, 1999; accepted May 17, 1999. From the Department of Health Care Policy, Harvard Medical School; DuPont Associates, Rockville, Md.; the Institute for Social Research, University of Michigan, Ann Arbor; and the Max Planck Institute of Psychiatry, Munich. Address reprint requests to Dr. Kessler, Department of Health Care Policy, Harvard Medical School, 180 Longwood Ave., Boston, MA 02115; Kessler@hcp.med.harvard.edu (e-mail).
Supported by NIMH grants MH-46376, MH-49098, and MH-52861; National Institute on Drug Abuse grant DA-11121; W.T. Grant Foundation grant 90135190 to Dr. Kessler (National Comorbidity Survey); the John D. and Catherine T. MacArthur Foundation Network in Successful Midlife Development (Midlife Development in the United States Survey); NIMH Research Scientist Award (MH-00507) to Dr. Kessler; and an unrestricted educational grant from Wyeth-Ayerst Laboratories.
The authors thank Philip Leaf and Paul Stang for their help on an earlier version of the article.

over the past decade on the basis of evidence that this type of comorbidity is very common (1), that it is associated with more impairment than either pure generalized anxiety disorder (2) or pure major depression (3), and that it predicts poor outcomes both among patients in treatment for generalized anxiety disorder (4) and among patients in treatment for major depression (5). There is also considerable interest in the relative impairment of pure generalized anxiety disorder and pure major depression. This interest can be traced to the controversy that has surrounded generalized anxiety disorder since its introduction in DSM-III in relation to the fact that the vast majority of patients with generalized anxiety disorder also carry one or more other psychiatric diagnoses (6). This high comorbidity has led to the suggestion that generalized anxiety disorder might be better conceptualized as a prodrome, residual, or severity marker of major depression or

35

other comorbid disorders than as an independent diagnosis (7, 8). An issue central to this nosological debate is whether generalized anxiety disorder itself is associated with role impairment or whether the impairment of patients with generalized anxiety disorder is due to depression or other comorbid disorders (9).

Some information about the relative impairment of generalized anxiety disorder and major depression can be gleaned from three studies of untreated mental disorders among primary care patients (10–12). All three of these studies found that both "pure" major depression and "pure" generalized anxiety disorder, defined as current episodes of these disorders in the absence of any of the other mood, anxiety, or substance use disorders assessed in the surveys, were associated with meaningful levels of impairment in a number of life domains. For example, Ormel et al. (10) found that mean numbers of disability days in the past month were much higher among primary care patients with pure generalized anxiety disorder (4.4 days) and pure major depression (6.3 days) than among patients with none of the psychiatric disorders assessed in their survey (1.7 days), whereas Schonfeld et al. (12) found that mean age-sex adjusted scores on the 36-item Medical Outcomes Study Short-Form General Health Survey (13) scale of social functioning (possible score of 0–100) were much lower (a high score is indicative of good functioning) among primary care patients with pure generalized anxiety disorder (71.0) and pure major depression (60.3) than among those with none of the psychiatric disorders assessed in their survey (83.6).

The impairment associated with pure major depression is greater and more varied than that associated with pure generalized anxiety disorder in two of these studies (11, 12). However, the reliability of these findings can be questioned based on the fact that the numbers of patients with pure disorders in these studies were quite small: only four cases in one study (11) and 14 in the other (12) with pure generalized anxiety disorder and only 25 in the one study (11) and 54 in the other (12) with pure depression. Differences in the magnitude of impairment associated with pure generalized anxiety disorder and pure major depression were much smaller in the study by Ormel et al. (10), which included considerably larger numbers of respondents with pure generalized anxiety disorder (N=272) and pure major depression (N=438). Aggregate impairment of generalized anxiety disorder and major depression was also quite similar in a large primary care study carried out by Spitzer et al. (14) that did not distinguish between pure and comorbid patient cases.

It is important to note that the evaluations of comorbidity in all of these studies included other psychiatric disorders in addition to generalized anxiety disorder and major depression. Given the much higher prevalence of comorbidity between generalized anxiety disorder and major depression than with other types of anxiety-mood comorbidity (15), it is desirable to obtain more focused general population data to evaluate

the separate and joint effects of these two disorders as well as to evaluate the effects of broader comorbidities in the general population. The current report presents data of this sort on work and social role impairment and perceived mental health status from two large nationally representative general population surveys, the National Comorbidity Survey (16) and the Midlife Development in the United States Survey (17).

METHOD

Samples

The National Comorbidity Survey is a nationally representative household survey of 8,098 persons age 15 to 54 years in the noninstitutionalized civilian population of the 48 coterminous United States, along with a representative supplemental sample of students living in campus group housing. The National Comorbidity Survey was administered to 8,098 respondents between September 1990 and February 1992 in face-to-face, in-home interviews. The response rate was 82.4%. A part two subsample of 5,877 respondents, consisting of all those with any Composite International Diagnostic Interview diagnosis and a random subsample of others, was administered a series of questions about the risk factors and consequences of psychiatric disorders. The data on impairment reported here are from the part two subsample. These data have been weighted to adjust for differential probabilities of selection and nonresponse. More details on the National Comorbidity Survey design, field procedures, and sample weights were reported elsewhere (16, 18).

The Midlife Development in the United States Survey is a nationally representative survey of 3,032 persons age 25–74 years in the noninstitutionalized civilian population of the 48 coterminous United States. The Midlife Development in the United States Survey was carried out by the John D. and Catherine T. MacArthur Foundation Network on Successful Midlife Development between January 1995 and January 1996. All respondents completed a 30-minute telephone interview (70.0% response rate) and filled out two mailed questionnaires estimated to take a total of about 90 minutes to complete (86.8% conditional response rate in the subsample of telephone respondents). The overall response rate (0.700×0.868) was 60.8%. The data reported here were weighted to adjust for differential probabilities of selection and nonresponse. More details on the Midlife Development in the United States Survey design, field procedures, and sampling weights are available elsewhere (17).

Diagnostic Assessment

National Comorbidity Survey diagnoses are based on a modified version of the Composite International Diagnostic Interview (19), a fully structured interview designed to be administered by interviewers who are not clinicians and to generate diagnoses according to the definitions and criteria of both DSM-III-R and ICD-10. The current report uses DSM-III-R criteria. Although the focus is on the prevalences of generalized anxiety disorder and major depression within the year prior to the interview (prevalences at 12 months), we also controlled for prevalences of the other disorders assessed in the National Comorbidity Survey at 12 months. These included other anxiety disorders (panic disorder, simple phobia, social phobia, agoraphobia, and posttraumatic stress disorder), mania, substance use disorders (alcohol and drug abuse and dependence), and nonaffective psychosis. Diagnoses were made without hierarchy rules. A National Comorbidity Survey clinical reappraisal study found good test-retest reliability and procedural validity of all of the diagnoses compared to clinical reassessments (20), with the exceptions of mania and nonaffective psychosis. On the basis of the finding that the Composite International Diagnostic Interview validly assesses only manic patients with a euphoric-grandiose symptom profile (21), our control for mania was limited to this subtype of manic patients. On the basis of the finding that the Composite International Diagnostic Interview substantially overdiagnoses nonaffective psychosis (22),

36

our control for nonaffective psychosis was based on clinical reinterviews with all National Comorbidity Survey respondents who screened positive for nonaffective psychosis in the Composite International Diagnostic Interview.

The DSM diagnostic hierarchy rule for generalized anxiety disorder and major depression stipulates that an episode of generalized anxiety that occurs exclusively within a major depressive episode is not classified as generalized anxiety disorder. This rule was put into use in the National Comorbidity Survey in a series of three questions asked of all respondents who met the criteria for generalized anxiety disorder without hierarchy and major depression. The first asked whether the generalized anxiety disorder never, sometimes, or always occurred during times when the respondent was depressed. If it occurred sometimes or always, the second question asked which syndrome started first during these episodes of overlapping symptoms—the depression, the anxiety, both at the same time, or it varied. The third question was similar to the second except that it asked which symptoms ended first when and if either of them ever resolved. Only 4.6% of the National Comorbidity Survey respondents with comorbid generalized anxiety disorder at 12 months (without hierarchy) and major depression reported that their episodes of generalized anxiety disorder occurred exclusively within their episodes of major depression.

The Midlife Development in the United States Survey diagnoses were based on the Composite International Diagnostic Interview Short Form scales (23), a series of diagnosis-specific scales that were developed from item-level analyses of the Composite International Diagnostic Interview questions in the National Comorbidity Survey. The Composite International Diagnostic Interview Short Form scales were designed to reproduce the full Composite International Diagnostic Interview diagnoses as exactly as possible with only a small subset of the original questions. Comparison of the Composite International Diagnostic Interview Short Form classifications of generalized anxiety disorder with the full Composite International Diagnostic Interview classifications in the National Comorbidity Survey yielded a sensitivity of 96.6%, a specificity of 99.8%, and 99.6% overall agreement. A comparison of the Composite International Diagnostic Interview Short Form classifications of major depression with the full Composite International Diagnostic Interview classifications in the National Comorbidity Survey yielded a sensitivity of 89.6%, a specificity of 93.9%, and an overall agreement of 93.2%. Additional Composite International Diagnostic Interview Short Form diagnoses at 12 months included in the Midlife Development in the United States Survey are panic disorder (with or without agoraphobia), alcohol abuse and dependence, and drug abuse and dependence.

Measures of Impairment

Three measures of impairment were considered in this study. The first dealt with perceived mental health on the basis of parallel questions in both surveys that asked respondents to rate their mental health as excellent, very good, good, fair, or poor. A separate dichotomous version of this scale was created as an outcome for logistic regression analysis by assigning respondents who reported either fair or poor mental health a code of one and all others a code of zero.

The next measure dealt with work role impairment on the basis of two parallel questions in which respondents were asked about work loss and work cutback in the past month. Work loss was assessed by asking respondents how many days in the past month they were totally unable to work or carry out their normal daily activities because of problems with their emotions, nerves, or mental health. Work cutback was assessed by asking respondents how many days in the past month, exclusive of work loss days, they had to cut back on the amount of work they got done or did not get as much done as usual because of problems with their emotions, nerves, or mental health. Responses to the two questions were summed and collapsed into the categories 0, 1 to 2, 3 to 5, and 6 or more work impairment days. A separate dichotomous variable was created as an outcome for logistic regression analysis by assigning respondents with six or more combined work loss and work cutback days a code of one and all others a code of zero.

The last measure dealt with social role impairment on the basis of previously developed six-item scales of social support and negative social interaction (24). These scales were used to assess impairment in relationships with friends and relatives. The social support scale asked respondents to rate the following items with response categories of a lot, some, a little, and not at all: "How much friends and relatives...1) really care about you, 2) understand the way you feel about things, and 3) appreciate you. 4) How much can you rely on them for help if you have a serious problem? 5) How much can you open up to them if you need to talk about your worries? and 6) How much can you relax and be yourself around them?" The negative social interaction scale asked respondents to rate the following items with response categories of often, sometimes, rarely, and never: "How often do your friends and relatives 1) make too many demands on you, 2) make you feel tense, 3) argue with you, 4) criticize you, 5) let you down when you are counting on them, and 6) get on your nerves?"

Scores on the social support scale were reversed, so that low support had the highest score, and scores were summed with the negative interaction scale. The total score was then divided into four discrete categories on the basis of total sample percentiles of 0%–50% (lowest social role impairment), 51%–80%, 81%–90%, and 91% or higher (highest social role impairment). A separate dichotomous measure of extreme social role impairment was also created as an outcome variable for logistic regression analysis by assigning respondents with answers in the 90%-or-higher range a code of one and all others a code of zero.

Analysis

Simple cross-tabulations were used to estimate the overlap between generalized anxiety disorder and major depression at 12 months. Conditional logistic regression analysis was then used to estimate the associations of generalized anxiety disorder and major depression at 12 months with measures of impairment in subsamples that differed in the presence or absence of the other disorder. All equations controlled for other DSM-III-R disorders assessed in the surveys as well as for sociodemographic variables (age, gender, education, race/ethnicity, employment status, marital status, and urbanicity). Finally, a series of equations was estimated in the subsample of National Comorbidity Survey respondents with comorbid generalized anxiety disorder and major depression at 12 months to investigate whether temporal priority of one disorder over the other in age at first onset or timing of onset or offset within episodes significantly predicted the impairment.

Significance tests for individual coefficients were computed by using jackknife repeated replications (25) to estimate standard errors that adjusted for design effects introduced by the clustering (only in the National Comorbidity Survey as there was no geographic clustering in the Midlife Development in the United States Survey because it used a telephone sampling frame rather than a multistage area frame) and weighting of observations. Jackknife repeated replication is one of several methods that uses simulations of coefficient distributions in subsamples to generate empirical estimates of standard errors and significance tests. These estimates were used to compute 95% confidence intervals for unstandardized linear regression coefficients as well as for odds ratios obtained by exponentiating logistic regression coefficients. Tests for the significance of sets of predictors taken together were computed by using Wald chi-square tests. Design effects were introduced into these calculations by basing the Wald tests on coefficient variance-covariance matrices obtained from jackknife repeated replication simulations. All evaluations of statistical significance were made at the 0.05 level by using z tests, two-tailed.

RESULTS

The majority of respondents with generalized anxiety disorder at 12 months in both the National Comorbidity Survey (58.1%) and the Midlife Development in

37

FIGURE 1. Prevalence and Comorbidity of Generalized Anxiety Disorder and Major Depression at 12 Months in Two National General Population Surveys

Generalized Anxiety Disorder
National Comorbidity Survey
Prevalence=3.1%, SE=0.3%
Midlife in the U.S. Survey
Prevalence=3.3%, SE=0.3%

Major Depression
National Comorbidity Survey
Prevalence=10.3%, SE=0.6%
Midlife in the U.S. Survey
Prevalence=14.1%, SE=0.9%

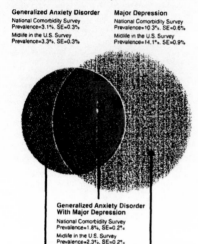

Generalized Anxiety Disorder With Major Depression
National Comorbidity Survey
Prevalence=1.8%, SE=0.2%
Midlife in the U.S. Survey
Prevalence=2.3%, SE=0.2%

Generalized Anxiety Disorder Without Major Depression
National Comorbidity Survey
Prevalence=1.3%, SE=0.2%
Midlife in the U.S. Survey
Prevalence=1.0%, SE=0.1%

Major Depression Without Generalized Anxiety Disorder
National Comorbidity Survey
Prevalence=8.5%, SE=0.6%
Midlife in the U.S. Survey
Prevalence=11.8%, SE=0.5%

the United States Survey (69.7%) also had major depression at 12 months, whereas 17.5% of the respondents with major depression also had generalized anxiety disorder in the National Comorbidity Survey and 16.3% in the Midlife Development in the United States Survey (figure 1).

Scores on the measures of impairment are presented in table 1. There is good consistency in results across the two surveys. In comparison with respondents in all three categories of disorder, the impairment of respondents with neither disorder is substantially lower than that of respondents with one or both disorders. Furthermore, the impairment of respondents with only one of the two disorders is consistently lower than that of respondents with both disorders, although this pattern is weak for social role impairment in the National Comorbidity Survey.

Data on the associations between pure generalized anxiety disorder and pure major depression and impairment, adjusted for other comorbid disorders and for sociodemographic variables, are presented in table 2. The first four columns report associations involving pure generalized anxiety disorder. Five of these six coefficients show that generalized anxiety disorder

is associated with higher impairment than that found among respondents who do not have generalized anxiety disorder. Three of these five coefficients are statistically significant at the 0.05 level. The exception is social role impairment in the Midlife Development in the United States Survey, where there is no meaningful elevation among respondents with generalized anxiety disorder. The next four columns report associations involving pure major depression. All of these coefficients show that major depression is associated with significantly higher impairment than that found among respondents who do not have major depression. Comparison of the impairment associated with pure generalized anxiety disorder and pure major depression is reported in the last four columns of the table. None of these differences is statistically significant.

Data on the incremental effects of generalized anxiety disorder or major depression in the subsample of respondents with the other disorder are presented in table 3. The first four columns report associations involving the incremental effects of generalized anxiety disorder over and above those of major depression. Five of the six coefficients show that generalized anxiety disorder and major depression are associated with higher impairment than that found among depressed respondents who do not have generalized anxiety disorder. Three of these five are significant at the 0.05 level. The exception is social role impairment in the National Comorbidity Survey, in which the odds ratio is not meaningfully different from 1.0. The next four columns report associations involving the incremental effects of major depression over and above those of generalized anxiety disorder. Five of the six coefficients show that generalized anxiety disorder and major depression are associated with higher impairment than that found among respondents with pure generalized anxiety disorder. Two of these coefficients are significant at the 0.05 level. The exception is social role impairment in the National Comorbidity Survey, in which the odds ratio is 1.0.

Finally, we carried out more detailed analyses of the National Comorbidity Survey data to consider the possibility that the impairment associated with comorbid generalized anxiety disorder and major depression differs depending on which of the two disorders is primary and which is secondary. Similar analyses could not be carried out in the Midlife Development in the United States Survey because data on the primary-secondary distinction were not collected in that survey. Because this distinction is defined in several different ways (26), the analyses were carried out by estimating a series of three different models to predict impairment in the subsample of respondents who had both generalized anxiety disorder and major depression at 12 months and controlling for other DSM-III-R disorders at 12 months and sociodemographic variables.

The first of these models introduced information about whether age at onset of generalized anxiety disorder was before, after, or at the same age at onset as major depression. This information is not significantly

38

TABLE 1. Impairment Associated With Generalized Anxiety Disorder and Major Depression at 12 Months in Two National General Population Surveys

Study and Measure of Impairment	Major Depression and Generalized Anxiety Disorder				Major Depression Only				Generalized Anxiety Disorder Only				Neither Major Depression nor Generalized Anxiety Disorder			
		Measure Present				Measure Present				Measure Present				Measure Present		
	N	%	SE		N	%	SE		N	%	SE		N	%	SE	
National Comorbidity Survey	99				489				92				5,217			
Perceived mental health																
Excellent		8.8	3.3			9.6	1.4			15.8	6.2			33.2	0.8	
Very good		17.8	4.7			30.9	2.1			24.8	6.0			41.0	1.0	
Good		37.9	4.1			39.7	2.4			30.1	4.9			21.1	0.1	
Fair or poor		35.5	3.7			19.7	1.8			29.3	6.0			4.7	0.4	
Past month's work impairment (days)																
0		58.2	6.2			75.3	2.1			78.2	4.2			94.7	0.3	
1 or 2		8.1	2.6			5.3	1.0			7.9	3.1			2.1	0.2	
3–5		11.8	3.9			9.4	1.8			2.6	1.8			1.6	0.2	
6 or more		21.9	4.3			10.0	1.3			11.3	4.2			1.5	0.2	
Social role impairment																
10%—high impairment		26.5	4.7			22.5	2.0			24.0	4.6			8.4	0.4	
10%		17.3	3.7			17.8	1.9			11.4	3.7			9.3	0.6	
30%		18.0	4.0			32.3	2.4			31.7	4.7			30.0	1.0	
50%—low impairment		38.2	5.3			27.4	2.0			32.9	6.2			52.3	1.0	
Midlife Development in the United States Survey	70				358				29				2,575			
Perceived mental health																
Excellent		7.2	2.9			9.8	1.3			19.0	6.1			24.8	0.7	
Very good		12.9	3.7			19.9	1.8			14.3	5.4			36.3	0.8	
Good		26.9	4.9			40.9	2.2			41.5	7.6			32.7	0.8	
Fair or poor		52.9	5.5			29.3	2.0			25.2	6.7			6.1	0.3	
Past month's work impairment (days)																
0		49.9	5.6			68.1	2.0			79.7	6.2			94.5	0.4	
1 or 2		9.2	3.2			9.1	1.3			9.5	4.5			3.1	0.3	
3–5		8.8	3.1			9.7	1.3			2.5	2.4			1.4	0.2	
6 or more		32.1	5.2			13.1	1.5			8.3	4.3			0.9	0.2	
Social role impairment																
10%—high impairment		33.3	5.2			17.2	1.7			15.5	5.6			9.4	0.5	
10%		10.7	3.4			10.1	1.3			8.5	4.3			8.6	0.5	
30%		30.3	5.1			32.3	2.1			41.1	7.8			30.1	0.8	
50%—low impairment		25.7	4.9			40.5	2.2			34.8	7.4			51.8	0.8	

TABLE 2. Independent Effects of Generalized Anxiety Disorder and Major Depression at 12 Months in Predicting Impairment in Two National General Population Surveys, With Controls for Sociodemographic Variables and Other DSM-III-R Disorders at 12 Months[a]

Measure of Impairment	Pure Generalized Anxiety Disorder				Pure Major Depression				Pure Generalized Anxiety Disorder and Pure Major Depression			
	National Comorbidity Survey		Midlife Development in the United States Survey		National Comorbidity Survey		Midlife Development in the United States Survey		National Comorbidity Survey		Midlife Development in the United States Survey	
	Odds Ratio	95% CI	Odds Ratio	95% CI	Odds Ratio	95% CI	Odds Ratio	95% CI	Odds Ratio	95% CI	Odds Ratio	95% CI
Mental health perceived as fair or poor	6.0[b]	2.7–13.8	4.8[b]	1.9–12.2	3.3[b]	2.5–4.3	5.2[b]	3.8–7.2	1.6	0.8–3.3	0.8	0.3–2.0
High level of work impairment	3.5	0.7–16.9	3.5	0.7–18.3	3.5[b]	2.1–5.6	8.5[b]	4.9–14.9	0.9	0.3–2.7	0.5	0.1–2.0
High level of social role impairment	2.5[b]	1.3–4.7	1.2	0.4–3.9	2.0[b]	1.6–2.6	1.6[b]	1.1–2.3	1.5	0.9–2.5	1.0	0.2–2.4

[a] Results based on separate regression equations controlled for age, gender, education, race/ethnicity, employment status, marital status, urbanicity, and other DSM-III-R disorders at 12 months. The disorders included as controls were more extensive in the National Comorbidity Survey (mania, panic disorder, simple phobia, social phobia, agoraphobia, posttraumatic stress disorder, alcohol and drug abuse and dependence, and nonaffective psychosis) than in the Midlife Development in the United States Survey (panic disorder and alcohol and drug abuse and dependence) because the latter survey assessed only a small number of disorders.
[b] Significant at the 0.05 level (z test, two-tailed).

39

TABLE 3. Incremental Effect of Comorbid Generalized Anxiety Disorder and Major Depression at 12 Months Compared to Separate Disorders in Predicting Impairment in Two National General Population Surveys, With Controls for Sociodemographic Variables and Other DSM-III-R Disorders at 12 Months[a]

| Measure of Impairment | Generalized Anxiety Disorder Over and Above Major Depression | | | | Major Depression Over and Above Generalized Anxiety Disorder | | | |
| | National Comorbidity Survey | | Midlife Development in the United States Survey | | National Comorbidity Survey | | Midlife Development in the United States Survey | |
	Odds Ratio	95% CI	Odds Ratio	95% CI	Odds Ratio	95% CI	Odds Ratio	95% CI
Mental health perceived as fair or poor	1.4	0.8–2.4	2.7[b]	1.5–4.9	1.2	0.5–2.9	5.2[b]	1.6–17.2
High level of work impairment	1.5	0.8–2.7	3.5[b]	1.7–7.2	2.2	0.6–7.9	40.7[b]	3.5–466.1
High level of social role impairment	0.8	0.5–1.5	2.4[b]	1.3–4.6	1.0	0.4–2.6	4.1	0.8–20.5

[a] Results based on separate regression equations controlled for age, gender, education, race/ethnicity, employment status, marital status, urbanicity, and other DSM-III-R disorders at 12 months.
[b] Significant at the 0.05 level (z test, two-tailed).

related to any of the impairment measures. The second model added information about whether the symptoms of generalized anxiety disorder usually begin first, the symptoms of major depression usually begin first, both syndromes usually begin at about the same time, or it varies at the onset of episodes of comorbid generalized anxiety disorder and major depression. This information is not significantly related to any of the impairment measures. Finally, the third model added information about the typical order in which symptoms remit during episodes of comorbid generalized anxiety disorder and major depression. This information is not significantly related to any of the impairment measures.

DISCUSSION

A number of limitations need to be noted. First, the Composite International Diagnostic Interview is a lay-administered diagnostic interview that only imperfectly captures the diagnostic distinctions made by experienced clinicians. This is of special concern in an analysis of the comorbidity of generalized anxiety disorder and major depression because the core symptoms of generalized anxiety disorder and major depression overlap. The evidence of good concordance between the Composite International Diagnostic Interview and independent clinical diagnoses argues against a pervasive bias (20), but it remains possible that imprecision in the Composite International Diagnostic Interview in distinguishing cases of generalized anxiety disorder and major depression plays a part in the results reported here. Second, the impairment measures are based on self-reports. Because mood disturbances can lead to distorted perceptions of role functioning (27), it is conceivable that the results reflect the influences of comorbidity on perceptions of impairment rather than on actual impairment. This is especially problematic for the measures of work impairment because respondents had to report not only days of work loss and work cutback, but they also had to make attributions as to whether these work impairments were due to problems with their emotions, nerves, or mental health.

Within the context of these limitations, our results are similar to those in previous studies in the general population (1, 28, 29), in primary care samples (11, 30), and in mental health specialty samples (31, 32) in showing that major depression is a good deal more common than generalized anxiety disorder, that there is a strong comorbidity between generalized anxiety disorder and major depression, that major depression occurs in the majority of people with generalized anxiety disorder, and that generalized anxiety disorder occurs in a substantial minority of people with major depression. This is not to say that generalized anxiety disorder and major depression are so strongly related that they cannot be distinguished—they can. For example, Brown et al. (33) tested several models of structural relationships between symptoms of anxiety and depression and found separate latent factors of positive affectivity, negative affectivity, and autonomic suppression (related to generalized anxiety disorder). This finding strongly argues that generalized anxiety disorder and major depression can be distinguished despite the overlap in many of their core symptoms. Consistent with this finding, analyses of twin data by using an additive behavior genetic model concluded that the environmental determinants of generalized anxiety disorder and major depression are distinct (34). In turn, this result is consistent with the finding in epidemiologic research that generalized anxiety disorder and major depression have significantly different sociodemographic predictors (35).

It is noteworthy that twin studies also suggest that the genes for generalized anxiety disorder and major depression are the same (34), raising the possibility that the two syndromes are different manifestations of the same underlying disorder. However, the model on which this conclusion is based assumes that the joint effects of genes and environment are additive—that is, the impact of environmental determinants is not influenced by the presence or absence of the genes. This is implausible. A more realistic interactive specification, which cannot be identified with conventional twin data, might well show a differentiation of genetic effects. Consistent with this possibility, family studies show a differential aggregation of mental disorders in the families of patients with general-

Am J Psychiatry 156:12, December 1999

40

ized anxiety disorder and major depression (36) and raise the possibility that comorbid generalized anxiety disorder and major depression might be a distinct disorder from pure generalized anxiety disorder or pure major depression (37).

We were able to go beyond simple bivariate analysis at 12 months with the National Comorbidity Survey data, but not with the Midlife Development in the United States Survey data (because of the absence of data on lifetime disorders and age at onset) to shed some light on two broader patterns of comorbidity. First, additional National Comorbidity Survey analysis not reported in this article shows that the absence of major depression at 12 months is uncommon among respondents with generalized anxiety disorder at 12 months and a lifetime history of major depression (8.3%). This result indirectly implies that generalized anxiety disorder and major depression covary over time within persons who have a history of both disorders. This is an implication that is consistent with previously reported direct evidence of a significant association between the persistence of generalized anxiety disorder and the persistence of major depression in the National Comorbidity Survey (15) and indirectly consistent with the suggestion that comorbid generalized anxiety disorder and major depression might be a distinct disorder. Second, further National Comorbidity Survey analysis, again not reported in this article, found that the majority (66.6%) of respondents with comorbid generalized anxiety disorder and major depression at 12 months also reported at least one other DSM-III-R anxiety disorder with an earlier age at onset than that of both generalized anxiety disorder and major depression. This means that the comorbidity of generalized anxiety disorder and major depression is often part of a larger anxiety-depression syndrome in which other anxiety disorders are temporally primary. This larger syndrome, which was not examined in the present report, warrants detailed examination in future research.

As noted in the introduction, some commentators have argued that comorbidity among patients with generalized anxiety disorder is so high that generalized anxiety disorder might more accurately be conceptualized as a prodrome, residual, or severity marker than as an independent disorder (6, 8). In evaluating this suggestion, it is important to appreciate that major depression is much more prevalent than generalized anxiety disorder (16). This means that the strong comorbidity between the two disorders translates into only a minority of people with major depression having comorbid generalized anxiety disorder but a majority of those with generalized anxiety disorder having comorbid major depression (15). The suggestion that generalized anxiety disorder is not an independent disorder fails to take a statistical artifact into consideration: less prevalent disorders, all else equal, have higher rates of comorbidity than more common disorders even when the strength of associations (odds ratios) of the two disorders with

other disorders are identical. It is noteworthy in this regard that the comparative odds ratios of generalized anxiety disorder and major depression with other disorders in the National Comorbidity Survey are not consistently larger for generalized anxiety disorder (15). Furthermore, when we look at overall lifetime comorbidities of generalized anxiety disorder and major depression with any of the DSM-III-R disorders assessed in the National Comorbidity Survey, the rates are not dramatically different: 91% lifetime comorbidity for generalized anxiety disorder and 83% for major depression. Rates of episode comorbidity, which have been the focus of recent studies in primary care samples, are also not dramatically different for the two disorders. For example, Ormel et al. (10) found 61% episode comorbidity for generalized anxiety disorder and 63% for major depression, whereas Olfson et al. (11) found 88% episode comorbidity for generalized anxiety disorder and 66% for major depression. These rates are not so different as to argue that major depression is a true independent disorder whereas generalized anxiety disorder is not.

The issue of primary importance in this report regards the comparative impairment of generalized anxiety disorder and major depression. We found, consistent with previous research, that comorbid generalized anxiety disorder and major depression are associated with more impairment than are pure generalized anxiety disorder or pure major depression. We also found that respondents with only one of these disorders have more impairment than do respondents who have neither disorder, after adjusting for additional diagnoses and sociodemographic differences. However, more important from a nosological perspective, we also found that the impairment of pure generalized anxiety disorder is equivalent in magnitude to the impairment of pure major depression. This is true even when we control for the co-occurrence of all the other DSM-III-R disorders assessed in the two surveys. The finding of equivalent effects suggests that generalized anxiety disorder is consequential in and of itself and that its impairment is not due to other disorders. It is also important to note, although the results are not reported here, that these conclusions are insensitive to variation in the specifications of functional form. Specifically, whereas we presented results for dichotomous versions of the impairment measures, similar results were found in linear regression analyses by using continuous versions of these measures and separating submeasures such as work loss versus work cutback and the quality of relationships with friends versus relatives (results available on request from Dr. Kessler).

A question can be raised regarding the inconsistency of our findings with the conclusions of Olfson et al. (11) and Schonfeld et al. (12) in primary care samples that pure generalized anxiety disorder is not associated with significant impairment. However, it must be remembered that Olfson et al. and Schonfeld et al. studied very small numbers of respondents with pure generalized anxiety disorder, which introduced instability into their findings. The fact that significant independent effects of generalized anxiety disorder were found in the much larger and nationally representative National Comorbidity Survey and Midlife Development in the United States Survey calls the findings of Olfson et al. and Schonfeld et al. into question. The inconsistency of the results certainly suggests that this issue should be reexamined in other available data sets. However, the weight of the evidence at the moment, on the basis of the results reported here, is clear that—contrary to the suggestion that generalized anxiety disorder is better conceptualized as a prodrome, residual, or severity marker of depression rather than as an independent disorder in its own right—a substantial proportion of the cases of generalized anxiety disorder in the general population occur independently of major depression. The role impairment due to generalized anxiety disorder is comparable to that due to major depression, even after adjusting for a wide range of other comorbid disorders.

REFERENCES

1. Kessler RC: The epidemiology of psychiatric comorbidity, in Textbook of Psychiatric Epidemiology. Edited by Tsuang M, Tohen M, Zahner G. New York, John Wiley & Sons, 1995, pp 179–197
2. Wittchen H-U, Zhao S, Kessler RC, Eaton WW: DSM-III-R generalized anxiety disorder in the National Comorbidity Survey. Arch Gen Psychiatry 1994; 51:355–364
3. Kessler RC, Nelson CB, McGonagle KA, Liu J, Swartz MS, Blazer DG: Comorbidity of DSM-III-R major depressive disorder in the general population: results from the US National Comorbidity Survey. Br J Psychiatry 1996; 168:17–30
4. Durham RC, Allan T, Hackett CA: On predicting improvement and relapse in generalized anxiety disorder following psychotherapy. Br J Clin Psychol 1997; 36:101–119
5. Brown C, Schulberg HC. Madonia MJ, Shear MK, Houck PR: Treatment outcomes for primary care patients with major depression and lifetime anxiety disorders. Am J Psychiatry 1996; 153:1293–1300
6. Breslau N, Davis GC: Further evidence on the doubtful validity of generalized anxiety disorder. Psychiatry Res 1985; 16:177–179
7. Gorman JM: Comorbid depression and anxiety spectrum disorders. Depress Anxiety 1996–1997; 4:160–168
8. Nisita C, Petracca A, Akiskal HS, Galli L, Gepponi I, Cassano GB: Delimitation of generalized anxiety disorder: clinical comparisons with panic and major depressive disorders. Compr Psychiatry 1990; 31:409–415
9. Roy-Byrne PP: Generalized anxiety and mixed anxiety-depression: association with disability and health care utilization. J Clin Psychiatry 1996; 57:86–91
10. Ormel J, Von Korff M, Ustun B, Pini S, Korten A, Oldehinkel T: Common mental disorders and disability across cultures: results from the WHO Collaborative Study on Psychological Problems in General Health Care. JAMA 1994; 272:1741–1748
11. Olfson M, Fireman B, Weissman MM, Leon AC, Sheehan DV, Kathol RG, Hoven C, Farber L: Mental disorders and disability among patients in a primary care group practice. Am J Psychiatry 1997; 154:1734–1740
12. Schonfeld WH, Verboncoeur CJ, Filer SK, Lipschutz RC, Lubeck DP, Buesching DP: The functioning and well-being of patients with unrecognized anxiety disorders and major depressive disorder. J Affect Disord 1997; 43:105–119
13. Stewart AL, Hays RD, Ware JE Jr: The MOS Short-Form General Health Survey: reliability and validity in a patient population. Med Care 1988; 26:724–735
14. Spitzer RL, Kroenke K, Linzer M, Hahn SR, Williams JB, deGruy FV III, Brody D, Davies M: Health-related quality of life in primary care patients with mental disorders. JAMA 1995; 274: 1511–1517
15. Kessler RC: The prevalence of psychiatric comorbidity, in Treatment Strategies for Patients With Psychiatric Comorbidity. Edited by Wetzler S, Sanderson WC. New York, John Wiley & Sons, 1997, pp 23–48
16. Kessler RC, McGonagle KA, Zhao S, Nelson CB, Hughes M, Eshleman S, Wittchen H-U, Kendler KS: Lifetime and 12-month prevalence of DSM-III-R psychiatric disorders in the United States: results from the National Comorbidity Survey. Arch Gen Psychiatry 1994; 51:8–19
17. Kessler RC, Mickelson KD, Zhao S: Patterns and correlates of self-help group membership in the United States. Soc Policy 1997; 27:27–46
18. Kessler RC, Little RJA, Groves RM: Advances in strategies for minimizing and adjusting for survey nonresponse. Epidemiol Rev 1995: 17:192–204
19. World Health Organization: Composite International Diagnostic Interview (CIDI), version 1.0. Geneva, WHO, 1990
20. Kessler RC, Wittchen H-U, Abelson JM, McGonagle KA, Schwarz N, Kendler KS, Knäuper B, Zhao S: Methodological studies of the Composite International Diagnostic Interview (CIDI) in the US National Comorbidity Survey. Int J Methods in Psychiatr Res 1998: 7:33–55
21. Kessler RC, Rubinow DR, Holmes C, Abelson JM, Zhao S: The epidemiology of DSM-III-R bipolar I disorder in a general population survey. Psychol Med 1997; 27:1079–1089
22. Kendler KS, Gallagher TJ, Abelson JM, Kessler RC: Lifetime prevalence, demographic risk factors, and diagnostic validity of nonaffective psychosis as assessed in a US community sample: the National Comorbidity Survey. Arch Gen Psychiatry 1996; 53:1022–1031
23. Kessler RC, Andrews G, Mroczek D, Ustun B, Wittchen H-U: The World Health Organization Composite International Diagnostic Interview Short Form (CIDI-SF). Int J Methods in Psychiatr Res 1998; 7:171–185
24. Schuster TL, Kessler RC, Aseltine RH Jr: Supportive interactions, negative interactions, and depressed mood. Am J Community Psychol 1990; 18:423–438
25. Kish L, Frankel MR: Inferences from complex samples. J Royal Statistical Society 1974; 36:1–37
26. Schuckit MA: Genetic and clinical implications of alcoholism and affective disorder. Am J Psychiatry 1986; 143:140–147
27. Morgado A, Smith M, Lecrubier Y, Widlocher D: Depressed subjects unwittingly over-report poor social adjustment which they reappraise when recovered. J Nerv Ment Dis 1991; 179: 614–619
28. Robins LN, Locke BZ, Regier DA: An overview of psychiatric disorders in America, in Psychiatric Disorders in America: The Epidemiologic Catchment Area Study. Edited by Robins LN, Regier DA. New York, Free Press, 1991, pp 328–366
29. Kendler KS, Walters EE, Neale MC, Kessler RC, Heath AC, Eaves LJ: The structure of the genetic and environmental risk factors for six major psychiatric disorders in women: phobia, generalized anxiety disorder, panic disorder, bulimia, major depression, and alcoholism. Arch Gen Psychiatry 1995; 52: 374–383
30. Sherbourne CD, Jackson CA, Meredith LS, Camp P, Wells KB: Prevalence of comorbid anxiety disorders in primary care outpatients. Arch Fam Med 1996; 5:27–34
31. Shores MM, Glubin T, Cowley DS, Dager SR, Roy-Byrne PP, Dunner DL: The relationship between anxiety and depression: a clinical comparison of generalized anxiety disorder, dysthymic disorder, panic disorder, and major depressive disorder. Compr Psychiatry 1992; 33:237–244
32. Pini S, Cassano GB. Simonini E, Savino M, Russo A, Montgomery SA: Prevalence of anxiety disorders comorbidity in bi-

42

polar depression, unipolar depression and dysthymia. J Affect Disord 1997; 42:145–153

33. Brown TA, Chorpita BF, Barlow DH: Structural relationships among dimensions of the DSM-IV anxiety and mood disorders and dimensions of negative affect, positive affect, and autonomic arousal. J Abnorm Psychol 1998; 107:179–192

34. Kendler KS, Neale MC, Kessler RC, Heath AC, Eaves LJ: Major depression and generalized anxiety disorder: same genes, (partly) different environments? Arch Gen Psychiatry 1992; 49:716–722

35. Skodal AE, Schwartz S, Dohrenwend BP, Levav I, Shrout PE: Minor depression in a cohort of young adults in Israel. Arch Gen Psychiatry 1994; 51:542–551

36. Reich J: Distinguishing mixed anxiety/depression from anxiety and depressive groups using the family history method. Compr Psychiatry 1993; 34:285–290

37. Reich J: Family psychiatric histories in male patients with generalized anxiety disorder and major depressive disorder. Ann Clin Psychiatry 1995; 7:71–78

43

Social Phobia Subtypes in the National Comorbidity Survey

Ronald C. Kessler, Ph.D., Murray B. Stein, M.D., and Patricia Berglund, M.B.A.

Objective: This article presents epidemiologic data on the distinction between social phobia characterized by pure speaking fears and that characterized by other social fears. Method: The data come from the National Comorbidity Survey (N=8,098). Social phobia was assessed with a revised version of the Composite International Diagnostic Interview. Results: Latent class analysis showed that the brief set of social fears assessed in the survey can be disaggregated into a class characterized largely by speaking fears and a second class characterized by a broader range of social fears. One-third of the people with lifetime social phobia exclusively reported speaking fears, while the other two-thirds also had at least one of the other social fears assessed. The vast majority of the latter had multiple social fears including, in most cases, both performance and interactional fears. The two subtypes were similar in age at onset distribution, family history, and certain sociodemographic correlates. However, the social phobia characterized by pure speaking fears was less persistent, less impairing, and less highly comorbid with other DSM-III-R disorders than was social phobia characterized by other social fears. Conclusions: Further general population research assessing more performance and interaction fears is needed to determine whether social phobia subtypes can be refined and whether the subtypes are better conceptualized as distinct disorders. In the meantime, people who have social phobia with multiple fears, some of which are nonspeaking fears, appear to have the most impairment and should be the main focus of prevention and intervention efforts.
(Am J Psychiatry 1998; 155:613–619)

S ocial phobia is a commonly occurring anxiety disorder (1–5) often associated with serious role impairment (3, 4, 6, 7). Distinct symptom profiles have been found in clinical samples of some patients suffering exclusively from performance fears (e.g., speaking in public) and others with a broader array of fears that include both performance and interactional fears (e.g., meeting new people) (8–10). The latter disorder is referred to as generalized social phobia (DSM-IV).

Generalized social phobia has been observed to be more severe and disabling than other social phobias (11). Therefore, in planning public health responses to the findings that social phobia affects more than one out of eight people in the population on a lifetime basis (3) and as many as 8% in a year (1, 2), it would be useful to know the proportion who have broad-based and seriously impairing social fears versus less extensive or impairing fears. This was the purpose of the present investigation. In this report we show that two empirically derived subtypes of social phobia can be found in a large general population survey that distinguish people with exclusively speaking fears from other people with social phobia. While it has previously been noted that many persons in the community suffer from public speaking fears that can be considered a form of social phobia (12), to our knowledge no previous epidemiologic study has examined this or other social phobia subtypes in the general population. We present data that compare these subtypes on family history, comorbidity, impairment, and sociodemographic correlates.

METHOD

Sample

The data come from the National Comorbidity Survey (1), a survey of 8,098 respondents in the age range 15–54 years who were selected from the noninstitutionalized household population of the coterminous United States; the sample included an equal-probability subsample of students in campus group housing. The survey was fielded between September 1990 and March 1992. Interviews were administered face-to-face in the homes of the respondents and averaged somewhat more than 2 hours to complete. The response rate was 82.4%. The data were weighted for differential probabilities of selection and differential nonresponse. More details on the design of the National Comorbidity Survey have been reported elsewhere (1, 13).

Received April 9, 1997; revision received Aug. 18, 1997; accepted Sept. 18, 1997. From the Department of Health Care Policy, Harvard Medical School; the Department of Psychiatry, University of California, San Diego, La Jolla, Calif.; and the Institute for Social Research, University of Michigan, Ann Arbor. Address reprint requests to Dr. Kessler, Department of Health Care Policy, Harvard Medical School, 180 Longwood Ave., Boston, MA 02115; kessler@hcp.med.harvard.edu (e-mail).

45

TABLE 1. Lifetime Prevalences of Social Fears and Social Phobia Among Respondents in the National Comorbidity Survey (N=8,098)

Social Fear	Lifetime Prevalence of Fear		Lifetime Prevalence of Social Phobia in Subsample With Lifetime Fear	
	%	SE	%	SE
Public speaking	30.2	0.9	37.5	1.5
Using a toilet away from home	6.6	0.5	35.4	2.4
Eating or drinking in public	2.7	0.3	47.7	5.1
Talking with others	13.7	0.7	49.3	2.5
Writing while someone watches	6.4	0.5	46.2	3.8
Talking in front of a small group	15.2	0.7	42.1	2.1
Any social fear	38.6	1.2	34.5	1.5

Diagnostic Assessment

The survey diagnoses were based on a modified version of the World Health Organization's Composite International Diagnostic Interview (14), a structured interview designed to be administered by trained interviewers who are not clinicians. The diagnoses included in the full National Comorbidity Survey were DSM-III-R anxiety disorders (social phobia, agoraphobia, simple phobia, panic disorder, generalized anxiety disorder), mood disorders (major depression, dysthymia, mania), addictive disorders (alcohol and drug abuse and dependence), and antisocial personality disorder. The WHO field trials of the Composite International Diagnostic Interview (15) and the National Comorbidity Survey clinical reappraisal study (16–20) both indicated good reliability and acceptable validity of these diagnoses.

Social phobia was assessed by asking the respondents whether there was ever a time when any of six situations always made them so afraid that they either tried to avoid it or felt very uncomfortable in the situation. The situations were speaking in public, having to use the toilet when away from home, eating or drinking in public, talking to people when you might have nothing to say or might sound foolish, writing while someone watches, and talking in front of a small group of people ("small" was not defined). The main change to the WHO Composite International Diagnostic Interview made in the National Comorbidity Survey was that respondents were asked to review this list visually as the interviewer read the items, in an effort to control the pace of review, to focus memory search, and to reduce the chance of inducing the "no" response set that has been documented as occurring when yes-or-no questions are presented in lists of this sort (21). Respondents who endorsed one or more of these situational descriptors were asked the remaining social phobia questions from the Composite International Diagnostic Interview. The National Comorbidity Survey clinical reappraisal study (20) showed acceptable agreement (kappa=0.68 with a standard error of 0.09) between DSM-III-R diagnoses based on these structured questions and diagnoses based on blind clinical reinterviews using the Structured Clinical Interview for DSM-III-R (22).

Other Measures

The sociodemographic variables evaluated for association with social phobia subtypes were age, sex, region, urbanicity, education, income, and marital status. Subtype differences in parent histories of depression, generalized anxiety disorder, antisocial personality disorder, and substance dependence were examined by using the Family History Research Diagnostic Criteria (FH-RDC) interview (23). As the latter does not include generalized anxiety disorder, questions developed by Kendler et al. (24) to assess generalized anxiety disorder in a format comparable to that of the FH-RDC interview were used.

The diagnoses made with the Composite International Diagnostic Interview were used to study the comorbidity of the social phobia subtypes with other DSM-III-R disorders. Finally, impairments were evaluated on the basis of self-reports of whether the respondent's phobia had ever interfered a lot with his or her life or activities, whether the respondent had ever sought treatment for the phobia, and whether he or she had ever taken medications for the phobia.

Analysis Procedures

Latent class analysis (25) was used to determine how many subtypes underlie the observed covariances among the six fears of social situations assessed in the National Comorbidity Survey. Latent class analysis is a categorical equivalent of factor analysis that postulates the existence of a discrete latent variable (as opposed to one or more continuous variables in factor analysis) defining classes that explain the covariances among observed variables (26). The Kaplan-Meier method (27) was used to calculate curves for age at onset and for time to "offset," the number of years between retrospectively reported age at onset and age at the time of the most recent phobic symptoms. Between-subtype differences in family history, comorbidity, and impairment were assessed with logistic regression models (28). These models began by comparing the subtypes with pure speaking fears and with nonspeaking fears and then evaluated differences within each by distinguishing cases with public speaking fears exclusively from others in the pure speaking subtype and cases based on number of social fears (one, two, or three or more) in the subtype with nonspeaking fears. Sociodemographic correlates were also studied by using logistic regression models.

The clustering and weighting of the National Comorbidity Survey makes it inappropriate to use conventional significance tests to evaluate parameter estimates because the latter underestimate the magnitude of standard errors. Therefore, the Taylor series linearization method (29) was used to adjust standard errors of means, and the method of jackknife repeated replications (30) was used to adjust the 95% confidence intervals of the odds ratios. Global significance tests comparing the five subsamples defined by the cross-classification of subtype and number of social fears were done by using Wald chi-square tests calculated on variance-covariance matrices, adjusted by the method of jackknife repeated replications, among the logistic regression coefficients.

RESULTS

Lifetime Prevalences of Social Fears and Social Phobia

As shown in table 1, the lifetime prevalences of the six social fears in the total sample ranged from 2.7% for fear of eating or drinking in public to 30.2% for fear of speaking in public. The lifetime prevalence of at least one fear was 38.6%. The speaking fears were the most common. The conditional probabilities of social phobia given a particular social fear (i.e., the proportion of people with a given fear who met the criteria for social phobia) had a much narrower range, from 35.4% for fear of using a toilet away from home to 49.3% for fear of talking with others, and they averaged 34.5% across all fears.

Latent Class Analysis of Lifetime Social Fears

Latent class analysis models for the six lifetime social fears were fit for between one and four classes. A three-class model was found to provide the best fit, as indicated by the improvement over a two-class model (χ^2=314.2, df=7, p<0.001) and the failure of a four-class model to

614

46

TABLE 2. Lifetime and 12-Month Prevalences of Pure Speaking Fears, Other Social Fears, and Social Phobia Among Respondents in the National Comorbidity Survey (N=8,098)

Type or Number of Social Fears	Lifetime Prevalence										12-Month Prevalence										
	Lifetime Prevalence of Fear		Lifetime Prevalence of Social Phobia in Subsample With Lifetime Fear		Lifetime Prevalence of Social Phobia in Total Sample		Proportion of Lifetime Social Phobia Diagnoses		12-Month Prevalence of Social Phobia in Subsample With Lifetime Fear		12-Month Prevalence of Social Phobia in Total Sample		Proportion of 12-Month Social Phobia Diagnoses	
	%	SE	%	SE	%	SE	%	SE	%	SE	%	SE	%	SE
Pure speaking fears														
Public speaking only	10.8	0.5	27.0	2.5	2.9	0.3	21.8	1.3	9.0	1.3	1.0	0.1	12.7	1.4
Others	7.0	0.4	26.7	2.8	1.9	0.2	14.0	1.1	11.6	1.7	0.8	0.1	10.1	1.3
Total	17.8	0.6	26.9	2.0	4.8	0.4	35.8	1.5	10.0	1.0	1.8	0.2	22.8	1.8
Other social fears														
One fear	5.3	0.4	21.4	2.7	1.1	0.2	8.5	0.8	15.1	2.1	0.8	0.1	10.1	1.7
Two fears	6.0	0.4	35.3	3.3	2.1	1.2	15.9	1.1	24.2	2.3	1.5	0.2	19.0	1.8
Three or more fears	9.6	0.6	55.1	2.7	5.3	0.4	39.6	1.5	39.8	2.1	3.8	0.3	48.1	2.8
Total	20.9	0.9	40.9	2.0	8.5	0.5	64.0	1.5	29.1	1.2	6.1	0.4	77.2	1.8
Any social fear	38.6	1.2	34.5	1.5	13.3	0.7	100.0		20.3	0.9	7.9	0.4	100.0	

improve over the three-class model ($\chi^2=0.01$, df=7, p= 1.00). Class 1 was characterized by low endorsement probabilities. Class 2 was characterized by a 93% probability of fear of speaking in public, a probability over 50% of fear of speaking in front of a small group, and a 32% probability of fear of talking with others. Class 3 was characterized by comparatively high probabilities of all six fears.

Lifetime and 12-Month Prevalences of Social Fear and Phobia Subtypes

On the basis of the results of the latent class analysis, the respondents with social fears were divided into two broad groups, those with pure speaking fears and those who endorsed at least one other social fear (with or without a speaking fear). Because of the much higher prevalence of public speaking fear than other social fears, the group with pure speaking fear was further divided into those with public speaking fear only and those with more extensive speaking fears. The group that endorsed other social fears, in comparison, was further divided into those with one, two, and three or more social fears in order to distinguish the effect of number from the effect of type of social fears.

The lifetime and 12-month prevalences of social fears and social phobia in these various subgroups are reported in table 2. Similar proportions of the total sample reported one or more lifetime pure speaking fears (17.8%) and other social fears (20.9%). Within the subsample with pure speaking fears, over one-half reported that their only social fear was public speaking. Within the group with other social fears, about one-fourth reported only one of the fears, while close to one-half reported three or more of the six social fears.

As shown in the third data column, a significantly lower proportion of those with pure speaking fears (26.9% of 1,441) than other social fears (40.9% of

1,691) (z=4.9, p<0.001) met the criteria for lifetime social phobia. As a result, even though the lifetime prevalences of pure speaking fears and other social fears were roughly equal, in the total sample the lifetime prevalence of social phobia with nonspeaking fears (8.5%) was much higher than the lifetime prevalence of social phobia with pure speaking fears (4.8%) (z=5.8, p< 0.001). There was an even larger difference between the conditional prevalences of 12-month social phobia in the subsamples of people with lifetime pure speaking fears (10.0% of 388) and those with other lifetime social fears (29.1% of 692) (z=12.3, p<0.001), suggesting that the former are less persistent than the latter. There was a significant association between the number of lifetime fears and the probability of lifetime phobia within the subsample having nonspeaking fears, from a low of 21.4% among the 429 respondents with only one fear to a high of 55.1% among the 777 with three or more fears (z=8.8, p<0.001). There was no significant difference, however, between the probability of lifetime social phobia in the subsample of respondents with pure fear of public speaking (27.0% of 875) and the probability for those with other pure speaking fears (26.7% of 567) (z=0.08, p=0.99).

Age at Onset and Time to Offset

Kaplan-Meier cumulative curves for age at onset based on retrospective reports were computed separately for social phobia with pure speaking fears and for subgroups of other social phobias defined on the basis of number and type of fears. No evidence was found for meaningful differences in the age-at-onset distributions of these subsamples.

Kaplan-Meier curves for time to offset were also computed for the same subsamples. Time to offset was the number of years between retrospectively reported age at onset and age at most recent phobic symptoms.

47

FIGURE 1. Kaplan-Meier Curves for Cumulative Time Between Age at Onset and Age at Most Recent Phobic Symptoms (Offset) for Subtypes of Social Phobia in the National Comorbidity Survey (N=8,098)

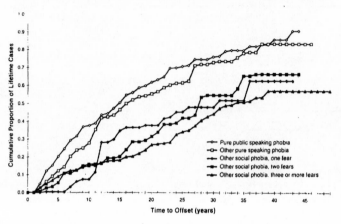

Time to Offset (years)

Legend:
- Pure public speaking phobia
- Other pure speaking phobia
- Other social phobia, one fear
- Other social phobia, two fears
- Other social phobia, three or more fears

However, we found a statistically significant difference between social phobia with pure speaking fears and other social phobia in only one of the measures of parental psychopathology, maternal generalized anxiety disorder (χ^2= 8.2, df=2, p<0.001); the prevalence was lower among those with pure speaking fears than among those with other social phobias.

Comorbidity

A previous report from the National Comorbidity Survey documented substantial comorbidity of lifetime social phobia and other lifetime DSM-III-R disorders assessed in the survey (3). The results in table 3 show that there was

As shown in figure 1, time to offset was significantly shorter for social phobia with pure speaking fears than for social phobia with other social fears (χ^2=86.2, df=1, p<0.001). There was no significant difference in time to offset, in comparison, among the subsamples defined by number of fears for either the respondents with social phobia and pure speaking fears (χ^2=3.0, df=2, p= 0.08) or those with social phobia with other social fears (χ^2=3.0, df=2, p=0.22).

Parental History of Psychopathology

There were consistently positive associations between parental history of depression, generalized anxiety disorder, substance dependence, and antisocial personality disorder and the respondents' lifetime social phobia.

also considerable variation in comorbidity across subtypes of social phobia. Histories of mood disorder, anxiety disorder, and antisocial personality disorder were all significantly more common among respondents who had social phobia with at least one nonspeaking fear than among those with social phobia and pure speaking fears. Among the respondents with social phobia and comorbid disorders, furthermore, those with pure speaking fears were significantly more likely than those with other social fears to report that social phobia was their earliest lifetime disorder (73.4% of 263 versus 59.4% of 570) (z=2.3, p=0.03). For the respondents with social phobia, there was less comorbidity with mood disorder and antisocial personality disorder among those with public speaking fears only than among those with other pure speaking fears. However, comorbidity

TABLE 3. Lifetime Comorbidity of Social Phobia Subtypes With Other DSM-III-R Disorders Assessed in the National Comorbidity Survey (N=8,098)

	Respondents With Social Phobia													Respondents Without Social Phobia	
	Pure Speaking Fears						Other Social Fears[a]								
	Public Speaking Only		Others		Total		One Fear		Two Fears		Three or More Fears		Total		Odds Ratio	
Other Disorder	%	SE	%	SE	%	SE	%	SE	%	SE	%	SE	%	SE		SE
Any mood disorder	26.9[b]	3.8	40.6[b]	5.9	32.3[c]	3.8	40.5	7.4	41.3	4.6	50.1	2.6	46.7[c]	2.4	15.9[d]	0.6
Any anxiety disorder	37.0	3.7	43.2	6.1	39.5[c]	3.3	57.9	6.7	55.9	3.4	63.4	3.1	60.8[c]	2.5	13.4[d]	0.5
Any addictive disorder	34.3	4.3	43.2	5.7	37.8	3.6	41.0	6.1	39.9	5.0	40.7	3.8	40.6	2.9	24.6[d]	0.9
Antisocial personality disorder	1.1[b]	0.6	6.7[b]	1.2	3.3[c]	0.6	7.7	3.3	10.1	2.8	9.7	1.9	9.5[c]	1.4	2.5[d]	0.2
Any disorder	65.7	4.1	71.3	4.5	67.9[c]	3.1	77.7	4.8	80.7	2.9	84.0	1.8	82.4[c]	1.5	39.9[d]	1.0

[a]None of the comorbid disorders varied significantly with number of fears (p≤0.05, adjusted Wald chi-square test).
[b]Significant difference between respondents with public speaking fear only and those with other pure speaking fears (p≤0.05, adjusted Wald chi-square test).
[c]Significant difference between total group with pure speaking fears and total group with other social fears (p≤0.05, adjusted Wald chi-square test).
[d]Significant difference between total group with social phobia and respondents without social phobia (p≤0.05, adjusted Wald chi-square test).

48

TABLE 4. Impairments Due to Lifetime Social Phobia Among Respondents in the National Comorbidity Survey (N=8,098)

	Respondents With Social Phobia												
	Pure Speaking Fears[a]						Other Social Fears						
	Public Speaking Only		Others		Total		One Fear		Two Fears		Three or More Fears		Total	
Impairment Indicator	%	SE	%	SE	%	SE	%	SE	%	SE	%	SE	%	SE
Phobia ever interfered a lot with life or activities	11.5	3.0	17.5	3.5	13.8[b]	2.5	22.3[c]	5.4	20.7[c]	2.9	41.6[c]	3.3	33.9[b]	2.7
Ever sought treatment from a medical doctor	10.7	2.4	15.6	4.3	12.7[b]	2.4	18.1	5.5	27.2	4.3	22.6	2.6	23.1[b]	2.2
Ever sought treatment from any other professional	2.6	1.4	7.5	3.9	4.5[b]	2.2	14.3	4.5	16.5	3.1	15.6	2.4	15.7[b]	2.0
Ever took medication more than once	0.3	0.3	1.5	1.0	0.8[b]	0.5	5.4	2.8	6.3	2.4	11.6	1.7	9.5[b]	1.3
Any impairment	21.2	3.4	27.9	4.7	23.8[b]	2.7	34.2[c]	6.4	40.6[c]	4.4	53.4[c]	3.5	47.7[b]	3.0

[a]None of the impairment indicators differed significantly between the group with public speaking fear only and the group with other pure speaking fears.
[b]Significant difference between total group with pure speaking fears and total group with other social fears (p≤0.05, adjusted Wald chi-square test).
[c]Significant difference among groups with one, two, and three or more fears (p≤0.05, adjusted Wald chi-square test).

was not associated with the number of social fears among those with social fears beyond speaking.

Impairment

The Composite International Diagnostic Interview includes four indicators of impairment in each diagnostic section: whether the disorder ever interfered a lot with the respondent's life or activities, whether the respondent ever sought treatment from a medical doctor, whether the respondent ever sought treatment from any other professional (e.g., social worker or clergy), and whether the respondent ever took medications more than once for the disorder. Of the respondents with lifetime social phobia, 39.1% endorsed at least one of these impairment statements. As shown in table 4, the percentage of endorsement was approximately twice as high for respondents with nonspeaking fears (47.7% of 388) as for those with pure speaking fears (23.8% of 692) (z=5.9, p<0.001). Within the subsample of respondents with social phobia having at least one nonspeaking fear, furthermore, the endorsement percentage was monotonically related to number of fears: 34.2% of the 92 with one fear, 40.6% of the 171 with two fears, and 53.4% of the 428 with three or more fears ($\chi^2=15.6$, df=2, p<0.001).

Sociodemographic Correlates

A previous report on the National Comorbidity Survey (3) documented several sociodemographic correlates of lifetime social phobia, the most powerful being low income, low education, and female gender. Disaggregated analyses showed no specification by subtype for the gender effect. However, there were significant findings for income and education, both of which were significantly inversely related to social phobia with nonspeaking fears (income: $\chi^2=36.2$, df=3, p<0.001; education: $\chi^2=88.3$, df=3, p<0.001). Social phobia with pure speaking fears, in comparison, was not significantly related to income ($\chi^2=2.6$, df=3, p=0.45) and was

nonmonotonically related to education; i.e., there were high rates among both high school graduates and those with some college education and low rates both among those with less than a high school education and among college graduates ($\chi^2=29.2$, df=3, p<0.001).

DISCUSSION

The finding of two social phobia subtypes is superficially consistent with theoretical speculation (11, 12, 31) and clinical observations that patients with social phobia can be divided into those with predominantly performance-type fears and those who also have a broader range of interactional fears (9, 32, 33). However, there are two important differences between the subtypes found in the National Comorbidity Survey and those found in clinical studies. First, persons with social phobia with pure speaking fears are rare in clinical samples because they have a low rate of service use. As a result, clinical studies have failed to identify the pure-speaking-fear subtype found here. Second, the pure-performance-fear subtype in clinical studies is usually characterized by a larger set of performance fears, such as fear of writing in public and fear of eating in public, in addition to speaking fears, while generalized social phobia is characterized by a combination of performance fears and interactional fears, such as fears of dating, of attending social gatherings, and of speaking with strangers.

We did not find a distinction between the latter two subtypes (broadly defined performance fear versus generalized fear) in the National Comorbidity Survey. Our failure to find this distinction is probably due to the fact that only one of the six questions in the Composite International Diagnostic Interview asked about an interactional fear (fear of talking to people because you might have nothing to say or might sound foolish). This highlights an important limitation in the National Comorbidity Survey for purposes of the current analysis: the survey assessed only six social fears. A much larger

49

set of social fears, including a wider range of performance fears plus interactional fears, is needed in future epidemiologic studies to carry out more fine-grained subtyping of social phobia.

Despite this limitation, it is worth noting that in the National Comorbidity Survey the subtype involving at least one nonspeaking fear was found to be more chronic, comorbid, and impairing than the pure-speaking-fear subtype and that this was especially true for respondents with three or more social fears. The vast majority of survey respondents with this subtype endorsed the statement about the one interactional fear included in the survey. The fact that these people reported the most impairment is consistent with the clinical observation that patients in treatment for social phobia who have fears of most social situations are more impaired than those who have fewer social fears (34). This finding presumably reflects the fact that situations that require public speaking can be avoided by most people with less impairment than situations that require other types of social performance or social interaction.

Our finding that socioeconomic status is inversely related to social phobia with nonspeaking fears could be due either to social causation (socioeconomic success protecting against social phobia), social selection (early-onset social phobia interfering with socioeconomic success), or some combination of these processes. The finding that social phobia with pure speaking fears is more prevalent among those with high school or some college education than either college graduates or people with less than a high school education is most plausibly interpreted as a mixture of processes that include lack of exposure to the phobic stimulus among people with little education (i.e., a low chance of the fear of public speaking ever being activated among people with low education because it is rare for them to be called on to speak in public) and social selection at higher levels of education (i.e., speaking phobia might interfere with subsequent educational attainment among high school graduates).

It is interesting to consider whether the apparently lower degree of impairment among respondents with social phobia with pure speaking fears than among those with other social phobia is simply a matter of number rather than type of fears. There is no way to answer this question definitely in the National Comorbidity Survey because the set of six social fear questions is too brief to permit confidence that people classified as having only one social fear would not have reported others if a longer list had been presented. Nonetheless, it is informative to compare the 35.8% of respondents with social phobia in the survey who were classified as have pure speaking fears with the 8.5% who had only one other fear among the six assessed. A comparison of these two subgroups showed that respondents with pure-speaking-fear social phobia had a weaker family history of the disorders considered here, less comorbidity, and less impairment than the respondents with social phobia who had only one nonspeaking social fear each.

This last result might mean that pure-speaking-fear social phobia is a different type of social phobia than social phobia characterized by nonspeaking fears. It would be a mistake, however, to conclude that social phobia with pure speaking fear is not real social phobia. As other studies have shown (11), some persons with pure-speaking-fear social phobia experience considerable impairment. Furthermore, it is possible that some of these persons experience more subtle forms of impairment than the measures used in the survey were able to detect. As already noted, it would be useful for future epidemiologic surveys to assess a broader range of social situations, both performance and interactional, than the six in the National Comorbidity Survey in order to assess this possibility and provide a rigorous definition of the DSM-IV requirement that generalized social phobia include fears of "most social situations." Despite this limitation, though, we can draw two useful conclusions from the results reported here. First, a substantial proportion of persons with social phobia in the general population have pure speaking fears, although a more in-depth assessment might show that fears of other social situations are also involved in some cases, while other people with social phobia generally have a greater number of fears that usually involve both performance and interaction. It is not clear from the results reported here whether these two represent distinct subtypes or, rather, different severity thresholds on a single dimension of extensiveness of social fears. It is clear, though, that speaking fears are much more prevalent than the other social fears considered here and that a substantial proportion of people with social phobia meet the criteria exclusively because of speaking fears.

Second, social phobia that involves more extensive fears is more persistent, is associated with more impairment, and is more frequently present with other DSM-III-R disorders than the subtype with pure speaking fears. For these reasons, social phobia involving multiple fears that are not exclusively fears of speaking should be the focus of the most intensive public health interest until more fine-grained subtyping can be done.

ACKNOWLEDGMENTS

The National Comorbidity Survey is a collaborative epidemiologic investigation of the prevalences, causes, and consequences of psychiatric morbidity and comorbidity in the United States supported by NIMH (MH-46376, MH-49098, MH-52861) with supplemental support from the National Institute on Drug Abuse (through a supplement to MH-46376) and the W.T. Grant Foundation (90135190), Ronald C. Kessler, principal investigator. Preparation for this report was also supported by an NIMH Research Scientist Award to Dr. Kessler (MH-00507). Collaborating National Comorbidity Survey sites (and investigators) are as follows: Addiction Research Foundation (Robin Room), Duke University Medical Center (Dan Blazer, Marvin Swartz), Harvard Medical School (Richard Frank, Ronald Kessler), Johns Hopkins University (James Anthony, William Eaton, Philip Leaf), Max Planck Institute of Psychiatry Clinical Institute (Hans-Ulrich Wittchen), Medical College of Virginia (Kenneth Kendler), University of Miami (R. Jay Turner), University of Michigan (Lloyd Johnston, Roderick Little), New York University (Patrick Shrout), State University of New York at Stony Brook (Evelyn Bromet), and Washington University School of Medicine (Linda Cott-

50

ler. Andrew Heath). A complete list of all National Comorbidity Survey publications along with abstracts, study documentation, interview schedules, and the raw National Comorbidity Survey public use data files can be obtained directly from the National Comorbidity Survey home page by using the URL http://www.umich.edu/~ncsum/ on the World Wide Web.

REFERENCES

1. Kessler RC, McGonagle KA, Zhao S, Nelson CB, Hughes M, Eshleman S, Wittchen H-U, Kendler KS: Lifetime and 12-month prevalence of DSM-III-R psychiatric disorders in the United States: results from the National Comorbidity Survey. Arch Gen Psychiatry 1994; 51:8–19
2. Stein MB, Walker JR, Forde DR: Setting diagnostic thresholds for social phobia: considerations from a community survey of social anxiety. Am J Psychiatry 1994; 151:408–412
3. Magee WJ, Eaton WW, Wittchen H-U, McGonagle KA, Kessler RC: Agoraphobia, simple phobia, and social phobia in the National Comorbidity Survey. Arch Gen Psychiatry 1996; 53:159–168
4. Schneier FR, Johnson J, Hornig C, Liebowitz M, Weissman M: Social phobia: comorbidity and morbidity in an epidemiologic sample. Arch Gen Psychiatry 1992; 49:282–288
5. Chapman TF, Mannuzza S, Fyer AJ: Epidemiology and family studies of social phobia, in Social Phobia: Diagnosis, Assessment, and Treatment. Edited by Heimberg RG, Liebowitz MR, Hope DA, Schneier FR. New York, Guilford Press, 1995, pp 21–39
6. Schneier FR, Heckelman LR, Garfinkel R, Campeas R, Fallon BA, Gitow A, Street L, Del Bene D, Liebowitz MR: Functional impairment in social phobia. J Clin Psychiatry 1994; 55:322–331
7. Davidson JRT, Hughes DL, George LK, Blazer DG: The epidemiology of social phobia: findings from the Duke Epidemiological Catchment Area Study. Psychol Med 1993; 23:709–718
8. Chapman TF, Mannuzza S, Fyer AJ: Epidemiology and family studies of social phobia, in Social Phobia: Diagnosis, Assessment, and Treatment. Edited by Heimberg RG, Liebowitz MR, Hope DA, Schneier FR. New York, Guilford Press, 1995, pp 21–39
9. Heimberg RG, Holt CS, Schneier FR, Liebowitz MR: The issue of subtypes in the diagnosis of social phobia. J Anxiety Disorders 1993; 7:249–269
10. Turner SM, Beidel DC, Townsley RM: Social phobia: a comparison of specific and generalized subtypes and avoidant personality disorder. J Abnorm Psychol 1992; 101:326–331
11. Stein MB: How shy is too shy? Lancet 1996; 347:1131–1132
12. Stein MB, Walker JR, Forde DR: Public speaking fears in a community sample: prevalence, impact on functioning, and diagnostic classification. Arch Gen Psychiatry 1996; 53:169–174
13. Kessler RC, Little RJA, Groves RM: Advances in strategies for minimizing and adjusting for survey nonresponse. Epidemiol Rev 1995; 17:192–204
14. World Health Organization: Composite International Diagnostic Interview (CIDI), version 1.0. Geneva, WHO, 1990
15. Wittchen H-U: Reliability and validity studies of the WHO-Composite International Diagnostic Interview (CIDI): a critical review. J Psychiatr Res 1994; 28:57–84
16. Blazer DG, Kessler RC, McGonagle KA, Swartz MS: The prevalence and distribution of major depression in a national community sample: the National Comorbidity Survey. Am J Psychiatry 1994; 151:979–986
17. Kessler RC, Crum RM, Warner LA, Nelson CB, Schulenberg J, Anthony JC: The lifetime co-occurence of DSM-III-R alcohol abuse and dependence with other psychiatric disorders in the National Comorbidity Survey. Arch Gen Psychiatry 1997; 54: 313–321
18. Warner LA, Kessler RC, Hughes M, Anthony JC, Nelson CB: Prevalence and correlates of drug use and dependence in the United States: results from the National Comorbidity Survey. Arch Gen Psychiatry 1995; 52:219–229
19. Wittchen H-U, Kessler RC, Zhao S, Abelson J: Reliability and clinical validity of UM-CIDI DSM-III-R generalized anxiety disorder. J Psychiatr Res 1995; 29:95–110
20. Wittchen H-U, Zhao S, Abelson JM, Abelson JL, Kessler RC: Reliability and procedural validity of UM-CIDI DSM-III-R phobic disorders. Psychol Med 1996; 26:1169–1177
21. Kessler RC, Wethington E: The reliability of life events reports in a community survey. Psychol Med 1991; 21:1–16
22. Spitzer RL, Williams JBW, Gibbon M, First MB: The Structured Clinical Interview for DSM-III-R (SCID), I: history, rationale, and description. Arch Gen Psychiatry 1992; 49:624–629
23. Endicott J, Andreasen N, Spitzer RL: Family History Research Diagnostic Criteria, 3rd ed. New York, New York State Psychiatric Institute, Biometrics Research, 1978
24. Kendler KS, Silberg JL, Neale MC, Kessler RC, Heath AC, Eaves LJ: The family history method: whose psychiatric history is measured? Am J Psychiatry 1991; 148:1501–1504
25. Lazarsfeld PR, Henry NW: Latent Structure Analysis. Boston, Houghton-Mifflin, 1968
26. Eaves LJ, Silberg JL, Hewitt JK, Rutter M, Meyer JM, Neale MC, Pickles A: Analyzing twin resemblance in multisymptom data: genetic applications of a latent class model for symptoms of conduct disorder in juvenile boys. Behav Genet 1993; 23:5–19
27. Kaplan EL, Meier P: Nonparametric estimation from incomplete observations. J Am Statistical Association 1958; 53:281–284
28. Hosmer DW, Lemeshow S: Applied Logistic Regression. New York, John Wiley & Sons, 1989
29. Woodruff RS, Causey BD: Computerized method for approximating the variance of a complicated estimate. J Am Statistical Association 1976; 71:315–321
30. Kish L, Frankel MD: Inferences from complex samples. J Am Statistical Association 1970; 65:1071–1094
31. Hazen AL, Stein MB: Clinical phenomenology and comorbidity, in Social Phobia: Clinical and Research Perspectives. Edited by Stein MB. Washington, DC, American Psychiatric Press, 1995, pp 3–42
32. Gelernter CS, Stein MB, Tancer ME, Uhde TW: An examination of syndromal validity and diagnostic subtypes in social phobia and panic disorder. J Clin Psychiatry 1992; 53:23–27
33. Heimberg RG, Hope DA, Dodge CS, Becker RE: DSM-III-R subtypes of social phobia. J Nerv Ment Dis 1990; 178:172–179
34. Mannuzza S, Schneier FR, Chapman TF, Liebowitz MR, Klein DF, Fyer AJ: Generalized social phobia: reliability and validity. Arch Gen Psychiatry 1995; 52:230–237

51

Patterns of Psychopathology and Dysfunction in High-Risk Children of Parents With Panic Disorder and Major Depression

Joseph Biederman, M.D.

Stephen V. Faraone, Ph.D.

Dina R. Hirshfeld-Becker, Ph.D.

Deborah Friedman, B.A.

Joanna A. Robin, B.A.

Jerrold F. Rosenbaum, M.D.

Objective: The purpose of the study was to evaluate 1) whether an underlying familial predisposition is shared by all anxiety disorders or whether specific risks are associated with specific disorders, and 2) whether panic disorder and major depression have a familial link.

Method: The study compared four groups of children: 1) offspring of parents with panic disorder and comorbid major depression (N=179), 2) offspring of parents with panic disorder without comorbid major depression (N=29), 3) offspring of parents with major depression without comorbid panic disorder (N=59), and 4) offspring of parents with neither panic disorder nor major depression (N=113).

Results: Parental panic disorder, regardless of comorbidity with major depression, was associated with an increased risk for panic disorder and agoraphobia in offspring. Parental major depression, regardless of comorbidity with panic disorder, was associated with increased risks for social phobia, major depression, disruptive behavior disorders, and poorer social functioning in offspring. Both parental panic disorder and parental major depression, individually or comorbidly, were associated with increased risk for separation anxiety disorder and multiple (two or more) anxiety disorders in offspring.

Conclusions: These findings confirm and extend previous results documenting significant associations between the presence of panic disorder and major depression in parents and patterns of psychopathology and dysfunction in their offspring.

(Am J Psychiatry 2001; 158:49–57)

Although several studies have shown that the young offspring of parents with anxiety disorders are at increased risk for anxiety disorders (1–6), uncertainties remain as to the nature of this risk. One question regards its specificity: is there an underlying familial predisposition shared by all anxiety disorders or are there specific risks for specific anxiety disorders?

The idea that a general "anxiety proneness" may be transmitted has been hypothesized by several authors (7–9). Support for this hypothesis derives from family (2, 10) and twin (7, 11) studies suggesting that familial or genetic diatheses confer risk for anxiety disorders in general but not for specific disorders. The high rates of comorbidity within the anxiety disorders observed among adults (12–14) and children (15), as well as findings documenting similar patterns of comorbidity between anxiety disorders of childhood and adulthood (16–19), lend further support. However, some data have suggested specificity of transmission for anxiety disorders. Evidence from family studies has suggested specific aggregation for panic disorder (10, 20, 21), generalized anxiety disorder (22, 23), social phobia (24, 25), and other phobic disorders (26). Still other studies either have supported contributions of both general and specific diatheses (27) or have suggested different patterns of association for different anxiety disorders (28,

29). Clearly, further work is needed to resolve this important issue.

A second and related question pertains to diagnostic homogeneity of parental groups. Some researchers combined data for offspring of parents with heterogeneous anxiety disorders (2, 4). However, if different parental anxiety disorders have different underlying diatheses, they may be associated with different patterns of risk to offspring. Therefore, the next phase of work ought to focus on diagnostically homogeneous parental groups, while examining a variety of anxiety disorders in the offspring as outcomes.

A third major question concerns the association between anxiety disorders and major depression, disorders that have been observed to be highly comorbid (30). The ambiguous relationship between these conditions is reflected in the literature on children at risk by the limited and somewhat contradictory data about the contribution of parental major depression to the risk for anxiety disorders in the offspring. For example, although Turner et al. (2) found that children of parents with agoraphobia or obsessive-compulsive disorder were more likely than children of parents with dysthymia to have childhood anxiety disorders, Sylvester et al. (5) and Beidel and Turner (4) reported similar rates of anxiety disorders in children of pa-

53

tients with anxiety disorders and major depression. Breslau et al. (31), in an epidemiological study, found that children of mothers with major depression, but not with generalized anxiety disorder, had increased rates of overanxious disorder and major depression.

On the other hand, our group reported that parental panic disorder with agoraphobia increased the risk for both anxiety disorders and major depression in the offspring, whereas parental major depression increased the risk selectively for major depression but not for anxiety disorders (3). Similar results were reported by Weissman et al. (1), who found an increased risk for anxiety disorders in children whose parents had a diagnosis of major depression and comorbid agoraphobia or panic disorder, while children of parents with major depression only or of normal comparison parents had very low rates of anxiety disorders. These contradictory findings call for more research.

Delineating the spectrum of psychopathology and dysfunction in children at risk for anxiety disorders has clinical, scientific, and public health implications. Clarifying the type and severity of anxiety and related disorders in children of parents with specific anxiety disorders may lead to the development of preventive interventions for children at high risk for specific anxiety disorders. Focusing on young offspring could allow the development of early interventions that could be administered before these conditions become chronic and difficult to treat. Moreover, clarifying the putative familial link between anxiety and depressive disorders in parents and children at risk may lead to a better understanding of the comorbidity between these disorders.

The present study sought to address the limitations of prior studies with a study of young high-risk children, selected through parents with panic disorder or major depression. The study evaluated multiple domains of functioning in these children and in comparison subjects whose parents had neither panic disorder nor major depression. On the basis of prior literature, we hypothesized that parental panic disorder would confer a risk for both panic disorder and major depression and that parental major depression would confer a risk for major depression but not panic disorder.

Method

Subjects

We recruited three groups of parents who had at least one child age 2–6 years: 1) 131 parents treated for panic disorder and their 227 children, 2) 61 comparison parents with neither major anxiety nor mood disorders and their 119 children, and 3) 39 parents treated for major depression who had no history of either panic disorder or agoraphobia and their 67 children. The children ranged in age from 2–25 years. Of the 131 panic disorder families, 113 had either one parent with comorbid panic disorder and major depression (N=102) or one parent with panic disorder and another with major depression (N=11). Assessments of psychopathology and/or dysfunction were available for 380 of the 413

children (92.0%). Therefore, comparisons were made between four groups: 1) children of parents with both panic disorder and major depression (N=179), 2) children of parents with panic disorder without comorbid major depression (N=29), 3) children of parents with major depression without comorbid panic disorder (N=59), and 4) children of parents with neither panic disorder nor major depression (N=113).

We recruited parents with panic disorder and major depression from clinical referrals and advertising by using a three-stage ascertainment procedure. The first stage was implicit in the patient's referral to a clinic or response to an advertisement calling for adults in treatment for panic disorder or major depression. The second step consisted of screening the patient by telephone to document the presence of the full DSM-III-R criteria for panic disorder or major depression. Patients who met the criteria for these disorders were recruited for a complete structured psychiatric interview. Only patients who received a positive lifetime diagnosis of panic disorder or major depression by psychiatric interview and who had been treated for these disorders were included.

We recruited comparison parents who were free of major anxiety disorders (panic disorder, agoraphobia, social phobia, or obsessive-compulsive disorder) or mood disorders (major depression, bipolar disorder, or dysthymia) through advertisements to hospital personnel and in community newspapers. We screened these adults in three stages. The first stage was implicit in the fact that hospital personnel or respondents to advertisements should have rates of panic disorder or major depression no higher than the rates in the general population. The second stage was the telephone screen described earlier. The prospective comparison subjects were then administered a psychiatric interview. This study was approved by the institutional review board of the hospital where the study was based, and all participants (parents) signed written consent.

Procedures

We conducted psychiatric assessments of children age 5 and older (N=312) by completing the Schedule for Affective Disorders and Schizophrenia for School-Age Children—Epidemiologic Version (K-SADS-E) (32) with the mothers. Children age 12 and older (N=11) were interviewed directly by a separate interviewer. We combined data from direct and indirect interviews and considered a diagnostic criterion positive if it was endorsed in either interview. We conducted direct psychiatric assessments with each parent by using the Structured Clinical Interview for DSM-III-R (33). We documented the degree of impairment associated with each diagnosis and the type of treatment obtained. We assessed socioeconomic status with the Hollingshead Four-Factor Index (34), which includes information about both parents' educational levels and occupations.

Interviews were conducted by raters with a bachelor's degree in psychology under the supervision of the two senior investigators (J.F.R. and J.B.). The raters underwent a training program in which they were required to 1) master the diagnostic instruments, 2) learn about DSM-III-R criteria, 3) watch training tapes, 4) participate in interviews performed by experienced raters, and 5) rate several subjects under the supervision of the project coordinator. The raters received continued supervision of their assessments from senior project staff and audiotaped all interviews for later random checking. Kappa coefficients of agreement were computed between the interviewers and the board-certified psychiatrists who listened to the audiotaped interviews. For 173 interviews, the median kappa was 0.86. Diagnoses for all subjects were made on the basis of a consensus judgment by the two senior investigators (J.B. and J.F.R.).

Children were evaluated by interviewers blind to the diagnostic status of the parents. Blinded evaluation was assured as follows:

50

1) only the project coordinator knew the diagnostic category of the parent; 2) psychiatric interviewers were blind to the ascertainment status of the parent (e.g., panic disorder patient, major depression patient, comparison subject, spouse), as well as to all information about the children; 3) interviewers who gathered data on children from the children's mothers or from the children themselves were blind to all diagnostic information about the parents, including their ascertainment status; and 4) the final diagnoses for all subjects (parents and children) were made by clinicians who were blind to the subjects' original recruitment group, to all nonpsychiatric data collected from the individual being diagnosed, and to all information about other family members.

In addition, we collected dimensional measures of psychopathology in children age 2 and older by having the mothers complete the Child Behavior Checklist in separate versions for preschoolers (2–3 years old) and for school-age children (4–18 years old) (35, 36). For the purpose of this analysis, we combined data from the corresponding scales in the two versions of the Child Behavior Checklist. One advantage of the Child Behavior Checklist as a measure of psychopathology is that, unlike diagnoses, which focus on clinically serious symptoms, the Child Behavior Checklist can also capture milder levels of symptoms. To capitalize on this feature of the Child Behavior Checklist, we used a T score of ≥ 60 (i.e., one standard deviation above the mean) to signify impairment.

We also assessed the following areas of functioning in children over age 5:

6. Social functioning was assessed with the Global Assessment of Functioning scale of DSM-III-R and the Social Adjustment Inventory for Children and Adolescents (37). The Social Adjustment Inventory for Children and Adolescents is a semistructured interview that assesses adaptive functioning in children and adolescents and covers the four major role areas of school functioning, spare time activities, peer relations, and home life.
7. School functioning was measured by three indices: placement in a special class, use of in-school resource-room tutoring, and having to repeat grades.
8. Treatment history information was obtained by inquiring while administering the K-SADS-E questions about the nature and duration of treatment the child had received.

Statistical Analyses

We first compared children from the four parental diagnostic groups on potentially confounding demographic variables (age, gender, socioeconomic status, size of sibship, intactness of family, and race/ethnicity). Then we examined differences in psychopathology and functioning between children from the four parental ascertainment groups while controlling for potential demographic confounds. Multiple members of a single family (i.e., members of the same sibship) cannot be considered independent of one another because they share genetic, cultural, and social risk factors. To deal with this problem, for all comparisons we used the generalized estimating equation method to estimate general linear models (38), controlling for one or more potentially confounding variables where necessary, as implemented in Stata (39). We used Wald's chi-square test to assess the statistical significance of individual regressors. We used Fisher's exact test in place of the generalized estimating equation when there were one or more zero frequencies in the two-way table defined by the categorical predictor and dichotomous outcome. All tests were two-tailed with alpha set at 0.05.

Results

Data for some children were missing because not all measures were collected for all children. For the 179 children of parents with both panic disorder and major depression, we had structured diagnostic interview data for 141 children and Child Behavior Checklist data for 150. For the 29 children of parents with panic disorder only, we had structured diagnostic interview data for 26 and Child Behavior Checklist data for 25. For the 59 children of parents with major depression only, we had structured diagnostic interview data for 46 and Child Behavior Checklist data for 50. For the 113 comparison children whose parents had neither panic disorder nor major depression, we had structured diagnostic interview data for 99 and Child Behavior Checklist data for 101.

Among children providing structured interview data, 195 were age 5–6, 75 were age 7–9, and 42 were over age 9. Among children for whom Child Behavior Checklist data were available, 111 were age 2–3, and 215 were age 4–18. As shown in Table 1, no significant differences between the children from the four parental diagnostic groups were found for age, gender, or sibship size. There were significant differences among groups for intactness of family and socioeconomic status and a difference that approached significance for race/ethnicity. Therefore, all analyses were corrected for these three variables.

Psychiatric Disorders in Children

Significant differences were detected between children from the four parental diagnostic groups in the mean number of anxiety disorders: mean=0.25 (SD=0.7) in the comparison children, and mean=0.65 (SD=1.3), mean=0.85 (SD=1.5), and mean=1.0 (SD=1.5) in the children of parents with major depression only, panic disorder only, and both panic disorder and major depression, respectively (χ^2=19.3, df=3, p<0.001). Children of all three groups of parents with psychopathology differed significantly from comparison children in the mean number of anxiety disorders (z=2.35, p<0.02; z=2.60, p=0.009; and z=4.32, p<0.001 for comparisons involving children of parents with major depression only, panic disorder only, and both panic disorder and major depression, respectively). Differences remained significant when demographic confounds were covaried.

Significant differences between groups were found for rates of multiple anxiety disorders (two or more anxiety disorders in the same child), separation anxiety disorder, agoraphobia, social phobia, panic disorder, and avoidant disorder (Figure 1). Although we found no significant differences among the children in various psychopathologic groups, each group showed some differences from the comparison children. Separation anxiety disorder and multiple anxiety disorders showed nonspecific effects inasmuch as the children of all three groups of parents with psychopathology showed significantly higher rates of

TABLE 1. Demographic Characteristics of Children in a Familial Study of Anxiety Disorders Whose Parents Had Both Panic Disorder and Major Depression, Panic Disorder Only, Major Depression Only, or Neither Disorder

Characteristic	Children of Parents With Both Panic Disorder and Major Depression (N=179)		Children of Parents With Panic Disorder Only (N=29)		Children of Parents With Major Depression Only (N=59)		Children of Parents Without Panic Disorder or Major Depression (N=113)		Analysis[a]		
	Mean	SD	Mean	SD	Mean	SD	Mean	SD	Value	df	p
Age of child at interview (years)	6.8	2.8	6.6	1.5	6.7	2.5	6.8	1.9	F=0.2	3, 196	0.90
Parents' social class[b,c]	2.3	1.0	1.8	0.6	2.2	1.0	1.8	0.9	Wald χ^2=14.6	3	0.002
Number of siblings in family	2.1	0.9	2.0	0.7	2.1	1.0	2.3	0.9	Wald χ^2=3.1	3	0.39
	N	%	N	%	N	%	N	%	Value	df	p
Female child	85	47.5	13	44.8	23	39.0	46	40.7	Wald χ^2=2.1	3	0.55
Intact family[d]	150	83.8	29	100.0	47	79.7	102	90.3			<0.02[e]
Race/ethnicity											<0.06[e,f]
Caucasian	171	95.5	29	100.0	54	91.5	100	88.5			
African American	5	2.8	0	0.0	3	5.1	4	3.5			
Hispanic	0	0.0	0	0.0	2	3.4	4	3.5			
Asian	3	1.7	0	0.0	0	0.0	5	4.4			

[a] Associations tested by using a generalized estimating equation model controlling for intrafamilial clustering. Fisher's exact test used when one or more cells had a zero frequency.
[b] Measured with the Hollingshead Four-Factor Index (34).
[c] Significant differences between the panic-plus-depression group and the neither-disorder group (p<0.01), the panic-plus-depression group and the panic-only group (p<0.01), and the depression-only group and the neither-disorder group (p<0.05).
[d] Significant differences between the panic-plus-depression group and the panic-only group (p<0.01), the depression-only group and the neither-disorder group (p<0.05), and the depression-only group and the panic-only group (p<0.01).
[e] Fisher's exact test.
[f] For comparison of Caucasian and non-Caucasian groups.

FIGURE 1. Rates of Individual and Multiple Anxiety Disorders in Children of Parents With Both Panic Disorder and Major Depression, Panic Disorder Only, Major Depression Only, or Neither Disorder[a]

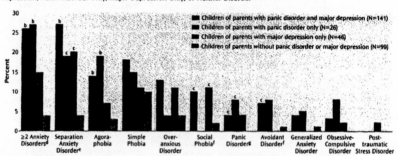

[a] Associations tested by using the generalized estimating equation model controlling for intrafamilial clustering. Fisher's exact test used when one or more cells had a zero frequency.
[b] Significantly different from children of parents with neither disorder (p<0.01).
[c] Significantly different from children of parents with neither disorder (p<0.05).
[d] Significant difference among groups (Wald χ^2=12.5, df=3, p=0.006).
[e] Significant difference among groups (Wald χ^2=13.4, df=3, p=0.004).
[f] Significant difference among groups (Fisher's exact test, p<0.03).
[g] Significant difference among groups (Fisher's exact test, p<0.05).

those disorders than the comparison children. After covarying demographic confounds, the significant difference in the rate of multiple anxiety disorders between the children of parents with major depression and the comparison children became nonsignificant (odds ratio=4.0, 95% confidence interval [CI]=0.92–17.8, z=1.85, p=0.06).

In contrast, other disorders showed some evidence for specificity. Higher rates of panic disorder and agoraphobia

56

than in the comparison children were found only in children of parents with panic disorder and of parents with both panic disorder and major depression. Higher rates of social phobia than in comparison children were found only in children of parents with major depression and of parents with both panic disorder and major depression. After controlling for demographic confounds, the overall difference in the rates of agoraphobia between groups dropped to nonsignificance (χ^2=10.8, df=6, p<0.10); however, the higher rates of agoraphobia in the children of parents with panic disorder (odds ratio=7.3, 95% CI=1.7–32.4, z=2.63, p=0.009) and in the children of parents with both panic disorder and major depression (odds ratio=5.5, 95% CI=1.6–19.0, z=2.67, p=0.008) retained significance. Although a higher rate of avoidant disorder was found in children of parents with panic disorder only and in children of parents with both panic disorder and major depression than in comparison children, the rate was significantly different only in the children of parents with both panic disorder and major depression.

As shown in Figure 2, rates of major depression were significantly higher than in the comparison children among children of parents with major depression only and with both panic disorder and major depression but not among children of parents with panic disorder only. After controlling for demographic confounds, the overall difference in the rates of major depression between groups became nonsignificant (χ^2=11.2, df=6, p=0.08); however, the higher rate in the children of parents with both panic disorder and major depression (odds ratio=5.1, 95% CI=1.1–24.4, z=2.04, p<0.05) and in the children of parents with major depression only (odds ratio=9.0, 95% CI=1.9–44.0, z=2.72, p=0.006) retained significance. A similar pattern was observed for disruptive behavior disorders, although the difference between the children of parents with major depression only and the comparison children failed to reach statistical significance (Figure 2).

The Child Behavior Checklist findings revealed significant differences among the groups in the frequency of scores indicating impairment (scores of 60 or higher) in scales measuring somatic problems (overrepresented in all high-risk groups); withdrawn, aggressive, and destructive behaviors (overrepresented in the children of parents with both panic disorder and major depression); and social interaction problems (overrepresented in children of parents with major depression only) (Figure 3). All comparisons retained significance when demographic confounds were covaried.

Psychosocial Functioning and Treatment in Children

We observed significant differences between groups on the Global Assessment of Functioning scale for both current and lifetime functioning (Table 2). Both the children of parents with major depression only and the children of parents with both panic disorder and major depression

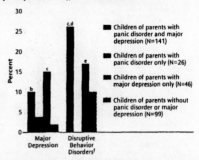

FIGURE 2. Rates of Major Depression and Disruptive Behavior Disorders in Children of Parents With Both Panic Disorder and Major Depression, Panic Disorder Only, Major Depression Only, or Neither Disorder[a]

- ■ Children of parents with panic disorder and major depression (N=141)
- ■ Children of parents with panic disorder only (N=26)
- ■ Children of parents with major depression only (N=46)
- ■ Children of parents without panic disorder or major depression (N=99)

[a] Associations tested by using the generalized estimating equation model controlling for intrafamilial clustering. Fisher's exact test used when one or more cells had a zero frequency.
[b] Significantly different from children of parents with neither disorder (p<0.05).
[c] Significantly different from children of parents with neither disorder (p<0.01).
[d] Significantly different from children of parents with panic disorder only (p<0.01).
[e] Significantly different from children of parents with panic disorder only (p<0.05).
[f] Significant difference among groups (Fisher's exact test, p=0.001).

showed poorer levels of functioning than the comparison children. Although we observed a similar pattern for the total score of the Social Adjustment Inventory for Children and Adolescents, differences between groups became nonsignificant after covarying demographic confounds (χ^2=10.5, df=6, p=0.10). As for school functioning, we found that the children of parents with both panic disorder and major depression had significantly higher frequencies of having repeated a grade than the comparison children. The groups did not differ in treatment history.

Discussion

Our results provide mixed support for the idea that the familial diathesis for anxiety disorders includes a nonspecific "anxiety proneness." If that had been the case, we would have expected high rates of all anxiety disorders among children of parents with panic disorder. Instead, parental panic disorder, regardless of comorbidity with major depression, predicted child panic disorder and agoraphobia, but not other anxiety disorders. This finding confirms prior reports of a specific aggregation for panic disorder (10, 20, 21).

But we also found 1) that parental major depression, regardless of comorbidity with panic disorder, predicted increased risks for social phobia and major depression in children and 2) that both parental panic disorder and pa-

FIGURE 3. Rates of Impairment in Functional Areas Measured by the Child Behavior Checklist in Children of Parents With Both Panic Disorder and Major Depression, Panic Disorder Only, Major Depression Only, or Neither Disorder[a]

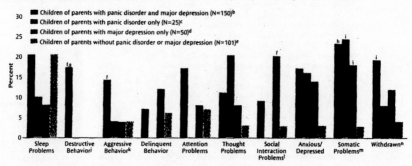

■ Children of parents with panic disorder and major depression (N=150)[b]
■ Children of parents with panic disorder only (N=25)[c]
■ Children of parents with major depression only (N=50)[d]
■ Children of parents without panic disorder or major depression (N=101)[e]

[a] T scores of ≥60 (i.e., one standard deviation above the mean) on the Child Behavior Checklist signified impairment. Responses for scales from both the version of the Child Behavior Checklist for 2–3-year-olds and the version for 4–18-year-olds were combined for this analysis. Data on sleep problems and destructive behavior are based on scales from the version for 2–3-year-olds; data on delinquent behavior, attention problems, thought problems, and social interaction problems are based on scales from the version for 4–18-year-olds; and data on the remaining variables are based on scales from both versions. Associations tested by using a generalized estimating equation model controlling for intrafamilial clustering. Fisher's exact test used when one or more cells had a zero frequency.
[b] For 2–3-year-olds, N=46; for 4–18-year-olds, N=104.
[c] For 2–3-year-olds, N=10; for 4–18-year-olds, N=15.
[d] For 2–3-year-olds, N=25; for 4–18-year-olds, N=25.
[e] For 2–3-year-olds, N=30; for 4–18-year-olds, N=71.
[f] Significantly different from children of parents with neither disorder (p<0.05).
[g] Significantly different from children of parents with major depression only (p<0.05).
[h] Significantly different from children of parents with neither disorder (p<0.001).
[i] Significantly different from children of parents with neither disorder (p<0.01).
[j] Significant difference among groups (Fisher's exact test, p=0.01).
[k] Significant difference among groups (Wald χ^2=9.0, df=3, p=0.03).
[l] Significant difference among groups (Fisher's exact test, p<0.04).
[m] Significant difference among groups (Wald χ^2=13.9, df=3, p=0.003).
[n] Significant difference among groups (Wald χ^2=9.8, df=3, p=0.02).

rental major depression, individually or comorbidly, were associated with increased risk for separation anxiety disorder. This familial line between major depression and some anxiety disorders is consistent with prior studies (4, 5).

Our results indicate heterogeneity within the group of anxiety disorders. Some disorders may share a common familial vulnerability, others may be associated with the risk for major depression, and others may possibly represent nonspecific manifestations of risk in offspring of parents with anxiety or major depression. In our study, the risks for panic disorder and major depression were not additive. Having parents with two disorders did not double the child's risk for having one. Instead, the pattern of risk was better predicted by which disorder had been diagnosed in the parent, regardless of the presence of other disorders. These findings stress the importance of considering specific anxiety disorders in studies of children at risk.

Equally consistent with the extant literature is our finding that separation anxiety disorder is associated with either anxiety or major depression in parents (40). This result, together with reports of others (41) failing to find

associations between adult panic or agoraphobia and childhood history of separation anxiety disorder, challenges the idea that separation anxiety disorder is a specific childhood antecedent of subsequent panic disorder or agoraphobia.

We also observed specificity of transmission of major depression between parents and children. Moreover, parental major depression increased the risk for major depression in the offspring irrespective of the presence of panic disorder in the parent. Similar findings have been reported by Weissman et al. (1). These findings suggest that there are separate familial vulnerabilities for panic disorder and major depression.

Notably, the risk for anxiety disorders in children of parents with panic disorder was not limited to the traditional childhood-onset disorders but also included the adult-type anxiety disorders panic disorder and agoraphobia. Although these adult-type disorders are not commonly assessed in pediatric studies, a body of literature has documented that these disorders occur and can be diagnosed in children (42, 43). Such findings support the value of considering the full spectrum of anxiety disorders in children.

54

58

TABLE 2. Functional Characteristics of Children of Parents With Both Panic Disorder and Major Depression, Panic Disorder Only, Major Depression Only, or Neither Disorder

Characteristic	Children of Parents With Both Panic Disorder and Major Depression			Children of Parents With Panic Disorder			Children of Parents With Major Depression			Children of Parents Without Panic Disorder or Major Depression			Analysis[a]	
	Total N	Mean	SD	Total N	Mean	SD	Total N	Mean	SD	Total N	Mean	SD	Wald χ^2 (df=3)	p
Social competence areas measured by the Child Behavior Checklist (T scores)														
Social relations	43	47.6	6.8	6	41.8	7.3	9	48.8	6.2	32	47.8	8.1	2.4	0.49
Activities	53	47.6	6.6	9	48.4	4.4	9	49.7	4.8	40	47.9	5.7	0.8	0.86
School functioning	36	46.2	8.2	7	45.0	7.8	8	46.9	6.8	28	48.1	7.6	3.2	0.36
Social Adjustment Inventory for Children and Adolescents score[b]	110	15.0	4.0	19	14.7	2.4	36	16.1	5.2	82	13.6	3.3	8.6	<0.04[c]
Global Assessment of Functioning score														
Current (past month)[d]	141	65.6	7.7	26	68.3	5.0	46	66.8	5.9	99	69.8	4.0	29.4	<0.001
Lifetime (worst functioning)[e]	141	63.7	8.7	26	66.3	5.9	46	64.9	6.8	99	68.7	5.7	24.9	<0.001
	N	%		N	%		N	%		N	%		Wald χ^2 (df=3)	p
School functioning														
Repeated grade[f]	141	9	6.4	26	1	3.8	46	1	2.2	99	0	0.0		<0.04[g]
Needed tutoring	141	17	12.1	26	3	11.5	46	8	17.4	99	9	9.1	1.7	0.64
Placed in special class	141	8	5.7	26	1	3.8	46	3	6.5	99	4	4.0	0.5	0.91
Treatment history														
Counseling only	125	28	22.4	24	8	33.3	40	10	25.0	88	10	11.4	6.6	<0.09
Pharmacotherapy only	125	1	0.8	24	0	0.0	40	0	0.0	88	0	0.0		1.00[g]
Counseling and pharmacotherapy	125	5	4.0	24	0	0.0	40	0	0.0	88	2	2.3		0.74[g]
Psychiatric hospitalization	125	1	0.8	24	0	0.0	40	0	0.0	88	0	0.0		1.00[g]

[a] Associations tested by using a generalized estimating equation model controlling for intrafamilial clustering. Fisher's exact test used when one or more cells had a zero frequency.
[b] Significant differences between the panic-plus-depression group and the neither-disorder group (p<0.05) and between the depression-only group and the neither-disorder group (p<0.05).
[c] Overall difference became nonsignificant after demographic confounds (age, gender, socioeconomic status, size of sibship, intactness of family, and race/ethnicity) were covaried.
[d] Significant differences between the panic-plus-depression group and the neither-disorder group (p<0.001), between the panic-plus-depression group and the panic-only group (p<0.05), and between the depression-only group and the neither-disorder group (p<0.01).
[e] Significant differences between the panic-plus-depression group and the neither-disorder group (p<0.001) and between the depression-only group and the neither-disorder group (p<0.01).
[f] Significant difference between the panic-plus-depression group and the neither-disorder group (p<0.01).
[g] Fisher's exact test.

In addition to increasing the risks for major depression and anxiety disorders in the offspring, parental major depression also increased the risk for disruptive behavior disorders both as a diagnosis and as measured by the Child Behavior Checklist. This finding is consistent with literature documenting a high degree of syndromatic overlap and familial co-aggregation between disruptive behavior and depressive disorders (44–46).

Despite these differences in psychopathology among the groups, we found few differences in levels of functioning. The strongest differences were for both current and lifetime functioning on the Global Assessment of Functioning scale, on which children of parents with major depression only or with both panic disorder and major depression showed poorer levels of functioning than the comparison children. There were small differences on the total score of the Social Adjustment Inventory for Children and Adolescents, but these were accounted for by intactness of family, socioeconomic status, and race/ethnicity.

We found no differences on Child Behavior Checklist measures of functioning and only one sign of school dysfunction, more repeated grades among children of parents with both panic disorder and major depression. Consistent with the minimal differences in functioning, treatment history findings revealed no significant differences among groups.

The low levels of treatment are consistent with the findings of Weissman et al. (47), who reported that one-third of depressed high-risk children had not been treated during a 10-year follow-up period despite impaired family and work functioning. Moreover, epidemiologic studies have suggested that underidentification is pervasive; only a small fraction of youth with mental disorders receive adequate treatment (48). These results call for increased efforts to identify emotional and behavioral difficulties in children of parents referred for anxiety and depression to adult psychiatry practices.

Our findings should be viewed in the context of the study's methodological limitations. Any interpretation of these findings must be tempered by the fact that these children are still early in the risk period for anxiety and depressive disorders. Future onset of illness may lead to different inferences about patterns of transmission. The assessment of psychopathology in the children was based mainly on interviews with the mothers. Psychiatric disorders in parents may have affected the reported rates of childhood symptoms. Psychiatric patients may exaggerate symptoms in their children, or, alternatively, mothers without psychopathology may underreport problem behaviors (49). Another concern is that the numbers of parents with major depression only and with panic disorder only (without comorbid major depression) were relatively small and so did not afford adequate statistical power for a thorough test of associations between major depression or panic disorder in parents and in their high-risk children. Because we conducted multiple statistical tests without a Bonferroni correction, some of our findings may be due to chance. Had we used a Bonferroni correction, psychopathology findings would have been significant at $p<0.004$ (Figure 1 and Figure 2), Child Behavior Checklist findings would have been significant at $p<0.005$ (Figure 3), and functional characteristics at $p<0.004$ (Table 2). Thus, our results should be viewed cautiously until confirmed in additional studies.

Because the proband parents were clinically referred, the generalizability of our findings is limited to offspring of referred patients. Also, the large majority of subjects were Caucasians from intact families and higher social classes. Further work is needed to determine if our results generalize beyond these constraints.

Despite these considerations, in a large group of children at risk we found that parental panic disorder and major depression conferred a significant risk for dysfunction and emotional distress in their offspring. A longitudinal follow-up of this group is needed to determine whether these difficulties will confer further vulnerability on these children as well as to identify risk and protective factors that influence the transition from childhood to adult anxiety disorders.

Received Sept. 29, 1999; revisions received May 17 and July 20, 2000; accepted Aug. 10, 2000. From the Pediatric Psychopharmacology Program and the Department of Psychiatry, Massachusetts General Hospital; the Department of Psychiatry, Harvard Medical School, Boston; and the Harvard Institute of Psychiatric Epidemiology and Genetics, Boston. Address reprint requests to Dr. Biederman, Clinical Psychopharmacology Unit, WACC 725, Massachusetts General Hospital, 15 Parkman St., Boston, MA 02114.
Supported by NIMH grant MH-47077.
The authors thank Jerome Kagan, Ph.D., Nancy Snidman, Ph.D., Allan Nineberg, M.D., and Daniel J. Gallery, Psy.D.

References

1. Weissman MM, Leckman JF, Merikangas KR, Gammon GD, Prusoff BA: Depression and anxiety disorders in parents and children: results from the Yale Family Study. Arch Gen Psychiatry 1984; 41:845–852

2. Turner SM, Beidel DC, Costello A: Psychopathology in the offspring of anxiety disorders patients. J Consult Clin Psychol 1987; 55:229–235

3. Biederman J, Rosenbaum JF, Bolduc EA, Faraone SV, Hirshfeld DR: A high risk study of young children of parents with panic disorder and agoraphobia with and without comorbid major depression. Psychiatry Res 1991; 37:333–348

4. Beidel DC, Turner SM: At risk for anxiety, I: psychopathology in the offspring of anxious parents. J Am Acad Child Adolesc Psychiatry 1997; 36:918–924

5. Sylvester CE, Hyde TS, Reichler RJ: Clinical psychopathology among children of adults with panic disorder, in Relatives at Risk for Mental Disorders. Edited by Dunner DL, Gershon ES, Barrett JE. New York, Raven Press, 1988, pp 87–102

6. Capps L, Sigman M, Sena R, Henker B, Whalen C: Fear, anxiety and perceived control in children of agoraphobic parents. J Child Psychol Psychiatry 1996; 37:445–452

7. Andrews G, Stewart G, Allen R, Henderson AS: The genetics of six neurotic disorders: a twin study. J Affect Disord 1990; 19:23–29

8. Barlow D: Anxiety and Its Disorders. New York, Guilford Press, 1988

9. Rosenbaum JF, Biederman J, Hirshfeld DR, Bolduc EA, Faraone SV, Kagan J, Snidman N, Reznick JS: Further evidence of an association between childhood inhibition and anxiety disorders: results from a family study of children from a non-clinical sample. J Psychiatr Res 1991; 25:49–65

10. Harris EL, Noyes R, Crowe RR, Chaudhry DR: A family study of agoraphobia: report of a pilot study. Arch Gen Psychiatry 1983; 40:1061–1064

11. Torgersen S: Genetic factors in anxiety disorders. Arch Gen Psychiatry 1983; 40:1085–1089

12. Barlow DH, DiNardo PA, Vermilyea JA: Co-morbidity and depression among the anxiety disorders: issues in diagnosis and classification. J Nerv Ment Dis 1986; 174:63–72

13. Stein MB, Shea CA, Uhde TW: Social phobic symptoms in patients with panic disorder: practical and theoretical implications. Am J Psychiatry 1989; 146:235–238

14. DeRuiter C, Rijkin H, Garssen B: Comorbidity among the anxiety disorders. J Anxiety Disord 1989; 3:57–68

15. Last CG, Strauss CC, Francis G: Comorbidity among childhood anxiety disorders. J Nerv Ment Dis 1987; 175:726–730

16. Deltito JA, Perugi G, Maremmani I, Mignani V, Cassano GB: The importance of separation anxiety in the differentiation of panic disorder from agoraphobia. Psychiatr Dev 1986; 4:227–236

17. Silove D, Manicavasagar V, Curtis J, Blaszczynski A: Is early separation anxiety a risk factor for adult panic disorder? a critical review. Compr Psychiatry 1996; 37:167–179

18. Lipsitz JD, Martin LY, Mannuzza S, Chapman TF, Liebowitz MR, Klein DF, Fyer AJ: Childhood separation anxiety disorder in patients with adult anxiety disorders. Am J Psychiatry 1994; 151:927–929

19. Otto MW, Pollock MH, Rosenbaum JF, Sachs GS, Asher RH: Childhood history of anxiety in adults with panic disorder: association with anxiety sensitivity and comorbidity. Harv Rev Psychiatry 1994; 1:288–293

20. Crowe RR, Noyes R, Pauls DL, Slymen D: A family study of panic disorder. Arch Gen Psychiatry 1983; 40:1065–1069

21. Noyes R, Crowe R, Harris E, Hamra B, McChesney C, Chaudhry D: Relationship between panic disorder and agoraphobia: a family study. Arch Gen Psychiatry 1986; 43:227–232

22. Weissman M: Panic and generalized anxiety: are they separate disorders? J Psychiatr Res 1990; 24:157–162

56

60

23. Kendler K, Walters E, Neale M, Kessler R, Heath A, Eaves L: The structure of the genetic and environmental risk factors for six major psychiatric disorders in women: phobia, generalized anxiety disorder, panic disorder, bulimia, major depression, and alcoholism. Arch Gen Psychiatry 1995; 52:374–383

24. Fyer A, Mannuzza S, Chapman T, Liebowitz M, Klein D: A direct interview family study of social phobia. Arch Gen Psychiatry 1993; 50:286–293

25. Stein MB, Chartier MJ, Hazen AL, Kozak MV, Tancer ME, Lander S, Furer P, Chubaty D, Walker JR: A direct-interview family study of generalized social phobia. Am J Psychiatry 1998; 155:90–97

26. Fyer AJ, Mannuzza S, Chapman TF, Martin LY, Klein DF: Specificity in familial aggregation of phobic disorders. Arch Gen Psychiatry 1995; 52:564–573

27. Kendler KS, Neale MC, Kessler RC, Heath AC, Eaves LJ: The genetic epidemiology of phobias in women: the interrelationship of agoraphobia, social phobia, situational phobia, and simple phobia. Arch Gen Psychiatry 1992; 49:273–281

28. Goldstein RB, Weissman MM, Adams PB, Horwath E, Lish J, Charney D, Woods S, Sobin C: Psychiatric disorders in relatives of probands with panic disorder and/or major depression. Arch Gen Psychiatry 1994; 51:383–394

29. Horwath E, Wolk SI, Goldstein RB, Wickramaratne P, Sobin C, Adams P, Lish JD, Weissman MM: Is the comorbidity between social phobia and panic disorder due to familial cotransmission or other factors? Arch Gen Psychiatry 1995; 52:574–582

30. Maser JD, Cloninger CR (eds): Comorbidity of Anxiety and Mood Disorders. Washington, DC, American Psychiatric Press, 1990

31. Breslau N, Davis GC, Prabucki K: Searching for evidence on the validity of generalized anxiety disorder: psychopathology in children of anxious mothers. Psychiatry Res 1987; 20:285–297

32. Orvaschel H, Puig-Antich J: Schedule for Affective Disorders and Schizophrenia for School-Age Children—Epidemiologic Version (K-SADS-E), 4th revision. Fort Lauderdale, Fla, Nova University, Center for Psychological Study, 1987

33. Spitzer RL, Williams JBW, Gibbon M, First MB: Structured Clinical Interview for DSM-III-R—Non-Patient Edition (SCID-NP, Version 1.0). Washington, DC, American Psychiatric Press, 1990

34. Hollingshead AB: Four-Factor Index of Social Status. New Haven, Conn, Yale University, Department of Sociology, 1975

35. Achenbach TM: Manual for the Child Behavior Checklist/4-18 and 1991 Profile. Burlington, University of Vermont, Department of Psychiatry, 1991

36. Achenbach TM: Manual for the Child Behavior Checklist/2-3 and 1992 Profile. Burlington, University of Vermont, Department of Psychiatry, 1992

37. John K, Gammon GD, Prusoff BA, Warner V: The Social Adjustment Inventory for Children and Adolescents (SAICA): testing of a new semistructured interview. J Am Acad Child Adolesc Psychiatry 1987; 26:898–911

38. Liang KY, Zeger SL: Longitudinal data analysis using generalized linear models. Biometrika 1986; 73:13–22

39. Stata Reference Manual: Release 5. College Station, Tex, Stata Corp, 1997

40. Zitrin CM, Ross DC: Early separation anxiety and adult agoraphobia. J Nerv Ment Dis 1988; 176:621–625

41. van der Molen G, van den Hout M, van Dieren A, Griez E: Childhood separation anxiety and adult-onset panic disorders. J Anxiety Disord 1989; 3:97–106

42. Biederman J, Faraone SV, Marrs A, Moore P, Garcia J, Ablon JS, Mick E, Gershon J, Kearns ME: Panic disorder and agoraphobia in consecutively referred children and adolescents. J Am Acad Child Adolesc Psychiatry 1997; 36:214–223

43. Moreau D, Weissman MM: Panic disorder in children and adolescents: a review. Am J Psychiatry 1992; 149:1306–1314

44. Puig-Antich J, Rabinovich H: Relationship between affective and anxiety disorders in childhood, in Anxiety Disorders of Childhood. Edited by Gittelman R. New York, Guilford Press, 1986, pp 136–156

45. Orvaschel H, Walsh-Allis G, Ye WJ: Psychopathology in children of parents with recurrent depression. J Abnorm Child Psychol 1988; 16:17–28

46. Faraone SV, Biederman J: Do attention deficit hyperactivity disorder and major depression share familial risk factors? J Nerv Ment Dis 1997; 185:533–541

47. Weissman MM, Warner V, Wickramaratne PJ, Moreau D, Olfson M: Offspring of depressed parents: 10 years later. Arch Gen Psychiatry 1997; 54:932–940

48. Bird HR, Canino G, Rubio-Stipec M, Gould MS, Ribera J, Sesman M, Woodbury M, Huertas-Goldman S, Pagan A, Sanchez-Lacay A, Moscoso M: Estimates of the prevalence of childhood maladjustment in a community survey in Puerto Rico: the use of combined measures. Arch Gen Psychiatry 1988; 45:1120–1126

49. Mick E, Santangelo S, Wypij D, Biederman J: Impact of maternal depression on ratings of comorbid depression in adolescents with attention-deficit/hyperactivity disorder. J Am Acad Child Adolesc Psychiatry 2000; 39:314–319

61

Vulnerability Factors among Children at Risk for Anxiety Disorders

Kathleen Ries Merikangas, Shelli Avenevoli, Lisa Dierker, and Christian Grillon

Background: *The high-risk strategy is one of the most powerful approaches for identifying premorbid risk factors and reducing etiologic and phenotypic heterogeneity characteristic of the major psychiatric disorders.*

Methods: *This paper reviews the methods of high-risk research and findings from previous high-risk studies of anxiety. The preliminary results of the 6–8 year follow-up of a high-risk study of 192 offspring of probands with anxiety disorders, substance abuse, and unaffected controls are presented. The key study measures include comprehensive diagnostic interviews, symptom ratings, indirect measures of brain functioning (neuropsychologic, neurologic and psychophysiologic function), developmental measures, and family functioning measures.*

Results: *The major findings reveal that there is specificity of familial aggregation of anxiety disorders among parents and children; children at high risk for anxiety have increased startle reflex, autonomic reactivity, and stress reactivity, higher verbal IQ, and deficits in paired associative learning as compared to other children.*

Conclusions: *The finding that family environment and parenting do not differ between children at risk for anxiety disorders and other children, when taken together with the strong degree of specificity of transmission of anxiety disorders, suggests that there may be temperamental vulnerability factors for anxiety disorders in general that may already manifest in children prior to puberty.* Biol Psychiatry 1999;46:1523–1535 © 1999 Society of Biological Psychiatry

Key Words: Anxiety, high risk, genetic, children

Introduction

Despite dramatic advances in the understanding of genetics, neurobiology, and the links between the environment and central nervous system functioning, the etiology of the anxiety disorders is still unknown. There are no patho-

gnomonic markers with which a presumptive diagnosis of an anxiety disorder may be made in the absence of a clinical interview. This paper will 1) provide a brief summary of evidence from family and twin studies regarding the role of genetic factors in the etiology of the anxiety disorders; 2) summarize controlled high-risk studies of anxiety disorders; 3) review evidence of vulnerability markers for anxiety disorders derived from high-risk studies; and 4) present preliminary data regarding vulnerability factors from a prospective high-risk study of anxiety disorders.

Familial Aggregation of Anxiety Disorders

All major subtypes of the anxiety disorders have been shown to aggregate in families. Panic disorder is the anxiety syndrome that has been shown to have the strongest degree of familial aggregation, with an average relative risk of approximately 9.4 (Weissman 1993), as well as the highest heritability (Kendler et al 1993, 1995; Skre et al 1993). In addition, early-onset panic has been shown to have a higher familial loading than later onset panic disorder (Goldstein et al 1997). Far fewer controlled studies of other anxiety subtypes exist, although specific phobia, social phobia, agoraphobia, and generalized anxiety disorder have also been shown to be familial (Fyer et al 1993, 1995; Noyes et al 1987; Stein et al 1998), and twin studies have revealed a small but significant degree of heritability for several of these subtypes (Kendler et al 1992, 1995; see reviews by Merikangas and Angst 1995, Woodman and Crowe 1996).

Based on indirect evidence implicating the adrenergic system in panic disorder (Goddard et al 1996), several linkage studies have investigated the role of mutations in adrenergic receptor loci on chromosomes 4; 5, or 10 (Wang et al 1992) without success. Other work has similarly excluded linkage with $GABA_A$ receptor genes (Schmidt et al 1993). Reports from a genomic survey of panic disorder using 600 markers have not yielded evidence of linkage (Nurnberger and Byerley 1995).

What Is Inherited?

Although most theories of anxiety assume some underlying genetic predisposition, the specific components of

From the Departments of Epidemiology and Public Health (KRM, SA, LD) and Psychiatry (KRM, CG), Yale University School of Medicine, New Haven and the Department of Psychology, Wesleyan University, Middletown (LD), Connecticut.

Address reprint requests to Dr. K.R. Merikangas, Yale University School of Medicine, Suite 7B, 40 Temple Street, New Haven, CT 06510.

Received March 23, 1999; revised June 22, 1999; accepted June 23, 1999.

0006-3223/99/$20.00
PII S0006-3223(99)00172-9

anxiety that may be heritable are unknown. The wide range of biochemical and physiologic measures that have been investigated as potential trait markers for anxiety disorders fall into the following three categories: 1) psychophysiologic function such as pulse, respiration rate, and galvanic skin response and other output of the sympathetic nervous system (e.g., Grillon et al 1994, 1999; Marks 1986); 2) biochemical factors as assessed by peripheral measures of putative central nervous system function, usually through challenge studies such as response to lactate, CO_2, and yohimbine; and 3) temperamental or personality traits including neuroticism, behavioral inhibition, and anxiety sensitivity. The only psychological trait that has been identified as a potential premorbid marker for the development of anxiety, particularly social phobia, is behavioral inhibition, which has been associated with anxiety states both prospectively (Kagan et al 1998) and among offspring of parents with anxiety (Biederman et al 1991; Rosenbaum et al 1988).

Recent reviews of this large body of research are presented by Johnson and Lydiard (1995), Goddard et al (1996), Coplan and Lydiard (1998), Fyer (1998), Stein et al (1998) and Kagan et al (1998). The general conclusion is that multiple systems and brain structures are involved in the pathophysiology of anxiety disorders (Goddard et al 1996; Johnson and Lydiard 1995). Most of these studies, however, did not provide adequate evidence of the extent to which the measures may serve as putative trait markers for anxiety disorders because of nonsystematically ascertained clinical samples and a lack of distinction between state and trait markers. Moreover, most studies have not accounted for the major sources of clinical heterogeneity of the anxiety disorders including the presence of multiple subtypes of anxiety, comorbidity with other disorders, and gender differences in the expression of anxiety.

Some recent work has begun to test the stability of these measures under various conditions (Wilkinson et al 1998), as well as the prognostic significance of these measures (Grillon et al 1997a, 1998; Schmidt et al 1997) and their presence in children (Grillon et al 1997a, 1998; Kagan et al 1998; Pine et al 1998). Progress in understanding the pathogenesis of anxiety will be critically dependent on further work in identifying the specific components of anxiety disorders that may be heritable.

Strategies for Identifying Vulnerability Factors for Anxiety Disorders

Etiologic and phenotypic heterogeneity may be the chief impediment to elucidation of the pathogenesis of anxiety disorders because unrelated patient samples are the primary source of data on the neurobiology of most major psychiatric disorders. The increasing trend toward adver-

tising for such samples raises serious concern regarding potential biases that may lead to erroneous inferences about the risk factors for these conditions. The family study approach, particularly when employed with systematic community-based samples, is one of the most powerful strategies to minimize heterogeneity because etiologic factors for the development of a particular disorder can be assumed to be relatively homotypic within families. There is a dearth of studies that have employed within-family designs to examine some of the putative biological factors underlying the major anxiety disorders. Perna et al (1996, 1995), for example, have shown that healthy relatives of probands with panic disorder have increased sensitivity to CO_2 challenge. This finding, when taken together with findings of similar sensitivity in children and adolescents with panic (Pine et al 1998), suggests that CO_2 sensitivity may be a promising trait marker for the development of panic.

High-Risk Design

An even more powerful strategy for identification of premorbid vulnerability factors for a particular disease is the high-risk design, which is comprised of a comparison between individual risk of a particular condition and those without the risk factor. By focusing on individuals with the greatest probability of developing specific disorders, the high-risk design 1) maximizes the potential case yield; 2) increases the power within a particular sample to observe hypothesized risk-factor associations; 3) minimizes the heterogeneity that is likely to characterize unrelated samples of youth enrolled in prospective studies; 4) increases the likelihood of observing the effects of mediating and moderating variables on the primary risk factor of interest (e.g., children of alcoholic parents with or without accompanying risk factors); and 5) identifies early patterns of disease given the exposure (e.g., parental psychopathology).

Limitations of the high-risk design include 1) the inability to identify which offspring are truly at risk (on average only 50% will possess the genetic vulnerability factors); 2) the wide age range and developmental level represented in the sample, which often precludes common assessment methods for the entire sample both cross-sectionally and longitudinally; and 3) the relatively low number of actual cases, despite maximizing potential caseness based on family history. Perhaps the most important limitation of high-risk studies is the inability to employ the wide range of tools to probe susceptibility in unaffected individuals, particularly in children, because of ethical concerns and the potential for triggering onset of the disorder. In addition, the disadvantages of any prospective longitudinal research also apply to the high-risk study design, namely the high expense and effort devoted

Table 1. Controlled High-Risk Studies of Anxiety

Study: Author (Year)	Sample: Proband Anxiety	Proband Other	Other	Spouse	Offspring N	Offspring Age	Relative Risk
Sylvester et al (1987)	Panic	MDD	—	No Dx	91	17	13.3
Turner et al (1987)	Agoraphobia/OCD	Dysthymia	—	Not Eval	43	7–12	4.8
Capps et al (1996)	Agoraphobia	Agoraphobia/Panic	—	Not Eval	43	8–24	—
Warner et al (1995)	Panic/MDD	Panic	Early-Onset MDD	Dx	145	6–29	1.3
Beidel et al (1997)	Anxiety and Depression	Anxiety	MDD	No Dx	129	7–12	4.0
Merikangas et al (1998)	Panic/Social Phob	Alcohol or Drug Use	Substance and ANX	Dx	192	7–17	2.0
Unnewehr et al (1998)	Panic	Simple		Not Eval	87	5–15	9.2

to tracking and assessing samples, high attrition rates, and the long duration before conclusive findings may be generated. Despite these limitations, the high-risk design remains one of the most valuable tools for studying premorbid risk factors.

High-Risk Studies of Psychiatric Disorders

The role of a family history of psychiatric disorders as one of the most potent risk factors for the development of psychopathology has generated a substantial body of research on offspring of parents with schizophrenia, alcoholism, anxiety disorders, and affective disorders (Downey and Coyne 1990; Erlenmeyer-Kimling et al 1983; Johnson and Lydiard 1995; Last et al 1991). These studies have attempted to identify the correlates and consequences of parental psychopathology and to map the complex developmental course of psychopathology during relevant periods of risk. Due to a lack of adequate controls, however, few of the high-risk studies to date have studied the specificity of associations between vulnerability markers. Such studies enable investigation of the specificity of familial factors as opposed to the impact of psychopathology in general (Laucht et al 1994).

There are several design issues that preclude aggregation across studies. First, the majority of high-risk studies have failed to consider either the characteristics of fathers or information provided by them, despite the important genetic and environmental contribution of fathers to their offspring. Second, the control groups are selected by diverse methods that often differ from the sampling of the probands. Third, the control group is often devoid of any psychopathology, thereby limiting the ability of the study to examine specificity. Fourth, siblings of the high-risk sample are often not assessed despite the important information they provide on familial transmission. Finally, many studies examine only the diagnostic entities of interest rather than a wide range of potential risk and protective factors.

High-Risk Studies of Anxiety Disorders

There are fewer high-risk studies of anxiety than of schizophrenia, alcoholism, or depression. Those high-risk studies of anxiety that have been conducted focused on parental panic disorder. A summary of controlled high-risk studies of anxiety disorders is presented in Table 1.

There are seven controlled studies of anxiety disorders among offspring of parents (primarily mothers) with anxiety disorders (Beidel 1988; Capps et al 1996; Merikangas et al 1998a; Sylvester et al 1987; Turner et al 1987; Unnewehr et al 1998; Warner et al 1995). The risk of anxiety disorders among offspring of parents with anxiety disorders compared to controls averages 3.5 (range 1.3–13.3), suggesting specificity of parent-child concordance within broad subtypes of anxiety disorders. The wide range of estimates is chiefly attributable to the diagnostic methods and sampling of the individual studies. Many studies did not evaluate the nonproband parent, whereas others excluded families in which the coparent had another psychiatric disorder. The age composition of the samples was also markedly different, as were the diagnostic methods.

Nonetheless, similar to studies of adults that show common familial and genetic risk factors for anxiety and depression (Kendler et al 1993; Merikangas 1990; Stavrakaki and Vargo 1986), these studies have revealed that there is a lack of specificity with respect to depression (Beidel and Turner 1997; Sylvester et al 1987; Turner et al 1987; Warner et al 1995). Studies that employed a comparison group of parent probands with depressive disorders have shown that rates of anxiety disorders are also increased among the offspring of these parents (Beidel and Turner 1997; Sylvester et al 1988; Turner et al 1987; Warner et al 1995); conversely, offspring of parents with anxiety disorders and depression have elevated rates of depression when compared to those of control subjects (Sylvester et al 1988) or to offspring of parents with anxiety disorders but without depression (Biederman et al 1991). Similar findings emerged from the family study by Last et al (1991), who found an increase in rates of major depression among the adult relatives of children with anxiety. These findings are usually interpreted as providing evidence for age-specific expression of common risk factors for anxiety in childhood and for depression with or without comorbid anxiety in adulthood.

The high rates of anxiety disorders among offspring of parents with anxiety suggest that there may be underlying psychological or biological vulnerability factors for anxiety disorders in general that may manifest in children prior to puberty. Previous research has shown that children at risk for anxiety disorders are characterized by behavioral inhibition (Rosenbaum et al 1988), autonomic reactivity (Beidel 1988), somatic symptoms (Reichler et al 1988; Turner et al 1987), and social fears (Sylvester et al 1988; Turner et al 1987). Fears involving social evaluation have been shown to be far more stable than other childhood fears that may be self-limited (Achenbach 1985).

Several studies have also suggested that there is an association between childhood medical conditions and the subsequent development of anxiety. Kagan et al (1984) reported an association between allergic symptoms, particularly hay fever, and inhibited temperament in young children. In a retrospective review of prenatal, perinatal, and early childhood risk factors for different forms of psychiatric disorders in adolescence and early adulthood, Allen et al (1998) found that anxiety disorders in adolescents were associated specifically with illness during the first year of life, particularly high fever. Taylor (1991) reported that immunologic diseases and infections were specifically associated with emotional disorders because children with developmental or behavioral disorders had no elevation in infections or allergic diseases. These findings suggest that it may be useful to examine links between immunologic function and the development of anxiety disorders.

Studies of Biological Vulnerability Factors

Despite an abundance of studies of biological correlates of anxiety in adults, there are almost no studies of biological function in high-risk youth, a key source of information regarding the underlying role of biological parameters in the development of anxiety disorders. Reichler et al (1988) assessed several biological factors in their high-risk study of panic disorder including lactate metabolism, mitral valve prolapse, urinary catecholamines, and monoamine oxidase, but none of these parameters discriminated high-risk youth from low-risk youth. The lack of differences may have been attributable to low statistical power.

Findings from Yale Family Study of Anxiety Disorders

This paper will report the preliminary results of a prospective study of offspring embedded in a larger family study of comorbidity of anxiety disorders and substance use, which examined the patterns of familial aggregation and comorbidity in the relatives of 165 probands selected for alcoholism, anxiety disorders, or both compared to those of 61 unaffected control subjects. The major findings of the adult family study with relevance to the anxiety disorders indicated that there was some specificity of familial aggregation of subtypes of anxiety disorders, particularly social phobia and panic. With respect to familial mechanisms for comorbidity of anxiety disorders and alcoholism, the patterns of coaggregation of alcohol dependence and anxiety disorders in families differed according to the subtype of anxiety disorder. Evidence existed for a partially shared diathesis underlying panic and alcoholism, whereas social phobia and alcoholism tended to aggregate independently (Merikangas et al 1998b).

Methods and Materials

Sample

ADULT PROBANDS. Controls and the 260 adult probands with anxiety disorders, substance use, or both were recruited from outpatient clinics and the community via a random telephone-calling procedure. All probands in the present study were Caucasian; separate family studies of similar diagnostic groups of African American and Hispanic probands are now underway. Probands and relatives were directly interviewed with the semistructured Schedule for Affective Disorders and Schizophrenia (SADS), current and lifetime versions (Endicott and Spitzer 1978), extensively modified to obtain DSM-III and DSM-III-R criteria (American Psychiatric Association 1987). Adult first-degree relatives and spouses were directly interviewed by experienced clinical interviewers who were blind to the diagnostic status of the proband. There were a total of 1218 adult first-degree relatives of the adult probands.

In order to be eligible for the high-risk study, the potential probands (cases and controls) were required to have offspring between the ages of 7 and 17 and to provide consent for their offspring to be interviewed. The families included in this subset of the larger family study consisted of 123 probands, three of whom had offspring with two different spouses, for a total of 126 couples. There was an approximately equal distribution of male and female probands, with an average age of 39. There was a broad range of social class representation with about one third falling in the lower two classes, one third in class three, and one third in classes one or two as defined by modified Hollingshead classification.

Parent probands consisted of 1) 52 individuals in the substance abuse/dependence group who were diagnosed with alcoholism, drug use disorders, or both including anxiolytic, sedative, or

BIOL PSYCHIATRY 1527
1999;46:1523–1535

benzodiazepine abuse, and marijuana abuse or dependence; 2) 36 probands in the anxiety group who were diagnosed with anxiety disorders including panic with or without agoraphobia, social phobia, generalized anxiety disorder (anxiety group), or any combination thereof; and 3) 35 control probands having no lifetime history of psychiatric disorder. Probands with comorbid affective disorders, antisocial personality disorder (ASP), or other nonpsychotic Axis I disorders were not excluded from the study.

OFFSPRING AGES 7–17.   There were 192 children assessed at the time of the original study. Thirty-eight were children of probands diagnosed with alcoholism and/or drug use disorders; 39 were children of probands diagnosed with both an anxiety disorder and a substance disorder; 58 were children of probands diagnosed with anxiety; and 57 were children of control probands. Probands were contacted at approximately 2-year intervals to obtain permission for follow-up of the offspring (Dierker et al 1999; Merikangas et al 1998a). Approximately 80% of the original sample participated at the second wave of data collection, and 72% of those who participated at Wave 2 were again interviewed at Wave 3. Ninety-one percent of the original sample participated in at least one subsequent assessment. In addition, younger siblings were interviewed at subsequent data collection points.

There were approximately equal proportions of males and females with an average age of 12 (range 7–17) at study entry and 18 (range 13–23) at follow-up. The distribution of social economic status was similar for children of probands with anxiety disorders and children of control probands; however, these groups differed from children of probands with substance disorder.

Assessment of Children

PSYCHIATRIC ASSESSMENT.   A modified version of the Kiddie-Schedule for Affective Disorders and Schizophrenia (K-SADS-E) was used for diagnostic assessment of the offspring (Orvaschel et al 1982), modified for DSM-III-R (Chambers et al 1985; Gammon et al 1983; Orvaschel et al 1982). The diagnostic interview was administered independently by experienced clinical interviewers (primarily clinical psychologists) with the offspring and with the mother about the offspring. Diagnoses were derived by an independent child psychiatrist, who was also blind to the diagnostic status of the parents and who was not involved in direct interviews, after review of all available information, including the diagnostic interview, family history reports on the offspring, teacher reports, and medical records. Diagnoses were coded on a four-point scale reflecting the level of certainty of diagnosis (i.e., none, possible, probable, definite). In the present report, DSM-III-R diagnoses were considered present if a subject met either a probable (criteria are met through the combination of parent and child report) or definite (criteria are fully met according to one or both reporters) level of certainty; diagnoses were characterized as absent at the "possible" level or when none of the criteria were met.

Domains of Assessment

Although the primary focus of most high-risk studies of psychiatric disorders is on the development of emotional, behavioral,

and cognitive symptoms and disorders, the present study also examined a comprehensive set of domains to examine premorbid risk factors or early manifestations of adulthood anxiety disorders, as described below.

FAMILY FUNCTIONING.   Family and parental functioning were measured by several instruments administered to the entire family. The Family Adaptability and Cohesion Scale III (FAC-ES) (Olson 1979, 1982, 1985) was used to evaluate familial cohesion and adaptability. The McMaster Family Assessment Device (FAD) (Epstein 1983) was used to assess overall family functioning, and the Parental Bonding Inventory (PBI) (Parker 1979) was collected to assess maternal and paternal care and protection.

ANXIETY SYMPTOMS AND TRAITS.   Measures of traits underlying anxiety include anxiety sensitivity with the Anxiety Sensitivity Index (ASI) (Reiss 1986), anxiety traits with the Revised-Children's Manifest Anxiety Scale (R-CMAS) (Reynolds 1978), behavioral inhibition with the Concurrent Self-Report of Child Inhibition (CSRCI) (Reznick 1992), and temperamental domains rated by the Dimension of Temperament Survey (DOTS) (Lerner 1982).

NEUROLOGICAL EXAMINATION.   A neurological examination was administered by experienced neurologists at each assessment of the sample. Individual test components include a physical examination, functions of the cardiovascular and autonomic systems, minor physical anomalies, sensorimotor function, handedness, a mini-mental examination, and neurological hard and soft signs (adapted in part from the Neurological Examination for Subtle Signs [NESS; Denckla 1985] and the Physical and Neurological Examination for Soft Signs [PAN-ESS; Denckla 1985]). The neurological examination was developed by Dr. James Merikangas, who established reliability with three neurologists during subsequent waves of the study.

NEUROPSYCHOLOGICAL TESTING.   The Peabody Picture Vocabulary Test (PPVT) was used to assess auditory comprehension of picture names. A full battery of traditional neuropsychological tests, including the Wechsler Intelligence Scale for Children (WISC), was also administered. The Cambridge Neuropsychological Test Automated Batteries (CANTAB) (Downes et al 1994) is a system of computerized neuropsychological tests developed at the University of Cambridge. The tests are run on an IBM-compatible personal computer with a touch screen. To assess cognitive function, six different tests are used to examine three main components: visual memory, attention, and spatial working memory and planning. The tests provide separate assessments of the relative integrity of different neurophysiological and neuroanatomical subsystems.

PSYCHOPHYSIOLOGIC ASSESSMENT.   In recent years, the startle reflex (a cross-species reflex to an abrupt unexpected stimulus) has emerged as an exceptional new tool for the study of anxiety and psychopathology in both adults and children. Startle has been shown to be extremely sensitive to fear, anxiety, and

Table 2. Lifetime Rates of Anxiety and Affective Disorders in Offspring by Parental Anxiety

| Anxiety in Offspring (%) | Parental Anxiety | | | | | | | | | |
| | Both Anxiety | | | One Anxiety | | | Neither Anxiety | | | |
	M $N = 10$	F $N = 12$	T $N = 22$	M $N = 52$	F $N = 52$	T $N = 104$	M $N = 14$	F $N = 12$	T $N = 26$	P
Overanxious	10.0	66.7	40.9[a]	9.62	15.4	12.5[b]	0	8.3	3.9[b]	<.01
Separation Anxiety	0	25.0	13.6	9.6	11.5	10.6	0	8.3	3.9	ns
Panic	0	16.7	9.1	0	7.7	3.9	0	0	0	ns
Specific Phobia	40.0	50.0	45.5[a]	5.8	17.3	11.5[b]	14.3	8.3	11.5[b]	<.01
Social Phobia	30.0	41.7	36.4[a]	7.7	17.3	12.5[b]	0	0	0[b]	<.05
Any Anxiety	**40.0**	**75.0**	**68.2[a]**	**23.1**	**34.6**	**33.7[b]**	**14.3**	**25.0**	**19.2[b]**	**<.05**
Major Depression	30.0	33.3	31.8	13.5	25.0	19.2	0	3.9	3.9	ns
Dysthymia	0	8.3	4.6'	1.9	1.9	1.9	0	0	0	ns
Any Depression	**30.0**	**41.7**	**36.4**	**15.4**	**26.9**	**21.2**	**0**	**8.3**	**3.9**	**ns**

Between-group differences are signified by superscript letters.

negative affects in a number of paradigms. The most compelling feature of the startle reflex is the abundant basic research that informs its underlying anatomic and functional basis, thereby shedding light on the biological pathways involved in fear and anxiety states. Studies suggest that startle can be potentiated by both explicit threat signals (e.g., a light that predicts a shock) and by multisensory contextual stimuli (e.g., a cage or an experimental room). Startle potentiation by these two types of stimuli appears to reflect different processes (i.e., fear vs. anxiety) mediated by distinct brain structures (i.e., amygdala vs. bed nucleus of the stria terminalis [Davis 1998]).

Two procedures were employed to potentiate startle based on the assumption that they were differentially sensitive to the pathways of fear/anxiety mentioned above. The first procedure examined anticipatory anxiety elicited by an explicit threat cue, a test of amygdala functioning. Subjects were told to anticipate a mildly unpleasant stimulus during threat periods but not during safe periods, signaled by lights of different colors. The aversive stimulus blast of air was administered through a plastic tubing to the throat at the level of the larynx. This procedure has been shown to produce a large and reliable potentiation of startle in children and adolescents in a collaborative study (Grillon et al 1999). Acoustic startle probes were delivered via headphones during the safe and threat periods. Psychophysiological measures included the eye-blink component of the startle reflex and the skin conductance response elicited by the onset of each period (i.e., colored lights).

The second procedure examined startle potentiation in the dark. In this experiment, startle probes were delivered during alternating periods when the experimental room was illuminated or when it was in complete darkness. It has been suggested elsewhere that the facilitation of startle by darkness was mediated by the bed nucleus of the stria terminalis (Grillon et al 1997a; Walker and Davis 1997).

Statistical Analyses

Data analyses included standard Chi-square tests for n-way tables of categorical level variables and analyses of variance (ANOVA) for continuous outcomes using the Duncan procedure

to test mean differences after controlling for multiple comparisons. The significance of analyses of categorical outcome variables were tested via logistic regression analyses, which controlled for gender and age of the child while investigating the effect of parent proband diagnostic group. Due to the low prevalence rates of most disorders, chi square analyses are presented and interpreted only for associations that were specified in advance.

Results

Family Factors

ASSOCIATION BETWEEN PARENTAL AND CHILD ANXIETY DISORDERS. Familial aggregation may be due to either common genetic factors in families or to familial environmental factors that serve as risk factors for the disorder of interest. The primary goal of the current study, and that of high-risk studies in general, was to examine the familial aggregation of the major subtypes of anxiety disorders and early signs and premorbid risk factors for the development of anxiety in youth. The findings from the most recent follow-up of the study are shown in Table 2, which presents the lifetime rates of anxiety disorders by parental concordance for anxiety disorders. For anxiety disorders in general as well as all of the subtypes of anxiety, a consistent increase exists in the rates of anxiety disorders according to the number of parents with anxiety disorders themselves (parents with substance disorders only were excluded from analyses). This effect is most pronounced for overanxious disorder and specific phobic states that tend to begin in middle childhood and for social phobia that has an average onset in this study during the midteen years. Offspring of one parent with an anxiety disorder have a threefold increased risk of overanxious disorder, and an additional threefold increased risk when both parents are affected. Likewise, offspring of two

68

BIOL PSYCHIATRY   1529
1999;46:1523-1535

parents with anxiety have a threefold increased risk of social phobia over offspring of one parent with anxiety and even greater risk when neither parent has an anxiety disorder. Inspection of the findings by gender reveals that the anxiety states were far more common among female offspring; in fact, all of the cases of panic were female offspring. This is similar to the results of the analyses of adult relatives, in whom the familial aggregation of anxiety states was primarily attributable to female relatives. When the criteria of impairment and avoidance were excluded, however, the patterns of familial aggregation of anxiety disorders were similar for both male and female relatives (Merikangas et al 1998). By contrast, rates of phobic states were approximately equivalent in male and female offspring. When only the definite diagnostic level was examined, rates of overanxious disorder, social phobia, and specific phobia decreased approximately 25%; however, patterns of risk remained the same.

Although panic disorder solely occurred among offspring of parents with anxiety disorders, particularly those with two affected parents, the absolute risk of this disorder is extremely low in this sample, despite the high-risk design. Follow-up should identify additional cases of panic and other anxiety disorders as this cohort continues to pass through the age of development of these conditions.

Because previous studies have shown a lack of specificity in familial transmission of anxiety and depression, we also assessed lifetime rates of depressive disorders in children of anxious parents (see Table 2). Although the data suggest that offspring of two parents with an anxiety disorder have increased risk of a depressive disorder, the differences in rates are not significant across groups after controlling for mother and father depression.

FAMILY FUNCTIONING. The relationship between family functioning and parental disorders was also investigated to examine the extent to which disorders in offspring may emerge from familial dysfunction in general as opposed to specific disorders in parents. The results of family adaptability and cohesion measures from the FACES, general functioning scale of the FAD, and care and protection scales of the PBI indicate that offspring of parents with anxiety disorders alone are not exposed to greater family disruption or poorer parenting than those of other parents. In fact, findings from the PBI suggest that anxious fathers actually exhibit more care than nonanxious fathers. By contrast, offspring of parents with substance use disorders tend to experience significantly poorer family cohesion than either offspring of parents with anxiety or of control parents.

Other Assessment Domains

A comprehensive review of the results of all the domains of assessment in the present study is beyond the scope of

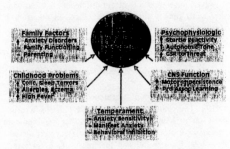

Figure 1. Vulnerability factors: Summary of findings.

this paper. Preliminary findings based on a priori hypotheses regarding each of the domains are summarized in Figure 1. The specific results of each domain are either in progress or have been published elsewhere.

DEVELOPMENTAL AND MEDICAL DISORDERS IN CHILDHOOD. The second major domain of inquiry in the present study involved early developmental factors: pre- and perinatal exposure to drugs, alcohol, or major illness or trauma, as well as childhood diseases, injuries, and major stressful life events. No differences were found between offspring of parents with anxiety disorders compared to control parents in any of the pre- and perinatal factors including drug or alcohol exposure, birth complications, or developmental anomalies as well as developmental milestones. Offspring of parents with anxiety did have more sleep terrors, however. In terms of childhood illnesses, a greater proportion of offspring of parents with anxiety had allergies, eczema, and high fever than those of control parents. As noted above, only those disorders that had been previously suggested as associated with anxiety were included in these analyses.

TEMPERAMENTAL FACTORS. The third major area of investigation as a risk domain for the development of anxiety involves temperamental factors such as behavioral inhibition, anxiety sensitivity, and fearfulness. These factors are believed to predispose individuals to the subsequent development of anxiety in adolescence and adulthood. Because the age composition of this sample was well beyond that in which temperament can be truly assessed, the retrospective measures employed herein are necessarily limited in their utility for examining links between temperament and anxiety. Nevertheless, some self-reported scales were employed, as well as parental and teacher reports, to examine shy and inhibited temperament in this sample, as described above. The offspring of parents with anxiety did not differ from those of the other proband groups with respect to any of the measures;

however, there were significant differences between children with anxiety disorders and others on all of these scales after controlling for gender and age. Thus, these measures tended to characterize children with anxiety states rather than those with vulnerability for the development of anxiety.

NEUROLOGIC AND NEUROPSYCHOLOGIC FUNCTION. The evaluation of neurologic function was undertaken to identify specific signs that may indicate central or motor disturbances associated with anxiety disorders. Results indicate that offspring of probands with anxiety exhibited greater motor impersistence and brisker patellar reflex than offspring of other proband groups. There were no differences in neurologic hard signs or left–right anomalies among those at risk for anxiety disorders compared to those at risk for substance use disorders or control probands.

In general, there were few differences between those at risk for anxiety and control probands on most of the neuropsychological tests. In fact, the offspring of parents with anxiety tended to have somewhat higher functioning in several domains compared to those of the substance abuse groups, particularly on the PPVT. The main difference among those with vulnerability to anxiety when compared to control probands emerged in the Paired Associative Learning Subtest of the CANTAB on which they performed more poorly on the memory task and made more errors than control probands.

PSYCHOPHYSIOLOGIC FUNCTION. Autonomic function assessment at baseline did not differ between the at-risk groups. There was, however, higher autonomic tone (i.e., background homeostatic regulation of the central and peripheral vascular systems against which reactivity to the environment occurs), lower sensitivity to orthostatic change, and greater galvanic skin response (GSR) among offspring of parents with anxiety compared to those of the other proband groups. Although the high-risk anxiety group had higher baseline GSR, the difference was far more pronounced under the threat condition. Similar to the other domains, those offspring with anxiety states exhibited greater differences on all of these measures than those without anxiety (Figure 2).

The results of the anticipatory anxiety experiment of this cohort were described in Grillon et al (1997b, 1998).

The high-risk group exhibited gender-specific abnormal startle reactivity. High-risk female offsprings showed enhanced baseline startle, whereas high-risk male offsprings exhibited elevated potentiated startle to the threat signal. High-risk female offspring also had increased

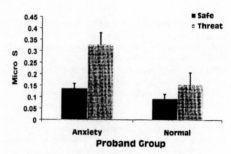

Figure 2. Galvanic skin response by proband group.

baseline startle in the dark/light experiment (Figure 3), whereas male offspring did not (Figure 4).

Discussion

These findings confirm the results of the earlier interviews of this sample in which there was a strong degree of specificity of expression of anxiety disorders among offspring of parents with anxiety disorders (Dierker et al 1999; Merikangas et al 1998a). As much as 8 years later, parental anxiety disorders were directly associated with anxiety disorders in offspring. Similar to previous studies, the findings of this study also yielded elevated rates of depression among the offspring of parents with anxiety; however, depression was more strongly associated with parental depression than with anxiety. The specificity of expression of anxiety and the direct relationship between the number of parents with anxiety and increased rates of anxiety disorders in offspring are consistent with the expectations of increased genetic propensity for anxiety. Biological and genetic explanations are further supported by the lack of evidence for impairment in either parenting or family function associated with parental anxiety. In fact, fathers with anxiety disorders were reported as

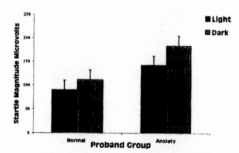

Figure 3. Startle reflex by proband group: Females.

BIOL PSYCHIATRY   1531
1999;46:1523–1535

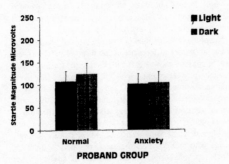

Figure 4. Startle reflex by proband group: Males.

having greater levels of care than those without. In contrast, both depression and substance abuse in parents were strongly associated with severe disruption in parental and family functioning, leading to increased behavioral disorders and depression in exposed youth. Evidence from the present study as well as others reveals that parental substance disorders and depression are more common in lower social classes and are associated with increased rates of disrupted family structure (Merikangas et al 1998b). Evidence for the latter has been suggested by a strong association between depression and environmental adversity (Rutter 1986), increased incidence of depression in youth after acute stress (Reinherz et al 1993), and increased rates of Conduct Disorder among offspring of parents concordant for psychiatric disorders in general (Dierker et al 1999).

The lack of pre- and perinatal risk factors for the development of anxiety disorders confirms the findings of Allen and Matthews (1997), who found that children who suffered from a variety of exposures ranging from prenatal substance use to postnatal injuries were more likely to develop behavior disorders (particularly attention deficit disorder and conduct problems) but not anxiety disorders.

The link between childhood allergies and eczema and behavioral inhibition was discussed by Kagan (1998), who proposed that the high levels of cortisol associated with anxiety may lead to immunologic sensitivity to environmental stimuli. Likewise, Allen and Matthews (1997) reported that adolescents and young adults with anxiety disorders were more likely to have suffered from infections during early childhood than others. Confirmation of this finding from the perspective of a sample of high-risk youth provides more compelling evidence for an association between enhanced vigilance of these children and environmental stimuli. In the present study, the prevalence of high fevers in childhood along with diseases associated with the immune system suggest future inquiry into the possible role of the immune system in anxiety states.

The lack of an association between the dimensional measures of anxiety sensitivity, behavioral inhibition, and manifest anxiety traits and parental anxiety was unexpected. Nonetheless, all of these constructs were strongly associated with anxiety disorders in children. The age sample of the cohort may partially explain the lack of increased behavioral inhibition because this trait is based on observational studies of infants and very young children (Kagan et al 1998). Additionally, assessment of these phenomena via questionnaire rather than observation may require a higher self-defined threshold for detection of inhibition in social settings that cause discomfort. Finally, the assessment of all of the temperamental and trait measures are based on the current state of the subject, another major difference between the diagnostic assessments and the self-reported constructs of the components of anxiety. Repeated assessments of these constructs over time would be far more likely to tap vulnerability unconfounded by current state. Nevertheless, the strong links with behavioral inhibition and anxiety sensitivity suggest that these traits are important features of some of the anxiety states.

Clues regarding the neural pathways underlying anxiety were provided by all of the indirect assessments of CNS function including the neurologic examination, the nonverbal computerized neuropsychological evaluation, and the psychophysiologic studies. Motor impersistence, which is a test of motor-cortical pathways, reflects an inability to suppress the motor system, which is an important component of anxiety (Joynt 1990). In the present study, nearly half of the high-risk subjects exhibited motor impersistence, which has most often been reported from lesions of the dorsolateral frontal lobes (Joynt et al 1962).

Although no direct biochemical or brain functioning measures were employed, the findings from these indirect measures may provide clues for future studies employing tools of neuroimaging or neurochemistry. Possible serotonergic mechanisms for vulnerability to anxiety in this study were suggested by the pattern of performance of the high-risk offspring on the neuropsychological testing. Based on prior studies of specific deficits in paired associative learning, but not other subtests of the CANTAB sensitive to frontal lobe dysfunction, after reduction of serotonin by tryptophan depletion in normal subjects, Park et al (1994) concluded that the serotonergic system may have a specific role in the processes of memory and learning not directly implicated in frontal lobe function. The role of serotonergic mechanisms in anxiety states has been reviewed by Goddard et al (1996); whether disturbance in serotonergic function was perturbed by the acute stressful circumstances rather than representing trait-related dysregulation was not deter-

1532   BIOL PSYCHIATRY
        1999;46:1523-1535

mined, suggesting a potentially exciting direction for future research.

The disturbances in autonomic and psychophysiologic function confirm the abundant research on both clinical samples of anxiety disorders and induced anxiety in experimental studies. To our knowledge, however, this is the first study that begins to yield indicators from a variety of tests tapping different aspects of fear, vigilance, and arousal in a high-risk sample. The increased patellar reflex taken together with far lower orthostatic changes in pulse and blood pressure may signify increased autonomic tone, another potential indicator of hypervigilance of the autonomic nervous system to environmental stimuli.

These results begin to test the pathways posited by Gray (1982), Kagan et al (1998), and others that implicated the projections from the amygdala that control the cognitive, motor, and autonomic systems involved in the fear response. Startle directly assesses amygdaloid processing of fearful or arousing discrete stimuli. This pathway has been posited to underlie the symptoms of cue-explicit fear (Davis 1998). An additional pathway might be involved in more generalized anxiety elicited by contextual stimuli that are not in themselves sources of immediate danger. This anxiety-like reaction has been linked to the bed nucleus of the stria terminalis (Davis 1998). Lesions of the amygdala in rats, for example, suppress cue-explicit potentiated startle but do not affect the facilitation of startle by bright lights. In contrast, lesions of the bed nucleus of the stria terminalis do block the facilitation of startle by bright light, but do not affect cue-explicit potentiated startle. Thus, fear and anxiety responses appear to emerge from distinct brain pathways.

Our results suggest that vulnerability to anxiety disorders involves a gender-specific differential sensitivity of these pathways, with the amygdala/fear and bed nucleus of the stria terminalis/anxiety pathways being more relevant to vulnerable male offspring and female offspring, respectively. Enhanced sensitivity of the bed nucleus of the stria terminalis/anxiety pathway in high-risk female offspring is suggested by their elevated baseline startle, which might reflect their fear of the threatening aversive context. Given the uneven distribution and the high rates of anxiety disorders among female offspring compared to male offspring, the present results should provide impetus for further research into the role of the bed nucleus of the stria terminalis in the development of anxiety.

Future analyses of the predictive significance of these findings and their specificity with respect to anxiety states may elucidate the involvement of these systems in the development of anxiety. If confirmed, these preliminary findings may provide leads regarding specific hypotheses to examine using the tools of neuroimaging and pharmacological challenges that may lead to the discovery of the biologic factors conveying vulnerability to the development of anxiety disorders and the environmental contexts that potentiate or suppress their expression.

Nosologic implications of the present study include the potential gender differences in the thresholds for expression of anxiety, as well as the importance of the diagnostic category of overanxious disorder. The finding that overanxious disorder was one of the most specific forms of expression associated with parental anxiety, particularly among younger offspring, suggests that the elimination of this diagnostic entity from the DSM-IV may not have been well based. There were nearly no children under 12 years of age who met criteria for generalized anxiety disorder, which taps physiologic manifestations of anxiety rather than the cognitive symptoms, particularly worry that characterized anxiety states reported by children in the current study.

Though preliminary, these findings demonstrate the relevance of the high-risk design to studying the etiologic pathways not only to anxiety disorders, but also to other psychiatric and nonpsychiatric disorders. The small number of studies employing this design, particularly the absence of a biological conceptualization of potential risk factors, suggests this as an extremely important future area of research. Such research will be critical to reducing the heterogeneity that underlies the development of the psychiatric disorders, as well as to defining more precise phenotypes that may be amenable to etiologic investigation using the powerful tools of genetics and neuroscience.

Research supported in part by grants AA07080, DA05348, MH30929, from Alcohol, Drug Abuse, and Mental Health Administration of the United States Public Health Service, a Research Scientist Development Award K02-DA 00293 (Dr. Merikangas), and a postdoctoral research training fellowship MH14235 (Dr. Dierker and Dr. Avenevoli).

We wish to acknowledge the contributions of the John D. and Catherine T. MacArthur Foundation, Research Network on Psychopathology and Development, for making available the CANTAB, Dr. James Merikangas for development and direction of the neurologic examination, Dr. Barbara Sahakian for interpretation of the CANTAB results, and Dr. Peter Szatmari and Dr. France Chaput for their work on the diagnostic evaluation of the sample.

This work was presented at the scientific satellite conference, "The Role of Biological and Psychological Factors on Early Development and Their Impact on Adult Life," that preceded the Anxiety Disorders Association of America (ADAA) annual meeting, San Diego, March 1999. The conference was jointly sponsored by the ADAA and the National Institute of Mental Health through an unrestricted educational grant provided by Wyeth-Ayerst Laboratories.

References

Achenbach TM (1985): Assessment of anxiety in children. In: Tuma AH, Maser J, editors. Anxiety and the Anxiety Disorders. Hilldale, NJ: Lawrence Erlbaum Associates Publishers, 707–734.

Allen M, Matthews K (1997): Hemodynamic responses to laboratory stressors in children and adolescents: the influences of age, race, and gender. *Psychophysiology* 34:329–339.

Allen NB, Lewinsohn PM, Seeley JR (1998): Prenatal and perinatal influences on risk for psychopathology in childhood and adolescence. *Dev Psychopathol* 10:513–529.

American Psychiatric Association (1987): *Diagnostic and Statistical Manual of Mental Disorders*, 3rd ed rev. Washington, DC: American Psychiatric Association.

Beidel D, Turner S (1997): At risk for anxiety: I. Psychopathology in the offspring of anxious parents. *J Am Acad Child Adolesc Psychiatry* 36:918–924.

Beidel DC (1988): Psychophysiological assessment of anxious emotional states in children. *J Abnorm Psychol* 97:80–82.

Biederman J, Rosenbaum JF, Bolduc EA, Faraone SV, Hirshfeld DR (1991): A high risk study of young children of parents with panic disorders and agoraphobia with and without comorbid major depression. *Psychiatr Res* 37:333–348.

Capps L, Sigman M, Sena R, Henker B (1996): Fear, anxiety and perceived control in children of agoraphobia. *J Child Psychol Psychiatry* 37:445–452.

Chambers W, Puig-Antich J, Tabrizi M, Davies M (1985): The assessment of affective disorders in children and adolescents by semi-structured interview: test-retest reliability of the Schedule for Affective Disorders and Schizophrenia for school age children, present episode version. *Arch Gen Psychiatry* 42:696–697.

Coplan JD, Lydiard RB (1998): Brain circuits in panic disorder. *Biol Psychiatry* 44:1264–1276.

Davis M (1998): Are different parts of the extended amygdala involved in fear versus anxiety? *Biol Psychiatry* 44:1239–1247.

Denckla MB (1985): Revised Neurological Examination for Subtle Signs (1985). *Psychopharmacol Bull* 21:773–789.

Dierker LC, Merikangas KR, Szatmari P (1999): Influence of parental concordance for psychiatric disorders on psychopathology in offspring. *J Am Acad Child Adolesc Psychiatry* 38:280–288.

Downes J, Evenden J, Morris R, et al (1994): *Cambridge Neurological Test Automated Battery (CANTAB): Instruction Manual*. Waterbeach, UK: Paul Fray Ltd.

Downey G, Coyne JC (1990): Children of depressed parents: An integrative review. *Psychological Bull* 108:50–76.

Endicott J, Spitzer RL (1978): A diagnostic interview: The Schedule for Affective Disorders and Schizophrenia-Lifetime version. *Arch Gen Psychiatry* 35:837–844.

Epstein NB, Baldwin LM, Bishop DS (1983): The McMaster Family Assessment Device. *J Marital Fam Ther* 9:171–180.

Erlenmeyer-Kimling L, Cornblatt B, Golden RR (1983): Early indicators of vulnerability to schizophrenia in children at high genetic risk. In: Guze SB, Earls FJ, Barrett JE, editors. *Childhood Psychopathology and Development*. New York: Raven Press, 247–264.

Fyer AJ (1998): Current approaches to etiology and pathophysiology of specific phobia. *Biol Psychiatry* 44:1295–1304.

Fyer AJ, Mannuzza S, Chapman TF, Liebowitz MR, Klein DF (1993): A direct interview family study of social phobia. *Arch Gen Psychiatry* 50:286–293.

Fyer AJ, Mannuzza S, Chapman TF, Martin LY, Klein DF (1995): Specificity in familial aggregation of phobic disorders. *Arch Gen Psychiatry* 52:564–573.

Gammon GD, John K, Rothblum ED, Mullen K, Tischler GL, Weissman MM (1983): Use of a structured diagnostic interview to identify bipolar disorder in adolescent inpatients: Frequency and manifestations of the disorder. *Am J Psychiatry* 140:543–547.

Goddard AW, Woods SC, Charney DS (1996): A critical review of the role of norepinephrine in panic disorder: Focus on its interaction with serotonin. In: Westenberg HGM, Den Boer JA, Murphy DL, editors. *Advances in the Neurobiology of Anxiety Disorders*. New York: John Wiley and Sons, 107–137.

Goldstein RB, Wickramaratne PJ, Horwath E, Weissman MM (1997): Familial aggregation and phenomenology of "early"-onset (at or before age 20 years) panic disorder. *Arch Gen Psychiatry* 54:271–278.

Gray JA (1982): Precis of the neuropsychology of anxiety: An inquiry into the function of the septo-hippocampal system. *Brain Sci* 5:469–534.

Grillon C, Ameli R, Goddard A, Woods S, Davis M (1994): Baseline and fear-potentiated startle in panic disorder patients. *Biol Psychiatry* 35:431–439.

Grillon C, Dierker L, Merikangas KR (1997a): Startle modulation in children at risk for anxiety disorders and/or alcoholism. *J Am Acad Child Adolesc Psychiatry* 36:925–932.

Grillon C, Dierker L, Merikangas KR (1998): Fear-potentiated startle in adolescent offspring of parents with anxiety disorders. *Biol Psychiatry* 44:990–997.

Grillon C, Merikangas KR, Dierker LC, et al (1999): Startle potentiation by threat of aversive stimuli and darkness in adolescents: A multi-site study. *Int J Psychophysiol* 32:63–73.

Grillon C, Morgan CA (1999): Fear-potentiated startle conditioning to explicit and contextual cues in Gulf war veterans with posttraumatic stress disorder. *J Abnorm Psychol* 108:134–142.

Grillon C, Pellowski M, Merikangas KR, Davis M (1997b): Darkness facilitates the acoustic startle in humans. *Biol Psychiatry* 42:453–460.

Johnson MR, Lydiard RB (1995): The neurobiology of anxiety disorders. *Psychiatr Clin North Am* 18:681–725.

Joynt RJ (1990): *Behavioral Aspects of Neurological Disease, Vol 2*. Philadelphia: J.B. Lippincott Company.

Joynt RJ, Benton AL, Fogel M (1962): Behavioral and pathological correlates of motor impersistence. *Neurology* 12:876.

Kagan J (1998): *Galen's Prophecy: Temperament in Human Nature*. Boulder, CO: Westview Press.

Kagan J, Reznick J, Clarke C, Snidman N, Garcia-Coll C (1984): Behavioral inhibition to the unfamiliar. *Child Dev* 55:2212–2225.

Kagan J, Snidman N, Arcus D (1998): Childhood derivatives of high and low reactivity in infancy. *Child Dev* 69:1483–1493.

Kendler KS, Neale MC, Kessler RC, Heath AC, Eaves LJ

(1992): The genetic epidemiology of phobias in women. *Arch Gen Psychiatry* 49:273-281.

Kendler KS, Neale MC, Kessler RC, Heath AC, Eaves LJ (1993): Major depression and phobias: The genetic and environmental sources of comorbidity. *Psychol Med* 23:361-371.

Kendler KS, Walters EE, Neale MC, Kessler RC, Heath AC, Eaves LJ (1995): The structure of the genetic and environmental risk factors for six major psychiatric disorders in women. *Arch Gen Psychiatry* 52:374-383.

Last C, Hersen M, Kazdin A, Orvaschel H, Perrin S (1991): Anxiety disorders in children and their families. *Arch Gen Psychiatry* 48:928-934.

Laucht M, Esser G, Schmidt MH (1994): Parental mental disorder and early child development. *Eur Child Adolesc Psychiatry* 3:125-137.

Lerner RM, Palermo M, Spiro A, Nesselroade A (1982): Assessing the dimension of temperamental individuality across the life span: The Dimensions of Temperament Survey (DOTS). *Child Dev* 53:149-157.

Marks IM (1986): Genetics of fear and anxiety disorders. *Brit J Psychiatry* 149:406-418.

Merikangas KR (1990): Co-morbidity for anxiety and depression: Review of family and genetic studies. In: Maser JD, Cloninger CR, editors. *Comorbidity of Mood and Anxiety Disorders*. Washington DC: American Psychiatric Press, 331-348.

Merikangas K, Angst J (1995): Comorbidity and social phobia: evidence from clinical, epidemiologic and genetic studies. *Eur Arch Psychiatry Clin Neurosci* 244:297-303.

Merikangas K, Dierker L, Szatmari P (1998a): Psychopathology among offspring of parents with substance abuse and/or anxiety: A high risk study. *J Child Psychol Psychiatry* 39:711-720.

Merikangas KR, Stevens DE, Fenton B, et al (1998b): Comorbidity and familial aggregation of alcoholism and anxiety disorders. *Psychol Med* 28:773-788.

Noyes RJ, Clarkson C, Crowe RR (1987): A family study of generalized anxiety disorder. *Am J Psychiatry* 144:1019-1024.

Nurnberger J, Byerley W (1995): Molecular genetics of anxiety disorders. *Psychiatr Genetics* 5:5-7.

Olson DH, Portner J, Bell R (1982): FACES II: Family Adaptability and Cohesion Evaluation Scales. Unpublished manuscript, University of Minnesota, Family Social Science, St. Paul.

Olson DH, Portner J, Lavee Y (1985): FACES III: Family Adaptability and Cohesion Evaluation Scales. Unpublished manuscript, University of Minnesota, Family Social Science, St. Paul.

Olson DH, Spenkle DH, Russell CS (1979): Complex model of martial and family systems. 1: Cohesion and adaptability dimensions, family types and clinical applications. *Fam Process* 18:3-78.

Orvaschel H, Thompson WD, Belanger A, Prusoff BA, Kidd KK (1982): Comparison of the family history method to direct interview: Factors affecting the diagnosis of depression. *J Affect Disord* 4:49-59.

Park SB, Coull RH, Young AH, Sahakian BJ, Robbins TW, Cowen PJ (1994): Tryptophan depletion in normal volunteers produces selective impairments in learning and memory. *Neuropharmacology* 33:575-588.

Parker G, Tupling H, Brown LB (1979): A parental bonding instrument. *Brit J Med Psychol* 52:1-10.

Perna G, Bertani A, Caldirola L (1996): Family history of panic disorder and hypersensitivity to CO_2 in patients with panic disorder. *Am J Psychiatry* 153:1060-1064.

Perna G, Brambilla F, Arancio C, Bellodi L (1995): Menstrual cycle related sensitivity to 35% CO_2 in panic patients. *Biol Psychiatry* 37:528-532.

Pine D, Cohen P, Gurley D, Brook J, Ma Y (1998): The risk for early-adulthood anxiety and depressive disorders in adolescents with anxiety and depressive disorders. *Arch Gen Psychiatry* 55:56-64.

Reichler RJ, Sylvester CE, Hyde TS (1988): Biological studies on offspring of panic disorder probands. In: Dunner DL, Gershon E, Barrett J, editors. *Relatives at Risk for Mental Disorders*. New York: Raven Press, 103-125.

Reinherz HZ, Giaconia RM, Pakiz B, Silverman AB, Frost AK, Lefkowitz ES (1993): Psychosocial risks for major depression in late adolescence: A longitudinal community study. *J Am Acad Child Adolesc Psychiatry* 32:1155-1163.

Reiss S, Pererson RA, Gursky DM, McNally RJ (1986): Anxiety sensitivity, anxiety frequency and the prediction of fearfulness. *Behav Res Ther* 24:1-8.

Reynolds CR, Richmond BO (1978): What I think and feel: A revised measure of children's manifest anxiety. *J Abnorm Child Psychol* 6:271-280.

Reznick S, Hegeman IM, Kaufman ER, Woods SWJA (1992): Retrospective and concurrent self-report of behavioral inhibition and their relation to adult mental health. *Dev Psychopathol* 4:301-321.

Rosenbaum J, Biederman J, Gersten M (1988): Behavioral inhibition in children of parents with panic disorder and agoraphobia: A controlled study. *Arch Gen Psychiatry* 45:463-470.

Rutter M (1986): *The Developmental Psychopathology of Depression: Issues and Perspectives*. New York: Guilford Press.

Schmidt LA, Fox NA, Rubin KH, et al (1997): Behavioral and neuroendocrine responses in shy children. *Dev Psychobiology* 30:127-140.

Schmidt SM, Zoega T, Crowe RR (1993): Excluding linkage between panic disorder and the gamma-aminobutyric acid beta I reactor locus in five Icelandic pedigrees. *Acta Psychiatr Scand* 88:225-228.

Skre I, Onstad S, Torgersen S, Lygren S, Kringlen E (1993): A twin study of DSM-III-R anxiety disorders. *Acta Psychiatr Scand* 88:85-92.

Stavrakaki C, Vargo B (1986): The relationship of anxiety and depression: A review of literature. *Br J Psychiatry* 149:7-16.

Stein MB, Chartier MJ, Hazen AL (1998): A direct-interview family study of generalized social phobia. *Am J Psychiatry* 155:90-97.

Sylvester C, Hyde T, Reichler R (1988): Clinical psychopathology among children of adults with panic disorder. In: Dunner D, Gershon E, Barrett J, editors. *Relatives at Risk for Mental Disorder*. New York: Raven Press, 87-102.

Sylvester CE, Hyde TS, Reichler RJ (1987): Clinical psychopathology among children of adults with panic disorder. *J Am Acad Child Psychiatry* 26:668-675.

BIOL PSYCHIATRY   1535
1999;46:1523-1535

Taylor EA, Sandberg SJ, Thorley G, Giles S (1991): *The Epidemiology of Childhood Hyperactivity.* Oxford, England: Oxford University Press/Maudsley Monographs.

Turner SM, Beidel DC, Costello A (1987): Psychopathology in the offspring of anxiety disorders patients. *J Consult Clin Psychol* 55:229–235.

Unnewehr S, Schneider S, Florin I, Margraf J (1998): Psychopathology in children of patients with panic disorder or animal phobia. *Psychopathology* 31:69–84.

Walker D, Davis M (1997): Double dissociation between the involvement of the bed nucleus of the stria terminalis and the central nucleus of the amygdala in startle increases produced by conditioned versus unconditioned fear. *J Neurosci* 17: 9375–9383.

Wang ZW, Crowe RR, Noyes RJ (1992): Adrenergic receptor genes as candidate genes for panic disorder: A linkage study. *Am J Psychiatry* 149:470–474.

Warner V, Mufson L, Weissman M (1995): Offspring at high risk for depression and anxiety: Mechanisms of psychiatric disorder. *J Am Acad Child Adol Psychiatry* 34:786–797.

Weissman M (1993): Family genetic studies of panic disorder. *J Psychiatric Res* 27:69–78.

Wilkinson DJC, Thompson JM, Lambert GW, et al (1998): Sympathetic activity in patients with panic disorder at rest, under laboratory mental stress, and during panic attacks. *Arch Gen Psychiatry* 55:511–520.

Woodman C, Crowe R (1996): The genetics of the anxiety disorders. *Bailliere's Clin Psychiatry* 2:47–57.

Early Childhood Predictors of Adult Anxiety Disorders

Jerome Kagan and Nancy Snidman

This paper considers the influence of temperamental factors on the development of anxious symptoms in children and adolescents.

About 20 percent of healthy children are born with a temperamental bias that predisposes them to be highly reactive to unfamiliar stimulation as infants and to be fearful of or avoidant to unfamiliar events and people as young children. Experiences act on this initial temperamental bias and, by adolescence, about one-third of this group is likely to show signs of serious social anxiety. These children are also likely to have one or more biological features, including a sympathetically more reactive cardiovascular system, asymmetry of cortical activation in EEG favoring a more active right frontal area, more power in the EEG in the higher frequency range, and a narrower facial skeleton. The data imply that this temperamental bias should be conceptualized as constraining the probability of developing a consistently fearful and spontaneous profile rather than as determining an anxious or introverted phenotype. Biol Psychiatry 1999;46:1536–1541 © 1999 Society of Biological Psychiatry

Key Words: Anxiety, inhibition, temperament

Introduction

One feature that distinguishes European-American conceptualizations of psychological variation during most of this century with the views of physicians and philosophers in ancient Athens, Rome, and Alexandria is the stigma the former group attributes to individuals who are excessively apprehensive over physical harm, task failure, or unfamiliar social settings. Citizens in ancient societies regarded anger, not anxiety, as the more harmful emotion that individuals should try to control. The contemporary judgment that chronic anxiety is a greater obstacle to adjustment than chronic anger, boredom, or sexual frustration is the product of historical factors. Conformity to authority and to the values of the local community were adaptive in early societies; worry over the evaluative judgments of others is easier if one is vulnerable to apprehension. These anxiety states are a burden in modern society because assuming risk, defending an unpopular opinion, engaging strangers, and meeting difficult obligations serve effective adaptation. Thus, the current concern with, and intensive study of, anxiety and its symptoms are understandable.

Current hypotheses regarding the causes of variation in susceptibility to this family of feelings have cycled back to the views of Hippocrates and Galen who claimed that some individuals inherited a constitutional vulnerability to anxious states, a quality called "temperament" by modern authors.

The suggestion by Thomas and Chess (1977) that temperamental factors render some children especially susceptible to fear and anxiety was followed by elegant discoveries in neuroscience laboratories that made it possible for scientists to speculate on the possible biological substrates for vulnerabilities to fear and anxiety. It took less than 50 years after the first Chess and Thomas publication to persuade the psychiatric and psychological community that some children inherited a biology that made it easier for them to feel uncertain, tense, or apprehensive to unfamiliarity and challenge and, as a result, to be more vulnerable to one or more of the anxiety disorders.

This paper summarizes what scholars have learned about these temperamental biases. My colleagues and I—especially Nancy Snidman, Doreen Arcus, J. Steven Reznick, and Mark McManis—have been studying this interesting problem for almost 20 years and much of the evidence to be summarized comes from my laboratory. Before presenting the data, however, it is necessary to make a methodological point.

The primary information in the work to be described came from direct observations rather than parental descriptions of children. Investigators who rely only on parental descriptions assume that these verbal reports correspond closely to what would be detected by direct behavioral observations. Unfortunately, the degree of correspondence between the two sources of information is modest at best; therefore, generalizations based only on parental descriptions have a special meaning and validity (Spiker et al 1992; Seifer et al 1994; Rosicky 1993; Klein 1991; Perrin and Last 1992; Kagan 1998).

From Harvard University, Cambridge, Massachusetts.
Address reprint requests to: Jerome Kagan, Department of Psychology, Harvard University, 33 Kirkland Street, Cambridge, MA 02138.
Received February 5, 1999; revised May 3, 1999; accepted May 4, 1999.

0006-3223/99/$20.00
PII S0006-3223(99)00137-7

BIOL PSYCHIATRY 1537
1999;46:1536–1541

Table 1. Differences between High Reactive and Low Reactive Infants from 14 Months to 7.5 Years

Variable	High Reactive[a]	Low Reactive[a]	
Mean fear at 14 months	4.2	2.5	$t(286) = 11.1, p < .001$
	(2.4)	(1.6)	
Mean fear at 21 months	3.4	2.0	$t(243) = 4.67, p < .001$
	(2.5)	(1.9)	
Mean spontaneous comments at 4.5 years	40.7	53.7	$t(191) = 1.96, p < .05$
	(39.3)	(47.5)	
Mean smiles at 4.5 years	17.8	27.7	$t(191) = 3.69, p < .01$
	(15.3)	(19.3)	
Percent inhibited with peers at 4.5 years	46%	10%	
Percent uninhibited with peers at 4.5 years	27%	67%	$\chi^2(1) = 35.5, p < .001$
Mean spontaneous comments at 7.5 years	19.6	32.8	$t(109) = 2.37, p < .01$
	(27.9)	(30.3)	
Mean smiles at 7.5 years	14.4	22.0	$t(109) = 1.97, p = .05$
	(18.2)	(21.5)	
Percent with anxious symptoms at 7.5 years	45%	15%	$\chi^2(2) = 12.8, p < .01$

[a]Numbers in parentheses are standard deviations.

Reactivity in Infancy

Research with animals reveals that the amygdala is responsive to unfamiliar events and, in addition, is a necessary structure for the acquisition of conditioned reactions that imply a fear state when aversive events, like shock, are the unconditioned stimuli (Davis et al 1995; Blanchard and Blanchard 1988; LeDoux 1996). The amygdala contains receptors for a large number of neurotransmitters and neuromodulators that are relevant to the display of fearful behavior, including GABA, opioids, norepinephrine, and corticotropin releasing hormone (Amaral et al 1992). The basolateral area of the amygdala sends projections to the ventral striatum and excitation of this structure induces limb movement in animals (Rolls 1992). Second, the amygdala is the origin of the amygdalofugal pathway whose projections to the central gray and anterior cingulate modulate distress cries. Thus, infants born with a low threshold in the amygdala and its projections should display vigorous limb movements and become easily distressed to unfamiliar stimulation. Further, as young children, these infants should be avoidant of, or fearful to, unfamiliar events. These children are called inhibited. In contrast, infants born with an amygdaloid neurochemistry that raised the threshold of these structures should display minimal motor activity and minimal crying to unfamiliar stimulation and should be minimally fearful to, or avoidant of, unfamiliar events. These children are called uninhibited.

The Consequences of Variation in Infant Reactivity

A sample of 462 healthy, Caucasian, middle-class, four-month-old infants were administered a battery of visual, auditory, and olfactory stimuli (Kagan 1994). About 20% of the sample showed a combination of frequent vigorous motor activity, including arching of the back, combined with fretting and crying. These infants were called high reactive. About 40% of the sample showed the opposite profile of low motor activity and minimal distress to the same battery and these children were classified as low reactive. The remaining infants belonged to other temperamental groups.

Almost 80% of the sample of children returned to the laboratory when they were 14- and 21- months old and encountered a variety of unfamiliar social and nonsocial events. The unfamiliar events included: interacting with an unfamiliar examiner, placement of heart rate electrodes and a blood pressure cuff, an unfamiliar liquid being placed on the child's tongue, and the appearance, in different episodes, of a stranger, a clown, and an odd-looking robot made of metal combined with requests by an adult to approach each of these discrepant objects. Each episode was scored for the display of an unambiguous fear reaction, where fear was defined strictly as a display of fretting or crying to any of the unfamiliar incentives or failure to approach the stranger, clown, or robot despite a friendly invitation to do so. The mean number of fears was 2.6 at 14 months and 2.7 at 21 months and about 30% of the sample showed 4 or more fears at both 14 and 21 months. The high reactive infants displayed significantly more fears than the low reactives and were more likely to show four or more fears at both ages (Table 1).

A majority of the high and low reactive children were evaluated again when they were 4.5 years of age. We assumed that inhibition of speech in an unfamiliar social setting is analogous to an animal's freezing in an unfamiliar context and, therefore, expected that the high reactive infants would be far less talkative than low reactives while interacting with an unfamiliar adult. Further, because the high reactive infants smiled less often during the evaluations at 14 and 21 months and spontaneous smiling in a social interaction requires a low level of uncertainty, we expected that high reactives should smile less often with the examiner than low reactives. The videotapes of a 60 min battery involving the child and an unfamiliar female examiner were coded for the number of spontaneous comments and smiles. In addition, between 3 and 6 weeks after the laboratory session, the child and parent returned for a play session with two other unfamiliar children of the same age and gender. The three parents sat on a couch in a large playroom while the three children played with age-appropriate toys.

The 4.5-year-olds who had been high reactive infants displayed significantly fewer comments and smiles with the examiner and, in addition, were more likely than the low reactives to be classified as shy/inhibited when playing with the unfamiliar peers (Table 1). Only 4% of the entire sample (9 children) displayed a profile at 4.5 years that was inconsistent with their original 4 month temperament. Three high reactive infants were spontaneous and sociable and 6 low reactive infants were shy. The majority of the children, both high and low reactive, were neither extremely inhibited nor uninhibited at 4.5 years (Kagan et al 1998).

Development of Signs of Anxiety

A group of 164 of the original sample of 462 children were evaluated again when they were 7.5 years old. Initially, all mothers were sent a questionnaire and asked to rate their child on a 3-point scale for descriptions of age-appropriate behavior. Twelve of the questions dealt with anxious symptoms (for example, "My child becomes quiet and subdued in unfamiliar places," "My child is afraid of thunder and lightning," "My child is afraid of animals," "My child has nightmares"). A score of 1 was assigned to the child if the mother said that the anxious behavior was sometimes true of the child, a score of 2 was assigned if the mother said the behavior was often true of her child. Children with a total score of 9 or more across the 12 questions were regarded as potential members of a category of anxious children. The mothers of these potentially anxious children were interviewed on the telephone and asked to provide specific examples to support their descriptions. These interviews often revealed that some mothers had exaggerated the seriousness of their child's behavior and these children were eliminated from the potentially anxious group. The teachers of the remaining children were interviewed on the telephone. Each teacher, who

had no knowledge of the child's prior behavior or the purpose of the interview, described and then ranked the child with respect to all children of the same gender in that classroom for the qualities of shyness and fearfulness.

The maternal questionnaire and the subsequent interviews with the mother and the teacher were then discussed by a trio of investigators. If all three agreed that the evidence indicated the child met criteria for anxious symptoms, the child was categorized as anxious (42 children or 26% of the group met that criterion). We selected 107 control children from the rest of the sample who did not meet criteria for any symptom and brought all 164 children to the laboratory where each was administered a variety of procedures. As at 4.5 years, the frequency of spontaneous comments and smiles was coded from videotapes.

More high than low reactive infants had acquired anxious symptoms—45% of high reactives but only 15% of low reactives and 21% of all remaining children were. classified as possessing anxious symptoms. Further, the high reactives displayed fewer spontaneous comments and smiles than the low reactives while interacting with an unfamiliar female examiner (Table 1). Only a modest proportion of children were consistently inhibited or consistently uninhibited on all assessments from 14 months to 7.5 years. Only 18% of the high reactives showed a combination of high fear scores at 14 and 21 months, inhibition with the examiner and inhibited behavior with same gender peers at 4.5 years, and, in addition, display of anxious symptoms at 7.5 years. Not one high reactive infant developed the complementary profile of low fear at 14 and 21 months, uninhibited behavior at 4.5 years, and no anxious symptoms at 7.5 years. Thus, the classification high reactive constrained the likelihood that a child would develop a consistently uninhibited phenotype. Most high reactive infants developed a profile in the average range (Kagan et al 1999).

The 23 high reactives who had anxious symptoms differed from the 27 high reactives who did not show signs of anxiety. More members of the former group had a narrow facial skeleton, higher sitting diastolic blood pressure, and a greater magnitude of cooling of the temperature of the fingertips while listening to a series of digits they were asked to remember. The latter 2 variables imply that these children had greater sympathetic influence on the cardiovascular system.

The predictive value of the facial skeleton was not a surprise. We had discovered earlier that the 14- and 21-month-old children who had a narrow facial skeleton were more inhibited than those with broad faces (Arcus and Kagan 1995). We interpret these results as implying that the genes that control the growth of the maxilla, which is a derivative of the neural crest and, therefore, ectodermal in origin, are correlated with the genetic factors that

BIOL PSYCHIATRY 1539
1999;46:1536–1541

contribute to inhibited behavior. It is relevant, therefore, that an allelomorph of the agouti gene, located on chromosome 2 in mice, is linked to craniofacial anomalies (Asher et al 1996). Both melanocytes, whose activity is modulated by the agouti gene, and facial bone are derivatives of the neural crest. Mice and rats who are homozygous for the recessive form of the agouti gene (called non-agouti) have all black fur and are tamer and less fearful than animals with the agouti gene (Cottle and Price 1987; Hayssen 1997).

Other data affirm an association between high reactivity as an infant and greater sympathetic activation of cardiovascular targets at 7.5 years. For example, an asymmetry in skin temperature between the fingertips of the index fingers of the left and right hand is a result of differential constriction of arteriovenous anastomoses. The index fingers typically have larger asymmetries than the middle or ring fingers (average asymmetry of $+0.3°C$ favoring a cooler left hand). When the distribution of asymmetries was divided into terciles, significantly more high than low reactives were either in the top or the bottom tercile (80% vs. 58%), and girls with large asymmetries were more likely to have anxious symptoms than girls with smaller asymmetries.

EEG Asymmetry

Davidson (1992) and Fox and Davidson (1988) have suggested that children who are avoidant of or fearful to unfamiliar events show greater desynchronization of alpha frequencies over the right frontal area compared with the left frontal area under resting conditions (Davidson 1995). In addition, high reactives showed greater activation of the right frontal area when they were 9- and 24-months-old, whereas low reactives showed greater activation over the left frontal area (Fox et al 1994). Because neural activity in the amygdala is transmitted to the frontal lobes via cholinergic fibers projecting from the basal nucleus of Meynert, it is possible that greater desynchronization of alpha frequencies in the right frontal area reflects greater activity in the right amygdala (Kapp et al 1994; Lloyd and Kling 1991). We have begun to evaluate the children from this longitudinal sample at 10 years of age. At the time of this writing, 28 high reactives and 24 low reactives have been measured and significantly more high than low reactives are showing greater EEG activation under resting conditions over the right frontal area (30% vs. 8%) whereas more low reactives are showing greater activation over the left frontal area (55% vs. 25%) (chi square = 4.0, $p < .05$). This replication of Fox and Davidson findings lends robustness to this empirical association. In addition, more high than low reactives had greater power in the 14- to 30-Hz range than in the 8- to 13-Hz range at frontal sites (eyes opened and relaxed) (chi square = 4.1, $p < .05$).

This result suggests greater cortical arousal in the children who had been high reactive infants.

Inhibition in Children of Panic Disorder Parents

An early study on a small sample suggested that children with a panic parent were more likely than controls to show inhibited behavior in a laboratory setting (Rosenbaum et al 1988). A subsequent collaboration involved an evaluation of two larger samples of Caucasian, middle-class children (65 4.5-year-olds and 83 6.5-year-olds), who had a parent with panic disorder or panic combined with depression. We compared the behavior and physiology of these children with that of 42 4.5-year-old and 36 6.5- year-old Caucasian children from middle-class families with no psychiatric symptoms. Each child was administered a battery by an examiner who was blind to the diagnostic status of the parent.

More panic than control children were emotionally subdued as they interacted with the unfamiliar female examiner. Nineteen percent of children with a panic parent, but only 5% of control children, had values in the lowest quartile of the distributions for both spontaneous smiles and comments while interacting with the female examiner. These behavioral differences between the panic and control children were clearer if the parent reported onset of panic disorder before 21 years of age.

The autonomic variable that best differentiated the panic from control children was a large temperature asymmetry ($\geq 1°C$) between the right and left index fingers while the child was watching film clips. It will be recalled that this sympathetically mediated measurement also differentiated high from low reactives in the longitudinal sample.

Thus, about 1 in 5 middle-class, Caucasian children living with a parent who had panic disorder was likely to become an inhibited child, compared with a probability of 1 in 20 for matched control children. If one adds the large temperature asymmetry as a diagnostic marker, then 1 in 10 children with a panic parent, but only 1 in 100 control children combined a subdued style of interaction with this sign of sympathetic lability.

A group of 10 girls living with a panic parent (15% of all girls) were extremely subdued—they displayed fewer than 10 spontaneous comments and 10 smiles across the battery. These extremely subdued girls were qualitatively different from the remaining girls living with a panic parent who were emotionally more spontaneous with the examiner. The 10 extremely subdued girls had higher resting heart rates, were more likely to have a very cool right compared with left index finger, and more likely to have very light blue eyes. These 3 features are more characteristic of extremely inhibited children in the larger longitudinal sample (Kagan 1994).

Implications

The major implication of this work is that high reactive infants, many of whom show an inhibited profile to unfamiliar events and situations in the second year, are at slightly higher than normal risk for the later development of some form of anxious symptomatology. This suggestion is affirmed by longitudinal study of an independent sample of 79 13-year-olds, who had been classified as inhibited or uninhibited in the second year of life (Kagan et al 1988b). These adolescents were interviewed by Carl Schwartz, a child psychiatrist, who had no knowledge of their initial temperamental classification or later laboratory behavior. More of the adolescents who had been classified as inhibited rather than uninhibited in the second year had symptoms of social anxiety (61% vs. 27%) (Schwartz et al, in press). These inhibited children were not more likely to have developed specific target phobias or separation anxiety, implying that inhibited children might be at special risk for the development of social phobia during the adolescent and adult years. College students who reported high levels of social anxiety remembered being very shy when they were young children (Mick and Telch 1998; van Ameringen et al 1998).

It is possible that inhibited children are especially susceptible to anxiety or PTSD after threatening events. Only 10 children from a large group of school children who were kidnaped and terrorized for 2 days developed post-traumatic stress disorder (Terr 1979); these 10 might have been temperamentally inhibited children. In 1984, a sniper in a building across the street from a Los Angeles elementary school fired at the children on the playground killing 1 and injuring 13 children. One month later a group of psychologists and psychiatrists who interviewed the victims of this event judged 38% of the group to be anxious. A primary quality that differentiated the anxious from the nonanxious children was a prior avoidant personality among the former group (Pynoos et al 1987).

It is important to appreciate, however, that the majority of inhibited children probably will not become anxiety disorder patients in later life. Given the frequency of anxiety disorder in the population, a variable that correctly predicted 90% of individuals with adult anxiety disorder and eliminated 90% of those who would not, would be correct in only one-third of the cases.

The Notion of Constraint

It will be recalled that only 18% of the high reactive infants were consistently inhibited at every evaluation, but not one member of the group was consistently uninhibited from 1–7 years of age. This fact suggests that the relation between infant reactivity and the later development of a consistently inhibited style is real, but modest. When the probability of one event following another is low, say the correlation is less than 0.4, it is likely that the relevant antecedent event is affecting the consequent either indirectly, only at extreme values, or in combination with other factors. Under these conditions, it is more accurate to use the verb "constrain" rather than "determine" to describe the relation between the earlier and later event. For example, consistent nurturance of young children during the first five years of life does not predict, with a high level of confidence, the quality of one's marriage, amount of education, or degree of professional accomplishment. Early nurturant care probably constrains, in a significant way, the likelihood that children raised in such families will become criminals. Because no high reactive infant became a consistently uninhibited child, it is more accurate to write that a high reactive temperament constrains the probability of the child becoming consistently uninhibited, rather than to claim that high reactivity determines the development of an inhibited or anxious profile. The replacement of the word "determine" with "constrain" is not idle word play for the connotations surrounding the two words are different.

Summary

The evidence and ideas presented in this paper support the usefulness of combining biological and behavioral evidence. During the first half of this century, psychiatrists and psychologists ignored the modest but significant contribution of temperament to personality profiles. The child's social history determines the meaning he or she will impose on an event; the combination of temperament and history determines the ease with which the event activates limbic structures and the subsequent emotional response. The fact that only a small proportion of high reactive infants became consistently fearful, anxious children implicates an important role for the environment. We must now search for the integrated profiles that emerge from particular temperamental dispositions encountering varied life histories and resist the desire to simplify the problem by proceeding as if we could eventually have a quantitative estimate of the separate contributions of temperament and life events.

The preparation of this article was supported by grants from the W. T. Grant Foundation, Foundation Bial, and NIMH Grant 47077. We thank Mark McManis, Donna Steinberg, Jenny Mongkolcheep, Melissa Lewis, Eric Peterson, and Vali Kahn for their contribution to this research.

This work was presented at the scientific satellite conference, "The Role of Biological and Psychological Factors on Early Development and Their Impact on Adult Life," that preceded the Anxiety Disorders Association of America (ADAA) annual meeting, San Diego, March 1999. The conference was jointly sponsored by the ADAA and the National Institute of Mental Health through an unrestricted educational grant provided by Wyeth-Ayerst Laboratories.

References

Amaral DG, Price JL, Pitkanen A, Carmichael ST (1992): Anatomical organization of the primate amygdaloid complex. In: Aggleton JP, editor. *The Amygdala*. New York: Wiley-Liss, 1–66.

Arcus DM, Kagan J (1995): Temperament and craniofacial skeleton in childhood. *Child Dev* 66:1529–1540.

Asher JH, Harrison RW, Morell R, Carey MC, Friedman TB (1996): Effects of Pax3 modifier genes on craniofacial morphology, pigmentation, and viability. *Genomics* 34:285–291.

Blanchard DC, Blanchard RJ (1988): Etho-experimental approaches to the biology of emotion. In: Rosenzweig MR, Porter LW, editors. *Annual Review of Psychology*. Palo Alto, California: Annual Reviews, 43–68.

Cottle CA, Price EO (1987): Effects of the nonagouti pelage-color allele on the behavior of captive wild Norway rats. *J Comp Psychol* 101:390–394.

Davidson RJ (1992): Anterior cerebral asymmetry and the nature of emotion. *Brain Cognit* 20:125–151.

Davidson RJ (1995): Cerebral asymmetry, emotion, and affective style. In: Davidson RJ, Hugdahl K, editors. *Brain Asymmetry*. Cambridge: MIT Press, 361–388.

Davis M, Gewirtz JC, McNish KA, Kim M (1995): The roles of amygdala and the bed nucleus of the stria terminalis in the acquisition of fear-potentiated startle using both explicit and contextual cues. Presented at the 25th meeting of the Society for Neuroscience, San Diego.

Fox NA, Davidson RJ (1988): Pattern of brain electrical activity during facial signs of emotion in ten month old infants. *Dev Psychol* 24:230–236.

Fox NA, Calkins SD, Bell MA (1994): Neural plasticity and development in the first two years of life. *Dev Psychopathol* 6:677–696.

Hayssen V (1997): Effects of the non-agouti coat-color allele on behavior of deer mice (*Peromyscus maniculatus*). *J Comp Psychol* 111:419–423.

Kagan J (1994): *Galen's Prophecy*. New York: Basic Books.

Kagan J (1998): Biology and the child. In: Eisenberg N, editor. *Handbook of Child Psychology, Vol. 3, 5th ed.* New York: Wiley, 177–236.

Kagan J, Snidman N, Arcus D (1998a): Childhood derivatives of high and low reactivity in infancy. *Child Dev* 69:1483–1493.

Kagan J, Reznick JS, Snidman N (1988b): Biological bases of childhood shyness. *Science 240:167–171.*

Kagan J, Snidman N, Zentner M, Peterson E (1999): Infant temperament and anxious symptoms in school age children. *Dev Psychopathol* 11:209–224.

Kapp BS, Supple WF, Whalen PJ (1994): Effects of electrical stimulation of the amygdaloid central nucleus on neurocortical arousal in the rabbit. *Behav Neurosci* 108:81–93.

Klein RG (1991): Parent-child agreement in clinical assessment of anxiety and other psychopathology. *J Anxiety Dis* 5:182–198.

LeDoux JE (1996): *The Emotional Brain*. New York: Simon & Schuster.

Lloyd RL, Kling AS (1991): Delta activity from amygdala in squirrel monkeys (*Saimiri sciureus*): Influence of social and environmental contexts. *Behav Neurosci* 105:223–229.

Mick MA, Telch MJ (1998): Social anxiety and the history of behavioral inhibition in young adults. *J Anxiety Dis* 12:1–20.

Perrin S, Last CG (1992): Do childhood anxiety measure anxiety? *J Abnorm Child Psychol* 25:567–578.

Pynoos RS, Frederick C, Neder K, Arroyo W, Steinberg A, Eth F, et al (1987): Life threat and post-traumatic stress disorder in school-age children. *Arch Gen Psychiatry* 44:1057–1063.

Rolls ET (1992): Neurophysiology and functions of the primate amygdala. In: Aggleton JP, editor. *The Amygdala*. New York: Wiley-Liss, 143–166.

Rosenbaum JF, Biederman J, Gersten M, Hirschfeld-Becker DR, Meninger SR, Herman JB, et al (1988): Behavioral inhibition in children of parents with panic disorder and agoraphobia: A control study. *Arch Gen Psychiatry* 45:463–470.

Rosicky J (1993, March): The assessment of temperamental fearfulness in infancy. Presented at the meeting of the Society for Research in Child Development, New Orleans.

Schwartz CE, Snidman N, Kagan J (1999): Adolescent social anxiety as an outcome of inhibited temperament in childhood. *J Am Acad Child Adolesc Psychiatry* 38:1008–1015.

Seifer R, Sameroff AJ, Barrett LC, Krafchuk E (1994): Infant temperament measured by multiple observations and mother report. *Child Dev* 65:1478–1490.

Spiker D, Kraemer HC, Constantine NA, Bryant D (1992): Reliability and validity of behavior problem checklists as measures of stable traits in low birth weight premature preschoolers. *Child Dev* 63:1481–1496.

Terr LC (1979): Children of Chowchilla. *Psychoanal Study Child* 34:547–627.

Thomas A, Chess S (1977): *Temperament and Development*. New York: Brunner Mazel.

Van Ameringen M, Mancini C, Oakman JM (1998): The relationship of behavioral inhibition and shyness to anxiety disorder. *J Nervous Ment Dis* 186:425–431.

0271-0749/98/1806-006S$03.00/0
Journal of Clinical Psychopharmacology
Copyright © 1998 by Lippincott Williams & Wilkins

Vol. 18, No. 6, Suppl. 2
Printed in U.S.A.

The Long-Term Course of Panic Disorder and Its Predictors

HEINZ KATSCHNIG, MD, AND MICHAELA AMERING, MD

Department of Psychiatry, University of Vienna, Vienna, Austria

Whereas lifetime prevalence rates of panic disorder—as established in epidemiologic surveys—range between 1.6 and 3.5%, 1-month rates usually amount to much less than one half of the lifetime rates. This finding indicates that a substantial proportion of patients who had panic disorder at some stage in their life must have remitted. In contrast to these results, clinicians tend to regard panic disorder as a chronic condition because, as a rule, they see panic patients only several years after onset of the disorder. A number of small, prospective, long-term studies of such clinical populations indicate that after several years, between 17 and 70% of patients still have panic attacks, and between 36 and 82% have phobic avoidance. In the largest and longest follow-up study published to date, 45% of all patients showed an unremitting—although in a certain proportion waxing and waning—course, 24% followed a pattern of remissions and relapses, whereas 31% went back into a stable remission. The evidence of factors predicting the course of panic disorder in clinical populations suggests that long duration and agoraphobia at baseline—not the severity and frequency of panic attacks—are predictors of an unfavorable course. Additional studies are needed to determine whether personality factors, depression, and other variables are also of predictive relevance. Also, factors working during follow-up, such as positive and negative life events, coping behaviors, and treatment, should be considered in future studies. (J Clin Psychopharmacol 1998;18[suppl 2]:6S–11S)

QUALITY-OF-LIFE ISSUES are becoming increasingly important in medicine today. In psychiatry, therefore, long-term outcomes of patients with mental disorders are becoming of equal interest as outcomes of short-term pharmacologic trials. Comprehensive databases of long-term outcomes exist for some psychiatric disorders, such as schizophrenia. However, for many other psychiatric disorders, similar databases are not as well established, often for the simple reason that the disorder was defined a relatively short time ago. Panic disorder, which only emerged as a specific disease entity in 1980 (DSM-III), is one of these latter disorders. In this article, we present evidence that we have collected regarding the course of panic disorder beyond the usual 6- or 8-week clinical trial period. We also attempt to answer the clinically most relevant question: Is it possible to identify, at an early stage of panic disorder, those persons who are at risk for an unfavorable course?

The usual clinical description of panic disorder begins with unexpected panic attacks, then expected or situational panic attacks develop, then phobic avoidance, and finally full-blown agoraphobia. Comorbid conditions, such as depression and substance abuse, often complicate the clinical pictures of the patients we usually see as clinicians, and comorbidity is often so prominent that the original disorder is not recognized. Approximately 80% of panic disorder patients seen by psychiatrists in clinical settings also have agoraphobia, and the average illness duration is approximately 5 years.[1] Therefore, if psychiatric practitioners draw conclusions from the patients they typically see, they will regard panic disorder as a chronic condition. However, only prospective studies can prove or disprove that the pattern of chronicity seen in clinical patients is valid for most or all patients who start having unexpected panic attacks.

Unfortunately, not many prospective studies have been conducted so far, and those that have been had methodologic disadvantages in one respect or another, such as small sample sizes, short duration of follow-up, insufficient outcome criteria selection, etc. In this article, we attempt to sketch a picture of the course of panic disorder, beginning with a startling epidemiologic observation, going on to describe the results of prospective studies, and finishing by essaying the task of identifying predictors of source and outcome once

Address correspondence to: Heinz Katschnig, MD, Department of Psychiatry, University of Vienna, Währinger Gürtel 18–20, A-1090 Vienna, Austria.

panic disorder has developed. Although the attempt is ambitious, we feel that it is justified in the effort to concentrate the ever-shrinking health care resources on those patients who need them most.

Conclusions About Course and Outcome of Panic Disorder from Cross-Sectional Epidemiologic Data

Epidemiologic data suggest that it is an oversimplification to regard panic disorder as a chronic condition. This is demonstrated in the comparison of lifetime, 12-month, and 1-month prevalence rates from the two large U.S. epidemiologic studies conducted over the last 15 years. Although all the rates in the more recent National Comorbidity Survey (NCS)[2, 3] are more than twice as high as those in the older Epidemiological Catchment Area (ECA) study,[4, 5] the relationship between lifetime, 12-month, and 1-month prevalence rates is strikingly similar. As shown in Figure 1, the 1-month prevalence rates are less than half of the lifetime prevalence rates. More precisely, the 1-month rate is less than one third of the lifetime rate in the ECA study, and approximately two fifths of the lifetime prevalence rate in the NCS. Therefore, according to the results of these large epidemiologic studies, at least three fifths to two thirds of those who had panic disorder at some period in their lives did not experience it during the month before the intake interviews.

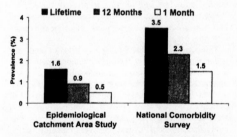

FIG. 1. Prevalence of panic disorder. (Sources: Regier DA, Boyd JH, Burke JD Jr, Rae DS, Myers JK, Kramer M, Robins LN, George LK, Karno M, Locke BZ. One-month prevalence of mental disorders in the United States. Arch Gen Psychiatry 1988;45:977–86; Eaton WW, Dryman A, Weissman MM. Panic and phobia: the diagnosis of panic disorder and phobic disorder. In: Robins LN, Regier DA, eds. Psychiatric disorders in America: the Epidemiologic Catchment Area study. New York: The Free Press, 1991:155–79; Kessler RC, McGonagle KA, Zhao S, Nelson CB, Hughes M, Eshleman S, Wittchen H-U, Kendler K. Lifetime and 12-month prevalence of DSM-III-R psychiatric disorders in the United States: results from the national comorbidity study. Arch Gen Psychiatry 1994;51:8–19; Eaton WW, Kessler RC, Wittchen HU, Magee WJ. Panic and panic disorder in the United States. Am J Psychiatry 1994;151:413–20.)

In a second approach to drawing conclusions about the course of panic disorder from prevalence data, lifetime prevalence data from the ECA study, as analyzed by Weissman[6] and Klerman and associates,[7] can be interpreted as providing the following hypothetical "longitudinal" picture: although approximately 10% of the general population experience at least one panic attack at some stage in their lives, only one in six of these persons fulfills diagnostic criteria for panic disorder (1.6% lifetime prevalence). One third of the latter group also had agoraphobia (i.e., in an epidemiologic sample, two thirds did not seem to develop agoraphobia) while fulfilling criteria for panic disorder, which is just the opposite of the picture seen in clinical samples—usually approximately 80% of those presenting for treatment of panic disorder have developed agoraphobia.[1]

However, hypothetical constructs notwithstanding, actual longitudinal data from epidemiologic studies are not available. We therefore have to rely on clinical populations when studying the course and outcome of panic disorder. Data on these populations are nevertheless useful as a guidance for clinicians, although selection criteria for inclusion into such studies vary to a considerable degree, and most studies use clinical trial populations as a starting point, which usually constitute a highly selective group.

Choosing Outcome Criteria

The epidemiologic studies just cited used operational diagnostic criteria, and we drew our conclusions from the presence or absence of these full criteria. But diagnostic criteria are crude, do not reflect the complex and varied structure of the disorder in individual patients, and usually do not say anything about severity. Diagnostic criteria may also miss relevant psychopathology. For instance, Katschnig and Amering,[8] in reference to data published by Weissman[6] and Klerman and associates,[7] have stressed that of all persons assessed in the ECA study, 1.2% experienced panic *attacks* with agoraphobia *without* fulfilling diagnostic criteria for panic *disorder*. These persons obviously were not included in the ECA prevalence data, but their daily life was nevertheless quite likely impaired to some degree.

Therefore, when following up a group of panic disorder patients to assess course and outcome, one inevitably is challenged by the great complexity of panic disorder. Spontaneous panic attacks, anticipatory anxiety, situational panic attacks, phobic avoidance, disabilities, comorbid depression, and substance abuse have to be considered. Some of these phenomena are persistent, others are not, as clinical experience shows. For instance, the outcome of "zero panic attacks" at follow-up is much more frequent than that of remission of other symptoms.[9, 10]

Many methodologic questions remain open today: Which of the different phenomena complicating panic disorder should be considered most important in assessing course and outcome? Furthermore, what are the critical time intervals? How often must panic attacks occur for the disorder to be considered active rather than remitted? Every day? Once a week? Once a month? What about two panic attacks within a single year? Furthermore, what about the disappearance of panic attacks because disabling avoidance behavior has developed? Because of the great complexity of these and other variables, Roy-Byrne and Cowley[9] and Shear and Maser,[11] as well as Starcevic,[12] indicate that it is necessary to use multiple measures in assessing outcome.

In view of these complex outcome criteria, simple conclusions, such as that panic disorder is or is not a chronic condition, are problematic. Panic disorder may be chronic in one respect but not in another (e.g., a patient might still be experiencing panic attacks but not have agoraphobia, or is agoraphobic but experiences no panic attacks). Also, because combinations of so many possible outcome criteria may lead to many different patterns, large samples are needed to properly describe at least the most frequent patterns.

Prospective Studies in Clinical Populations

Twenty-five years ago, Marks and Lader[13] reviewed six follow-up studies of anxiety neurosis, observing that between 41 and 59% of patients were considered unrecovered after an average of 19 years. The results of these early studies cannot be generalized, both because of the less stringent research methodology at that time and because the diagnosis of anxiety neurosis was a mixture of today's general anxiety disorder and panic disorder. Marks and Lader, however, certainly brought up the idea of chronicity.

In a recent review of 16 prospective studies, which fulfilled minimum methodologic standards, Roy-Byrne and Cowley[9] concluded that "despite the availability of effective antipanic treatments, panic disorder remains a chronic condition." We contend that this is an oversimplification. According to the Roy-Byrne and Cowley review, between 17 and 70% of patients (mean, 46%) still had panic attacks at follow-up, and between 36 and 82% had phobic avoidance (mean, 69%). Disabilities were still present in every second patient. However, these results also mean that between 30 and 83% of patients ceased to experience panic attacks, and between 18 and 64% were not agoraphobic at follow-up.[9] Clearly, there is a subgroup of panic disorder patients whose condition is "chronic," but there is also a large subgroup

whose condition is not. Also, given that multiple outcome criteria have to be used, there is clearly a need for a differentiated view, and the terms "chronic" and "not chronic" need specification.

Therefore, instead of aiming at gross generalizations, we contend that our task is to identify and describe subgroups of panic disorder patients to determine the characteristics of patients who might be expected to undergo a more or less unfavorable course. Questions to be answered in this regard are the following: Are there two or even more types of panic disorder? Does choice of treatment during follow-up make a difference, or does it not? Furthermore, what is the effect of adverse experiences during the follow-up period on course and outcome?

Sample sizes in the studies reviewed by Roy-Byrne and Cowley are rather small (5 studies with enrollment of up to 40 patients,[14–18] 8 studies with between 41 and 77 patients,[19–26] 1 study with 89 patients,[27] and 1 study with 107 patients[28]). Only one of these studies was large enough for detailed analysis (N = 394)[29] and in that study, 55% of patients who had panic disorder with agoraphobia and 68% of patients who had uncomplicated panic disorder were panic-free after 1 year. If one considers the variable proportions of patients lost to follow-up—in the most recent study more than 50% of the original group could not be followed up[30]—there is little room left for describing subtypes of course and outcome. Despite these methodologic drawbacks, which Roy-Byrne and Cowley[9] painstakingly analyze and identify in most of their 16 reviewed studies, they nevertheless come to the abovementioned conclusion that "panic disorder remains a chronic condition."

The largest and longest follow-up study of panic disorder, which because of the large number of patients allowed for the definition of possible subtypes of course and outcome, was carried out by Katschnig and associates.[10] In this study, 423 patients (a 1-in-4 sample of all patients who had taken part in a clinical drug trial[1]) were followed up over nearly 4 years on average. This study also assessed fluctuations over time; only 2 of the 16 studies reviewed by Roy-Byrne and Cowley[9] actually addressed this question.[26, 27]

Figure 2 shows the subtypes of course we identified (as defined by DSM-III-R criteria at a given point in time). In 45% of all patients, panic disorder had not remitted in the clinical drug trial and had persisted throughout follow-up, although in many patients there was a fluctuation in severity. Two fifths (18.6% of the total sample) of this group had a severe chronic course. On the other hand, 31% of the total group remitted and stayed well. Approximately one quarter had an episodic course with free intervals. These find-

N = 220, Follow-up ⏲ 4 Years

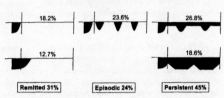

FIG. 2. Patterns of course of panic disorder in Cross-National Collaborative Study. (Source: Katschnig H, Amering M, Stolk JM, Klerman GL, Ballenger JC, Briggs A, Buller R, Cassano G, Garvey M, Roth M, Solyom C. Long-term follow-up after a drug trial for panic disorder. Br J Psychiatry 1995;167:487–94.)

ings were reflected in the analyses of status at follow-up, with roughly one in five patients performing badly on most outcome criteria, especially on disability measures.

Our study confirms the finding from other studies that the course of panic disorder over the long term can best be described as following different patterns in different subgroups of patients. But which patients do well, and which do not? The answer to this question, applied to early-stage patients, would be of considerable practical importance.

Predicting the Course and Outcome of Panic Disorder

Both unforeseeable external influences, such as negative and positive life events and other stressors, and unpredictable changes in personal coping behavior (because of new experiences) do not allow for the exclusive use of baseline variables as predictors of course and outcome in disorders such as panic disorder or schizophrenia.

The "vulnerability stress model"[31] and the "interactive developmental model"[32] are more in accordance with these observations than the "natural history" model. For instance, Telch and associates[33] and Mavissakalian[34] have convincingly shown that self-exposure to phobic stimuli is therapeutic for patients with panic disorder with agoraphobia, and it is unclear to what extent patients inadvertently or purposely practiced such exposure during follow-up. Another variable that we cannot control in naturalistic follow-up studies is the use of therapeutic resources by the patients, let alone the quality of their treatments. When trying to identify the predictors for course and outcome of panic disorder, one has to keep these caveats in mind. Unfortunately, there is a paucity of follow-up studies that monitor course and study external influence *during* the long-term development of the disorder, as well as treatments.

O'Rourke and associates[35] analyzed 25 outcome studies. Twelve of these studies were conducted before the publication of the DSM-III and are therefore not strictly comparable with DSM-III studies. O'Rourke and associates found that the most consistent predictors of unfavorable course and outcome were severity of illness at baseline, personality disorder, chronicity, comorbid states of depression, alcohol and substance abuse, and clinical status on discharge. They also conducted their own 5- to 6-year follow-up study of 79 patients who had received drug and behavioral counseling in a clinical trial; they found that 34% of all patients followed up went into remission and remained asymptomatic throughout follow-up. The authors could not confirm the prognostic value of severity at baseline, but showed that personality disorder was a factor. Long duration at baseline was a significant but weak predictor of an unfavorable outcome.

In the prospective Harvard/Brown Anxiety Disorders Research Program study of 412 subjects who were in episodes of DSM-III-R panic, Warshaw and associates[36] found that panic severity at intake was not predictive of time to remission, but that severity of agoraphobia was. Follow-up duration was between 6 months and 5 years. Depression was not found to be predictive of outcome if other variables were controlled for, a finding also reported by Maier and Buller.[25]

Most of these findings are in accordance with our own results in 423 panic disorder patients followed up over an average of 46.5 (±10.3) months.[10, 37] Panic attack frequency at baseline, which is often taken as an indicator of severity, was not predictive of any outcome measure at follow-up, neither of occurrence of panic attacks, nor phobic avoidance, nor disabilities in everyday life. Agoraphobia at baseline, however, predicted agoraphobia and disabilities at outcome. Longer duration of illness at baseline predicted a worse phobic avoidance outcome. Disabilities at baseline were predictive of disabilities at follow-up, but these were only domain-specific, e.g., work disabilities at baseline predicted work disabilities at follow-up, etc.

In this study, intermittent treatments received during the follow-up period were also recorded. Because this was a naturalistic follow-up study, treatments were not randomly allocated. One unexpected finding, that contact with or treatment by a psychiatrist or a psychologist was related to an unfavorable outcome, may thus be a consequence of patient self-selection, i.e., only the most severely ill might have used services. Also, the fact that continuous psychotropic medication was not related to a better outcome might be explained by the naturalistic design of the follow-up.

Conclusions

Usually panic disorder patients still wait many years before receiving state-of-the-art, specialized clinical treatment. As a result, clinicians see an overwhelming proportion of patients with a long duration of their disorder and therefore tend to regard panic disorder as a chronic condition. In retrospect, these patients do indeed follow a course progressing from unexpected to situational panic attacks, phobic avoidance, and full-blown agoraphobia, with disabilities in several life domains and comorbidity from depression and substance abuse. Today we know that these patients constitute a biased sample of all persons suffering from panic disorder. This observation is supported by the finding that although four of five panic disorder patients in clinical samples have agoraphobia, this percentage is only one third in panic disorder samples of the general population.

Research in recent years has shown that panic disorder tends to follow the pattern shown for the long-term course of schizophrenia. Although Kraepelin, who derived his knowledge from observing asylum patients, assumed that a chronic and progressive course was characteristic of the disorder (his "dementia praecox" concept), later research identified several types of long-term course, including a large proportion of patients with full remission.

The fact that panic disorder was only defined in 1980 prevents us from conducting studies on its lifelong course. The available evidence for shorter follow-up periods (up to 6 years) suggests that full remission might occur in approximately one third of patients who have undergone clinical treatment, i.e., in patients with rather long duration and higher severity. From comparing lifetime and 6-month prevalence data in epidemiologic studies, it can be concluded that the remission rate in general population samples is greater than one third. At the other end of the spectrum, in those panic disorder patients who have received specialized psychiatric care, it seems that approximately one in five follows an unremitting and severe chronic course.

The identification of those panic patients who might follow such a severe chronic and unremitting course is an important challenge, especially now, when health care resources are becoming more and more restricted. Unfortunately, empirical data about the prediction of the course and outcome of panic disorder are only available for clinical samples and are still missing for primary care patients and panic sufferers identified in general population surveys. Taken together, the results of long-term studies suggest that the frequency and intensity of panic attacks at baseline have no predictive importance. Instead, a longer dura-

tion of the disorder and the presence of agoraphobia at baseline seem to be connected with a less favorable course and outcome. Results regarding the predictive value of comorbid depression and personality disorder are ambiguous.

As Roy-Byrne and Cowley[9] have shown, many methodologic issues are unresolved or treated differently in different studies, and many questions regarding the long-term course and outcome of panic disorder have not yet been properly addressed. These issues include the following:

- The selection of patients to be followed up
  Those who have participated in a clinical drug trial? Unselected consecutive clients of a specialized anxiety clinic? Patients of general practitioners? General population samples?
- The choice of outcome domains
  Panic attacks? (Unexpected, situational?) Agoraphobia? Disabilities? Anticipatory anxiety? Quality of life?
- The outcome measure
  Mean values? Proportions of patients having reached a certain level of outcome, e.g., zero panic attacks?
- The design
  Prospective follow-up studies with regular, frequent assessments to actually describe the course? Outcome measures recorded only at follow-up?
- The influence of different treatments during follow-up
  Pharmacologic? Cognitive? Self-selection of those receiving treatment during follow-up in naturalistic studies?
- The influence of life changes on course and outcome

As long as there is no uniformity in these and other issues of design and method, conclusions about the long-term course and outcome of panic disorders must remain tentative.

One thing, however, is already clear: panic disorder is not a uniformly chronic and progressive disorder. Rather, it follows a course pattern known to us from many psychiatric and somatic disorders (for instance, hepatitis); a substantial proportion of patients achieve complete remission, whereas another group has a clearly unfavorable course. What happens to the group in-between probably depends largely on therapeutic efforts. Therefore, we require not only more naturalistic long-term follow-up studies with a uniform methodology, but also more long-term clinical trials, contrasting and combining pharmacologic and behavioral/cognitive treatments.

References

1. Drug treatment of panic disorder: comparative efficacy of alprazolam, imipramine and placebo. Cross-National Collaborative Panic Study, Second Phase Investigators. Br J Psychiatry 1992; 160:191–202.
2. Kessler RC, McGonagle KA, Zhao S, Nelson CB, Hughes M, Eshleman S, Wittchen H-U, Kendler K. Lifetime and 12-month prevalence of DSM-III-R psychiatric disorders in the United States: results from the national comorbidity study. Arch Gen Psychiatry 1994;51:8–19.
3. Eaton WW, Kessler RC, Wittchen HU, Magee WJ. Panic and panic disorder in the United States. Am J Psychiatry 1994;151:413–20.
4. Regier DA, Boyd JH, Burke JD Jr, Rae DS, Myers JK, Kramer M, Robins LN, George LK, Karno M, Locke BZ. One-month prevalence of mental disorders in the United States. Arch Gen Psychiatry 1988;45:977–86.
5. Eaton WW, Dryman A, Weissman MM. Panic and phobia: the diagnosis of panic disorder and phobic disorder. In: Robins LN, Regier DA, eds. Psychiatric disorders in America: the epidemiologic catchment area study. New York: The Free Press, 1991: 155–79.
6. Weissman MM. The epidemiology of panic disorder and agoraphobia. In: Frances AJ, Hales RE, eds. American Psychiatric Press review of psychiatry. Vol 7. Washington, DC: American Psychiatric Press, Inc., 1988:54–66.
7. Klerman GL, Weissman MM, Ouellette R, Johnson J, Greenwald S. Panic attacks in the community: social morbidity and health care utilization. JAMA 1991;265:742–6.
8. Katschnig H, Amering M. The long-term course of panic disorder. In: Wolf BE, Maser JD, eds. Treatment of panic disorder: a consensus development conference. Washington, DC: American Psychiatric Press, Inc., 1994:196–206.
9. Roy-Byrne PP, Cowley DS. Course and outcome in panic disorder: a review of recent follow-up studies. Anxiety 1995;1:151–60.
10. Katschnig H, Amering M, Stolk JM, Klerman GL, Ballenger JC, Briggs A, Buller R, Cassano G, Garvey M, Roth M, Solyom C. Long-term follow-up after a drug trial for panic disorder. Br J Psychiatry 1995;167:487–94.
11. Shear MK, Maser JD. Standardized assessment for panic disorder research: a conference report. Arch Gen Psychiatry 1994;51: 346–54.
12. Starcevic V. Treatment goals for panic disorder. J Clin Psychopharmacol 1998;18[suppl 2];19S–26S.
13. Marks I, Lader M. Anxiety states (anxiety neurosis): a review. J Nerv Ment Dis 1973;156:3–18.
14. Craske MG, Brown TA, Barlow DH. Behavioral treatment of panic disorder: a two-year follow-up. Behav Ther 1991;22:289–304.
15. Beck AT, Sokol L, Clark DA, Berchick R, Wright F. A crossover study of focused cognitive therapy for panic disorder. Am J Psychiatry 1992;149:778–83.
16. Nagy LM, Krystal JH, Charney DS, Merikangas KR, Woods SW. Long-term outcome of panic disorder after short-term imipramine and behavioral group treatment: 2.9-year naturalistic follow-up study. J Clin Psychopharmacol 1993;13:16–24.
17. Vollrath M, Angst J. Outcome of panic and depression in a seven-year follow-up: results of the Zurich study. Acta Psychiatr Scand 1989;80:591–6.
18. Lelliott PT, Marks IM, Monteiro WO, Tsakiris F, Noshirvani H. Agoraphobics 5 years after imipramine and exposure. J Nerv Ment Dis 1987;175:599–605.
19. Mavissakalian M, Michelson L. Two-year follow-up of exposure and imipramine treatment of agoraphobia. Am J Psychiatry 1986; 143:1106–12.
20. Nagy LM, Krystal JH, Woods SW, Charney DS. Clinical and medication outcome after short-term alprazolam and behaviorial group treatment in panic disorder. Arch Gen Psychiatry 1989;46: 993–9.
21. Lepola UM, Rimón RH, Riekkinen PJ. Three-year follow-up of patients with panic disorder after short-term treatment with alprazolam and imipramine. Int Clin Psychopharmacol 1993; 8:115–8.
22. Albus M, Scheibe G. Outcome of panic disorder with or without concomitant depression: a 2-year prospective follow-up study. Am J Psychiatry 1993;150:1878–80.
23. Pollack MH, Otto MW, Tesar GE, Cohen LS, Meltzer-Brody S, Rosenbaum JF. Long-term outcome after acute treatment with alprazolam or clonazepam for panic disorder. J Clin Psychopharmacol 1993;13:257–63.
24. Faravelli C, Albanesi G. Agoraphobia with panic attacks: 1-year prospective follow-up. Compr Psychiatry 1987;28:481–7.
25. Maier W, Buller R. One-year follow-up of panic disorder. Eur Arch Psychiatry Neurol Sci 1988;238:105–9.
26. Noyes R Jr, Clancy J, Woodman C, Holt CS, Suelzer M, Christiansen J, Anderson D. Environmental factors related to the outcome of panic disorder: a seven-year follow-up study. J Nerv Ment Dis 1993;181:529–38.
27. Noyes R Jr, Reich J, Christiansen J, Suelzer M, Pfohl B, Coryell A. Outcome of panic disorder: relationship to diagnostic subtypes and comorbidity. Arch Gen Psychiatry 1990;47:809–18.
28. Noyes R, Garvey MJ, Cook BL. Follow-up study of patients with panic disorder and agoraphobia with panic attacks treated with tricyclic antidepressants. J Affect Dis 1989;16:249–57.
29. Keller MB, Yonkers KA, Warshaw MG, Pratt LA, Gollan JK, Massion AO, White K, Swartz AR, Reich J, Lavori PW. Remission and relapse in subjects with panic disorder and panic with agoraphobia: a prospective short-interval naturalistic follow-up. J Nerv Ment Dis 1994;182:290–6.
30. Cowley DS, Flick SN, Roy-Byrne PP. Long-term course and outcome in panic disorder: a naturalistic follow-up study. Anxiety 1996;2:13–21.
31. Zubin J, Spring B. Vulnerability a new view of schizophrenia. J Abnorm Psych 1977;86:103–26.
32. Strauss JS, Hafez H, Liebermann P, Harding CM. The course of psychiatric disorders. III. Longitudinal principles. Am J Psychiatry 1985;142:289–96.
33. Telch MJ, Agras WS, Taylor CB, Roth WT, Gallen CC. Combined pharmacological and behavioral treatment for agoraphobia. Behav Res Ther 1985;23:325–35.
34. Mavissakalian M. The mutually potentiating effects of imipramine and exposure in agoraphobia. In: Hand I, Wittchen HU, eds. Panic and phobias. Berlin: Springer, 1988.
35. O'Rourke D, Fahy TJ, Brophy J, Prescott P. The Galway Study of Panic Disorder. III. Outcome at 5 to 6 years. Br J Psychiatry 1996;168:462–9.
36. Warshaw MG, Massion AO, Shea MT, Allsworth J, Keller MB. Predictors of remission in patients with panic with and without agoraphobia: prospective 5-year follow-up data [brief report]. J Nerv Ment Dis 1997;185:517–9.
37. Katschnig H, Amering M, Stolk JM, Ballenger JC. Predictors of quality of life in a long-term follow-up study in panic disorder patients after a clinical drug trial. Psychopharmacol Bull 1996;32:149–55.

Prospective Study of Posttraumatic Stress Disorder and Depression Following Trauma

Arieh Y. Shalev, M.D., Sara Freedman, M.A., Tuvia Peri, Ph.D., Dalia Brandes, M.Sc., Tali Sahar, M.Sc., Scott P. Orr, Ph.D., and Roger K. Pitman, M.D.

Objective: The purpose of this study was to prospectively evaluate the onset, overlap, and course of posttraumatic stress disorder (PTSD) and major depression following traumatic events. _Method:_ The occurrence of PTSD and major depression and the intensity of related symptoms were assessed in 211 trauma survivors recruited from a general hospital's emergency room. Psychometrics and structured clinical interview (the Structured Clinical Interview for DSM-III-R and the Clinician-Administered PTSD Scale) were administered 1 week, 1 month, and 4 months after the traumatic event. Heart rate was assessed upon arrival at the emergency room for subjects with minor physical injury. Twenty-three subjects with PTSD and 35 matched comparison subjects were followed for 1 year. _Results:_ Major depression and PTSD occurred early on after trauma; patients with these diagnoses had similar recovery rates: 63 survivors (29.9%) met criteria for PTSD at 1 month, and 37 (17.5%) had PTSD at 4 months. Forty subjects (19.0%) met criteria for major depression at 1 month, and 30 (14.2%) had major depression at 4 months. Comorbid depression occurred in 44.5% of PTSD patients at 1 month and in 43.2% at 4 months. Comorbidity was associated with greater symptom severity and lower levels of functioning. Survivors with PTSD had higher heart rate levels at the emergency room and reported more intrusive symptoms, exaggerated startle, and peritraumatic dissociation than those with major depression. Prior depression was associated with a higher prevalence of major depression and with more reported symptoms. _Conclusions:_ Major depression and PTSD are independent sequelae of traumatic events, have similar prognoses, and interact to increase distress and dysfunction. Both should be targeted by early treatment interventions and by neurobiological research.

(Am J Psychiatry 1998; 155:630–637)

An extensive literature associates the exposure to traumatic events with the occurrence of posttraumatic stress disorder (PTSD). Major depression has also been associated with stressful life events and with PTSD (table 1) (1–16). The co-occurrence of depression and PTSD (concurrent: up to 56%; lifetime: 95% [16]) exceeds the expected effect of simple coincidence. Alternative explanations include similarity in symptoms, common causation, and sequential causation, in which depression is assumed to be secondary to prolonged PTSD. Specific attributes of traumatic events may contribute to the occurrence of either PTSD or depression.

Symptoms of depression are frequently observed among survivors but seem to be more intense in those with PTSD. For example, Holocaust survivors with PTSD report more depressive symptoms than those without PTSD (17). Vietnam veterans hospitalized for PTSD had higher Hamilton Depression Rating Scale scores than veterans admitted for major depression (18). A significant correlation between the intensity of early PTSD symptoms and the occurrence of depression 19 months later has been documented in survivors of a marine disaster (19). The presence of comorbid depression has been shown to predict chronicity of PTSD (10, 20).

Studies evaluating the onset of PTSD and major depression following trauma arguably associate chronological order with causality. Most of these studies are retrospective and therefore rely on memory for sequence of remote events. Nevertheless, they suggest that depression is often "secondary" to PTSD. In the National Comorbidity Study, for example, 78.4% of subjects with comorbid major depression and PTSD reported that the onset of their affective disorder followed

Received June 18, 1997; revision received Oct. 30, 1997; accepted Dec. 11, 1997. From the Center for Traumatic Stress, Department of Psychiatry, Hadassah University Hospital; and Manchester VA Research Service, Harvard Medical School, Manchester, N.H. Address reprint requests to Dr. Shalev, Department of Psychiatry, Hadassah University Hospital, P.O. Box 12000, Jerusalem, 91120, Israel; ashalev@cc.huji.ac.il (e-mail).
Supported by NIMH research grant MH-50379.

88

TABLE 1. Studies Evaluating the Prevalence and Co-occurrence of PTSD and Depression

Study	Study Group	N	Design and Instruments[a]	Percent With PTSD	Depression	
					Percent	Percent of Subjects With PTSD
Sierles et al. (1), 1983	War veterans with PTSD (inpatients)	25	SADS	100	8[b]; 72[c]	8[b]; 72[c]
Davidson et al. (2), 1990	War veterans with PTSD	44	SADS-L.	100	59[c]	59[c]
Shore et al. (3), 1989	Community sample (Mt. St. Helens)	274	DIS	3[c]	—	51[b]
Green et al. (4), 1990	Vietnam veterans	200	Cross-section; SCID; SADS-L.	29[b]	15[b]	35[b]
Engdahl et al. (5), 1991	World War II prisoners of war	62	Cross-section	29[b]	26[b]	61[b]
Lima et al. (6), 1991	Earthquake survivors	102	Survey at 8 months; clinical interviews	42[d]	13[d]	—
Carlson and Rosser-Hogan (7), 1991	Cambodian refugees	50	Survey; Dissociation Experiences Scale; SCL-90	86[d]	80[d]	—
Mellman et al. (8), 1992	Veterans (outpatients)	60	Survey; SADS-L.	82[c]	68[c]	—
Roca et al. (9), 1992	Patients in burn unit	31	4-month follow-up; SCID	23[b]	—	29[b]
McFarlane and Papay (10), 1992	Firefighters	398	Cross-section at 42 months; DIS	18[d]	10[d]	51[d]
Smith et al. (11), 1990	Survivors of air crash disaster	46	Survey at 4–6 weeks; DIS	22[b]	41[b]	—
Ramsay et al. (12), 1993	Survivors of state violence	100	Retrospective case notes	31[d]	42[d]	65[d]
North et al. (13), 1989	Survivors of mass shooting	136	Cross-section at 1 month; DIS	26[b]	10[b]	30[b]
Blanchard et al. (14), 1996	Help-seeking survivors of motor vehicle accidents	158; 93	Case-control; Clinician-Administered PTSD Scale; SCID	39[b]	23[b]	53[b]
Kessler et al. (15), 1995	Population sample	5,877	Survey; DIS; Composite International Diagnostic Interview	8[c]	18[c]	48[c]
Bleich et al. (16), 1997	War veterans; help seeking	60	Cross-section at 7 years; SADS	87[b]; 100[c]	50[b]; 95[c]	56[b]; 95[c]

[a]SADS=Schedule for Affective Disorders and Schizophrenia, L.=Lifetime; DIS=Diagnostic Interview Schedule; SCID=Structured Clinical Interview for DSM-III-R.
[b]Current.
[c]Lifetime.
[d]Since trauma.

that of PTSD (15). Vietnam combat veterans similarly reported that the onset of phobias, major depression, and panic disorder followed that of PTSD (8). In a study of Israeli combat veterans, however, PTSD and depression started together in 65% of the cases, major depression preceded PTSD in 16% of the cases, and PTSD preceded major depression in 19% (16). The last study, however, addressed depression in help-seeking PTSD patients, examined 4–6 years after the war.

Psychiatric morbidity before the traumatic event seems to increase the likelihood of developing both PTSD and depression upon exposure (21, 22). However, Smith et al. (11) found that predisaster depression predicted depression but not PTSD. Prior mental disorders may interact with trauma intensity: Resnick et al. (23) found a positive association between precrime depression and PTSD in rape victims exposed to high crime stress but not in those exposed to low crime stress. Conversely, Foy et al. (24) found that family history of psychiatric disorders predicted PTSD in low combat exposure but not in high combat exposure.

The contribution of gender to development of PTSD has been evaluated by several authors (15, 20, 21). Differences in type of exposure have been found; female subjects are more frequently exposed to rape and molestation, and males are more frequently exposed to

combat, accidents, and physical attacks and have a higher prevalence of exposure in general (15, 20). The likelihood of developing PTSD upon exposure, however, was found to be higher in female subjects (15, 21).

The degree of exposure during a traumatic event has been specifically associated with the occurrence of PTSD. Exposure to atrocities was a specific predictor of PTSD, but not of depression, among Vietnam veterans (25). The intensity of torture predicted PTSD in civilians exposed to state violence (12, 26). Finally, in young Cambodian refugees, stressors that followed the trauma were associated with depression, whereas trauma intensity predicted PTSD (7).

The previous studies are limited by design and method. Specifically, most are retrospective, some have evaluated acute and others chronic PTSD, many have addressed help-seeking survivors, and few have used both continuous and categorical measures. Hence, they leave the following questions unanswered (27): Are major depression and PTSD independent consequences of trauma, each having its own course and prognosis? Which symptoms are shared, and which others separate the two disorders? Is there a hierarchy, such that prolonged PTSD is the cause of subsequent major depression or otherwise "dominates"? The present study addresses these questions, using a longitudinal design,

89

starting at the time of the traumatic event and following subjects into the stage of chronicity.

METHOD

As previously described in detail (28), patients arriving at the emergency room of a general hospital were recruited over a period of 3 years. Patients were examined by a research psychiatrist and were considered for inclusion if they were between 16 and 65 years old and had experienced an event meeting DSM-III-R criterion A for PTSD. Patients were not included if they suffered from head injury, burn injury, current or lifetime abuse of alcohol or illicit drugs (relatively rare in Israel), past or present psychosis, or life-threatening medical illness.

Subject candidates received information describing the study, were invited to participate, and gave written informed consent. They were subsequently assessed 1 week, 1 month, and 4 months after the traumatic event. A selected subgroup was assessed again 1 year after the traumatic event (see later discussion). The assessments included structured clinical interviews and self-reported and interviewer-generated psychometric material. Heart rate was recorded upon the subjects' arrival at the emergency room (see later discussion and reference 29).

Structured clinical interviews included the Clinician-Administered PTSD Scale (30) and the Hebrew version of the Structured Clinical Interview for DSM-III-R (SCID) (31). Both instruments had been validated and used in previous studies (28, 29, 32, 33), and both were administered by clinicians with extensive experience in diagnosis and treatment of PTSD. PTSD status was determined according to DSM-III-R criteria as measured by the Clinician-Administered PTSD Scale. Current and lifetime diagnoses of major depression were identified through use of the SCID.

Psychometric instruments included the Impact of Event Scale (34), State-Trait Anxiety Inventory (35), Beck Depression Inventory (36), Hamilton Depression Rating Scale (37), the civilian version of the Mississippi Scale for Combat-Related Posttraumatic Stress Disorder (38), and Peritraumatic Dissociation Experiences Questionnaire (39). The Impact of Event Scale, State-Trait Anxiety Inventory, Mississippi scale, Hamilton depression scale, Peritraumatic Dissociation Experiences Questionnaire, and Beck inventory have been used in previous studies and will not be described here (for details regarding the Peritraumatic Dissociation Experiences Questionnaire see references 28 and 33). An immediate response questionnaire included 14 items to assess the intensity of physical (e.g., pain), emotional (fear, anger), and negative cognitive (e.g., expecting doom) experiences during the traumatic event. Each item was rated 1 to 10 (1=none, 10=highest possible intensity), yielding response intensity scores ranging from 14 to 140. Finally, 12 professional raters, blind to the subjects' diagnostic status, listened to audiotaped scripts describing the traumatic events, as reported by each subject 1 week after the trauma (for details on script generation and recording see references 32 and 40), and rated event severity on a 1–10-point scale (1=not severe at all, 10=extreme severity). Event severity scores were averaged across the 12 raters.

Upon the subject's presentation to the emergency room, a registered nurse used a vital signs monitor to obtain heart rate. In order to avoid confounds related to physical injury, only subjects with minor injuries, who were released to their home within 12 hours of arrival at the emergency room, were included in the analyses of heart rate responses (N=84).

In order to evaluate the long-term outcome of early PTSD, subjects with PTSD at 4 months (N=37) were invited to attend an evaluation session 1 year after their traumatic events; 32 (86.5%) were located, and 23 (62.2%) were interviewed. Subjects with PTSD who were not assessed (N=9) included seven who did not wish to attend and two who were in the midst of litigation and wanted to use their follow-up visit to support their legal case. Thirty-five age- and gender-matched comparison subjects, without PTSD at 4 months, were also assessed 1 year after the trauma.

During the 1-week interview (mean=7.6 days after the trauma, SD=3.0), subjects provided a detailed description of the traumatic event and completed the Impact of Event Scale, state scale of the State-Trait Anxiety Inventory, Beck inventory, Hamilton depression scale, and Peritraumatic Dissociation Experiences Questionnaire. One-month interviews (mean=32.9 days following trauma, SD=6.4) and 4-month interviews (mean=116.7 days following trauma, SD= 29.4) also included the Mississippi scale and the Clinician-Administered PTSD Scale. The Peritraumatic Dissociation Experiences Questionnaire, which evaluated reactions at the time of the trauma, was not repeated.

RESULTS

Subjects, Noncompletion, and Exclusion

Of 420 traumatized individuals whose agreement was sought in the emergency room, 270 (64.3%) initially agreed to participate in the study, and 211 of those (78.1%; 103 men and 108 women) completed all interviews. Traumatic events among those who completed all interviews included road traffic accidents (N=181, 85.8%), work and domestic accidents (N=15, 7.1%), terrorist acts (N=9, 4.3%), combat events (N=4, 1.9%), and physical assault (N=2, 0.9%). The distribution of traumatic events among subjects who completed all interviews resembles that observed among 4,514 trauma survivors seen in the emergency room over a year in that the majority of traumatic events (N=3,670, 81.3%) were road traffic accidents, followed by 748 (16.6%) work and domestic accidents and 96 (2.1%) war events and terrorist attacks.

Subjects who did and did not complete all interviews had similar age and gender distribution, had undergone similar traumatic events, and had similar response-intensity scores. The groups differed, however, in 1-week psychometric scores (F=3.20, df=4, 267, p=0.03, multivariate analysis of variance [MANOVA]), with post hoc tests (Tukey's honestly significant difference for unequal sample sizes) showing lower 1-week scores on the Impact of Event Scale for subjects who did not complete all interviews than for those who did (mean=18.9, SD= 12.1, versus mean=27.9, SD=8.7) (p<0.01). Thus, subjects who did not complete the interviews tended to report fewer symptoms than those who did.

Occurrence of PTSD and Comorbidity

Sixty-three subjects (29.9%) met diagnostic criteria for PTSD at 1 month, and 37 (17.5%) had PTSD at 4 months. Forty subjects (19.0%) met criteria for major depression at 1 month, and 30 (14.2%) had major depression at 4 months. Comorbidity between major depression and PTSD was present at 1 month, and its frequency remained stable across time, affecting 28 (44.4%) of 63 PTSD patients at 1 month and 16 (43.2%) of 37 PTSD patients at 4 months. PTSD and major depression also occurred in isolation; between 1 and 4 months 30 individuals met criteria for PTSD without ever meeting criteria for major depression (42.2% of all PTSD), while 17 individuals had major depression without ever having PTSD (29.3% of all major depression). Forty-one individuals met criteria for both disorders at 1–4 months.

632

90

TABLE 2. Psychometric Test Scores for Survivors of Trauma (N=211) 1–4 Months After the Traumatic Event, by Diagnosis

	Score								ANOVA		
Variable and Time of Assessment	PTSD (N=30)		Major Depression (N=17)		PTSD and Major Depression (N=41)		No PTSD or Major Depression (N=123)		F (df=3, 207)	p	Post Hoc Least Significant Difference[a]
	Mean	SD	Mean	SD	Mean	SD	Mean	SD			
Event-related variables											
Event severity	5.26	1.74	5.11	1.87	5.47	1.65	4.56	1.49	3.7	0.02	PTSD, PTSD/MD > N
Response intensity	78.05	29.24	71.77	23.38	83.68	28.82	56.68	23.95	13.8	0.0001	PTSD, PTSD/MD > N
Peritraumatic Dissociation Experiences Questionnaire	22.73	7.30	18.67	7.45	25.85	5.92	16.96	5.93	21.8	0.0001	PTSD/MD > PTSD > MD, N
1 Week											
State-Trait Anxiety Inventory state scale	55.78	11.13	53.16	10.72	56.82	12.15	42.59	12.96	18.9	0.0001	All > N
Impact of Event Scale	39.91	10.88	25.93	11.72	40.83	14.00	20.71	12.34	36.3	0.0001	PTSD, PTSD/MD > MD, N
Beck Depression Inventory	20.06	11.58	12.88	7.35	23.49	10.81	8.01	7.05	39.1	0.0001	PTSD/MD, PTSD > MD > N
1 Month											
State-Trait Anxiety Inventory state scale	51.53	14.74	48.55	15.48	56.78	14.39	36.37	11.04	31.7	0.0001	All > N; PTSD/MD > MD
Impact of Event Scale	36.94	12.21	18.76	10.52	38.00	13.94	15.32	13.00	43.2	0.0001	PTSD/MD, PTSD > MD, N
Beck Depression Inventory	15.14	9.73	12.06	8.27	19.48	11.46	5.35	5.90	35.9	0.0001	PTSD/MD > PTSD, MD > N
Mississippi Scale for Combat-Related Posttraumatic Stress Disorder—civilian version	95.72	23.51	82.57	19.00	105.77	22.16	70.12	15.23	41.9	0.0001	PTSD/MD > PTSD > MD > N
SCID Global Assessment of Functioning Scale	81.86	12.16	82.58	14.08	73.50	16.69	87.67	7.19	12.1	0.0001	N > All; MD > PTSD/MD
4 Months											
State-Trait Anxiety Inventory state scale	44.34	14.37	41.54	14.49	51.44	13.49	33.29	10.06	26.7	0.0001	PTSD/MD > PTSD, MD > N
Impact of Event Scale	27.83	12.40	19.95	11.11	31.85	12.51	10.67	9.78	46.9	0.0001	PTSD/MD, PTSD > MD > N
Beck Depression Inventory	11.48	8.46	12.66	11.76	16.53	10.49	4.03	5.40	31.4	0.0001	All > N; PTSD/MD > PTSD
Mississippi Scale for Combat-Related Posttraumatic Stress Disorder—civilian version	90.48	22.31	83.26	20.34	101.25	23.38	66.59	14.72	42.0	0.0001	PTSD/MD > PTSD, MD > N
SCID Global Assessment of Functioning Scale	80.54	13.53	85.00	12.43	75.12	14.48	89.23	3.80	21.3	0.0001	N > PTSD/MD, PTSD; PTSD, MD > PTSD/MD

[a] "PTSD/MD" represents the group with PTSD and major depression; "N" represents the group with no PTSD or major depression.

Mobility within the diagnostic categories was very similar in that it consisted primarily of progressive recovery (the term recovery is used here in the restricted sense of not meeting full diagnostic criteria for a disorder). The recovery rate of subjects with major depression did not differ statistically from that of subjects with PTSD. By 4 months 27 (67.5%) of 40 subjects with major depression at 1 month had recovered from major depression, and 34 (54.0%) of those with PTSD at 1 month had recovered from PTSD (p=0.49, Fisher's exact probability test). Finally, 13 (9.6%) of 136 individuals without mental disorder at 1 month developed diagnosable disorders at 4 months, including PTSD (N= 2, 1.5%), major depression (N=3, 2.2%), and comorbid PTSD and major depression (N=8, 5.9%).

Recovery among subjects with comorbid disorders at 1 month did not differ from that observed among subjects without comorbidity. Nineteen subjects with comorbid PTSD and major depression at 1 month (67.9% of 28) had recovered from PTSD by 4 months, compared with 20 (57.1%) of 35 without comorbid major depression (χ^2=0.76, df=1, p=0.38). Similarly, 19 subjects with comorbid disorders at 1 month (67.9%) had recovered from major depression by 4 months, compared with eight (66.7%) of 12 subjects with major depression alone (χ^2=0.01, df=1).

Subjects' gender did not affect the frequency of PTSD and major depression at 1 month or 4 months. The ratios of men to women were as follows: at 1 month— PTSD, 29:34, and major depression, 17:23 (maximum

91

TABLE 3. Clinician-Administered PTSD Scale Scores for Survivors of Trauma (N=51) 4 Months After the Traumatic Event, by Diagnosis

	Score						ANOVA		
DSM-III-R Criterion	PTSD (N=21)		Major Depression (N=14)		PTSD and Major Depression (N=16)		F (df=2, 48)	p	Post Hoc Least Significant Difference[a]
	Mean	SD	Mean	SD	Mean	SD			
B: reexperiencing									
Intrusive recollections	1.52	1.73	0.14	1.79	2.27	1.64	9.75	0.0005	PTSD/MD > PTSD > MD
Recurrent intrusive dreams	0.95	1.46	0.14	0.89	1.00	1.74	2.60	0.09	PTSD/MD, PTSD > MD
Acting as if event is recurring	0.43	0.98	0.14	0.53	0.75	1.39	1.28	0.29	
Distress upon reexposure	2.52	1.29	1.50	2.05	3.00	1.03	4.41	0.02	PTSD/MD, PTSD > MD
Physiological reactivity	1.57	1.59	0.79	2.05	1.20	1.53	1.29	0.29	
C: avoidance									
Efforts to avoid thoughts or feelings associated with the trauma	2.24	1.39	0.36	0.87	1.93	1.64	6.16	0.005	PTSD/MD, PTSD > MD
Efforts to avoid activities that arouse recollections of the trauma	1.95	1.70	0.36	1.79	1.80	1.62	4.69	0.02	PTSD/MD, PTSD > MD
Inability to recall	1.00	1.54	1.07	1.95	1.47	1.19	0.27	0.74	
Diminished interest	2.81	1.72	0.79	0.89	2.87	1.18	14.82	0.0001	PTSD/MD, PTSD > MD
Detachment or estrangement	2.00	1.69	0.50	1.79	1.93	1.71	4.62	0.02	PTSD/MD, PTSD > MD
Restricted range of affect	1.62	1.33	0.21	2.19	2.07	1.78	6.13	0.005	PTSD/MD, PTSD > MD
Sense of foreshortened future	0.00		0.29	1.06	1.00	1.73	3.68	0.04	PTSD/MD > PTSD
D: hyperarousal									
Difficulty falling or staying asleep	2.24	1.40	2.07	1.79	3.13	0.92	2.00	0.15	
Irritability or anger	2.43	1.69	2.07	1.79	3.60	1.32	2.92	0.07	
Difficulty concentrating	2.14	1.82	1.50	1.54	2.20	1.51	0.98	0.38	
Hypervigilance	1.48	1.58	0.93	2.00	1.13	1.41	0.65	0.53	
Exaggerated startle	1.86	1.71	0.50	1.67	2.13	1.72	6.50	0.005	PTSD/MD, PTSD > MD

[a] "PTSD/MD" represents the group with PTSD and major depression.

likelihood χ^2=1.66, df=4, p=0.80); at 4 months—PTSD, 22:15, and major depression, 13:17 (maximum likelihood χ^2=6.09, df=4, p=0.19).

Symptom Severity

Subjects with comorbid PTSD and major depression tended to report more symptoms and were judged to have lower functioning (Global Assessment of Functioning Scale from the SCID). Table 2 provides means, analyses of variance (ANOVAs), and post hoc comparisons among four diagnostic groups: PTSD, major depression, comorbid PTSD and major depression, and those with neither PTSD nor major depression between 1 and 4 months. Given the large differences between subjects with a mental disorder and those without, MANOVAs comparing the three groups with diagnoses (PTSD, major depression, comorbid disorders) were performed on all psychometric interviews, at each stage of the study, yielding significant differences at 1 week (F=3.63, df=6, 170, p<0.002), 1 month (F=3.71, df=8, 168, p<0.001), and 4 months (F=1.94, df=8, 168, p<0.05).

Stepwise logistic regression evaluated the relative contribution of 1-month diagnostic status to PTSD at 4 months. Having PTSD at 1 month significantly predicted PTSD at 4 months (χ^2=15.53, df=1, p<0.0001); having major depression did not improve significantly that prediction (difference in χ^2=1.51, df=2, p=0.22); and having comorbid PTSD and major depression added significantly to predictions made from both PTSD and major depression status (added χ^2=35.95, df=3, p<0.0001).

Symptom Overlap and Specificity

In order to compare the diagnostic groups on symptoms of PTSD and depression, 4-month Clinician-Administered PTSD Scale frequency scores and Hamilton depression scale scores are reported: symptoms at 4 months were less likely to reflect an acute response to the trauma than were those recorded at 1 month. As shown in table 3, the groups with PTSD alone and comorbid PTSD and major depression differed from the major depression group on several Clinician-Administered PTSD Scale items. MANOVA for clusters B, C, and D yielded the following: F=2.37, df=10, 88, p<0.02; F=3.71, df=14, 82, p<0.0001; and F=1.98, df=12, 82, p<0.05, respectively. The PTSD and major depression groups differed in PTSD symptoms that are typically thought to reflect depression (i.e., diminished interest, detachment or estrangement, restricted range of affect, and sense of a foreshortened future). The groups had similar levels of hyperarousal symptoms (with the exception of exaggerated startle). As for depressive symptoms, the groups had comparable Hamilton depression scale scores (MANOVA F<1), although the PTSD group reported more insomnia and the major depression group reported greater loss of appetite (table 4).

Heart Rate Responses

The occurrence of posttraumatic disorders among subjects evaluated for heart rate (N=84) did not differ from that among the four diagnostic groups: At 4

92

TABLE 4. Hamilton Depression Rating Scale Scores for Survivors of Trauma (N=51) 4 Months After the Traumatic Event, by Diagnosis

	Score						ANOVA		
Hamilton Scale Item	PTSD (N=21)		Major Depression (N=14)		PTSD and Major Depression (N=16)		F (df=2, 43)	p	Post Hoc Least Significant Difference[a]
	Mean	SD	Mean	SD	Mean	SD			
Depressed mood	1.82	1.38	2.17	1.40	2.66	1.27	1.58	0.21	
Guilt feelings	0.42	0.90	0.41	1.16	0.80	1.26	0.61	0.55	
Suicidal ideation	0.16	0.68	0.67	1.07	0.20	0.56	1.80	0.18	
Initial insomnia	1.84	1.70	1.33	1.61	2.77	1.48	3.01	0.06	PTSD/MD > MD
Middle insomnia	1.32	1.42	0.52	1.24	2.40	1.68	5.73	0.01	PTSD/MD > PTSD > MD
Delayed insomnia	1.23	1.51	0.25	0.87	1.67	1.87	2.99	0.06	PTSD/MD > MD
Work and interest	1.73	1.48	1.75	1.60	2.53	1.55	1.35	0.27	
Retardation	0.58	1.02	0.67	1.07	0.87	1.88	0.29	0.74	
Agitation	0.63	0.76	0.58	0.79	0.87	1.87	0.39	0.68	
Anxiety—psychological	1.50	1.20	1.92	1.31	1.85	1.21	0.62	0.54	
Anxiety—somatic	0.47	1.02	0.67	1.23	0.86	1.29	0.43	0.65	
Loss of appetite	0.63	0.83	1.58	1.73	1.33	1.23	2.51	0.09	MD > PTSD
Anergia	1.79	1.23	1.25	1.36	2.47	1.06	3.43	0.05	PTSD/MD > MD
Loss of libido	1.37	1.57	1.25	1.54	1.66	1.54	0.26	0.76	
Hypochondriasis	0.00		0.00		0.00				
Weight loss	0.47	0.90	0.66	0.98	0.80	1.21	0.43	0.65	
Loss of insight	0.00		0.00		0.00				

[a]"PTSD/MD" represents the group with PTSD and major depression.

months 15 subjects (17.9%) had developed PTSD, 23 (27.4%) had comorbid PTSD and major depression, four (4.7%) had major depression, and 42 (50.0%) had no disorder (total χ^2=3.93, df=3, p=0.27). The mean heart rate levels at the emergency room were as follows: for patients with PTSD, mean=94.6 bpm, SD=18.1; for comorbid PTSD and major depression, mean=87.3, SD=12.4; for major depression, mean=83.5, SD=4.8; and for no disorder, mean=82.3, SD=9.9. ANOVA for heart rate was significant (F=3.83, df=3, 80, p<0.02), with post hoc tests (Tukey's honestly significant difference) showing significantly higher heart rate for subjects with PTSD than for subjects with no disorder (p< 0.05). This difference remained significant when event severity was controlled by means of analysis of covariance (F=2.82, df=3, 77, p<0.05; post hoc [PTSD versus no disorder] p<0.04).

Effect of Prior Depression

Forty-eight individuals (22.8% of 211) had suffered from major depression before the traumatic event. Subjects with prior depression did not differ from all others in age and trauma severity but had higher Beck inventory scores at 1 week (mean=19.47, SD=11.64, versus mean=11.06, SD=9.72) (t=4.98, df=209, p<0.0001), 1 month (mean=15.42, SD=11.71, versus mean=8.36, SD=8.69) (t=4.40, df=209, p<0.0001), and 4 months (mean=12.74, SD=9.78, versus mean=6.81, SD=8.60) (t=4.02, df=209, p<0.0001) and higher Mississippi scale scores at 1 month (mean=96.52, SD=22.94, versus mean=77.42, SD=21.93) (t=4.93, df=209, p<0.0001) and 4 months (mean=91.93, SD=32.12, versus mean= 73.74, SD=21.53) (t=4.95, df=209, p<0.0001).

Within 4 months of the traumatic event eight of the

subjects with prior depression (16.6%) had developed major depression, 15 (31.3%) had developed comorbid depression and PTSD, and seven (14.6%) had developed PTSD. PTSD, major depression, and comorbid major depression and PTSD following trauma occurred more frequently in subjects with prior depression than in those without prior depression (for PTSD: χ^2=4.13, df=1, p<0.05; for major depression: χ^2=13.04, df=1, p< 0.0005; for comorbid major depression and PTSD: χ^2= 5.02, df=1, p<0.03).

1-Year Follow-Up

The subgroup of subjects followed for 1 year (N=58; 28 men and 30 women) did not differ from those who were not followed (N=153) in type of traumatic event (road traffic accidents in 50 [86.2%] and 131 [85.6%], respectively) and in symptom intensity at 1 week, 1 month, and 4 months. MANOVAs for all psychometric interviews at each stage showed no main effect of being in the 1-year follow-up group, a consistent main effect of having PTSD at 4 months (for 1 week: F=9.14, df=5, 197, p<0.0001; for 1 month: F=14.13, df=6, 199, p< 0.0001; for 4 months: F=35.72, df=8, 195, p<0.0001), and no interaction between PTSD status at 4 months and being in the 1-year follow-up group.

Thirteen subjects who were followed for 1 year had comorbid PTSD and major depression at 4 months, and 10 had PTSD alone. Comorbidity at 1 year was very similar, with eight (61.5%) of 13 subjects having PTSD and major depression (χ^2<1). Recovery from comorbid PTSD and major depression at 4 months was somewhat lower (yet statistically nonsignificant) than that from PTSD or major depression alone: 40.0% versus 54.5% for PTSD and 62.5% for major depression (χ^2=2.08,

93

df=6, p=0.36). Finally, prior depression (N=16) was associated with a greater risk of having major depression at 1 year and with higher 1-year Beck inventory and Mississippi scale scores (Beck inventory: mean=16.82, SD=14.59, versus mean=6.68, SD=9.28 [t=2.80, df=57, p<0.01]; Mississippi scale: mean=104.28, SD=30.75, versus mean=76.25, SD=25.54 [t=3.29, df=57, p<0.002]).

DISCUSSION

The results of this study show that extreme events can be associated with the early and simultaneous development of both PTSD and major depression or a combination thereof. The remission rates of these disorders were similar. The intensity of depressive symptoms in PTSD resembles that of major depression, yet the disorders differed in symptoms of insomnia, intrusion, and auditory startle. Individuals with comorbid PTSD and major depression reported more symptoms. Prior depression was associated with a greater risk for developing major depression and with reporting more symptoms across time.

In contrast with most previous studies (8, 15) but consistent with that of Bleich et al. (16), this study does not show a chronological development leading from PTSD to major depression. Our results support the idea (10, 20) that within PTSD depressive symptoms predict severity, but clear prediction of chronicity was not observed. Event severity and response intensity did not differentiate PTSD from major depression (as would be predicted given previous studies [7, 10, 11, 25, 26]), but this may be explained by similarity between the traumatic events (short incidents, followed by immediate rescue) in this study. Global Assessment of Functioning Scale scores for subjects with mental disorders, in this study, were relatively high, yet this may be because of the early stage of the disorder and lack of chronic impairment.

Elevated heart rate levels at the emergency room were specifically associated with PTSD. These data suggest that early autonomic activation may be specifically linked with subsequent PTSD, while the mechanisms that mediate the occurrence of depression may be of a different nature.

In reading these results one should be aware of the study's limitations, which include a relatively short follow-up period, a group of survivors of single and short events, and sampling from an emergency room of a general hospital. Other traumatic circumstances, such as rape, disaster, captivity, or torture, may involve different degrees of loss, humiliation, relocation, or prolonged exposure and may result in different ratios of depression and PTSD. However, the occurrence of depression at the early stages of such short events argues that these widely acceptable predictors of sadness and helplessness are not necessary in order to trigger depressive disorders among survivors.

Indeed, the salient finding of this study is the co-occurrence of PTSD and major depression following

trauma and their complex interaction. Such knowledge argues for a broader conceptualization of the response to traumatic events, going beyond the present emphasis on PTSD. Future studies should, therefore, address the occurrence of mood and anxiety disorders among survivors. They should also go beyond categorical outcome measures to include continuous dimensions of the response to trauma, such as symptoms and bodily responses. Finally, early treatment interventions should target both PTSD and depression.

REFERENCES

1. Sierles FS, Chen J-J, McFarland RE, Taylor MA: Posttraumatic stress disorder and concurrent psychiatric illness: a preliminary report. Am J Psychiatry 1983; 140:1177–1179
2. Davidson JR, Kudler HS, Saunders WB, Smith RD: Symptom and comorbidity patterns in World War II and Vietnam veterans with posttraumatic stress disorder. Compr Psychiatry 1990; 31: 162–170
3. Shore JH, Vollmer WM, Tatum EL: Community patterns of posttraumatic stress disorders. J Nerv Ment Dis 1989; 177:681–685
4. Green BL, Grace MC, Lindy JD, Gleser GC, Leonard A: Risk factors for PTSD and other diagnoses in a general sample of Vietnam veterans. Am J Psychiatry 1990; 147:729–733
5. Engdahl BE, Speed N, Eberly RE, Schwartz J: Comorbidity of psychiatric disorders and personality profiles of American World War II prisoners of war. J Nerv Ment Dis 1991; 179:181–187
6. Lima BR, Pai S, Santacruz H, Lozano J: Psychiatric disorders among poor victims following a major disaster: Armero, Columbia. J Nerv Ment Dis 1991; 179:420–427
7. Carlson EB, Rosser-Hogan R: Trauma experiences, posttraumatic stress, dissociation, and depression in Cambodian refugees. Am J Psychiatry 1991; 148:1548–1551
8. Mellman TA, Randolph CA, Brawman-Mintzer O, Flores LP, Milanes FJ: Phenomenology and course of psychiatric disorders associated with combat-related posttraumatic stress disorder. Am J Psychiatry 1992; 149:1568–1574
9. Roca RP, Spence RJ, Munster AM: Posttraumatic adaptation and distress among adult burn survivors. Am J Psychiatry 1992; 149:1234–1238
10. McFarlane AC, Papay P: Multiple diagnoses in posttraumatic stress disorder in the victims of a natural disaster. J Nerv Ment Dis 1992; 180:498–504
11. Smith EM, North CS, McCool RE, Shea JM: Acute postdisaster psychiatric disorders: identification of persons at risk. Am J Psychiatry 1990; 147:202–206
12. Ramsay R, Gorst Unsworth C, Turner S: Psychiatric morbidity in survivors of organised state violence including torture. A retrospective series. Br J Psychiatry 1993; 162:55–59
13. North CS, Smith EM, McCool RE, Shea JM: Short-term psychopathology in eyewitnesses to mass murder. Hosp Community Psychiatry 1989; 40:1293–1295
14. Blanchard EB, Hickling FJ, Taylor AE, Loos WR, Forneris CA, Jaccard J: Who develops PTSD from motor vehicle accidents? Behav Res Ther 1996; 34:1–10
15. Kessler RC, Sonnega A, Bromet E, Hughes M, Nelson CB: Posttraumatic stress disorder in the National Comorbidity Survey. Arch Gen Psychiatry 1995; 52:1048–1060
16. Bleich A, Koslowsky M, Dolev A, Lerer B: Post-traumatic stress disorder and depression. Br J Psychiatry 1997; 170:479–482
17. Yehuda R, Kahana B, Southwick SM, Giller EL Jr: Depressive features in Holocaust survivors with post-traumatic stress disorder. J Trauma Stress 1994; 7:699–704
18. Southwick SM, Yehuda R, Giller EL Jr: Characterization of depression in war-related posttraumatic stress disorder. Am J Psychiatry 1991; 148:179–183
19. Joseph S, Yule W, Williams R: The Herald of Free Enterprise

94

disaster: the relationship of intrusion and avoidance to subsequent depression and anxiety. Behav Res Ther 1994; 32:115–117

20. Breslau N, Davis GC, Andreski P, Peterson E: Traumatic events and posttraumatic stress disorder in an urban population of young adults. Arch Gen Psychiatry 1991; 48:216–222

21. Breslau N, Davis GC: Posttraumatic stress disorder in an urban population of young adults: risk factors for chronicity. Am J Psychiatry 1992; 149:671–675

22. McFarlane AC: The aetiology of post-traumatic morbidity: predisposing, precipitating and perpetuating factors. Br J Psychiatry 1989; 154:221–228

23. Resnick HS, Kilpatrick DG, Best CL, Kramer TL: Vulnerability-stress factors in development of posttraumatic stress disorder. J Nerv Ment Dis 1992; 180:424–430

24. Foy DW, Resnick HS, Sipprelle R, Carroll EM: Premilitary, military, and postmilitary factors in the development of combat-related posttraumatic stress disorder. Behav Therapist 1987; 10:3–9

25. Breslau N, Davis GC: Posttraumatic stress disorder: the etiologic specificity of wartime stressors. Am J Psychiatry 1987; 144:578–583

26. Basoglu M, Paker M, Paker O, Ozmen E, Marks I, Incesu C, Sahin D, Sarimurat N: Psychological effects of torture: a comparison of tortured with nontortured political activists in Turkey. Am J Psychiatry 1994; 151:76–81

27. Keane TM, Wolfe J: Comorbidity in post-traumatic stress disorder: an analysis of community and clinical studies. J Appl Soc Psychol 1990; 20:1776–1788

28. Shalev AY, Freedman S, Peri T, Brandes D, Sahar T: Predicting PTSD in civilian trauma survivors: prospective evaluation of self report and clinician administered instruments. Br J Psychiatry 1997; 170:558–564

29. Shalev AY, Sahar T, Freedman S, Peri T, Glick N, Brandes D, Orr SP, Pitman RK: A prospective study of heart rate responses following trauma and the subsequent development of PTSD. Arch Gen Psychiatry (in press)

30. Blake DD, Weathers FW, Nagy LM, Kaloupek DG, Klauminzer G, Charney DS, Keane TM: A clinician rating scale for assessing current and lifetime PTSD: the CAPS-1. Behavior Therapist 1990; 13:187–188

31. Spitzer RL, Williams JBW, Gibbon M: Structured Clinical Interview for DSM-III-R (SCID). New York, New York State Psychiatric Institute, Biometrics Research, 1987

32. Shalev AY, Orr SP, Pitman RK: Psychophysiologic assessment of traumatic imagery in Israeli civilian patients with posttraumatic stress disorder. Am J Psychiatry 1993; 150:620–624

33. Shalev AY, Peri T, Canetti L, Schreiber S: Predictors of PTSD in injured trauma survivors: a prospective study. Am J Psychiatry 1996; 153:219–225

34. Horowitz MJ, Wilner N, Alvarez W: Impact of Event Scale: a measure of subjective stress. Psychosom Med 1979; 41:209–218

35. Speilberger CD: Manual for State-Trait Anxiety Inventory. Palo Alto, Calif, Consulting Psychologists Press, 1983

36. Beck AT, Ward CH, Mendelson M, Mock J, Erbaugh J: An inventory for measuring depression. Arch Gen Psychiatry 1961; 4:561–571

37. Hamilton M: A rating scale for depression. J Neurol Neurosurg Psychiatry 1960; 23:56–62

38. Keane TM, Caddell JM, Taylor KL: Mississippi Scale for Combat-Related Posttraumatic Stress Disorder: three studies in reliability and validity. J Consult Clin Psychol 1988; 56:85–90

39. Marmar CR, Weiss DS, Schlenger WE, Fairbank JA, Jordan BK, Kulka RA, Hough RL: Peritraumatic dissociation and posttraumatic stress in male Vietnam theater veterans. Am J Psychiatry 1994; 151:902–907

40. Pitman RK, Orr SP, Forgue DF, Altman B, de-Jong JB, Herz LR: Psychophysiologic assessment of posttraumatic stress disorder imagery in Vietnam combat veterans. Arch Gen Psychiatry 1987; 44:970–975

95

Psychological Medicine, 1998, **28**, 773–788.   Printed in the United Kingdom
© 1998 Cambridge University Press

Co-morbidity and familial aggregation of alcoholism and anxiety disorders

K. R. MERIKANGAS,[1] D. E. STEVENS, B. FENTON, M. STOLAR, S. O'MALLEY, S. W. WOODS AND N. RISCH

From the Departments of Epidemiology and Psychiatry, Yale University School of Medicine and Department of Genetics, Stanford University School of Medicine, CT, USA

ABSTRACT

Background. This study examined the patterns of familial aggregation and co-morbidity of alcoholism and anxiety disorders in the relatives of 165 probands selected for alcoholism and/or anxiety disorders compared to those of 61 unaffected controls.

Methods. Probands were either selected from treatment settings or at random from the community. DSM-III-R diagnoses were obtained for all probands and their 1053 first-degree relatives, based on direct interview or family history information.

Results. The findings indicate that: (1) alcoholism was associated with anxiety disorders in the relatives, particularly among females; (2) both alcoholism and anxiety disorders were highly familial; (3) the familial aggregation of alcoholism was attributable to alcohol dependence rather than to alcohol abuse, particularly among male relatives; and (4) the pattern of co-aggregation of alcohol dependence and anxiety disorders in families differed according to the subtype of anxiety disorder; there was evidence of a partly shared diathesis underlying panic and alcoholism, whereas social phobia and alcoholism tended to aggregate independently.

Conclusions. The finding that the onset of social phobia tended to precede that of alcoholism, when taken together with the independence of familial aggregation of social phobia and alcoholism support a self-medication hypothesis as the explanation for the co-occurrence of social phobia and alcoholism. In contrast, the lack of a systematic pattern in the order of onset of panic and alcoholism among subjects with both disorders as well as evidence for shared underlying familial risk factors suggests that co-morbidity between panic disorder and alcoholism is not a consequence of self-medication of panic symptoms. The results of this study emphasize the importance of examining co-morbid disorders and subtypes thereof in identifying sources of heterogeneity in the pathogenesis of alcoholism.

INTRODUCTION

Association between alcoholism and anxiety

An association between alcoholism and the anxiety disorders has been observed in both clinical and epidemiological samples (see reviews of George *et al.* 1990*a*; Kushner *et al.* 1990; Wesner, 1990; Schuckit & Hesselbrock, 1994; Crowley & Riggs, 1995). The strength of this association in recent large-scale epidemiological studies suggests that co-morbidity between alcoholism and anxiety states is not attributable to an increased frequency of treatment-seeking among those with co-morbidity (Helzer & Pryzbeck, 1988; Regier *et al.* 1990; Angst, 1993; Kessler *et al.* 1996). However, the nature of this association remains unclear, largely because of the heterogeneity of both disorders and partly as a result of the disparate methodologies employed among the studies that have been conducted so far.

Studies that have investigated co-morbidity according to specific subtypes of anxiety and alcoholism reveal that the association is greater

[1] Address for correspondence: Dr Kathleen R. Merikangas, Genetic Epidemiology Research Unit, Yale University School of Medicine, 40 Temple Street, New Haven, CT 06510, USA.

for phobic disorders than for panic and generalized anxiety states, and for alcohol dependence than for abuse (Mullaney & Trippett, 1979; Bowen *et al.* 1984; Smail *et al.* 1984; Stockwell *et al.* 1984; Hesselbrock *et al.* 1985; Roelofs, 1985; Weiss & Rosenburg, 1985; Chambless *et al.* 1987; Helzer & Pryzbeck, 1988; Ross *et al.* 1988; Kushner *et al.* 1990; Regier *et al.* 1990; Kessler *et al.* 1996). However, Schuckit & Hesselbrock (1994) concluded that the rates of co-morbid primary anxiety disorders and alcoholism do not significantly exceed population base rates of these disorders.

Comorbidity in family study data

Although the familial aggregation of both alcoholism (Cotton, 1979; Merikangas, 1990*a*; McGue, 1994; Merikangas *et al.* 1994) and anxiety disorders (Carey & Gottesman, 1981; Torgersen & Philos, 1986; Skre *et al.* 1994; Woodman & Crowe, 1996) has been demonstrated in numerous studies, only a few have systematically and simultaneously examined the patterns of co-aggregation of both of these disorders among first-degree relatives of affected probands. Numerous family studies of both alcoholism and anxiety disorders have reported elevated rates of the other condition among relatives (Cohen *et al.* 1951; Noyes *et al.* 1978; Munjack & Moss, 1981; Harris *et al.* 1983; Leckman *et al.* 1983; Merikangas *et al.* 1985). The classic family study of neurocirculatory asthenia by Cohen and colleagues (1951) revealed increased rates of alcoholism among the fathers and brothers of patients compared with those of controls. Indeed, Cohen and colleagues (1951) considered alcoholism as a *forme fruste* of neurocirculatory asthenia, believed to be equivalent to the contemporary concept of panic disorder. However, because comorbidity was not the major focus of these studies, the rates of co-morbid disorders among the relatives were not presented according to comorbidity in the proband. Without such stratification, one cannot determine whether the disorders were transmitted independently.

After removal of artefactual sources of comorbidity such as exclusive use of uncontrolled clinic-based samples, overlap in diagnostic criteria, or failure to consider the effect of confounding factors which may induce comorbidity (e.g. gender), the two possible

mechanisms for associations between disorders are: (1) common aetiology, with the index and co-morbid disorders representing alternative manifestations of the same underlying factors, or different stages of the same disease; and (2) causal, in which an index disorder 'causes', or predisposes to the development of the co-morbid disorder.

The chief methods for examining mechanisms for co-morbidity are prospective longitudinal studies of the stability, order of onset and course of co-morbid disorders, treatment studies that discriminate differential treatment response by patterns of co-morbidity, and family and twin studies which examine whether co-morbidity is attributable to common familial or genetic factors. The present study employs the family study method to discriminate between alternative mechanisms for the co-occurrence of two or more disorders by examining patterns of expression of co-morbid and non-co-morbid forms of the disorders among the relatives of probands with co-morbid and non-co-morbid disorders (Merikangas, 1990*b*).

If the two disorders were manifestations of common underlying risk factors, relatives of probands with either disorder alone should have elevated rates of the other disorder alone as compared with expected population rates. Therefore, relatives of probands with anxiety alone should have an increased risk of alcoholism alone and the converse. In contrast, if the relationship between two disorders were aetiological (one condition causing the other) it would be expected that relatives would manifest an increased risk of the causal disorder and the combination of the two syndromes, but not the other disorder alone.

In order to discriminate between these alternatives, family studies must include sufficient numbers of probands with each of the disorders under investigation without a history of the other conditions, and a sample of controls without either of the disorders under study in order to estimate the differences in rates of disorders among the relatives of affected probands *versus* controls using similar sampling and diagnostic procedures.

There are few family studies which were designed specifically to investigate patterns of co-morbidity. We have previously employed family study data to address mechanisms for co-morbidity of depression and migraine (Merikangas *et al.* 1988) as well as alcoholism, anxiety and depression (Merikangas *et al.* 1994).

Background to the present study

Application of the family study method to our previous work which examined the co-morbidity and co-aggregation of alcoholism, anxiety and depression in a family study of depression with secondary anxiety or alcoholism, yielded evidence for the aggregation of alcoholism and anxiety as well as evidence for the co-aggregation of both disorders within families (Merikangas *et al.* 1994). In a similar study, Maier and colleagues (1993; Maier & Merikangas, 1994) concluded that there are shared susceptibility factors for alcoholism and panic based on an elevated risk of alcoholism among the relatives of probands with pure panic disorder.

METHOD

Sample characteristics

A total of 226 probands were selected from out-patient speciality clinics for alcoholism and/or anxiety disorders at the Connecticut Mental Health Center (New Haven, Connecticut) or through a random digit dialling procedure in the greater New Haven area. The probands were assigned to one of four lifetime diagnostic groups based on an algorithm designed to reflect predominant level of psychopathology: 47 probands and a DSM-III-R diagnosis of alcohol dependence with a DSM-III-R anxiety disorder; 42 probands with a DSM-III-R diagnosis of alcohol dependence without an anxiety disorder; 76 probands with a DSM-III-R diagnosis of anxiety disorders; and 61 normal controls with no lifetime history of a DSM-III-R Axis I disorder. Assignment to the anxiety groups was based on the presence of either DSM-III-R panic disorder with or without agoraphobia or social phobia. Probands assigned to alcohol groups must have had alcohol dependence for at least 1 year with an age of offset greater than 25 years of age in order to rule out episodic experimentation during the high-school, college and post-college years.

Based upon review by clinicians with expertise in substance abuse, probands were excluded from the study if there was evidence of significant organic mental impairment, schizoaffective dis-order, schizophrenia or a significant history of drug dependence, particularly intravenous drug use. Probands with a lifetime history of drug abuse or dependence that overshadowed that of alcoholism (e.g. based on an algorithm taking into consideration substance of choice, age of onset, duration, severity, number of symptoms, quantity, frequency and chronicity) were assigned to a separate diagnostic group and will be analysed separately in conjunction with a series of probands in treatment for drug abuse (e.g. marijuana, cocaine and/or opioid abuse/dependence). The normal controls were recruited using a random digit dialling procedure in which they were drawn from the same general population as those of the affected probands. The control group was subjected to the same protocol as the treatment groups. They were considered to be controls if there was no evidence of DSM-III-R psychopathology. The rationale for including a combination of clinically referred probands and those recruited at random from the community was to minimize bias associated with treatment-seeking (e.g. Berkson's bias). All probands were interviewed directly according to the procedures described below.

Interview procedures

Probands

Direct interviews were conducted with all probands and a pedigree was generated that identified spouses, ex-spouses with whom probands have children and first-degree biological relatives. The proband also provided family history information on all his/her first-degree relatives. Permission to contact first-degree relatives as well as their addresses and phone numbers was obtained at the initial interview.

An independent interviewer, blind to the diagnosis of the proband, was then assigned to contact the spouse or first-degree relatives of the proband. Children of the proband under age 18 were enrolled in a longitudinal high-risk component of the study using parallel as well as additional measures. Relatives were directly interviewed either by telephone or in person. In general, studies that have compared the reliability of telephone *versus* personal interviews have found that there was no significant difference in reporting in the two types of interviews (Colombotos, 1969; Aneshensel *et al.* 1982; Weeks *et al.* 1983). Hochstim (1963) found that the telephone interview may even be more reliable than direct interviews when the questions are comprised of socially undesirable topics, such as drinking behaviour. Indeed, Rohde (1997) found excellent agreement between face-to-face and telephone interviews for the diagnoses of anxiety disorders (kappa = 0·87); major depression (kappa = 0·96) and substance use disorders (kappa = 1·0).

Relatives

The total sample used for the familial aggregation analyses included 224 probands who had 1053 adult first-degree relatives. Approximately equal proportions of relatives were interviewed across proband groups. Entry criteria required that at least one relative and child under 18 participate. Sixty-five per cent (80 % parents, 30 % siblings and 90 % offspring) of the relatives of probands who met study criteria were interviewed directly. Fifty-six per cent of the relatives were queried face-to-face. These rates did not differ significantly by proband diagnostic group and are in accordance with previous family studies of psychiatric disorders (Weissman *et al.* 1986; Mirin *et al.* 1991), and generally compare favourably with previous family studies of alcoholism. The refusal rate for participation of first-degree relatives was approximately 20 %. Biases resulting from lack of consent of probands in family studies are discussed by Norden *et al.* (1995). Interview status was controlled in the analytic models presented below.

Diagnostic assessments

Direct interview

The diagnostic interview for adults was the semi-structured Schedule for Affective Disorders and Schizophrenia (SADS), current and lifetime version (Endicott & Spitzer, 1978), which was modified to obtain DSM-III and DSM-III-R criteria (American Psychiatric Association, 1980, 1987). The major modifications of this instrument include: (*a*) addition of an open-ended section designed to obtain a more close approximation of the clinical interview, to facilitate rapport between the interviewer and subject and to identify key diagnostic sections to be completed; (*b*) addition of questions on the inter-relationships of disorders in terms of temporal sequence and shared symptomatology

(for subjects meeting less than full criteria); (*c*) elicitation of information on psychiatric disorders and subthreshold manifestations for multiple diagnostic systems; and (*d*) expansion of the substance abuse section to obtain more detailed information on the patterns of use of each drug class, their inter-relationships, and on the course of substance use and abuse. Each diagnostic section of the instrument contained a question regarding whether co-morbid symptoms occurred exclusively in the context of drinking.

Family history information

The method employed for obtaining information on the family history of psychiatric disorders was the Family History-Research Diagnostic Criteria (FH-RDC) developed by Andreasen and colleagues for the collaborative family study of affective disorders (Andreasen *et al.* 1977). The interview, which was modified to enable collection of DSM-III and DSM-III-R criteria, is comprised of the following sections: questions regarding the degree of familiarity and contact with the index relative; an open-ended summary of the history of emotional and behavioural problems and social adjustment of the index relative or spouse; and key probes regarding each major diagnostic area of the DSM-III-R, Axis I adult disorders, antisocial personality disorder, and history of childhood disorders including conduct disorder, attention deficit hyperactivity disorder, and childhood anxiety. Symptoms, severity, impairment, age at onset and treatment history were obtained regarding each syndrome for which the key phenomenological probe was endorsed. The reliability of the diagnostic interview has been investigated by comparing the results of direct interviews of the index person to those obtained by family history. The kappa values for substance abuse and behaviour disorders are in the excellent range, whereas those for specific emotional disorders are acceptable, but far less reliable than those for more observable behaviours.

Training and reliability of interviewers

The interviewers were either psychologists or psychiatric social workers with clinical experience in psychiatric settings. Extensive effort was devoted to establishing the reliability of the diagnostic assessments in several phases of variable length until satisfactory levels of agreement were obtained. Kappas derived from joint ratings of individual interviews were generally higher for substance abuse (0·72–0·94) than for anxiety or affective disorders which ranged from (0·54–0·78) across the first three series of training sessions.

Diagnostic procedures

The final diagnoses were based upon all available information, including the diagnostic interview, family history reports, and medical records using a best estimate diagnostic procedure. Age of onset of each disorder was defined as the age at which the criteria for the disorder were first met. Although retrospective information was used to estimate ages of onset of diagnostic criteria for each disorder, treatment records and family reports were often used for corroboration to enhance the reliability of the estimates. At a minimum, this ancillary information could clarify the temporality of the onsets of alcoholism and anxiety disorders.

Statistical analysis

Data analysis included standard chi-square tests for two-way tables of categorical level variables and analyses of variance for continuous data. In order to reduce Type I error, a Bonferroni multiple comparison procedure was utilized whereby an alpha level of 0·0063 was determined. Comparisons with significance levels from 0·10 to 0·006 are noted as trends.

The multi-way contingency tables for the association between diagnoses in probands and relatives were analysed via logistic regression. This type of categorical analysis allows an independent assessment of the contribution of several potential predictors on a binary outcome variable, such as the presence or absence of a specific diagnosis. The main effects of the following variables on the risk of alcoholism and anxiety in relatives were examined: (*a*) alcoholism in proband; (*b*) anxiety disorders in proband; (*c*) sex of proband; (*d*) presence of co-morbid disorders in relatives (anxiety disorders for models to predict alcoholism in relatives; alcoholism for models to predict anxiety in relatives); (*e*) sex of relative; (*f*) age of relative (continuous); and (*g*) interview status of relative (direct interview *v.* family history information). Interaction terms involving proband and relative

co-morbid diagnoses as well as the gender and co-morbid diagnoses of relatives on the outcome of alcoholism were also examined.

Proportional hazard models

The risk for psychiatric disorders in relatives according to the presence of disorders in probands was calculated using proportional hazard (PH) models, which are general quasi-parametric models (Kaplan & Meier, 1958; Cox, 1972; Bishop *et al.* 1975) where the antilogarithm of the β and its confidence limits yields a hazard ratio and its confidence limits, which are interpreted as relative risks. The PH procedure yields the regression coefficient β (and its standard error) of an independent variable in estimating the age-specific incidence of the outcome variable (i.e. diagnosis of relatives) while simultaneously controlling for other independent variables which may be related to the outcome. In these models, the age of onset of alcoholism in relatives was used as the dependent variable. If the age of onset was pending, the age at assessment was used as the survival time for the censored observations. The model for alcohol dependence considers dependence onset as the event of interest, with abusers and non-alcoholics as censored outcomes. The model for alcohol abuse considers abuse onset to be the event of interest, with non-alcoholics as censored outcomes and those with alcohol dependence excluded. The age of the relatives was maintained in the models to assess a potential cohort effect. The computer analyses were conducted using the PHREG procedure for proportional hazard models from the Statistical Analysis System (Reinhardt, 1980).

Cumulative logit models

A logistic regression model for ordered categorical outcomes with more than two levels called a cumulative logit model was also applied (McCullagh, 1980) because the outcome variable (alcoholism) could also be categorized ordinally from the least to the most severe: normal, alcohol abuse, alcohol dependence. Rather than modeling the log-odds at a given response level, the cumulative logit models the log-odds of a response less than or equal to a given level. The model incorporates the order of the response levels without giving them arbitrary numerical values of questionable validity. A common slope but different intercepts are estimated for each of the outcomes, abuse and dependence.

The form of the cumulative logit model for a variable with three ordered outcome levels is an extension of the binary logit:

(1) $\log\{\text{ODDS of being at or below level } j\}$
$= \theta_j - \beta'\mathbf{X}$
where $j = 1,2$ for first and second outcome
　　　　levels respectively (dependence,
　　　　abuse),
$\mathbf{X}$ = covariates (e.g. normal v. affected
　　　　proband),
β = rate of change in log ODDS per unit
　　　　change in covariate (e.g. normal = 0
　　　　v. affected = 1),
θ_j = log ODDS of being at or below level
　　　　j where $\mathbf{X} = 0$ (baseline).

The model shown above (1) is known as the proportional-odds model because the log odds ratio between two values of X, say X_1 and X_2, is proportional to $X_1 - X_2$ and is independent of the level j:

$\log\{\text{ODDS RATIO of being at or below level}$
$j \text{ when } \Delta X = X_1 - X_2\}$
$= (\theta_j - \beta'X_1) - (\theta_j - \beta'X_2)$
$= (\theta_j - \theta_j) - \beta'(X_2 - X_2)$
$= -\beta'(X_1 - X_2).$

Similar to the proportional hazard models, a significant association between proband anxiety and alcoholism in the relative is consistent with common risk contributing to the two conditions, whereas a lack of an association is consistent with a causal association between the two disorders.

RESULTS

1　Characteristics of the probands

Demographic characteristics of the probands are presented in Table 1. Although there were no significant differences in age across the four diagnostic groupings, there were more females in the anxiety disorder group and fewer females in the alcohol group ($\chi^2 = 43\cdot1$, df = 3, $P < 0\cdot0001$). The distribution of probands by recruitment source (i.e. treatment v. community ascertained) was such that approximately 50% of the subjects with anxiety disorders and approximately 20% of the alcohol groups were ascertained through random digit dialling. No

significant differences emerged in the rates of the major diagnostic categories derived from in-person compared to telephone interviews. Alcoholics with or without anxiety disorders were more likely to be divorced at the time of the interview ($\chi^2 = 45\cdot2$, $P < 0\cdot0001$), and have lower socioeconomic status ($\chi^2 = 35\cdot1$, $P < 0\cdot0001$).

Probands with a lifetime history of co-morbid antisocial personality or major depression were not excluded from the study. Rather, the effects of these conditions on the association between alcoholism and anxiety in the probands and relatives were examined in multivariate analyses. Approximately 50% of the probands had a current alcohol disorder and 32% had a current diagnosis of social phobia or panic disorder. Eighty-three per cent of the probands with social phobia and alcoholism developed social phobia prior to alcoholism. In contrast, only 47·4% of probands developed panic disorder prior to alcoholism.

2　Unadjusted rates of disorders in relatives by proband diagnostic group

Diagnoses in relatives are presented by proband diagnostic group and sex of relative in Table 2. The diagnoses in relatives are not mutually exclusive with the exception of alcohol abuse and dependence as well as bipolar and unipolar depression. In general, higher rates of the anxiety disorders and affective disorders were observed among the female relatives of affected probands, whereas the rates of alcoholism were higher among the male relatives of affected probands.

Rates of alcoholism were higher in the relatives of probands with alcoholism and anxiety disorder as well as alcoholism alone compared with those of controls ($\chi^2 = 36\cdot3$, df = 3, $P < 0\cdot0001$). Rates of alcohol dependence but not abuse were significantly greater among relatives of probands with either alcoholism alone or alcoholism plus anxiety ($\chi^2 = 34\cdot6$, df = 3, $P < 0\cdot0001$). When the rates were examined separately by sex of relative, the male relatives of probands with alcohol and anxiety or alcohol only had significantly higher rates of alcoholism than the male relatives of the anxiety probands ($\chi^2 = 8\cdot3$, df = 3, $P < 0\cdot01$) and normal controls ($\chi^2 = 20\cdot9$, df = 3, $P < 0\cdot0001$). These findings were similar for females although it was only marginally significant for relatives of alcoholics

Table 1. *Description of the proband sample*

Sociodemographic characteristics	Disorders in probands				
	Alcoholism and anxiety disorders $N = 47$	Alcoholism $N = 42$	Anxiety disorders $N = 76$	Controls $N = 61$	P
Sex					
Males (%)	55	88	26	43	< 0·001
Socio-economic status (%)					
Hollingshead† > 3	50	56	28	25	0·001
Marital status (%)					
Married/remarried	53	66	86	96	< 0·001
Single	4	5	3	2	
Divorced	34	29	12	2	
Source (%)					
Clinics	85	79	53	—	NS
First-degree relatives ($N = 1053$)	230	195	359	269	NS

† 1,2 = Upper *v.* 3–5 = Lower.

Table 2. *Unadjusted rates of disorders in relatives by proband diagnostic group and sex of relative*

	Disorders in probands												Significance		
	Alcoholism and anxiety disorders			Alcoholism			Anxiety disorders			Controls					
Sex of relatives	M	F	Total	M	F	Total	M	F	Total	M	F	Total	M	F	Total
Relatives (N)	103	127	230	103	92	195	177	182	359	139	133	269			
Disorders in relatives															
Alcoholism (All)	48	26	36	47	16	33	33	15	24	24	4	14	***	***	***
Abuse	11	11	11	17	6	12	12	7	10	13	2	7	NS	*	NS
Dependence	37	16	25	30	10	21	21	8	14	12	2	7	***	**	***
Anxiety disorders (All)	13	34	24	16	21	18	18	36	27	16	15	16	NS	***	**
Panic	0	10	5	2	1	2	2	12	7	0	2	1	NS	***	***
Social phobia	9	17	13	6	9	7	8	17	13	7	7	7	NS	*	*
Agoraphobia (±panic)	0	9	5	2	3	3	1	11	6	1	4	2	NS	*	+
Generalized anxiety	5	20	13	6	9	7	11	21	16	7	6	6	NS	**	***
Simple phobia	3	11	7	4	6	5	4	11	7	2	5	4	NS	NS	NS

⁺ $P < 0·10$; * $P < 0·05$; ** $P < 0·01$; *** $P < 0·001$.

v. anxiety probands ($\chi^2 = 3·03$, df = 3, $P < 0·10$) and normal controls ($\chi^2 = 11·9$, df = 3, $P < 0·001$).

Rates of anxiety disorders in general as well as specific anxiety disorders were significantly greater among relatives of probands with anxiety themselves compared with relatives of those without anxiety (e.g. alcoholism alone, controls). Significant differences in the rates of generalized anxiety disorder and panic disorder in relatives occurred across proband groups. However, these differences were primarily limited to female relatives. With the exception of the trends observed for dysthymia and bipolar disorder, anxiety and affective disorders in male relatives were not associated with anxiety or alcoholism in probands. There was an increase in the rates of bipolar disorder among the male relatives of probands with alcoholism alone. Rates of affective disorders and antisocial personality were elevated among the relatives of all affected probands.

Ages of onset (i.e. age at which full diagnostic criteria were met) were examined among relatives

Table 3. *Co-morbidity of alcohol dependence and psychiatric disorders in male and female relatives (adjusted odds ratios ±95% confidence limits controlled for age and interview status)*

	Alcoholism				
	Male		Female		
Sex of relative	Dependence	Abuse	Dependence	Abuse	Total
Anxiety (All)	2·0 (1·2–3·3)**	1·6 (0·7–3·5)	3·7 (1·9–7·0)***	0·7 (0·3–1·7)	2·5 (1·7–3·7)***
Panic disorder	0·6 (0·1–5·2)	3·4 (1·1–10·0)*	4·2 (1·8–9·8)***	1·2 (0·1–11·0)	2·7 (1·2–5·8)*
Generalized anxiety	2·3 (1·1–4·5)*	1·6 (0·6–4·4)	2·8 (1·4–5·7)**	0·4 (0·1–1·9)	2·5 (1·5–4·1)***
Social phobia	1·7 (0·8–3·4)	2·1 (0·8–5·6)	4·1 (2·0–8·6)***	0·4 (0·1–1·7)	2·4 (1·5–4·0)***
Agoraphobia	—	5·0 (1·7–14·2)**	2·4 (0·9–6·2)	5·0 (0·7–36·6)	1·5 (0·6–3·8)
Affective (All)	5·2 (3·2–8·5)***	2·6 (1·2–5·7)*	5·3 (2·7–10·2)***	1·3 (0·6–2·9)	5·1 (3·5–7·6)***
Major depression	5·5 (3·1–9·6)***	1·9 (0·8–4·6)	2·1 (1·1–4·3)*	1·2 (0·4–3·3)	3·6 (2·3–5·5)***
Bipolar disorder	2·4 (0·4–14·6)	13·0 (2·4–695)**	9·6 (2·8–33·4)***	11·2 (1·0–128·0)*	5·8 (2·0–16·4)***
Dysthymia	3·7 (1·8–7·6)***	1·3 (0·4–3·9)	3·4 (1·7–7·0)***	0·7 (0·2–3·2)	3·5 (2·1–5·8)***
Substance abuse or dependence	10·5 (5·0–21·9)***	2·2 (0·6–7·7)	13·1 (4·9–35·3)***	6·0 (1·6–22·5)**	10·6 (5·8–19·6)***
Antisocial personality	34·5 (7·9–151·7)***	22·1 (1·9–26·0)*	36·8 (9·0–149·8)***	—	36·3 (13·2–100·3)***

NB: These are non-mutually exclusive diagnoses.
* $P < 0.05$; ** $P < 0.01$; *** $P < 0.001$.

who had a specific anxiety disorder and alcoholism. Approximately 74% of relatives with social phobia and alcoholism developed social phobia prior to alcoholism. In contrast, only 12·5% of relatives developed panic disorder prior to alcoholism.

3 Co-morbidity in relatives

Table 3 provides the sex-specific odds ratios adjusted for age and interview status of the relative for the co-occurrence of anxiety and affective disorders with alcohol dependence in relatives. Differential risks for the co-occurrence of these disorders exist between males and females, with the exception of dysthymia and antisocial personality disorder. The risk of co-morbid anxiety and alcohol dependence was higher in females, whereas the co-occurrence of major depression and alcohol dependence appeared higher in males.

4 Multivariate modelling of co-morbidity and co-transmission

Alcoholism and anxiety

In order to control for multiple potential confounders in the simultaneous investigation of the co-aggregation and co-morbidity of alcoholism and anxiety disorders, proportional hazard models were applied to the data. Covariates previously identified as important in earlier family studies of alcoholism and psycho-pathology were included in these analyses (i.e. sex of proband and sex, age, and interview status of relative). The specificity of familial aggregation of alcoholism and anxiety disorders in relatives was examined by inclusion of the corresponding disorder in probands, while cross-aggregation was examined simultaneously by the inclusion of the alternate disorder in probands. For the prediction of alcohol disorders in relatives, co-morbidity within relatives was included in the models.

Alcohol dependence in the proband was significantly associated with alcohol dependence in relatives, after controlling for proband anxiety, anxiety in the relative, interview status, sex and age of the relative. The association between these two factors was stronger in models in which the alcohol case definition in the relatives was subset to alcohol dependence (risk ratio = 2·8, $P < 0.0001$) and in this case an anxiety disorder (risk ratio = 1·5, $P < 0.04$) in the proband was also significantly associated with alcohol dependence in the relative (Table 4). Consistent with the bivariate associations, the rate of co-morbidity of anxiety disorders and alcohol dependence was higher in female relatives (risk ratio = 3·6, $P < 0.0002$). The risk of alcoholism was found to decrease with increasing age of relative (earlier birth cohort) and males were more likely to be alcoholic than females (risk ratio = 3·6, $P < 0.0001$).

Alcoholism and specific anxiety disorders

In order to examine the co-transmission of the two major anxiety disorders (i.e. social phobia

Table 4. *Co-morbidity and co-aggregation of alcohol dependence and abuse and anxiety disorders among probands and relatives: results of proportional hazard models*

Factors in models	Alcoholism in relatives (hazard ratios ± 95 % CI)	
	Alcohol dependence (N = 996)	Alcohol abuse (N = 821)
Disorders in probands		
Alcohol dependence v. Not	2·83 (2·0–4·0)***	1·61 (0·94–2·8)+
Anxiety v. Not	1·46 (1·0–2·1)*	0·99 (0·59–1·6)
Disorders in relatives		
Anxiety v. Not	2·07 (1·4–3·0)***	0·89 (0·53–1·6)
Covariates for relatives		
Interviewed v. Not	1·24 (0·83–1·8)	1·81 (1·0–3·1)*
Age (current in years)+	0·98 (0·97–0·99)***	0·96 (0·94–0·98)***
Female v. Male	0·28 (0·19–0·41)***	0·42 (0·25–0·71)**
Covariates for probands		
Female v. Male	1·43 (0·99–2·1)	0·91 (0·53–1·5)

† Increase per year.
‡ Analyses controlling for antisocial personality disorder and major depression in probands yielded similar results.
+ P < 0·1; * P < 0·05; ** P < 0·01; *** P < 0·001.

Table 5. *Co-morbidity and co-aggregation of alcohol dependence and specific anxiety disorders among probands and relatives (hazard ratios ± 95 % CI)†*

Factors in models	Alcohol dependence in relatives (N = 996)
	Hazard ratios (CI)
Disorders in probands	
Alcohol dependence v. Not	3·01 (2·1–4·3)***
Panic disorder	1·63 (1·1–2·4)**
Social phobia	0·99 (0·69–1·4)
Disorders in relatives	
Panic disorder	1·44 (0·71–2·9)
Social phobia	1·87 (1·2–3·0)**
Covariates for relatives	
Interviewed v. Not	1·22 (0·82–1·8)
Age	0·98 (0·97–0·99)***
Female v. Male	0·28 (0·19–0·42)***
Covariates for probands	
Females v. Male	1·37 (0·94–2·0)

† Analyses controlling for co-morbid antisocial personality disorder and major depression in the proband yielded similar results.
** P < 0·01; *** P < 0·001.

two major anxiety disorders (i.e. social phobia and panic), mutually exclusive categories were created for probands based upon fulfilment of diagnostic criteria for these specific disorders and anxiety group assignment (i.e. social phobia and panic, social phobia, panic, other anxiety and none).

In proportional hazard models (Table 5) which included panic disorder and social phobia, both alcohol dependence (risk ratio = 3·01, P < 0·0001) and panic disorder (risk ratio = 1·63, P < 0·01) in the proband independently increased the risk of alcohol dependence in relatives, whereas social phobia in the proband was not associated with an increased the risk of alcohol dependence in relatives (risk ratio = 0·99, NS). Panic in the relatives was not associated with alcohol dependence whereas relative sex and age were significantly associated with alcohol dependence.

Because of the low base rates of anxiety disorders in male relatives, we examined subthreshold cases, defined as meeting the key diagnostic probe as well as full symptom criteria, but excluding the duration and impairment criteria (Angst *et al.* 1997). This yielded a strong association between alcohol dependence and panic in both genders. Adjusting for major depression and generalized anxiety in probands changed neither the parameter estimates nor conclusions regarding statistical significance. Additional analyses controlling for antisocial personality disorder in the relatives did not affect the relationship between alcoholism in the probands and alcoholism and/or anxiety disorders in the relatives. In order to determine whether the results were stable across recruitment source (e.g. clinic v. community ascertainment) and interview mode (direct in-person v. telephone) we entered a dummy variable into the analyses. The results showed that neither recruitment source nor interview mode were confounders of the relationship between alcoholism and/or anxiety disorders in the family transmission analyses.

Simultaneous assessment of alcohol abuse and dependence

The final multivariate models used to examine these data were cumulative logit models. In this type of model, alcohol abuse and dependence were examined simultaneously by treating them as ordinal outcomes with dependence considered

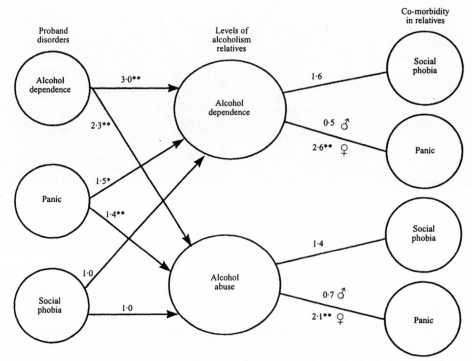

FIG. 1. Adjusted odds ratios of levels of alcoholism (abuse/dependence) of relatives from cumulative logit models of alcoholism and anxiety in probands and relatives. The 95% confidence limits are: proband alcohol dependence–relative alcohol dependence (2·2, 4·2); proband panic–relative alcohol dependence (1·1, 2·2); proband social phobia–relative alcohol dependence (0·7, 1·4); proband alcohol dependence–relative alcohol abuse (1·8–3·1); proband panic–relative alcohol abuse (1·1, 1·8); proband social phobia–relative alcohol abuse (0·85, 1·26). For relatives: relative social phobia–alcohol dependence (1·0, 2·6); relative panic–relative alcohol dependence (0·1, 2·8) male – (1·2, 5·5) female; relative panic–relative alcohol abuse (0·43, 2·19) male – (1·15–4·06) female; relative social phobia–alcohol abuse (0·99–2·04).
Each odds ratio controls for: (1) the other six proband and relative diagnoses shown including a panic by sex interaction; and (2) proband sex, relative sex, relative age and interview status. (* $P < 0.05$; ** $P < 0.01$.)

as a more severe type of alcoholism than abuse. In addition, *a priori* statistical interactions between sex of relative and co-morbid conditions as well as interactions between proband diagnoses were tested. In each case, the goodness-of-fit statistic indicated that the data supported the proportional-odds assumption. The odds ratios from the final model are presented in Fig. 1.

We observed that proband alcohol dependence predicted both alcohol abuse (OR = 2·3) and alcohol dependence (OR = 3·0) in relatives ($\chi^2 = 44·4$, df = 1, $P < 0·0001$). We also observed that panic disorder in probands predicted alcoholism in relatives (OR = 1·4 for alcohol

abuse and OR = 1·5 for alcohol dependence; $\chi^2 = 6·2$, df = 1, $P = 0·0124$). With respect to co-morbidity in relatives, panic and alcohol disorders were significantly associated in female relatives only (OR = 2·1 for alcohol abuse and OR = 2·6 for alcohol dependence; $\chi^2 = 6·2$, df = 1, $P = 0·0126$), while social phobia was associated with alcoholism in the overall relative sample (OR = 1·4 for alcohol abuse and OR = 1·6 for alcohol dependence; $\chi^2 = 3·6$, df = 1, $P = 0·0572$). The addition of affective disorders to the cumulative logit model did not substantially alter our conclusions. Although the statistical significance of the association between social phobia and alcoholism decreased, the effect size

106

remained relatively fixed. In order to examine whether interview status was important in influencing the relationship between alcoholism and anxiety as described in the final models, we ran an additional set of analyses using only the directly interviewed relatives. The association between alcoholism and anxiety disorders remained the same.

DISCUSSION

Familial aggregation of alcoholism and anxiety

The results of the present study confirm the well-established familial aggregation of both the anxiety disorders and alcoholism (Cohen *et al.* 1951; Noyes *et al.* 1978; Munjack & Moss, 1981; Harris *et al.* 1983; Leckman *et al.* 1983). There was a three-fold increased risk of alcoholism among the relatives of probands with alcoholism and a two-fold increased risk of anxiety disorders among the relatives of probands with anxiety. However, this study also revealed that the familial transmission of alcoholism can be primarily attributed to alcohol dependence, rather than abuse, thereby validating the DSM-III-R and ICD-10 distinction between alcohol abuse and dependence (Edwards & Gross, 1976). Similar conclusions were drawn from the results of a twin study of Pickens and colleagues (1991) and the longitudinal study of Hasin *et al.* (1990). Although familial transmission of alcohol dependence was far greater than that of abuse in the present study, there was still evidence for transmission of alcohol abuse in female relatives. Hence, the abuse–dependence distinction may be more important in discriminating alcoholism in males than in females.

Previous twin and adoption studies of alcoholism have been inconclusive with respect to the role of genetic factors in the gender differences in alcoholism. Twin studies have suggested greater heritability for early onset male alcoholism than for female alcoholism (McGue *et al.* 1992) and for alcohol dependence than for abuse in women (Pickens *et al.* 1991). In contrast, the most recent large-scale twin study of a population-based sample revealed equal levels of heritability of alcohol dependence among males and females (Heath *et al.* 1997). The study of female twin pairs by Kendler *et al.* (1992) revealed that genetic influences were

important for alcoholism for both narrow and broad definitions of alcoholism.

Association between alcoholism and anxiety

The present study confirms the association between alcoholism and anxiety disorders as reported in previous clinical and epidemiological studies (Regier *et al.* 1990; Wesner, 1990; Kessler *et al.* 1996). Our further investigation of potential sex-specific patterns and pathways revealed that these associations between alcohol dependence and anxiety disorders were primarily a function of the effect in female relatives. Otto *et al.* (1992) reported that alcoholism among patients with panic disorder was primarily due to co-morbidity in women. Existing studies have frequently yielded inconsistent results regarding gender-specific co-morbidity (Smail *et al.* 1984; Chambless *et al.* 1987; Otto *et al.* 1992).

In the present study, the association between the specific subtypes of anxiety disorders and alcohol dependence was greater for females than for males, possibly due to the extremely low rates of threshold-level anxiety disorders among the males. As shown in previous studies, we found a more consistent association between alcoholism and social phobia across gender than between alcoholism and panic disorder, for which there was no evidence for co-morbidity in males. However, when repetitive spontaneous panic attacks with full symptomatic criteria were considered, a strong association emerged in both genders. Examination of the sex-specific parameters (without respect to their statistical significance) show that the association is not a function of the relative number of cases in males *v.* females. Different patterns of co-morbidity between alcoholism and specific subtypes of anxiety as well as sex differences may explain the discrepant conclusions regarding co-morbidity between alcoholism and anxiety (Schuckit & Hesselbrock, 1994). However, Schneier *et al.* (1992), Angst *et al.* (1993) and Kessler *et al.* (1997) have all reported associations between alcoholism and social phobia and panic in large-scale epidemiological studies in both men and women.

Inspection of data on retrospective recall of the order of onset of alcoholism and anxiety disorders in the subjects with co-morbidity revealed that the majority of those with social phobia reported the onset of social phobia prior to that of alcoholism. This concurs with several previous clinical studies in which social phobia tended to precede that of alcoholism in patients with co-morbidity (Mullaney & Trippett, 1979; Bowen *et al.* 1984; Weiss & Rosenburg, 1985; Stravynski, *et al.* 1986). In contrast, similar to the results of previous studies in which there appeared to be no specific pattern of onset of panic with respect to alcoholism (Powell *et al.* 1982; Hesselbrock *et al.* 1985; Chambless *et al.* 1987; Ross *et al.* 1988; George *et al.* 1990); nearly equal proportions of subjects with co-morbid panic disorder and alcoholism reported the onset of panic earlier, simultaneous to, or later than the onset of alcoholism. The findings from retrospective studies were recently confirmed by the results of a prospective longitudinal cohort study of young adults selected from the general community in Zurich, Switzerland in which the onset of panic and alcohol misuse either tended to occur in close temporal proximity or with alcohol misuse preceding the onset of panic (Degonda & Angst, 1993).

Association between alcoholism and specific subtypes of anxiety

The findings of the present study suggest two pathways for co-morbidity between alcoholism and anxiety disorders. The rates of alcoholism were increased only among relatives of social phobics who themselves manifested social phobia. This suggests that the two disorders are transmitted independently despite the large degree of co-morbidity between them. When taken together with the patterns of onset of these conditions reported in this study as well as in numerous other clinical and epidemiological studies, the findings are consistent with a self-medication model in which alcoholism develops as a consequence of social phobia.

In contrast, co-morbidity between panic disorder and alcoholism is partially attributable to shared aetiological factors. The non-systematic patterns of onset of panic and alcoholism suggest that panic and alcohol disorders may represent manifestations of the same underlying risk factors. These findings are remarkably similar to those of Maier and colleagues (1993) who found evidence for increased risk of 'pure' alcoholism in the relatives of probands with 'pure' panic disorder, but no significant symmetric effect for

panic disorder in relatives of probands with alcoholism. Indeed, the adjusted odds ratios for the association between alcoholism and panic disorder were nearly identical to those in the present study. However, it is likely that the lack of symmetry results from diminished statistical power. Likewise, in their twin study of females, Kendler *et al.* (1995) found a genetic factor with high loadings on major depression and generalized anxiety disorder that also included modest loadings for both panic disorder and alcoholism. Aside from common genetic factors, shared aetiological factors leading to alcoholism or panic may include common biological or psychosocial environmental risk factors. The manifestation of a particular disorder may be a function of the timing of risk factors and/or additional mediating genetic or environmental factors.

Alcoholism may have differential associations with specific anxiety disorders in that the underlying physiological mechanism or vulnerability involved with each type of disorder may react differently to the anxiolytic properties of alcohol (Kushner *et al.* 1990). Our data suggest that subjects with social phobia admit to using alcohol to assuage anxiety when confronted with the phobic stimulus, confirming the conclusions of several previous clinical studies of both alcoholics and phobics. Subjects with panic disorder were far less likely to report using alcohol for self-medication of anxiety; rather, panic attacks may be precipitated by physiological changes resulting from alcoholism. This could result from differences in the core phenomenology of these anxiety disorders, based on the fairly predictable occurrence of exposure to provocative situations by social phobics, particularly those with specific social phobia, in contrast to the unpredictable occurrence of panic attacks in patients with panic disorder, particularly during the early manifestations of this syndrome.

Strengths and limitations of present study

The strengths of this investigation are the application of a family study design to address specifically mechanisms for co-morbidity, selection of probands from both clinical and community settings to enhance the generalizability of the findings, investigation of co-morbidity and co-aggregation of specific subtypes of these conditions, and the use of multivariate techniques in order to control for potential confounders. The use of a longitudinal design to investigate the order of onset of psychiatric disorder in the high risk component of this study will help to clarify the order of the onset of these disorders without bias inherent in retrospective recall. In addition, this is the first family study designed specifically to examine co-morbidity of specific subtypes of alcoholism and the specific subtypes of anxiety disorders including both panic disorder and social phobia.

The application of the cumulative logit model for this ordinal response variable (alcoholism) is an important advance over alternative modelling strategies. Use of one model for several different outcome levels yields statistically efficient estimates, allows for direct comparison of effect sizes, and incorporates the order of the outcomes simultaneously on all subjects in the analysis.

The selection of optimal control and comparison groups for family studies has been discussed extensively; selection of controls without psychopathology (i.e. 'super-normal') and probands with 'pure' disorders have been criticized because they may exaggerate the difference between relatives of cases and controls for all psychiatric disorders rather than only the disorder under study (Kendler, 1990). However, Klein (1993) argued that the careful screening of both case and control probands and appropriate multivariate analyses can minimize bias arising from sampling of unaffected controls. Additionally, Hill & Neiswanger (1997) argue that unaffected controls minimize heterogeneity in genetic linkage and association studies. Comparison of the results of the present study using a control group without substance abuse, anxiety or depression, with a control group which included depression (who were excluded from the study) did not alter the findings reported herein. Moreover, the comparability between the rates of disorders in relatives of controls in the present study and those reported in recent epidemiological studies suggests that they comprise an unbiased comparison group (Kessler, *et al.* 1996).

One methodological limitation of the present study is the lack of direct interview data on all of the relatives necessitating the derivation of best estimate diagnoses based on family history information. However, Graham & Jackson (1993) have reported that proxy sources are unlikely to lead to biased estimates of alcohol consumption. Another limitation is the lack of power to investigate specificity and co-morbidity of subtypes of the rarer conditions in this sample, particularly co-morbid disorders not directly under investigation herein.

Implications of findings of the present study

These findings have important implications for the diagnostic classification, and for the course, treatment and prevention of these disorders. As described above, the distinction between alcohol abuse and dependence in the current diagnostic classification systems was validated by our findings.

As highlighted by the originators of the term co-morbidity, characterization of subjects according to all disorders rather than to the presenting disorder or more significant disorder is critical for adequate prediction of course and outcome (Kaplan & Feinstein, 1974). Numerous studies have revealed that the course of substance abuse is worse in the presence of psychiatric disorders (Rounsaville *et al.* 1987). Alcoholics with co-morbid anxiety have been shown to experience more severe alcohol withdrawal, an increased tendency to relapse, greater impairment levels, and worse prognosis than those without anxiety disorders (Johnston, *et al.* 1991; LaBounty *et al.* 1992; Lotufo-Neto & Gentil, 1994).

The co-morbidity of alcoholism and anxiety disorders may also affect the evaluation and treatment of individuals with these conditions, irrespective of the disorder for which they seek treatment. Alcohol disorders resulting from self-medication may often go unrecognized in treatment settings for anxiety disorders. Indeed, alcohol withdrawal can closely mimic the symptoms of panic and generalized anxiety. Moreover, persons with co-morbid anxiety and alcoholism often manifest additional co-morbid disorders, particularly affective disorders. Consequently, it is essential to evaluate potential manifestations of anxiety and depression during alcohol withdrawal and subsequent abstinence when designing long-term treatment strategies (Anthenelli & Shuckit, 1993).

The differential relationships between panic and phobic states with alcoholism are also relevant to the development of alcohol treatment programmes. Whereas treatment of alcoholics with social phobia should focus on the amelioration of the underlying social phobia using the highly efficacious methods demonstrated for this condition in contemporary psychiatry (Marks & Lader, 1973; Liebowitz *et al.* 1988; Heimberg & Juster, 1995; Potts & Davidson, 1995), treatment of panic in the context of alcoholism could be more appropriately directed at abstinence to determine whether panic attacks are potentiated by ethanol. Treatment strategies that address both conditions may ultimate yield greater efficacy than those that focus solely on the index condition for which the subject sought treatment.

The relationships between alcoholism and anxiety disorders described in this article also provide key information for both primary and secondary prevention of these disorders. A family history of these conditions is an important indicator of an increased risk to the offspring in these families. The potential aetiological pathway from anxiety disorders to alcoholism suggests that children with high levels of anxiety symptoms or anxiety disorders have a heightened risk for the use of alcohol to self-medicate the symptoms of anxiety, particularly in the presence of other known risk factors for the development of alcoholism. The early identification and treatment of these children could help to prevent the development of alcohol abuse and dependence.

Conclusion

These findings illustrate the importance of the use of family studies to investigate the mechanisms underlying co-morbidity. Compared with other experimental approaches, family studies examining high-risk relatives (i.e. relatives of probands with a specific diagnosis) remove some of the selection biases associated with analysing clinical treatment samples and increase the number of potential subjects with the desired co-morbidity. Thus, family studies can produce more stable estimates of the risk of co-morbidity. Twin studies are also a powerful approach to investigate mechanisms for co-morbidity since they permit estimation of the degree to which genetic and environmental factors may contribute to the joint expression of several syndromes (see Kendler *et al.* 1993, 1995).

Finally, these results suggest that family studies of alcoholism should discriminate between families with panic and those with social phobia. In the former case, alcoholism could represent a manifestation of the same underlying diathesis, whereas in the latter case, social phobia would be the chief phenomenon of interest. Clarifying mechanisms for co-morbidity is essential for the accurate classification of subjects for genetic studies, or for any study that seeks to gain understanding of the pathophysiology of alcoholism or anxiety disorders.

This work was supported in part by grants AA07080, AA09978, DA09055, DA05348, MH36197 from Alcohol, Drug Abuse and the Mental Health Administration of the United States Public Health Services and a Research Scientist Development Award from the National Institute of Mental Health (KO2 MH00499 and K02DA00293). The authors are grateful to the late Dr Brigitte A. Prusoff for her significant contribution to this work.

REFERENCES

American Psychiatric Association (1980). *Diagnostic and Statistical Manual of Mental Disorders, 3rd edn.* APA: Washington, DC.
American Psychiatric (1987). *Diagnostic and Statistical Manual of Mental Disorders, 3rd edn.* Revised. APA: Washington, DC.
Andreasen, N. C., Endicott, J., Spitzer, R. L. & Winokur, G. (1977). The family history method using diagnostic criteria, reliability and validity. *Archives of General Psychiatry* 34, 1229–1235.
Aneshensel, C., Frerichs, R., Clark, V. & Yokopanic, P. (1982). Telephone vs. in-person surveys of community health surveys. *American Journal of Public Health* 72, 1017–1021.
Angst, J. (1993). Comorbidity of anxiety, phobia, compulsion, and depression. *International Clinical Psychopharmacology* 8, 21–25.
Angst, J., Merikangas, K. R. & Preisig, M. (1997). Subthreshold syndromes of depression and anxiety in the community. *Journal of Clinical Psychiatry* 58 (suppl. 8), 6–10.
Anthenelli, R. M. & Schuckit, M. A. (1993). Affective and anxiety disorders and alcohol and drug dependence: diagnosis and treatment. In *Cormorbidity of Addictive and Psychiatric Disorders* (eds N. S. Miller and B. Stimmel), pp. 73–87: The Haworth Press, Inc.: New York.
Bishop, Y., Fienberg, S. & Holland, P. (1975). *Discrete Multivariate Analysis.* MIT Press: Cambridge, MA.
Bowen, R., Cipywnyk, D., D'Arcy, C. & Keegan, D. (1984). Alcoholism, anxiety disorders, and agoraphobia. *Alcoholism: Clinical and Experimental Research* 8, 48–50.
Carey, G. & Gottesman, I. I. (1981). *Twin and Family Studies of Anxiety, Phobic, and Obsessive Disorders* (D. F. Klein and J. Rabkin eds.). Raven Press: New York.
Chambless, D., Cherney, J., Caputo, G. & Rheinstein, B. J. (1987). Anxiety disorders and alcoholism: a study with inpatient alcoholics. *Journal of Anxiety Disorders* 1, 29–40.
Cohen, M. E., Badal, D. W., Kilpatrick, A., Reed, E. W. & White, P. D. (1951). The high familial prevalence of neurocirculatory asthenia (anxiety neurosis, effort syndrome). *American Journal of Human Genetics* 3, 126–158.
Colombotos, J. (1969). Personal vs. telephone interviews: effect on response. *Public Health Reports* 84, 773–782.

Cotton, N. S. (1979). The familial incidence of alcoholism. *Journal of Studies on Alcohol* 40, 89–116.

Cox, D. R. (1972). Regression models and life tables. *Journal of the Royal Statistical Society* Bull. 34, 187–220.

Crowley, T. J. & Riggs, P. D. (1995). Adolescent substance use disorder with conduct disorder and comorbid conditions. *NIDA Research Monograph* 156, 49–111.

Degonda, M., Angst, J. (1993). The Zurich study. XX. Social phobia and agoraphobia. *European Archives of Psychiatry and Clinical Neuroscience* 243, 95–102.

Edwards, G. & Gross, M. M. (1976). Alcohol dependence: provisional description of a clinical syndrome. *British Medical Journal* i, 1058–1061.

Endicott, J. & Spitzer, R. L. (1978). A diagnostic interview: the Schedule for Affective Disorders and Schizophrenia – lifetime version. *Archives of General Psychiatry* 35, 837–844.

George, D. T., Nutt, D. J., Dwyer, B. A. & Linnoila, M. (1990). Alcoholism and panic disorder: is the comorbidity more than coincidence. *Acta Psychiatrica Scandinavica* 81, 97–107.

Graham, P. & Jackson, R. (1993). Primary versus proxy respondents: comparability of questionnaire data on alcohol consumption. *American Journal of Epidemiology* 138, 443–452.

Harris, E. L., Noyes, R., Jr., Crowe, R. R. & Chaudhry, D. R. (1983). A family study of agoraphobia. *Archives of General Psychiatry* 40, 1061–1064.

Hasin, D. S., Grant, B. & Endicott, J. (1990). The natural history of alcohol abuse: implications for definitions of alcohol use disorders. *American Journal of Psychiatry* 147, 1537–1541.

Heath, A. C., Bucholz, K. K., Madden, P. A., Dinwiddie, S. H., Slutske, W. S., Bierut, L. J., Statham, D. J., Dunne, M. P., Whitfield, J. B. & Martin, N. G. (1997). Genetic and environmental contributions to alcohol dependence risk in a national twin sample: consistency of findings in men and women. *Psychological Medicine* 27, 1381–1396.

Heimberg, R. G. & Juster, H. R. (1995). Cognitive–behavioral treatments: literature review. In *Social Phobia: Diagnosis, Assessment, Treatment* (ed. R. G. Heimberg, M. R. Liebowitz, D. A. Hope), pp. 261–309. Guilford: New York.

Helzer, J. & Pryzbeck, T. (1988). The co-occurrence of alcoholism with other psychiatric disorders in the general population and its impact on treatment. *Journal of Studies on Alcohol* 49, 219–224.

Hesselbrock, M., Meyer, R. & Keener, J. (1985). Psychopathology in hospitalized alcoholics. *Archives of General Psychiatry* 42, 1050–1055.

Hill, S. W. & Neiswanger, K. (1997). The value of narrow psychiatric phenotypes and 'super' normal controls. In *Handbook of Psychiatric Genetics* (ed. K. Blum and E. P. Noble). CRC Press: New York.

Johnston, A. L., Thevos, A. K., Randall, C. L. & Anton, R. F. (1991). Increased severity of alcohol withdrawal in in-patient alcoholics with a co-existing anxiety diagnosis. *British Journal of Addiction* 86, 719–725.

Kaplan, E. L. & Meier, P. (1958). Nonparametric estimations from incomplete observations. *Journal of the American Statistical Association* 53, 459–482.

Kaplan, M. H. & Feinstein, A. R. (1974). The importance of classifying initial co-morbidity in evaluating the outcome of diabetes mellitus. *Journal of Chronic Disease* 27, 387–404.

Kendler, K. S. (1990). The super-normal control group in psychiatric genetics: post artifactual evidence for aggregation. *Psychiatric Genetics* 1, 45–53.

Kendler, K. S., Health, A. C. & Neale, M. C. (1992). A population-based twin study of alcoholism in women. *Journal of the American Medical Association* 268, 1877–1882.

Kendler, K. S., Heath, A. C., Neale, M. C., Kessler, R. C. & Eaves, L. J. (1993). Alcoholism and major depression in women. *Archives of General Psychiatry* 50, 690–698.

Kendler, K. S., Walters, E., Neale, M., Kessler, R. C., Heath, A. C. & Eaves, L. J. (1995). The structure of the genetic and environmental risk factors for six major psychiatric disorders in women. *Archives of General Psychiatry* 52, 374–383.

Kessler, R. C., Nelson, M. B., McGonagle, K. A. & Edlund, M. J. (1996). The epidemiology of co-occuring mental disorders and substance use disorders in the National Comorbidity Survey: implications for prevention and service utilization. *American Journal of Orthopsychiatry* 66, 17–31.

Kessler, R. C., Crum, R., Warner, L., Nelson, C. B., Schulenberg, J. & Anthony, J. C. (1997). Lifetime co-occurrence of DSM-III-R alcohol abuse and dependence with other psychiatric disorders in the National Comorbidity Survey. *Archives of General Psychiatry* 54, 313–321.

Klein, D. (1993). The utility of the super-normal control group in psychiatric genetics. *Psychiatric Genetics* 3, 17–19.

Kushner, M., Sher, K. & Beitman, B. (1990). The relationship between alcohol problems and the anxiety disorders. *American Journal of Psychiatry* 147, 685–695.

LaBounty, L. P., Hatsukami, D., Morgan, S. F. & Nelson, L. (1992). Relapse among alcoholics with phobic and panic symptoms. *Addictive Behaviors* 17, 9–15.

Leckman, J. F., Weissman, M. M., Merikangas, K. R., Pauls, D. L. & Weissman, M. M. (1983). Panic disorder and major disorder and major depression. Increased risk of depression, alcoholism, panic, and phobic disorders in families of depressed probands with panic disorder. *Archives of General Psychiatry* 40, 1055–1060.

Liebowitz, M. R., Gorman, J. M., Fyer, A. J., Campeas, R., Levin, A. P., Sandberg, D., Hollander, E., Papp, L. & Goetz, D. (1988). Pharmacotherapy of social phobia: an interim report of a placebo-controlled comparison of phenelzine and atenolol. *Journal of Clinical Psychiatry* 49, 252–257.

Lotufo-Neto, F. & Gentil, V. (1994). Alcoholism and phobic anxiety – a clinical-demographic comparison. *Addiction* 89, 447–453.

McCullagh, P. (1980). Regression models for ordinal data. *Journal of the Royal Statistical Society* B 42, 109–142.

McGue, M. (1994). Genes, environment, and the etiology of alcoholism. In *The Development of Alcohol Problems: Exploring the Biopsychosocial Matrix* (eds. R. Zucker, G. Boyd and J. Howard), pp. 1–39. US Dept. Health, Human Services Research Monograph No. 26: Rockville.

McGue, M., Pickens, R. W. & Svikis, D. S. (1992). Sex and age effects on the inheritance of alcohol problems: a twin study. *Journal of Abnormal Psychology* 101, 3–17.

Maier, W. & Merikangas, K. (1994). Co-occurrence and co-transmission of affective disorders and alcoholism in families. In *Genetic Research in Psychiatry* (ed. J. Medlewicz and W. Hippius), pp. 210–224. Springer Verlag: New York.

Maier, W., Minges, J. & Lichtermann, D. (1993). Alcoholism and panic disorder: co-occurrence and co-transmission in families. *European Archives of Psychiatry and Clinical Neuroscience* 243, 205–211.

Marks, I. & Lader, M. (1973). Anxiety states (anxiety neurosis): a review. *Journal of Nervous and Mental Disease* 156, 3–18.

Merikangas, K. R. (1990a). The genetic epidemiology of alcoholism. *Psychological Medicine* 20, 11–22.

Merikangas, K. R. (1990b). Co-morbidity for anxiety and depression: review of family and genetic studies. In *Comorbidity of Mood and Anxiety Disorders* (ed J. D. Maser and C. R. Cloninger), pp. 331–348. American Psychiatric Press Inc.: Washington, DC.

Merikangas, K. R., Leckman, J., Prusoff, B., Pauls, D. L. & Weissman, M. M. (1985). Familial transmission of depression and alcoholism. *Archives of General Psychiatry* 42, 367–372.

Merikangas, K. R., Risch, N. J., Merikangas, J. R., Weissman, M. M. & Kidd, K. (1988). Migraine and depression: association and familial transmission. *Journal of Psychiatric Research* 22, 119–129.

Merikangas, K. R., Risch, N. & Weissman, M. (1994). Comorbidity and co-transmission of alcoholism, anxiety, and depression. *Psychological Medicine* 24, 69–80.

Mirin, S. M., Weiss, R. D., Griffin, M. L. & Michael, J. L. (1991). Psychopathology in drug abusers and their families. *Comprehensive Psychiatry* 32, 36–51.

Mullaney, J. A. & Trippett, C. J. (1979). Alcohol dependence and phobias: clinical description and relevance. *British Journal of Psychiatry* 135, 565–573.

Munjack, D. J. & Moss, H. B. (1981). Affective disorder and alcoholism in families of agoraphobics. *Archives of General Psychiatry* 38, 869–871.

Norden, K. A., Klein, D. N., Ferro, T. & Kasch, K. (1995). Who participates in a family study? *Comprehensive Psychiatry* 36, 199–206.

Noyes, R., Jr., Clancy, J., Crowe, R. R., Hoenk, P. R. & Slymen, D. J. (1978). The family prevalence of anxiety neurosis. *Archives of General Psychiatry* 35, 1057–1059.

Otto, M. W., Pollack, M. H., Sachs, G. S., O'Neil, C. A. & Rosenbaum, J. F. (1992). Alcohol dependence in panic disorder patients. *Journal of Psychiatric Research* 26, 29–38.

Pickens, R. W., Svikis, D. S., McGue, M., Lykken, D. T., Heston, L. I. & Clayton, P. J. (1991). Heterogeneity in the inheritance of alcoholism: a study of male and female twins. *Archives of General Psychology* 48, 19–28.

Potts, N. & Davidson, J. (1995). Pharmacologic treatments: literature review. In *Social Phobia: Diagnosis, Assessment and Treatment* (ed. R. G. Heimberg, M. R. Liebowitz, A. Hope), pp. 334–365. Guilford: New York.

Powell, B. J., Penick, E., Othmer, E. & Bingham, S. F. (1982). Prevalence of additional psychiatric syndromes among male alcoholics. *Journal of Clinical Psychiatry* 43, 404–407.

Regier, D., Farmer, M., Rae, D., Locke, B. Z., Keith, J. J., Judd, L. L. & Goodwin, F. K. (1990). Comorbidity of mental disorders with alcohol and other drug abuse: results from the Epidemiologic Catchment Area (ECA) Study. *Journal of the American Medical Association* 264, 2511–2518.

Reinhardt, P. (1980). *SAS Supplemental Library User's Guide.* SAS Institute: Cary, NC.

Roelofs, S. (1985). Hyperventilation, anxiety, craving for alcohol: a subacute alcohol withdrawal syndrome. *Alcohol* 2, 501–505.

Rohde, P., Lewinsohn, P. M. & Seeley, J. R. (1997). Comparability of telephone and face-to-face interviews: Assessing Axis I and II Disorders. *American Journal of Psychiatry* 154, 1593–1598.

Ross, H. E., Glaser, F. B. & Germanson, T. (1988). The prevalence of psychiatric disorders in patients with alcohol and other drug problems. *Archives of General Psychiatry* 45, 1023–1032.

Rounsaville, B. J., Dolinsky, Z. S., Babor, T. F. & Meyer, R. E. (1987). Psychopathology as a predictor of treatment outcomes in alcoholics. *Archives of General Psychiatry* 44, 505–513.

Schneier, F. R., Johnson, J., Hornig, C. D., Liebowitz, M. R. & Weissman, M. M. (1992). Social phobia: comorbidity and morbidity in an epidemiologic sample. *Archives of General Psychiatry* 49, 282–288.

Schuckit, M. & Hesselbrock, V. (1994). Alcohol dependence and anxiety disorders: what is the relationship? *American Journal of Psychiatry* 151, 1723–1734.

Skre, I., Onstad, S., Edvardsen, J., Torgerson, S. & Kringlen, E. (1994). A family study of anxiety disorders: familial transmission and relationship to mood disorder and psychoactive substance use disorder. *Acta Psychiatrica Scandinavica* 90, 366–374.

Smail, P., Stockwell, T., Canter, S. & Hodgson, R. (1984). Alcohol dependence and phobic anxiety states. I. A prevalence study. *British Journal of Psychiatry* 144, 53–57.

Stockwell, T., Smail, P., Hodgson, R. & Canter, S. (1984). Alcohol dependence and phobic anxiety states. II. A retrospective study. *British Journal of Psychiatry* 144, 58–63.

Stravynski, A., Lamontagne, Y. & Lavallee, Y. J. (1986). Clinical phobias and avoidant personality disorder among alcoholics admitted to an alcoholism rehabilitation setting. *Canadian Journal of Psychiatry* 31, 714–719.

Torgersen, S. & Philos, D. (1986). Childhood and family characteristics in panic and generalized anxiety disorders. *American Journal of Psychiatry* 143, 530–632.

Warner, L. A., Kessler, R. C., Hughes, M., Anthony, J. C. & Nelson, C. B. (1995). Prevalence and correlates of drug use and dependence in the United States. *Archives of General Psychiatry* 52, 219–229.

Weeks, M., Kulka, R., Lessler, J. & Whitmore, R. (1983). Personal versus telephone surveys for collecting household data at the local level. *American Journal of Public Health* 73, 1389–1394.

Weiss, K. J. & Rosenberg, D. J. (1985). Prevalence of anxiety disorder among alcoholics. *Journal of Clinical Psychiatry* 46, 3–5.

Weissman, M. M., Merikangas, K. R., John, K., Wickramaratne, P., Prusoff, B. A. & Kidd, K. K. (1986). Family-genetic studies of psychiatric disorders: developing technologies. *Archives of General Psychiatry* 43, 1104–1116.

Wesner, R. B. (1990). Alcohol use and abuse secondary to anxiety. In *Psychiatric Clinics of North America* (ed. R. B. Wesner and G. Winokur), pp. 699–714. W. B. Saunders Company: Philadelphia, PA.

Woodman, C. & Crowe, R. (1996). The genetics of the anxiety disorders. *Bailliere's Clinical Psychiatry* 2, 47–57.

Annu. Rev. Psychol. 1998. 49:377–412

COMORBIDITY OF ANXIETY AND UNIPOLAR MOOD DISORDERS

Susan Mineka

Department of Psychology, Northwestern University, Evanston, Illinois 60208;
e-mail: mineka@nwu.edu

David Watson and Lee Anna Clark

Department of Psychology, The University of Iowa, Iowa City, Iowa 52242-1407

KEY WORDS: depression, anxiety, comorbidity

ABSTRACT

Research on relationships between anxiety and depression has proceeded at a rapid pace since the 1980s. The similarities and differences between these two conditions, as well as many of the important features of the comorbidity of these disorders, are well understood. The genotypic structure of anxiety and depression is also fairly well documented. Generalized anxiety and major depression share a common genetic diathesis, but the anxiety disorders themselves are genetically hetergeneous. Sophisticated phenotypic models have also emerged, with data converging on an integrative hierarchical model of mood and anxiety disorders in which each individual syndrome contains both a common and a unique component. Finally, considerable progress has been made in understanding cognitive aspects of these disorders. This work has focused on both the cognitive content of anxiety and depression and on the effects that anxiety and depression have on information processing for mood-congruent material.

CONTENTS

377

MEANINGS AND IMPLICATIONS OF ANXIETY-DEPRESSION COMORBIDITY

Background

Comorbidity is currently one of the "hot" topics in psychopathology research (Kendall & Clarkin 1992). According to Klerman (1990), a neo-Kraeplinian belief in the existence of discrete mental disorders clearly reemerged in the Third Edition of the *Diagnostic and Statistical Manual of Mental Disorders* (*DSM-III*) (American Psychiatric Association 1980), fueled in part by the success of research into diagnostic classification afforded by such developments as the Research Diagnostic Criteria (RDC) (Spitzer et al 1978). Consistent with this belief, the framers of *DSM-III* included extensive exclusionary criteria. However, criticism of these exclusionary rules soon followed on both conceptual and empirical grounds (First et al 1990), and they were largely eliminated in *DSM-III-R* (American Psychiatric Association 1987). Freed from these exclusionary rules, ensuing research documented extensive comorbidity across the entire spectrum of psychopathology (Clark et al 1995, Kendall & Clarkin 1992) and sparked numerous discussions on the meaning and implications of comorbidity in psychopathology.

With regard to anxiety and depression, the modern history of their classification (Clark 1989, Clark & Watson 1991a,b) and the surrounding controversies (Cole et al 1997, Feldman 1993, King et al 1991, Lonigan et al 1994) have been reviewed previously. Throughout the century, the anxiety and depressive disorders have been treated as separate diagnostic classes in official nosologies; many researchers have argued that these disorders are distinct entities (Akiskal 1985, Cox et al 1993). Nonetheless, other researchers have asserted that they represent a single underlying dimension, or that together they form a more general class of mood disorders (Feldman 1993, Hodges 1990). This latter, unitary construct, view has been particularly prominent in Europe where even the term "mood disorders" subsumes both anxiety and depression. In turn, the former, dual construct, view may reflect a more general tendency on the part of American psychiatry toward diagnostic "splitting" rather than "lumping" (Frances et al 1990).

In *DSM-III* exclusion rules limited co-diagnosis both within and across the anxiety and depressive disorders, but as mentioned, early research that ignored these exclusion rules revealed extensive comorbidity. Moreover, research based on the *DSM-III-R* and *DSM-IV* (American Psychiatric Association 1994), in which the exclusion rules were largely eliminated, documented that the anxiety and depressive disorders were among the most notable examples of overlapping disorders (Clark et al 1995). Ironically, insofar as this research is leading some researchers to argue that diagnostic splitting has gone too far and that certain disorders should be recollapsed into a single category, it may serve ultimately to justify the view of the *DSM-III* framers that certain coexisting syndromes actually reflect the same underlying disorder and should not be diagnosed separately.

More generally, researchers gradually have begun to realize that the controversy over the unitary versus dual models is both unnecessary and unproductive. These models increasingly are being replaced by a more nuanced view in which anxiety and depression are posited to have both shared, common components and specific, unique components (Clark & Watson 1991b). We discuss these developments in a subsequent section.

The Meaning of Comorbidity: Current Controversies

The term *comorbidity* was coined in the context of chronic disease (Feinstein 1970) to refer to "any distinct additional clinical entity that has existed or that may occur during the clinical course of a patient who has the index disease under study" (pp. 456–57). Attempts to extend this definition of comorbidity to psychiatric disorder, however, quickly run into difficulties in delineating the concept of a "distinct clinical entity" (Lilienfeld et al 1994). If the presence of Disorder A significantly increases the likelihood of the occurrence of Disorder B, various reasons may explain this increased co-occurrence. Kaplan & Feinstein (1974) described several types of comorbidity in medical disorders in which the development of Disorder B was specifically related to the presence of Disorder A. For example, Disorder A may be a risk factor for B (prognostic comorbidity), or Disorder B may be a secondary complication of A (pathogenic comorbidity) (for discussions, see Lilienfeld et al 1994, Maser & Cloninger 1990a, Spitzer 1994). But what if Disorder A [(e.g. major depressive disorder (MDD)] is frequently comorbid not only with B [e.g. general anxiety disorder (GAD)] but also with Disorders C, D, E, F, G, and H (e.g. the other anxiety and mood disorders) and further, what if these disorders themselves substantially co-occur? Given these conditions, the concept of a distinct clinical entity is decidedly fuzzy; yet data from the National Comorbidity Survey (NCS) reveal precisely this pattern (e.g. Kessler 1997).

Discussions of this topic have been wide ranging. Frances et al (1990) present a series of methodological issues that affect determination of the degree of comorbidity. For example, they note that higher rates of comorbidity tend to be found in more recent studies using structured interviews. To discount the phenomenon of comorbidity based on this fact, however, would be to blame the messenger for the message. Another issue commonly raised is that the presence of the same symptom in two or more diagnoses (e.g. sleep disturbance in MDD and GAD] artifactually raises the co-occurrence of the disorders (e.g. Caron & Rutter 1991). A key word here is "artifactually." Certainly no one would argue that the presence of fever in the diagnosis of chicken pox and measles artifactually raises their co-occurrence, or that "headaches" should be removed from the list of symptoms of either brain tumors or concussions in order to improve differential diagnosis; nevertheless, similar arguments have been made for overlapping psychological symptoms, perhaps reflecting differential levels of knowledge about the etiology of medical versus mental disorders.

Excessive diagnostic splitting also has been noted as an artifactual "cause" of comorbidity, usually with regard to highly similar disorders (e.g. overanxious disorder and GAD in children; Caron & Rutter 1991). However, the separation of phenotypically diverse syndromes (e.g. MDD and GAD) into distinct categories may reflect the same phenomenon. Thus, the greatest challenge that the extensive comorbidity data pose to the current nosological system concerns the validity of the diagnostic categories themselves—do these disorders constitute distinct clinical entities? Even when one psychological syndrome temporally precedes another (e.g. GAD preceding MDD), the earlier syndrome may represent a prodromal manifestation of the latter.

Lilienfeld et al (1994) advocate avoiding the term "psychiatric comorbidity" because it implies greater knowledge about disorders than currently exists and will lead to reification of the *DSM* syndromes. Others, however, argue that the term is less important than the phenomena it reveals (Robins 1994). Certainly, the challenge is to make sense of surface-descriptive comorbidity data, and to recognize that more extensive information about underlying mechanisms and causal relationships is needed for this purpose (Frances et al 1990).

Impact of Comorbidity

Numerous studies have documented the negative effects of anxiety-depression comorbidity on various aspects of psychopathology, such as course, chronicity, recovery and relapse rates (Brown et al 1996, Rief et al 1995; however, a few studies report no effects, e.g. Hoffart & Martinsen 1993), treatment seeking (Lewinsohn et al 1995, Sartorius et al 1996), and psychosocial functioning (Lewinsohn et al 1995, Reich et al 1993). Insofar as comorbidity rates tend to be substantially higher in individuals with more severe conditions (Kendall et al 1992, Kessler et al 1994), and severity of disorder is also a negative prognostic indicator (Keller et al 1992), it may be impossible at this stage of our knowledge to disentangle the issues of comorbidity and severity of disorder (Clark et al 1995). We next illustrate the negative impact of comorbidity involving anxiety and depression by reviewing evidence related to suicide potential.

SUICIDE POTENTIAL   Multiple studies in a range of settings have found increased rates of suicidal ideation, suicide attempts, and completed suicide in cases with comorbid anxiety and depression compared to those with a single disorder. In general, the risk of suicide is greater in patients with depression than any other single diagnosis (Wilson et al 1996) with the possible exception of substance abuse (Conwell 1996). However, the increased risk associated with comorbidity cannot be attributed simply to the presence of depression (Clark et al 1995). For instance, the co-presence of anxiety in patients with depression, or vice versa, increases the risk of suicide over the risk associated with pure depression (Bronisch & Wittchen 1994, Reich et al 1993). Moreover, the direction of causality is not simply from comorbidity to increased suicide risk: Newly abstinent substance abuse patients were more likely to develop a comorbid anxiety disorder if they had a history of suicidal ideation (Westermeyer et al 1995).

Increased rates of suicide attempts in individuals with comorbid depression and anxiety disorders have been reported in community samples (Angst 1993, Bronisch & Wittchen 1994, Lewinsohn et al 1995, Schneier et al 1992) as well as patient samples (Fawcett et al 1993, Reich et al 1993). Many studies have also examined comorbidity of anxiety and depression with other disorders and found increased suicide risk regardless of the comorbid disorder (e.g. personality disorder, Zisook et al 1994). Similarly, age does not appear to be a factor: Similar findings have been reported in children (Shafii et al 1988), adolescents (Lewinsohn et al 1995), and the elderly (Kunik 1993).

SYMPTOM CO-OCCURRENCE AND DIAGNOSTIC COMORBIDITY

Symptom Co-occurrence

The term "comorbidity" probably should be reserved to designate co-occurring disorders (or at least syndromes), but investigation of anxiety-depression comorbidity begins with the observation that key symptoms that define these theoretically distinct syndromes or disorders often co-occur. These symptoms can be divided into those that are unique to each type of disorder (e.g. panic attacks versus feelings of worthlessness) and those that are shared (e.g. difficulty concentrating). However, few of these symptoms clearly differentiate patients with one type of disorder versus the other (Clark 1989). When rated by clinicians, panic attacks, agoraphobic avoidance, and overall autonomic symptoms (but, surprisingly, not anxious mood) tend to be found more frequently in anxiety disorder patients, whereas depressed mood, anhedonia, psychomotor retardation, suicidal behavior, early-morning wakening, and pessimism (but not loss of libido, loss of appetite, feelings of worthlessness, or guilt) are generally found to be more frequent in depressed patients. However, when self-ratings are compared, depressed patients tend to report more symptoms of both types than do those with anxiety disorders (Clark 1989).

A similar picture is obtained at the syndromal level. The psychometric properties of measures assessing syndromal depression and anxiety are generally good in terms of convergent validity for both self- and clinician ratings, but the discriminant validity of self-ratings is poor in both adults (Clark & Watson 1991b) and children (Brady & Kendall 1992). Clinician ratings are notably more discriminating, suggesting that clinicians give more weight to factors that distinguish anxiety from depression than do patients. It is unclear, however, whether this represents (a) sensitivity to subtle cues that patients discount or are unaware of, or (b) rating biases on the part of clinicians. However, ratings of anxiety and depression in children by clinicians, teachers, and parents also show poor discrimination: Analyses of behavioral and observational rating scales typically yield a single anxiety-depression factor in children. It is unclear whether (a) the syndromes are less differentiated in children or (b) the scales used to assess them are less adequate than those available for use with adults (Brady & Kendall 1992).

Diagnostic Comorbidity

ANXIETY AND DEPRESSION   As noted, lifetime diagnoses of anxiety and depression show extensive comorbidity. In Clark's (1989) meta-analysis, depressed patients had an overall rate of 57% for any anxiety disorder. The NCS found a remarkably similar 58% lifetime prevalence rate (Kessler et al 1996) and an only slightly lower (51.2%) 12-month prevalence rate. In general, the likelihood of a particular anxiety disorder co-occurring with depression mirrors the base-rate prevalence of the anxiety disorder (Kessler et al 1994). That is, social and simple phobias have both higher overall base rates and the highest rates of occurrence in depressed individuals, whereas panic disorder has the lowest rate in both cases. Nonetheless, the odds ratio (OR) in all cases far exceeds co-occurrence due simply to base rates (overall OR = 4.2; Kessler et al 1996). Moras et al (1996) reported a similar phenomenon but at notably lower levels for strictly defined *current* comorbidity across 10 studies.

As for depression comorbid with anxiety, the overall average is the same (e.g. 56% in Clark's 1989 meta-analysis), but with rates widely varying by diagnosis: 67% in panic/agoraphobia, 33% in *DSM-III* GAD, 20% in social and simple phobias. The rates obtained for *DSM-III-R* GAD are considerably higher, however, in both the NCS data (62.4% for MDD, 39.5% for dysthymia; Wittchen et al 1994) and the one study (73% MDD) reported in Clark (1989), which reflects the major changes in GAD criteria between the two versions. Again, Moras et al (1996) reported lower rates for *current* comorbidity of a mood disorder with a principal anxiety disorder (24%, ranging from 15% for simple phobia to 66% for obsessive-compulsive disorder). The various anxiety disorders are also highly comorbid with each other (Brown & Barlow 1992, Brown et al 1997), but anxiety disorders in the NCS were as—or more—comorbid with depression (M OR = 6.6) as among themselves (M OR = 6.2) (Kessler 1997).

The literature on children yields similar results. Angold & Costello's (1993) review reported that comorbidity with anxiety disorders was high, ranging from 30% to 75%. Data from adolescents (e.g. DB Clark et al 1994) and from other countries (King 1990) lead to similar conclusions.

Anxiety and depression with other disorders   Our focus is on the comorbidity between anxiety and depressive disorders, but these disorders also show extensive comorbidity with other types of psychopathology. For example, anxiety and/or depressive disorders have been found to be strongly comorbid with substance-use disorders (e.g. Kendler et al 1995, Kessler 1997, Mulder 1991, Westermeyer et al 1995, Wittchen et al 1994), hypochondriasis, somatization and other somatoform disorders (e.g. Rief et al 1995), eating disorders (Braun et al 1994, Castonguay et al 1995, Herpertz-Dahlmann et al 1996), conduct and attention deficit disorders (Angold & Costello 1993, Jensen et al 1993, Loeber & Keenan 1994, Milberger et al 1995), and personality disorder (Farmer & Nelson-Gray 1990, Flick et al 1993, Mulder 1991, Shea et al 1992). This sampling of published research includes both epidemiological and clinic-based studies; draws from populations of children, adolescents, adults, and the elderly; and focuses only on the major classes of disorders for which comorbidity with anxiety and depression have been studied. Throughout this review, therefore, it is important to keep in mind that the data focused on anxiety and depression represent but one piece of a puzzle.

OTHER IMPORTANT FEATURES OF COMORBIDITY

In 1990, Alloy & Mineka and colleagues identified three "tentative" phenomena that any comprehensive theory of comorbidity in anxiety and depression should ideally be able to explain: (*a*) the sequential relationship between anxiety and depression, (*b*) the differential comorbidity of depression with various anxiety disorders, and (*c*) the relative infrequency of pure depression compared with pure anxiety (Alloy et al 1990). These phenomena were labeled "tentative" because knowledge about comorbidity was relatively sparse at that time. We now examine the current status of these phenomena.

The Sequential Relationship of Anxiety and Depression Both Within and Across Episodes

The sequential relationship between anxiety and depression has been observed both within episodes and across the lifetime. Within a single episode of illness, anxiety symptoms are more likely to precede depressive symptoms than the reverse (Alloy et al 1990). Such observations stemmed initially from both human and nonhuman primate research examining infants' responses to separation and loss, where there is typically a biphasic response of protest followed by despair or depression (e.g. Bowlby 1973, Mineka & Suomi 1978). Bowlby (1980) later argued that this initial protest response is a prototype for anxiety in adults, whereas the despair response is a prototype for depression. He noted that adults show a similar pattern in response to loss, starting with a brief period of numbness and disbelief, followed by a phase of searching and yearning (cf intense anxiety), and then often by a phase of disorganization and despair (cf severe depression). The experimental literature on response to uncontrollable aversive events also suggests that anxiety symptoms are much more likely to precede depressive symptoms than vice versa (Alloy et al 1990).

Regarding lifetime comorbidity, Alloy et al (1990) also reviewed evidence that an anxiety disorder is significantly more likely to precede a mood disorder than the reverse. This phenomenon is now well established. For example, in the International WHO/ADAMHA CIDI field trials, of the 242 individuals with comorbid anxiety and mood disorders, 59% had had the onset of the first anxiety disorder at least a year before the onset of the first mood disorder, only 15% had experienced the onset of a mood disorder before the onset of the first anxiety disorder, and another 26% experienced the onset of both within the same year (Lepine et al 1993).

Similarly, in the NCS data, Kessler et al (1997) found that all the anxiety disorder diagnoses are associated with an elevated risk of a later diagnosis of minor or major depression. The ORs were especially high for severe major depression (7–9 symptoms), ranging from 2.86 for social phobia to 12.87 for GAD. Kessler (1997) also reported that anxiety disorders were more likely to be temporally primary. For example, nearly 83% of patients with one or more lifetime anxiety disorders reported that one of these was their first disorder; in contrast, only about 44% of those with a mood disorder reported that it was their first disorder. In fact, most cases (roughly 62%) of lifetime major depression are secondary to other *DSM-III-R* disorder(s), with anxiety disorders being the most common primary conditions (about 68% of cases with secondary depression are associated with a temporally primary anxiety disorder) (Kessler et al 1996). The elevated risk of depression in those with a temporally primary anxiety disorder endures for many years without changing in magnitude.

Similarly, recent reanalyses of the ECA study (approximately 18,000 adults) indicated that of the participants with comorbid depression and social phobia, the latter was temporally primary for nearly 71% (Schneier et al 1992). Lewinsohn et al (1997) reported similar findings in a study of over 10,000 high school students. Finally, Kovacs et al (1989) reported that anxiety tends to precede depression in children (reviewed in Brady & Kendall 1992).

The Differential Comorbidity Between Depression and Different Anxiety Disorders

Alloy et al's (1990) early review also suggested that individuals who received the diagnoses of panic disorder, agoraphobia, obsessive-compulsive disorder, and post-traumatic stress disorder were more likely to experience depression than were those with generalized anxiety disorder, social phobia, or simple phobia. The NCS data generally confirmed this conclusion through the use of OR that take into account the large base-rate differences for the different disorders (Kessler et al 1996). Specifically, lifetime comorbidity data for major depression revealed OR of 2.9 for social phobia, 3.1 for simple phobia, 3.4 for agoraphobia, 4.0 for panic disorder and post-traumatic stress disorder, and 6.0 for GAD (results for obsessive-compulsive disorder are not presented). Thus, the one exception to the pattern observed by Alloy et al (1990) was that GAD was the anxiety disorder *most* likely to co-occur with MDD. Lepine et al (1993) also largely replicated these results, except that social phobia was nearly as highly associated with MDD as were agoraphobia and panic disorder. Finally, Brown & Barlow (1992) reported results from a clinical sample in which obsessive-compulsive disorder and severe agoraphobia were most highly associated with MDD and dysthymia, whereas simple phobia was least associated, and social phobia and GAD were intermediate.

Thus, results seem to confirm that obsessive-compulsive disorder, panic disorder and agoraphobia, and post-traumatic stress disorder are highly associated with MDD and that simple phobia is either less or not associated with it. The results for social phobia and GAD are less consistent, with more recent data suggesting a significantly stronger association with depression. The inconsistent results for GAD likely reflect the major changes in diagnostic criteria made between *DSM-III* and *DSM-III-R*.

The Relative Infrequency of Pure Depression

Alloy et al (1990) also summarized evidence that cases of pure depression without concomitant anxiety were rarer than cases of pure anxiety without concomitant depression. This pattern can be observed at the purely symptomatic level: Individuals with a diagnosis of MDD typically show levels of anxiety on self-report or clinical rating scales that are as high as—or higher than—those of patients with a diagnosis of GAD or panic disorder (e.g. DiNardo & Barlow 1990). It also occurs at the diagnostic level: The likelihood that someone with a mood disorder also will receive an anxiety-disorder diagnosis (either concurrently or subsequently) appears to be greater than the reverse. In the ECA study, 43% of individuals with a mood disorder also received an anxiety diagnosis at some time in their lives, whereas only 25% of those with an anxiety disorder also received a lifetime mood disorder diagnosis (Regier et al 1990). In the NCS data, 58% of those with a lifetime diagnosis of a depressive disorder also had an anxiety disorder (Kessler et al 1996). Finally, in eight of the nine studies of children and adolescents reviewed by Angold & Costello (1993), the rates of mood disorder in those with an anxiety disorder were substantially lower than vice versa.

Theoretical Perspectives on These Important Features of Comorbidity

THE HELPLESSNESS/HOPELESSNESS PERSPECTIVE   Alloy, Mineka, and colleagues proposed a helplessness/hopelessness perspective to clarify these important features of anxiety-depression comorbidity (Alloy et al 1990, see also Garber et al 1980). Their model integrates Abramson et al's (1989) hopelessness theory of depression with extensive research documenting the importance of perceived uncontrollability in the etiology of anxiety (e.g. Barlow 1988, Barlow et al 1996, Mineka 1985, Mineka & Kelly 1989, Mineka & Zinbarg 1996). Uncontrollable, stressful life events were originally implicated as playing a central etiological role in depression (e.g. Seligman 1974). However, later reformulations of the helplessness theory of depression deemphasized uncontrollability per se and focused on the central role that key cognitive variables play in determining vulnerability to depression following negative life events (Abramson et al 1978). In a later reformulation, expectations of hopelessness were hypothesized to serve as proximal and sufficient causal factors for the onset of depression (Abramson et al 1989). Concurrently, anxiety researchers—based in large part on animal research—were recognizing the central role that perceptions of uncontrollability play in creating vulnerability to anxiety as well as depression (e.g. Barlow 1988, Mineka 1985, Mineka & Kelly 1989).

Alloy et al (1990) proposed that the interplay of three cognitive components of helplessness and hopelessness may determine, at least in part, whether a person experiences pure anxiety, a mixed anxiety-depression syndrome, or hopelessness depression. Specifically, they proposed that the interplay of helplessness expectancies, negative-outcome expectancies, and the certainty of these expectancies influences which of these states will be experienced. Individuals uncertain about their ability to control important outcomes would be most likely to experience pure anxiety. In contrast, those who are more certain about their helplessness—but still uncertain about whether a negative outcome will actually occur—will experience a mixed anxiety-depressive state. Finally, individuals who are certain of both their helplessness and the occurrence of a negative outcome will experience hopelessness depression, characterized by despair, loss of interest, and suicidality. Thus, anxiety and depression share expectations of helplessness but differ in negative-outcome expectancies (see also Garber et al 1980). Numerous other theorists have also argued that anxiety is characterized by helplessness (e.g. Beck & Emery 1985, Mandler 1972), whereas depression is centered on hopelessness (e.g. Beck 1967, Brown & Harris 1978).

Alloy et al (1990) argued that this perspective is useful in accounting for the three important features of comorbidity discussed. The sequential relationship between anxiety and depressive symptoms is explained by noting that expectancies of helplessness (certain or uncertain) are likely to precede the development of certain negative-outcome expectancies when efforts to exert control may all fail. The across-episode sequential relationship between anxiety and depression may occur because prior experiences with uncertain helplessness (and anxiety) may increase one's vulnerability to more certain helplessness and even hopelessness (and hopelessness depression) in the face of future severe stressors, perhaps especially when an individual has a pessimistic attributional style (i.e. attributing negative outcomes to stable and global causes). This perspective is also consistent with findings that anxiety is associated with anticipated threat or danger, whereas depression is often preceded by a major loss event (e.g. Brown et al 1993, Monroe 1990). Loss events are more likely to lead to hopelessness and depression given that a bad outcome has occurred; threat events have an inherent uncertainty and are more likely to lead to a sense of helplessness and therefore anxiety.

Regarding the differential comorbidity of depression with the different anxiety disorders, Alloy et al (1990) hypothesized that those anxiety disorders characterized by more chronic and pervasive feelings of helplessness would show higher rates of comorbidity with depression. They therefore argued that panic disorder and agoraphobia, obsessive-compulsive disorder, and post-traumatic stress disorder should show a particularly strong degree of overlap with depression, which has been supported by more recent evidence. Alloy et al further argued that the more pervasive feelings of helplessness associated with these disorders might stem, in part, from the intrusive and terrifying nature of many of their symptoms (e.g. panic attacks, obsessions, compulsions, flashbacks, nightmares, etc). To the extent that such symptoms are perceived as uncontrollable, over prolonged periods a state of certain helplessness would be expected to emerge, which would then lead to depression. Individuals with a pessimistic attributional style who have these anxiety disorders (Heimberg et al 1989, Mineka et al 1995) may be particularly prone to developing depression in response to the experience of uncontrollable anxiety symptoms.

Social phobia and simple phobia, by contrast, should be expected to be associated with a more circumscribed sense of helplessness, perhaps accounting for the lower rates of comorbidity of these disorders with depression. Individuals with generalized social phobia, as opposed to specific social phobia, should show higher levels of depression given that their lives are far more restricted in terms of the social situations they fear and avoid. Holt et al (1992) and Turner et al (1992) both reported such findings.

However, Alloy et al (1990) did not predict the recent findings of high rates of comorbidity between GAD and MDD, given that chronic worry and other generalized anxiety symptoms would not generally be expected to lead to as pervasive a sense of uncontrollability as would panic disorder, obsessive-compulsive disorder, and post-traumatic stress disorder. However, below we review evidence for a common genetic diathesis for GAD and MDD that may be the important key to this relationship rather than any factor posited by Alloy et al's perspective.

Finally, the relative infrequency of pure depression is explained by the observation that the cognition of hopelessness is a subset of helplessness cognitions. That is, people who are hopeless also perceive that they are helpless but the reverse is not necessarily true. This could account for why pure anxiety is much more likely to be observed than is pure depression.

BOWLBY'S ATTACHMENT-OBJECT LOSS THEORY   Bowlby wrote extensively about the relationship between anxiety and depression from the vantage point of attachment theory (1973, 1980) and later incorporated ideas from cognitive psychology into his perspective (1980). Attachment theory views attachment behavior in evolutionary/functional terms, with a young infant's attachment behavior serving to create a secure base from which to explore the environment. When separation from the attachment object occurs, a biphasic protest-despair response occurs. Early experiences with separation and loss (as well as the nature of the attachment relationships per se) are postulated to have major effects on adult attachment relationships as well as on response to adulthood stressors. The effects of these early experiences are thought to be mediated through the development of cognitive schemata that later affect an adult's response to disruptions in attachment relationships.

Bowlby's perspective can explain various aspects of comorbidity. First, the sequential relationship between anxiety and depressive symptoms (within episode) is explicitly predicted; indeed, his observations of children and adults in response to separation and loss are key findings documenting this phenomenon (Bowlby 1973). Second, pure depression is infrequent because people first become anxious about the threat of a loss (or as an initial response to an actual loss); however, if the loss does not occur, or does not persist, or if a substitute attachment occurs, then depression may never occur. In this regard, the importance of social support in buffering against depression in the face of major life stressors has received considerable support in the literature (e.g. Brown et al 1993). Bowlby (1980) also noted, however, that once the depression phase occurs, it is usually interspersed with phases of anxiety and longing for the lost attachment object (mixed anxiety-depression). Finally, Bowlby's perspective (1973, 1980) explicitly predicts the high levels of comorbidity between panic disorder/agoraphobia and depression, in that disordered attachment relationships (early in life and/or in adulthood) play a central role in both conditions, and both are often precipitated by a major loss.

STRUCTURAL MODELS OF ANXIETY AND DEPRESSION

As mentioned, the unitary versus dual construct debate has gradually given way to more sophisticated views of the anxiety-depression relationship. Investigators have used a variety of multivariate techniques to isolate common and unique features of the two constructs and have developed structural models to conceptualize the findings that emerged. We now review the evolution of structural models at both the genotypic and phenotypic levels.

The Genotypic Structure of Depression and Anxiety

SYMPTOM LEVEL ANALYSES   Beginning in the 1980s, numerous studies have examined the genetic links between anxiety and depression, primarily investigating whether a common genetic diathesis renders certain individuals vulnerable to the development of both types of disorder. The first major analysis investigated self-reported anxious and depressive symptoms in a large, community-based sample of Australian twins (Jardine et al 1984). These analyses indicated that the observed phenotypic covariation between the two types of symptoms was largely due to a single common genetic factor (see also Kendler et al 1987). Moreover, this same genetic factor was shared with neuroticism, a broad personality trait that reflects individual differences in subjective distress

125

and dissatisfaction (see Kendler et al 1993a, Watson et al 1994). Thus, anxiety, depression, and neuroticism could be linked to a single genetic diathesis that apparently represents an underlying vulnerability to subjective distress and negative affectivity.

Subsequent analyses of these same data, however, revealed that symptoms of a panic attack (e.g. breathlessness or heart pounding) reflected unique genetic variance that differentiated them from other symptoms of depression and anxiety (Kendler et al 1987) and from neuroticism (Martin et al 1988). Thus, these symptom-level data revealed an important distinction between the cognitive/affective versus somatic symptoms of anxiety, with the former being more closely related to depression and neuroticism than the latter.

DIAGNOSTIC ANALYSES   More recently, a number of genetic studies have examined the issue at the diagnostic level and again have revealed evidence of both commonality and specificity, with the level of overlap varying systematically across the individual anxiety disorders. At one extreme, analyses consistently have found that major depression and GAD are genetically indistinguishable; that is, the genetic correlation between these disorders is essentially unity, indicating that they reflect a single, common genetic diathesis (Kendler 1996, Kendler et al 1992, Roy et al 1995). Moreover, replicating results at the symptom level, Kendler et al (1993a) found that this common genetic diathesis was also strongly linked to neuroticism, suggesting that this shared genetic factor represents a general tendency to respond poorly to stress and, therefore, to experience frequent and intense episodes of distress and negative affect (Kendler et al 1992, 1995).

In contrast, anxiety disorders other than GAD are more modestly related to depression. Panic disorder, for example, is genetically distinguishable from both GAD and depression (Kendler 1996, Kendler et al 1995, Woodman 1993), a finding that replicates the symptom-level results. Similarly, Kendler et al (1993b) found that major depression shared a moderate amount of genetic variance with agoraphobia, social phobia, and animal phobia but was genetically unrelated to situational phobias (e.g. fears of tunnels, bridges, heights). Other evidence indicates that obsessive-compulsive disorder is genetically distinct from major depression, GAD, panic, and the phobias (Pauls et al 1994); in fact, unlike these other syndromes, obsessive-compulsive disorder appears to have a strong genetic link to Tourette's syndrome (Pauls 1992, Pauls et al 1995).

To date, Kendler et al (1995) have reported the most comprehensive analysis of the genetic architecture of depression and the anxiety disorders, examining the associations among major depression, GAD, panic, and the phobias. They found evidence of two significant genetic factors. One factor was primarily defined by major depression and GAD (loadings of .64 and .47, respectively); panic disorder also had a moderate loading (.35) on this factor, but the phobias were largely unrelated to it (a loading of only .14). In contrast, the second factor was defined primarily by panic disorder and the phobias (loadings of .58 and .57, respectively).

SUMMARY AND IMPLICATIONS   The genetic evidence has important implications for our understanding of the mood and anxiety disorders. First, it is clear that the anxiety disorders themselves are genetically heterogeneous (Kendler 1996, Kendler et al 1995). Thus, one cannot posit a single invariant relation between depression and the anxiety disorders; rather, the nature of the relation necessarily will depend on the type of anxiety that is examined. Consistent with this view, the accumulating data indicate that depression is genetically indistinguishable from GAD, moderately related to panic, and more modestly related to the phobias (which are themselves heterogeneous) (Kendler et al 1993b, 1995). In addition, major depression and GAD both are closely linked to the broad personality trait of neuroticism (LA Clark et al 1994, Jardine et al 1984, Kendler et al 1993a). Taken together, these data suggest that the observed covariation between depression and anxiety is largely attributable to a shared genetic factor that reflects general individual differences in subjective distress and negative affectivity. However, the precise nature of this shared genetic factor remains unclear (for discussions, see Carey & DiLalla 1994, Neale & Kendler 1995, Roy et al 1995).

Finally, these data have potentially important implications for the classification of these disorders within the *DSM*, in that they indicate that GAD is more closely linked to major depression than to the other anxiety disorders (Kendler et al 1995). It is noteworthy, moreover, that comorbidity and structural-modeling data demonstrate this same pattern at the phenotypic level (Brown et al 1995, 1997). Therefore, maximum clarity in this area might be achieved by rearranging the mood and anxiety disorders to place greater emphasis on the close affinity between distress-based disorders such as major depression and GAD.

The Phenotypic Structure of Depression and Anxiety

TWO-FACTOR AFFECTIVE MODEL   Paralleling the genetic data, phenotypic models increasingly have emphasized that depression and anxiety are characterized by both common and distinctive features. An early example of this approach was a two-factor model based on the seminal work of Tellegen (1985) that emphasized the role of basic dimensions of affect. Extensive research has demonstrated that affective experience is characterized by two general factors:

Negative Affect and Positive Affect (Tellegen 1985, Watson & Clark 1997, Watson & Tellegen 1985). Negative Affect reflects the extent to which a person is experiencing negative mood states such as fear, sadness, anger, and guilt, whereas Positive Affect reflects the extent to which one reports positive feelings such as joy, enthusiasm, energy, and alertness.

These two general dimensions are differentially related to depression and anxiety. Specifically, depression and anxiety both are strongly related to measures of general Negative Affect. In contrast, measures of Positive Affect are consistently negatively correlated with depressed mood and symptomatology but are largely unrelated to anxious mood and symptomatology (Dyck et al 1994, Jolly et al 1994, Tellegen 1985, Watson et al 1988). Thus, in this two-factor model Negative Affect represents a *nonspecific* factor common to depression and anxiety, whereas Positive Affect is a *specific* factor that is related primarily to depression.

TRIPARTITE MODEL   Clark & Watson (1991b) extended this model by proposing a second specific factor—physiological hyperarousal—that is relatively specific to anxiety. They therefore argued that a "tripartite model" offered a more accurate characterization of anxious and depressive phenomena. In this model, symptoms of depression and anxiety can be grouped into three basic subtypes. First, many symptoms are strong indicators of a general distress or Negative Affect factor. This nonspecific group includes both anxious and depressed mood, as well as other symptoms (insomnia, poor concentration, etc) that are prevalent in both types of disorder. However, each syndrome also is characterized by its own cluster of symptoms: somatic tension and hyperarousal (e.g. shortness of breath, dizziness and lightheadedness, dry mouth) are relatively specific to anxiety, whereas manifestations of anhedonia and the absence of Positive Affect (e.g. loss of interest, feeling that nothing is interesting or enjoyable) are relatively specific to depression.

BARLOW'S THREE-FACTOR MODEL   Recently, Barlow and his colleagues have articulated a very similar three-factor model (Barlow et al 1996, Chorpita et al 1997). This model emphasizes that the mood and anxiety disorders are fundamentally disorders of emotion (Barlow 1988, 1991) and so relates these disorders to processes associated with the three basic emotions of anxiety (or "anxious apprehension"), fear, and depression. At the symptom level, Barlow and colleagues argue that (*a*) general distress and Negative Affect are manifestations of *anxiety* (anxious apprehension), (*b*) autonomic arousal is an expression of *fear/panic*, and (*c*) anhedonia, low Positive Affect, and hopelessness are indicators of *depression*. Paralleling the tripartite model of Clark & Watson (1991b), autonomic arousal and anhedonia/low Positive Affect are viewed as unique symptom clusters that are relatively specific to the anxiety and mood disorders, respectively, whereas general distress and Negative Affect are relatively nonspecific symptoms that are strongly characteristic of both types of disorder.

TESTS OF THE THREE-FACTOR MODELS   The formulation of these three-factor models has stimulated a new wave of research into the phenotypic structure of anxious and depressive symptoms. Several early studies subjected existing psychometric instruments to traditional exploratory factor analyses. Consistent with the tripartite model, these studies found clear evidence of three factors: a specific anxiety factor, a specific depression factor, and a general factor that subsumed both types of phenomena (DA Clark et al 1990, Jolly & Dykman 1994, Jolly & Kramer 1994).

One limitation of these studies is that they relied on measures that were laden with items assessing general distress/Negative Affect, and that covered the two hypothesized specific symptom groups (i.e. somatic hyperarousal and anhedonia/low Positive Affect) less satisfactorily. This meant that the nonspecific factor tended to be quite large relative to the two specific factors; moreover, the paucity of good hyperarousal and/or anhedonia items (particularly the latter) made it difficult to identify specific factors that closely matched the predictions generated by the three-factor models. Nevertheless, several investigators obtained structures that offered strong support for these models (DA Clark et al 1994; Steer et al 1994, 1995), with the exception that the third somatic factor was sometimes broader than expected (Dyck et al 1994).

To address these measure-based limitations, Watson & Clark (1991) created the Mood and Anxiety Symptom Questionnaire (MASQ). Watson et al (1995b) tested the prediction that symptoms of somatic arousal and anhedonia offer the best differentiation of anxiety and depression using two specific scales—Anhedonic Depression and Anxious Arousal—composed of items assessing anhedonia/low Positive Affect and somatic arousal, respectively. Consistent with the tripartite model, these specific scales provided the best differentiation of the constructs in each of five samples, with correlations ranging from .25 to .49 ($M = .34$). In contrast, measures of anxious and depressed mood—which, according to the tripartite model, should demonstrate much poorer specificity—consistently showed a much higher level of overlap, with correlations ranging from .61 to .78 ($M = .69$).

Watson et al (1995a) subjected the 90 MASQ items to separate factor analyses in each of five samples (three student, one adult, one patient). Consistent with the model, three large and replicable dimensions could be identified: a nonspecific general distress factor, a bipolar dimension of positive mood versus anhedonia, and a factor defined largely by somatic manifestations of anxiety. However, the specific anxiety factor was somewhat broader than expected and included several somatic symptoms that do not clearly reflect sympathetic arousal (e.g. nausea, diarrhea). Consequently, this third factor is better characterized as "somatic anxiety" rather than the hypothesized dimension of "anxious arousal." Importantly, the same three factors emerged in each of the five data sets, indicating that symptom structure in this domain is reasonably robust across diverse samples.

Several recent studies have broadened the empirical support for the tripartite model in notable ways. For instance, Joiner et al (1996) showed that the three hypothesized factors emerged in a sample of child and adolescent psychiatric inpatients, thereby extending the model to younger respondents. Joiner (1996) explicitly tested the viability of the model in college students using confirmatory factor analysis; he found that the hypothesized three-factor structure provided a good fit to the observed data, whereas one- and two-factor structures did not. Chorpita et al (1997) replicated and extended these findings in a clinical sample of children and adolescents, conducting confirmatory factor analyses on both self- and parent ratings; again, the hypothesized three-factor model best fit the data. Similarly, Brown et al (1997) reported evidence supporting the tripartite model in LISREL analyses using both self-report and interview-based data.

Psychophysiological analyses offer further support for the tripartite model by demonstrating that the three hypothesized symptom groups reflect highly distinctive patterns of brain activity. Specifically, individuals reporting elevated levels of general Negative Affect consistently show augmented base startle reactivity (Cook et al 1991, Lang et al 1993); this exaggerated basal startle response is thought to be mediated by the bed nucleus of the stria terminalis (Cuthbert et al 1996, Davis et al 1997) and can be distinguished from the cue-based reactivity characteristic of phobics (Cuthbert & Melamed 1993, McNeil et al 1993), which appears to be mediated by the base nucleus of the amygdala (Cuthbert et al 1996, Davis et al 1997). Other evidence has linked heightened levels of Negative Affect to increased activity in the right frontal cortex (Bruder et al 1997, Tomarken & Keener 1997).

The two hypothesized specific factors—anhedonia and anxious arousal—show markedly different patterns of psychophysiological activity. Anxious arousal consistently has been linked to *hyper*activation of the right parietotemporal region; in sharp contrast, anhedonia and low Positive Affect are associated with *hypo*activation of this same region (Bruder et al 1997, Heller 1993, Heller et al 1995), as well as hypoactivation of the left prefrontal area (Larsen et al 1995, Tomarken & Keener 1997). It is noteworthy that formerly depressed patients who were currently euthymic also showed left frontal hypoactivation (Henriques & Davidson 1990, see also Allen et al 1993), as did asymptomatic adolescent children of depressed mothers (Tomarken & Keener 1997).

On the basis of these data, Davidson, Tomarken, and their colleagues have argued that left frontal hypoactivation reflects a characterological deficit in a reward-oriented approach system that clinically manifests itself as a loss of interest and motivation (i.e. anhedonia; see Henriques & Davidson 1991, Tomarken et al 1992, Tomarken & Keener 1997). Further evidence links this frontal asymmetry to activity in the mesolimbic dopaminergic system, which also has been related to individual differences in positive emotionality versus anhedonia (Depue et al 1994, Tomarken & Keener 1997).

CLARIFYING THE RELATION AMONG THE THREE FACTORS Although an impressive array of evidence demonstrates the existence of three separable factors, the nature of the relations among these factors remains an unresolved and somewhat controversial issue. Investigators in some of the earlier studies extracted highly correlated lower order factors corresponding to depression and anxiety, which then gave rise to a second order dimension of general distress or Negative Affect (e.g. DA Clark et al 1994, Steer et al 1995). These results suggest a hierarchical three-factor model in which the traditional syndromes of anxiety and depression represent narrow, lower order constructs that are highly interrelated; in this hierarchical model, the Negative Affect dimension emerges as a broader, more general construct that represents the strong degree of overlap between the lower order syndromes. In other studies, however, general distress, anhedonia/low Positive Affect, and somatic arousal have emerged as three separable first order factors. In some analyses, the somatic anxiety and Negative Affect factors are moderately to strongly interrelated (e.g. Brown et al 1997, Chorpita et al 1997, Joiner 1996), but in other cases all three factors are largely independent of one another (Joiner et al 1996, Watson et al 1995b). These data suggest a nonhierarchical model in which the three hypothesized symptom factors exist at the same basic level of generality.

To a considerable extent, these apparently inconsistent findings reflect the types of variables that were included in these structural analyses. That is, studies using traditional assessment instruments, instruments laden with items tapping general Negative Affect have tended to support a hierarchical model with a dominant higher order factor. In contrast, analyses using carefully selected items that are explicitly linked to the tripartite model have yielded greater support for a nonhierarchical arrangement (see Joiner 1996, Joiner et al 1996). Still, these factors alone cannot account for all of the reported inconsistencies, and further investigations of this issue (e.g. using techniques such as LISREL) are needed. To date, Brown et al (1997) reported the most compelling analysis. They tested various alternative structural models and found evidence of two higher order factors; one of these (Positive Affect) was specifically related to depression, whereas the other (Negative Affect) was nonspecific. The third component of the tripartite model—anxious arousal—emerged as a specific lower order factor.

An Integrative Hierarchical Model of Anxiety and Depression

HETEROGENEITY OF THE ANXIETY DISORDERS   It has become increasingly apparent that at both the genotypic and phenotypic levels, the anxiety disorders are heterogeneous and subsume a diverse array of symptoms (Brown et al 1997, Kendler 1996, Kendler et al 1995, Zinbarg & Barlow 1996). This heterogeneity has important implications for structural models. First, as reviewed earlier, the individual anxiety disorders clearly are differentially related to depression, with certain types of anxiety showing much greater overlap than others. Second, the individual anxiety disorders are differentially related to one another; for example, panic disorder is much more highly related to GAD than to obsessive-compulsive disorder (Brown et al 1997). Third, it is increasingly clear that a single specific factor—such as the anxious arousal or somatic anxiety component of the tripartite model—is insufficient to account fully for the diversity of symptoms subsumed by the anxiety disorders.

BARLOW'S HIERARCHICAL MODEL OF THE ANXIETY DISORDERS   To address this last problem, Barlow and colleagues have proposed a hierarchical model of the anxiety disorders (Barlow 1991, Brown & Barlow 1992, Zinbarg & Barlow 1996). They assert that each of the individual anxiety disorders contains a shared component that represents the higher order factor in a two-level hierarchical scheme. In earlier treatments of the model, this higher order factor usually was described as "anxious apprehension" (e.g. Barlow 1991, Brown & Barlow 1992); in more recent papers, however, Barlow and colleagues have acknowledged that it essentially represents the general Negative Affect component of the tripartite model (Brown et al 1997, Zinbarg & Barlow 1996). Accordingly, this higher order factor not only is common across the anxiety disorders but is shared with depression; therefore, it primarily is responsible for the observed overlap both among the individual anxiety disorders and between depression and anxiety. In addition to this shared component, however, each of the anxiety disorders also contains a specific, unique component that distinguishes it from all the others (for a parallel analysis of the childhood anxiety disorders, see Spence 1997).

Several recent structural analyses, which use both self-report and interview-based data, have yielded strong support for this hierarchical view (Brown et al 1997, Spence 1997, Zinbarg & Barlow 1996). The results of Brown et al (1997) are especially noteworthy: They found that the anxious arousal component of the tripartite model was not generally characteristic of the anxiety disorders but instead represented the specific, unique component of panic disorder.

132

AN INTEGRATIVE HIERARCHICAL MODEL OF ANXIETY AND DEPRESSION   We suggest that a more accurate and comprehensive structural model, one that is consistent with both the genotypic and phenotypic data, is one that integrates key features of Clark & Watson's (1991b) tripartite model with Barlow's (1991, Zinbarg & Barlow 1996) hierarchical model of the anxiety disorders. In this integrative, hierarchical model, each individual syndrome can be viewed as containing both a common and a unique component. The shared component represents broad individual differences in general distress and Negative Affect; it is a pervasive higher order factor that is common to both the mood and anxiety disorders and is primarily responsible for the overlap among these disorders. In addition, each disorder also includes a unique component that differentiates it from all the others. For instance, anhedonia, disinterest, and the absence of Positive Affect comprise the specific, unique component of depression.

Thus far, all of these propositions are fully consistent with the original tripartite model. The major change, which is necessitated by the marked heterogeneity of the anxiety disorders, is that anxious arousal no longer is viewed as broadly characteristic of all anxiety disorders; rather, it assumes a more limited role as the specific component of panic disorder (see Brown et al 1997). Note that each of the other anxiety disorders—with the possible exception of GAD, which clearly contains an enormous amount of general distress variance (e.g. Brown & Barlow 1992, Brown et al 1997)—includes its own unique component that is differentiable from anxious arousal. An important task for future research is to specify the nature of these unique components more precisely. In this regard, Brown et al (1997) have demonstrated that one obtains a clearer and more accurate view of these specific components after the influence of the general Negative Affect factor is eliminated.

Both the scope and the precision of this integrative model can be enhanced with three additional considerations. First, the size of the general and specific components differs markedly across the various anxiety disorders. For example, the genetic and phenotypic data both establish that depression and GAD are distress-based disorders containing an enormous amount of variance attributable to general Negative Affect; in contrast, obsessive-compulsive disorder, social phobia, and specific phobia all appear to contain a more modest component of general distress (e.g. Brown et al 1997, Kendler 1996, Kendler et al 1995). Thus, future research must move beyond the simple truism that each disorder is characterized by both a common and a unique component and specify the proportions of general and specific variance that are characteristic of each syndrome.

Second, it now is obvious that this general Negative Affect dimension is not confined solely to the mood and anxiety disorders, but is even more broadly related to psychopathology (e.g. Hinden et al 1997). Significant elevations in Negative Affectivity and neuroticism have been reported in a wide array of syndromes, including substance use disorders, somatoform disorders, eating disorders, personality and conduct disorders, and schizophrenia (e.g. Krueger et al 1996, Trull & Sher 1994, Watson & Clark 1994). Indeed, Widiger & Costa (1994) recently concluded that "neuroticism is an almost ubiquitously elevated trait within clinical populations" (p. 81). Thus, this integrative model clearly need not be confined to the mood and anxiety disorders, and we encourage future investigators to expand its scope to include a broad range of associated phenomena, such as the personality and somatoform disorders.

Third, symptom specificity must be viewed in relative rather than absolute terms. It is highly unlikely that any group of symptoms will be found to be unique to a single disorder across the entire *DSM*, if for no other reason than that the current taxonomic system contains many problematic diagnoses with overlapping symptoms and unclear boundaries (see Clark et al 1995). Moreover, it is clear that symptoms do not conform neatly to existing diagnostic categories but instead tend to characterize clusters of related disorders. For instance, anhedonia and low Positive Affect are not confined solely to depression, but also characterize—to a lesser degree, perhaps—schizophrenia, social phobia, and other disorders (e.g. Brown et al 1997, Watson & Clark 1995, Watson et al 1988). This suggests that we need to move toward more complex, multilevel hierarchical models in which groups of symptoms are classified at varying levels of specificity. Furthermore, it may be best to view individual disorders as representing unique *combinations* of different types of symptoms, with each type showing varying degrees of nonspecificity and with no type being entirely unique to any single disorder.

COGNITIVE APPROACHES TO ANXIETY AND DEPRESSION

Beck's Cognitive-Content Specificity Approach

In 1976, Beck expanded his cognitive model of depression into a more general model of psychopathology, focusing especially on similarities and differences between the anxiety and mood disorders. The theory holds that these disorders are characterized by specific kinds of cognitions (Beck 1976, Beck & Emery 1985). The automatic thoughts of depressed people tend to focus on themes of self-depreciation and negative attitudes about the world and the future and are fueled by underlying depressogenic schemas that are organized around themes of loss, personal deficiency, worthlessness, and hopelessness. By contrast, the automatic thoughts of anxious individuals are focused on anticipated future harm or danger and are fueled by schemas organized around themes of danger, uncertainty, and future threat.

Several studies have provided important tests of this cognitive-content specificity approach, as well as of its relationship to the tripartite model of anxiety and depression discussed earlier. An initial test of the theory (Beck et al 1987) involved the development of a Cognition Checklist (CCL) that measured automatic thoughts considered to be relevant to depression (e.g. "I'm worthless," "I don't deserve to be loved") and anxiety (e.g. "I might be trapped," "I am going to have an accident"). The CCL was administered to outpatients at the Center for Cognitive Therapy, together with the Hamilton Rating Scales and structured diagnostic interviews. As predicted, depressed patients had higher scores on the CCL-Depression scale, whereas anxious patients scored more highly on the CCL-Anxiety scale. Moreover, the CCL-Depression scale was significantly correlated with the Hamilton Depression scale, even when controlling for anxiety, and vice versa for the CCL-Anxiety scale.

DA Clark et al (1990) subsequently conducted a similar study of another large outpatient sample, using several additional self-report measures. This study also provided a preliminary test of the extent to which Beck's cognitive-content specificity approach to anxiety and depression was complementary (vs contradictory) to the two-factor affective model discussed previously. An initial factor analysis of the anxiety and depression measures revealed a large general factor, which could be interpreted as negative affectivity, that accounted for roughly 40% of the variance. However, a second analysis in which two factors were extracted, one that clearly represents depression and the other anxiety, provided a better fit to the data. Moreover, depressed patients reported significantly more hopelessness, lower self-worth, and more negative thoughts involving failure and loss; anxious patients had more thoughts of anticipated danger and harm. Not surprisingly, patients with comorbid anxiety-depression diagnoses showed a mixed cognitive profile.

Three recent studies from the same research group (one with 844 outpatients, one with 1000 outpatients, and one with 420 undergraduates) tested the complementarity of the cognitive-content specificity approach with the tripartite model (DA Clark et al 1994, Steer et al 1995). Separate analyses of the three samples yielded a very large second order factor in each case (accounting for approximately 40–50% of the variance), which clearly could be interpreted as the general distress/Negative Affect dimension of the tripartite model. However, each analysis also revealed specific first order factors corresponding to depression and anxiety. Consistent with Beck's model, cognitive content centered on personal loss and failure loaded strongly on the lower order depression factor and more modestly on the higher order Negative Affect factor. Specific motivational and behavioral symptoms of depression (e.g. fatigability, social withdrawal) also were significant markers of the specific depression factor, although they were modestly related to the general distress factor as well. Moreover, consistent with the tripartite model, a measure of positive emotionality was strongly negatively correlated with scores on the specific depression factor (DA Clark et al 1990). Finally, as predicted by the tripartite model, physiological symptoms of anxiety were most strongly related to the first order anxiety factor. Interestingly, the cognitive symptoms of anxiety were more strongly related to the higher order distress factor than to the specific anxiety factor. These results parallel the genetic analyses described earlier, which also revealed cognitive/affective symptoms of anxiety to be more closely related to neuroticism than were somatic symptoms. Overall, analyses of all three samples yielded broad support for both the tripartite and cognitive-content specificity models and clearly establish the compatibility of these approaches.

Information Processing Approaches: Cognitive Biases for Emotion-Relevant Material

In addition to work comparing the thought *content* of anxious and depressed people, the past decade also has seen much interest in the effects that these disorders have on cognitive *processing*. Researchers have been particularly interested in the role that cognitive biases may play in the etiology and/or maintenance of these disorders. The term "cognitive bias" refers to any selective or nonveridical processing of emotion-relevant information (e.g. Mineka 1992, Mineka & Tomarken 1989). Although the idea that both anxiety and depression can disrupt efficient cognitive processing in a general way has a long history (MacLeod & Mathews 1991), the focus of this research has been to delineate how these disorders often selectively affect processing of *emotion-relevant* material. More than a decade of research has shown that anxiety and depression have prominent effects on different aspects of information processing; most of the research has focused on attentional and memory biases, with a smaller amount addressing judgmental biases. In the current context, it is of particular interest to determine the similarity vs distinctiveness of the biases associated with these disorders.

ATTENTIONAL BIASES   Many studies show that anxiety is associated with an attentional bias for threatening information, such that anxious patients' attention is drawn toward threatening cues when both threatening and nonthreatening cues are available. Nonanxious individuals tend, if anything, to show the opposite bias. These studies have used a number of different paradigms, ranging from the emotional Stroop or interference tasks to various attentional probe tasks. The bias appears to occur preconsciously, that is, without awareness (for reviews, see MacLeod & Mathews 1991, Mathews & MacLeod 1994, Mineka &

Sutton 1992). Many researchers believe that this attentional bias for threat may play a role in the maintenance of anxiety. That is, having one's attention automatically drawn toward threatening information may help to maintain or exacerbate anxiety. Results from at least one experiment suggest that the tendency to exhibit this bias may serve as a risk factor for the development of emotional distress symptoms in response to a major stressor (MacLeod & Hagan 1992).

In sharp contrast to the anxiety data, there is little evidence for a similar attentional bias for negative information in depression. There are a few studies suggesting that depressed individuals may show interference on the emotional Stroop task (e.g. Gotlib & Cane 1987, Williams & Nulty 1986); however, a study that directly compared depression and generalized anxiety failed to find such interference in depression (Mogg et al 1993). Moreover, emotional Stroop interference itself is not generally considered to be a pure measure of attentional bias, and the studies that have reported the bias did not rule out the possibility that the depressed patients' elevated levels of anxiety may be responsible for the effect (Mathews & MacLeod 1994). In contrast, attentional probe tasks provide a purer assessment of attentional bias; studies using this paradigm have sometimes found a relative bias, with depressed patients attending to positive and negative material equally, whereas nondepressed individuals show a bias toward positive material (e.g. Gotlib et al 1988). Again, however, one cannot rule out the possibility that anxiety actually is responsible for any observed effects (see Mogg et al 1991).

There are two recent exceptions to this generally negative pattern. Mathews et al (1996) found evidence for attention to social threat information in depression using an attentional probe task, but primarily when the words were clearly visible, suggesting it was a strategic process rather than the automatic preconscious bias seen with anxiety (see also Mogg et al 1995). At present, it is unclear how these findings can be reconciled with the largely negative results of prior studies; moreover, to clarify their meaning, it will be important to replicate these findings using more of the same paradigms used to study attentional biases in anxiety.

MEMORY BIASES   For the most part, the data on memory biases show a pattern opposite to that attentional biases. That is, a great deal of research demonstrates the presence of mood-congruent memory biases in depression, whereas the evidence for anxiety is relatively sparse and inconsistent (e.g. MacLeod & Mathews 1991, Mathews & MacLeod 1994, Mineka & Nugent 1995). Studies of mood-congruent memory in depression typically compare the performance of depressed and nondepressed participants on various memory tasks (free recall, recognition, autobiographical memory, etc), in which the materials to be remembered vary in affective content (positive vs negative vs neutral). A 1992 meta-analysis indicated that clinically depressed participants consistently show a significant bias to recall negative information, especially when it is self-referential (Matt et al 1992). Nondepressed individuals typically show a trend toward an opposite bias, favoring positive material. Teasdale (1988) argued that this memory bias creates a "vicious cycle of depression": When one is already depressed, having one's memory biased toward remembering negative events can only serve to perpetuate the depression. Results of several studies have demonstrated that such memory biases are indeed significant predictors of greater levels of depression three to seven months later, even when controlling for initial depression (e.g. Brittlebank et al 1993, Dent & Teasdale 1988).

More recent studies have also examined whether depression is associated with implicit or nonconscious memory biases for negative information. Unlike explicit memory tasks in which participants are asked specifically to reflect upon prior experiences, in implicit memory tasks the participants' memory is tested indirectly. Several more recent studies have provided convincing support for the presence of implicit memory biases (e.g. Bradley et al 1995, 1996; Watkins et al 1996). Such findings are of particular interest because they suggest a possible explanation for why depressed individuals so often have negative information entering into their consciousness without any conscious effort to recall such information.

In sharp contrast to the depression data, there is relatively little evidence indicating that similar biases are associated with anxiety (e.g. Mathews & Mac-Leod 1994, Mineka & Nugent 1995). Moreover, even when significant findings have been reported, they often have failed to replicate. Two studies did suggest the presence of an autobiographical memory bias in anxiety (Burke & Mathews 1992, Richards & Whitaker 1990), but these results are somewhat suspect because of significant methodological problems (Levy & Mineka 1997). Using improved methodology, Levy & Mineka (1997) found no evidence for an autobiographical memory bias in individuals high in trait anxiety.

Furthermore, although an early study suggested the presence of an implicit memory bias for threatening information in anxiety (Mathews et al 1989a), subsequent studies failed to replicate that finding (e.g. Bradley et al 1995, Mathews et al 1995, Nugent & Mineka 1994). One later study did report a significant implicit memory bias using a perceptual identification task, but no attempt was made to determine if the bias was because the anxious participants also had elevated depression levels (MacLeod & McLaughlin 1995). Overall, the pattern of largely negative findings for anxiety—using a wide range of memory bias paradigms—stands in rather striking contrast to the positive findings seen with depression.

Thus, although the results are not entirely consistent, the weight of the evidence suggests that anxiety and depression have different effects on cognitive

processing. Interesting theories have emerged to explain these apparent disso-
ciations between the cognitive processes associated with the two syndromes
(e.g. Oatley & Johnson-Laird 1987, Williams et al 1988), but none at present can
account for all of the findings that have emerged (e.g. Bradley et al 1996, Mineka & Nugent 1995). Nevertheless, the different modes of cognitive operation
associated with the different primary emotions may reflect the fact that these
emotions evolved to meet different environmental demands (Oatley & Johnson-Laird 1987). Anxiety, like fear, is important for vigilance and preparation
for impending danger; it therefore requires a cognitive system that facilitates a
quick scanning for—and perception of—cues for danger (Mathews 1993). The
attentional biases seen in anxiety seem well suited for this purpose. Depression, by contrast, involves a rather more reflective consideration of events that
have led to perceived failure and loss; a cognitive system adept at remembering important information that might have led to such failures or losses certainly would facilitate such reflection. The mood-congruent memory biases
we see in depression seem well suited for this purpose as well (Mathews 1993,
Mineka 1992). In this context it is noteworthy that over a decade ago, Tellegen
(1985) in a broad-ranging article specifically described anxiety as an engaged,
"orienting" mode characterized by a focus on the future, and contrasted it with
the disengaged, "oriented," past-focusing mode of depression.

JUDGMENTAL OR INTERPRETIVE BIASES   Both anxiety and depression are associated with several forms of judgmental or interpretive biases. For example,
relative to normal controls, anxious and depressed subjects show biased judgments of the likelihood that negative events will occur (Butler & Mathews
1983, Krantz & Hammen 1977). More recently, AK MacLeod & Byrne (1996)
compared anxious and depressed individuals on their anticipation of both future positive and future negative experiences. Those with relatively pure anxiety showed greater anticipation of future negative experiences than controls,
whereas those with depression (who also had elevated anxiety levels) showed
both greater anticipation of negative experiences and reduced anticipation of
positive experiences. The authors associated the heightened anticipation of future negative experiences with negative affect and the reduced anticipation of
future positive experiences with low positive affect (Clark & Watson
1991a,b).
    Anxious individuals also show an increased likelihood of interpreting am-
biguous information in a negative manner. This occurs both with ambiguous
homophones (e.g. die/dye, pain/pane) (Mathews et al 1989b) and with ambiguous sentences ("The doctor examined Little Emma's growth" or "They
discussed the priest's convictions") (Eysenck et al 1991). The most elegant
study to date involved a text comprehension paradigm; the results demon-

strated that these interpretive biases were occurring while the anxious individuals were reading the text rather than afterward (MacLeod & Cohen 1993).

SUMMARY   Depression and anxiety both are associated with cognitive biases for emotion-relevant material. Judgmental and interpretive biases (which have received the least attention) occur with both conditions. Attentional biases for threatening information are more prominent in anxiety than in depression; this conclusion seems especially clear for preconscious automatic biases. Depression, by contrast, is more clearly associated with memory biases for mood-congruent information than is anxiety. From the evolutionary perspective of Oatley & Johnson-Laird (1987), these differences make some sense. However, from the perspective of the structural models and comorbidity viewed earlier, they are somewhat surprising. For example, in nearly all the studies of attentional bias in depression, the depressed individuals show very high levels of anxiety as well as of depression; nevertheless, they do not generally show the patterns of attentional bias seen with anxiety. What is it about the co-occurrence of depressed and anxious mood that seems to mask attentional biases? Future work in this area would profit from using measures with improved discriminant validity, such as the MASQ developed to test the tripartite model (Watson & Clark 1991).

CONCLUSIONS

Interest in the relationships between anxiety and depression has a long history but only began to receive serious attention from researchers and theoreticians in the mid to late 1980s. Since that time considerable progress has been made in documenting the similarities and differences between these two conditions. In addition, we now have a more sophisticated understanding of many of the important features of both the concurrent and the lifetime comorbidity of these disorders. Major progress also has been made in understanding the genotypic structure of anxiety and depression, with considerable evidence indicating that generalized anxiety and major depression share a common genetic diathesis but that the anxiety disorders themselves are genetically heterogeneous, reflecting multiple genetic diatheses. Phenotypic models also have become quite sophisticated, with data converging on an integrative hierarchical model of mood and anxiety disorders in which each individual syndrome contains both a common and a unique component. The shared component of Negative Affect is common to both the mood and the anxiety disorders. Anxious arousal, one of the components of the tripartite model, seems to be the specific component of panic disorder, whereas the other anxiety disorders have their own unique components that are differentiable from anxious arousal. Finally, considerable progress also has been made in understanding the cognitive components of the anxiety and mood disorders. This work has focused on both the cognitive content of anxiety and depression and the effects that anxiety and depression have on information processing. The majority of evidence suggests that anxiety is associated with automatic attentional biases for emotion-relevant (threatening) material, that depression is associated with memory biases for emotion-relevant (negative) information, and that both anxiety and depression are associated with judgmental or interpretive biases. Much work remains to be done, however, to understand how this pattern of cognitive biases can be related to the hierarchical structural model of the anxiety and mood disorders that has emerged.

> Visit the *Annual Reviews home page* at
> http://www.AnnualReviews.org.

Literature Cited

Abramson LY, Metalsky GL, Alloy LB. 1989. Hopelessness depression: a theory based subtype of depression. *Psychol. Rev.* 96: 358–72

Abramson LY, Seligman MEP, Teasdale JD. 1978. Learned helplessness in humans: critique and reformulation. *J. Abnorm. Psychol.* 87:49–74

Akiskal HS. 1985. Anxiety: definition, relationship to depression, and proposal for an integrative model. See Tuma & Maser 1985, pp. 787–97

Allen JL, Iacono WG, Depue RA, Arbisi P. 1993. Regional EEG asymmetries in bipolar seasonal affective disorder before and after phototherapy. *Biol. Psychiatry* 33: 642–46

Alloy L, Kelly K, Mineka S, Clements C. 1990. Comorbidity in anxiety and depressive disorders: a helplessness/hopelessness perspective. See Maser & Cloninger 1990, pp. 499–543

American Psychiatric Association. 1980. *Diagnostic and Statistical Manual of Mental Disorders.* Washington, DC: Am. Psychiatr. Assoc. 3rd ed.

American Psychiatric Association. 1987. *Diagnostic and Statistical Manual of Mental Disorders.* Washington, DC: Am. Psychiatr. Assoc. 3rd ed. Rev.

American Psychiatric Association. 1994. *Diagnostic and Statistical Manual of Mental*

Disorders. Washington, DC: Am. Psychiatr. Assoc. 4th ed.

Angold A, Costello EJ. 1993. Depressive comorbidity in children and adolescents: empirical, theoretical, and methodological issues. *Am. J. Psychiatry* 150:1779–91

Angst J. 1993. Comorbidity of anxiety, phobia, compulsion and depression. *Int. Clin. Psychopharmacol.* 8(Suppl.):21–25

Barlow DH. 1988. *Anxiety and Its Disorders: The Nature and Treatment of Anxiety and Panic.* New York: Guilford

Barlow DH. 1991. The nature of anxiety: anxiety, depression, and emotional disorders. In *Chronic Anxiety: Generalized Anxiety Disorder and Mixed Anxiety-Depression,* ed. RM Rapee, DH Barlow, pp. 1–28. New York: Guilford

Barlow DH, Chorpita BF, Turovsky J. 1996. *Fear, panic, anxiety and disorders of emotion. Nebr. Symp. Motiv.* 43:251–328

Beck AT. 1967. *Depression: Clinical, Experimental, and Theoretical Aspects.* New York: Harper & Row

Beck AT. 1976. *Cognitive Therapy and the Emotional Disorders.* New York: Int. Univ. Press

Beck AT, Brown G, Steer RA, Eidelson JI, Riskind JH. 1987. Differentiating anxiety and depression: a test of the cognitive content-specificity hypothesis. *J. Abnorm. Psychol.* 96:179–83

Beck AT, Emery G. 1985. *Anxiety Disorders and Phobias: A Cognitive Perspective.* New York: Basic Books

Bowlby J. 1973. *Attachment and Loss,* Vol. 2: *Separation.* New York: Basic Books

Bowlby J. 1980. *Attachment and Loss,* Vol. 3: *Loss.* New York: Basic Books

Bradley BP, Mogg K, Millar N. 1996. Implicit memory bias in clinical and nonclinical depression. *Behav. Res. Ther.* 34:865–79

Bradley BP, Mogg K, Williams R. 1995. Implicit and explicit memory for emotion-congruent information in clinical depression and anxiety. *Behav. Res. Ther.* 33: 755–70

Brady EU, Kendall PC. 1992. Comorbidity of anxiety and depression in children and adolescents. *J. Consult. Clin. Psychol.* 111:244–55

Braun DL, Sunday SR, Halmi KA. 1994. Psychiatric comorbidity in patients with eating disorders. *Psychol. Med.* 24:859–67

Brittlebank AD, Scott J, Williams JM, Ferrier IN. 1993. Autobiographical memory in depression: State or trait marker? *Br. J. Psychiatry* 162:118–21

Bronisch T, Wittchen HU. 1994. Suicidal ideation and suicide attempts: comorbidity with depression, anxiety disorders, and substance abuse disorder. *Eur. Arch. Psychiatry Clin. Neurosci.* 244:93–98

Brown C, Schulberg HC, Madonia MJ, Shear MK. 1996. Treatment outcomes for primary care patients with major depression and lifetime anxiety disorders. *Am. J. Psychiatry* 153:1293–300

Brown GW, Harris TO. 1978. *Social Origins of Depression.* New York: Free

Brown GW, Harris TO, Eales MJ. 1993. Aetiology of anxiety and depressive disorders in an inner-city population. 2. Comorbidity and adversity. *Psychol. Med.* 23: 155–65

Brown TA, Antony MM, Barlow DH. 1995. Diagnostic comorbidity in panic disorder: effect on treatment outcome and course of comorbid diagnoses following treatment. *J. Consult. Clin. Psychol.* 63:408–18

Brown TA, Barlow DH. 1992. Comorbidity among anxiety disorders: implications for treatment and DSM-IV. *J. Consult. Clin. Psychol.* 60:835–44

Brown TA, Chorpita BF, Barlow DH. 1997. Structural relationships among dimensions of the DSM-IV anxiety and mood disorders and dimensions of negative affect, positive affect, and autonomic arousal. *J. Abnorm. Psychol.* In press

Bruder GE, Fong R, Tenke CE, Leite P, Towey JP, et al. 1997. Regional brain asymmetries in major depression with or without an anxiety disorder: a quantitative EEG study. *Biol. Psychiatry.* In press

Burke M, Mathews A. 1992. Autobiographical memory and clinical anxiety. *Cogn. Emot.* 6:23–35

Butler G, Mathews A. 1983. Cognitive processes in anxiety. *Adv. Behav. Res. Ther.* 5:51–62

Carey G, DiLalla DL. 1994. Personality and psychopathology: genetic perspectives. *J. Abnorm. Psychol.* 103:32–43

Caron C, Rutter M. 1991. Comorbidity in child psychopathology: concepts, issues and research strategies. *J. Child. Psychol. Psychiatry* 32:1063–80

Castonguay LG, Eldredge KL, Agras WS. 1995. Binge eating disorder: current state and future directions. *Clin. Psychol. Rev.* 15:865–90

Chorpita BF, Albano AM, Barlow DH. 1997. The structure of negative emotions in a clinical sample of children and adolescents. *J. Abnorm. Psychol.* In press

Clark DA, Beck AT, Stewart B. 1990. Cognitive specificity and positive-negative affectivity: complementary or contradictory views on anxiety and depression? *J. Abnorm. Psychol.* 99:148–55

Clark DA, Steer RA, Beck AT. 1994. Common and specific dimensions of self-reported anxiety and depression: implications for the cognitive and tripartite models. *J. Abnorm. Psychol.* 103:645–54

Clark DB, Smith MG, Neighbors BD, Skerlec LM. 1994. Anxiety disorders in adolescence: characteristics, prevalence, and comorbidities. *Clin. Psychol. Rev.* 14: 113–37

Clark LA. 1989. The anxiety and depressive disorders: descriptive psychopathology and differential diagnosis. In *Anxiety and Depression: Distinctive and Overlapping Features,* ed. PC Kendall, D Watson, pp. 83–129. San Diego: Academic

Clark LA, Watson D. 1991a. Theoretical and empirical issues in differentiating depression from anxiety. In *Psychosocial Aspects of Depression,* ed. J Becker, A Kleinman, pp. 39–65. Hillsdale, NJ: Erlbaum

Clark LA, Watson D. 1991b. Tripartite model of anxiety and depression: evidence and taxonomic implications. *J. Abnorm. Psychol.* 100:316–36

Clark LA, Watson D, Mineka S. 1994. Temperament, personality, and the mood and anxiety disorders. *J. Abnorm. Psychol.* 103:103–16

Clark LA, Watson D, Reynolds S. 1995. Diagnosis and classification of psychopathology: challenges to the current system and future directions. *Annu. Rev. Psychol.* 46: 121–53

Cole DA, Truglio R, Peeke L. 1997. Relation between symptoms of anxiety and depression in children: a multitrait-multimethod-multigroup assessment. *J. Consult. Clin. Psychol.* 65:110–19

Conwell Y. 1996. Relationship of age and Axis I diagnoses in victims of completed suicide: a psychological autopsy study. *Am. J. Psychiatry* 153:1001–8

Cook EW III, Hawk LW Jr, Davis TL, Stevenson VE. 1991. Affective individual differences and startle reflex modulation. *J. Abnorm. Psychol.* 100:5–13

Cox BJ, Swinson PP, Kuch K, Reichman JT. 1993. Self-report differentiation of anxiety and depression in an anxiety disorders sample. *Psychol. Assess.* 5:484–86

Cuthbert BN, Melamed BG. 1993. Anxiety and clinical psychophysiology: three decades of research on three response systems in three anxiety disorders. In *The Structure of Emotion*, ed. N Birbaumer, A Öhman, pp. 93–109. Seattle: Hofgrebe & Huber

Cuthbert BN, Bradley MM, Lang PJ. 1996. Fear and anxiety: theoretical distinction and clinical test. *Psychophysiology* 33 (Suppl. 1):S15

Davis M, Walker DL, Yee Y. 1997. Amygdala and bed nucleus of the stria terminalis: differential roles in fear and anxiety measured with the acoustic startle reflex. In *Biological and Psychological Perspectives on Memory and Memory Disorders*, ed. L Squire, D Schacter. Washington, DC: Am. Psychiatr.

Dent J, Teasdale J. 1988. Negative cognition and the persistence of depression. *J. Abnorm. Psychol.* 97:29–34

Depue R, Luciana M, Arbisi P, Collins P, Leon A. 1994. Dopamine and the structure of personality: relation of agonist-induced dopamine activity to positive emotionality. *J. Pers. Soc. Psychol.* 67:485–98

DiNardo PA, Barlow DH. 1990. Symptom and syndrome co-occurrence in the anxiety disorders. See Maser & Cloninger 1990, pp. 205–30

Dyck MJ, Jolly JB, Kramer T. 1994. An evaluation of positive affectivity, negative affectivity, and hyperarousal as markers for assessing between syndrome relationships. *Pers. Individ. Differ.* 17:637–46

Eysenck M, Mogg K, May J, Richards A, Mathews A. 1991. Bias in interpretation of ambiguous sentences related to threat in anxiety. *J. Abnorm. Psychol.* 100:144–50

Farmer R, Nelson-Gray RO. 1990. Personality disorders and depression: hypothetical relations, empirical findings, and methodological considerations. *Clin. Psychol. Rev.* 10:453–76

Fawcett J, Clark DC, Busch KA. 1993. Assessing and treating the patient at risk for suicide. *Psychiatr. Ann.* 23:244–55

Feinstein AR. 1970. The pretherapeutic classification of co-morbidity in chronic disease. *J. Chronic Dis.* 23:455–68

Feldman LA. 1993. Distinguishing depression and anxiety in self-report: evidence from confirmatory factor analysis on nonclinical and clinical samples. *J. Consult. Clin. Psychol.* 61:631–38

First MB, Spitzer RL, Williams JBW. 1990. Exclusionary principles and the comorbidity of psychiatric diagnoses: a historical review and implications for the future. See Maser & Cloninger 1990, pp. 83–109

Flick SN, Roy-Byrne PP, Cowley DS, Shores MM, Dunner DL. 1993. DSM-III-R personality disorders in a mood and anxiety disorders clinic: prevalence, comorbidity, and clinical correlates. *J. Affect. Disord.* 27:71–79

Frances A, Widiger TA, Fyer MR. 1990. The influence of classification methods on comorbidity. See Maser & Cloninger 1990, pp. 41–59

Garber J, Miller SM, Abramson LY. 1980. On the distinction between anxiety states and depression: perceived control, certainty, and probability of goal attainment. In *Human Helplessness: Theory and Applications*, ed. J Garber, MEP Seligman. New York: Academic

Gotlib IH, Cane DB. 1987. Construct accessibility and clinical depression: a longitudinal approach. *J. Abnorm. Psychol.* 96: 199–204

Gotlib IH, MacLachlan A, Katz A. 1988. Biases in visual attention in depressed and nondepressed individuals. *Cogn. Emot.* 2: 185–200

Heimberg RG, Klosko JC, Dodge CS, Becker RE, Barlow DH. 1989. Anxiety disorders, depression, and attributional style: a further test of the specificity of depressive attributions. *Cogn. Ther. Res.* 13:21–36

Heller W. 1993. Neuropsychological mechanisms of individual differences in emotion, personality, and arousal. *Neuropsychol.* 7: 476–89

Heller W, Etienne MA, Miller GA. 1995. Patterns of perceptual asymmetry in depression and anxiety: implications for neuropsychological models of emotion and psychopathology. *J. Abnorm. Psychol.* 104: 327–33

Henriques JB, Davidson RJ. 1990. Regional brain electrical asymmetries discriminate between previously depressed subjects and healthy controls. *J. Abnorm. Psychol.* 99: 22–31

Henriques JB, Davidson RJ. 1991. Left frontal hypoactivation in depression. *J. Abnorm. Psychol.* 100:535–45

Herpertz-Dahlmann BM, Wewetzer C, Schulz E, Remschmidt H. 1996. Course and outcome in adolescent anorexia nervosa. *Int. J. Eating Disord.* 19:335–45

Hinden BR, Compas BE, Howell DC, Achenbach TM. 1997. Covariation of the anxious-depressed syndrome during adolescence: separating fact from artifact. *J. Consult. Clin. Psychol.* 65:6–14

Hodges K. 1990. Depression and anxiety in children: a comparison of self-report questionnaires to clinical interview. *Psychol. Assess.* 2:376–81

Hoffart A, Martinsen EW. 1993. The effect of personality disorders and anxious-depressive comorbidity on outcome in patients with unipolar depression and with panic disorder and agoraphobia. *J. Pers. Disord.* 7:304–11

Holt CS, Heimberg RG, Hope DA. 1992. Avoidant personality disorder and the generalized subtype of social phobia. *J. Abnorm. Psychol.* 101:318–25

Jardine R, Martin NG, Henderson AS. 1984. Genetic covariation between neuroticism and the symptoms of anxiety and depression. *Genet. Epidemiol.* 1:89–107

Jensen PS, Shervette RE, Xenakis SN, Richters J. 1993. Anxiety and depressive disorders in attention deficit disorder with hyperactivity: new findings. *Am. J. Psychiatry* 150:1203–9

Joiner TE Jr. 1996. A confirmatory factor-analytic investigation of the tripartite model of depression and anxiety in college students. *Cogn. Ther. Res.* 20:521–39

Joiner TE Jr, Catanzaro SJ, Laurent J. 1996. Tripartite structure of positive and negative affect, depression, and anxiety in child and adolescent psychiatric inpatients. *J. Abnorm. Psychol.* 105:401–9

Jolly JB, Dyck MJ, Kramer TA, Wherry JN. 1994. Integration of positive and negative affectivity and cognitive-content specificity: improved discriminations of anxious and depressive symptoms. *J. Abnorm. Psychol.* 103:544–52

Jolly JB, Dykman RA. 1994. Using self-report data to differentiate anxious and depressive symptoms in adolescents: cognitive content specificity and global distress? *Cogn. Ther. Res.* 18:25–37

Jolly JB, Kramer TA. 1994. The hierarchical arrangement of internalizing cognitions. *Cogn. Ther. Res.* 18:1–14

Kaplan MH, Feinstein AR. 1974. The importance of classifying initial comorbidity in evaluating the outcome of diabetes mellitus. *J. Chronic Dis.* 27:387–404

Keller MB, Lavori PW, Mueller TI, Endicott J, Coryell W, et al. 1992. Time to recovery, chronicity, and levels of psychopathology in major depression: a 5-year prospective follow-up of 431 subjects. *Arch. Gen. Psychiatry* 49:809–16

Kendall PC, Clarkin JF. 1992. Introduction to special section: comorbidity and treatment implications. *J. Consult. Clin. Psychol.* 60: 833–34

Kendall PC, Kortlander E, Chansky TE, Brady EU. 1992. Comorbidity of anxiety and depression in youth: treatment implications. *J. Consult. Clin. Psychol.* 60:869–80

Kendler KS. 1996. Major depression and generalised anxiety disorder: same genes, (partly) different environments—revisited. *Br. J. Psychiatry* 168(Suppl. 30):68–75

Kendler KS, Heath AC, Martin NG, Eaves LJ. 1987. Symptoms of anxiety and symptoms of depression: same genes, different environments? *Arch. Gen. Psychiatry* 44: 451–57

Kendler KS, Neale MC, Kessler RC, Heath AC, Eaves LJ. 1992. Major depression and generalized anxiety disorder: same genes, (partly) different environments? *Arch. Gen. Psychiatry* 49:16–22

Kendler KS, Neale MC, Kessler RC, Heath AC, Eaves LJ. 1993a. A longitudinal twin study of personality and major depression in women. *Arch. Gen. Psychiatry* 50: 853–62

Kendler KS, Neale MC, Kessler RC, Heath AC, Eaves LJ. 1993b. Major depression and phobias: the genetic and environmental sources of comorbidity. *Psychol. Med.* 23:361–71

Kendler KS, Walters EE, Neale MC, Kessler RC, Heath AC, Eaves LJ. 1995. The structure of the genetic and environmental risk factors for six major psychiatric disorders in women: phobia, generalized anxiety disorder, panic disorder, bulimia, major depression, and alcoholism. *Arch. Gen. Psychiatry* 52:374–83

Kessler RC. 1997. The prevalence of psychiatric comorbidity. In *Treatment Strategies for Patients with Psychiatric Comorbidity*, ed. S Wetzler, WC Sanderson, pp. 23–48. New York: Wiley

Kessler RC, McGonagle KA, Zhao S, Nelson CB, Hughes M, et al. 1994. Lifetime and

12-month prevalence of DSM-III-R psychiatric disorders in the United States: results from the National Comorbidity Survey. *Arch. Gen. Psychiatry* 51:8–19

Kessler RC, Nelson CB, McGonagle KA, Liu J, Swartz M, Blazer DG. 1996. Comorbidity of DSM-III-R major depressive disorder in the general population: results from the US National Comorbidity Survey. *Br. J. Psychiatry* 168(Suppl. 30):17–30

Kessler RC, Zhao S, Blazer DG, Swartz MD. 1997. Prevalence, correlates, and course of minor depression and major depression in the National Comorbidity Survey. *J. Affect Disord.* In press

King NJ. 1990. Childhood anxiety disorders and depression: phenomenology, comorbidity, and intervention issues. *Scand. J. Behav. Ther.* 19:59–70

King NJ, Ollendick TH, Gullone E. 1991. Negative affectivity in children and adolescents: relations between anxiety and depression. *Clin. Psychol. Rev.* 11:441–59

Klerman GL. 1990. Approaches to the phenomena of comorbidity. See Maser & Cloninger 1990, pp. 13–37

Kovacs M, Gatsonis C, Paulaskas SL, Richards C. 1989. Depressive disorders in childhood. *Arch. Gen. Psychiatry* 46: 776–82

Krantz S, Hammen C. 1977. Assessment of cognitive bias in depression. *J. Abnorm. Psychol.* 88:611–19

Krueger RF, Caspi A, Moffitt TE, Silva PA, McGee R. 1996. Personality traits are differentially linked to mental disorders: a multitrait-multidiagnosis study of an adolescent birth cohort. *J. Abnorm. Psychol.* 105:299–312

Kunik ME. 1993. Personality disorders in elderly inpatients with major depression. *Am. J. Geriatr. Psychiatry* 1:38–45

Lang PJ, Bradley MM, Cuthbert BN, Patrick CJ. 1993. Emotion and psychopathology: a startle probe analysis. In *Progress in Experimental Personality and Psychopathology Research,* ed. LJ Chapman, JP Chapman, DC Fowles, 16:163–99. New York: Springer

Larsen CL, Davidson RJ, Abercrombie HC. 1995. Prefrontal brain function and depression severity: EEG differences in melancholic and nonmelancholic depressives. *Psychophysiology* 32:S49

Lepine JP, Wittchen H-U, Essau CA. 1993. Lifetime and current comorbidity of anxiety and affective disorders: results from the International WHO/ADAMHA CIDI field trials. *Int. J. Methods Psychiatr. Res.* 3:67–77

Levy E, Mineka S. 1997. *Anxiety and mood-congruent autobiographical memory.* Presented at Midwest. Psychol. Assoc., May

Lewinsohn PM, Rohde P, Seeley JR. 1995. Adolescent psychopathology. III. The clinical consequences of comorbidity. *J. Am. Acad. Child Adolesc. Psychiatry* 34: 510–19

Lewinsohn PM, Zinbarg R, Seeley JR, Lewinsohn M, Sack WH. 1997. Lifetime comorbidity among anxiety disorders and between anxiety disorders and other mental disorders in adolescents. *J. Anxiety Disord.* In press

Lilienfeld SO, Waldman ID, Israel AC. 1994. Critical examination of the use of the term and concept of comorbidity in psychopathology research. *Clin. Psychol. Sci. Pract.* 1:71–83

Loeber R, Keenan K. 1994. Interaction between conduct disorder and its comorbid conditions: effects of age and gender. *Clin. Psychol. Rev.* 14:497–523

Lonigan CJ, Carey MP, Finch AJ Jr. 1994. Anxiety and depression in children and adolescents: negative affectivity and the utility of self-reports. *J. Consult. Clin. Psychol.* 62:1000–8

MacLeod AK, Byrne A. 1996. Anxiety, depression, and the anticipation of future positive and negative experiences. *J. Abnorm. Psychol.* 105:286–89

MacLeod C, Cohen I. 1993. Anxiety and the interpretation of ambiguity: a text comprehension study. *J. Abnorm. Psychol.* 102: 238–47

MacLeod C, Hagan R. 1992. Individual differences in the selective processing of threatening information, and emotional responses to a stressful life event. *Behav. Res. Ther.* 30:151–61

MacLeod C, Mathews AM. 1991. Cognitive-experimental approaches to the emotional disorders. In *Handbook of Behavior Therapy and Psychological Science,* ed. P Martin, pp. 116–50. New York: Pergamon

MacLeod C, McLaughlin K. 1995. Implicit and explicit memory bias in anxiety: a conceptual replication. *Behav. Res. Ther.* 33: 1–14

Mandler G. 1972. Helplessness: theory and research in anxiety. In *Anxiety: Current Trends in Theory and Research,* Vol. 3, ed. CD Spielberger. New York: Academic

Martin NG, Jardine R, Andrews G, Heath AC. 1988. Anxiety disorders and neuroticism: Are there genetic factors specific to panic? *Acta Psychiatr. Scand.* 77:698–706

Maser JD, Cloninger CR. 1990. Comorbidity

of anxiety and mood disorders: introduction and overview. In *Comorbidity of Mood and Anxiety Disorders*, ed. JD Maser, CR Cloninger, pp. 3–12. Washington, DC: Am. Psychiatr. Press

Mathews A. 1993. Anxiety and the processing of emotional information. In *Models and Methods of Psychopathology: Progress in Experimental Personality and Psychopathology Research*, ed. L Chapman, J Chapman, D Fowles, pp. 254–80. New York: Springer

Mathews A, MacLeod C. 1994. Cognitive approaches to emotion and emotional disorders. *Annu. Rev. Psychol.* 45:25–50

Mathews A, Mogg K, Kentish J, Eysenck M. 1995. Effect of psychological treatment on cognitive bias in generalized anxiety disorder. *Behav. Res. Ther.* 33:293–303

Mathews A, Mogg K, May J, Eysenck M. 1989a. Implicit and explicit memory bias in anxiety. *J. Abnorm. Psychol.* 98:236–40

Mathews A, Richards A, Eysenck M. 1989b. Interpretation of homophones related to threat in anxiety states. *J. Abnorm. Psychol.* 98:31–34

Mathews A, Ridgeway V, Williamson D. 1996. Evidence for attention to threatening stimuli in depression. *Behav. Res. Ther.* 34:695–705

Matt G, Vazquez C, Campbell WK. 1992. Mood-congruent recall of affectively toned stimuli: a meta-analytical review. *Clin. Psychol. Rev.* 12:227–55

McNeil DW, Vrana SR, Melamed BG, Cuthbert BN, Lang PJ. 1993. Emotional imagery in simple and social phobia: fear versus anxiety. *J. Abnorm. Psychol.* 102:212–25

Milberger S, Biederman J, Faraone SV, Murphy J, Tsuang MT. 1995. Attention deficit hyperactivity disorder and comorbid disorder: issues of overlapping symptoms. *Am. J. Psychiatry* 152:1793–99

Mineka S. 1985. Animal models of anxiety-based disorders: their usefulness and limitations. See Tuma & Maser 1985, pp. 199–244

Mineka S. 1992. Evolutionary memories, emotional processing and the emotional disorders. In *The Psychology of Learning and Motivation*, ed. D Medin, 28:161–206. New York: Academic

Mineka S, Kelly K. 1989. The relationship between anxiety, lack of control, and loss of control. In *Stress, Personal Control and Health*, ed. A Steptoe, A Appels, pp. 163–91. New York: Wiley

Mineka S, Nugent K. 1995. Mood-congruent memory biases in anxiety and depression.

In *Memory Distortion: How Minds, Brains, and Societies Reconstruct the Past*, ed. D Schacter, pp. 173–93. Cambridge, MA: Harvard Univ. Press

Mineka S, Pury C, Luten A. 1995. Explanatory style in anxiety versus depression. In *Explanatory Style*, ed. G Buchanan, MEP Seligman, pp. 135–58. Hillsdale, NJ: Erlbaum

Mineka S, Suomi SJ. 1978. Social separation in monkeys. *Psychol. Bull.* 85:1376–400

Mineka S, Sutton S. 1992. Cognitive biases and the emotional disorders. *Psychol. Sci.* 3:65–69

Mineka S, Tomarken A. 1989. The role of cognitive biases in the origins and maintenance of fear and anxiety disorders. In *Aversion, Avoidance, and Anxiety: Perspectives on Aversively Motivated Behavior*, ed. T Archer, L Nilsson, pp. 195–221. Hillsdale, NJ: Erlbaum

Mineka S, Zinbarg R. 1996. Conditioning and ethological models of anxiety disorders: Stress-in-dynamic-context anxiety models. *Perspectives on anxiety, panic, and fear. Nebr. Symp. Motiv.* 43:135–211

Mogg K, Bradley BP, Williams R. 1995. Attentional bias in anxiety and depression: the role of awareness. *Br. J. Clin. Psychol.* 43:17–36

Mogg K, Bradley BP, Williams R, Mathews AM. 1993. Subliminal processing of emotional information in anxiety and depression. *J. Abnorm. Psychol.* 102:304–11

Mogg K, Mathews AM, May J, Grove M, Eysenck M, Weinman J. 1991. Assessment of cognitive bias in anxiety and depression using a colour perception task. *Cogn. Emot.* 5:221–38

Monroe SM. 1990. Psychosocial factors in anxiety and depression. See Maser & Cloninger 1990, pp. 463–98

Moras K, Clark LA, Katon W, Roy-Byrne R, Watson D, Barlow D. 1996. Mixed anxiety-depression. In *DSM-IV Sourcebook*, ed. TA Widiger, AJ Frances, HA Pincus, R Ross, MB First, WW Davis, pp. 623–43. Washington, DC: Am. Psychiatr.

Mulder RT. 1991. The comorbidity of anxiety disorders with personality, depressive, alcohol and drug disorders. *Int. Rev. Psychiatr.* 3:253–63

Neale MC, Kendler KS. 1995. Models of comorbidity for multifactorial disorders. *Am. J. Hum. Genet.* 57:935–53

Nugent K, Mineka S. 1994. The effects of high and low trait anxiety on implicit and explicit memory tasks. *Cogn. Emot.* 8:147–63

Oatley K, Johnson-Laird P. 1987. Towards a

cognitive theory of emotions. *Cogn. Emot.* 1:29–50

Pauls DL. 1992. The genetics of obsessive compulsive disorder and Gilles de la Tourette's syndrome. *Psychiatr. Clin. North Am.* 15:759–66

Pauls DL, Alsobrook JP II, Goodman W, Rasmussen S, Leckman JF. 1995. A family study of obsessive-compulsive disorder. *Am. J. Psychiatry* 152:76–84

Pauls DL, Leckman JF, Cohen DJ. 1994. Evidence against a genetic relationship between Tourette's syndrome and anxiety, depression, panic and phobic disorders. *Br. J. Psychiatry* 164:215–21

Regier DA, Burke JD, Burke KC. 1990. Comorbidity of affective and anxiety disorders in the NIMH Epidemiologic Catchment Area Program. See Maser & Cloninger 1990, pp. 113–22

Reich J, Warshaw M, Peterson LG, White K. 1993. Comorbidity of panic and major depressive disorder. *J. Psychiatr. Res.* 27 (Suppl.):23–33

Richards A, Whitaker TM. 1990. Effects of anxiety and mood manipulation in autobiographical memory. *Br. J. Clin. Psychol.* 29:145–53

Rief W, Hiller W, Geissner E, Fichter MM. 1995. A two-year follow-up study of patients with somatoform disorders. *Psychosomatics* 36:376–86

Robins LN. 1994. How recognizing "comorbidities" in psychopathology may lead to an improved research nosology. *Clin. Psychol. Sci. Pract.* 1:93–95

Roy M-A, Neale MC, Pedersen NL, Mathé AA, Kendler KS. 1995. A twin study of generalized anxiety disorder and major depression. *Psychol. Med.* 25:1037–49

Sartorius N, Ustun TB, Lecrubier Y. 1996. Depression comorbid with anxiety: Results from the WHO study on "Psychological disorders in primary health care." *Br. J. Psychiatry* 168(Suppl. 30):38–43

Schneier FR, Johnson J, Hornig CD, Liebowitz MR. 1992. Social phobia: comorbidity and morbidity in an epidemiologic sample. *Arch. Gen. Psychiatry* 49:282–88

Seligman MEP. 1974. Depression and learned helplessness. In *The Psychology of Depression: Contemporary Theory and Research*, ed. RJ Friedman, MM Katz, pp. 83–113. New York: Winston-Wiley

Shafii M, Steltz-Lenarsky J, Derrick AM, Beckner C. 1988. Comorbidity of mental disorders in the post-mortem diagnosis of completed suicide in children and adolescents. *J. Affect. Disord.* 15:227–33

Shea MT, Widiger TA, Klein MH. 1992.

Comorbidity of personality disorders and depression: implications for treatment. *J. Consult. Clin. Psychol.* 60:857–68

Spence SH. 1997. Structure of anxiety symptoms among children: a confirmatory factor-analytic study. *J. Abnorm. Psychol.* 106:280–97

Spitzer RL. 1994. Psychiatric "co-occurrence"? I'll stick with "comorbidity." *Clin. Psychol. Sci. Pract.* 1:88–92

Spitzer RL, Endicott J, Robins E. 1978. Research Diagnostic Criteria: rationale and reliability. *Arch. Gen. Psychiatry* 35: 773–82

Steer RA, Clark DA, Beck AT, Ranieri WF. 1995. Common and specific dimensions of self-reported anxiety and depression: a replication. *J. Abnorm. Psychol.* 104: 542–45

Steer RA, Clark DA, Ranieri WF. 1994. Symptom dimensions of the SCL-90-R: a test of the tripartite model of anxiety and depression. *J. Pers. Assess.* 62:525–36

Teasdale JD. 1988. Cognitive vulnerability to persistent depression. *Cogn. Emot.* 2: 247–74

Tellegen A. 1985. Structures of mood and personality and their relevance to assessing anxiety, with an emphasis on self-report. See Tuma & Maser 1985, pp. 681–706

Tomarken AJ, Davidson RJ, Wheeler RE, Doss RC. 1992. Individual differences in anterior brain asymmetry and fundamental dimensions of emotion. *J. Pers. Soc. Psychol.* 62:676–87

Tomarken AJ, Keener AD. 1997. Frontal brain asymmetry and depression: a self-regulatory perspective. *Cogn. Emot.* In press

Trull TJ, Sher KJ. 1994. Relationship between the five-factor model of personality and Axis I disorders in a nonclinical sample. *J. Abnorm. Psychol.* 103:350–60

Tuma AH, Maser J, eds. 1985. *Anxiety and the Anxiety Disorders*. Hillsdale, NJ: Erlbaum

Turner SM, Beidel DC, Townsley RM. 1992. Social phobia: a comparison of specific and generalized subtypes and avoidant personality disorder. *J. Abnorm. Psychol.* 101:326–32

Watkins PC, Vache K, Verney SP, Muller S, Mathews A. 1996. Unconscious mood-congruent memory bias in depression. *J. Abnorm. Psychol.* 105:34–41

Watson D, Clark LA. 1991. The mood and anxiety symptom questionnaire. Univ. Iowa, Dep. Psychol. Unpubl. manuscr.

Watson D, Clark LA. 1994. Introduction to the special issue on personality and psychopathology. *J. Abnorm. Psychol.* 103:3–5

Watson D, Clark LA. 1995. Depression and

the melancholic temperament. *Eur. J. Pers.* 9:351–66

Watson D, Clark LA. 1997. Measurement and mismeasurement of mood: recurrent and emergent issues. *J. Pers. Assess.* 68: 267–96

Watson D, Clark LA, Carey G. 1988. Positive and negative affectivity and their relation to anxiety and depressive disorders. *J. Abnorm. Psychol.* 97:346–53

Watson D, Clark LA, Harkness AR. 1994. Structures of personality and their relevance to psychopathology. *J. Abnorm. Psychol.* 103:18–31

Watson D, Clark LA, Weber K. Assenheimer JS, Strauss ME, McCormick RA. 1995a. Testing a tripartite model: II. Exploring the symptom structure of anxiety and depression in student, adult, and patient samples. *J. Abnorm. Psychol.* 104:15–25

Watson D, Tellegen A. 1985. Toward a consensual structure of mood. *Psychol. Bull.* 98:219–35

Watson D, Weber K, Assenheimer JS, Clark LA, Strauss ME, McCormick RA. 1995b. Testing a tripartite model: I. Evaluating the convergent and discriminant validity of anxiety and depression symptom scales. *J. Abnorm. Psychol.* 104:3–14

Westermeyer J, Tucker P, Nugent S. 1995. Comorbid anxiety disorder among patients with substance abuse disorders. *Am. J. Ad-dict.* 4:97–106

Widiger TA, Costa PT Jr. 1994. Personality and the personality disorders. *J. Abnorm. Psychol.* 103:78–91

Williams JMG, Nulty DD. 1986. Construct accessibility, depression and the emotional Stroop task: transient mood or stable structure? *Pers. Individ. Differ.* 7:485–91

Williams JMG, Watts FN, MacLeod C, Mathews AM. 1988. *Cognitive Psychology and the Emotional Disorders,* pp. 1–226. Chichester, NY: Wiley

Wilson GT, Nathan PE, O'Leary KD, Clark LA. 1996. *Abnormal Psychology: Integrating Perspectives,* pp. 1–778. Boston: Allyn & Bacon

Wittchen H-U, Zhao S, Kessler RC, Eaton WW. 1994. DSM-III-R generalized anxiety disorder in the National Comorbidity Survey. *Arch. Gen. Psychiatry* 51:355–64

Woodman CL. 1993. The genetics of panic disorder and generalized anxiety disorder. *Ann. Clin. Psychiatry* 5:231–40

Zinbarg RE, Barlow DH. 1996. Structure of anxiety and the anxiety disorders: a hierarchical model. *J. Abnorm. Psychol.* 105: 181–93

Zisook S. Goff A, Sledge P, Shuchter SR. 1994. Reported suicidal behavior and current suicidal ideation in a psychiatric outpatient clinic. *Ann. Clin. Psychiatry* 6: 27–31

Prevalence of anxiety disorders and their comorbidity with mood and addictive disorders

D. A. REGIER, D. S. RAE, W. E. NARROW, C. T. KAELBER
and A. F. SCHATZBERG

Background   The co-occurrence of anxiety disorders with other mental, addictive, and physical disorders has important implications for treatment and for prediction of clinical course and associated morbidity.

Method   Cross-sectional and prospective data on 20 291 individuals from the Epidemiologic Catchment Area (ECA) study were analysed to determine one-month, current disorders, one-year incidence, and one-year and lifetime prevalence of anxiety, mood, and addictive disorders, and to identify the onset and offset of disorders within the one-year prospective period.

Results   Nearly half (47.2%) of those meeting lifetime criteria for major depression also have met criteria for a comorbid anxiety disorder. The average age of onset of any lifetime anxiety disorder (16.4 years) and social phobia (11.6 years) among those with major depression was much younger than the onset age for major depression (23.2 years) and panic disorder.

Conclusions   Anxiety disorders, especially social and simple phobias, appear to have an early onset in adolescence with potentially severe consequences, predisposing those affected to greater vulnerability to major depression and addictive disorders.

The co-occurrence of anxiety disorders with other mental, addictive, and physical disorders is of considerable clinical interest both because of the treatment implications and the ability to predict the likely clinical course and morbidity associated with these interacting conditions. Family and clinical studies have noted increased rates of comorbidity between anxiety and affective (mood) disorders and the transmission of vulnerablility for mixed disorder types from parent to child (Leckman et al, 1984; Weissman et al, 1984; Coryell et al, 1988). Concern about the significance of mixed anxiety/depressive disorder led to a separate classification of such a condition in ICD–10 (World Health Organization, 1992) and DSM–IV (American Psychiatric Association, 1994) listed potential research diagnostic criteria for this condition. In addition, both ICD–10 and DSM–IV include substance-induced anxiety disorders and anxiety disorders due to a general medical condition.

Epidemiologists and clinicians have different yet complementary interests in the relationship between specific anxiety and mood disorders. From an epidemiological perspective, it is important to identify risk factors for the development of any mental disorder. The potential risk that one disorder may pose for development of a second disorder also offers an opportunity for generating aetiological hypotheses as well as preventive intervention approaches. For the·clinician, however, the treatment issues involve an assessment of probable clinical course and judgements about the effectiveness of interventions for the full range of symptoms.

To address the linkage of anxiety and mood disorders, we have completed a comparison between an epidemiologically defined population from the Epidemiologic Catchment Area (ECA) study and a clinical sample of patients with major depression at the McLean Hospital, Boston, Massachusetts (Schatzberg et al, 1998). Epidemio-

logical findings should complement data from clinical investigations by providing information on more representative samples of the population and by identifying disorders with a wider range of severity. Since the identification of multiple conditions in patients is statistically more likely in clinical settings, a logical phenomenon known as Berkson's bias (Berkson, 1946), the patterns of comorbidity identified in epidemiological samples can be tested without the confound of a treatment-seeking bias. Likewise, the sequence of onset and offset of multiple disorders can be defined in both types of studies as a means of identifying early indicators of these disorders which can facilitate early treatment or preventive strategies.

Anxiety disorders were recognised as one of the most prevalent diagnostic mental disorder groups in the early single wave-I interview reports of the ECA study (Robins et al, 1984; Myers et al, 1984; Regier et al, 1990). As a lifetime diagnosis, they were found in 14.6% of the adult US population aged 18+ years. By comparison, affective or mood disorders were found in 8.3%, and any addictive disorder in 16.7% of US adults – one or more mental/addictive disorder was found in 32.7% of the population. In a more recent analysis of both wave-I and wave-II interviews, spaced one year apart, the prospective one-year prevalence of one or more mental/addictive disorders was found to be 28.1% (Regier et al, 1993). Following completion of the ECA study, the National Institute of Mental Health was able to support a follow-up study to examine the prevalence and temporal sequence of mental and addictive disorders in greater detail. The National Comorbidity Study (NCS) was directed by Ronald Kessler at the University of Michigan with a modified version of the WHO Composite International Diagnostic Interview, which is an international version of the Diagnostic Interview Schedule used in the ECA. Based on a more intensive memory enhancement strategy, a younger age group (15–54 years), a true representative sample of the US population, and a revised version of the diagnostic criteria (DSM–III–R), the NCS found a considerably higher rate of lifetime disorders from a single interview, and about the same rate of one-year disorders as was found in two waves of interviews in the ECA (Kessler et al, 1994, 1996). For example, one or more anxiety disorder was found in 24.9%, mood disorders in 19.3% and addictive disorders

Table 5 Comorbidity of any anxiety, mood and substance use disorders

	Prevalence (s.e.)	% with anxiety disorder (s.e.)	% with mood disorder (s.e.)	% with substance use disorder (s.e.)	% with all three (s.e.)
Any anxiety disorder	12.6 (0.3)	–	26.1 (1.2)	14.0 (1.0)	5.4 (0.6)
Any mood disorder	9.5 (0.3)	34.5 (1.5)	–	17.3 (1.2)	7.1 (0.8)
Any substance use disorder	9.5 (0.3)	18.6 (1.4)	17.5 (1.2)	–	7.2 (0.8)

Table 6 Comorbidity of social phobia, major depression and substance use disorders

	Prevalence (s.e.)	% with social phobia (s.e.)	% with major depression (s.e.)	% with any substance use disorder (s.e.)	% with all three (s.e.)
Social phobia	4.2 (0.2)	–	23.7 (2.4)	14.3 (1.9)	6.2 (1.4)
Major depression	5.7 (0.2)	21.7 (2.3)	–	19.1 (1.6)	5.6 (1.3)
Any substance use disorder	9.5 (0.3)	6.2 (0.9)	11.6 (1.0)	–	2.7 (0.6)

this sequence is most likely to occur over several years, it was also interesting to use the prospective design of the ECA to examine the sequence of occurrence within a one-year period. As can be seen in Table 7, slightly less than 1% of the population (a total of 148 unweighted subjects) either started with or developed one or more disorders in all three categories of anxiety, mood, and addictive disorder in one year. About one-third (35%) started the year with all three, while the second largest group (22.8%) began with both an anxiety and a mood disorder at the start of the year. Some combination of a mood disorder with other anxiety or substance use disorders was most prominent at the beginning of the year (about 40%), and the development of a substance use disorder in about the same percentage (39.3%) was the most likely

new disorder to develop in this triad over the course of the year.

DISCUSSION

When rates from the ECA community sample were compared with the McLean Hospital cohort of 85 patients with current major depression, aged 17–65 years, we note a lifetime history of any anxiety disorder in 34%, simple phobia 5%, agoraphobia 5%, social phobia 15%, panic disorder 12% and OCD in 7% of this clinical sample (Schatzberg et al, 1998). Current anxiety disorder rates were only slightly lower than the lifetime rates for social phobia (13%) and any anxiety disorder (29%).

Hence, the rates of any lifetime anxiety disorder (47%) are somewhat higher in the community sample with major depression, as are the rates of simple and agoraphobia. In contrast, almost identical rates of a lifetime history of social phobia were found in the community (13.6%) and clinical (15%) samples of subjects with major depression. When the one-year prospective sample of subjects with major depression was evaluated, almost 22% were found to have a diagnosis of social phobia in the same one-year period. The age of onset was also found to be significantly earlier for social phobia in both clinical and community samples with an average age of onset of 11.6 years for social phobia and 13.5 years for simple phobia.

In summary, anxiety disorders in general, and social and simple phobias in particular, appear to have an early onset in adolescence with potentially severe consequences. Aside from the distress and disability they cause children at this age, they also appear to predispose them to a greater vulnerability to major depression and addictive disorders. Given the strong support for the linkage of the social and simple phobias to major depression in both clinical and epidemiological studies, there is added impetus for untangling the potential pathophysiology of these relationships as noted by Schatzberg et al (1998). A challenge for both epidemiology and clinical psychiatry is to be able to identify these children early and to offer effective early intervention or preventive strategies to reduce the risk and morbidity inherent in these conditions.

Table 7 Persons with any anxiety, any mood and any substance abuse/dependence in one year sequence of comorbid disorder occurrence

Start	Develop	Weighted %	n
All	–	35.2	53
Anxiety	Mood, substance	8.4	14
Anxiety, substance	Mood	4.2	5
Anxiety, mood	Substance	22.8	37
Mood	Anxiety, substance	8.1	10
Mood, substance	Anxiety	9.0	10
Substance	Anxiety, mood	4.7	4
	All	7.4	15
Total		100.0	148

Note: Start with one-month at wave I; develop one-year at wave II.

151

Table 2 Lifetime prevalence of various anxiety disorders among persons with major depression

Anxiety disorder	With major depression (s.e.)
Any anxiety disorder	47.2 (2.3)
Simple phobia	25.6 (1.8)
Agoraphobia	20.4 (1.7)
Social phobia	13.6 (1.6)
Panic disorder	13.0 (1.4)
Obsessive–compulsive disorder	14.4 (1.5)

before the onset of major depression. An age of onset of at least two years prior to depression was found in 69–72% of those with phobias and in 43% of those with OCD. The statistical significance of the earlier age of onset for anxiety disorders is demonstrated by the high odds ratios for all of the anxiety disorders and for social phobia in particular, where the odds are more than five times greater that a prior anxiety disorder will precede the onset of major depression. However, for panic disorder, about equal percentages (29%) had a prior onset of either depression or panic disorder with about 40% having an onset within the same two-year time span.

Odds ratios for major depression preceding anxiety disorders were also calculated and showed no elevation for social or simple phobias. However, they were 1.2 for any anxiety disorder, 4.2 for panic disorder and 3.4 for OCD. Such symmetrical odds ratios for panic and OCD indicate that they are about as likely to follow the onset of major depression as they are to precede it, with a substantial proportion starting both disorders within the same two-year time frame.

The time relationship between anxiety and mood disorders can readily be understood by observing, in Table 4, that the average age of onset of any lifetime anxiety disorder is 16.4 years, with social phobia beginning earliest at an average of 11.6 years, and panic disorder much later at an average age of 23.8 years. In contrast, the average age of onset for major depression among those with an anxiety disorder ranges from 23.6 years to 25 years for subjects with comorbid social phobia, panic disorder, or any anxiety disorder.

One-year prevalence comorbidity

Since most clinical decision-making is concerned with prognoses and treatment plans

of less than an entire future lifetime, we will also focus on the degree of comorbidity that tends to occur in a single year. In the same one-year prospective analysis that identified 28.1% of the population as having a mental or addictive disorder, we found a one-month prevalence of 7.3% with any anxiety disorder at wave I, a one-year incidence/recurrence rate of 5.3%, and a total one-year prevalence rate of 12.6%. Although this one-year rate is considerably below the 17.2% one-year rate reported in the NCS, it is almost as high as the wave-I, single-interview lifetime ECA rate reported previously. From these findings, one can deduce that a large proportion of individuals meeting DSM–III or DSM–III–R criteria for anxiety and mood disorders tend to have relatively brief episodes which may be recurrent.

Comorbidity rates in the one-year period are somewhat lower than those found in the lifetime prevalence analyses. However, more than one-third (34%) of subjects with a mood disorder will have an anxiety disorder, 17% a substance use disorder, and 7% all three disorders. These rates are much closer to those found in a clinical population of patients with mood disorders – a clinical state in which the relative significance of other lifetime dis-

orders may be less appreciated (Schatzberg et al, 1998). About one-quarter of those with an anxiety disorder will also have a mood disorder and 15% a substance use disorder. Among the 9.5% of the population with a one-year diagnosis of substance abuse or dependence, about an equal number (18–19%) will have an anxiety or a mood disorder during the year.

In Table 6, a more detailed analysis of social phobia, major depression and substance abuse is provided to assist in examining this significant clinical triad for its developmental sequence as well as for the pattern of comorbidity. Among those with major depression during one year, more than one-fifth (21.7%) have a social phobia episode during the same year, and almost as many (19.1%) a substance use disorder. Because of the slightly lower base rate of social phobia (4.2%) than major depression (5.7%), the proportion of subjects with social phobia during the year who have major depression comorbidity (23.7%) is slightly higher than the comorbidity rates of the cohort with major depression – an important statistical issue addressed previously (Regier et al, 1990).

The early onset of social phobia may be considered a risk factor for subsequent substance abuse or depression. Although

Table 3 Relative age of onset among persons with both major depression and anxiety disorders

Anxiety disorder	Depression first	Anxiety first	Odds ratio[1]
Any anxiety	18%	55%	3.72
Simple phobia	10%	71%	2.39
Social phobia	5%	72%	5.35
Agoraphobia	9%	69%	3.74
Panic disorder	29%	29%	4.66
Obsessive–compulsive disorder	25%	43%	4.31

1. Odds of developing depression at least two years after the development of given anxiety disorder.
Note: remainder of persons in each row had onset of both disorders within two years of each other.

Table 4 Mean ages of onset of major depression and anxiety disorders among persons with comorbid disorders

Anxiety disorder	Mean age of onset of depression (s.e.)	Mean age of onset of anxiety (s.e.)
Any anxiety disorder	24.7 (0.6)	16.4 (0.7)
Simple phobia	24.5 (1.0)	13.5 (1.0)
Social phobia	23.6 (1.3)	11.6 (1.0)
Agoraphobia	24.1 (1.0)	15.7 (1.2)
Panic disorder	25.0 (1.4)	23.8 (1.5)
Obsessive–compulsive disorder	21.5 (1.06)	22.3 (1.4)

26

Table 5 Comorbidity of any anxiety, mood and substance use disorders

	Prevalence (s.e.)	% with anxiety disorder (s.e.)	% with mood disorder (s.e.)	% with substance use disorder (s.e.)	% with all three (s.e.)
Any anxiety disorder	12.6 (0.3)	–	26.1 (1.2)	14.0 (1.0)	5.4 (0.6)
Any mood disorder	9.5 (0.3)	34.5 (1.5)	–	17.3 (1.2)	7.1 (0.8)
Any substance use disorder	9.5 (0.3)	18.6 (1.4)	17.5 (1.2)	–	7.2 (0.8)

Table 6 Comorbidity of social phobia, major depression and substance use disorders

	Prevalence (s.e.)	% with social phobia (s.e.)	% with major depression (s.e.)	% with any substance use disorder (s.e.)	% with all three (s.e.)
Social phobia	4.2 (0.2)	–	23.7 (2.4)	14.3 (1.9)	6.2 (1.4)
Major depression	5.7 (0.2)	21.7 (2.3)	–	19.1 (1.6)	5.6 (1.3)
Any substance use disorder	9.5 (0.3)	6.2 (0.9)	11.6 (1.0)	–	2.7 (0.6)

this sequence is most likely to occur over several years, it was also interesting to use the prospective design of the ECA to examine the sequence of occurrence within a one-year period. As can be seen in Table 7, slightly less than 1% of the population (a total of 148 unweighted subjects) either started with or developed one or more disorders in all three categories of anxiety, mood, and addictive disorder in one year. About one-third (35%) started the year with all three, while the second largest group (22.8%) began with both an anxiety and a mood disorder at the start of the year. Some combination of a mood disorder with other anxiety or substance use disorders was most prominent at the beginning of the year (about 40%), and the development of a substance use disorder in about the same percentage (39.3%) was the most likely

new disorder to develop in this triad over the course of the year.

DISCUSSION

When rates from the ECA community sample were compared with the McLean Hospital cohort of 85 patients with current major depression, aged 17–65 years, we note a lifetime history of any anxiety disorder in 34%, simple phobia 5%, agoraphobia 5%, social phobia 15%, panic disorder 12% and OCD in 7% of this clinical sample (Schatzberg *et al*, 1998). Current anxiety disorder rates were only slightly lower than the lifetime rates for social phobia (13%) and any anxiety disorder (29%).

Hence, the rates of any lifetime anxiety disorder (47%) are somewhat higher in the community sample with major depression, as are the rates of simple and agoraphobia. In contrast, almost identical rates of a lifetime history of social phobia were found in the community (13.6%) and clinical (15%) samples of subjects with major depression. When the one-year prospective sample of subjects with major depression was evaluated, almost 22% were found to have a diagnosis of social phobia in the same one-year period. The age of onset was also found to be significantly earlier for social phobia in both clinical and community samples with an average age of onset of 11.6 years for social phobia and 13.5 years for simple phobia.

In summary, anxiety disorders in general, and social and simple phobias in particular, appear to have an early onset in adolescence with potentially severe consequences. Aside from the distress and disability they cause children at this age, they also appear to predispose them to a greater vulnerability to major depression and addictive disorders. Given the strong support for the linkage of the social and simple phobias to major depression in both clinical and epidemiological studies, there is added impetus for untangling the potential pathophysiology of these relationships as noted by Schatzberg *et al* (1998). A challenge for both epidemiology and clinical psychiatry is to be able to identify these children early and to offer effective early intervention or preventive strategies to reduce the risk and morbidity inherent in these conditions.

Table 7 Persons with any anxiety, any mood and any substance abuse/dependence in one year sequence of comorbid disorder occurrence

Start	Develop	Weighted %	n
All	–	35.2	53
Anxiety	Mood, substance	8.4	14
Anxiety, substance	Mood	4.2	5
Anxiety, mood	Substance	22.8	37
Mood	Anxiety, substance	8.1	10
Mood, substance	Anxiety	9.0	10
Substance	Anxiety, mood	4.7	4
	All	7.4	15
Total		100.0	148

Note: Start with one-month at wave I; develop one-year at wave II.

REFERENCES

American Psychiatric Association (1994) *Diagnostic and Statistical Manual of Mental Disorders* (4th edn) *(DSM-IV)*. Washington, DC: APA.

Berkson, J. (1946) Limitations of the application of four-fold tables to hospital data. *Biometric Bulletin*, **2**, 47-53.

Coryell, W., Endicott, J., Andreasen, N. C., et al (1988) Depression and panic attacks: the significance of overlap as reflected in follow-up and family study data. *American Journal of Psychiatry*, **145**, 293-300.

Kessler, R. C., McGonagle, K. A., Zhao, S., et al (1994) Lifetime and 12-month prevalence of DSM-III-R psychiatric disorders in the United States: results from the National Comorbidity Survey. *Archives of General Psychiatry*, **51**, 8-19.

—, Nelson, C. B., McGonagle, K. A., et al (1996) The epidemiology of co-occurring addictive and mental disorders: Implications for prevention and service utilization. *American Journal of Orthopsychiatry*, **66**, 7-31.

Leckman, J. F., Weissman, M. M., Prusoff, B. A., et al (1984) Subtypes of depression: Family study perspective. *Archives of General Psychiatry*, **41**, 833-838.

Myers, J. K., Weissman, M. M., Tischler, G. L., et al (1984) Six-month prevalence of psychiatric disorders in three communities. *Archives of General Psychiatry*, **41**, 959-967.

DARREL A. REGIER, MD, DONALD S. RAE, MA, WILLIAM E. NARROW, MD, CHARLES T. KAELBER, MD, Division of Epidemiology and Services Research, National Institute of Mental Health, National Institutes of Health, Rockville, Maryland; ALAN F. SCHATZBERG, MD, Department of Psychiatry and Behavioral Sciences, Stanford University Medical Center, Stanford, California

Correspondence: Dr D. A. Regier, National Institute of Mental Health, Parklawn Building, Room 10-105, 5600 Fishers Lane, Rockville, MD 20857, USA

Regier, D. A., Farmer, M. E., Rae, D. S., et al (1990) Comorbidity of mental disorders with alcohol and other drug abuse. *Journal of the American Medical Association*, **264**, 2511-2518.

—, Narrow, W. E., Rae, D. S., et al (1993) The de facto US Mental and Addictive Disorders Service system: Epidemiologic Catchment Area prospective 1-year prevalence rates of disorders and services. *Archives of General Psychiatry*, **50**, 85-94.

—, Kaelber, C. T., Rae, D. S., et al (1998) Limitations of diagnostic criteria and assessment instruments for mental disorders: implications for research and policy. *Archives of General Psychiatry*, **55**, 109-115.

Robins, L. N., Helzer, J. E., Weissman, M. M., et al (1984) Lifetime prevalence of specific psychiatric disorders in three sites. *Archives of General Psychiatry*, **41**, 949-958.

— & Regier, D. A. (eds) (1991) *Psychiatric Disorders in America*. New York: Free Press.

Schatzberg, A. F., Samson, J. A., Rothschild, A. J., et al (1998) McLean Hospital Depression Research Facility: early-onset phobic disorders and adult-onset major depression. *British Journal of Psychiatry*, **173**, (suppl. 34), 29-34.

Weissman, M. M., Leckman, J. F., Merikangas, K. R., et al (1984) Depression and anxiety disorders in parents and children: Results from the Yale family study. *Archives of General Psychiatry*, **41**, 845-852.

World Health Organization (1992) *The Tenth Revision of the International Classification of Diseases and Related Health Problems* (ICD-10). Geneva: WHO.

ORIGINAL ARTICLES

Fear and Fitness: An Evolutionary Analysis of Anxiety Disorders

Isaac M. Marks
Institute of Psychiatry, London

Randolph M. Nesse
University of Michigan Medical School, Department of Psychiatry, Ann Arbor

This article reviews the evolutionary origins and functions of the capacity for anxiety, and relevant clinical and research issues. Normal anxiety is an emotion that helps organisms defend against a wide variety of threats. There is a general capacity for normal defensive arousal, and subtypes of normal anxiety protect against particular kinds of threats. These normal subtypes correspond somewhat to mild forms of various anxiety disorders. Anxiety disorders arise from dysregulation of normal defensive responses, raising the possibility of a bypophobic disorder (too little anxiety). If a drug were discovered that abolished all defensive anxiety, it could do harm as well as good. Factors that have shaped anxiety-regulation mechanisms can explain prepotent and prepared tendencies to associate anxiety more quickly with certain cues than with others. These tendencies lead to excess fear of largely archaic dangers, like snakes, and too little fear of new threats, like cars. An understanding of the evolutionary origins, functions, and mechanisms of anxiety suggests new questions about anxiety disorders.

KEY WORDS: Fear, phobias, anxiety disorders, obsessive-compulsive disorder, agoraphobia, social phobia, prepotency, preparedness

INTRODUCTION

Nearly everyone recognizes that anxiety is a useful trait that has been shaped by natural selection. Even good things, however, cease to be good when they become excessive. Too much anxiety can be disabling. If a drug were found that abolished all anxiety for ail time it could be as harmful as a drug that

Received January 23, 1994; revised September 17, 1994.

Address reprint requests and correspondence to: Isaac M. Marks, M.D., Institute of Psychiatry, London, SE5 8AF, U.K., or to Randolph M. Nesse, M.D., The University of Michigan Medical School, Department of Psychiatry, C440, Med-Inn Bldg., Ann Arbor, MI 48109-0840, U.S.A. E-mail: Nesse@um.ccumich.edu

Ethology and Sociobiology 15: 247-261 (1994)
0 Elsevier Science Inc., 1994
655 Avenue of the Americas, New York, NY 10010

0162-3095/94/$7.00

155

induced anxiety of crippling degree. Adaptive modulation is the keynote to success. This point is best understood from an evolutionary perspective on the origins and functions of anxiety. Such a framework can illuminate current clinical and research issues.

Anxiety is one kind of emotion, Why do emotions play such a central part in our lives? Many researchers now view emotions as response patterns shaped by natural selection to offer selective advantages in certain situations (Plutchik and Kellerman 1980; Marks 1987; Lelliott et al. 1989). The bodily, behavioral, and cognitive responses that constitute emotions are a preprogrammed pattern of responses that increase ability to cope with threats or seize opportunities.

Each emotion can be thought of as a computer program designed to accomplish some specific fitness task particularly well (Nesse 1990). If the current task is courtship, romantic love is helpful. If one is being betrayed, anger is useful. If a tiger is attacking, then fearful flight and avoidance are best. If people are disapproving, then social anxiety may be appropriate. Different emotions, however, must be orchestrated, just as endocrine function must be coordinated in an endocrine orchestra. Emotional responses must fit changing adaptive challenges, with each emotion fitting a particular kind of situation.

Anxiety increases fitness in dangerous situations which threaten a loss of reproductive resources. Such resources include not only life and health, but also relationships, property, status, reputation, skill, and anything else that could increase Darwinian fitness. Given this function of anxiety, we would expect it to be aroused by any cues that indicate a risk of loss. If each subtype of anxiety evolved to deal with a particular kind of danger (as we will suggest), then the features of each anxiety subtype and the signals that arouse it should match the corresponding danger.

Prior Work on Evolution and Anxiety

The utility of fear and anxiety has long been recognized. Darwin's book on emotions emphasized the communication aspect of fear (Darwin 1872). The function of separation anxiety was pointed out by Bowlby (1973), Marks (1987), Ainsworth (Ainsworth et al. 1978), Klein (1981, p. 248), and many others. The adaptive functions of components of the stress response were laid out long ago by Cannon (1929) and later by Frankenhaeuser (Konner 1990). It has also long been known that fear is more easily linked to certain cues than to others (Marks 1969; Seligman 1970; Paley 1970 [1802]; Ruse 1988; Mineka et al. 1980).

We still lack, however, a systematic analysis of the evolutionary origins and functions of anxiety. Little research has demonstrated the advantages of anxiety, and almost no one has looked for disorders characterized by too little anxiety. There are several reasons for these gaps in our knowledge. Most writings on the functions of anxiety apologize about "speculatively" addressing such "teleological" issues, even though biologists have known for 30 years that questions about the evolutionary function of a trait are not teleological at all and that hypotheses about such functions can be tested just like any others (Mayr 1974). Complex traits can be shaped by natural selection only if they serve functions that increase fitness. Hypotheses about these functions are not matters for speculation but for clear formulation and rigorous testing.

Testing of evolutionary hypotheses is now the focus of most research into animal behavior (Alcock 1989), especially by behavioral ecologists (Krebs and Davies 1991), who emphasize the functional significance of behavior, not just the descriptions dwelt on by earlier ethologists. These methods are only just beginning to be applied to the study of human behavior (Howard 1991; Barkow et al. 1992; Smith 1982). Therefore, few data-based studies of humans are available as yet. By highlighting the value of this approach and its clinical and research significance, we hope to encourage work on human anxiety that builds on the models provided by behavioral ecology. Even before then, we suggest that this perspective can provide some guidance in answering current questions about anxiety and its disorders.

Subtypes of Anxiety

A question of major concern is how to split (or lump) the various kinds of anxiety disorders, and how to justify the taxonomy. Some researchers emphasize the similarities of all anxieties and postulate the unity of all anxiety disorders. Others stress the differences between different kinds of anxiety, positing several distinct disorders, each with its own etiology, phenomenology, and treatment. An evolutionary perspective suggests a middle ground between these two extremes. General anxiety probably evolved to deal with threats whose nature could not be defined very clearly. Subtypes of anxiety probably evolved to give a selective advantage of better protection against a particular kind of danger.

To illustrate this, consider another defense, the immune response. Humans have a capacity for both a general immune response and for specialized immune responses. Antigens arouse general responses, such as lymphocyte monitoring for the presence of foreign material, inflammation, fever, pain, and malaise. They also arouse specific responses, such as immunoglobulins to bacterial infection, interferon to viral invasion, eosinophils to parasites, and natural killer cells to cancer.

Like antigens, other external threats also arouse both general and more specific responses. General threats arouse general anxiety-inducing vigilance, physiological arousal, and planning for defense. Specific threats elicit specific patterns of behavioral defense (Edmunds 1974; Janzen 1981). High places evoke freezing; social threats arouse submission; predators provoke flight. An evolutionary view suggests that different types of fear should share many aspects because reactions (e.g., rise in heart rate) that are useful in one kind of danger are likely to also help other kinds. Furthermore, the presence of one threat makes it likely that others are present too. A hunter-gatherer who is excluded from the group becomes more vulnerable not only to predators but also to starvation, climatic extremes, and falling off cliffs and into holes in unknown   territory.

The utility of different kinds of anxiety depends in part on the four ways in which anxiety can give protection (Marks 1987). Two of them parallel the body's ways of dealing with foreign material: (1) *Escape (flight) or avoidance (preflight)* distances an individual from certain threats in the way that vomiting, disgust, diarrhea, coughing, and sneezing put physical space between the organism and a pathogen. (2) *Aggressive* defense (anger, clawing, biting, or spraying with noxious substances) harms the source of the danger just as the immune system attacks bacteria. (3) *Freezing/immobility* may benefit by (a) aiding location and assessment of the danger, (b) concealment, and (c) inhibiting the predator's attack reflex. (4) *Submission/appeasement* is useful when the threat comes from one's own group. Inhibition of impulses probably fits best under this category.

Multiple strategies can, of course, be used together, Squid escape by jet propulsion in a cloud of concealing ink. Puffer fish look ferocious, and their spines harm the predator's mouth. Agoraphobics   freeze in panic and then dash for home. Social phobics avoid or escape from authority figures if they can, and submit if they cannot. Obsessive-compulsives avoid "contamination" if possible; if they can't, they try to escape from it by washing. Any of the above four strategies can involve deception (Krebs and Dawkins 1984). An escaping rabbit runs straight ahead, but then circles furtively behind the pursuer. When a cat is threatened, its fur stands on end, making it seem larger. A possum plays dead.

In summary, the anxiety subtypes probably exist because of the benefits of having responses specialized to deal with particular dangers, but it is unlikely that anxiety subtypes have differentiated into completely unrelated response patterns. To the extent that various anxiety disorders are exaggerations of various subtypes of normal anxiety, anxiety disorders can likewise be expected to be partially, not fully, differentiated.

The Relationship Between General Anxiety and Panic

Can an evolutionary perspective illuminate the relationship between general anxiety and panic? Are anxiety and panic separate, or on a continuum? Mild threat causes a general increase in anxiety that helps to locate the source and type of danger and to plan possible ways to deal with it, Extreme or sudden danger is more likely to produce panic. General anxiety commonly precedes panic. A similar relationship is observed with the two related defenses of nausea and vomiting. Nausea stops one from eating (useful if the food being ingested is toxic), and leads one to avoid foods that induced nausea (also useful). Extreme nausea culminates in vomiting, which expels the contents of the stomach. Occasionally there can be projectile vomiting without preceding nausea, just as there can be sudden panic without preceding anxiety,

Many components of the anxiety and panic response are those which

Cannon recognized as useful in situations in which "fight or flight" are the adaptive responses (Cannon, 1929). Cannon noted the functions of many of these components. Epinephrine acts on platelet beta receptors to enhance clotting and on the liver to release glucose. Cardiovascular changes speed blood circulation. Circulation patterns change so that less blood goes to the skin and gut, and more to the muscles. Hyperventilation raises oxygen import and carbon dioxide export. Sweating cools the body and makes it slippery. A sense of imminent doom galvanizes preventive action and forestalls dawdling. These components form a reliable constellation in the anxiety/panic response, which is partly mediated by adrenergic receptors (a proximate explanation). They act together to increase fitness in the face of danger (the evolutionary explanation that is needed in addition to the proximate one).

These aspects of anxiety and panic are largely similar whether cued by heights, animals, thunderstorms, darkness, public places, separation, or social scrutiny. Their similarity reflects the value of this defense against a wide array of threats.

Other Subtypes of Anxiety and Specific Threats

The features of many anxiety subtypes are well matched to the task of defending against particular types of threats. On the hypothesis that anxiety disorders represent extremes of normal forms of anxiety, we will not distinguish here between normal and pathological states.

1. Fear:
   a. Heights induce freezing instead of wild flight, thus making one less liable to fall.
   b. Blood or injury cues produce a diphasic vasovagal response ending in bradycardic syncope. Such fainting may reduce blood loss after injury and, like death feigning, inhibit further attack by a predator (Marks 1988).
   c. Public places and being far from home arouse a cluster of mild fears that guard against the many dangers encountered outside the home range of any territorial species. Agoraphobia can be seen as an intensification of such extraterritorial fear (Nesse 1987; Lelliott et al. 1989).
   d. Traumas are followed by fear and avoidance of anything reminiscent of the original trauma. A natural tendency to such seeming "overreaction" is understandable given the high cost of failure to avoid any possibility of reexperiencing a mortal danger.
   e. Social threats evoke responses that promote group acceptance, for example, submission to dominants and to norms of dress, mien, odor, speech, customs, beliefs. This prevents dangerous extrusion from the group. Mild shyness and embarrassment can promote acceptance. If shyness and embarrassment are excessive, however, then fitness suffers, as in several anxiety disorders: pervasive shyness in avoidant personality disorder; gaze aversion and fear of scrutiny, of shaking, and of blushing in social

phobia; fear of excreting near others in sphincteric phobias (Marks 1987, pp. 362-371); terror of looking or smelling abnormal in dysmorphopho- bia; fear of behaving antisocially in obsessive-compulsive disorder. Impulses to behave in ways that would cause social rejection may arouse general anxiety without the subject being aware of those punishable impulses, thus helping to conceal them from others (Nesse 1990). We do not emphasize a distinction between fear of specific dangers and anxiety aroused by nonspecific dangers or unconscious impulses, because in all cases the state, whether anxiety or fear, is aroused by a cue that indicates a threat to reproductive resources,

2. Fear-like Patterns:
   Some threats evoke specific discomforts not usually called anxiety.
   a. Food aversions are conditioned much less easily to anxiety and to pain than to nausea and vomiting.
   b. Threat of losing one's mate to a rival evokes jealousy that includes not only anxiety but also seeking of reassurance and aggression to try to avert loss. This pattern is intensified in morbid jealousy, which often includes obsessive ruminations and ritualistic checking on possible infi- delity of the partner.
   c. The normal gag reflex stops material entering the upper respiratory tract. Hypersensitivity of this reflex may cause undue gagging with intense pharyngeal discomfort (Wilks and Marks 1983).

3. Obsessive-compulsive (OC) behaviors
   The anxiety and sense of compulsion in obsessive-compulsive disorder (OCD) may be a caricature of the motivational mechanisms that drive and prioritize normal behavioral routines. Such routines are parodied by OC rituals, which distort priorities.
   a. Many behavioral sequences are best completed to their functional end; if left unfinished, time and energy are likely to be wasted. Tension moti- vates persistence until closure is effected. Many obsessive-compulsives seem to lack the "fiat" we experience that marks the end of one sequence of thoughts or actions (James 1893). Such patients feel tense and must continue repeating thoughts or actions until they "feel right."
   b. Many behavioral sequences are best executed one at a time, otherwise energy may be frittered away on disparate tasks, none of which are completed. The excess orderliness of OCD also wastes energy by doing tasks one by one to perfection, regardless of their importance, while leaving vital tasks undone.
   c. Parasitism and infection are reduced in mammals by grooming and in birds by preening (Hart 1990). In many primate species, grooming also smoothes social interaction as when a defeated baboon grooms the victor intensely after a fight. Many obsessive-compulsives wash and groom endlessly; if not allowed to do this, they often feel disgust or other discomfort rather than anxiety.
   d. Group membership requires attention to others' needs. Disregard of these

makes ostracism likely. In OCD, there is maladaptive overconcern with the risk of harming others.

e. Hoarding guards against future shortages and is protective in environments of scarcity. It is grotesquely exaggerated in some obsessive compulsives.

It is unclear why obsessive-compulsives explain (rationalize) their fears and rituals in a more complex manner than do phobics. Perhaps different cognitive mechanisms are deranged in obsessive-compulsives as compared to phobics.

To summarize this section, the features of anxiety disorder subtypes largely correspond to various dangers humans have faced during their evolution. As noted above, subtypes of anxiety are not completely distinct because multiple threats are common, and because so many aspects of anxiety defend against many, not just one, kinds of danger. The most recent genetic evidence is consistent with this view. A study of 2,163 female twin pairs concludes: "[We] found strong evidence of the existence both of genetic and environmental risk factors unique to each kind of phobia and for genetic and environmental risk factors that influenced all phobia subtypes. Our results were midway between the two extreme hypotheses regarding the interrelationship of the subtypes of phobias: (1) the subtypes of phobias are distinct, unrelated syndromes and (2) the subtypes of phobias represent minor variations of a single disorder." (Kendler 1992, p. 279).

It should be possible to create a taxonomy for anxiety disorders that reflects the origin and functions of normal anxieties. Just as various components of the normal immune response can respond too much (anaphylaxis), too little (hypoimmune disorders), or to the wrong cue (allergy) or wrong target (autoimmune disease), so anxiety can be excessive (as in general anxiety or panic disorder), deficient (hypophobia), or in response to a stimulus that is not dangerous (simple/specific phobias). The immune disorders are being unraveled by increasing understanding of the normal functions and mechanisms of the immune system. The anxiety disorders will also make more sense as we learn about the normal functions of the components of the anxiety system and the mechanisms that mediate them.

Defense Regulation

Defenses enhance survival only when appropriate to the degree and type of threat. If a defense is deficient, excessive, or inappropriate in form, then fitness suffers. People who lack the capacity for pain die young because their tissues get damaged (Stevens 1981); those with excessive pain are also disabled. Suppressing the cough reflex makes pneumonia likely; too much coughing can cause cerebral hemorrhage. Stopping vomiting or diarrhea may lead to death by toxin absorption (DuPont and Hornick 1973); too much vomiting or diarrhea can kill by dehydration. The systems that regulate these defenses have been fine-tuned to detect the form and amount of threat and respond appropriately.

Anxiety, too, is beneficial only if carefully regulated. Too much disables. Too little anxiety leads to behavior that makes us more likely to fall off a cliff, be attacked by a wild beast, hurt by other humans, or to act in ways that lead to social exclusion. People with too little anxiety do not come to psychiatrists complaining of deficient fear, so their disorders, the "hypophobias," still await formal   description.

The regulation of anxiety is an example of the benefit-cost tradeoffs that make every organism "a bundle of selective compromises" (Alexander 1975). While a grazing deer that lifts its head every few seconds to scan for predators has less time to eat, mate, and care for offspring, one that lifts its head too little may eat more, but is at greater risk of being eaten itself. How are such factors balanced?

The law of diminishing returns applies to anxiety, as to so much else. A little anxiety may yield marked protective gains but more fear may not be worth the costs. Selection pressure for fearfulness tapers off at the point where the incremental cost of further fear starts to rise above the incremental protection it yields. Evolved defenses often seem over-responsive (Marks 1987) because repeated false alarms may cost less than a single failure to respond when the danger is great (Nesse 1990). Anxiety at the mere hint of danger is therefore common, even though it may appear needless to a casual observer. Because the costs of erring on the side of caution are usually less than those of risk taking, it is no wonder that anxiety disorders are frequent.

Different environments select for different degrees of fear. On long-isolated islands, without predators many species lost their tendency to flee, fight, or hide. When humans arrived and brought in predators, the tame indigenous species were often killed off rapidly. The point is captured in the phrase "Dead as a dodo."

Regulation of Anxiety by Cues of Danger

It would be grossly inefficient to become anxious only after actual pain or loss. Instead, the nervous system has been shaped so that anxiety arises in response to cues that denote potential threats. Most of the dangers an individual is likely to encounter have already been survived by its forebears. Individuals who recognized and responded to a hint of such threats lived longer and had more descendants than those who had to learn from bitter experience. Selection thereby shaped a nervous system that makes us attend intently to certain cues--this is *prepotency* (Marks 1969; Ohman and Dimberg 1984) or *salience.* For instance, snake- or eye-like patterns arouse anxiety more easily than do other patterns. We are also predisposed to learn certain reactions to certain stimuli-this is *preparedness* (Seligman 1970). For instance, heights and snakes evoke fear rather than nausea, while bad food produces nausea rather than fear. *Prepotent* attention to particular patterns of stimulation is the first step on the path to *prepared* reactions to those patterns.

Fear develops quickly to minimal cues that reflect ancient dangers. As with imprinting, where experience inscribes the precise parental features that the offspring recognizes, so it is often better to convey the specifics of danger by rapid learning than by rigid genetic encoding. This avoids wasteful defense against safe stimuli. African plains' animals are less fearful of predators' presence per se than of their approach, their hunting intent, and other signs of danger (Marks 1987).

Prepared rapid learning of fear is partly mediated by the reactions of caretakers and peers. Keen observation and imitation of them is itself a prepared response. When an infant sees a visual cliff or a stranger, it looks at mother frequently to monitor her response (Marks 1987). If she smiles, this reassures; if she shows alarm, this augments her baby's fear. Rhesus monkeys are born without snake fear. Enduring fear develops after a few observations of another rhesus taking fright at a snake, but not after seeing it take the same fright at a flower (Mineka et al. 1984). Likewise, a fawn is not born with fear of a wolf, but lifelong panic is conditioned by seeing its mother flee just once from a wolf.

Prepared fears tend to manifest at the age when they become adaptive (Marks 1987). Height fear emerges in infants shortly before they start crawling at six months (Scan: and Salapatek 1970) and rises with crawling experience (Berthenthal et al. 1983). As the two-year-old child explores further afield, animal fears emerge. As young people leave home, agoraphobia arises.

Both prepotency and preparedness lead to a nonrandom distribution of fears (Marks 1987). Stimuli that come to be feared are mostly ancient threats: snakes, spiders, heights, storms, thunder, lightning, darkness, blood, strangers, social scrutiny, separation, and leaving the home range. Most phobias are exaggerations of these natural fears.

Unlike the prepared fears and phobias just noted, we rarely fear cues that have been harmless in our past, for example, wood, leaves, flowers, stones, or shallow water. Aversion therapists found it hard to induce fear of alcohol in alcoholics, or of women's clothes in transvestites (Gelder and Marks 1970). Nor do we easily develop fear of evolutionarily recent dangers (Cook et al. 1986). Few fear motor cars, guns, cigarettes, or alcohol, despite knowing that these now kill far more people than do snakes, spiders, or sharks. Not having been present long enough to materially alter our genetic endowment, such modem perils are feared too little. It is difficult for even the great intelligence of humans to override genetic predispositions. Head and heart unite more easily when new threats relate to earlier ones. When they do, then fears of those threats may develop easily, but often in unmodulated fashion. Excessive fears of dentists and of AIDS grow out of ancient fears of injury and of infection,

Two tales show how food aversion conditions more easily when a novel food is paired with nausea than with pain. The first is of biased learning. Seligman (1970) developed nausea and vomiting some hours after a meal that included his first tasting of bernaise   sauce. Despite knowing that his affliction was probably viral, he acquired a lasting aversion to bernaise   sauce. His learning overrode his logic. The second tale is of failure to condition. Marks developed intense epigastric pain but no nausea while eating catfish for the first time. After 14 hours of agony, intestinal obstruction from an intussuscepted Meckel's diverticulum was found and corrected. No aversion to catfish followed. Such conditioning of food aversion to nausea rather than pain makes evolutionary sense; gastrointestinal toxins give rise to nausea and vomiting more than to pain.

Parents have difficulty training their offspring to fear evolutionarily recent dangers. It is hard for parents to "shift (children's) attitudes toward fear of matches, knives, bottles, dangerous sports, and the like, or toward tolerance and affection for uncles, aunts, physicians, cod liver oil, green vegetables, keeping on mittens and the like. Progress is slow" (Thorndike 1935). Thorndike here describes prepotency and preparedness for both fear and attraction. Our nervous system is neither a tabula rasa nor a clockwork machine. In addition to built-in biases, it has flexibility; its preexisting pathways can be strengthened or weakened according to certain rules that make it able to fine-tune its responses to various environments.

Benefits and Costs

There is an interesting tradeoff between biases and flexibility. Biases allow swift response to old threats with a minimum of experience, but at the cost of false alarms to cues that no longer indicate danger. The lack of other biases also has costs: We adapt slowly to some evolutionarily recent dangers. Though we fear much that now carries little risk, we accept many new perils with equanimity. We have too much fear of spiders, but too little fear of driving fast, saturated fat, and very loud music.

Our brain's flexibility does help us to (slowly) learn anxiety to totally new dangers, but this carries the cost of frequent misconnections   of anxiety to cues that do not signal danger. We make inappropriate connections, thrust meaning on random sequences, and develop superstitious fears. We make false correlations between events (Mineka and Tomarken 1989) and misattribute them, particularly when anxious. People who are poor judges of probability report more experiences of illusory causality (Blackmore 1990a,b).

Cognitive Biases

Our cognitive mechanisms seem to have built-in biases shaped by natural selection. These biases usually give the right answer in daily life, but they can go wrong in circumstances that were rare in our evolutionary past. We attend to and fear rare events more than common ones: a jumbo jet crash more than daily road deaths, a rare new syndrome more than heart disease (Tversky and Kahneman 1974). We undervalue base rates in calculating risk (Kahneman et al. 1982). We attend unduly to superficial similarities to the problem at hand (Nisbett and Ross 1980). We remember recent events more than those long past. We use accessible information that is unreliable rather than search for more valid data further afield. Abstract learning is more domain-specific than previously believed (Fodor 1983; Cosmides and Tooby 1987). This specificity is beneficial, because the possibilities for action are infinite. As Cosmides and Tooby (1987, p. 296) put it: "When a tiger bounds toward you, what should your response be? Should you file your toenails? Do a cartwheel? Sing a song? Is this the moment to run an uncountable number of randomly generated response possibilities through the decision rule? And again, how could you compute which possibility would result in more grandchildren? The alternative: Darwinian algorithms specialized for predator avoidance, that err on the side of false positives in predator detection, and, upon detecting a potential predator, constrain your responses to flight, fight or hiding." Emotions are good examples of domain-specific mechanisms. Anxiety evolved to deal efficiently with the domain of danger and its subtypes differentiated to avert specific threats within that domain.

Implications for Research and Treatment

Current anxiety research often seeks syndrome-specific neurophysiological defects. Although such defects undoubtedly exist for some patients with some syndromes, exclusive reliance on this approach leads to three difficulties. First, if anxiety is a normal defense, then some marked anxiety is likely to be, like being very tall, at the tail end of a Gaussian distribution. Different anxiety thresholds may often reflect, not specific defects, but individual polygenic variation similar to that which accounts for variation in susceptibility to cough, vomiting, or fever.

Second is the difficulty in neatly dividing anxiety disorders into mutually exclusive subtypes when each may in fact correspond to a particular danger but none is completely differentiated from any other. If this is correct, then attempts to delineate mutually exclusive anxiety disorders are likely to fail.

Third is the problem in deciding which physiological aspects of anxiety reflect abnormalities and which merely reflect normal operation of the anxiety system. The sites, pathways, and neurotransmitters that regulate anxiety, like those that regulate normal vomiting, are its cause only in the superficial sense of being part of a long mediating chain. Anxiolytic drugs may correct no primary defect but rather block defensive responses well downstream from the initiating problem. Likewise, "[B] rain imaging data do not address the cause of OCD in any way whatsoever. , . . [Mental activity as well as motor behavior, regardless of 'cause,' is mediated by the biochemical processes of the brain. Brain imaging data merely provide clues to some of the sites of abnormal cerebral *activity of complex mentation and behavioral patterns of [OCD]" (Baxter 1990).

"Pharmacological dissection" seeks to delineate specific syndromes on the basis of response to particular drugs. But a single drug, even one that affects only a specific brain system, can affect many etiologically diverse conditions. Just as the analgesic effects of aspirin are not a sound basis for classifying arthritis, so antidepressants do not help us classify the many, conditions in which they reduce dysphoria-anxiety, depression, schizophrenia, Alzheimer's disease, multiple sclerosis, and carcinoma. Current drugs for anxiety may be more like aspirin for pain than like insulin for juvenile-onset diabetes.

Exposure therapy is similarly nonspecific in its effects. Prolonged and repeated nontraumatic exposure to anxiety cues activates the evolved habituation mechanism that down-regulates fear. Without habituation to repeated stimulation, continual overresponding would prevent normal living. The lasting improvement from exposure therapy tells us little about how a phobia began but perhaps something about how avoidance maintains the established disorder.

The Heuristic Value of an Evolutionary Perspective

An evolutionary view can help explain otherwise puzzling features of anxiety by suggesting new and testable hypotheses about its function, and a search for relevant evidence. To take an example, stranger fear arises worldwide in infants at about six months of age. In trying to explain this, Marks when writing *Fears, Phobias,* and *Rituals* (1987) reasoned that a fear that is so transcultural is likely to be adaptive. At age six months, babies start to crawl away from mother and encounter strangers more often. Were strangers especially dangerous to infants in our recent evolutionary past? A search for relevant evidence found much that was emerging. Infanticide by strangers turned out to be so common that it is a strong selective force in primates as well as other species (Hrdy 1977). Abundant documentation also emerged that even today human infants are far more likely to be killed or abused by strangers than by familiars (Daly and Wilson 1989).

Without an evolutionary perspective the above hypothesis would not have been thought of and the evidence not have been sought. It was not a post hoc prediction; Marks did not know that such evidence was emerging at the time he began to look for it. Had infanticide turned out to be rare, the hypothesis would have been falsified.

Another new testable hypothesis arising out of an evolutionary view concerns agoraphobia. Mild "normal" agoraphobia seems homologous to fear of leaving the home range in territorial animals, a situation fraught with danger in the wild. Being away from home should thus be a prepotent cue for fear in normal young adults. An aversive event such as the hearing of repeated screams should evoke more anxiety (indicating prepotency) and condition more avoidance (showing preparedness) when it occurs in a public place far from, rather than near, home, even when familiarity has been controlled. Marks suggested this test to van den Hout; the results bore out the prediction (van den Hout, unpublished).

An evolutionary perspective might also explain why general anxiety is' not always aversive and can even be pleasurable. Millions flock to be thrilled by horror movies, the big wheel, tightrope walkers, and the like. Perhaps this is a form of play behavior, like so many other enjoyable games that help us deal better with real problems when the time comes. Young mammals spend much time in play that teaches them the game of life (Smith 1982). Hypotheses to test this view should be formulable.

The four defensive strategies noted earlier-escape, aggression, freezing, and submission-are deployed to varying degrees in different subtypes of anxiety, in accordance with their utility. Examples include the greater prominence of nausea rather than anxiety in food phobias, and of syncope rather than flight in blood/injury phobias. Predictions yet to be tested include these hypotheses: (a) Submission is more marked in social than animal phobias, (b) freezing is more pronounced in fear of heights than of animals, and (c) flight is more pronounced in fear of animals than in fear of heights. Close matching of the features of anxiety subtypes to the threats they defend against demands the testing of many such predictions. This major research program is likely to reveal unsuspected facets of anxiety and its disorders.

CONCLUSION

The capacity for anxiety, like other normal defenses, has been shaped by natural selection. Anxiety disorders, like disorders of other defensive systems, are mainly disorders of regulation that entail excessive or deficient responses. As we steadily unravel the neurophysiology of the mediating mechanisms we need to remember that even if we knew every connection of every neuron, every action of every transmitter, our understanding would remain inadequate until we also knew the function for which those mechanisms were shaped. If we find drugs that offer reduction of anxiety without major side effects or dependency, then we will urgently need to know more about when anxiety is useful and when it is not. In the meantime, more knowledge about the adaptive significance of anxiety and its subtypes, and the normal mechanisms that regulate them, will help us make even more rapid progress in understanding and treating anxiety disorders.

Helena Cronin made many valuable criticisms of the manuscript, as did members of the Evolution and Psychiatry Project at the Department of Psychiatry at the University of Michigan,

REFERENCES

Ainsworth, M.D., Blehar, M.C., Waters, E., and Wall, S. *Patterns of Attachment: A Psychological Study of the Strange Situation,* Hillsdale, NJ: Erlbaum, 1978.

Alcock, J. *Animal Behavior: An Evolutionary Approach,* Sunderland, MA: Sinauer, 1989.

Alexander, R.D. The search for a general theory of behavior. *Behavioral Science 20: 77-100,* 1975.

Barkow, J., Cosmides, L., and Tooby, J. (Eds.) *The Adapted Mind,* New York: Oxford University Press, 1992.

Baxter, L. Neuroimaging in obsessive compulsive disorder: seeking the mediating neuroanatomy. *Obsessive Compulsive Disorder.* 167-188, 1990.

Berthenthal, B.I., Campos, J.J., and Caplovitz, KS. Self-produced locomotion: an organizer of emotional, cognitive, and social development in infancy. In *Continuities and Discontinuities in Development,* R.M. Emde and Harmon, R. (Eds.). New York: Plenum, 1983.

Blackmore, S. Living in a nonrandom world. *The Guardian.* London, 1990a.

Blackmore, S. The lure of the paranormal. New *Scientist. 62-69,* 1990b.

Bowlby, J. *Separation: Anxiety and Anger,* New York: Basic Books, Inc, 1973.

Cannon, W.B. *Bodily Changes in Pain. Hunger, Fear, and Rage: Researches into the Function of Emotional Excitement,* New York: Harper and Row, 1929.

Cook, E.W., Hodes, R.L., and Lang, P.J. Preparedness and phobia: effects of stimulus content on human visceral conditioning. *Journal of Abnormal Psychology 95(3): 195-207,* 1986.

Cosmides, L., and Tooby, J. From evolution to behavior: evolutionary psychology as the missing link. In *The Latest on the Best: Essays on Evolution and Optimality,* J. Dupre (Ed.). Cambridge, MA: MIT Press, 1987.

Daly, M. and Wilson, M. *Homicide,* New York: Aldine, 1989.

Darwin, C. *The Expression of the Emotions in Man and Animals,* Chicago: University of Chicago Press, 1965 [1872].

DuPont, H.L., and Hornick, R.B. Adverse effect of Lomotil therapy in shigellosis. *Journal of the American Medical Association 226:* 1525-1528, 1973.

Edmunds, M. *Defence in Animals,* Harlow, Essex, England: Longman, 1974.

Fodor, J. *Modularity of Mind,* Cambridge, MA: MIT Press, 1983.

Gelder, M.G., and Marks, I.M. Transsexualism and faradic stimulation. In *Transsexualism and Sex Reassignment,* R. Green (Ed.). Baltimore, MD: Johns Hopkins University Press, 1970.

Hart, B.L. Behavioral adaptations to pathogens and parasites: five strategies. *Neuroscience and Biobehavioral Reviews* 14: 273-294, 1990.

Howard, J.C. Disease and evolution. *Nature* 352: 565-567, 1991.

Hrdy, S.B. Infanticide as a primate reproductive strategy. *American Scientist* 65: 40-49, 1977.

James, W. *The Principles of Psychology,* New York: Holt, 1893.

Janzen, D.H. Evolutionary physiology of personal defense. In *Physiological Ecology: An Evolutionary Approach to Resource* Use, C.R. Townsend and P. Calow (Eds.). Oxford: Blackwell, 1981, pp. 145-164.

Kahneman, D., Slovic, P. and Tversky, A. *Judgment Under Uncertainty: Heuristics and Biases,* Cambridge: Cambridge University Press, 1982.

Kendler, K.S., Neale, MC., et al. The genetic epidemiology of phobias in women: the interrelationship of agoraphobia, social phobia, situational phobia, and simple phobia. *Archives of General Psychiatry 49:* 273-281, 1992.

Klein, D.F. *Anxiety Reconceptualized,* New York: Raven Press, 1981.

Konner, M. *Why the Reckless Survive,* London: Penguin, 1990.

Krebs, J., and Davies, N. *Behavioral Ecology: An Evolutionary Approach,* Oxford: Blackwell, 1991.

Krebs, J.R. and Dawkins, R.D. Animal signals: mind-reading and manipulation. In *Behavioral Ecology: An Evolutionary Approach,* J.R. Krebs and N.B. Davies (Eds.). Sunderland, MA: Sinauer, 1984, pp. 380-402.

Lelliott, P., Marks, I., McNamee, G., and Tobena, A. Onset of panic disorder with agoraphobia: toward an integrated model. *Archives of General Psychiatry* 46(11): 1000-1004, 1989.

Marks, I.M. *Fears and Phobias,* New York Academic Press, 1969.

Marks, I.M. *Fears, Phobias, and Rituals,* New York Oxford University Press, 1987.

Marks, I.M. Blood-injury phobia: a review. *American Journal of Psychiatry* 145(10): 1207-1213, 1988.

Mayr, E. Teleological and teleonomic, a new analysis. *Boston Stud. Philo. Sci.* 14: 91-117, 1974.

Mineka, S., Davidson, M., Cook, M., and Keir, R. Observational conditioning of snake fear in rhesus monkeys. *Journal of Abnormal Psychology* 93: 355-372, 1984.

Mineka, S., Keir, R., and Price, V. Fear of snakes in wild and laboratory-reared rhesus monkeys (*Macaca mulatta*). *Anim. Lrn. Behav. 8(4): 653-663,* 1980.

Mineka, S., and Tomarken, A. The role of cognitive biases in the origins and maintenance of fear and anxiety disorders. In *Aversion, Avoidance, and Anxiety: Perspectives on Aversely Motivated Behavior,* L. Nilsson and T. Archer (Eds.), Hillsdale, NJ: Erlbaum, 1989.

Nesse, R.M. An evolutionary perspective on panic disorder and agoraphobia. *Ethology and Sociobiology 8: 73S43S,* 1987.

Nesse, R.M. Evolutionary explanations of emotions. *Human Nature* l(3): 261-289, 1990a.

Nesse, R.M. The evolutionary functions of repression and the ego defenses. *Journal of the American Academy of Psychoanalysis* 1 S(2): 260-285, 1990b.

Nisbett, R., and Ross, L. *Human Inference: Strategies and Shortcomings of Social Judgment,* Englewood Cliffs, NJ: Prentice-Hall, Inc., 1980.

Ohman, A., and Dimberg, U. An evolutionary perspective on human social behavior. In *Sociopsychology,* W.M. Waid (Ed.). New York: Springer, 1984.

Paley, W. *Natural* Theology, Westmead, England: Gregg International Publications, 1970 [18021.

Plutchik, R. and Kellerman, H. *Theories Of Emotion,* Orlando: Academic Press, Inc., 1980.

Ruse, M. *Philosophy of Biology Today,* . Albany, NY: State University of New York, 1988.

Scarr, S., and Salapatek, P. Patterns of fear development during infancy. *Merrill-Palmer Quarterly* 16: 53-90, 1970.

Seligman, M. On the generality of the laws of learning. *Psychological Review* 77: 406-418, 1970.

Smith, P.K. Does play matter? The functional and evolutionary aspects of animal and human play. *Behavioral & Bruin Sciences 5:* 139-184, 1982.

Stevens, K.M. Pain: evolutionary background and primary stimulus. *Medical Hypotheses 7:* 51-54, 1981.

Thorndike, E.L. *The Psychology of Wants, Interests, and Attitudes,* London: Appleton-Century, 1935.

Toft, CA., Aeschlimann, A., and Bolis, L. (Eds.) *Parasite-Host Associations: Coexistence or Conflict?* New York: Oxford University Press, 1991.

Tversky, A., and Kahneman, D. Heuristics and biases. *Science* 185: 1124-l 131, 1974.

vanden Hout, M. Agoraphobia: an extraterritorial fear. Unpublished manuscript.

Wilks C.G.W., and Marks, I.M. Reducing hypersensitive gagging. *British Dental Journal 155:* 263-265, 1983.

Psychological Review
2001, Vol. 108, No. 1, 4–32

A Modern Learning Theory Perspective on the Etiology of Panic Disorder

Mark E. Bouton
University of Vermont

Susan Mineka
Northwestern University

David H. Barlow
Boston University

Several theories of the development of panic disorder (PD) with or without agoraphobia have emerged in the last 2 decades. Early theories that proposed a role for classical conditioning were criticized on several grounds. However, each criticism can be met and rejected when one considers current perspectives on conditioning and associative learning. The authors propose that PD develops because exposure to panic attacks causes the conditioning of anxiety (and sometimes panic) to exteroceptive and interoceptive cues. This process is reflected in a variety of cognitive and behavioral phenomena but fundamentally involves emotional learning that is best accounted for by conditioning principles. Anxiety, an anticipatory emotional state that functions to prepare the individual for the next panic, is different from panic, an emotional state designed to deal with a traumatic event that is already in progress. However, the presence of conditioned anxiety potentiates the next panic, which begins the individual's spiral into PD. Several biological and psychological factors create vulnerabilities by influencing the individual's susceptibility to conditioning. The relationship between the present view and other views, particularly those that emphasize the role of catastrophic misinterpretation of somatic sensations, is discussed.

Early learning theorists such as Pavlov (1927), Watson (J. B. Watson & Rayner, 1920), and later Mowrer (1947) and Solomon (e.g., Solomon, Kamin, & Wynne, 1953) were highly interested in the relevance of their work on conditioning and learning to understanding the genesis of what was then called neurotic behavior in humans. Other investigators, using a variety of experimental paradigms that induced so-called experimental neurosis in animals (e.g., Pavlov, Gantt, Liddell, and Masserman, to name a few; see Mineka & Kihlstrom, 1978), also assumed that their work would be directly relevant to human neurotic behavior. Unfortunately, enthusiasm for this work on the part of psychopathology research-

Mark E. Bouton, Department of Psychology, University of Vermont; Susan Mineka, Department of Psychology, Northwestern University; David H. Barlow, Department of Psychology and Center for Anxiety and Related Disorders, Boston University.

Preparation of this article began while the authors were Fellows at the Center for Advanced Study in the Behavioral Sciences (CASBS) during 1997–1998 (supported by John D. and Catherine T. MacArthur Foundation Grant 95-32005-0). David H. Barlow was also supported by the CASBS Foundations Fund for Research in Psychiatry as a Fritz Redlich Fellow. The final phases of article preparation were supported by National Science Foundation Grant IBN 9727992. We thank the Center and its staff for providing an ideal environment that made unplanned collaborations attractive and possible. We also thank David M. Clark, Anke Ehlers, Michael Fanselow, Chris Hayward, Peter Lovibond, Colin MacLeod, Richard McNally, C. Barr Taylor, Richard Zinbarg, and two anonymous reviewers for their comments on drafts of the article at various stages.

Correspondence concerning this article should be addressed to Mark E. Bouton, Department of Psychology, University of Vermont, Burlington, Vermont 05405. Electronic mail may be sent to mbouton@zoo.uvm.edu.

ers began to wane in the 1970s as criticisms of the applicability of this earlier work to human neuroses mounted (see Rachman, 1977, 1990, for reviews).

At the same time, a virtual revolution in the field of learning was occurring, focusing on the development of new paradigms and new theoretical developments about the nature of the associative learning process. However, most later learning theorists were not as interested as the founding fathers in the relevance of their findings for understanding psychopathology, and the two fields went their separate ways with little cross-fertilization of ideas. Over the past 15 years, a goal of some of our work has been to reinvigorate this cross-fertilization by demonstrating the relevance of newer perspectives on learning theory to understanding anxiety and the anxiety disorders (e.g., Barlow, 1988; Barlow, Chorpita, & Turovsky, 1996; Bouton, 1988, 1991b, 2000; Bouton & Nelson, 1998b; Bouton & Swartzentruber, 1991; Chorpita & Barlow, 1998; Mineka, 1985a, 1985b; Mineka & Zinbarg, 1991, 1995, 1996, 1998). The major goal of the present article is to spell out the relevance of some contemporary work on classical conditioning, and learning theory more broadly, to understanding the etiology and maintenance of anxiety disorders with an emphasis on one of the more common anxiety disorders: panic disorder (PD).

The study of anxiety disorders and their treatment expanded steadily in the 1970s and 1980s; the National Institute of Mental Health dubbed the 1980s the "decade of anxiety" (e.g., Rachman & Maser, 1988; Tuma & Maser, 1985). The efficacy of treatments for most of these disorders represents one of the great success stories of applied psychological science (e.g., Barlow & Lehmann, 1996). However, although our understanding of basic behavioral and cognitive processes underlying panic and anxiety likewise advanced significantly, the underlying development of theories

4

focused on the etiology of panic disorder has not advanced appreciably since the 1980s. In our view, psychological theories of PD remain in an early developmental stage, as is the case with more biological theories, at least in part because they have not incorporated the latest developments in the basic behavioral, cognitive, and neural sciences or the integration of any of these fields. As noted, this is one purpose of this article. After briefly describing the disorder, as well as current theoretical perspectives on it, we proceed to an articulation of a new contemporary learning theory perspective on PD that does incorporate developments from these other fields.

PD is a clinical syndrome that provides a particularly appropriate context in which to examine the relevance of basic principles of conditioning and learning for the development and maintenance of psychopathology. In this anxiety disorder, the fundamental emotional constructs of anxiety, panic, and consequent phobic avoidance come together in an intricate relationship that can devastate the lives of those who develop it in severe form. Some patients are confined to their homes as virtual prisoners for years on end.

To meet criteria for PD, a person must experience recurrent unexpected panic attacks that occur without any obvious cues or triggers, such as encounters with a frightening object or experiencing a traumatic event. In other words, the panic attack seems to come out of the blue. A panic attack is an abrupt experience of intense fear or discomfort accompanied by a number of physical and mental symptoms, most usually heart palpitations, chest pain, sensations of shortness of breath, dizzy feelings, and thoughts of going crazy, losing control, or dying. Significantly, the attack must develop abruptly and reach a peak within 10 min (American Psychiatric Association, 1994).

The experience of unexpected panic attacks is not enough to meet criteria for PD, however. In addition, the individual must develop substantial anxiety or concern over the possibility of having another attack or about the implications of the attack or its consequences (such as the attack leading to a heart attack, to "going crazy," or to "losing control"). This is an important criterion, because we now know that numerous individuals experience "nonclinical panic attacks," in which a susceptible individual under stress may experience a sudden jolt of unexpected panic but fail to develop anxiety about a possible subsequent attack and its consequences, attributing it instead to benign events of the moment.

Many people with PD develop the complication of agoraphobia, which literally refers to fear of the marketplace. Agoraphobia, the most severe of all phobias, describes anxiety about being in places or situations from which escape might be difficult or embarrassing or in which help may not be available in the event of an unexpected panic attack (or panic-like symptoms). Typically, agoraphobic fears occur in clusters of situations that include being outside of the home alone, being in a crowded church or shopping mall, or being on public transportation (buses, trains, or airplanes). Agoraphobic avoidance behavior is simply one of the learned consequences of having severe unexpected panic attacks. If you have an unexpected panic attack and are afraid you may have another one, it is not surprising that you want to be in a safe place or at least with a safe person who either can help or knows what you are experiencing in the event another attack occurs.

Not everyone develops agoraphobia, and in those who do, agoraphobic avoidance may develop along a continuum from mild to severe. Thus, PD may occur with or without agoraphobic avoidance. For those individuals who do not develop agoraphobic avoidance, it is characteristic to find other associated behavioral coping tendencies such as resorting to the use (and often the abuse) of drugs and/or alcohol to self-medicate anxiety and panic. Avoidance of behaviors or activities that might provoke somatic symptoms similar to those that occur during panic is also common. For example, patients may avoid exercising (which may produce breathlessness or trembling and perspiration), sexual relations (which may produce other similar physical symptoms), or frightening movies (which may produce emotional symptoms that are reminiscent of panic attacks). PD is fairly common; approximately 3.5% to 5.3% of the population meet the criteria for PD at some point during their lives (Kessler et al., 1994). Onset usually occurs in early adult life from the midteenage years to about 40 years, although it can occur in children as well (Barlow, in press).

Current Theories of PD

Currently, there are at least three prominent psychological theories about the origins of PD. Two of them (cognitive theory and anxiety sensitivity theory) emphasize cognitive aspects of the disorder. An earlier conditioning theory was heavily criticized and has stimulated less research in recent years. We now briefly review these approaches and illustrate the criticisms that have been raised for each (see Thorn, Chosak, Baker, & Barlow, 1999, for a more detailed review).

Cognitive Theories

Cognitive theories, which are most closely associated with D. M. Clark (1986, 1988, 1996) and Beck (e.g., Beck & Emery, 1985), see an individual's "catastrophic misinterpretations" of somatic and other sensations as crucial to the development and maintenance of PD (see also Salkovskis, 1988). Specifically, an individual will experience panic when his or her focus on internal bodily sensations (whether produced by anxiety or not) leads to catastrophic thoughts about their imminent meaning (e.g., "I am going to have a heart attack"). Such catastrophic thoughts, which are anxiety-producing themselves, lead to further bodily sensations, which provide more fuel for more catastrophic thoughts, and thus a vicious cycle culminating in a panic attack. The internal focus on somatic and other sensations leads to chronic vigilance and increased sensitivity to otherwise normal physical sensations. Evidence in support of this theory includes the effects of direct manipulations of catastrophic cognitions in the laboratory. If such cognitions are hypothetically stimulated (as, e.g., by reading pairs of words consisting of various combinations of bodily sensations and catastrophes, such as palpitations-die or breathless-suffocate), the probability of panic increases (D. M. Clark et al., 1988). If such cognitions are reduced, the probability of panic in response to panic-provocation agents decreases (Clark, 1996). Further indirect evidence stems from the success of cognitive therapy in alleviating PD (e.g., D. M. Clark et al., 1994).

Problems for cognitive theory include the fact that panic attacks can occur in panic patients in the absence of detectable catastrophic cognitions. For example, patients may experience nocturnal panic attacks (usually during the transition from Stage 2 to Stage 3 sleep rather than during rapid eye movement sleep, when most dreaming occurs). Alternatively, they may sometimes have diurnal attacks without antecedent cognitions when the cognitions should have been readily detectable (e.g., Rachman, Lopatka, & Levitt, 1988; Zucker et al., 1989), even in studies using prospective self-monitoring of panic attacks (e.g., Kenardy, Fried, Kraemer, & Taylor, 1992; Kenardy & Taylor, 1999). The phenomenon of "nonfearful" panic, in which patients develop the disorder without having cognitions of danger or threat, also seems problematic for this theory (Barlow, Brown, & Craske, 1994; Kushner & Beitman, 1990). Proponents of the cognitive model might respond by suggesting that catastrophic misinterpretations in these cases may be very quick and below the threshold of awareness, even occurring during the transition between Stage 2 and Stage 3 sleep. However, without an independent measure of catastrophic misinterpretations (other than the panic attacks themselves), this sort of response begins to make the theory appear untestable (McNally, 1994, 1999).

It has also been claimed that cognitive models are somewhat vague in specifying or operationalizing terms such as "catastrophic misinterpretations" (Seligman, 1988; Teasdale, 1988). These terms, noted D. M. Clark (1996), "are expressed in everyday language rather than in the more precise technical terms that characterize many models in cognitive psychology (see Teasdale, 1988). . . . the advantage of such a model is the ease with which it suggests specific clinical procedures. The disadvantage is that it can be more difficult to test because it is not always clear how to operationalize key terms in a way that allows them to be precisely measured and manipulated" (p. 319). We suggest that the vagueness is not in the content of the cognitions, but rather how they are acquired, who acquires them, how they can be measured independently of panic itself, and under what conditions they become "catastrophic."

Two other problems with this approach are worth noting. First, as we discuss later, although catastrophic cognitions often may occur in panic patients, it is not necessarily clear that they play a causal role in creating panic attacks. Second, the cognitive model sees little need to distinguish between the emotional states of panic and anxiety, despite growing evidence to the contrary, described below.

Anxiety Sensitivity Theory

Anxiety sensitivity (AS) theory posits the existence of a traitlike belief in some individuals, especially including patients with panic disorder. The essence of this belief is that anxiety and its associated symptoms, particularly somatic symptoms, may cause deleterious physical, psychological, or social consequences that extend beyond any immediate physical discomfort during an episode of anxiety or panic itself. Proponents of AS theory, such as Reiss (1991) and McNally (1994), differentiate this theory from other perspectives in several ways. First, they clearly see AS as an enduring traitlike tendency. Second, AS theorists argue that individuals with PD are often fully aware of the causes of their sensations (i.e., they do not misinterpret them) and yet are frightened by them because they still hold an inherent belief that the sensations are harmful to their body or mental state. (Cognitive

theorists might claim that it is the sensations and/or the immediate consequences of the sensations, e.g., fainting, heart attack, that are "misinterpreted.") Moreover, the two theories clearly emphasize different time perspectives regarding the consequences of the sensations, with cognitive theory emphasizing the idea of immediate impending disaster and AS theory emphasizing that harm or danger from the symptoms may accumulate over time.

The AS model has generated a widely used measure, the Anxiety Sensitivity Index (ASI; Reiss, Peterson, Gursky, & McNally, 1986) and much thoughtful research. Generally, AS has been found to be normally distributed in the population, suggesting that it is a dimensional construct, and it is seen as a vulnerability factor that increases the likelihood of developing an anxiety disorder, especially PD (Reiss, 1991). Yet questions remain about the cause of this trait as well as its precise role in the subsequent etiology of PD (as well as other anxiety disorders).

Three studies lend support to anxiety sensitivity as a vulnerability factor for panic attacks. In the first study, Schmidt, Lerew, and Jackson (1997) found that higher initial scores on the ASI (but not trait anxiety scores) in military recruits predicted more anxiety and depressive symptoms and a greater number of unexpected panic attacks after a very stressful course of basic military training. Although the investigators noted that the relationships were relatively weak in this sample of well-adjusted military recruits, accounting for a rather small percentage of the variance, this study helps to confirm AS as reflecting at least one possible vulnerability for later anxiety, panic attacks, and depressive symptoms, triggered by extreme stress. However, this study did not provide evidence of a unique relationship between AS and panic attacks (or PD), in that high AS scores also predicted later anxiety and depressive symptoms more generally. In a similar second study, Schmidt et al. (1999) replicated these findings and found that anxiety sensitivity was more specifically related to anxiety/panic symptoms compared with depressive symptoms, although the findings accounted for only 2% of the variance in predicting unexpected panic attacks. Finally, Hayward, Killen, Kraemer, and Taylor (2000), in a 4-year prospective study of high school adolescents, found that AS was a significant predictor of onset of panic attacks as defined by the *Diagnostic and Statistical Manual of Mental Disorders*, 3rd edition, revised (*DSM-III-R*; American Psychiatric Association, 1994) but not of major depression when changes in panic were measured while controlling for changes in depression. Although AS predicted changes in panic attacks but not major depression in this study, it was not the best predictor of panic attacks; instead, negative affectivity was the single biggest predictor of panic attacks (and major depression). (See also Ehlers, 1995.) Thus, questions remain both about the specificity of what AS predicts and about whether it is a better predictor of unexpected panic than negative affectivity (the Hayward et al. study suggests that it is not).

Conditioning Theories

Conditioning theory has a long and distinguished tradition in helping to understand the etiology of anxiety disorders (e.g., Eysenck, 1979; Marks, 1969; Wolpe & Rowan, 1988), and it was one of the first types of theory applied to the cause of PD (e.g., Eysenck, 1960; Eysenck & Rachman, 1965). Generally, conditioning theories suggest that when stimuli, events, or situations (conditioned stimuli [CSs]) are paired with a panic attack (and all of its associated physiological sensations), the learning that may occur can allow the CSs to trigger panic and anxiety when they are encountered again. This sort of theory has taken a number of different forms when applied to PD. Early conditioning theories focused on the role of conditioning in the onset of agoraphobia or situational panic attacks (i.e., conditioning to external or exteroceptive cues). However, perhaps the best known version of conditioning theory applied to PD originated in an important article by Goldstein and Chambless (1978) that described a process they termed "fear of fear." Citing Razran (1961), Goldstein and Chambless reintroduced the notion of *interoceptive conditioning*, in which low-level somatic sensations of anxiety or arousal effectively became CSs associated with higher levels of anxiety or arousal. Thus, they posited that early somatic components of the anxiety response can come to elicit significant bursts of anxiety or panic. (These were also expected to generalize to other stimuli.) Thus, the focus of conditioning theory changed from exteroceptive conditioning in explaining agoraphobia and situational panics to interoceptive conditioning in explaining the cause of more "spontaneous" or apparently uncued panic attacks.

Criticisms of conditioning theories are presented in more detail under Clarifying the Role of Classic Conditioning in PD. To summarize briefly, interoceptive conditioning has been criticized as being conceptually confusing because anxiety or panic seem to serve somewhat indiscriminately as CS, unconditioned stimulus (US), conditioned response (CR), and unconditioned response (UR; McNally, 1990, 1994; Reiss, 1987). According to Reiss (1987), for example, anxiety seems to become conditioned to itself, but what does that mean? In addition, conditioning theory seems to lead to an overprediction of panic, because a fear or panic response should theoretically occur every time the CS (e.g., a somatic sensation, such as a quickened heart rate) is encountered (e.g., D. M. Clark, 1988). A third criticism stemmed from the observation that the fear or panic response does not seem subject to extinction after numerous natural trials in which arousal and the somatic cues it generates are not followed by panic (Rachman, 1991; Seligman, 1988; Van den Hout, 1988). However, a major point of the present article is that all of these concerns fall away when one considers a more modern perspective on classical conditioning and its many effects on emotion and behavior.

Summary and Overview

PD is a common anxiety disorder in which unexpected panic attacks lead to excessive anxiety about future attacks. The approaches sketched previously also contain a number of unmentioned common elements, such as vague allusions to biological vulnerabilities as well as fundamental cognitive or psychological vulnerabilities predating the development of the panic attacks, or PD, but these elements are seldom elaborated. Moreover, each approach tends to highlight one aspect or another of the process, such as interoceptive fear conditioning, catastrophic misinterpretations of physical sensations, or beliefs about the dangers of anxiety, as though they are mutually exclusive.

The present article provides an integrative theory of the etiology of PD that uses contemporary learning theory as its base. On the basis of information that is available in the psychometric, ethological, and neurobiological literatures, we distinguish between two aversive motivational states: anxiety and panic. Further, on the basis of the conditioning literature, we expect that a major effect of early experience with panic is the conditioning of anxiety to cues that are associated with the episode. One result is that, in the presence of the interoceptive or exteroceptive cues associated with panic, anxiety now occurs. As is widely recognized, the classical conditioning of anxiety also makes it possible for new operant behaviors to be reinforced when they escape or reduce it (e.g., Mowrer, 1947).

Conditioning of anxiety can also have other major consequences that are emphasized here. As we show later, the presence of conditioned anxiety may serve to exacerbate or potentiate the next panic attack, beginning the vicious spiral into PD. A second factor that can exacerbate the next panic attack is that panic itself may come to be elicited by a more specific set of cues associated with panic. The conditioning of panic responses to some cues may occur in parallel with the conditioning of anxiety to other cues; conditioning is a multifaceted process in which a range of interacting stimuli can acquire the ability to control a constellation or system of different emotions, cognitions, and behaviors. These themes, coupled with a modern understanding of conditioning processes that will further modulate and influence the course of conditioning, constitute the core of our approach to the development of PD. Other biological and psychological processes that are thought to influence PD (including catastrophic thoughts, AS, and other processes that appear to make certain individuals vulnerable) may be seen as operating through their interaction with this core conditioning process.

Introduction to a Modern Learning Theory Perspective on PD

Panic and Anxiety

Any theory of PD must acknowledge the strong and growing network of evidence suggesting fundamental differences between the emotional phenomena of panic and anxiety. Panic attacks have been defined as a subjective sense of extreme fear or impending doom accompanied by a massive autonomic surge and strong flight-or-fight behavioral action tendencies (Barlow, Brown, & Craske, 1994; American Psychiatric Association, 1994). Anxiety has been defined as an apprehensive anticipation of future danger, often accompanied by somatic symptoms of tension or feelings of dysphoria. The focus of anticipated danger can be internal or external. Phenomenological as well as neurobiological evidence suggests that panic attacks are descriptively and functionally distinct events when compared with anxiety. Some of this evidence comes from detailed analyses of fear and anxiety in normal populations, in which the findings support these constructs as being partially overlapping and yet partially distinctive at a psychometric level. In early studies, fear emerged as a partially distinct primary (lower order) factor, but it also loaded on the higher order factor of negative affect (L. A. Clark & Watson, 1991; Tellegen, 1985; D. Watson & Clark, 1984). These lower and higher order factors not only seem separable but also relate in rather different ways to other anxiety disorders and depression. For example, more recent structural equation modeling and factor analyses of symptomatology exploring the dimensions of panic, anxiety, and depression in clinically anxious patients have also uncovered two different factors. One, which is characterized by a subjective sense of extreme fear or impending doom, strong autonomic arousal, and strong flight-or-fight behavioral action tendencies, seems best described as panic. The other is characterized by the kinds of apprehension and worry accompanied by tension that are best described as anxiety (T. A. Brown, Chorpita, & Barlow, 1998; Joiner et al., 1999; Mineka, Watson, & Clark, 1998; Zinbarg et al., 1994). Anxiety, a principal component of generalized anxiety disorder, is very closely related to depression. Spikes of strong autonomic arousal characteristic of panic, in contrast, are substantially restricted in patients experiencing more generalized anxiety (T. A. Brown et al., 1998; Borkovec, 1994; Hoehn-Saric, McLeod, & Zimmerli, 1989; Zinbarg et al., 1994). Also, these different emotional experiences may produce differential regional brain activity as measured by electroencephalography (Heller, Nitschke, Etienne, & Miller, 1997).

Ethological evidence concerning specific defensive reactions such as the flight-or-fight response points to their survival value and heritability as well as their distinctiveness (and partial separateness at the level of heritability; Kendler, Walters, et al., 1995) compared with more diffuse states analogous to generalized anxiety or depressed mood. Fanselow and Lester (1988), among others, noted the qualitative differences in animal defensive behavior that occur depending on the "imminence" or proximity of threat (see also D. C. Blanchard, 1997; R. J. Blanchard & D. C. Blanchard, 1987). In rodents, freezing may occur after a potential threat has been detected, whereas more active behaviors occur when a predator actually attacks. Ethologists have pointed to hierarchical arrangements between action tendencies of freezing and heightened vigilance, which may represent anxiety (see later discussion), and other more proximal action tendencies that may be associated with fear and panic (e.g., Gallup & Maser, 1977; Gray & McNaughton, 1996). That is, freezing (anxiety) may antedate and potentiate other behaviors that occur as a threatening predator approaches more closely.

There is also increasing evidence from neurobiology supporting the existence of at least two negative emotional states mediated by different brain circuits and potentially representing anxiety and panic (Charney, Grillon, & Bremner, 1998; Heller et al., 1997; Lang, Davis, & Öhman, 2000; White & Depue, 1999). A great deal of evidence suggests the role of the amygdala and related areas of the brain in fear and defensive behavior (e.g., Davis, 1992; Fanselow, 1994; Kapp, Whalen, Supple, & Pascoe, 1992; LeDoux, 1996; Rosen & Schulkin, 1998). Fanselow (1994) proposed two related but separable brain circuits that are implicated in different defensive emotional reactions. The first circuit, involving the central amygdala and the ventral periaqueductal gray, mediates freezing and opiate-mediated analgesia. (Other output from the amygdala mediates autonomic responses [see Kapp et al., 1992] and potentiated startle responses [see Davis, 1992]). These behaviors and autonomic responses correspond to anxiety in our approach. The second circuit identified by Fanselow, involving the dorsolateral periaqueductal gray and superior colliculus, mediates more active defensive behaviors, such as flight-or-fight and non-opiate-mediated analgesia. These behaviors are associated with what Fanselow called "circa-strike" defense, which has evolved to deal with actual predatory attack and corresponds to panic in our approach.

Other investigators, including Davis (e.g., Davis, Walker, & Yee, 1997; see also Rosen & Schulkin, 1998) and Gray and McNaughton (1996; McNaughton & Gray, in press) have also recently distinguished between two aversive motivational systems and circuits. Although there are differences in these various approaches, it is now common to distinguish between at least two negative emotional neural systems and the corresponding behavioral systems they control. Thus, many neuroscientists would now agree with psychopathologists that there are important distinctions to be made between emotional states that may correspond to anxiety and panic.

True Alarms, False Alarms, and Learned Alarms

Barlow (1988; Barlow et al., 1996) proposed a conditioning theory of clinical anxiety disorders that accepts the distinction between panic and anxiety. This theory, which has come to be known as "alarm theory" (Carter & Barlow, 1995; Forsyth & Eifert, 1996), begins with the observation that the experience of unexpected panic attacks seems to be relatively common in the population at large (e.g., Norton, Cox, & Malan, 1992; Norton, Dorward, & Cox, 1986; Telch, Brouillard, Telch, Agras, & Taylor, 1989; Wittchen & Essau, 1991). Evidence suggests that these attacks seldom progress to PD and, therefore, are referred to as "nonclinical" attacks. Individuals experiencing nonclinical panic attacks show little or no concern over the possibility of experiencing additional attacks. Rather, they seem to dismiss the attacks, for the most part, as associated with some trivial and potentially controllable event. Other evidence suggests that panic attacks may be a nonspecific response to stress, similar to hypertension or headaches, that runs in families (Barlow et al., 1996).

Individuals with PD are clearly discriminable from nonclinical panickers in that they develop anxiety focused on the next potential panic attack. These individuals anticipate the next attack apprehensively, perceive the attacks as uncontrollable and unpredictable, and are extremely vigilant for somatic symptoms that might signal the beginning of the next attack. In this formulation, the crucial step in the development of PD is the conditioning of anxiety focused on the next panic attack, occurring most often in those with a preexisting vulnerability to make this association (see later discussion).

The model assumes that a panic attack (the flight-or-fight response) is the fundamental emotion of unconditioned fear occurring at the wrong time. When the danger is real, these responses are "true alarms." Thus, alarms are "false" if they occur when there is nothing to fear (no danger). Because there is nothing to fear, a false alarm often occurs to the great surprise of the individual experiencing one. It has been widely recognized that it is adaptive to learn to associate emotional responses very quickly with both discrete and contextual cues. When these alarms, true or false, are associated with, or conditioned to, external or internal cues, they become "learned alarms."

When the clinical disorder is a specific phobia, it seems clear that fear or anxiety is conditioned to an otherwise harmless object or situation. In contrast, in PD the cues eliciting fear or anxiety are often more diffuse (being away from a safe place or a safe person) or difficult to pinpoint. Thus, following Goldstein and Chambless (1978), Barlow proposed that false alarms could be conditioned to internal physiological stimuli reflecting the process of interoceptive conditioning (Razran, 1961). The occurrence of false alarms and subsequent learned alarms need not be pathological if the alarms are infrequent and anxiety focused on the possible occurrence of future alarms does not develop. It is the development of anxiety that fundamentally produces vigilance for somatic sensations, increased tension and arousal, a resulting increase in somatic cues, and a spiraling of anxiety and panic. Anxiety focused on a possible future panic attack is now part of the defining *DSM-IV* criteria for PD (American Psychiatric Association, 1994).

As noted earlier, the role of conditioning in PD has produced much controversy and confusion, which was not explicitly addressed by alarm theory. Therefore, we now consider some recent developments in our knowledge of conditioning and emotional learning for a fuller explication of this aspect of development of PD and other clinical anxiety disorders.

Clarifying the Role of Classical Conditioning in PD

Although panic attacks do not inevitably lead to conditioning, we assume that a crucial element in the origin of PD is a conditioning episode (or episodes) involving early panic attacks (usually false alarms as opposed to true alarms reflecting confrontation with a traumatic event), often enabled or potentiated by biological factors and/or the presence of stress (e.g., Barlow, 1988; Barlow et al., 1996). As we review later, a large percentage of patients with PD do point to an initial panic attack at the beginning of the disorder (e.g., Craske, Miller, Rotunda, & Barlow, 1990; Öst & Hugdahl, 1983). Either the panic attack itself (e.g., Forsyth & Eifert, 1996, 1998) or the event that actually triggers it (if indeed there is an identifiable one) then becomes associated with initially neutral cues through the associative learning process known as classical conditioning. Those cues could include proximal or distal cues, such as specific social situations (e.g., eating in restaurants, going to church) or entering general shopping malls or sports arenas, and also interoceptive and exteroceptive stimuli that are more directly involved in panic, such as the bodily sensations arising from the increase in respiration that occurs with hyperventilation. Most likely, both types of cues are involved.

The consequences of this conditioning are spelled out in detail in the next sections. As a preliminary to this discussion, we note that classical conditioning has many characteristics and consequences that are not widely understood outside a relatively small community of specialists. Many psychologists now know that modern views of conditioning are "cognitive" in the sense that they use theoretical constructs like attention, surprise, information value, short-term memory, rehearsal, and so forth to explain even simple conditioning (e.g., Mackintosh, 1975; Pearce & Hall, 1980; Rescorla & Wagner, 1972; Wagner, 1976, 1981). We accept and embrace this view. However, we do not accept the idea that a modern view of conditioning implies that conditioning trials inevitably give rise to a kind of propositional, declarative knowledge that is the same as that created by verbal input (e.g., Lovibond, 1993). Conditioning theories themselves are agnostic on the issue. We suspect that, although conditioning and propositional systems may sometimes interact (e.g., Grings, Schell, & Carey, 1973), the extent to which they do will depend on the type of conditioning system, the specific conditioning procedure, and the brain systems they engage (Bechara et al., 1995; R. E. Clark & Squire, 1998; LeDoux, 1996).

LeDoux (1996) and Öhman, Flykt, and Lundqvist (2000) argued that aversive emotional learning can occur without any conscious representation of the learning. This means that implicit emotional memories can activate the fear system without the person necessarily having any conscious recollection or awareness of why they are aroused. A number of findings are consistent with this possibility, such as the fact that classically conditioned emotional responses are not always influenced by verbal instruction (e.g., Bridger & Mandel, 1964; Hamm & Vaitl, 1996) and that emotional conditioning does not appear to depend on conscious awareness (see LeDoux, 1996; Öhman et al., 2000; Öhman & Mineka, 2001). Data reported by Bechara et al. (1995) provide an especially compelling dissociation between emotional conditioning and verbal, declarative knowledge. When given a classical conditioning experience, a patient with a damaged amygdala did not acquire classical autonomic conditioning but was able to report what CSs predicted the US. Conversely, a patient with a damaged hippocampus acquired the autonomic responding but was unable to report what CSs predicted the US. Such findings encourage the view that conscious, declarative, or propositional knowledge about conditioning contingencies is not necessary or sufficient for emotional conditioning.

This is not to claim that cognitions are irrelevant in PD, however. We have already noted that PD may often involve catastrophic thoughts in which the patient believes that the somatic symptoms will lead to a heart attack, death, and so forth. Whether such cognitions have a truly causal role in creating panic attacks is not currently clear. However, the idea that they may sometimes play a causal role (albeit through a mechanism different from the one posited by cognitive theory) would not necessarily be inconsistent with a learning theory perspective on PD. Such thoughts may first arise during a panic attack either because they are an inherent component of a panic attack or because they are instrumental acts (i.e., operants) that have been reinforced in similar situations in the past. (We later review evidence that PD may be correlated with a childhood in which sick role behaviors were modeled and reinforced in the presence of panic symptoms by parents in the home; Ehlers, 1993). Once the thought occurs during a panic attack, it may become a verbal CS associated with the rest of the panic attack. Through a process of verbal conditioning, thought CSs could become capable of eliciting panic themselves: when the thoughts now occur, they might help cause panic, just as other CSs do. It is often productive to think of cognitions as responses or stimuli within the terms of learning theory (e.g., Baldwin & Baldwin, 1998). Thus, there may be nothing particularly unique about their role in PD.

As noted earlier, a variety of critiques of conditioning theories have been made in the past. We believe that many stem from the fact that modern issues and findings in conditioning and learning have not been communicated adequately to clinical scientists. One critique is that the conditioning approach lacks conceptual clarity when applied to PD (e.g., McNally, 1990, 1994, 1999; Reiss, 1987). For example, McNally argued that confusion exists about what constitutes the CS, US, CR, and UR, and that defining two arbitrary points on a continuum of arousal "blurs" the distinction between the CS and CR. He also argued that the distinction between the US and the UR is problematic. "Because certain bodily sensations are designated as CSs, by definition, they must have been established as such through association with a US.

What, then, is this US and what UR does it elicit?" (1994, p. 107). He concluded, "The interoceptive conditioning hypothesis- ... constitutes little more than a misleading metaphor for the mechanisms underlying panic" (1994, p. 108). In the next sections, we show that modern conditioning research has done much to blur the old distinctions between these different terms. Thus, we argue that this critique of conditioning theory is neither compelling nor valid.

A second criticism of conditioning theories is that they seem to "overpredict" panic (e.g., D. M. Clark, 1988). For example, while referring to early simplistic statements (e.g., Wolpe & Rowan, 1988), Clark argued that a conditioning theory should predict that every time a person experienced certain bodily sensations (CSs) that had been associated with panic, he or she should have a panic attack, and yet this is clearly not the case. We show that this argument loses force when one recognizes that the effects of CSs are routinely modulated by other stimuli in the background. A third criticism is that interoceptively conditioned responses should ex-tinguish when the internal CS (such as a pounding heart) is not followed by panic, as might be the case when the patient runs up a flight of stairs (e.g., van den Hout, 1988). As we discuss in detail later, however, modern research on extinction, and particularly on what may be the inherent context specificity of extinction (Bouton, 1991a, 1993), obviates this criticism. Emotional responses extin-guished in the context of athletic exertion would not be eliminated in other contexts.

In summary, learning theory sheds important light on the de-velopment of panic disorder, and earlier critiques of early condi-tioning theories of PD may be met by an analysis of the current research literature. We believe that the complex state of affairs surrounding the origins of PD is consistent with modern concep-tualizations of classical conditioning. Several points seem espe-cially salient as we consider the role of conditioning in the behav-ioral events surrounding the development of PD.

Conditioning Allows the CS to Trigger Constellations of Behavior and Emotion That Are Not Necessarily the Same as the UR

In textbook descriptions of Pavlov's original experiment, there is a focus on a single response, such as salivation. In fact, Pavlov's results were undoubtedly more interesting and complex than this. If one could stand back and look at what Pavlov's dogs were actually doing, one would find the bell eliciting not only drooling but other digestive reflexes (including gastric acid, pancreatic enzymes, and insulin secretion) as well as behavioral responses that are designed to help the animal to get ready for food (Powley, 1977; Woods & Strubbe, 1994). A similar complexity is true of defensive conditioning in animals. Thus, the CR has many com-ponents, including freezing and other natural defensive behaviors, changes in respiration, blood pressure, and heart rate, and the release of endogenous opiates that reduce pain (Bolles & Fanselow, 1980; Davis, 1992; Hollis, 1982). The general role of this constellation of behaviors is to prepare the organism to deal with an upcoming dangerous event (e.g., Hollis, 1982, 1997). So it may be with the conditioning involved with PD; conditioned anxiety is a complex set of responses, including ones correspond-ing to vigilance, that essentially help the person prepare for another panic attack.

Viewed this way, there is no reason to expect that the CR and the UR will necessarily be identical. One example of the difference between CR and UR is a common result seen in defensive condi-tioning in rats. Freezing is a common measure of conditioned anxiety (often referred to as conditioned "fear" in this literature, although here we maintain Barlow's distinction between anxiety and fear [panic]). Notably, freezing does not appear to be a component of the rat's unconditioned reaction to footshock. If the animal is shocked and then moved immediately to a different location, freezing is not observed; rather, freezing occurs only if the animal is returned to the place where the shock was encoun-tered (Blanchard & Blanchard, 1969; Fanselow, 1980). It is a CR that may involve heightened vigilance (e.g., "risk assessment," D. C. Blanchard, R. J. Blanchard, & Rodgers, 1991), but it un-doubtedly also functions to decrease attack or detection from predators (Hirsch & Bolles, 1980). The unconditioned reaction to shock is a very different burst of activity (Fanselow, 1994). Thus, even in basic aversive learning situations, there is often no identity relation between the UR and the CR.

Another classic example of different CRs and URs is some well-known work on drug conditioning that began in the 1970s (e.g., for reviews see Cunningham, 1998; Siegel, 1989). In this literature, there is a difference between the response one observes to the drug US and the response one observes to the CS that signals it. Specifically, the CR often appears to be "opposite" to the UR: it compensates for the upcoming drug effect, another example of a get-ready response. One widely studied example is conditioning with morphine injection as a US. Although the unconditioned effect of morphine itself is to reduce pain, the CR to cues associ-ated with it may be hyperalgesia, an increase in sensitivity to pain (e.g., Siegel, 1975). This and other related drug-conditioning phe-nomena (e.g., Siegel, 1989) have helped elucidate the complex relationship between the CR and the UR, a complete review of which is outside the scope of this article (for further discussion, see Eikelboom & Stewart, 1982; Hollis, 1982; Ramsay & Woods, 1997).

The CR Is Often Determined by the Nature of the CS

In the 1970s, conditioning researchers also discovered that dif-ferent CSs associated with the same US (and thus the same UR) can come to evoke very different CRs (e.g., Holland, 1977; Tim-berlake & Grant, 1975). For example, when presentation of a rat is used as a CS to signal food, the subject rat responds not merely with drooling but with social contact behaviors directed at the CS (Timberlake & Grant, 1975). Conditioning is now thought to engage whole *behavior systems*, or sets of behaviors that are functionally organized to deal with different USs (e.g., Domjan, 1994; Fanselow, 1994; Timberlake, 1994; Timberlake & Silva, 1995). Once a behavior system is engaged, different CSs provide "support" (Tolman, 1932) for particular behaviors in the same sense that a hallway makes it possible to walk and a swimming pool makes it possible to swim. A particularly interesting and potentially relevant example is the sexual conditioning system in Japanese quail (e.g., Domjan, 1994, 1997). In this research, a CS is presented to a male quail before a female US is presented and copulation ensues. The type of CR evoked by the CS depends on the CS's duration and qualitative nature. For example, when a 30-s presentation of a foam block with feathers signals the female, the male begins to approach the CS; in contrast, when the foam block CS is presented for 20 min, the male instead paces back and forth when it is presented (Akins, Domjan, & Gutierrez, 1994). However, a CS can also come to elicit copulation as the CR (i.e., same as the UR), but only if it is a taxidermically prepared model that contains plumage and other features of the female quail (e.g., Domjan, Huber-McDonald, & Holloway, 1992).

Such research suggests that different CSs can support quite different CRs and that only certain cues may actually support a CR that resembles the UR. As mentioned earlier, studies of defensive conditioning in rats with footshock USs have tended to uncover CRs that mostly consist of freezing (e.g., Fanselow, 1989; Fanselow & Lester, 1988; here the freezing CR is very different from the activity-burst UR. Nevertheless, because the form of the CR in other systems depends on both the qualitative nature of the CS as well as its timing (see also Silva, Timberlake, & Koehler, 1996; Timberlake, Wahl, & King, 1982), we should remain open to the possibility that different types of CRs will develop with different types of CSs predicting the US at different delays. In a classic study of defensive conditioning in rabbits, VanDercar and Schneiderman (1967) signaled a shock US delivered near the eye with tone CSs of various durations. In this method, the shock US elicits a closure of the rabbit's nictitating membrane (which protects the eye) and also an increase in heart rate. Short CSs (e.g., less than 1 s) that ended with the US elicited the nictitating membrane response (i.e., a CR that resembled the UR) and caused a modest decrease in heart rate. In contrast, longer CSs (e.g., 6.75 s) supported no nictitating membrane response at all but elicited a strong decrease in heart rate. Thus, in some examples of aversive conditioning, qualitatively different CRs can emerge with cues associated with the US at different time intervals. One implication for PD is that the nature of the CR elicited by a CS (i.e., anxiety or panic) may depend on the CS's temporal proximity to the US.

The form of the CR in human fear conditioning also depends on the qualitative nature of the CS. For example, if interoceptive cues are "prepared" or "fear relevant" in the same way that evolutionarily based cues for phobias are (cf. Öhman & Mineka, 2001), then there is some evidence in humans that the CR may resemble the UR more so than is the case with unprepared or fear-irrelevant CSs. Cook, Hodes, and Lang (1986) showed that the CR using prepared CSs (slides of snakes) was heart rate acceleration rather than deceleration, as is more typically seen in human autonomic conditioning with fear-irrelevant or unprepared CSs (i.e., the CR is isodirectional to the UR in response to a US of shock). Dimberg (1987) also showed that with fear-relevant angry faces paired with shock, the CR was an accelerated heart rate response and an increase in activity in the corrugator muscle, which controls the eyebrow when frowning; neither of these response occurred in individuals who received conditioning with fear-irrelevant or happy faces. Finally, Forsyth and Eifert (1998; see also Forsyth, Eifert, & Thompson, 1996) reported related results. One of their fear-relevant stimuli to which heart rate acceleration (rather than deceleration) was conditioned was a video clip of a heart beating arrhythmically, an exteroceptive representation of an interoceptive stimulus.

Given the variability in the form of the CR, it is easy to imagine that CSs associated with a panic attack will evoke responses that may often differ substantially from panic itself. However, it is also conceivable, given what we know about many conditioning systems, that certain CSs and/or certain CS–US intervals may condition a CR that resembles the UR, a conditioned panic attack. Anxiety and panic reactions are functionally different; a functional perspective on conditioning actually causes us to anticipate that different conditions could support conditioning of different responses. Panic is an immediate response to an insult to the organism; although it may involve cognitions about impending doom, it must have temporal and other properties that help the organism deal with a terrifying event that is already in progress. Anxiety, in contrast, is functionally organized to help the organism prepare for a possible upcoming insult. It is more "forward looking" in this sense (Barlow, 1988, 1991). Given their different functional roles, it is not surprising that panic and anxiety are different. Our perspective thus accepts a qualitative distinction between the two, whereas other approaches to PD either do not make one or certainly do not focus on its importance (cf. Beck & Emery, 1985; D. M. Clark, 1996; McNally, 1994).

Interoceptive Conditioning

An important component of the conditioning approach to PD is the idea that interoceptive conditioning is involved (Barlow, 1988; Goldstein & Chambless, 1978). The occurrence of a panic attack is itself a conditioning trial that allows the patient to associate internal bodily sensations that accompany the early onset of the attack with the rest of the attack; the result is that modest changes in heart rate and respiration become signals and can later elicit a full-blown attack. One relevant example is a classic Soviet dog experiment described by Razran (1961, p. 86). Distension of the intestine, an interoceptive CS, was paired with presentation of a mixture of 10% carbon dioxide administered directly to the trachea (the US). When these two events were paired, the intestinal distension (CS) quickly acquired the ability to elicit hypercapnic respiratory changes (CR) that were the same as the UR. The phenomenon might parallel what happens when and if internal sensations (such as intestinal contractions) are paired with hyperventilation, which often occurs during a panic attack; one might expect in the future that the intestinal contractions alone might become sufficient to trigger respiration changes and possibly panic. Interestingly, Razran (1961), in summarizing the Soviet literature, claimed that interoceptive conditioning is especially resistant to extinction, lending further plausibility to its likely role in the etiology of PD.

Little interoceptive conditioning research seems to have followed the methods used in the Soviet heyday described in Razran's (1961) classic monograph (see Dworkin, 1993). However, once again, the literature on classical conditioning with drug stimuli is relevant. Here, interoceptive events clearly do become associated. For example, Siegel (1988) showed that an injection of pentobarbital that signaled an injection of morphine caused a classical CR to pentobarbital: The rats were more tolerant to morphine when pentobarbital was present than when it was not. Evidently, they had learned to associate the morphine US with the pentobarbital CS, two interoceptive events. The reader might recognize this experiment as an example of "state-dependent learning," the well-known phenomenon in which learning is best when it is tested in the presence of the drug state (or mood state, see Eich, 1995) in which it originally occurred. To the extent that such states are interoceptive, state-dependent learning is an effect indicating that interoceptive events can be associated with their consequences.

The idea that internal cues can be associated with interoceptive aversive events is also consistent with some research in humans. Human participants were exposed to three pairings of mental images with a US of 5.5% carbon dioxide (CO_2)-enriched air (Stegen, De Bruyne, Rasschaert, Van de Woestijne, & Van den Bergh, 1999). The images were either fear relevant or fear irrelevant (being stuck in an elevator or sauna vs. reading a book or overlooking the sea). Participants exposed to the fear-relevant images (but not those exposed to the fear-irrelevant images) showed significant conditioning of both subjective symptoms of anxiety as well as altered respiratory behavior and cardiac/warmth symptoms similar to those produced by the US. That fear-relevant imagery can elicit such interoceptive and subjective CRs after only three conditioning trials has implications for our argument regarding the role of interoceptive conditioning in PD. The authors noted that "a little stress-induced hyperventilation in association with a phobia-relevant place or an image thereof may evoke the experience of similar symptoms and anxiety on next confrontations, even without apparent hyperventilation" (p. 150). Moreover, as noted earlier, the nature of the CR in animal conditioning can depend on the qualitative nature of the CS and the interstimulus interval (ISI). Thus, it is possible that a true panic CR might become conditioned with the right CS and the right ISI. Definitive tests of this idea must await future research.

A particularly interesting type of interoceptive conditioning is the case in which a low dose of a drug signals a higher dose of the same drug. Greeley, Lê, Poulos, and Cappell (1984) injected a small dose of ethanol in rats before administering a larger dose. Tolerance to the larger dose subsequently depended on the small dose preceding it, but only if the two injections had been paired. Pairings also enabled the small injection to initiate a stronger compensatory response. Thus, a small dose of ethanol acquired the ability to signal more of itself. Comparable results have been reported for morphine-morphine pairings (Cepeda-Benito & Short, 1997). Thus, animals can associate a strong interoceptive event with a weaker version of the same event. More recently, Kim, Siegel, and Patenall (1999) found evidence of a similar kind of learning occurring within single administrations of morphine. They found that rats given long exposures to morphine show a conditioned compensatory response to a short "probe" injection that deliberately mimicked the early-onset properties of the longer injection. Apparently, interoceptive cues corresponding to the onset of a long interoceptive stimulus can indeed become associated with the remainder of the stimulus. It is not difficult to imagine that early-onset properties of a panic attack can, therefore, come to signal the rest of the event as it continues to unfold in time.

Conditioning in which the onset of an event signals the rest of the event clearly blurs the traditional distinction between CS and US. Nonetheless, we believe this form of conditioning is probably very common. In an extended discussion of the relationship between learning and regulatory physiology, Dworkin (1993) reached a similar conclusion. Dworkin gave the type of conditioning in which early onset is associated with an event's later aspects a name, the *homoreflex*, and contrasted it with the better known arrangement in which CS and US are different, the *heteroreflex*. One example of a homoreflex is a baroreceptor that detects a small increase in blood pressure coming to predict a further increase in

blood pressure. Learning this sort of relationship presumably allows other parts of the system to respond and adapt to the blood pressure change more quickly. Because the "CS" and "US" are so similar, there are grounds for expecting this kind of learning to be robust: Similarity between signals and the things they signal can allow especially strong conditioning (e.g., Rescorla & Furrow, 1977; Rescorla & Gillan, 1980; Testa, 1975). Dworkin (1993) noted that if this is correct, then "homoreflexes should turn out to be even more common than heteroreflexes" (Dworkin, 1993, p. 79).

Interestingly, there is a sense in which the earliest conditioning experiments in Pavlov's own laboratory probably also involved the dog associating early and late aspects of a single event. Pavlov's students first noted that, after introducing sand into the dog's mouth, which caused salivation, the mere sight of sand itself soon came to cause anticipatory salivation (Domjan, 1998). The dog was associating the sight of sand with its later properties. This type of learning is undoubtedly common as organisms learn about events and objects in their world. Therefore, to understand this learning process better, Pavlov devised a method in which the signal and the signaled event were separated so that they could be manipulated independently. That is, the bell-food experiment we now know so well can be seen as a technique used to break down and analyze learning about dynamic individual events that naturally flow and change over time.

We suggest that this type of conditioning is fundamental to understanding PD. That is, the patient with PD has learned to associate weak and early panic symptoms with the remainder of the full-blown panic episode. Mere exposure to a US may inevitably allow cues that correspond to its early onset to become associated with its later aspects, allowing conditioning of anxiety and possibly panic itself. A panic attack can be seen as an opportunity to associate early "warning signs" with the full-blown emotional reaction. Furthermore, because early-onset cues are presumably similar to the US's later effects, they may be especially easy to condition (see prior discussion); theoretically, they might, therefore, overshadow learning about other perfectly valid predictors of the US, such as other predictive external cues. This scenario suggests that interoceptive conditioning may be a major contributor to the development of PD.

Of course, not all of the body's reactions during early panic onset are necessarily interoceptive. Shortness of breath, for example, may have exteroceptive as well as interoceptive aspects. It is easy to find evidence of related US–US conditioning with USs that have exteroceptive effects. Goddard (e.g., 1996, 1997; Goddard & Jenkins, 1988) reported a number of experiments in which food USs signaled the occurrence of additional USs (see Goddard, 1999, for a review and implications). When food USs are delivered close together in time, the first pellet comes to signal others to follow. Similar learning occurs with aversive stimuli. For example, a weak shock can become more aversive through pairings with a stronger shock (Crowell, 1974). In addition, exposure to long shocks can increase the aversiveness of shorter shocks, apparently because shock onset becomes associated with the later aspects of the long event (Anderson, Crowell, DePaul, & McEachin, 1997). Interestingly, US–US conditioning can be extinguished by presenting the predictive stimulus (e.g., shock-onset cues or the first pellet) on many trials alone (e.g., Anderson et al., 1997; Goddard, 1997). Clearly, with both interoceptive or exteroceptive stimuli, nominal USs can signal other USs; one panic attack, or early aspects of a panic attack, can signal other panic attacks. It is not difficult to imagine this sort of learning contributing to the development and maintenance of PD.

CSs Do Not Just Trigger Responses; They Also "Modulate" Other Responses Controlled by Other Events

A case can thus be made for a role for interoceptive conditioning in PD as well as for the idea that the behaviors elicited by a CS will be multiple, complex, and not necessarily the same as the panic reaction itself. However, CSs have additional important means of influencing emotions and behavior; they also modulate other types of behavior. Historically, theorists (e.g., Mowrer, 1947, 1960) emphasized that aversive CSs that elicit anxiety can also modulate or influence the strength of ongoing operant or instrumental behaviors. According to two-process theory (e.g., Rescorla & Solomon, 1967), anxiety CSs should exaggerate avoidance behavior and weaken appetitively motivated behavior that occurs in their presence (see also Overmier & Lawry, 1979; Trapold & Overmier, 1972; see also Colwill, 1994). By this mechanism, conditioned anxiety might increase or potentiate instrumental acts that have been learned through negative reinforcement (e.g., escape or avoidance responses) to potentially keep the organism out of trouble. The tendency to carry "talismans" such as pill bottles, even if they are empty, and other safety signals or "safety behaviors" (Salkovskis, Clark, & Gelder, 1996) are presumably examples of avoidance or escape behaviors that have been reinforced by anxiety reduction or safety. The idea that anxiety CSs can modulate these behaviors means that heightened anxiety may exaggerate them, even if they appear "irrational" (i.e., an empty pill bottle has no objective effect on anxiety). As with all avoidance responses, they may serve to prevent extinction of the CR (which would include preventing disconfirmation of catastrophic thoughts).

Interestingly, modulation effects of CSs on instrumental behaviors can sometimes be specific. That is, CSs sometimes seem to arouse expectancies of the specific US with which they are associated and, therefore, mainly modulate instrumental behaviors that are connected with the same US (e.g., Colwill & Motzkin, 1994; Colwill & Rescorla, 1988; Delamater, 1996; Kruse, Overmier, Konz, & Rokke, 1983). In principle, then, a CS may arouse anxiety about a particular US (e.g., fainting and falling to the floor), and thereby selectively increase seemingly bizarre or idiosyncratic behaviors that have been reinforced for avoiding that particular US (e.g., clutching door handles, walls). Other behaviors connected with other USs (e.g., taking a spouse or trusted companion along for fear of panicking while driving) might not be affected.

Another important modulating effect of CSs is to exaggerate or potentiate the strength of URs or CRs that are elicited in their presence by other stimuli. This point has been emphasized by Wagner, Brandon, and their associates (e.g., Wagner & Brandon, 1989). Following Konorski (1967), they emphasized the fact that CSs enter into associations with both emotive and sensory aspects of the USs with which they are paired. The emotive CR (generated by the emotive association) functions to augment other responses, such as an eyeblink CR elicited by a second CS (Bombace, Brandon, & Wagner, 1991; Brandon, Betts, & Wagner, 1994; Brandon & Wagner, 1991) or an eyeblink or startle reflex evoked by other stimuli (Brandon, Bombace, Falls, & Wagner, 1991;

McNish, Betts, Brandon, & Wagner, 1997). The latter effect is consistent with the well-known fact that anxiety CSs also potentiate startle responses elicited by sudden bursts of noise (e.g., J. S. Brown, Kalish, & Farber, 1951; see Davis, 1992, for a review). In the presence of a CS controlling anxiety, we may become more reactive to sudden stimuli that evoke startle responses.

These modulating effects of emotions and emotional CSs have been emphasized in discussions of human emotion (e.g., Lang, 1994, 1995; Lang, Bradley, & Cuthbert, 1990) and anxiety disorders (Cook, Hawk, Davis, & Stevenson, 1991; Grillon, Ameli, Goddard, Woods, & Davis, 1994; Grillon, Ameli, Woods, Merikangas, & Davis, 1991; Morgan, Grillon, Southwick, Davis, & Charney, 1995). They may also be especially important to an understanding of PD. Through conditioning, anxiety cues may augment and exacerbate minor panic reactions that are triggered by other stimuli. This may be a key difference between patients who suffer from PD and other individuals who may occasionally experience nonclinical panic episodes without anxiety. Conditioned anxiety may lower the threshold of (or exaggerate) subsequent panic reactions. The modulating effects of anxiety CSs could thus cause, at a level below conscious awareness, the kind of exaggerated panic that cognitive theorists would assume requires catastrophic misinterpretations (e.g., D. M. Clark, 1986, 1988). A "floater," or floating object observed in the visual field, may mean nothing to a normal individual. However, to a person sensitized by anxiety, it could elicit another panic attack. In other words, classical conditioning may conceivably allow CSs to potentiate panic either through the modulating effect described here or through a more direct, traditional, eliciting effect described earlier in the section on interoceptive conditioning. Thus, by virtue of the modulating function, we can accept and retain the distinction between panic and anxiety but still find the state of anxiety exacerbating panic attacks.

The Effects of CSs Are Also Further Modulated by Other Stimuli

We have just emphasized how CRs and URs can be modulated by the presence of another stimulus; the CR to one CS can be potentiated by the emotional effect controlled by another. The general idea that the CR evoked by a CS is quite commonly modulated by the effects of other stimuli has received a great deal of attention in the conditioning literature (e.g., Swartzentruber, 1995). It introduces another layer to a conditioning theory of PD. Because responding is always viewed as the product of a CS as well as other modulating cues in the background, the CR cannot be assumed to be evoked automatically by a CS. This explains why a conditioning theory of PD does not "overpredict" panic in the presence of interoceptive (or exteroceptive) cues associated with panic attack. The conditioning experience creates a potential for a CS to evoke a CR, but the actual strength of the response always further depends on other stimuli in the situation.

Learning theory now recognizes several types of CR modulation. One is the potentiation-style effect described previously, in which the emotional properties of a CS can energize CRs, URs, or instrumental actions that are controlled by other stimuli. An even simpler modulation effect is summation. The strength of the CR observed in any situation is determined by the summed value of all the CSs that are currently present. The idea is captured by the

Rescorla-Wagner model (Rescorla & Wagner, 1972), which gives excitatory CSs (those that predict USs) positive values and inhibitory CSs (those that, in general, predict no US) negative values. When put together, the strength of the response is determined by the summed value of all the CSs that are present. Thus, when two excitatory CSs are put together, the response is larger than when either is presented alone (e.g., Hendersen, 1975; Reberg, 1972; Van Houten, O'Leary, & Weiss, 1970; S. J. Weiss & Emurian, 1970). Importantly, when an excitatory CS and an inhibitory CS (e.g., a safety signal) are put together, there will be less responding than to the excitor alone (e.g., Rescorla & Holland, 1977).[1]

Another implication of the Rescorla-Wagner model's summation mechanism is worth mentioning. According to the model, learning is an adjustment that occurs when there is a discrepancy between the outcome predicted on a conditioning trial (e.g., US or no US) and the actual outcome that occurs. The outcome predicted is determined by the sum of all stimuli present on the trial, as just discussed. This simple idea has several straightforward but remarkable implications. For example, when there is no US, and extinction would ordinarily occur, the presence of an inhibitor along with a to-be-extinguished excitor will subtract from and may cancel the excitor's prediction of a US, eliminating the discrepancy between prediction and actual outcome and thus leaving the excitor unextinguished. The inhibitor is said to "protect" the excitor from extinction (Chorazyna, 1962; Soltysik, Wolfe, Nicholas, Wilson, & Garcia-Sanchez, 1983). To the extent that agoraphobic "safety" behaviors such as carrying pill bottles also operate by canceling an excitatory CS's prediction of danger, combining the pill bottle with a trip to the shopping mall (an anxiety-evoking CS) may similarly protect the shopping mall CS from extinction (e.g., Soltysik, 1960). The converse of protection from extinction is also possible: During extinction, the addition of extra excitatory CSs that predict the US (instead of predicting no US, as an inhibitor does) would sum to yield an overprediction of the US, increasing the discrepancy between prediction and actual outcome and thus facilitating any associative loss to all the CSs resulting from extinction (Rescorla, 2000; Wagner, 1969). Therefore, extinguishing multiple excitatory CSs together should be more effective than extinguishing any one in isolation. The implication is that, to facilitate extinction of the shopping mall, it would be best to combine that CS with other CSs (e.g., elevators, a fast heart rate, shortness of breath) during exposure. Clinically, this is often used as an approach during cognitive–behavioral therapy for agoraphobia, although a different rationale is usually given (e.g., Barlow & Craske, 2000). A complete explication of the Rescorla-Wagner model is beyond the scope of this article. However, our discussion illustrates the extent to which all cues present at any time are important in determining anxiety and learning.

A related, and equally important, modulating effect is provided by contextual stimuli that are present but even further in the background when the CS is presented. In the conditioning laboratory, contextual cues are often operationally defined as the room or apparatus in which CSs and USs are presented; however, they can include a variety of other cues, including drug states, mood states, cues correlated with the passage of time, and the memory of recent events (e.g., Bouton & Nelson, 1998b; Bouton & Swartzentruber, 1991). Although such cues are indeed in the background, they can have potent effects on the CR that are relevant to any disorder in

which classical conditioning plays a role (e.g., see Bouton & Nelson, 1998b).

Bouton and colleagues showed that contextual stimuli are especially important in determining performance after extinction (e.g., Bouton, 1991a) or other situations in which learning in a second phase replaces or interferes with something learned first (Bouton, 1993). For example, anxiety evoked by a CS that has been through extinction is "renewed" if the context is changed after extinction (e.g., Bouton & King, 1983; Bouton & Ricker, 1994). This effect and others related to it have important implications for understanding relapse or return of fear (e.g., Bouton, 1988, 1991b; Bouton & Swartzentruber, 1991; see Mineka, Mystkowski, Hladek, & Rodriguez, 1999, for a preliminary example in humans). Somewhat surprisingly, in contrast to extinction, anxiety itself often generalizes almost perfectly between contexts: If anxiety is conditioned to a CS (by pairing it with shock) in one context and then the CS is tested in a second context, conditioned anxiety there is just as strong (e.g., Bouton & King, 1983; Hall & Honey, 1989; Lovibond, Preston, & Mackintosh, 1984). Thus, if a panic attack on a crowded bus conditioned anxiety to the feeling of dizziness, dizziness should elicit anxiety quite well in other contexts, such as the home, an airplane, or a ski lift. However, because extinction does not generalize as well between contexts, if anxiety were extinguished to dizziness in the context of the home, then dizziness would stop eliciting anxiety at home but could still evoke anxiety in other contexts (on the ski lift, the airplane, or the bus). The generalization of anxiety and the lack of generalization of extinction would contribute to the persistence of the disorder.

Interestingly, the psychological mechanism through which contexts control performance is different from the other modulating mechanisms described earlier. Instead of working through its direct association with the US, a context often modulates performance to the CS by signaling or retrieving the CS's own current connection with the US. It is as though the context disambiguates the CS (i.e., gives it its current meaning) in a manner analogous to the way in which contexts determine the meanings of words (e.g., Bouton, 1988, 1994b). This view has a number of implications for the persistence and treatment of anxiety disorders (e.g., Bouton, 1991b; Bouton & Nelson, 1998b; Bouton & Swartzentruber, 1991). For present purposes, what we view as the inherent context specificity of extinction performance is another reason why a conditioning model does not overpredict the occurrence of panic attacks: Anxiety elicited by an interoceptive CS may extinguish in some contexts without eliminating its impact in others.

The disambiguating effect of context is theoretically linked to a final form of modulation known as occasion setting (e.g., Holland, 1992; Schmajuk & Holland, 1998; Swartzentruber, 1995). Occasion setters are discrete stimuli (such as tones or lights) that can turn on or turn off responding to other CSs through some mechanism besides their direct association with the US and thus without necessarily evoking behavior on their own. Although their mechanism of action is currently a matter of debate, they are clearly

---

[1] It is worth noting that summation might not occur in all Pavlovian methods or response systems (e.g., Bouton, 1984; Bouton & King, 1986; Rescorla & Coldwell, 1995). One factor (among others) that appears to facilitate summation is similarity between the separate CSs and the compound (Pearce, Aydin, & Redhead, 1997).

connected with the theoretical issues concerning contextual control (e.g., Bouton & Swartzentruber, 1986; see also Bouton & Nelson, 1998a). Because neither contexts nor occasion setters operate through their direct associations with the US, simple extinction of an occasion setter (or a context) that "turns on" responding to a CS may not influence its ability to modulate responding to the CS (Bouton & Swartzentruber, 1986; Holland, 1989; Rescorla, 1985). Thus, we may find that the reaction of a patient with PD to his or her own racing heart (a CS) is especially problematic during visits to a shopping mall (a possible context or occasion setter). Exposure to the shopping mall alone may not weaken its ability to modulate the response to the heart racing. What is needed is extinction of the CS and the context together (e.g., Rescorla, 1986). This final example should make clear why so-called modulatory mechanisms are relevant to our understanding of PD. This may also be why many cognitive–behaviorial therapists find it useful to encourage their patients to bring on frightening bodily sensations (such as by hyperventilating) while engaging in exteroceptive exposure to their agoraphobic situations (Barlow & Craske, 2000).

Some Pertinent Clinical Evidence

Evidence that anxiety potentiates panic. From the perspective we are taking here, anxiety often potentiates panic rather than panic attacks truly coming out of the blue, as was originally thought to occur in most cases (Klein, 1981; Sheehan, 1983). As Basoglu, Marks, and Sengün (1992) argued, the problem with most prior studies suggesting that panic attacks come out of the blue is that they were based on retrospective recall. They noted that patients may not recall episodes of anxiety that preceded their panic episodes. Thus, Basoglu et al. (1992) conducted a prospective study of panic and anxiety in 39 patients who had PD with agoraphobia. Each patient recorded in a diary using an event-sampling technique the duration and intensity of episodes of panic and anxiety over three 24-hr periods, including their anxiety levels before panic episodes. Episodes of anxiety and panic were also classified as "situational/expected/predictable" versus "spontaneous/unexpected/unpredictable" based on whether the episode was expected and/or clearly linked to a situation that usually triggered such episodes (p. 58). Several results are of primary interest for our purposes. First, of 117 panic episodes recorded, 80% were situational/expected/predictable, and only 20% were spontaneous/unexpected/unpredictable. Moreover, of the 32 patients who reported at least one panic, 69% reported that their panics surged from an already heightened plateau of anxiety. Only 13% of the 32 who panicked had not reported a preceding period of anxiety. Another 18% reported anxiety preceding some panics but not others. In other words, more than 66% reported that anxiety had always preceded their panics on these recorded days, and 87% reported that this happened some or all of the time. Moreover, longer and more intense prepanic baseline anxiety was correlated with more intense panic (including number of episode symptoms). These results are consistent with our view that anxiety may often precede and potentiate the intensity of a panic attack.

Two other somewhat different prospective studies using computer-assisted self-monitoring techniques both reported related findings. Kenardy et al. (1992) followed 20 female panic patients for a 1-week period in a study of the psychological precursors of

panic attacks (not differentiating between predicted and unpredicted attacks). Patients answered a variety of questions every hour and whenever they believed they were having a panic attack. Anxiety in the hours preceding panic attacks (based on the question "How anxious do you feel?") was higher than in control hours (preceding no panic), although not significantly so. However, the participants' estimates of "the likelihood of panic this hour" (a more cognitive but conceptually related concept to anxiety) were significantly elevated in the hour preceding panic attacks relative to control hours. The authors deemed these elevated estimates of the likelihood of panic to support Barlow's (1988) position that "an underlying apprehension is a precursor to panic" and that such expectancies "can be thought of as developing from a conditioned fear of panic attacks" (Kenardy et al., 1992, p. 672).

Another related study (Kenardy & Taylor, 1999) had a somewhat different goal of determining the accuracy of predictions with predicted panic attacks (i.e., the sensitivity and specificity of the predictions) and whether psychological precursors (such as anxiety and perception of physical symptoms) were associated with panic attack prediction versus panic attack occurrence. In this study, 10 female panic patients monitored their panic attacks for 7 days, making predictions every hour about whether they would have a panic attack in that hour as well as their sense of threat or danger, their level of anxiety, number of physical symptoms of panic, and so on at the time of the ratings. Unpredicted panic attacks were only preceded by reports of elevated physical symptoms. Predictions that a panic attack would occur (whether or not it occurred) were associated with both physical symptoms and an elevated sense of threat or danger and anxiety. Thus, elevated physical symptoms and anxiety (only the former for unpredicted attacks) commonly preceded panic attacks, although they also occurred frequently at other times when no panic attacks occurred. (The only related finding reported in the Kenardy et al., 1992, study was that some panic symptoms—about one on average—frequently occurred in hours not associated with panic attacks.) Together, these results are consistent with our learning theory perspective that posits anxiety or physical symptoms as CSs—or potentiating factors—for panic.

Other evidence that anxiety precipitates panic comes from laboratory research on panic provocation, in which it has long been recognized that the single best predictor of panic in response to a variety of panic provocation agents is the baseline level of anxiety (e.g., Barlow, 1988; Margraf, Ehlers, & Roth, 1986). For example, Liebowitz et al. (1984) reported that patients who experienced panic attacks during lactate infusions in the laboratory experienced heightened anxiety before the infusion compared with the patients who did not panic. In another study (Liebowitz et al., 1985), heart rate averaged 83.98 beats per minute (bpm) during baseline for patients who went on to panic as opposed to 75.30 bpm during baseline for patients who did not go on to panic. Heart rate in control participants was 62.79 bpm. In fact, baseline differences in levels of anxiety between patients and controls before panic provocation have been reported in almost all studies dating back to the 1940s (e.g., Cohen & White, 1947, 1950). Breggin (1964) suggested current baseline anxiety as one of four principal factors accounting for the production of panic attacks in panic provocation experiments, thus anticipating our contemporary learning theory account by more than 35 years.

Interestingly, although anxiety seems to play a role, the specific somatic responses capable of provoking panic may differ markedly from patient to patient. This has never been better illustrated than in the data reported long ago by Lindemann and Finesinger (1938), in which individual patients responded with panic to infusions of either adrenaline or acetylcholine but not both. These substances produce very different, and almost opposing, sets of somatic sensations and have very different underlying neurobiological mechanisms of action. That individuals are specifically sensitive to dissimilar provocation procedures, a finding that characterizes the panic provocation literature (e.g., Barlow, 1988; van den Hout, 1988), suggests that individuals have learned a specific association between panic and certain discrete somatic sensations possibly associated with an earlier major alarm reaction.

Evidence that PD starts with a panic attack conditioning episode. Most patients report that PD usually starts with an initial panic attack followed by one or more attacks within a matter of weeks or months. It is generally over the course of these initial attacks that anxious apprehension about the possible occurrence of further attacks begins to develop. During this early stage, agoraphobic avoidance of situations that provide a possible setting for the attack may also begin to develop. For example, as noted earlier, Öst and Hugdahl (1983) gave detailed questionnaires to 80 people with PD and found that approximately 91% could recall the initial episode of panic (or vicarious experience of panic) after which the disorder began to develop; only 10% could not recall a conditioning event. Of these 91% with a conditioning mode of onset (as Öst & Hugdahl referred to it), more than 50% said that, after the first panic attack, the initial development of agoraphobia was rapid (i.e., fully developed agoraphobia within 2 weeks), and only 14% described a slow onset. Other investigators reported similar findings (Craske et al., 1990; Merckelbach, de Ruiter, Van den Hout, & Hoeckstra, 1989; Thyer & Himle, 1985; Uhde et al., 1985).

Although Öst and Hugdahl (1983) acknowledged that the US (i.e., the specific trigger) for the first panic attack could be identified in only a minority of cases, they shared our opinion, as well as that of Forsyth and Eifert (1996), that identifying a specific US is not essential in determining that conditioning plays a crucial role here. They noted that the attack itself was generally terrifying, with thoughts of losing control, fainting, or dying as core symptoms, and that this is sufficient to allow conditioning to occur. It is perhaps worth noting here that critics of this view, such as Menzies and Clarke (1995), have claimed that a US must be identified to ascribe a role to conditioning, but this argument is based on an unnecessarily restrictive view of conditioning. As argued elsewhere (e.g., Barlow, 1988; Carter & Barlow, 1995; see also Forsyth & Eifert, 1996), all that is needed for conditioning to occur is that either a true alarm or a false alarm reaction (activation of the flight-or-fight response) occurs in the presence of some potential interoceptive or exteroceptive CS.

The percentage of panic patients who claim to recall an initial panic attack conditioning episode might actually be considered impressive in light of evidence suggesting that emotional conditioning can occur without declarative memory of the conditioning experience. We have already described evidence suggesting that patients without an intact hippocampus can show emotional conditioning even though they cannot report the conditioning contingency (Bechara et al., 1995). Research by Öhman and colleagues has shown that the exteroceptive conditioning sometimes involved

in the origins of phobic fears may occur outside of conscious awareness if fear-relevant stimuli are involved (e.g., Öhman, 1996, 1997; Öhman, et al., 2000). In addition, it is worth noting that interoceptive conditioning has historically been thought to occur unconsciously and in the absence of an overt specifiable US because the US is internal (e.g., Razran, 1961). Together, these considerations suggest that accurate self-report data depending on conscious awareness may provide an inherently conservative estimate of the extent to which conditioning processes may be involved in the etiology of anxiety disorders. We should also note, however, that although the extant self-report data are consistent with a conditioning account of PD, there is a clear need for more objective data on the involvement of early conditioning trials.

Factors That May Affect the Potency of Panic Attacks and Hence the Strength of Conditioning

Several factors may further affect the potency of panic attacks and thus the likelihood that they will lead to PD through classical conditioning. These factors, which we now review, include whether the attacks are perceived as controllable and predictable, whether they occur in the presence or absence of safety cues, and whether separate experience with panic attacks has increased their emotional impact through some sensitization process.

Full-blown panic attacks are themselves experienced by people with PD as unpredictable and uncontrollable aversive (even terrifying) events. They are perceived as uncontrollable in the sense that there is nothing that can be done to abort an ongoing attack. However, they are also sometimes perceived as unpredictable in the sense that they seem to come from out of the blue, even if they may actually be triggered by unconscious interoceptive cues. First, consider the controllability dimension. The animal conditioning literature indicates that uncontrollable shock conditions anxiety to neutral CSs more powerfully than does the same amount of controllable shock (e.g., Mineka, Cook, & Miller, 1984; Mowrer & Viek, 1948). Indeed, Mineka et al. (1984) found that levels of anxiety conditioned with inescapable shock were twice as high as levels of anxiety conditioned with the exact same amount of escapable shock. In fact, there is evidence that initial panic attacks occurring in difficult-to-escape situations (e.g., driving on a highway, flying, being in a formal meeting) condition more anxiety than panics that occur in more escapable locations, such as being home alone or with a significant other (Barlow, 1988; Craske et al., 1990). Moreover, prior experiences with uncontrollable aversive events can later potentiate the conditioning of defensive reactions. Given this, and that initial panic attacks often occur during periods of uncontrollable stressors, we would expect them to be especially powerful sources of conditioning (e.g., see Maier, 1990).[2]

Sanderson, Rapee, and Barlow (1989) demonstrated that a sense of control may be important in influencing the occurrence of a panic attack itself. Using a 5% CO_2 panic provocation procedure, Sanderson et al. divided patients with PD into two groups. Both

---

[2] As discussed extensively elsewhere (e.g., Mineka et al., 1984; Mineka & Henderson, 1985), the mechanisms through which controllability operates may functionally be mediated by the added predictability over offset of a US that controllability affords (namely, when the US will end). However, for our purposes, the precise mechanisms through which controllability exerts its effects are not important and are not detailed here.

groups were told to inhale the CO_2; they were also told that if the sensations created by it were sufficiently bothersome, if and when a red light came on, they could turn a dial to reduce the rate of infusion of the CO_2 if they felt they had to. The two groups differed only in whether the red light actually came on during the CO_2 inhalation, affording one group the perception of control. Although no one in the perceived control group attempted to turn the dial, the dial was actually inoperative (it did not affect levels of CO_2). Thus, the two groups experienced equal amounts of CO_2. Nevertheless, there were substantial group differences in physiological reactivity to the CO_2; the perceived control group showed lower levels of physiological responding to the CO_2 than the no perceived control group. Moreover, 8 of 10 patients in the no perceived control group reported experiencing a panic attack compared with only 2 of 10 in the perceived control group.

Turning to unpredictability, there is evidence in the animal literature that unpredictable aversive events are perceived as more stressful than predictable aversive events (and that when given a choice, humans and animals generally prefer predictable to unpredictable aversive events; cf. Mineka & Hendersen, 1985). There is also evidence that unpredicted panics lead to more anxiety in a clinical population. On the basis of hypotheses developed from the animal conditioning literature, Craske, Glover, and Decola (1995) hypothesized that patients with PD would experience greater levels of anxiety on days that happened to follow an unpredicted panic than on days after a predicted panic. Although there were no differences between the group who only experienced predicted panic attacks and the group who only experienced unpredicted attacks, among the group who experienced a combination of the two this hypothesis was upheld. That is, patients with PD who experienced a mixture of the two kinds of attacks showed higher levels of anxiety and worry on days after an unpredicted attack than on days after a predicted attack. The authors also noted that these findings might be related to findings from the animal literature on experimental neurosis suggesting that having a history of predictability may exacerbate the effects of lack of predictability (Mineka & Kihlstrom, 1978; see also Mineka & Zinbarg, 1996). This is because the prediction was only upheld among those who had some history of predicted attacks intermixed with unpredicted attacks.

Another factor affecting the potency of a panic attack may be the anxiety-inhibiting presence of having a safe person present. Clinical observations have long suggested that patients with PD show a far greater range of activity and are less prone to panic when a safe person (often a spouse but sometimes a trusted companion of another sort) is with them than when they are alone. This phenomenon has been studied and documented in a laboratory study. Patients with PD showed fewer panic symptoms (distress symptoms, catastrophic cognitions, and physiological arousal) in response to CO_2 if a safe person was with them than in the absence of a safe person (Carter, Hollon, Carson, & Shelton, 1995).

The potency of panic attacks might also change as a function of previous experience with panic. Such experience might increase the intensity of later panics by engaging sensitization processes, including the neurobiological process recently described by Rosen and Schulkin (1998). Rosen and Schulkin argued that animal laboratory experiments on sensitization (in which exposure to uncontrollable stressors increases the organism's reactions to later stressors) serve as a model for similar observations in humans, showing that either distal or proximal exposure to uncontrollable stressors sensitizes them to the effects of subsequent stress, possibly including panic itself. They emphasized nonassociative (unlearned) neurobiological processes that might occur in the amygdala as underlying these effects. We would note that associative processes might also be involved. For example, as noted earlier, through repeated exposure to the stressor, the organism might learn to associate onset of the event with the rest of the event (e.g., Anderson et al., 1997). Event onset (including panic attack onset) could thus acquire a stronger and stronger emotional impact. Thus, either nonassociative or associative mechanisms could allow early panic attacks or other stressors to make later attacks more intense. Thus, in turn, sensitization to panic attacks could increase the strength of conditioning that results when a panic attack is subsequently associated with new CSs.

Sensitization of panic attacks might also influence the strength of anxiety reactions that have been conditioned previously. For example, inflation effects, first discovered by Rescorla (1974) and later replicated (at least through clinical case studies) in humans by Davey, de Jong, and Tallis (1993), are said to occur when a mild fear that is first conditioned to some cue using a mild unconditioned stressor later grows in magnitude when the animal or person is exposed noncontingently to a more powerful unconditioned stressor (not paired with the CS). Thus, a rat at first experiencing a tone paired with a mild shock shows a weak conditioned fear response, but if the rat is later exposed to a noncontingent strong shock on its own, the rat's level of fear of the tone is increased. By analogy, if a person experienced several mild panic attacks that were preceded by an upset or growling stomach, some conditioned excitatory strength might accrue to the stomach cues. However, this excitatory strength might later be inflated through the experience of other more severe panic attacks that were not accompanied by the same stomach cues. Bouton (1984) showed that such inflation effects are not context specific; that is, the inflation events need not occur in the same context in which the original conditioning took place, or where fear is tested, for inflation to occur. In addition, Hendersen (1985) also showed that inflation effects are often larger when the strong stressors are experienced a long time after the initial conditioning experience.

Summary

PD begins in individuals with certain psychological and biological vulnerabilities (to be discussed next) when early panic attacks occur and condition anxiety, a functional, forward-looking constellation of responses that prepares the person for the next panic attack. Several psychological factors that influence the perceived intensity of panic (e.g., its perceived controllability or predictability) may influence the potency of the US and thus the degree of conditioning. Panic may be associated with the setting or environment in which it occurs, and with interoceptive and/or exteroceptive correlates of early stages of panic itself. Anxiety can have a number of consequences. We have emphasized the possibility that it can potentiate or exaggerate the effects of other triggering events (other CSs, USs, or perhaps endogenous events) that may stimulate the next panic. Importantly, these potentiating effects are further modulated by other CSs and contextual cues that may be present in the background. It is plausible to suppose that conditioned anxiety is an essential process that allows early panics to spiral into PD. The idea is further consistent with clinical evidence suggesting that anxiety often precedes panic attacks and that anxiety seems to contribute to the evocation of panic in the laboratory. It is also consistent with evidence suggesting that PD often begins with panic experiences that can provide potent conditioning trials.

We have tended to emphasize the conditioning of anxiety CRs over panic CRs. This emphasis is consistent with the conditioning literature in animals such as rats, in which defensive CRs (e.g., freezing and endogenous analgesia) are not the same as the UR to footshock (activity bursting and pain). However, we believe it is likely that panic itself can also become a CR when certain fear-relevant interoceptive or exteroceptive cues are associated with panic attacks. From a functional perspective, panic reactions, unlike anxiety reactions, are designed to deal with an aversive US that is already in progress. Therefore, cues that are especially proximal in time to panic, such as the interoceptive correlates of panic onset, may be more likely than other kinds of cues to evoke this kind of CR. Support for this idea is largely indirect at this point, coming from a few animal and human conditioning experiments in which the CR is the same as the UR with certain CSs or certain interstimulus intervals (e.g., Cook et al., 1986; Dimberg, 1987; Domjan et al., 1992; Forsyth & Eiffert, 1996, 1998; Stegen et al., 1999; VanDercar & Schneiderman, 1967). Nonetheless, the idea that panic itself can be a CR is also an implication of what we know about conditioning in other behavior systems (e.g., Domjan, 1994, 1997). Further research is necessary before it can be determined what kinds of conditions allow panic itself to be a CR.

Importantly, conditioning processes and reactions like those we are describing here may often occur without conscious awareness, perhaps reflecting the operation of neurobiological emotional systems that are dissociable from declarative knowledge systems (see Bechara et al., 1995; R. E. Clark & Squire, 1998; see also LeDoux, 1996; Öhman, 1996, 1997; Öhman et al., 2000). As noted earlier, evidence suggests that emotional conditioning may be independent of declarative memory and conscious awareness. This aspect of emotional conditioning may obviate the well-known problem that cognitive perspectives have in explaining why panics can occur in the absence of catastrophic thoughts or ideas (e.g., Kenardy et al., 1992; Rachman et al., 1988). We believe that conditioning processes may go a considerable distance in explaining the major features of PD.

Vulnerabilities for the Development of PD

As noted earlier, not everyone who experiences occasional stress-related false alarms goes on to develop PD. Indeed, a majority do not. What makes some people who experience panic more vulnerable to developing PD than others? We have already noted that certain psychological concomitants of early panic attacks, such as their perceived controllability and predictability, can influence their perceived intensity and hence their ability to initiate conditioning. Moreover, multiple genetic, temperamental, and experiential factors have some empirical support as contributing to vulnerability to PD, and we now review what we consider to be three of the most prominent sets of factors. Two of these vulnerability factors (one biological and one psychological) are rather

nonspecific and may cause vulnerability to many different anxiety, mood, and related disorders. One additional set of psychosocial (experiential) factors is more specific for PD. Each may have an impact by influencing the conditioning process, described previously, that we view as central to the development of PD.

Nonspecific Biological (Genetic) Factors

There is clear evidence of the heritability of the trait variously referred to as "trait anxiety," "neuroticism," or "negative affect" (e.g., Eysenck, 1967; Gray & McNaughton, 1996; McGuffin & Reich, 1984; Plomin, DeFries, McClearn, & Rutter, 1997). It is unlikely that a single gene will be identified that relates to this heritability, but behavior genetic methods are at least beginning to identify the role of genetic contributions to anxiety and mood disorders. Nonetheless, although there is clear evidence for the heritability of each of these disorders, it should be emphasized that it is only modest in magnitude. For example, Kendler, Neale, Kessler, Heath, and Eaves, (1992), in a large female twin study, estimated that 35% to 39% of the variance in liability to agoraphobia and PD was due to genetic factors.

There is also evidence that the genetic vulnerability factors for PD and specific phobias (among other related disorders) may overlap (Kendler, Walters, et al., 1995). The possible genetic overlap between panic and phobias discussed by Kendler, Kessler, et al. (1995) is interesting in light of our learning theory perspective on the etiology of PD. Classical conditioning has long been implicated in the etiology of many specific phobias (e.g., Mineka, 1985a, 1985b; Mineka & Zinbarg, 1996; Öst & Hugdahl, 1981; J. B. Watson & Rayner, 1920), and we are making a parallel argument for PD here. In both specific phobias and PD, anxiety is conditioned to either exteroceptive cues or interoceptive cues, and conditioning of the flight-or-fight response may also occur. There is a long history of documenting the contribution of genetic and temperamental variables such as neuroticism or trait anxiety to classically conditioned aversive emotional responses (e.g., Brush, 1985; Levey & Martin, 1981; Pavlov, 1927), and this may be how the partially overlapping genetic diatheses between phobias and panic disorder may operate. Alternatively, another possible explanation for this partially shared genetic vulnerability may be for the frequency or intensity of experiencing panic attacks themselves, which sets the stage for conditioning of anxiety and/or panic.

Some evidence also suggests that genetic contributions to panic and generalized anxiety may differ, at least to some degree (Barlow, 1988; Kendler, Walters, et al., 1995). Elsewhere (Barlow, 1988) we have articulated how separate but perhaps overlapping biological vulnerabilities to anxiety and panic may increase the synergy between anxiety and panic (in which the presence of anxiety increases the probability of the occurrence of panic), long noted by ethologists (Maser & Gallup, 1974) and now emphasized here.

Thus, although having a genetically based vulnerability does not cause either panic or anxiety directly, it may well create the appropriate conditions for the occurrence of anxiety or panic or both in people undergoing stress. (Similarly, the tendency to react to stress with specific psychophysiological responses other than panic, e.g., headaches or irritable bowel syndrome, also seems to run in families and may have a somewhat heritable component; Barlow, 1991.) These overlapping genetic vulnerabilities could conceivably influence the onset of PD in one or more of three different ways. First, as already noted, they might influence the potency of panic attacks, making some people more prone to experiencing especially terrifying panic episodes. Second, they might influence the salience of fear-relevant CSs. For example, patients with PD are known to differentially attend to bodily sensations that occur when aroused (e.g., Ehlers & Breuer, 1992, 1996; see Craske, 1999, for a review). This heightened awareness of, or attention to, somatic sensations of arousal could increase their salience and, in turn, increase the probability of developing conditioned anxiety to subsequent panic attacks (see Mackintosh, 1974, for a review of the effects of CS salience on conditioning). Finally, as already noted, genetic vulnerabilities might influence the conditionability of panic and anxiety just as genetic and temperamental variables are known to influence other forms of conditioning (see Mineka & Zinbarg, 1991, 1995, for reviews).

With regard to temperamental or personality variables influencing conditioning, it is interesting to speculate that observed sex differences in neuroticism and trait anxiety (cf. Feingold, 1994, for a meta-analysis) could at least partially mediate the corresponding sex differences in PD (approximately 2:1 female:male) and agoraphobia (4:1 for severe agoraphobia). For example, in a meta-analysis, the average effect size (d) for sex differences in trait anxiety across 28 studies was −.30 (Feingold, 1994). Trait anxiety (or neuroticism) is the major personality variable known to be a risk factor for both anxiety and mood disorders (L. A. Clark, Watson, & Mineka, 1994), including PD (Hayward et al., 2000). Furthermore, as discussed earlier, trait anxiety has been consistently shown to increase the conditionability of aversive emotional reactions (e.g., Levey & Martin, 1981; Spence & Spence, 1966; Zinbarg & Mohlman, 1998). If higher trait anxiety in females were to lead to greater vulnerability to emotional conditioning, then PD would be more likely to develop in females even if females and males have the same probability of having initial panic attacks, as a number of studies indicate (e.g., King, Gullone, Tonge, & Ollendick, 1993; Telch et al., 1989).

Nonspecific Psychological Factors

The genetic and temperamental vulnerabilities just discussed do not operate in isolation, but must combine with psychological vulnerabilities emanating from early experiences to create a diathesis for the development of an anxiety disorder. Two of these early experiential factors seem to be nonspecific, serving as vulnerabilities for most anxiety and mood disorders; another seems to be more specific to PD.

Prior experience with control and mastery. There is reason to believe that people who have grown up with a sense of mastery or control over their environments (including their emotional lives) may be less likely to develop anxiety (and subsequently PD) when and if they have an unexpected panic attack than people who have grown up with a relatively impoverished sense of control and mastery over their environment. Developmental psychologists have long argued that an infant's experience with control over important aspects of his or her environment promotes exploration of novel events and less fearful reactions to strange or arousing stimuli. Infants and young children can gain such a sense of mastery if they have parents who respond to their needs, requests, and initiatives in a contingent way; this is in contrast to the

impoverished sense of mastery (or helplessness) that occurs in infants and young children with unresponsive parents who respond to their child in a relatively noncontingent manner. Chorpita, Brown, and Barlow (1998) investigated this general idea in a retrospective study. They operationalized the degree of experience with control or mastery that school-age children had received by using a measure of parenting style that assessed the degree to which the parent discourages autonomy and shows high protection of the child. Previous work had shown that this parenting style may influence the child's locus of control (i.e., high overprotectiveness is associated with external locus of control in the child; Schneewind, 1995). This parenting style is also associated with anxious and depressive symptoms in the child (e.g., Parker, 1983). In a cross-sectional study, Chorpita et al. found that parental overprotectiveness predicted external locus of control in the children (replicating Schneewind, 1995) and that the locus of control variable mediated the effects of parental overprotectiveness on clinical symptoms of anxiety and depression.

Unfortunately, these ideas regarding the role of mastery in reducing susceptibility to panic and anxiety are difficult to study experimentally in human infants and children because it is unethical to manipulate directly the controllability of a child's environment for significant periods of time. However, experimental evidence generally supports this idea in a study conducted in infant monkeys that were reared in controllable versus uncontrollable environments for the first year of life (Mineka, Gunnar, & Champoux, 1986). In the controllable environments, the master monkeys had levers to press and chains to pull to deliver themselves food, water, and treats. In the uncontrollable environments, the yoked monkeys received access to the same food, water, and treats, but these were delivered uncontrollably whenever a master monkey earned a reinforcer. When tested in several frightening and novel situations between 7 and 11 months of age, the master monkeys reared with control adapted more quickly in several different fear-provoking situations compared with the yoked monkeys reared without control. Thus, early experience with control and mastery over positive reinforcers appears to affect the level of fear that novel and frightening events evoke, paralleling what is thought to occur in early human development. By decreasing the intensity of reactions to frightening events or by increasing the rate of habituation to them, having a sense of control or mastery may thereby decrease the conditioning of panic or anxiety.

One thing that makes this example especially noteworthy is that the sense of mastery generalized across domains (in this case, from appetitive to aversive). Related findings have also been found in several other animal studies in the learned helplessness tradition. For example, Joffe, Rawson, and Mulick (1973) reported that rats raised in environments in which they had control over access to food, water, and visual stimulation later showed less emotionality and more exploratory behavior in a novel situation (known to evoke some anxiety) than did rats reared in yoked-uncontrollable environments. Hannum, Rosellini, and Seligman (1976) also showed that immunization effects (at least within an aversive domain) could be demonstrated over a substantial time frame. They found that immunization (or mastery) experiences with controllable shock given to young weanling rats had a protective effect when rats were later exposed as adults to inescapable shocks. Finally, J. Williams and Maier (1977) found immunization effects even when different kinds of aversive stimuli were used in the immunization (mastery) and helplessness induction phases (e.g., experiencing escaping from cold water immunized rats against the effects of subsequent exposure to uncontrollable footshocks). In combination, these studies suggest that learning a sense of mastery or control in one or more areas of life (but not necessarily related to control over aversive stimuli or emotions) could generalize to situations in which aversive stimuli or emotions are involved, such as coping with a few unexpected panic attacks.

Thus far, we have emphasized the ways in which an enhanced sense of mastery and control may immunize against later anxiety and possibly depression relative to some normative level of controllability. Conversely, high levels of prior experience with uncontrollable stressors may also enhance vulnerability to anxiety and depression relative to some normative baseline of experience with stress. Relevant to this latter line of research, stressful life events have been found to play two somewhat distinctive roles in the etiology of PD. First, stressful life events such as early parental death, separation, or divorce have been found in many, but not all, studies to enhance vulnerability to development of some of these disorders, most notably PD and agoraphobia (e.g., Kendler et al., 1992; Tweed, Schoenback, George, & Blazer, 1989). Second, for PD (and major depression), higher than normal levels of stressful life events have been found to precede and possibly precipitate the onset of the disorder in vulnerable individuals (e.g., see reviews by Monroe & Simons, 1991, for depression; Craske, 1999, for anxiety disorders).

Neurobiological mechanisms might also be involved in these effects. One possible mechanism is the one proposed by Rosen and Schulkin (1998), who argued that both distal (e.g., early childhood) and proximate (e.g., past few months) stressful life events, both physical and psychological, may serve to sensitize fear circuits in the brain (primarily the amygdala), making them "hyperexcitable" or easier to trigger for a long time. Such hyperexcitability might also occur simply as a function of the experience of panic attacks themselves, which are often perceived as terrifying life-threatening events. In addition, building on the pioneering efforts of Ader and Denenberg, Nemeroff et al. (e.g., Heim & Nemeroff, 1999; Ladd et al., 2000) noted permanent effects on brain function of early stressful experiences (separation) in rat pups. Specifically, early stressful experiences exert a significant impact on the developing hypothalamic-pituitary-adrenal (HPA) axis, causing an increase in the organism's response to psychologically stressful events as adults (e.g., exposure to a novel environment, restraint) but not physical stress (e.g., hemorrhage). This very specific heightened responsiveness to psychological stress in adulthood seems to be a function of hyperreactive HPA axis responding to these stressors as indexed by markedly elevated corticosterone and adrenocorticotropic hormone. Thus, early experience with uncontrollable stress may create a nonspecific diathesis for later life events perceived as unpredictable and/or uncontrollable.

Prior experience with unpredictability. Lack of control over one's environment often implies lack of predictability as well (i.e., if one cannot control an event, one often does not know when it will occur or terminate). As noted earlier, a good deal of research shows that the predictability versus unpredictability of uncontrollable events (possibly including panic attacks, cf. Craske et al., 1995) has a large impact on the amount of stress generated (e.g., Overmier, 1985; Seligman & Binik, 1977; J. Weiss, 1971; see

Mineka & Hendersen, 1985, for a review). Unfortunately, there is very little in the way of longitudinal research during early development on the effects of being raised in a highly unpredictable versus predictable environment. However, one important study in monkeys investigated this issue. Coplan et al. (1996) found that infant monkeys whose mothers experienced unpredictable foraging conditions (food sometimes scarce and sometimes abundant) showed higher levels of corticotropin-releasing factor (one of the major stress hormones) in cerebrospinal fluid as adults than did infants whose mothers had either a predictable overabundance of food or chronically (i.e., predictably) scarce food.

In summary, these findings regarding the effects of early experience with uncontrollable or unpredictable events, in conjunction with a larger web of related findings from developmental psychology, may have considerable relevance for understanding an individual's vulnerability to PD (Barlow, 1988; Barlow et al., 1996; Chorpita & Barlow, 1998; Mineka, 1985a; Mineka & Kelly, 1989; Mineka & Zinbarg, 1991, 1995, 1996). The mechanisms for these effects may be consistent with a traditional learned helplessness account (e.g., Maier & Seligman, 1976; Peterson, Maier, & Seligman, 1993). Specifically, learning that one does not have control over important life events at one point in time can produce associative and motivational deficits that result in failure to learn control at future points at which control is indeed possible. Alternatively or additionally, a nonassociative neurobiological sensitization mechanism may also operate (e.g., Heim & Nemeroff, 1999; Rosen & Schulkin, 1998). Once again, this vulnerability is viewed as nonspecific to PD and most likely undergirds the development of all or most anxiety and mood disorders as well as related disorders.

Specific Psychological Factors: Vicarious and Instrumental Learning

We have discussed both nonspecific biological and nonspecific psychological vulnerabilities for anxiety and mood disorders. In addition, there also seem to be some specific early vulnerability factors that may predispose only some people who experience a panic attack to develop PD as opposed to other anxiety disorders or no disorder. One rather specific set of psychological factors not yet reviewed concerns early learning experiences regarding the potential dangers of unexplained bodily sensations and how to respond to them based on observations of one's parents' behavior (see Levy, 1998, for a review). In an early study of these influences in the realm of medical illness, Turkat (1982) studied 27 diabetics whose parents had not been chronically ill while they were growing up. Two thirds of these individuals reported that their parents had engaged in sick role behavior (such as not going to work, canceling activities, or receiving special attention) when temporarily ill. Of the individuals with diabetes whose parents had shown sick role behavior when ill, 66% reported illness-related avoidance as adults themselves. Another 33% reported that their parents had not engaged in sick role behavior when they were ill while they were growing up; only 22% of these people with diabetes reported illness-related avoidance themselves. Thus, diabetics whose parents showed sick role behavior appeared much more likely to demonstrate similar illness behavior themselves as well as work and responsibility avoidance, leading Turkat to conclude that "parental reactions to illness may be transmitted to their offspring as well" (1982, p. 522). In addition, the individuals with diabetes whose parents had engaged in sick role behavior made more visits to their doctors and had more hospital admissions and more days ill than the other group, even though there was no evidence that they were more seriously ill based on physiological measures.

In another large-scale study, Whitehead, Winget, Fedoravicius, Wooley, and Blackwell (1982) found that adults were more likely to miss school or work as a result of illness and to seek medical help if their parents had reinforced them (e.g., with toys or special food) when they were ill as children. Moreover, in a later study of women, Whitehead, Bush, Heller, and Costa (1986) showed some correlational specificity to such relationships. For example, if the women had been encouraged to be cautious as children when they had colds, they were more likely to seek help for nongynecological problems. However, if they had been reinforced for sick role behavior for menstrual symptoms while growing up, they were more likely to miss school or work and seek medical attention for menstrual symptoms as adults.

Turning to PD, Ehlers (1993) suggested that any learning experience encouraging sick role behavior and/or negative evaluations of somatic symptoms associated with panic attacks may create a potential specific vulnerability factor for PD. In a retrospective study, Ehlers (1993) assessed 121 panic patients (including 24 in remission for at least 6 months), 86 infrequent panickers, 38 patients with other anxiety disorders (mostly specific phobias), and 61 normal controls for learning experiences when they were children and adolescents with respect to somatic symptoms. All individuals were asked about parental encouragement of sick role behavior when they were experiencing panic symptoms (as well as their frequency of occurrence), observation of parental sick role behavior and of frequency of parental panic symptoms, parental encouragement of sick role behavior when sick with colds, number of chronically ill family members (where chronic illness was defined as six months in duration or longer), and frequency of uncontrolled behavior of household members (because of rage or being drunk). Ehlers reported that the frequency of uncontrolled behavior was assessed because of the clinical observation that patients with PD who report fear of loss of control often have parents who abuse substances.

No differences were found between patients with PD and infrequent panickers on most variables, and the patterns of correlations between the groups were identical. All three anxiety groups reported greater frequency of uncontrolled behavior in their parents compared with controls. In addition, patients with PD and infrequent panickers reported having observed parents experiencing panic symptoms more frequently than anxiety disorder or normal controls; all three anxious groups also reported more panic symptoms in themselves while growing up than controls. The four groups had comparable parental encouragement of sick role behavior during the experience of panic-like symptoms (e.g., special attention and instructions to take special care of themselves and to avoid strenuous activities or social engagements). However, because of the differences in frequency with which actual symptoms were experienced across the four groups, there was more parental reinforcement of panic symptoms in the participants in the three anxiety groups relative to controls and more parental engagement in sick role behavior when the parents had panic symptoms in the two panic groups relative to the other groups. In contrast, there

were no differences between anxiety disorder groups and controls in reported parental encouragement of sick role behavior in the event of colds. Moreover, among the two panic groups combined, there were some modest but significant correlations between a combined index of this encouragement of sick role behavior and responses on two widely used measures of fear of bodily sensations: the Body Sensations Questionnaire and the Agoraphobic Cognitions Questionnaire (Chambless, Caputo, Bright, & Gallagher, 1984; Ehlers, Margraf, & Chambless, 1992). Overall, the results suggest that both clinical and nonclinical panickers had a history of sick role encouragement when experiencing panic symptoms (but not cold symptoms); controls reported significantly fewer symptoms in themselves and their parents, although when such symptoms occurred sick role behavior was also reinforced.

Ehlers (1993) also found that patients with PD and infrequent panickers reported a higher number of chronic illnesses in their households while growing up compared with those with other anxiety disorders or controls. She noted, "Observing physical suffering can also contribute to the evaluation that somatic symptoms are dangerous and that special care is needed" (p. 276). Whether this learning should be interpreted as an instance of vicarious classical conditioning (cf. Mineka & Cook, 1993), in which the child associates his or her own distress at watching the parent's distress with symptoms they are showing, or instrumental learning, in which the child observes the parent's reinforcement for doing certain things in response to certain symptoms, awaits further analysis (although these two possibilities are not mutually exclusive). In the former, illness cues might become associated with negative affect through evaluation of somatic symptoms as dangerous. In the latter, family members might have reinforced attributions about being sick and sick role behavior more directly.

Finally, there is some evidence that prior experience causes individuals to focus their anxiety on specific constellations of responses within a panic attack, such as respiratory symptoms (e.g., breathlessness), vestibular symptoms (e.g., dizziness), cardiovascular symptoms (e.g., increased heart rate), or symptoms of dissociation (e.g., depersonalization). Reports of a preexisting and presumably learned sensitivity to suffocation cues differentially predicts panic attacks to respiratory challenges such as breathing through a straw (e.g., Taylor & Rachman, 1994) or breathing into a paper bag (McNally & Eke, 1996). In addition, Craske (1999) reviewed some evidence that early experience with specific chronic illness in family members (e.g., chronic obstructive pulmonary disease) may lead to enhanced sensitivity to specific constellations of sensations such as respiratory symptoms. Also, Barrett, Rapee, Dadds, and Ryan (1996) observed parents of socially anxious children unwittingly reinforcing specific avoidant behavior associated with hypothetically threatening social situations, and this behavior increased after family discussions of ambiguously threatening social situations. Barrett et al. also found that parents of children with specific phobias reinforced their children for avoidance of hypothetically physically threatening situations. These results suggest that parents convey specific fear information to children including, perhaps, information about specific somatic sensations.

Of course, many of the studies we have discussed in this section have major methodological limitations in that they are retrospective in nature, and recall of early learning experiences may be colored by the participant's current emotional tendencies and symptomatology. Moreover, given the genetic vulnerabilities contributing to PD. one must consider the possible role of genetic factors in some of the associations described here, and some may be. they do suggest that early learning factors (including vicarious ones) may contribute to a specific vulnerability for PD by sensitizing individuals to the potential danger of somatic sensations. Thus. when a stress-related panic attack occurs in someone with such specific vulnerabilities, certain somatic sensations may be especially salient for that person. leading to especially robust conditioning of anxiety and/or panic to those cues.

Summary

Vulnerability factors for PD seem to include a variety of general and specific factors; that is, some vulnerability factors may predispose to other anxiety and related disorders, and some may be rather specific for PD. Genetic evidence on the specificity issue is somewhat inconsistent, but Kendler, Walters et al.'s large twin study (e.g., 1995) suggests that there may be some shared vulnerability between PD and specific phobias, which would be consistent with the theory proposed here. This is because the shared vulnerability could either be for experiencing especially intense or frequent panic-fear episodes, which set the stage for conditioning of specific phobias or for the onset of PD, or because of enhanced conditionability to exteroceptive or interoceptive cues. In addition. early experience with uncontrollable and unpredictable events is likely to serve as a psychosocial vulnerability factor for many anxiety disorders (Barlow, 1988; Barlow et al., 1996; Chorpita & Barlow, 1998; Mineka, 1985a, 1985b; Mineka & Zinbarg, 1995, 1996). Finally, vicarious learning of anxiety focused on certain bodily sensations and/or reinforcement of illness behavior while growing up may serve as a more specific vulnerability factor for PD but not other anxiety disorders (Ehlers, 1993).

Relationships Between a Learning Theory Perspective and Other Accounts of PD

A contemporary learning theory perspective appears to be consistent with much that is known about PD. It is also broadly consistent with what we view as the positive aspects of the other approaches and theories reviewed at the beginning of this article. For example, the data supporting the role of AS in the development of PD fit with the notion of a specific psychological vulnerability based. perhaps, on vicarious learning encouraging sick role behavior or negative evaluation of somatic symptoms such as those occurring during panic attacks. In our approach. individuals who go on to develop PD would learn AS or, more specifically, that somatic symptoms are potentially dangerous. In support of this idea, a reanalysis of data from the Barlow laboratory (Zinbarg, Brown, Barlow, & Rapee, in press) suggests that the physical harm factor of the ASI (anxiety focused on somatic sensations), in contrast to other factors derived from this scale, accounts for almost all of the variance in predicting whether panic attacks will occur in patients with PD who are provoked with CO_2 inhalations. In addition. Hayward et al. (2000) also found that the physical harm factor of the ASI was the only significant predictor from the ASI of naturally occurring panic attacks, when controlling for depression, in their 4-year prospective study of adolescents. However, as noted earlier, high scores on the ASI do not invariably

predict the development of panic attacks (and in the Hayward et al., 2000, study, high negative affectivity was a substantially better predictor). Moreover, no study has yet shown them to predict onset of full-blown PD in an unselected population. Thus. in our view AS plays an important role in the development of PD but at the level of only one of our three hypothetical vulnerabilities.

We also believe that an approach based on contemporary learning theory is consistent with data that seem to support cognitive theories emphasizing a role for catastrophic misinterpretation (e.g., Beck & Emery, 1985; D. M. Clark, 1986, 1988, 1996). As we noted earlier, catastrophic misinterpretations may indeed accompany many panic attacks. This may be because such thoughts are a natural part of the constellation of responses involved in panic or because they might have been encouraged and reinforced in a manner analogous to the sick role behaviors and negative evaluations identified by Ehlers (1993) during earlier experience of panic-like symptoms during childhood and adolescence. If they actually play a causal role in generating or exacerbating panic, they may do so because they serve as CSs that have been associated with panic. Through classical conditioning, they may come to elicit anxiety and panic when they occur again. Although a causal role for catastrophic cognition is thus not outside the scope of a learning theory analysis, we are less convinced than other theorists that catastrophic thoughts are necessary to generate panic attacks. Whether they are sufficient remains to be determined. It is worth noting that the modal observation during panic attacks or extreme fear during confrontation with a phobic situation (as opposed to the period of anxiety preceding the confrontation) is an absence. or substantial diminishment, of cognitive activity such as catastrophic cognitions or other conscious appraisals of danger (Craske, 1999; Last, O'Brien, & Barlow, 1985; S. L. Williams, Kinney, Harap, & Liebmann, 1997).

D. M. Clark (e.g., 1996) and others (Beck & Emery, 1985; Salkovskis, 1988) have. of course, emphasized the role of catastrophic cognitions in causing panic attacks as well as several threads of evidence that seem to justify their importance. However, few of the threads truly force one to accept a causal role. For example, D. M. Clark (e.g., 1996) reviewed evidence from a variety of studies supporting the idea that panic patients are more likely to choose negative interpretations of ambiguous internal events than are normals and other anxiety-disordered controls. Although such results are consistent with cognitive theory, he acknowledged that they do not show that catastrophic cognitions play a causal role in creating panic but rather may be epiphenomenal. For example, these cognitions may be one manifestation of a preexisting psychological vulnerability that facilitates the conditioning of anxiety to CSs signaling subsequent panic attacks. D. M. Clark (1996) also cited a study by Ehlers. Margraf. Roth, Taylor. and Birbaumer (1988) in which panic patients were given false auditory feedback indicating a sudden increase in heart rate to determine whether activating patients' catastrophic cognitions would increase their anxiety more than that in normal controls. Panic patients did show greater increases in heart rate, blood pressure, skin conductance, and self-reported anxiety than normals. However, there is no need to invoke catastrophic misinterpretations to explain these findings, even though they may well occur. That is, one can easily construe the false heart rate feedback as an exteroceptive CS similar to a conditioned interoceptive CS (increased heart rate); conditioned anxiety may merely generalize to it. Moreover, one would expect signs of an elevated heart rate to be an effective stimulus for anxiety in patients with PD, but not in normal controls who do not have the same conditioning history.

Cognitive theorists (e.g., D. M. Clark, 1996) have also cited a study from Clark's laboratory (D. M. Clark, Salkovskis, & Anastasiades, 1990) in which panic patients, recovered panic patients, and normal controls read pairs of words that involved combinations of bodily sensations and catastrophes (e.g., palpitations-dying, breathless-suffocate, numbness-stroke) and were asked to rate their anxiety and occurrence of any *DSM-III* panic symptoms. The results indicated that 83% of the panic patients (but none of the recovered controls or normal controls) had a *DSM*-defined panic attack while reading the cards with these pairs of words. Although these results were seen as evidence that catastrophic misinterpretations were sufficient to provoke panic attacks, a role for catastrophic misinterpretations per se was not directly established. For example, the word pairs might alternatively evoke thoughts and images that have been associated with panic and thus have become CSs capable of evoking panic.

A learning theory perspective accepts the role of other cognitive factors. It is undoubtedly true that certain kinds of cognitive processes other than catastrophic cognitions can also influence the perceived intensity of panic and thus influence its impact as a US on the development of conditioning. The learning literature has long emphasized predictability and controllability, which may be mediated by cognitions that modulate the perceived intensity of aversive events. Two experiments that have been interpreted to suggest the role of catastrophic cognitions may merely emphasize the importance of the perception of predictability and controllability. Panic patients were given virtually no explanation of what to expect before inhaling 5% CO_2 (Rapee, Mattick, & Murrell, 1986) or infusing sodium lactate (D. M. Clark et al., 1990), or they were given detailed information about what sensations to expect and that these sensations were due to the experimental agent. In both studies, the patients given the detailed explanations were significantly less likely to report panicking than those not given much explanation of what to expect. As discussed earlier, predictable aversive events are generally perceived as less stressful than are unpredictable aversive events. One way of making an event predictable is by providing extensive information about it ahead of time, as was done in these experiments (see Leventhal, 1982; Leventhal, Brown, Shacham, & Engquist, 1979; Mineka & Hendersen, 1985). Thus, panic patients, like normal controls, find predictable stressors to be far less stressful (and, therefore, less likely to provoke panic) than they find unpredictable stressors. The effect is cognitively mediated, but prior researchers have not found it necessary to invoke catastrophic misinterpretations to explain it. The Sanderson et al. (1989) study, already discussed, is also consistent with this point: The effects of perceived control (rather than predictability) over the rate of CO_2 infusion underscore the importance of a sense of control in reducing vulnerability to anxiety. Controllability and predictability are cognitive constructs that are relatively easy to operationalize and are connected with a long tradition of experimental research (e.g., Mineka & Hendersen, 1985; Minor, Dress, & Overmier, 1991; Peterson et al., 1993; Seligman, Maier, & Solomon, 1971).

We should also acknowledge that, as mentioned earlier, classical conditioning itself may sometimes give rise to cognitive processes that may permit input from other cognitive sources. Al-

though we have emphasized the idea that conditioning processes can be engaged without consciousness or awareness, many forms of human classical conditioning may involve the acquisition of explicit expectancies of the US. In such cases, it might be possible to influence conditioned responding with verbal information or cognition. Consistent with this idea, Lovibond (e.g., 1993) argued that verbal information about the nature of the US can be sufficient to cause changes in conditioned electrodermal responses elicited by conditioned stimuli (e.g., see Grings et al., 1973). We believe that this sort of verbal influence on conditioning is probably not universal and depends on the type of conditioning and the brain system involved. There is a need for more research on the interaction between verbal input and conditioning processes. Nonetheless, at this point we should expect some overlap between conditioning and these overtly "cognitive" processes (see also Öhman & Mineka, 2001).

A modern view of conditioning may also suggest reinterpretation of other evidence sometimes cited in favor of the catastrophic misinterpretation view. In an important early study suggesting the role of cognitive factors in determining panic reactions, D. M. Clark and Hemsley (1982) had normal participants hyperventilate. There was variability in their responses to this event. Participants who recalled experiencing the sensation during sex or while they were high on a pleasant drug rated the sensations as positive; those who recalled an unpleasant experience (e.g., fainting) rated the sensations as negative. To us, this result implies a clear role for the participant's associative learning history, the subject matter of conditioning. Memory retrieval is part of what the associative learning process represented by conditioning is all about (e.g., Bouton, 1994a). Like classical conditioning itself, the Clark and Hemsley result looks to us like another interesting example of associative learning.

Finally, there has also been an emphasis on the idea that the success of any treatment will depend on cognitive changes having occurred during the course of therapy (D. M. Clark, 1996, p. 322). In a treatment study, D. M. Clark et al. (1994) compared the effects of cognitive therapy for panic with the effects of applied relaxation treatment and imipramine. Collapsing across the three groups, misinterpretation of bodily sensations at the end of treatment was a significant predictor of a composite measure of panic/anxiety at follow-up even when partialing out the level of panic-anxiety at the end of treatment. Moreover, among those patients who were panic free at the end of treatment, misinterpretations of bodily sensations at the end point predicted subsequent relapse. On this point, we note that catastrophic cognitions seem to be part of a "context" or constellation of cues that have been associated with panic or are even part of the response itself, and may signal or mark residual anxiety conditioned specifically to panic attacks. If they are not extinguished, PD could well return. In addition, several treatment studies have shown that extensive exteroceptive and interoceptive exposure therapy may be equally effective as cognitive therapy in reducing panic disorder, in both the short term and long term (Margraf & Schneider, 1995; Telch, 1995). A contemporary learning theory perspective may uniquely accommodate these different forms and mechanisms of therapy.

In summary, many findings that seem uniquely interpretable from the perspective of cognitive theory (e.g., Beck & Emery, 1985; D. M. Clark, 1986; 1988, 1996) are not incompatible with contemporary learning theory. The evidence favoring the idea that catastrophic cognitions cause panic is weak. A learning theory perspective has advantages, moreover, in that it can account for panic attacks that occur apparently without identifiable catastrophic misinterpretations, including nocturnal panic (e.g., Craske, 1999; Kenardy & Taylor, 1999; Rachman et al., 1988). This perspective also recognizes the distinction between anxiety and panic, which seem central to current psychometric (e.g., T. A. Brown et al., 1998) and neurobiological work (e.g., Fanselow, 1994; Gray & McNaughton, 1996). In addition, it allows prediction of return of fear and anxiety based on a thorough analysis of context and conditioning (e.g., Bouton, 1991b) and a more explicit analysis of factors modulating the acquisition of fear, panic, and PD based on well-established paradigms in the laboratories of experimental psychology.

Implications and Conclusion

We are in a good position at this point to summarize our argument and mention some of its major implications. First, in keeping with earlier approaches to PD, our perspective emphasizes a fundamental role for early conditioning episodes in the etiology of the disorder. This idea can be seen as a strength of a learning perspective, because it constitutes a testable explanation of PD etiology. Prospective data on early panic attacks and their associative and psychological consequences are needed. We would expect, for example, that after an initial panic attack, people—especially those with one or more of the general or specific vulnerabilities discussed earlier—would show more anxiety to cues associated with the first attack. Such results could theoretically be obtained from prospective diary monitoring studies in vulnerable adolescents or young adults (similar to those reported by Basoglu et al., 1992; Kenardy et al., 1992; Kenardy & Taylor, 1999, although with additional measures). However, we also emphasize the fact that current learning theory does not regard conditioning as an inevitable consequence of CS–US pairings. Instead, the extent to which conditioning develops depends on many additional factors, including the person's previous experience with the CS and the US and with the "informativeness" of the various CSs present on the conditioning trial and on other modulating factors in the background, and so on. As we have emphasized throughout this article, laboratory research on conditioning and learning has progressed considerably since the 1960s, and it suggests a surprisingly nuanced perspective on the associative learning involved in panic and other anxiety disorders (see also Mineka, 1985a; Mineka & Zinbarg, 1996).

A second important aspect of our approach is that anxiety and panic are seen as separable aspects of PD. Anxiety is not merely a weak version of panic, and panic is not merely a strong form of anxiety. We see each state, and the constellation of behaviors and physiological responses connected with each, as serving different functions. Anxiety prepares the system for an anticipated trauma, whereas panic deals with one that is already in progress. Anxiety and panic are thus different. This perspective is consistent with data addressed early in this article suggesting that anxiety and panic seem at least in good part phenomenologically, psychometrically, ethologically, and neurobiologically distinct.

Anxiety and panic do interact, however, and our approach assumes that their interaction is central to the development of PD. We propose that anxiety potentiates panic, and the development

and presence of conditioned anxiety, therefore, serve to exacerbate subsequent panic attacks. A third crucial feature of our perspective, then, is the idea that the conditioned anxiety that comes to be elicited by interoceptive and exteroceptive cues associated with panic serves to augment future panic reactions. Anxiety thus becomes a precursor of panic. The approach fits conditioning research, which suggests that anxiety is perhaps the major response learned in aversive conditioning situations, and that anxiety can function to exacerbate CRs and URs elicited while in that state (e.g., Lang, 1994, 1995; Lang et al., 1990; Wagner & Brandon, 1989). It is also consistent with available data that suggest that panic attacks are very often preceded by anxiety in patients with PD (e.g., Barlow, 1988; Basoglu et al., 1992; Kenardy & Taylor, 1999). We expect that prospective data sets would show that, once conditioned anxiety develops as a consequence of the first panic attack, it would potentiate and exacerbate subsequent panics and thus begin the spiral into PD.

It should also be noted that the conditioned elicitation of anxiety does not rely on conscious processing (e.g., LeDoux, 1996; Öhman et al., 2000). Therefore, we predict that panic can be potentiated in the absence of conscious thought or reflection, as is more consistent with functioning in largely subcortical emotional networks connected to defensive motivational systems (Barlow, in press; Lang, 1995).

Although we believe that the conditioning of anxiety is a major consequence of the conditioning made possible by panic attacks, we also suspect that panic itself may become conditioned directly to certain kinds of cues. That is, although anxiety is a prevalent CR, panic itself, instead of anxiety, may also emerge as a CR to some of the available CSs. As we reviewed earlier, laboratory research suggests that the nature of the CR depends on a number of factors, including the qualitative nature of the CS and its temporal proximity to the US. We predict that proximal, fear-relevant cues, which might include early somatic aspects of panic itself, are especially likely to have the ability to elicit panic CRs. However, this issue needs more research: we need a more complete understanding of the kinds of cues or circumstances that allow a CS associated with an aversive US to control a CR that resembles the UR. We also predict that those CSs that do elicit panic should do so more strongly when they are presented after the evocation of anxiety. That is, anxiety should potentiate panic whether it is a CR or UR.

A fourth implication of our analysis concerns treatment. Like other conditioning perspectives, we expect that treatments that involve extinction or counterconditioning exposure to the interoceptive and exteroceptive CSs influencing the disorder are the most likely to yield success. However, we explicitly accept many different kinds of events and cues—interoceptive, exteroceptive, verbal, and cognitive—as potential CSs involved in the disorder. Therefore, we predict that approaches that entail extinction or counterconditioning exposure to all of these kinds of events will be most successful, particularly if they are conducted in a way that recognizes the crucial role of context in controlling extinction and other retroactive interference effects (e.g., Bouton, 1991b; Bouton & Nelson, 1998b; Bouton & Swartzentruber, 1991). Moreover, we also predict that treatments designed in part to extinguish the anxiety-reducing properties of safety behaviors (such as carrying a pill bottle or an umbrella) will be very useful (for preliminary evidence see Salkovskis et al., 1996). In our view, this is because such safety behaviors serve to protect fear of various exteroceptive cues (and potentially interoceptive cues as well) from extinction. If therapists endeavor to expose the anxiety-providing cues without allowing safety behaviors, fear of those cues should extinguish more fully.

In the last analysis, a good theory is a useful tool to guide future scientific exploration of a given topic. Unfortunately, early learning theory approaches to the etiology of panic and other anxiety disorders were overly simplistic, leading to some of the confusion regarding the usefulness of these approaches (e.g., McNally, 1990, 1994). However, the underlying science has developed rapidly over the decades and has been enriched by increasingly important developments in the biological and cognitive bases of learning reviewed here. In our view, a modern learning theory approach will provide the soundest base for future theoretical and empirical developments in the study of PD. Thus, we look forward to precise experimental tests of the various components of our approach, some of which have been suggested here. It is this kind of activity that will ultimately best advance our understanding.

We also believe that contemporary learning theory, perhaps integrated with related research on neurobiology, will continue to provide an essential framework for studying the development and maintenance of other anxiety and emotional disorders. Many of the processes described here in the context of PD are equally applicable to other anxiety and emotional disorders, although each has distinctive features (Barlow, 1988, in press; T. A. Brown et al., 1998; Mineka, 1985a; Mineka & Zinbarg, 1995, 1996, 1998). Although we have touched on evidence supporting the existence of both biological and psychological vulnerabilities, it is the etiological process that occurs in the context of these vulnerabilities on which we have focused most intently (i.e., what happens during and after the first panic attack). Finally, efforts at prevention, one ultimate goal of the study of psychopathology, will benefit from a greater understanding not only of etiological processes but also of the development of various vulnerabilities. Thus, we have attempted to point out how modern learning theory conceptualizes psychosocial vulnerabilities that, when combined with biological vulnerabilities, set the stage for the development of PD. In so doing, we have attempted to reflect the complexity of modern learning theory and of the psychopathology of PD as well as the enormous task, both theoretical and empirical, that remains before us before we fully understand the genesis of PD.

References

Akins, C. K., Domjan, M., & Gutierrez, G. (1994). Topography of sexually conditioned behavior in male Japanese quail (Coturnix japonica) depends on the CS-US interval. *Journal of Experimental Psychology: Animal Behavior Processes, 20*, 199–209.

American Psychiatric Association. (1994). *Diagnostic and statistical manual of mental disorders* (4th ed.). Washington, DC: Author.

Anderson. D. C., Crowell, C. R., DePaul, M., & McEachin, J. (1997). Intensification of punishment effects through exposure to prolonged, fixed-duration shocks: The role of shock cues as a stimulus for fear. *Animal Learning & Behavior, 25*, 68–83.

Baldwin, J. D., & Baldwin, J. I. (1998). *Behavior principles in everyday life* (3rd ed.). Englewood Cliffs, NJ: Prentice Hall.

Barlow, D. H. (1988). *Anxiety and its disorders: The nature and treatment of anxiety and panic.* New York: Guilford Press.

Barlow, D. H. (1991). The nature of anxiety: Anxiety, depression, and emotional disorders. In R. M. Rapee & D. H. Barlow (Eds.), *Chronic anxiety: Generalized anxiety disorder and mixed anxiety-depression* (pp. 1–28). New York: Guilford Press.

Barlow, D. H. (in press). *Anxiety and its disorders: The nature and treatment of anxiety and panic* (2nd ed.). New York: Guilford Press.

Barlow, D. H., Brown, T. A., & Craske, M. G. (1994). Definitions of panic attacks and panic disorder in the *DSM-IV:* Implications for research. *Journal of Abnormal Psychology, 103*, 553–564.

Barlow, D. H., Chorpita, B. F., & Turovsky, J. (1996). Fear, panic, anxiety, and disorders of emotion. In D. A. Hope (Ed.), *Perspectives on anxiety, panic, and fear* (The 43rd Annual Nebraska Symposium on Motivation) (pp. 251–328). Lincoln: Nebraska University Press.

Barlow, D. H., & Craske, M. G. (2000). *Mastery of your anxiety and panic: Client workbook for anxiety and panic (MAP-3).* San Antonio, TX: Graywind Publications.

Barlow, D. H., & Lehman, C. L. (1996). Advances in the psychosocial treatment of anxiety disorders: Implications for national health care. *Archives of General Psychiatry, 53*, 727–735.

Barrett, P. M., Rapee, R. M., Dadds, M. M., & Ryan, S. M. (1996). Family enhancement of cognitive style in anxious and aggressive children. *Journal of Abnormal Child Psychology, 24*, 187–203.

Basoglu, M., Marks, I., & Sengun, S. (1992). A prospective study of panic and anxiety in agoraphobia with panic disorder. *British Journal of Psychiatry, 160*, 57–64.

Bechara, A., Tranel, D., Damasio, H., Adolphs, R., Rockland, C., & Damasio, A. R. (1995). Double dissociation of conditioning and declarative knowledge relative to the amygdala and hippocampus in humans. *Science, 269*, 1115–1118.

Beck, A. T., & Emery, T. (1985). *Anxiety disorders and phobias.* New York: Basic Books.

Blanchard, D. C. (1997). Stimulus, environmental, and pharmacological control of defensive behaviors. In M. E. Bouton & M. S. Fanselow (Eds.), *Learning, motivation, and cognition: The functional behaviorism of Robert C. Bolles* (pp. 283–303). Washington, DC: American Psychological Association.

Blanchard, D. C., Blanchard, R. J., & Rodgers, R. J. (1991). Risk assessment and animal models of anxiety. In B. Olivier, J. Mos, & J. L. Slangen (Eds.), *Animal models in psychopharmacology* (pp. 117–134). Basel, Switzerland: Birkhäuser.

Blanchard, R. J., & Blanchard, D. C. (1969). Crouching as an index of fear. *Journal of Comparative & Physiological Psychology, 67*, 370–375.

Blanchard, R. J., & Blanchard, D. C. (1987). An ethoexperimental approach to the study of fear. *The Psychological Record, 37*, 305–316.

Bolles, R. C., & Fanselow, M. S. (1980). A perceptual-defensive-recuperative model of fear and pain. *Behavioral & Brain Sciences, 3*, 291–323.

Bombace, J. C., Brandon, S. E., & Wagner, A. R. (1991). Modulation of a conditioned eyeblink response by a putative emotive stimulus conditioned with hindleg shock. *Journal of Experimental Psychology: Animal Behavior Processes, 17*, 323–333.

Borkovec, T. D. (1994). The nature, functions, and origins of worry. In G. Davey & F. Tallis (Eds.), *Worrying: Perspectives on theory, assessment, and treatment* (pp. 5–35). Sussex, England: Wiley.

Bouton, M. E. (1984). Differential control by context in the inflation and reinstatement paradigms. *Journal of Experimental Psychology: Animal Behavior Processes, 10*, 56–74.

Bouton, M. E. (1988). Context and ambiguity in the extinction of emotional learning: Implications for exposure therapy. *Behaviour Research & Therapy, 26*, 137–149.

Bouton, M. E. (1991a). Context and retrieval in extinction and in other examples of interference in simple associative learning. In L. Dachowski & C. F. Flaherty (Eds.), *Current topics in animal learning: Brain, emotion, and cognition* (pp. 25–53). Hillsdale, NJ: Erlbaum.

Bouton, M. E. (1991b). A contextual analysis of fear extinction. In P. R.

Martin (Ed.), *Handbook of behavior therapy and psychological science: An integrative approach* (pp. 435–453). New York: Pergamon Press.

Bouton, M. E. (1993). Context, time, and memory retrieval in the interference paradigms of Pavlovian learning. *Psychological Bulletin, 114,* 80–99.

Bouton, M. E. (1994a). Conditioning, remembering, and forgetting. *Journal of Experimental Psychology: Animal Behavior Processes, 20,* 219–231.

Bouton, M. E. (1994b). Context, ambiguity, and classical conditioning. *Current Directions in Psychological Science, 3,* 49–53.

Bouton, M. E. (2000). A learning theory perspective on lapse, relapse, and the maintenance of behavior change. *Health Psychology, 19* (Suppl.), 57–63.

Bouton, M. E., & King, D. A. (1983). Contextual control of the extinction of conditioned fear: Tests for the associative value of the context. *Journal of Experimental Psychology: Animal Behavior Processes, 9,* 248–265.

Bouton, M. E., & King, D. A. (1986). Effect of context on performance to conditioned stimuli with mixed histories of reinforcement and nonreinforcement. *Journal of Experimental Psychology: Animal Behavior Processes, 12,* 4–15.

Bouton, M. E., & Nelson, J. B. (1998a). Mechanisms of feature-positive and feature-negative discrimination learning in an appetitive conditioning paradigm. In N. A. Schmajuk & P. C. Holland (Eds.), *Occasion setting: Associative learning and cognition in animals* (pp. 69–112). Washington, DC: American Psychological Association.

Bouton, M. E., & Nelson, J. B. (1998b). The role of context in classical conditioning: Some implications for cognitive behavior therapy. In W. T. O'Donohue (Ed.), *Learning and behavior therapy* (pp. 59–84). Boston: Allyn & Bacon.

Bouton, M. E., & Ricker, S. T. (1994). Renewal of extinguished responding in a second context. *Animal Learning & Behavior, 22,* 317–324.

Bouton, M. E., & Swartzentruber, D. (1986). Analysis of the associative and occasion-setting properties of contexts participating in a Pavlovian discrimination. *Journal of Experimental Psychology: Animal Behavior Processes, 12,* 333–350.

Bouton, M. E., & Swartzentruber, D. (1991). Sources of relapse after extinction in Pavlovian and instrumental learning. *Clinical Psychology Review, 11,* 123–140.

Brandon, S. E., Betts, S. L., & Wagner, A. R. (1994). Discriminated lateralized eyeblink conditioning in the rabbit: An experimental context for separating specific and general associative influences. *Journal of Experimental Psychology: Animal Behavior Processes, 20,* 292–307.

Brandon, S. E., Bombace, J. C., Falls, W. A., & Wagner, A. R. (1991). Modulation of unconditioned defensive reflexes by a putative emotive Pavlovian conditioned stimulus. *Journal of Experimental Psychology: Animal Behavior Processes, 17,* 312–322.

Brandon, S. E., & Wagner, A. R. (1991). Modulation of a discrete Pavlovian conditioned reflex by a putative emotive Pavlovian conditioned stimulus. *Journal of Experimental Psychology: Animal Behavior Processes, 17,* 299–311.

Breggin, P. R. (1964). The psychophysiology of anxiety with a review of the literature concerning adrenaline. *Journal of Nervous and Mental Disease, 139,* 558–568.

Bridger, W. H., & Mandel, I. J. (1964). A comparison of GSR fear responses produced by threat and electric shock. *Journal of Psychiatric Research, 2,* 31–40.

Brown, J. S., Kalish, H. I., & Farber, I. E. (1951). Conditioned fear as revealed by magnitude of startle response to an auditory stimulus. *Journal of Experimental Psychology, 41,* 317–327.

Brown, T. A., Chorpita, B. F., & Barlow, D. H. (1998). Structural relationships among dimensions of the *DSM-IV* anxiety and mood disorders and dimensions of negative affect, positive affect, and autonomic arousal. *Journal of Abnormal Psychology, 107,* 179–192.

Brush, F. R. (1985). Genetic determinants of avoidance learning: Mediation by emotionality? In F. R. Brush & J. B. Overmier (Eds.), *Affect, conditioning, and cognition: Essays on the determinants of behavior* (pp. 27–42). Hillsdale, NJ: Erlbaum.

Carter, M. M., & Barlow, D. H. (1995). Learned alarms: The origins of panic. In W. O'Donohue & L. Krasner (Eds.), *Theories of behavior therapy: Exploring behavior change* (pp. 209–228). New York: Guilford Press.

Carter, M. M., Hollon, S., Carson, R., & Shelton, R. (1995). Effects of a safe person on induced distress following a biological challenge in panic disorder with agoraphobia. *Journal of Abnormal Psychology, 104,* 156–163.

Cepeda-Benito, A., & Short, P. (1997). Morphine's interoceptive stimuli as cues for the development of associative morphine tolerance in the rat. *Psychobiology, 25,* 236–240.

Chambless, D., Caputo, G., Bright, P., & Gallagher, R. (1984). Assessment of fear of fear in agoraphobics: The Body Sensations Questionnaire and the Agoraphobic Cognitions Questionnaire. *Journal of Consulting and Clinical Psychology, 52,* 1090–1097.

Charney, D. S., Grillon, C., Bremner, J. D. (1998). The neurobiological basis of anxiety and fear: Circuits, mechanisms, and neurochemical interaction, part I. *The Neuroscientist, 4,* 35–44.

Chorazyna, H. (1962). Some properties of conditioned inhibition. *Acta Biologiae Experimentalis, 22,* 5–13.

Chorpita, B. F., & Barlow, D. H. (1998). The development of anxiety: The role of control in the early environment. *Psychological Bulletin, 124,* 3–21.

Chorpita, B. F., Brown, T., & Barlow, D. (1998). Perceived control as a mediator of family environment in etiological models of childhood anxiety. *Behavior Therapy, 29,* 457–476.

Clark, D. M. (1986). A cognitive approach to panic. *Behaviour Research and Therapy, 24,* 461–470.

Clark, D. M. (1988). A cognitive model of panic attacks. In S. Rachman & J. D. Maser (Eds.), *Panic: Psychological perspectives* (pp. 71–89). Hillside, NJ: Erlbaum.

Clark, D. M. (1996). Panic disorder: From theory to therapy. In P. M. Salkovskis (Ed.), *Frontiers of cognitive therapy* (pp. 318–344). New York: Guilford Press.

Clark, D. M., & Hemsley, D. (1982). The effects of hyperventilation: Individual variability and its relation to personality. *Journal of Behavior Therapy and Experimental Psychiatry, 13,* 41–47.

Clark, D. M., Salkovskis, P., & Anastasiades, P. (1990, November). Cognitive mediation of lactate induced panic. In R. Rapee (Chair), *Experimental investigations of panic disorder. Symposium at the Association for Advancement of Behavior Therapy.* San Francisco, CA.

Clark, D. M., Salkovskis, P. M., Gelder, M. G., Koehler, C., Martin, M., Anastasiades, P., Hackman, A., Middleton, H., & Jeavons, A. (1988). Tests of a cognitive theory of panic. In I. Hand & H. U. Wittchen (Eds.), *Panic and phobias II.* New York: Springer-Verlag.

Clark, D. M., Salkovskis, P. M., Hackmann, A., Middleton, H., Anastasiades, P., & Gelder, M. (1994). A comparison of cognitive therapy, applied relaxation and imipramine in the treatment of panic disorder. *British Journal of Psychiatry, 164,* 759–769.

Clark, L. A., & Watson, D. (1991). Tripartite model of anxiety and depression: Psychometric evidence and taxonomic implications. Special issue: Diagnoses, dimensions, and *DSM-IV*: The science of classification. *Journal of Abnormal Psychology, 100,* 316–336.

Clark, L. A., Watson, D., & Mineka, S. (1994). Temperament and personality in mood and anxiety disorders. *Journal of Abnormal Psychology, 103,* 103–116.

Clark, R. E., & Squire, L. R. (1998). Classical conditioning and brain systems: The role of awareness. *Science, 280,* 77–81.

Cohen, M. E., & White, P. D. (1947). Studies of breathing, pulmonary ventilation, and subjective awareness of shortness of breath (dyspnea) in neurocirculatory asthenia, effort syndrome, anxiety neurosis. *Journal of Clinical Investigation, 26,* 520.

Cohen, M. E., & White, P. D. (1950). Life situations, emotions, and neurocirculatory asthenia (anxiety neurosis, neurasthenia, effort syndrome). In H. G. Wolff (Ed.), *Life stress and bodily disease* (Nervous and Mental Disease, Research Publication No. 29). Baltimore, MD: Williams & Wilkins.

Colwill, R. M. (1994). Associative representations of instrumental contingencies. In D. L. Medin (Ed.), *The psychology of learning and motivation: Advances in research and theory,* (Vol. 31, pp. 1–72). San Diego, CA: Academic Press.

Colwill, R. M., & Motzkin, D. K. (1994). Encoding of the unconditioned stimulus in Pavlovian conditioning. *Animal Learning & Behavior, 22,* 384–394.

Colwill, R. M., & Rescorla, R. A. (1988). Associations between the discriminative stimulus and the reinforcer in instrumental learning. *Journal of Experimental Psychology: Animal Behavior Processes, 14,* 155–164.

Cook, E. W., Hawk, L. W., Davis, T. L., & Stevenson, V. E. (1991). Affective individual differences and startle reflex modulation. *Journal of Abnormal Psychology, 100,* 5–13.

Cook, E. W., Hodes, R. L., & Lang, P. J. (1986). Preparedness and phobia: Effects of stimulus content on human visceral conditioning. *Journal of Abnormal Psychology, 95,* 195–207.

Coplan, J. D., Andrews, M. W., Rosenblum, L. A., Owens, M. J., Friedman, S., Gorman, J. M., & Nemeroff, C. B. (1996). Persistent elevations of cerebrospinal fluid concentrations of corticotropin-releasing factor in adult nonhuman primates exposed to early-life stressors: Implications for the pathophysiology of mood and anxiety disorders. *Proceedings of the National Academy of Sciences, 93,* 1619–1623.

Craske, M. G. (1999). *Anxiety disorders: Psychological approaches to theory and treatment.* Boulder, CO: Westview Press.

Craske, M. G., Glover, D., & DeCola, J. (1995). Predicted versus unpredicted panic attacks: Acute versus general distress. *Journal of Abnormal Psychology, 104,* 214–223.

Craske, M. G., Miller, P. P., Rotunda, R., & Barlow, D. H. (1990). A descriptive report of features of initial unexpected panic attacks in minimal and extensive avoiders. *Behaviour Research & Therapy, 28,* 395–400.

Crowell, C. R. (1974). Conditioned-aversive aspects of electric shock. *Learning and Motivation, 5,* 209–220.

Cunningham, C. L. (1998). Drug conditioning and drug-seeking behavior. In W. T. O'Donohue (Ed.), *Learning and behavior therapy* (pp. 518–544). Boston: Allyn & Bacon.

Davey, G., de Jong, P., & Tallis, F. (1993). UCS inflation in the etiology of a variety of anxiety disorders: Some case histories. *Behaviour Research and Therapy, 31,* 495–498.

Davis, M. (1992). The role of the amygdala in conditioned fear. In J. P. Aggleton (Ed.), *The amygdala: Neurobiological aspects of emotion, memory, and mental dysfunction* (pp. 255–305). New York: Wiley-Liss.

Davis, M., Walker, D. L., & Yee, Y. (1997). Amygdala and bed nucleus of the stria terminalis: Differential roles in fear and anxiety measured with the acoustic startle reflex. In L. Squire & D. Schacter (Eds.), *Biological and psychological perspectives on memory and memory disorders.* Washington, DC: American Psychiatric Association.

Delamater, A. R. (1996). Effects of several extinction treatments upon the integrity of Pavlovian stimulus-outcome associations. *Animal Learning & Behavior, 24,* 437–449.

Dimberg, U. (1987). Facial reactions, autonomic activity, and experienced emotion: A three-component model of emotional conditioning. *Biological Psychology, 24,* 105–122.

Domjan, M. (1994). Formulation of a behavior system for sexual conditioning. *Psychonomic Bulletin & Review, 1,* 421–428.

Domjan, M. (1997). Behavior systems and the demise of equipotentiality:

Historical antecedents and evidence from sexual conditioning. In M. E. Bouton & M. S. Fanselow (Eds.), *Learning, motivation, and cognition: The functional behaviorism of Robert C. Bolles* (pp. 31–51). Washington, DC: American Psychological Association.

Domjan, M. (1998). *The principles of learning and behavior* (4th ed.). Pacific Grove, CA: Brooks/Cole.

Domjan, M., Huber-McDonald, M., & Holloway, K. S. (1992). Conditioning copulatory behavior to an artificial object: Efficacy of stimulus fading. *Animal Learning & Behavior, 20,* 350–362.

Dworkin, B. R. (1993). *Learning and physiological regulation.* Chicago: University of Chicago Press.

Ehlers, A. (1993). Somatic symptoms and panic attacks: A retrospective study of learning experiences. *Behaviour Research and Therapy, 31,* 269–278.

Ehlers, A. (1995). A 1-year prospective study of panic attacks: Clinical course and factors associated with maintenance. *Journal of Abnormal Psychology, 104,* 164–172.

Ehlers, A., & Breuer, P. (1992). Increased cardiac awareness in panic disorder. *Journal of Abnormal Psychology, 101,* 371–382.

Ehlers, A., & Breuer, P. (1996). How good are patients with panic disorder at perceiving their heartbeats? *Biological Psychology, 42,* 165–182.

Ehlers, A., Margraf, J., & Chambless, D. (1992). *Fragebögen zu körperbezogenen Ängsten, Kognitionen and Vermeidung.* Weinheim: Beltz.

Ehlers, A., Margraf, J., Roth, W. T., Taylor, C. B., & Birbaumer, N. (1988). Anxiety induced by false heart rate feedback in patients with panic disorder. *Behaviour Research and Therapy, 26,* 1–11.

Eich, E. (1995). Searching for mood dependent memory. *Psychological Science, 6,* 67–75.

Eikelboom, R., & Stewart, J. (1982). Conditioning of drug-induced physiological responses. *Psychological Review, 89,* 507–528.

Eysenck, H. J. (Ed.). (1960). *Behavior therapy and the neuroses.* Oxford, England: Pergamon Press.

Eysenck, H. J. (1967). *The biological basis of personality.* Springfield, IL: Charles C Thomas.

Eysenck, H. J. (1979). The conditioning model of neurosis. *Behavioral and Brain Sciences, 2,* 155–199.

Eysenck, H. J., & Rachman, S. (1965). *The causes and cures of neurosis.* London: Routledge & Kegan Paul.

Fanselow, M. S. (1980). Conditional and unconditional components of postshock freezing. *Pavlovian Journal of Biological Science, 15,* 177–182.

Fanselow, M. S. (1989). The adaptive function of conditioned defensive behavior: An ecological approach to Pavlovian stimulus-substitution theory. In R. J. Blanchard, P. F. Brain, D. C. Blanchard, & S. Parmigiani (Eds.), *Ethoexperimental approaches to the study of behavior* (pp. 151–166). Dordrecht, the Netherlands: Kluwer Academic.

Fanselow, M. S. (1994). Neural organization of the defensive behavior system responsible for fear. *Psychonomic Bulletin & Review, 1,* 429–438.

Fanselow, M. S., & Lester, L. S. (1988). A functional behavioristic approach to aversively motivated behavior: Predatory imminence as a determinant of the topography of defensive behavior. In R. C. Bolles & M. D. Beecher (Eds.), *Evolution and learning* (pp. 185–212). Hillsdale, NJ: Erlbaum.

Feingold, A. (1994). Gender differences in personality: A meta-analysis. *Psychological Bulletin, 116,* 429–456.

Forsyth, J. P., & Eifert, G. H. (1996). Systemic alarms in fear conditioning I: A reappraisal of what is being conditioned. *Behavior Therapy, 27,* 441–462.

Forsyth, J. P., & Eifert, G. H. (1998). Response intensity in content-specific fear conditioning comparing 20% versus 13% CO-sub-2-enriched air as unconditioned stimuli. *Journal of Abnormal Psychology, 107,* 291–304.

Forsyth, J. P., Eifert, G. H., & Thompson, R. N. (1996). Systemic alarms in fear conditioning: II. An experimental methodology using 20% carbon dioxide inhalation as an unconditioned stimulus. *Behavior Therapy, 27,* 391–415.

Gallup, G. G., Jr., & Maser, J. D. (1977). Tonic immobility: Evolutionary underpinnings of human catalepsy and catatonia. In J. D. Maser & M. E. P. Seligman (Eds.), *Psychopathology: Experimental models* (pp. 334–357). San Francisco: Freeman.

Goddard, M. J. (1996). Effect of US signal value on blocking of a CS-US association. *Journal of Experimental Psychology: Animal Behavior Processes, 22,* 258–264.

Goddard, M. J. (1997). Spontaneous recovery in US extinction. *Learning & Motivation, 28,* 118–128.

Goddard, M. J. (1999). The role of US signal value in contingency, drug conditioning, and learned helplessness. *Psychonomic Bulletin & Review, 6,* 412–423.

Goddard, M. J., & Jenkins, H. M. (1988). Blocking of a CS-US association by a US-US association. *Journal of Experimental Psychology: Animal Behavior Processes, 14,* 177–186.

Goldstein, A. J., & Chambless, D. L. (1978). A reanalysis of agoraphobia. *Behavior Therapy, 9,* 47–59.

Gray, J. A., & McNaughton, N. (1996). The neuropsychology of anxiety: Reprise. In D. A. Hope (Ed.), *Perspectives on anxiety, panic, and fear* (The 43rd Annual Nebraska Symposium on Motivation) (pp. 61–134). Lincoln: Nebraska University Press.

Greeley, J., Lê, D. A., Poulos, C. X., & Cappell, H. (1984). Alcohol is an effective cue in the conditional control of tolerance to alcohol. *Psychopharmacology, 83,* 159–162.

Grillon, C., Ameli, R., Goddard, A., Woods, S. W., & Davis, M. (1994). Baseline and fear-potentiated startle in panic disorder patients. *Biological Psychiatry, 35,* 431–439.

Grillon, C., Ameli, R., Woods, S. W., Merikangas, K., & Davis, M. (1991). Fear-potentiated startle in humans: Effects of anticipatory anxiety on the acoustic blink reflex. *Psychophysiology, 28,* 588–595.

Grings, W. W., Schell, A. M., & Carey, C. A. (1973). Verbal control of an autonomic response in a cue reversal situation. *Journal of Experimental Psychology, 99,* 215–221.

Hall, G., & Honey, R. C. (1989). Contextual effects in conditioning, latent inhibition, and habituation: Associative and retrieval functions of contextual cues. *Journal of Experimental Psychology: Animal Behavior Processes, 15,* 232–241.

Hamm, A. O., & Vaitl, D. (1996). Affective learning: Awareness and aversion. *Psychophysiology, 33,* 698–710.

Hannum, R., Rosellini, R., & Seligman, M. (1976). Retention of learned helplessness and immunization in the rat from weaning to adulthood. *Developmental Psychology, 12,* 449–454.

Hayward, C., Killen, J. D., Kraemer, H. C., & Taylor, C. B. (2000). Predictors of panic attacks in adolescence. *Journal of the American Academy of Child and Adolescent Psychiatry, 39,* 207–214.

Heim, C., & Nemeroff, C. B. (1999). The impact of early adverse experiences on brain systems involved in the pathophysiology of anxiety and affective disorders. *Biological Psychiatry, 46,* 1509–1522.

Heller, W., Nitschke, J. B., Etienne, M. A., & Miller, G. A. (1997). Patterns of regional brain activity differentiate types of anxiety. *Journal of Abnormal Psychology, 106,* 376–385.

Hendersen, R. W. (1975). Compounds of conditioned fear stimuli. *Learning & Motivation, 6,* 28–42.

Hendersen, R. W. (1985). Fearful memories: The motivational significance of forgetting. In F. R. Brush & J. B. Overmier (Eds.), *Affect, conditioning and cognition: Essays on the determinants of behavior* (pp. 43–52). Hillsdale, NJ: Erlbaum.

Hirsch, S. M., & Bolles, R. C. (1980). On the ability of prey to recognize predators. *Zeitschrift Fuer Tierpsychologie, 54,* 71–84.

Hoehn-Saric, R., McLeod, D. R., & Zimmerli, W. D. (1989). Somatic manifestations in women with generalized anxiety disorder: Psycho-

physiological responses to psychological stress. *Archives of General Psychiatry, 46,* 1113–1119.

Holland, P. C. (1977). Conditioned stimulus as a determinant of the form of the Pavlovian conditioned response. *Journal of Experimental Psychology: Animal Behavior Processes, 3,* 77–104.

Holland, P. C. (1989). Feature extinction enhances transfer of occasion setting. *Animal Learning & Behavior, 17,* 269–279.

Holland, P. C. (1992). Occasion setting in Pavlovian conditioning. In G. Bower (Ed.), *The psychology of learning and motivation* (Vol. 28, pp. 69–125). Orlando, FL: Academic Press.

Hollis, K. L. (1982). Pavlovian conditioning of signal-centered action patterns and autonomic behavior: A biological analysis of function. *Advances in the Study of Behavior, 12,* 131–142.

Hollis, K. L. (1997). Contemporary research on Pavlovian conditioning: A "new" functional analysis. *American Psychologist, 52,* 956–965.

Joffe, J., Rawson, R., & Mulick, J. (1973). Control of their environment reduces emotionality in rats. *Science, 180,* 1383–1384.

Joiner, T. E., Jr., Steer, R. A., Beck, A. T., Schmidt, N. B., Rudd, M. D., & Catanzaro, S. J. (1999). Physiological hyperarousal: Construct validity of a central aspect of the tripartite model of depression and anxiety. *Journal of Abnormal Psychology, 108,* 290–298.

Kapp, B. S., Whalen, P. J., Supple, W. F., Jr., & Pascoe, J. P. (1992). Amygdaloid contributions to conditioned arousal and sensory information processing. In J. P. Aggleton (Ed.), *The amygdala: Neurobiological aspects of emotion, memory, and mental dysfunction* (pp. 229–254). New York: Wiley.

Kenardy, J., Fried, L., Kraemer, H. C., & Taylor, C. B. (1992). Psychological precursors of panic attacks. *British Journal of Psychiatry, 160,* 668–673.

Kenardy, J., & Taylor, C. B. (1999). Expected versus unexpected panic attacks: A naturalistic prospective study. *Journal of Anxiety Disorders, 13,* 435–445.

Kendler, K. S., Kessler, R. C., Walters, E. D., MacLean, C., Neale, M. C., Heath, A. C., & Eaves, L. J. (1995). Stressful life events, genetic liability, and onset of an episode of major depression in women. *American Journal of Psychiatry, 152,* 833–842.

Kendler, K. S., Neale, M., Kessler, R., Heath, A., & Eaves, L. (1992). The genetic epidemiology of phobias in women: The interrelationship of agoraphobia, social phobia, situational phobia, and simple phobia. *Archives of General Psychiatry, 49,* 273–281.

Kendler, K. S., Walters, E. E., Neale, M. C., Kessler, R. C., Heath, A. C., & Eaves, L. J. (1995). The structure of the genetic and environmental risk factors for six major psychiatric disorders in women: Phobia, generalized anxiety disorder, panic disorder, bulimia, major depression, and alcoholism. *Archives of General Psychiatry, 52,* 374–382.

Kessler, R. C., McGonagle, K. A., Zhao, S., Nelson, C. B., Hughes, M., Eshleman, S., Wittchen, H.-U., & Kendler, K. S. (1994). Lifetime and 12-month prevalence of DSM-III-R psychiatric disorders in the United States: Results from the National Comorbidity Survey. *Archives of General Psychiatry, 51,* 8–19.

Kim, J. A., Siegel, S., & Patenall, V. R. A. (1999). Drug-onset cues as signals: Intra-administration associations and tolerance. *Journal of Experimental Psychology: Animal Behavior Processes, 25,* 491–504.

King, N. J., Gullone, E., Tonge, B. J., & Ollendick, T. H. (1993). Self-reports of panic attacks and manifest anxiety in adolescents. *Behaviour Research and Therapy, 31,* 111–116.

Klein, D. F. (1981). Anxiety reconceptualized. In D. F. Klein & J. Rabkin (Eds.), *Anxiety: New research and changing concepts* (pp. 235–264). New York: Raven Press.

Konorski, J. (1967). *Integrative activity of the brain.* Chicago: University of Chicago Press.

Kruse, J. M., Overmier, J. B., Konz, W. A., & Rokke, E. (1983). Pavlovian conditioned stimulus effects upon instrumental choice behavior are reinforcer specific. *Learning and Motivation, 14,* 165–181.

Kushner, M. G., & Beitman, B. D. (1990). Panic attacks without fear: An overview. *Behaviour Research and Therapy, 28,* 469–479.

Ladd, C. O., Huot, R. L., Thrivikraman, K. V., Nemeroff, C. B., Meaney, M. J., & Plotsky, P. M. (2000). Long-term behavioral and neuroendocrine adaptations to adverse early experience. In E. A. Mayer & C. B. Saper (Eds.), *Progress in brain research: The biological basis for mind body interactions* (Vol. 122, pp. 81–103). Amsterdam: Elsevier.

Lang, P. J. (1994). The varieties of emotional experience: A meditation on James-Lange theory. *Psychological Review, 101,* 211–221.

Lang, P. J. (1995). The emotion probe: Studies of motivation and attention. *American Psychologist, 50,* 372–385.

Lang, P. J., Bradley, M. M., & Cuthbert, B. N. (1990). Emotion, attention, and the startle reflex. *Psychological Review, 97,* 377–395.

Lang, P. J., Davis, M., & Öhman, A. (2000). Fear and anxiety: Animal models and human cognitive psychophysiology. *Journal of Affective Disorders, 61,* 137–159.

Last, C. G., O'Brien, G. T., & Barlow, D. H. (1985). The relationship between cognitions and anxiety. *Behavior Modification, 9,* 235–241.

LeDoux, J. E. (1996). *The emotional brain: The mysterious underpinnings of emotional life.* New York: Simon & Schuster.

Leventhal, H. (1982). The integration of emotion and cognition: A view from the perceptual-motor theory of emotion. In M. Clark & S. Fiske (Eds.), *Affect and Cognition: The 17th Annual Carnegie Symposium on Cognition.* Hilldale, NJ: Erlbaum.

Leventhal, H., Brown, D., Shacham, S., & Engquist, G. (1979). Effects of preparatory information about sensations, threat of pain, and attention on cold pressor distress. *Journal of Personality and Social Psychology, 37,* 688–714.

Levey, A., & Martin, I. (1981). Personality and conditioning. In H. Eysenck (Ed.), *A model for personality* (pp. 123–168). Berlin: Springer-Verlag.

Levy, E. (1998). *Learning experiences and vulnerability to panic disorder: Possible origins of high anxiety sensitivity and acquisition of catastrophic misinterpretation of sensations.* Unpublished doctoral dissertation, Northwestern University.

Liebowitz, M. R., Fyer, A. J., Gorman, J. M., Dillon, D., Appleby, I. L., Levy, G., Anderson, S., Levitt, M., Palij, M., Davies. S. O., & Klein, D. F. (1984). Lactate provocation of panic. *Archives of General Psychiatry, 41,* 764–770.

Liebowitz, M. R., Gorman, J. M., Fyer, A. J., Levitt, M., Dillon, D., Levy, G., Appleby, I. L., Anderson, S., Palij, M., Davies, S. O., & Klein, D. F. (1985). Lactate provocation of panic attacks: II. Biochemical and physiological findings. *Archives of General Psychiatry, 42,* 709–719.

Lindemann, E., & Finesinger, J. E. (1938). The effect of adrenaline and mecholyl in states of anxiety in psychoneurotic patients. *American Journal of Psychiatry, 95,* 353–370.

Lovibond, P. F. (1993). Conditioning and cognitive-behaviour therapy. *Behaviour Change, 10,* 119–130.

Lovibond, P. F., Preston, G. C., & Mackintosh, N. J. (1984). Context specificity of conditioning, extinction, and latent inhibition. *Journal of Experimental Psychology: Animal Behavior Processes, 10,* 360–375.

Mackintosh, N. J. (1974). *The psychology of animal learning.* San Diego, CA: Academic Press.

Mackintosh, N. J. (1975). A theory of attention: Variations in the associability of stimuli with reinforcement. *Psychological Review, 82,* 276–298.

Maier, S. F. (1990). Role of fear in mediating shuttle escape learning deficit produced by inescapable shock. *Journal of Experimental Psychology: Animal Behavior Processes, 16,* 137–149.

Maier, S. F., & Seligman, M. E. P. (1976). Learned helplessness: Theory and evidence. *Journal of Experimental Psychology: General, 105,* 3–46.

Margraf, J., Ehlers, A., & Roth, W. T. (1986). Sodium lactate infusions and panic attacks: A review and critique. *Psychosomatic Medicine, 48,* 23–51.

Margraf, J., & Schneider, S. (1995, July). *Psychological treatment of panic: What works in the long run?* Paper presented at the World Congress of Behavioural and Cognitive Therapies, Copenhagen, Denmark.

Marks, I. (1969). *Fears and phobias.* London: Heineman Medical Books.

Maser, J. D., & Gallup, G. G. (1974). Tonic immobility in the chicken: Catalepsy potentiation by uncontrollable shock and alleviation by imipramine. *Psychosomatic Medicine, 36,* 199–205.

McGuffin, P., & Reich, T. (1984). Psychopathology and genetics. In H. Adams & P. Sutker (Eds.), *Comprehensive handbook of psychopathology.* New York: Plenum.

McNally, R. J. (1990). Psychological approaches to panic disorder: A review. *Psychological Bulletin, 108,* 403–419.

McNally, R. J. (1994). *Panic disorder: A critical analysis.* New York: Guilford Press.

McNally, R. J. (1999). Theoretical approaches to the fear of anxiety. In S. Taylor (Ed.), *Anxiety sensitivity: Theory, research, and treatment of the fear of anxiety.* Hillsdale, NJ: Erlbaum.

McNally, R. J., & Eke, M. (1996). Anxiety sensitivity, suffocation fear, and breath-holding duration as predictors of response to carbon dioxide challenge. *Journal of Abnormal Psychology, 105,* 146–149.

McNaughton, N., & Gray, J. A. (in press). Anxiolytic action on the behavioural inhibition system implies multiple types of arousal contribute to anxiety. *Journal of Affective Disorders.*

McNish, K. A., Betts, S. L., Brandon, S. E., & Wagner, A. R. (1997). Divergence of conditioned eyeblink and conditioned fear in backward Pavlovian training. *Animal Learning & Behavior, 25,* 43–52.

Menzies, R., & Clarke, J. (1995). The etiology of phobias: A nonassociative account. *Clinical Psychology Review, 15,* 23–48.

Merckelbach, H., de Ruiter, C., van den Hout, M., & Hoekstra, R. (1989). Conditioning experiences and phobias. *Behaviour Research and Therapy, 27,* 657–662.

Mineka, S. (1985a). Animal models of anxiety-based disorders: Their usefulness and limitations. In A. H. Tuma & J. Maser (Eds.), *Anxiety and the anxiety disorders* (pp. 199–244). Hillsdale, NJ: Erlbaum.

Mineka, S. (1985b). The frightful complexity of the origins of fears. In F. R. Brush & J. B. Overmier (Eds.), *Affect, conditioning, and cognition: Essays on the determinants of behavior* (pp. 55–73). Hillsdale, NJ: Erlbaum.

Mineka, S., & Cook, M. (1993). Mechanisms underlying observational conditioning of fear in monkeys. *Journal of Experimental Psychology: General, 122,* 23–38.

Mineka, S., Cook, M., & Miller, S. (1984). Fear conditioned with escapable and inescapable shock: Effects of a feedback stimulus. *Journal of Experimental Psychology: Animal Behavior Processes, 10,* 307–323.

Mineka, S., Gunnar, M., & Champoux, M. (1986). Control and early socioemotional development: Infant rhesus monkeys reared in controllable versus uncontrollable environments. *Child Development, 57,* 1241–1256.

Mineka, S., & Hendersen, R. (1985). Controllability and predictability in acquired motivation. *Annual Review of Psychology, 36,* 495–530.

Mineka, S., & Kelly, K. (1989). The relationship between anxiety, lack of control, and loss of control. In A. Steptoe (Ed.), *Stress, personal control and health* (pp. 163–191). New York: Wiley.

Mineka, S., & Kihlstrom, J. F. (1978). Unpredictable and uncontrollable events: A new perspective on experimental neurosis. *Journal of Abnormal Psychology, 87,* 256–271.

Mineka, S., Mystkowski, J., Hladek, D., & Rodriguez, B. (1999). The effects of context on return of fear following successful exposure treatment for spider phobia. *Journal of Consulting and Clinical Psychology, 67,* 599–604.

Mineka, S., Watson, D., & Clark, L. A. (1998). Comorbidity of anxiety and unipolar mood disorders. *Annual Review of Psychology, 49,* 377–412.

Mineka, S., & Zinbarg, R. (1991). Animal models of psychopathology. In

C. E. Walker (Ed.), *Clinical psychology: Historical and research foundations* (pp. 51–86). New York: Plenum.

Mineka, S., & Zinbarg, R. (1995). Conditioning and ethological models of social phobia. In R. Heimberg, M. Liebowitz, D. Hope, & F. Schneier (Eds.), *Social phobia: Diagnosis, assessment and treatment* (pp. 1134–1162). New York: Guilford Press.

Mineka, S., & Zinbarg, R. (1996). Conditioning and ethological models of anxiety disorders: Stress-in-dynamic-context anxiety models. In D. A. Hope (Ed.), *Perspectives on anxiety, panic, and fear. Nebraska Symposium on Motivation* (Vol. 43, pp. 135–210). Lincoln: Nebraska University Press.

Mineka, S., & Zinbarg, R. (1998). Experimental approaches to understanding the mood and anxiety disorders. In J. Adair (Ed.), *Advances in psychological research, volume 2* (pp. 429–454). Hove, England: Psychology Press.

Minor, T., Dess, N., & Overmier, J. B. (1991). Inverting the traditional view of "learned helplessness." In R. Denny (Ed.), *Fear, avoidance, and phobias* (pp. 87–133). Hillsdale, NJ: Erlbaum.

Monroe, S. M., & Simons, A. E. (1991). Diathesis-stress theories in the context of life stress research: Implications for the depressive disorders. *Psychological Bulletin, 110,* 406–425.

Morgan, C. A., Grillon, C., Southwick, S. M., Davis, M., & Charney, D. (1995). Fear-potentiated startle in posttraumatic stress disorder. *Biological Psychiatry, 36,* 378–385.

Mowrer, O. H. (1947). On the dual nature of learning—A re-interpretation of "conditioning" and "problem-solving." *Harvard Educational Review, 17,* 102–148.

Mowrer, O. H. (1960). *Learning theory and behavior.* New York: Wiley.

Mowrer, O. H., & Viek, P. (1948). An experimental analogue of fear from a sense of helplessness. *Journal of Abnormal Social Psychology, 83,* 193–200.

Norton, G. R., Cox, B. J., & Malan, J. (1992). Nonclinical panickers: A critical review. *Clinical Psychology Review, 12,* 121–139.

Norton, G. R., Dorward, J., & Cox, B. J. (1986). Factors associated with panic attack in non-clinical subjects. *Behavior Therapy, 17,* 239–252.

Öhman, A. (1996). Preferential pre-attentive processing of threat in anxiety: Preparedness and attentional biases. In R. Rapee (Ed.), *Current controversies in the anxiety disorders* (pp. 253–290). New York: Guilford Press.

Öhman, A. (1997). Unconscious pre-attentive mechanisms in the activation of phobic fear. In G. C. L. Davey (Ed.), *Phobias: A handbook of theory, research, and treatment* (pp. 349–374). Chichester: Wiley.

Öhman, A., Flykt, A., & Lundqvist, D. (2000). Unconscious emotion: Evolutionary perspectives, psychophysiology and neuropsychological mechanisms. In R. Lane & L. Nadel (Eds.), *The cognitive neuroscience of emotion* (pp. 296–327). New York: Oxford University Press.

Öhman, A., & Mineka, S. (2001). Revisiting preparedness: Toward an evolved module of fear learning. *Psychological Review.* Manuscript submitted for publication.

Öst, L.-G., & Hugdahl, K. (1981). Acquisition of phobias and anxiety response patterns in clinical patients. *Behaviour Research and Therapy, 19,* 439–447.

Öst, L.-G., & Hugdahl, K. (1983). Acquisition of agoraphobia, mode of onset, and anxiety response patterns. *Behaviour Research and Therapy, 19,* 439–447.

Overmier, J. B. (1985). Toward a reanalysis of the causal structure of the learned helplessness syndrome. In F. R. Brush & J. B. Overmier (Eds.), *Affect, conditioning, and cognition: Essays on the determinants of behavior* (pp. 211–227). Hillsdale, NJ: Erlbaum.

Overmier, J. B., & Lawry, J. A. (1979). Pavlovian conditioning and the mediation of behavior. In G. H. Bower (Ed.), *The psychology of learning and motivation* (Vol. 13, pp. 1–55). New York: Academic Press.

Parker, G. (1983). *Parental overprotection: A risk factor in psychosocial development.* New York: Grune & Stratton.

Pavlov, I. P. (1927). *Conditioned reflexes.* London: Oxford University Press.

Pearce, J. M., Aydin, A., & Redhead, E. S. (1997). Configural analysis of summation in autoshaping. *Journal of Experimental Psychology: Animal Behavior Processes, 23,* 84–94.

Pearce, J. M., & Hall, G. (1980). A model for Pavlovian learning: Variations in the effectiveness of conditioned but not of unconditioned stimuli. *Psychological Review, 87,* 532–552.

Peterson, C., Maier, S. F., & Seligman, M. E. P. (1993). *Learned helplessness: A theory for the age of personal control.* New York: Oxford University Press.

Plomin, R., DeFries, J., McClearn, G., & Rutter, M. (1997). *Behavioral genetics, third edition.* New York: Freeman.

Powley, T. L. (1977). The ventromedial hypothalamic syndrome, satiety, and a cephalic phase hypothesis. *Psychological Review, 84,* 89–126.

Rachman, S. (1977). The conditioning theory of fear-acquisition: A critical examination. *Behaviour Research and Therapy, 15,* 375–387.

Rachman, S. (1990). *Fear and courage.* New York: Freeman.

Rachman, S. (1991). Neo-conditioning and the classical theory of fear acquisition. *Clinical Psychological Review, 11,* 155–173.

Rachman, S., Lopatka, C., & Levitt, K. (1988). Experimental Analyses of panic: II. Panic patients. *Behaviour Research and Therapy, 26,* 33–40.

Rachman, S. J., & Maser, J. (1988). *Panic and cognition.* Hillsdale, NJ: Erlbaum.

Ramsay, D. S., & Woods, S. C. (1997). Biological consequences of drug administration: Implications for acute and chronic tolerance. *Psychological Review, 104,* 170–193.

Rapee, R., Mattick, R., & Murrell, E. (1986). Cognitive mediation in the affective component of spontaneous panic attacks. *Journal of Behavior Therapy and Experimental Psychiatry, 17,* 245–253.

Razran, G. (1961). The observable unconscious and the inferable conscious in current Soviet psychophysiology: Interoceptive conditioning, semantic conditioning, and the orienting reflex. *Psychological Review, 58,* 81–147.

Reberg, D. (1972). Compound tests for excitation in early acquisition and after prolonged extinction of conditioned suppression. *Learning & Motivation, 3,* 246–258.

Reiss, S. (1987). Theoretical perspectives on the fear of anxiety. *Clinical Psychology Review, 7,* 585–596.

Reiss, S. (1991). Expectancy model of fear, anxiety, and panic. *Clinical Psychology Review, 11,* 141–153.

Reiss, S., Peterson, R. A., Gursky, D. M., & McNally, R. J. (1986). Anxiety sensitivity, anxiety frequency, and the prediction of fearfulness. *Behaviour Research and Therapy, 24,* 1–8.

Rescorla, R. A. (1974). Effect of inflation of the unconditioned stimulus value following conditioning. *Journal of Comparative and Physiological Psychology, 86,* 101–106.

Rescorla, R. A. (1985). Conditioned inhibition and facilitation. In R. R. Miller & N. E. Spear (Eds.), *Information processing in animals: Conditioned inhibition* (pp. 299–326). Hillsdale, NJ: Erlbaum.

Rescorla, R. A. (1986). Extinction of facilitation. *Journal of Experimental Psychology: Animal Behavior Processes, 12,* 16–24.

Rescorla, R. A. (1990). Extinction can be enhanced by a concurrent excitor. *Journal of Experimental Psychology: Animal Behavior Processes, 25,* 251–260.

Rescorla, R. A., & Coldwell, S. E. (1995). Summation in autoshaping. *Animal Learning & Behavior, 23,* 314–326.

Rescorla, R. A., & Furrow, D. R. (1977). Stimulus similarity as a determinant of Pavlovian conditioning. *Journal of Experimental Psychology: Animal Behavior Processes, 3,* 203–215.

Rescorla, R. A., & Gillan, D. J. (1980). An analysis of the facilitative effect of similarity on second-order conditioning. *Journal of Experimental Psychology: Animal Behavior Processes, 6,* 339–351.

Rescorla, R. A., & Holland, P. C. (1977). Associations in Pavlovian conditioned inhibition. *Learning & Motivation, 8,* 429–447.

Rescorla, R. A., & Solomon, R. L. (1967). Two-process learning theory: Relationships between Pavlovian conditioning and instrumental learning. *Psychological Review, 74,* 151–182.

Rescorla, R. A., & Wagner, A. R. (1972). A theory of Pavlovian conditioning: Variations in the effectiveness of reinforcement and nonreinforcement. In A. H. Black & W. F. Prokasy (Eds.), *Classical conditioning: II. Current research and theory* (pp. 64–99). New York: Appleton-Century-Crofts.

Rosen, J. B., & Schulkin, J. (1998). From normal fear to pathological anxiety. *Psychological Review, 105,* 325–350.

Salkovskis, P. M. (1988). Phenomenology, assessment, and the cognitive model of panic. In S. M. J. D. Rachman (Ed.), *Panic: Psychological perspectives* (pp. 111–136). Hillsdale, NJ: Erlbaum.

Salkovskis, P. M., Clark, D. M., & Gelder, M. G. (1996). Cognition-behaviour links in the persistence of panic. *Behaviour Research & Therapy, 34,* 453–458.

Sanderson, W., Rapee, R., & Barlow, D. (1989). The influence of an illusion of control on panic attacks induced via inhalation of 5.5% carbon dioxide-enriched air. *Archives of General Psychiatry, 46,* 157–162.

Schmajuk, N. A., & Holland, P. C. (Eds.). (1998). *Occasion setting: Associative learning and cognition in animals.* Washington, DC: American Psychological Association.

Schmidt, N. B., Lerew, D. R., & Jackson, R. J. (1997). The role of anxiety sensitivity in the pathogenesis of panic: Projective evaluation of spontaneous panic attacks during acute stress. *Journal of Abnormal Psychology, 106,* 355–364.

Schmidt, N. B., Lerew, D. R., Jackson, R. J. (1999). Prospective evaluation of anxiety sensitivity in the pathogenesis of panic: Replication and extension. *Journal of Abnormal Psychology, 108,* 532–537.

Schneewind, K. (1995). Impact of family processes on control beliefs. In A. Bandura (Ed.), *Self-efficacy in changing societies* (pp. 114–148). New York: Cambridge Press.

Seligman, M. E. P. (1988). Competing theories of panic. In S. Rachman & J. D. Maser (Eds.), *Panic: Psychological perspectives* (pp. 321–329). Hillsdale, NJ: Erlbaum.

Seligman, M. E. P., & Binik, Y. (1977). The safety signal hypothesis. In H. Davis & H. M. B. Hurwitz (Eds.), *Operant-Pavlovian interactions* (pp. 165–188). Hillsdale, NJ: Erlbaum.

Seligman, M. E. P., Maier, S., & Solomon, R. (1971). Unpredictable and uncontrollable aversive events. In F. Brush (Ed.), *Aversive conditioning and learning* (pp. 347–400). New York: Academic Press.

Sheehan, D. (1983). *The anxiety disease.* New York: Bantam Books.

Siegel, S. (1975). Evidence from rats that morphine tolerance is a learned response. *Journal of Comparative and Physiological Psychology, 89,* 498–506.

Siegel, S. (1988). State dependent learning and morphine tolerance. *Behavioral Neuroscience, 102,* 228–232.

Siegel, S. (1989). Pharmacological conditioning and drug effects. In A. J. Goudie & M. W. Emmett-Oglesby (Eds.), *Psychoactive drugs: Tolerance and sensitization* (pp. 115–180). Clifton, NJ: Humana Press.

Silva, F. J., Timberlake, W., & Koehler, T. L. (1996). A behavior systems approach to bidirectional excitatory serial conditioning. *Learning and Motivation, 27,* 130–150.

Solomon, R. L., Kamin, L. J., & Wynne, L. C. (1953). Traumatic avoidance learning: The outcomes of several extinction procedures with dogs. *Journal of Abnormal and Social Psychology, 48,* 291–302.

Soltysik, S. S. (1960). Studies on avoidance conditioning: III. Alimentary conditioned reflex model of the avoidance reflex. *Acta Biologiae Experimentalis, 20,* 183–191.

Soltysik, S. S., Wolfe, G. E., Nicholas, T., Wilson, W. J., & Garcia-Sanchez, L. (1983). Blocking of inhibitory conditioning within a serial conditioned stimulus-conditioned inhibitor compound: Maintenance of acquired behavior without an unconditioned stimulus. *Learning & Motivation, 14,* 1–29.

Spence, J. T., & Spence, K. (1966). The motivational components of manifest anxiety: Drive and drive stimuli. In C. Spielberger (Ed.), *Anxiety and behavior* (pp. 291–326.) New York: Academic Press.

Stegen, K., De Bruyne, K., Rasschaert, W., Van de Woestijne, K., & Van den Bergh, O. (1999). Fear-relevant images as conditioned stimuli for somatic complaints, respiratory behavior, and reduced end-tidal pCO_2. *Journal of Abnormal Psychology, 108,* 143–152.

Swartzentruber, D. (1995). Modulatory mechanisms in Pavlovian conditioning. *Animal Learning & Behavior, 23,* 123–143.

Taylor, S., & Rachman, S. (1994). Klein's suffocation theory of panic. *Archives of General Psychiatry, 51,* 505–506.

Teasdale, J. (1988). Cognitive models and treatments for panic. A critical evaluation. In S. Rachman & J. D. Maser (Eds.), *Panic: Psychological perspectives* (pp. 189–203). Hillsdale, NJ: Erlbaum.

Telch, M. J. (1995, July). *Singular and combined efficacy of in vivo exposure and CBT in the treatment of panic disorder with agoraphobia.* Paper presented at the World Congress of Behavioural and Cognitive Therapies, Copenhagen, Denmark.

Telch, M. J., Brouillard, M., Telch, C. F., Agras, W. S., & Taylor, C. B. (1989). Role of cognitive appraisal in panic related avoidance. *Behaviour Research and Therapy, 27,* 373–383.

Tellegen, A. (1985). Structure of mood and personality and their relevance to assessing anxiety, with an emphasis on self-report. In A. H. Tuma & J. D. Maser (Eds.), *Anxiety and the anxiety disorders* (pp. 681–706). Hillsdale, NJ: Erlbaum.

Testa, T. J. (1975). Effects of similarity of location and temporal intensity pattern of conditioned and unconditioned stimuli on the acquisition of conditioned suppression in rats. *Journal of Experimental Psychology: Animal Behavior Processes, 1,* 114–121.

Thorn, G. R., Chosak, A., Baker, S. L., & Barlow, D. H. (1999). Psychological theories of panic disorder. In D. J. Nutt, J. C. Ballenger, & J.-P. Lepine (Eds.), *Panic disorder: Clinical diagnosis, management, and mechanisms* (pp. 93–108). London: Martin Dunitz.

Thyer, B., & Himle, J. (1985). Temporal relationships between panic attack onset and phobic avoidance in agoraphobia. *Behaviour Research and Therapy, 23,* 607–608.

Timberlake, W. (1994). Behavior systems, associationism, and Pavlovian conditioning. *Psychonomic Bulletin & Review, 1,* 405–420.

Timberlake, W., & Grant, D. L. (1975). Auto-shaping in rats to the presentation of another rat predicting food. *Science, 190,* 690–692.

Timberlake, W., & Silva, K. M. (1995). Appetitive behavior in ethology, psychology, and behavioral systems. In N. S. Thompson (Ed.), *Perspectives in ethology* (Vol. 11, pp. 211–253). New York: Plenum.

Timberlake, W., Wahl, G., & King, D. (1982). Stimulus and response contingencies in the misbehavior of rats. *Journal of Experimental Psychology: Animal Behavior Processes, 8,* 62–85.

Tolman, E. C. (1932). *Purposive behavior in animals and men.* New York: Century.

Trapold, M. A., & Overmier, J. B. (1972). The second learning process in instrumental learning. In A. H. Black & W. F. Prokasy (Eds.), *Classical conditioning. II: Current research and theory* (pp. 427–452). New York: Appleton-Century-Crofts.

Tuma, A. H., & Maser, J. D. (Eds.). (1985). *Anxiety and the anxiety disorders.* Hillsdale, NJ: Erlbaum.

Turkat, I. (1982). An investigation of parental modeling in the etiology of diabetic illness behavior. *Behaviour Research and Therapy, 20,* 547–552.

Tweed, D. L., Schoenbach, V. J., George, L. K., & Blazer, D. G. (1989).

The effects of childhood parental death and divorce on six-month history of anxiety disorders. *British Journal of Psychiatry, 154,* 823–828.

Uhde, T., Boulenger, J., Roy-Byrne, P., Geraci, M., Vittone, B., & Post, R. (1985). Longitudinal course of panic disorder: Clinical and biological considerations. *Progressive-Neuro-psychopharmacology & Biological Psychiatry, 9,* 39–51.

Van den Hout, M. A. (1988). The explanation of experimental panic. In S. Rachman & J. D. Maser (Eds.), *Panic: Psychological perspectives.* Hillsdale, NJ: Erlbaum.

Van Houten, R., O'Leary, K. D., & Weiss, S. J. (1970). Summation of conditioned suppression. *Journal of the Experimental Analysis of Behavior, 13,* 75–81.

VanDercar, D. H., & Schneiderman, N. (1967). Interstimulus interval functions in different response systems during classical discrimination conditioning of rabbits. *Psychonomic Science, 9,* 9–10.

Wagner, A. R. (1969). Stimulus selection and a modified continuity theory. In G. H. Bower & J. T. Spence (Eds.), *The psychology of learning and motivation* (Vol. 36, pp. 1–41). New York: Academic Press.

Wagner, A. R. (1976). Priming in STM: An information-processing mechanism for self-generated or retrieval-generated depression in performance. In T. R. Tighe & R. N. Leaton (Eds.), *Habituation: Perspectives from child development, animal behavior, and neurophysiology* (pp. 95–128). Hillsdale, NJ: Erlbaum.

Wagner, A. R. (1981). SOP: A model of automatic memory processing in animal behavior. In N. E. Spear & R. R. Miller (Eds.), *Information processing in animals: Memory mechanisms* (pp. 5–47). Hillsdale, NJ: Erlbaum.

Wagner, A. R., & Brandon, S. E. (1989). Evolution of a structured connectionist model of Pavlovian conditioning (AESOP). In S. B. Klein & R. R. Mowrer (Eds.), *Contemporary learning theories: Pavlovian conditioning and the status of traditional learning theory* (pp. 149–189). Hillsdale, NJ: Erlbaum.

Watson, D., & Clark, L. A. (1984). Negative affectivity: The disposition to experience negative emotional states. *Psychological Bulletin, 96,* 465–490.

Watson, J. B., & Rayner, R. (1920). Conditioned emotional reactions. *Journal of Experimental Child Psychology, 3,* 1–14.

Weiss, J. (1971). Effects of coping behavior in different warning-signal conditions on stress pathology in rats. *Journal of Comparative and Physiological Psychology, 77,* 1–13.

Weiss, S. J., & Emurian, H. H. (1970). Stimulus control during the summation of conditioned suppression. *Journal of Experimental Psychology, 85,* 204–209.

White, T. L., & Depue, R. A. (1999). Differential association of traits of

fear and anxiety with norepinephrine- and dark-induced pupil reactivity. *Journal of Personality and Social Psychology, 77*(4), 863–877.

Whitehead, W. W., Bush, C., Heller, B., & Costa, P. (1986). Social learning influences of menstrual symptoms and illness behavior. *Health Psychology, 5,* 13–23.

Whitehead, W. W., Winget, C., Fedoravicius, A., Wooley, S., & Blackwell, B. (1982). Learned illness behavior in patients with irritable bowel syndrome and peptic ulcer. *Digestive Diseases and Science, 27,* 202–208.

Williams, J., & Maier, S. (1977). Transituational immunization and therapy of learned helplessness in the rat. *Journal of Experimental Psychology: Animal Behavior Processes, 3,* 240–252.

Williams, S. L., Kinney, P. H., Harap, S. T., & Liebmann, M. (1997). Thoughts of agoraphobic people during scary tasks. *Journal of Abnormal Psychology, 106,* 511–520.

Wittchen, H. U., & Essau, C. A. (1991). The epidemiology of panic attacks, panic disorder and agoraphobia. In J. R. Walker, G. R. Norton, & C. A. Ross (Eds.), *Panic disorder and agoraphobia* (pp. 103–149). Monterey, CA: Brooks/Cole.

Wolpe, J., & Rowan, V. C. (1988). Panic disorder: A product of classical conditioning. *Behaviour Research and Therapy, 26,* 441–450.

Woods, S. C., & Strubbe, J. H. (1994). The psychobiology of meals. *Psychonomic Bulletin & Review, 1,* 141–155.

Zinbarg, R. E., Barlow, D. H., Liebowitz, M., Street, L., Broadhead, E., Katon, W., Roy-Byrne, P., Lepine, J. P., Teherani, M., Richard, J., Brantley, P. J., & Kraemer, H. (1994). The *DSM-IV* field trial for mixed-anxiety depression. *The American Journal of Psychiatry, 151,* 1153–1162.

Zinbarg, R., Brown, T., Barlow, D., & Rapee, R. (in press). Fear responses to hyperventilation and 5.5% carbon dioxide enriched air and anxiety sensitivity: A reanalysis of Rapee, Brown, Antony, & Barlow (1992). *Journal of Abnormal Psychology.*

Zinbarg, R., & Mohlman, J. (1998). Individual differences in the acquisition of affectively valenced associations. *Journal of Personality and Social Psychology, 74,* 1024–1040.

Zucker, D., Taylor, C. B., Brouillard, M., Ehlers, A., Margraf, J., Telch, M., Roth, W. T., & Agras, W. S. (1989). Cognitive aspects of panic attacks: Content, course, and relationship to laboratory stressors. *British Journal of Psychiatry, 155,* 86–91.

Received May 17, 1999
Revision received April 10, 2000
Accepted April 11, 2000 ■

Neuron, Vol. 20, 947–957, May, 1998, Copyright ©1998 by Cell Press

Brain Systems Mediating Aversive Conditioning: an Event-Related fMRI Study

Christian Büchel,*‡ Jond Morris,*
Raymond J. Dolan,*† and Karl J. Friston*
*The Wellcome Department of Cognitive Neurology
Institute of Neurology
12 Queen Square
London WC1N 3BG
†The Royal Free Hospital School of Medicine
Rowland Street
London NW3 2PF
United Kingdom

Summary

We have used event-related functional magnetic resonance imaging (fMRI) to characterize neural responses associated with emotional learning. Employing a classical conditioning paradigm in which faces were conditioned by pairing with an aversive tone (US), we compared responses evoked by conditioned (CS+) and nonconditioned (CS−) stimuli. Pairing 50% of the CS+ with the US enabled us to constrain our analysis to responses evoked by a CS+ not followed by a US. Differential evoked responses, related to conditioning, were found in the anterior cingulate and the anterior insula, regions with known involvement in emotional processing. Differential responses of the amygdalae were best characterized by a time by stimulus interaction indicating a rapid adaptation of CS+-specific responses in this region.

Introduction

In classical conditioning paradigms, a previously neutral stimulus (conditioned stimulus or CS) comes to elicit a behavioral response through temporal pairing with an unconditioned stimulus (US). In many paradigms, the US is aversive and the behavioral response is measured in terms of changes in skin conductance (skin conductance response [SCR] or galvanic skin response [GSR]), pupil diameter, or some other measure such as freezing behavior (LeDoux, 1996). Hence, classical conditioning is a form of associative learning involving linkage between a neutral stimulus and a stimulus with high intrinsic behavioral significance.

Classical conditioning embodies elements of memory and emotional processing, a fact reflected by the associated functional anatomy. Lesion studies suggest a critical role for medial temporal lobe structures, especially the amygdala, in the acquisition of conditioned emotional responses (LaBar and LeDoux, 1996). For example, lesions restricted to bilateral amygdalae impair the acquisition of conditioned autonomic responses but leave declarative knowledge of stimulus contingencies intact. The opposite dissociation has been reported in association with bilateral hippocampal damage (Bechara et al., 1995).

‡ To whom correspondence should be addressed.

In classical conditioning, the close temporal proximity of US and CS pairings is essential. To achieve selective conditioning of some stimuli but not others, the intertrial interval (ITI) between neutral and conditioned stimuli has to be long compared to the time between CS and US. Several functional neuroimaging studies have investigated human classical conditioning (Fredrikson et al., 1995; Schreurs et al., 1997). Positron emission tomography (PET) functional neuroimaging (Morris et al., 1997) has implicated an extended system including the pulvinar, medial thalamic nuclei, and amygdala in aversive classical conditioning of emotionally expressive faces. Notably, functional imaging studies, using PET and functional magnetic resonance imaging (fMRI), employ blocked designs, in which subjects undergo an initial conditioning block by presenting the CS *with* the US and the effect is then assessed in a (test) second block by presenting the CS *alone* (Morris et al., 1997). Unfortunately, this procedure is confounded by the fact that during the test block, when the CS is always presented alone, there may also be an extinction component where the associated functional neuroanatomy may differ from that of conditioning per se (Rolls et al., 1994).

The optimal prerequisites for studying the neurobiology of classical conditioning in humans, using functional neuroimaging, are met by event-related (mixed/single trial) fMRI technique (Buckner et al., 1996; Dale and Buckner, 1997; Josephs et al., 1997). This novel technique resembles that used to record event-related potentials in electrophysiology, where different stimuli are presented repeatedly over time. Recent methodological advances (Josephs et al., 1997) have enabled us to study evoked hemodynamic responses for the whole brain to conditioned and neutral stimuli in a manner compatible with mixed trial classical conditioning paradigms. In this study, we used a partial reinforcement strategy in which one half of the CS+ presentations were paired with the US (CS+_paired) and the other half were not paired (CS+_unpaired), to compare evoked hemodynamic responses elicited by the CS+ in the absence of the US.

Results

We chose four neutral faces, two male and two female, taken from the Ekman series (Ekman, 1982). Faces were presented for 3 s. Subjects were scanned during two distinct phases: in an initial familiarization phase, all four faces were presented in randomized order (52 faces were presented over 10 min), and in a second conditioning phase, two (one male, one female) of the four faces were paired with an unpleasant tone (1 kHz) and consequently became CS+. The amplitude of the tone was adjusted to 10% above each subject's aversive threshold (~100 dB; estimated by self report during gradient switching). The 500 ms tone followed at the end of the 3 s presentation time of the face (Figure 1). Faces presented during the first and second phases of the experiment were identical.

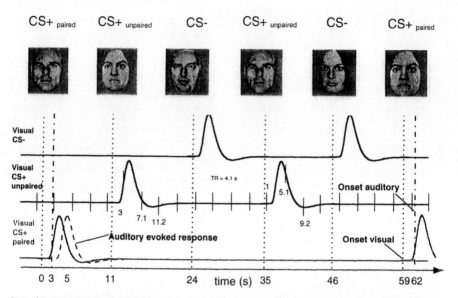

Figure 1. Illustration of the Experimental Design

The top row shows the four images used in the experiment. Two faces (first and second) were conditioned with an aversive tone. According to a 50% partial reinforcement, only one-half of the presentations were followed by the tone (e.g., first and last [CS+$_{paired}$] versus second and fourth [CS+$_{unpaired}$] presentation). Dotted and dash-dotted vertical lines indicate the onset of the visual and auditory stimuli, respectively. The three plots below the images show the modeled hemodynamic responses. Responses are time-locked to the onset of the face stimuli (CS−, CS+$_{unpaired}$, and CS+$_{paired}$). The dashed response in the last row is an example for a hypothetical auditory evoked response. Note the overlap in time of hemodynamic responses for the paired CS+ and the auditory response. The timescale indicates that the ITI was randomized to introduce a phase shift between sampling and stimulus onset (see Experimental Procedures for details). Thin vertical lines in the second row demonstrate the relation between the acquisition of fMRI volumes and the presentation of stimuli.

Skin Conductance Responses

The SCR time series confirmed that subjects acquired conditioned autonomic responses to the conditioned stimuli. Figure 2 (top) shows an example of the time course of the skin conductance signal for two subjects during MR scanning over a 100 s period. Statistical analysis was performed separately for data generated during scanning and for data of the remaining four subjects acquired in a separate study session. We found a significant difference between SCR for CS− compared to CS+ trials for both analyses (Figure 2, bottom). This demonstrates that subjects were successfully conditioned during the fMRI experiment. As with our fMRI analysis, we analyzed only CS+ that were not paired with the US.

We employed a 50% partial reinforcement strategy to assess the evoked hemodynamic response to the CS+ in the absence of the US (tone); that is, only half of the presentations of the two CS+ were paired with the tone (CS+$_{paired}$). In total, we presented 104 stimuli over ~20 min. 52 were neutral stimuli, 26 were CS+ paired with noise (CS+$_{paired}$) and 26 were CS+ not paired (CS+$_{unpaired}$) with noise. Figure 1 (top) gives an example of the scanning procedure. Using two CS+ and two CS− allowed a more balanced presentation of CS−, CS+$_{paired}$, and CS+$_{unpaired}$ in the context of the 50% partial reinforcement employed.

In contrast to evoked responses in electrophysiology, the sampling rate (i.e., TR) in event-related fMRI is restricted. To characterize hemodynamic responses following an indexed stimulus, it is necessary to sample data points after the onset of many stimuli at different peri-stimulus time points. This can be achieved by the introduction of a fixed or random jitter between ITI and TR. In this experiment, we chose a random jitter, to ensure an equal distribution of data points after each event type. The ITI was randomized in the range of 3 ± 0.5 TR, leading to ITIs that ranged between 10.25 and 14.35 s. The example in Figure 1 (second row) illustrates the relationship between fMRI volume acquisition and trials: image volumes were acquired continuously. For example, scans took place 3, 7.1, and 11.2 s after the first CS+$_{unpaired}$ stimulus onset. After the second CS+$_{unpaired}$ trial, volumes were acquired 1, 5.1, and 9.2 s after the onset of the stimulus.

Functional Neuroimaging
Visual and Auditory Evoked
Hemodynamic Responses

A first analysis addressed that event-related fMRI, with a TR of 4.1 s, is capable of detecting evoked responses elicited by sensory stimulation (i.e., visual and auditory).

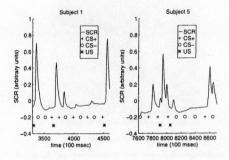

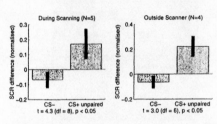

Figure 2. Skin Conductance Responses Are Shown for Two Subjects

The top graphs show the processed SCR (see text) for the presentation of face stimuli used in the experiment. Plus signs indicate the onset of a CS+ stimulus. Circles indicate the onset of a CS− stimulus. Asterisks indicate the onset of the aversive tone (US), following 50% of CS+. The two bottom graphs show the statistical analysis of the SCR. The left graph demonstrates the difference and the significance of that difference for SCR data acquired during scanning. Normalized differences between a baseline and the SCR response for CS+$_{unpaired}$ and CS− are plotted with their standard errors of the mean (SEM). The right graph shows the same analysis for SCR data recorded with the identical paradigm but outside the MR scanner. The difference between CS− and CS+$_{unpaired}$ is similar for both groups, indicating that subjects were reliably conditioned during the acquisition of fMRI volumes.

We compared hemodynamic responses evoked by visual face stimuli pooled over all categories (CS+$_{paired}$, CS+$_{unpaired}$, and CS−) to baseline. Activated areas were confined to bilateral striate (axial slice in Figure 3A) and extrastriate cortices. Visual evoked responses in right primary visual cortex are plotted for two of the six subjects (Figure 3A).

The second part of the analysis compared auditory evoked responses to baseline. This comparison, comprising only 26 auditory stimuli per subject, showed significant (p < 0.05, corrected) activations of primary auditory cortex and subcortical auditory structures. Figure 3B shows the activation of primary auditory cortex and the associated evoked hemodynamic responses in left primary auditory cortex for two subjects.

Comparison of CS+$_{unpaired}$ to CS− Stimuli during Conditioning

In a CS+$_{paired}$ trial, the peak of the visual evoked response occurred *after* delivery of the auditory stimulus (first

event in the third row in Figure 1). This can give rise to interaction effects in regions that respond to both the US and the CS+. To fully disambiguate the effects of CS+ and US, we compared only responses evoked by the conditioned face stimuli when they were *not* followed by a tone (CS+$_{unpaired}$). Consequently, the critical comparison in this experiment was that between the CS+$_{unpaired}$ visually evoked responses and those evoked by the CS− during conditioning. This comparison revealed differential activation of bilateral anterior cingulate gyri, bilateral anterior insulae, and medial parietal cortex. Further differential responses were detected in the supplementary motor area (SMA) and bilateral premotor cortices. Activation in the right (Z = 4.6) and left red nucleus (Z = 3.6) did not reach a significance criterion of p < 0.05 corrected, though it nevertheless achieved an uncorrected significance level at p < 0.001. We report these results for descriptive purposes in view of the bilaterality of the activations and their previously reported involvement in conditioning (Desmond and Moore, 1991; Thompson and Krupa, 1994). Coordinates and significance levels of activations are summarized in Table 1. Figure 4A shows the location of the left anterior cingulate activation overlaid on the template T1 MRI used for spatial normalization. This coronal slice also shows activation in bilateral insulae. In Figure 4, the peri-stimulus responses are plotted for three of the nine subjects. To best characterize the data, we plotted the responses evoked by the CS− (blue ± standard error), the response evoked by the CS+$_{unpaired}$ (red ± standard error), and the difference between the two (green). Figure 4B shows activation of bilateral insulae together with the right red nucleus and individual plots of the associated peri-stimulus responses for the left anterior insula.

Rapid habituation of amygdala responses in the context of classical conditioning has been demonstrated in animal studies (Quirk et al., 1997) and human imaging (Breiter et al., 1996; Whalen et al., 1998). Such temporal effects would be disguised in a simple categorical comparison of the CS+$_{unpaired}$ and CS−. We therefore explicitly tested for the presence of a time by event type interaction in an additional analysis. This analysis tests for areas in which neural responses evoked by CS+$_{unpaired}$ decrease over time, and at the same time this pattern is significantly different from the pattern for the responses evoked by the CS−. In effect, this analysis shows voxels with a differential adaptation for the CS+$_{unpaired}$ relative to the CS−.

In this group analysis, amygdala activations were significant bilaterally at p < 0.05 (left Z = 4.6 and right Z = 3.2, p values corrected for the volume of interest and smoothness of the underlying statistical parametric map [SPM; Worsley et al., 1996]). The exact coordinates and statistics of amygdalae activations are given in Table 1.

Figure 5 shows significant voxels for this group analysis of the left amygdala on a coronal section of the T1 MRI template that was used for spatial normalization. The right amygdala response is more posterior and does not show on this selected slice. The top panels show the fitted response for the CS+$_{unpaired}$ trials. These data for two subjects indicate that amygdala responses to CS+$_{unpaired}$ show a rapid habituation. The associated statistics indicate the significance of the difference of this interaction in comparison to the CS− responses.

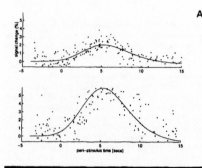
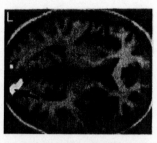

A

V1, p<0.05 corrected

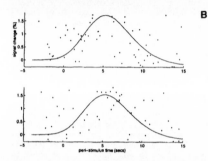
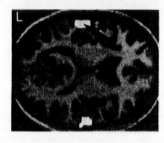

B

A1, p<0.05 corrected

Figure 3. Visual and Auditory Event-Related Hemodynamic Responses

(A) Visual evoked hemodynamic responses following the presentation of faces for a subgroup of six subjects. Activations in right primary visual cortex are shown overlaid on an axial slice of the template MRI used for spatial normalization. On the left, the fitted response and adjusted data are plotted as a function of peri-stimulus time for the most significant voxel in right primary visual cortex for two subjects. Activations are thresholded at p < 0.05 (corrected).

(B) Auditory evoked hemodynamic responses due to the presentation of an unpleasant 1 kHz tone for a subgroup of six subjects. Activation of primary auditory cortices are overlaid on the normalization template. On the left, the fitted response and adjusted data are plotted as a function of peri-stimulus time for the most significant voxel in the left primary auditory cortex for two subjects. Activations are thresholded at p < 0.05 (corrected).

We further investigated whether this temporally limited amygdala response is reflected in our behavioral SCR data. SCR for the first 8 and last 12 min of the conditioning phase were analyzed separately and contrasted. Figure 5D shows the differences of SCR for CS− and CS+$_{unpaired}$ for the early and late part of the conditioning phase, similar to Figure 2. The significant interaction (t[18] = 2.5, p < 0.05) indicates a relationship between lateral amygdala activation and behavioral measurements.

Comparison of CS+ and CS− Stimuli
before Conditioning

We assessed systematic effects related to the faces themselves by comparing responses elicited by the two conditioned and two neutral faces during the familiarization (preconditioning) phase, *before* any conditioning took place. This analysis confirmed that regions showing a significant activation for the CS+$_{unpaired}$ relative to the CS− in the conditioning phase showed

tested the robustness of our principal findings by performing an interaction analysis, looking for differences between CS+$_{unpaired}$ and CS− in the familiarization relative to the conditioning phase. Although Z scores were in general smaller (as expected for interactions), this analysis confirmed the conditioning-specific effects reported above. We also tested for significant differences in amygdala adaptation (i.e., time by event interaction) between the conditioning phase and the familiarization phase, again looking explicitly for a difference between the familiarization and conditioning phases. This was again significant (p < 0.001, uncorrected). It should be emphasized that comparing activations during the conditioning relative to the familiarization phase (i.e., interaction) is only a supplementary analysis and could be confounded by temporal order effects. The more important comparison is between CS+$_{unpaired}$ and CS− presented within the same trial. Furthermore, systematic

Table 1. Coordinates and Magnitudes of Main Activations

Coordinates	Z	p value	Coordinates	Z	p value
Anterior cingulate left			right		
−3, 15, 33	6.3	<0.05*	6, 30, 42	6.6	<0.05*
Red nucleus left			right		
−6, −9, −6	3.6	<0.001	9, −21, −12	4.6	= 0.08*
Anterior insula left			right		
−33, 27, −12	8.0	<0.05*	51, 24, −9	8.0	<0.05*
Medial parietal			right		
			15, −66, 36	5.6	<0.05*
Premotor left			right		
−39, 3, 54	4.6	= 0.08*	48, 12, 39	5.2	<0.05*
SMA			right		
			6, 6, 54	5.9	<0.05*
Time by condition interaction					
Amygdala left			right		
−24, 3, −24	4.6	<0.05**	27, −3, −24	3.2	<0.05**

Differential activations comparing visual evoked responses for conditioned stimuli in the absence of an unconditioned stimulus (CS+$_{unpaired}$) and CS−. Coordinates are in mm according to Talairach and Tournoux (1988) and are based on spatial normalization to a template provided by the Montreal Neurological Institute (Evans et al., 1994).
* p value corrected for entire brain volume.
** p value corrected for volume of interest.

Discussion

In this study, we used event-related whole brain fMRI. This required a TR of 4.1 s and meant that we could only sample two to three time points per stimulus. We were, nevertheless, able to demonstrate sensory evoked responses in the visual and auditory system. Furthermore, we were able to demonstrate differential hemodynamic responses elicited by conditioned and neutral stimuli divorced from confounding effects of an associated aversive stimulus. These differences must reflect learning the association between a neutral stimulus and an aversive tone. The purely sensory characteristics of the stimuli themselves evoked identical responses in a familiarization phase. Activations revealed by comparing CS+$_{unpaired}$ against CS− within the same session are unlikely to reflect factors such as motivation. Although this might confound blocked designs, in the context of mixed trials as employed here motivation should affect all event types equally.

Anterior Cingulate

Bilateral, significant differentially evoked hemodynamic responses were found in the anterior cingulate cortex. This structure plays a crucial role in assessing the motivational content of internal and external stimuli and in regulating context-dependent behaviors (Devinsky et al., 1995) such as approach and avoidance learning (Freeman et al., 1996). Direct evidence for the participation of the anterior cingulate in classical conditioning comes from animal (Powell et al., 1996; Everitt and Robbins, 1997) and human (Schreurs et al., 1997) functional imaging studies. The latter study described positive correlations between changes in regional cerebral blood flow (rCBF) and percent conditioned responses. Cingulo-thalamic neuronal plasticity may be crucial for the acquisition of avoidance responses in the context of conditioning, and it has been suggested that amygdala projections play an important role in the modulation of these plastic changes (Poremba and Gabriel, 1997a, 1997b).

The affective role of the anterior cingulate has been dissociated from any perceptual stimulus-processing role (Rainville et al., 1997). This latter experiment demonstrated that rCBF in the anterior cingulate is linearly correlated to the affective intensity of mediated pain. A similar response behavior of the anterior cingulate is suggested by our results: the presentation of the unpaired CS+ is not painful, but it has, through conditioning, become a predictor of pain (i.e., the expected ensuing unpleasant tone). In contrast to the study by Rainville et al. (1997), where hypnosis was used to downregulate pain affect, our experiment can be construed as effecting the reverse, namely, an upregulation of pain anticipation leading to a neural response in the absence of physical pain (for the CS+$_{unpaired}$).

This similarity of systems differentially activated in our experiment to those implicated in pain processing is remarkable. The activation of anterior insulae with anterior cingulate cortices is a prominent feature in most functional imaging studies of pain (Coghill et al., 1994; Rainville et al., 1997). It has been suggested that the anterior cingulate cortex together with the anterior insula provides one route through which nociceptive input is integrated with memory to allow appropriate responses to stimuli that predict future adversities (Coghill et al., 1994). This linkage of nociception with memory receives further support from our results. Activation of the red

203

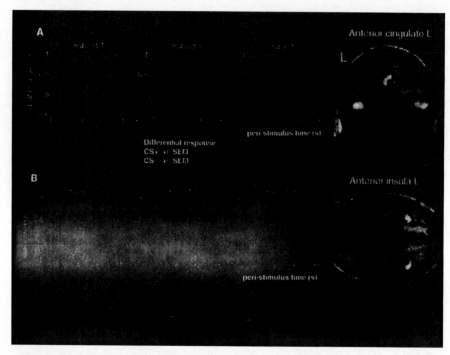

Figure 4. Neural Responses during Conditioning

(A) Significant differential visual evoked responses for conditioned versus neutral faces in the left anterior cingulate cortex (x = −3, y = 15, z = 33 mm). The coronal slice of the template T1 weighted MRI used for normalization shows differential responses in bilateral anterior insulae and right anterior cingulate. Images are thresholded at p < 0.001 uncorrected for visualization. The significances for individual activations are given in Table 1. The peri-stimulus time plots are shown for three out of nine subjects. Instead of plotting raw data, we show the fitted response ± the standard error of the mean (SEM) for CS− (blue) and CS+ unpaired (red) events. Dash-dotted lines represent the fitted response; dotted lines represent the mean ± SEM. Statistical inference is based on the difference between the two responses, shown in green.

(B) Significant differential visual evoked responses for conditioned versus neutral faces in the left anterior insula (x = −33, y = 27, z = −12). The axial slice of a mean T1 weighted group MRI also shows differential responses in the right red nucleus and right anterior insula. Peri-stimulus time plots are shown for three out of nine subjects. Fitted responses ± the standard error of the mean (SEM) for the CS− (blue) and CS+ unpaired (red) events are shown. Statistical inference is based on the difference between the two responses, shown in green.

nuclei in this regard suggests that projections from the cingulate, which assimilate the value of a stimulus, interact with an efferent motor system as a means of regulating context-dependent behaviors.

Anterior Insula

Several studies suggest a role for the anterior insula in processing emotionally relevant contexts, for instance, disgust (Phillips et al., 1997), pain (Casey et al., 1995), and the recollection of affect-laden autobiographical information (Fink et al., 1996). This functional characterization is in keeping with known insular projections to anterior cingulate, perirhinal, entorhinal, and periamygdaloid cortices and various amygdaloid nuclei (Mesulam and Mufson, 1982). This pattern of connectivity, together with neurophysiological data, has led to a conceptualization of the insula as an area functionally associated

with emotional processing (Casey et al., 1995; Augustine, 1996). In our study, the insula may provide information about primary reinforcers received from the sensory system (Rolls, 1994).

Amygdala

The initial analysis comparing CS+ unpaired with CS− over the entire conditioning phase did not reveal amygdala activation. However, based on recent evidence from an electrophysiological study showing habituation of amygdala single cell responses *during* conditioning in the rat (Quirk et al., 1997), we performed a further analysis to explicitly test for habituation (time by event type interaction) of amygdala responses. In line with Quirk et al. (1997), the a priori hypothesis for this analysis was restricted to the amygdala. Correction for multiple comparisons in this analysis was based on the size of the

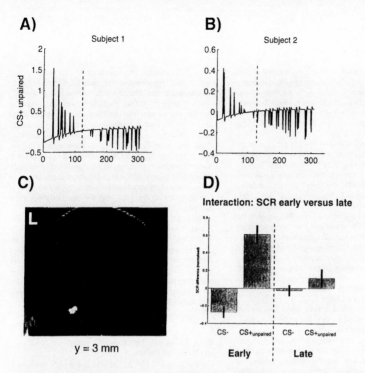

A)

Subject 1

CS+ unpaired

B)

Subject 2

C)

L

y = 3 mm

D)

Interaction: SCR early versus late

SCR difference (normalised)

CS- CS+unpaired CS- CS+unpaired

Early | Late

Figure 5. Time-Dependent Neural Responses in the Amygdala with Conditioning

Rapid habituation of amygdala responses to CS+unpaired stimuli. (A) and (B) show the fitted response for the CS+unpaired events for two subjects in left amygdala. Responses evoked by CS+unpaired stimuli are initially positive and then decrease to become deactivations (relative to baseline) after 120 scans (8.2 min) for subject 1 and after 100 scans (6.8 min) for subject 2. (C) shows the activation of the left amygdala (Z = 4.6) overlaid on a template T1 MRI. Statistical inference is based on the difference between the time by condition interaction shown in (A) and (B) relative to responses evoked by CS− stimuli. (D) shows differences in SCR responses comparing the first 8 min to the last 12 min of the conditioning phase. The difference between SCR elicited by CS+unpaired versus CS− is clearly larger for the first 8 min of the experiment. This interaction is significant (t[18] = 2.5, p < 0.05). The vertical dashed lines in (A) and (B) indicate the cutoff between early and late (117 volumes = 8 min) used for the SCR interaction analysis shown in (D).

amygdala as used by others (Breiter et al., 1996; Whalen et al., 1998). This anatomical constraint is justified on the grounds that ignoring this a priori evidence could lead to type II errors (Worsley et al., 1996).

In this additional analysis, the focus of maximal activation in the amygdala was seen in its rostrolateral part. Comparison of this location with response foci in other fMRI studies (Breiter et al., 1996; Whalen et al., 1998) reveals a difference in the z coordinate values (ventral–dorsal). Amygdala coordinates from these studies project into the striatum when using the template from the Montreal Neurological Institute as in our analysis. Therefore, we conclude that this difference is most likely due to differences in spatial normalization, for example, a different template. The activation of the lateral amygdala in classical conditioning is in accord with reciprocal projections between the medial geniculate nucleus and this

part of the amygdala (LeDoux et al., 1990b). Furthermore, the lateral amygdala is strongly implicated in classical conditioning as shown by single cell recordings (Quirk et al., 1997) and lesion experiments (LeDoux et al., 1990a) in rats.

Amygdala responses to CS+unpaired stimuli showed rapid habituation. This accords with results from other neuroimaging studies showing rapid habituation of amygdala responses in the context of viewing emotionally expressive faces (Breiter et al., 1996; Whalen et al., 1998). Our results extend these observations to human classical conditioning and are in accord with animal data of amygdala responses to acoustic stimuli (Bordi and LeDoux, 1992; Bordi et al., 1993) and lateral amygdala responses in classical conditioning in the rat (Quirk et al., 1997). The transient response characteristic further suggests an important role for the amygdala during the early phase of aversive conditioning, consistent with the suggestion that the amygdala serves as a rapid subcortical information processing pathway for behaviorally relevant (e.g., dangerous) stimuli (LeDoux, 1996). This early versus late dissociation, initially suggested for the hippocampus (Alvarez and Squire, 1994), may also apply to the amygdala.

Lesion studies have stressed the importance of the amygdala in acquisition and expression of conditioned fear (Campeau and Davis, 1995). However, NMDA antagonist administration impairs acquisition and the associated emergence of plastic changes but not expression of conditioned responses (Miserendino et al., 1990), highlighting potential differences in underlying mechanisms. Recent studies of single neuron responses in the amygdala of awake, behaving rats also reveal striking temporal dynamics of amygdala responses (Quirk et al., 1997). Recordings from lateral amygdala show temporally limited neuronal responses during conditioning (Quirk et al., 1997), whereas cortical responses remain elevated throughout the conditioning phase. Amygdala responses in our experiment show similar temporally limited response characteristics.

However, the temporal pattern of amygdala responses in our study seems at odds with the lesion literature, where an intact amygdala is necessary not only for acquisition but also for expression of conditioned responses. One possibility is that plastic changes occurring during the early phase of conditioning are related to increased amygdala activity. In this context, the initial increases in amygdala activity might represent plastic changes, necessary for the acquisition of the conditioned response. Although the integrity of the amygdala is essential for the continued expression of conditioned responses, a refined connectivity within the amygdala and between the amygdala and other regions leads to lower mean firing rates and synaptic activity during later stages of conditioning.

Another possible explanation for the habituation of amygdala responses is based on the concept of negative feedback in classical conditioning (Fanselow, 1998). It has been demonstrated that fear conditioning using electric shocks as USs produces an amygdala-dependent analgesic state mediated by endogenous opioids (Fanselow, 1984). This can be seen as a negative feedback since analgesia leads to a reduced ability of the US to condition and explains habituation of amygdala responses in the study by Quirk et al. (1997). In our experiment, where an aversive tone serves as the US, engagement of the stapedius reflex might decrease sound transmission at the level of the middle ear and mediate negative feedback that reduces the impact of the US (Cacace et al., 1992). This conjecture accords with our behavioral data showing time-dependent differences in SCR to CS− versus CS+$_{unpaired}$. These suggestions are necessarily speculative, and the functional significance of time-limited amygdala activations clearly warrants further investigations.

It has been speculated that the lateral amygdala serves as a differentiator and is therefore sensitive to changes in the CS–US relationship as it occurs at the beginning of conditioning (Quirk et al., 1997). On the other hand, ongoing selective activation of cortical areas throughout conditioning is in accord with the proposal that cortical regions act as integrators. Our data showing habituation to the CS in the lateral amygdala and ongoing activation in cortical areas (e.g., anterior cingulate and insular) support this hypothesis and suggest a similar model for human associative learning. As already noted, the amygdala habituation is mirrored by the temporal characteristics of SCR, showing smaller differences between SCR to CS− versus CS+$_{unpaired}$ after 8 min of conditioning. This relation to behavioral measurements is in accord with a neuroimaging study showing correlations of amygdala activation during viewing emotionally arousing film clips with the number of recalled film clips after 3 weeks (Cahill et al., 1996).

The contribution of amygdala to conditioning may be linked to early modulation of cingulo-thalamic connectivity (Poremba and Gabriel, 1997a, 1997b). All of these observations suggest that with time, mnemonic representations of behaviorally salient contexts are expressed in *cortical* regions other than medial temporal lobe structures (McGaugh et al., 1996). Proposed candidate structures, including the anterior cingulate and insular cortices, were all activated in our study (Everitt and Robbins, 1997).

Motor Structures: Red Nucleus, SMA, and Premotor Cortex

Activation of the red nucleus together with premotor structures is typically associated with the efferent motor component of eyeblink conditioning (Clark and Lavond, 1993; Krupa et al., 1993; Thompson and Krupa, 1994; Logan and Grafton, 1995). The involvement of the red nucleus in this context has been established in animal studies of eyeblink conditioning (Desmond and Moore, 1991; Thompson and Krupa, 1994) and by functional imaging of humans (Logan and Grafton, 1995). Further evidence for an important role in conditioning comes from experiments in which reversible inactivation of the red nucleus blocked the *expression* of conditioned responses (Krupa et al., 1993). This is in contrast to cerebellar inactivation, which impairs *acquisition* of conditioned responses (Krupa et al., 1993; Ramnani and Yeo, 1996).

Subcortical motor nuclei and premotor activations raise the question of a relationship between classical conditioning, as employed in our experiment, and eyeblink conditioning. Lid closure in eyeblink conditioning is an obligatory defensive mechanism to avoid the impact of a US (e.g., air puff to the cornea). After conditioning, a previously neutral stimulus can elicit the same defensive response (i.e., blink). In our paradigm, subjects' ability to react was restricted by positioning in a tight head holder as well as by the instruction not to move during imaging. Although almost no actual movements occurred (confirmed by the estimated head motion of <1.5 mm), it is likely that generating a preparatory motor response is obligatory in this setting. In keeping with this suggestion, cortical activation patterns involving motor regions can be observed when movements are prepared or imagined but not executed (Decety et al., 1994; Stephan et al., 1995).

Conclusion

Exploiting the high spatiotemporal resolution of fMRI for an event-related experimental design, our results illustrate the contribution of different cortical and subcortical areas to the rapid learning that mediates the behavioral effects of classical conditioning. Interpreting our results in the light of animal studies, we propose a central integrative role for the human "rostral limbic system," including anterior cingulate and insular cortices, which receive input from the amygdala, processing the behavioral relevance of sensory stimuli. Projections of the anterior cingulate to premotor regions and subcortical motor nuclei suggest a potential role for these structures in the formation of context-dependent adaptive behavioral responses.

Experimental Procedures

Subjects and Imaging

We studied nine healthy right-handed volunteers (seven male and two female). Written informed consent was obtained prior to MRI scanning. Data were acquired with a 2 Tesla Magnetom VISION whole body MRI system (Siemens, Erlangen, Germany) equipped with a head volume coil. Contiguous multi-slice T2* weighted echoplanar images (TE = 40 ms, 80.7 ms/image, 64 × 64 pixels [19.2 cm × 19.2 cm]) were obtained in an axial orientation. This sequence enhances blood oxygenation level–dependent (BOLD) contrast (Kwong et al., 1992). The volume acquired covered the whole brain (48 slices; slice thickness 3 mm, giving a 14.4 cm vertical field of view). The effective repetition time (TR) was 4.1 s/volume.

During scans, subjects looked at a translucent screen through a 45° angled mirror. The distance between eyes and screen was ~300 mm. Visual stimuli (i.e., faces) were back-projected onto the screen by an LCD video-projector, subtending 17° vertically and 8° horizontally in the visual field. The screen refresh rate was set to 67/s. During the ITI, the screen was dark. Computer-generated auditory stimuli were delivered through plastic tubes, sealed by foam ear inserts. To further decrease the influence of the gradient switching noise from the scanner, the sound delivery system was shielded by plastic ear defenders. To minimize head motion, subjects were restrained with bitemporal pressure pads.

Skin Conductance Responses

We measured online SCRs in all subjects during fMRI scanning. Unfortunately, SCR traces in four out of nine subjects could not be analyzed due to artifacts caused by gradient switching and radio frequency transmission from the MR scanner. SCRs were measured from two electrodes on the index and middle finger of the left hand using silver electrodes and electrode gel. The signal was amplified and sampled at 100 Hz. Further offline processing was performed with MATLAB (The MathWorks, Natick, MA). Data were detrended and temporally smoothed (Gaussian kernel with full width at half maximum of 2 s), and remaining MRI scanning artifacts were eliminated. Finally, the time series were resampled at 10 Hz using sinc interpolation. For quantitative analysis of SCRs (similar to Esteves et al., 1994), evoked SCR responses were characterized by the maximum of the SCR signal in the interval between stimulus onset and 5 s after stimulus onset. Extending this window beyond the onset of the US (3 s) was possible since we only analyzed CS− and CS+$_{unpaired}$. This value was then subtracted from a baseline, the mean of the SCR in the second before the onset of the stimulus, to account for residual baseline fluctuations. For statistical analysis, the differences were normalized to zero mean and standard deviation of unity. The significance of SCR differences for CS− and CS+$_{unpaired}$ was assessed by a t test. We analyzed both groups (SCRs acquired during fMRI scanning and SCRs acquired in a separate session) separately to demonstrate that conditioning took place during scanning. The group of subjects that was tested after fMRI scanning comprised three of the fMRI study participants. The fourth imaging

volunteer being unavailable, we substituted him with another subject.

Image Processing and Statistical Analysis

Image processing and statistical analysis were carried out using SPM97 (Worsley and Friston, 1995; Friston et al., 1995b; see also http://www.fil.ion.ucl.ac.uk/spm). The problem of medial temporal lobe susceptibility artifacts was addressed by looking at animated sequences of raw images. This procedure revealed no event-related changes in susceptibility. All volumes were realigned to the first volume (Friston et al., 1995a). Residual motion effects were eliminated at each and every voxel by regressing a periodic function of the estimated movement parameters at each voxel on the time course of this voxel. Actual head movements were <1.5 mm for all subjects. To account for the different sampling times of different slices, voxel time series were interpolated using sinc interpolation and resampled using the slice at the AC–PC line as the reference. A mean image was created using the realigned volumes. An anatomical MRI, acquired using a standard three-dimensional T1 weighted sequence (1 × 1 × 1.5 mm voxel size), was coregistered to this mean (T2*) image. This measure ensured that the functional and structural images were spatially aligned. Finally, the structural image was spatially normalized (Friston et al., 1995a) to a standard template (Talairach and Tournoux, 1988; Evans et al., 1994), using nonlinear basis functions. The nonlinear transformation mapping the structural T1 MRI scan onto the template was also applied to the fMRI data. The data were smoothed using an 8 mm (full width at half maximum) isotropic Gaussian kernel to compensate for residual variability after spatial normalization and to permit application of Gaussian random field theory to provide corrected statistical inference (Friston et al., 1995c).

Conditioning

The data were analyzed by modeling the evoked hemodynamic responses for different stimuli as delta functions convolved with a synthetic hemodynamic response function in the context of the general linear model as employed by SPM97 (Josephs et al., 1997). We defined three different event types: all were time-locked to the onset of the presentation of a face. The events were subdivided into (1) CS− (2) CS+ paired (CS+$_{paired}$), and (3) CS+ unpaired (CS+$_{unpaired}$) face stimuli (Figure 1). Specific effects were tested by applying appropriate linear contrasts to the parameter estimates for each event, resulting in a t statistic for every voxel. These t statistics (transformed to Z statistics) constitute an SPM. The contrast used in the main analysis tested for greater responses evoked by CS+$_{unpaired}$ stimuli relative to CS−.

Sensory (Auditory and Visual) Evoked Responses

In this analysis, we added a fourth event type to the main analysis, which was time-locked to the presentation of the US (1 kHz tone). The contrasts for the auditory evoked responses tested for the comparison of these events to baseline. For the visual evoked responses, the contrast resembles the grouped comparison between CS−, CS+$_{unpaired}$ and CS+$_{paired}$ to baseline. For this analysis, only the first six subjects were considered.

Interaction Analysis Including Familiarization Trials

We also combined the data for the familiarization phase and the conditioning phase and defined two additional events for the familiarization phase (fCS− and fCS+) for the faces that will become CS− and CS+. The contrast in this analysis modeled the difference between fCS+ versus fCS− and CS+$_{unpaired}$ versus CS−, that is, the interaction.

Time by Event Interaction Analysis

In addition to the main analysis, we defined three new regressors representing the time by event interactions. These three additional regressors were created by multiplying the regressors for CS−, CS+$_{paired}$ and CS+$_{unpaired}$ with a mean corrected exponential function with a time constant of one-fourth of the session length. Contrasts tested for the difference of the interaction terms between the CS− and CS+$_{unpaired}$.

Ensuing SPMs were interpreted by referring to the probabilistic behavior of Gaussian random fields. The data for all nine subjects were analyzed as a group, modeling evoked responses in a subject-specific way. To demonstrate individual effects, we display the evoked hemodynamic response for contrasts of interest for subjects individually. In the case of the amygdala, where we had a region-specific hypothesis, correction for multiple comparisons was based on the volume of interest (Filipek et al., 1994) and the smoothness of the underlying SPM (Worsley et al., 1996). For the remaining brain, where we had no a priori regional hypothesis, correction was for the entire volume analyzed (i.e., whole brain). Thus, in all cases the threshold was set to p < 0.05.

Acknowledgments

We thank A. Kleinschmidt, N. Ramnani, D. McGonigle, and R. Frackowiak for helpful comments. We would also like to thank the Functional Imaging Laboratory physics group and the radiographers for their support and help. C. B., J. M., R. D., and K. J. F. are funded by the Wellcome Trust.

Received February 4, 1998; revised April 29, 1998.

References

Alvarez, P., and Squire, L.R. (1994). Memory consolidation and the medial temporal lobe: a simple network model. Proc. Natl. Acad. Sci. USA 91, 7041–7045.

Augustine, J.R. (1996). Circuitry and functional-aspects of the insular lobe in primates including humans. Brain Res. Rev. 22, 229–244.

Bechara, A., Tranel, D., Damasio, H., Adolphs, R., Rockland, C., and Damasio, A.R. (1995). Double dissociation of conditioning and declarative knowledge relative to the amygdala and hippocampus in humans. Science 269, 1115–1118.

Bordi, F., and LeDoux, J. (1992). Sensory tuning beyond the sensory system—an initial analysis of auditory response properties of neurons in the lateral amygdaloid nucleus and overlying areas of the striatum. J. Neurosci. 12, 2493–2503.

Bordi, F., LeDoux, J., Clugnet, M.C., and Pavlides, C. (1993). Single-unit activity in the lateral nucleus of the amygdala and overlying areas of the striatum in freely behaving rats—rates, discharge patterns, and responses to acoustic stimuli. Behav. Neurosci. 107, 757–769.

Breiter, H.C., Etcoff, N.L., Whalen, P.J., Kennedy, W.A., Rauch, S.L., Buckner, R.L., Strauss, M.M., Hyman, S.E., and Rosen, B.R. (1996). Response and habituation of the human amygdala during visual processing of facial expression. Neuron 17, 875–887.

Buckner, R.L., Bandettini, P.A., Ocraven, K.M., Savoy, R.L., Petersen, S.E., Raichle, M.E., and Rosen, B.R. (1996). Detection of cortical activation during averaged single trials of a cognitive task using functional magnetic-resonance-imaging. Proc. Natl. Acad. Sci. USA 93, 14878–14883.

Cacace, A.T., Margolis, R.H., and Relkin, E.M. (1992). Short-term poststimulatory response characteristics of the human acoustic stapedius reflex—monotic and dichotic stimulation. J. Acoust. Soc. Am. 91, 203–214.

Cahill, L., Haier, R.J., Fallon, J., Alkire, M.T., Tang, C., Keator, D., Wu, J., and McGaugh, J.L. (1996). Amygdala activity at encoding correlated with long-term, free-recall of emotional information. Proc. Natl. Acad. Sci. USA 93, 8016–8021.

Campeau, S., and Davis, M. (1995). Involvement of the central nucleus and basolateral complex of the amygdala in fear conditioning measured with fear-potentiated startle in rats trained concurrently with auditory and visual conditioned-stimuli. J. Neurosci. 15, 2301–2311.

Casey, K.L., Minoshima, S., Morrow, T.J., Koeppe, R.A., and Frey, K.A. (1995). Imaging the brain in pain—potentials, limitations, and implications. Adv. Pain Res. Ther. 22, 201–211.

Clark, R.E., and Lavond, D.G. (1993). Reversible lesions of the red nucleus during acquisition and retention of a classically-conditioned behavior in rabbits. Behav. Neurosci. 107, 264–270.

Coghill, R.C., Talbot, J.D., Evans, A.C., Meyer, E., Gjedde, A., Bushnell, M.C., and Duncan, G.H. (1994). Distributed-processing of pain and vibration by the human brain. J. Neurosci. 14, 4095–4108.

Dale, A.M., and Buckner, R.L. (1997). Selective averaging of rapidly presented individual trials using fMRI. Hum. Brain Map. 5, 329–340.

Decety, J., Perani, D., Jeannerod, M., Bettinardi, V., Tadary, B., Woods, R., Mazziotta, J.C., and Fazio, F. (1994). Mapping motor representations with positron emission tomography. Nature 371, 600–602.

Desmond, J.E., and Moore, J.W. (1991). Single-unit activity in red nucleus during the classically-conditioned rabbit nictitating-membrane response. Neurosci. Res. 10, 260–279.

Devinsky, O., Morrell, M.J., and Vogt, B.A. (1995). Contributions of anterior cingulate cortex to behavior. Brain 118, 279–306.

Ekman, P. (1982). Emotion in the Human Face (Cambridge: Cambridge University Press).

Esteves, F., Parra, C., Dimberg, U., and Ohman, A. (1994). Nonconscious associative learning—pavlovian conditioning of skin-conductance responses to masked fear-relevant facial stimuli. Psychophysiology 31, 375–385.

Evans, A.C., Kamber, M., Collins, D.L., and Macdonald, D. (1994). An MRI-based probabilistic atlas of neuroanatomy. In Magnetic Resonance Scanning and Epilepsy, S. Shorvon, D. Fish, F. Andermann, G. M. Bydder, H. Stefan, eds. (New York: Plenum Press), pp. 263–274.

Everitt, B.J., and Robbins, T.W. (1997). Central cholinergic systems and cognition. Annu. Rev. Psych. 48, 649–684.

Fanselow, M.S. (1984). What is conditioned fear. Trends Neurosci. 7, 460–462.

Fanselow, M.S. (1998). Pavlovian conditioning, negative feedback, and blocking: mechanisms that regulate association formation. Neuron 20, 625–627.

Filipek, P.A., Richelme, C., Kennedy, D.N., and Caviness, V.S. (1994). Young-adult human brain—an MRI-based morphometric analysis. Cerebral Cortex 4, 344–360.

Fink, G.R., Markowitsch, H.J., Reinkemeier, M., Bruckbauer, T., Kessler, J., and Heiss, W.D. (1996). Cerebral representation of ones own past—neural networks involved in autobiographical memory. J. Neurosci. 16, 4275–4282.

Fredrikson, M., Wik, G., Fischer, H., and Andersson, J. (1995). Affective and attentive neural networks in humans—a pet study of pavlovian conditioning. Neuroreport 7, 97–101.

Freeman, J.H., Cuppernell, C., Flannery, K., and Gabriel, M. (1996). Limbic thalamic, cingulate cortical and hippocampal neuronal correlates of discriminative approach learning in rabbits. Behav. Brain Res. 80, 123–136.

Friston, K.J., Ashburner, J., Frith, C.D., Poline, J.-B., Heather, J.D., and Frackowiak, R.S.J. (1995a). Spatial registration and normalization of images. Hum. Brain Map. 2, 1–25.

Friston, K.J., Holmes, A.P., Poline, J.-B., Grasby, P.J., Williams, S. C. R., Frackowiak, R.S.J., and Turner, R. (1995b). Analysis of fMRI time series revisited. NeuroImage 2, 45–53.

Friston, K.J., Holmes, A.P., Worsley, K.P., Poline, J.-B., Frith, C.D., and Frackowiak, R.S.J. (1995c). Statistical parametric maps in functional imaging: a general linear approach. Hum. Brain Map. 2, 189–210.

Josephs, O., Turner, R., and Friston, K. (1997). Event-related fMRI. Hum. Brain Map. 5, 243–248.

Krupa, D.J., Thompson, J.K., and Thompson, R.F. (1993). Localization of a memory trace in the mammalian brain. Science 260, 989–991.

Kwong, K.K., Belliveau, J.W., Chesler, D.A., Goldberg, I.E., Weisskoff, R.M., Poncelet, B.P., Kennedy, D.N., Hoppel, B.E., Cohen, M.S., Turner, R., et al. (1992). Dynamic magnetic resonance imaging of human brain activity during primary sensory stimulation. Proc. Natl. Acad. Sci. USA 89, 5675–5679.

LaBar, K.S., and LeDoux, J.E. (1996). Partial disruption of fear conditioning in rats with unilateral amygdala damage—correspondence with unilateral temporal lobectomy in humans. Behav. Neurosci. 110, 991–997.

LeDoux, J. (1996). A few degrees of separation. In The Emotional Brain. (New York: Simon and Schuster), pp. 138–178.

LeDoux, J.E., Cicchetti, P., Xagoraris, A., and Romanski, L.M. (1990a). The lateral amygdaloid nucleus: sensory interface of the amygdala in fear conditioning. J. Neurosci. *10*, 1062–1069.

LeDoux, J.E., Farb, C.F., and Ruggiero, D.A. (1990b). Topographic organization of neurons in the acoustic thalamus that project to the amygdala. J. Neurosci. *10*, 1043–1054.

Logan, C.G., and Grafton, S.T. (1995). Functional-anatomy of human eyeblink conditioning determined with regional cerebral glucose-metabolism and positron-emission tomography. Proc. Natl. Acad. Sci. USA *92*, 7500–7504.

McGaugh, J.L., Cahill, L., and Roozendaal, B. (1996). Involvement of the amygdala in memory storage-interaction with other brain systems. Proc. Natl. Acad. Sci. USA *93*, 13508–13514.

Mesulam, M.M., and Mufson, E.J. (1982). Insula of the old-world monkey. 3. Efferent cortical output and comments on function. J. Comp. Neurol. *212*, 38–52.

Miserendino, M.J.D., Sananes, C.B., Melia, K.R., and Davis, M. (1990). Blocking of acquisition but not expression of conditioned fear-potentiated startle by NMDA antagonists in the amygdala. Nature *345*, 716–718.

Morris, J.S., Friston, K.J., and Dolan, R.J. (1997). Neural responses to salient visual stimuli. Proc. R. Soc. Lond. B. *264*, 769–775.

Phillips, M.L., Young, A.W., Senior, C., Brammer, M., Andrew, C., Calder, A.J., Bullmore, E.T., Perrett, D.I., Rowland, D., Williams, S.C.R., et al. (1997). A specific neural substrate for perceiving facial expressions of disgust. Nature *389*, 495–498.

Poremba, A., and Gabriel, M. (1997a). Amygdalar lesions block discriminative avoidance learning and cingulothalamic training-induced neuronal plasticity in rabbits. J. Neurosci. *17*, 5237–5244.

Poremba, A., and Gabriel, M. (1997b). Medial geniculate lesions block amygdalar and cingulothalamic learning-related neuronal activity. J. Neurosci. *17*, 8645–8655.

Powell, D.A., Maxwell, B., and Penney, J. (1996). Neuronal-activity in the medial prefrontal cortex during pavlovian eyeblink and nictitating-membrane conditioning. J. Neurosci. *16*, 6296–6306.

Quirk, G.J., Armony, J.L., and LeDoux, J.E. (1997). Fear conditioning enhances different temporal components of tone-evoked spike trains in auditory cortex and lateral amygdala. Neuron *19*, 613–624.

Rainville, P., Duncan, G.H., Price, D.D., Carrier, B., and Bushnell, M.C. (1997). Pain affect encoded in human anterior cingulate but not somatosensory cortex. Science *277*, 968–971.

Ramnani, N., and Yeo, C.H. (1996). Reversible inactivations of the cerebellum prevent the extinction of conditioned nictitating-membrane responses in rabbits. J. Physiol. *495*, 159–168.

Rolls, E.T. (1994). A theory of emotion and consciousness, and its application to understanding the neural basis of emotion. In The Cognitive Neurosciences, M.S. Gazzaniga, ed. (Cambridge, MA: MIT Press), pp. 1091–1106.

Rolls, E.T., Hornak, J., Wade, D., and McGrath, J. (1994). Emotion-related learning in patients with social and emotional changes associated with frontal-lobe damage. J. Neurol. Neurosurg. Psychiatry *57*, 1518–1524.

Schreurs, B.G., McIntosh, A.R., Bahro, M., Herscovitch, P., Sunderland, T., and Molchan, S.E. (1997). Lateralization and behavioral correlation of changes in regional cerebral blood flow with classical conditioning of the human eyeblink response. J. Neurophysiol. *77*, 2153–2163.

Stephan, K.M., Fink, G.R., Passingham, R.E., Silbersweig, D., Ceballosbaumann, A.O., Frith, C.D., and Frackowiak, R.S.J. (1995). Functional-anatomy of the mental representation of upper extremity movements in healthy-subjects. J. Neurophysiol. *73*, 373–386.

Talairach, P., and Tournoux, J. (1988) A Stereotactic Coplanar Atlas of the Human Brain (Stuttgart: Thieme).

Thompson, R.F., and Krupa, D.J. (1994). Organization of memory traces in the mammalian brain. Annu. Rev. Neurosci. *17*, 519–549.

Whalen, P.J., Rauch, S.L., Etcoff, N.L., McInerney, S.C., Lee, M.B., and Jenike, M.A. (1998). Masked presentations of emotional facial expressions modulate amygdala activity without explicit knowledge. J. Neurosci. *18*, 411–418.

Worsley, K.J., and Friston, K.J. (1995). Analysis of fMRI time series revisited—again. NeuroImage *2*, 173–181.

Worsley, K.J., Marrett, P., Neelin, A.C., Friston, K.J., and Evans, A.C. (1996). A unified statistical approach for determining significant signals in images of cerebral activation. Hum. Brain Mapp. *4*, 58–73.

The Effects of Early Rearing Environment on the Development of GABA$_A$ and Central Benzodiazepine Receptor Levels and Novelty-Induced Fearfulness in the Rat

Christian Caldji, B.Sc., Darlene Francis, B.Sc., Shakti Sharma, M.Sc., Paul M. Plotsky, Ph.D., and Michael J. Meaney, Ph.D.

We compared the effects of handling or maternal separation from the day following birth until postnatal day 14 on behavioral responses to novelty and on GABA$_A$ and central benzodiazepine (CBZ) receptor levels in the rat. As adults, handled animals showed reduced startle responsivity, increased exploration in a novel open field, and decreased novelty-induced suppression of feeding relative to the handled (H) and/or maternal separation (MS) groups. As compared with handled animals, both nonhandled (NH) and MS animals displayed: (1) reduced GABA$_A$ receptor levels in the locus coeruleus (LC) and the n. tractus solitarius (NTS); (2) reduced CBZ receptor sites in the central and lateral n. of the amygdala, the frontal cortex, and in the LC and NTS; and (3) reduced levels of the mRNA for the γ2 subunit of the GABA$_A$ receptor complex, which confers high affinity BZ binding, in the amygdaloid nuclei as well as in the LC and NTS. Both the amygdala and the ascending noradrenergic systems have been considered as critical sites for the anxiolytic effects of benzodiazepines. These data suggest that early life events influence the development of the GABA$_A$ receptor system, thus altering the expression of fearfulness in adulthood.
[Neuropsychopharmacology 22:219–229, 2000]
© 2000 American College of Neuropsychopharmacology. Published by Elsevier Science Inc.

KEY WORDS: Fear; Novelty; GABA$_A$ receptor; Central benzodiazepine receptor; Maternal separation; Early experience

The development of behavioral and endocrine responses to acute stress is greatly influenced by the early postnatal rearing environment (for reviews see Levine

From the Developmental Neuroendocrinology Laboratory (CC, DF, SS, MJM), Douglas Hospital Research Centre, Departments of Psychiatry, Neurology, and Neurosurgery, McGill University, Montreal, Quebec, Canada; and Department of Psychiatry and Behavioral Sciences (PMP), Emory University, Atlanta, Georgia.
Address correspondence to: Michael J. Meaney, Ph.D., Douglas Hospital Research Center, 6875 LaSalle Blvd., Montreal, Quebec, Canada H4H 1R3. Tel.: (514) 762-3048. Fax: (514) 762-3034. E-mail: mdmm@musica.mcgill.ca
Received March 3, 1999; revised July 22, 1999; accepted August 17, 1999.

1975; Denenberg 1964; Meaney et al. 1996). These environmental effects persist throughout the life of the animal, resulting in stable individual differences in stress reactivity. Indeed, there is considerable plasticity in the development of these systems. Postnatal handling during the first week of life greatly decreases behavioral fearfulness and hypothalamic-pituitary-adrenal (HPA) responses to stress; whereas, repeated periods of prolonged maternal separation produce enhanced reactivity. Increased stress reactivity has been associated with an enhanced risk for several forms of illness, including affective disorders, diabetes, autoimmune disorders, and coronary heart disease (Chrousos and Gold 1992; Higley et al. 1991; McEwen and Steller 1993; Seckl and Meaney 1994). Thus, in determining the magnitude of behavioral and endocrine responses to stress, early life events

NEUROPSYCHOPHARMACOLOGY 2000–VOL. 22, NO. 3
© 2000 American College of Neuropsychopharmacology
Published by Elsevier Science Inc.
655 Avenue of the Americas, New York, NY 10010

0893-133X/00/$–see front matter
PII S0893-133X(99)00110-4

contribute to vulnerability to disease in later life (Seckl and Meaney 1994). The critical question, then, concerns the mechanisms for these early environmental effects on the development of behavioral and endocrine responses to stress.

Postnatal handling has been shown to decrease fearfulness to novelty (Levine 1962, 1957; Denenberg 1964; Bodnoff et al. 1987). As adults, handled (H) rats show reduced novelty-induced suppression of appetitive behavior and increased exploration in novel environments. The behavioral effects of repeated maternal separation in rats are less documented, although, in primates, there is considerable evidence for enhanced fearfulness in animals exposed to maternal separation in early life (Sackett 1969).

The mechanisms underlying these early environmental effects on behavioral responses to novelty are unclear. Bodnoff et al. (1987) reported that neonatal handling increased forebrain central benzodiazepine (CBZ) receptor levels, with no indication of where in the forebrain such differences might exist. Nevertheless, these data are certainly consistent with the well-established, anxiolytic effects of benzodiazepines on behavioral responses to novelty (see File 1995 for a review). Moreover, these findings are also consistent with human data showing decreased CBZ receptor sensitivity in panic disorder patients (Roy-Byrne et al. 1996).

We report here the results of behavioral and pharmacological studies examining various behavioral responses to novelty as well as differences in CBZ and GABA$_A$ receptor binding levels in adult animals exposed to either handling or maternal separation during the first 2 weeks of life. The results of these studies are consistent with the idea that the early environment can regulate the development of GABA$_A$/CBZ receptor systems and that these effects, in turn, partially mediate the differences in behavioral responses to stress.

MATERIALS AND METHODS

Subjects

The animals used in these studies were the male offspring of Long–Evans, hooded rat dams obtained from Charles River (St. Constant, Quebec or Boston, MA) and mated in our animal colony. Handling consisted of removing the mother and then the pups from the home cage by gloved hand and placing the pups into a plastic container lined with bedding material for 15 minutes. The pups, followed by the mother, were then returned to their home cage. Handling occurred once per day between postnatal days (PND) 1 (Day 0 = day of birth) and 14 of life. Maternal separation involved the same procedures; however, the pups remained away from the dam for 180 minutes. In the course of normal

mother–pup interactions in the laboratory rat, the mother is routinely off the litter for periods of 20–25 minutes (the internest bout interval, see Leon et al. 1978; Jans and Woodside 1990). Thus, the maternal separation paradigm, unlike handling, represents the deprivation of maternal care. The nonhandled (NH) animals were left completely undisturbed throughout this period. For all animals, routine cage maintenance did not begin before PND 14.

On PND 22, the animals were weaned and housed in same-sex, same-treatment groups of three animals per cage. The animals were maintained on a 12:12 light:dark schedule (lights on at 0800 h) with free access to food (Purina Lab Chow) and water. The animals used in these experiments were 3 to 4 months of age (300–350 gm) at the time of testing and were randomly selected from approximately five litters per treatment group. There were no group differences in body weights. The experiments were conducted in accordance with the guidelines of the Canadian Council on Animal Care and the McGill University Animal Care Committee and in accordance with the Guide for the Care and Use of Laboratory Animals of the National Institutes of Health.

Behavioral Testing

For all behavioral testing, observers were blind as to the treatment condition of the animal. Each behavioral experiment was performed with a separate set of animals that were not exposed to any previous testing.

Animals were tested one at a time using a modified version of the Britton and Thatcher-Britton paradigm as a measure of novelty-induced suppression of appetitive behavior (see Britton and Thatcher-Britton 1981; Bodnoff et al. 1987,1989). Animals were food deprived for 24 hours before testing. The animals were then provided with food either in a novel environment or in the home cage. The novel environment was a 180 × 180 × 30 cm arena with food provided in a cylindrical wire-mesh hopper located in the center of the novel arena. To begin the test, all animals were placed one at a time into the periphery of the arena at the same starting point. The test session lasted for 360 seconds, and during this period, the experimenter scored the latency (s) to begin feeding, the total amount of time spent feeding, and the latency to first "visit" the food (i.e., to move within a 5-cm radius of the food container). If an animal did not eat within the test period, a score of 360 was assigned for latency measures and 0 for the amount of food consumed. The novel arena was cleaned with ethanol following the testing of each animal. A separate group of animals were tested in the same manner, with the exception that food was provided in the home cage, using the same food hopper, rather than in the novel environment. Although normally housed in groups, for the sake of testing, animals were tested alone in the home cage. The partner was removed 1 hour before testing.

Another set of animals was examined in an open-field test of exploration. Individual animals were placed, one at a time, into the same location of the periphery of a novel circular open field, 1.6 m in diameter. The critical measure was the time (s) the animal spent exploring the inner area of the novel arena. Exploration was defined as the entire body of the animal being away from the immediate vicinity of the wall (>10 cm) enclosing the open field. Each rat was tested for 10 min in the novel environment. The open field was cleaned between each subject to prevent olfactory cues from affecting the behavior of subsequently tested rats.

Finally, a third set of animals was tested for startle responses using two startle chambers (San Diego Instruments, San Diego, CA), each consisting of a *Plexiglas* chamber mounted on a *Plexiglas* base within a sound-attenuating chamber. A piezoelectric strain meter attached to the base transduced the startle response. Stabilimeter readings were rectified, digitized on a 4095 scale, and recorded by computer. An average of 100 1-ms readings, beginning at stimulus onset, was used as the measure of startle amplitude for each trial. A test session consisted of placing an animal in the startle chamber for a 5-min acclimatization period, after which it was exposed to five presentations of an 80 to 120 dB acoustic startle stimulus (30 ms) in a random sequence, separated by variable interstimulus intervals that averaged 15 s. The startle chambers were cleaned with a 70% alcohol solution between animals.

In Vitro GABA$_A$/Central Benzodiazepine Receptor Autoradiography

Handled, nonhandled, and maternal separation animals (n = 6/group) were rapidly decapitated less than 1 minute following removal from the home cage in order to avoid the dynamic effects of acute stress on BZ receptor expression (see Medina et al. 1983). Brains were quickly removed, frozen in −70°C isopentane, and stored at −80°C. Brains were sectioned at 15 μm, and sections were thaw-mounted onto gel-coated slides. Slides were then stored at −80°C until the time of assay.

Central benzodiazepine (CBZ) receptors were first examined using a procedure described by Bureau and Olsen (1993) with unfixed, frozen sections. Slides were thawed and pre-incubated in assay buffer (0.17 m Tris-HCl, pH 7.4) for 30 min at 4°C. The slides were then incubated with a saturating 0.5 nm concentration of [³H]flunitrazepam (84.5Ci/mmol, New England Nuclear, Boston, MA) in assay buffer for 60 min at 4°C. Nonspecific, background binding was determined in parallel sections using 1 μm clonazepam. Postassay washes (2 × 30 s) were performed using assay buffer. The sections were left to dry overnight and then were apposed to tri-

tium-sensitive Ultrafilm (Amersham Canada Inc., Montreal, Canada) along with ³H microscales for 14 days.

Type I CBZ receptor binding was quantified using [³H]zolpidem (50.8 Ci/mmol, New England Nuclear), following procedures described in Ruano et al. (1993). Slides were thawed and pre-incubated in 50 mm Tris-HCl assay buffer (120 mm NaCl, 5 mm KCl, pH 7.4) for 30 min at room temperature. Sections were then incubated in assay buffer containing a saturating 5 nm concentration of [³H]zolpidem (5 nm) for 30 min at 4°C. Nonspecific binding was determined in parallel sections incubated with buffer containing 50 μm of cold zolpidem (purchased from RBI, Natick, MA). Sections were then washed (2 × 3 min) in ice-cold assay buffer, rinsed in cold, distilled water, and dried rapidly under a stream of cold air. Autoradiograms were generated by apposing slides to tritium-sensitive ultrafilm with the appropriate [³H] microscales for a period of 14 days, a period that provided for linearity of microscales and maximal binding.

GABA$_A$ receptor levels were quantified using [³H]GABA according to the procedure of Chu et al. (1990). After thawing, slides were pre-incubated in 50 mm Tris-HCl buffer (pH 7.4) for 60 min at room temperature. Slides were then incubated with 30 nm [³H]GABA and 10 mm baclofen, to block binding to GABA$_B$ receptor sites, at 4°C for 45 min in 50 mm Tris-HCl 50 mm buffer (pH 7.4) containing 2.5 mm CaCl . Nonspecific background binding was determined on parallel sections by the addition of 10 mm isovagine. Following incubation, slides were washed (2 × 5 min) in ice cold 50 mm Tris-HCl buffer. The slides were then dipped quickly in acetone:glutaraldehyde 2.5% and dried under a gentle stream of air. Autoradiograms were generated by exposure to ³H-sensitive ultrafilm along with ³H microscale standards for 21 days.

Autoradiograms were analyzed by obtaining optical densities (expressed as mean ± SEM in fmol/mg protein) determined by computer-assisted densitometry using an MCID image analysis system (Imaging Research Inc., St. Catherine's, Ontario, Canada) and low activity tritium standards. For each brain region, nonspecific binding was assessed using analysis of the same brain region from sections prepared as described above. Sections were coded, and the analysis was performed by individuals unaware of the treatment origin of the sections.

In Situ Hybridization

Brains were obtained as described above, and 15 μm coronal sections were prepared under RNase-free conditions and stored at −80°C. In preparation for the hybridization experiments, sections were prefixed in a 4% paraformaldehyde solution for 10 min. Sections were then washed in 2 × SSC buffer (2 × 5 min) and in 0.25%

acetic anhydride and 0.1 m triethanolamine solution (pH 8.0; 1 × 10 min). Sections were then dehydrated using a 50 to 100% ethanol gradient, placed in choloroform for 10 min, followed by a rehydration in 95% ethanol. Sections were then incubated overnight at 37°C with 75 μl/section of hybridization buffer containing 50% deionized formamide, 10 mm dithiothreitol, 10 mm Tris (Ph 7.5), 600 mm sodium chloride, 1 mm EDTA, 10% dextran sulfate, 1 × Denhardt's solution, 100 μg salmon sperm DNA, 100 μg/ml yeast tRNA, with 1 × 10^6 CPM [^{35}S] ddATP labeled γ_2 oligonucleotide probe. The γ_2 oligonucleotide probe (5'–3': GTC ATA GCC ATA TTC TTC ATC CCT CTC TTG AAG GTG GGT GGC; Shivers et al. 1989) was synthesized (Beckman 1000 DNA Synthesizer, Beckman, USA) and labeled using a DNA 3'-end labeling kit (Boehringer Mannheim, USA). Preliminary studies using a scrambled version of the probe yielded no specific signal on brain sections (data not shown). The slides were then dipped in NTB-2 emulsion (Kodak, Rochester, NY), stored at 4°C for 8 weeks, and developed. Following counterstaining with Cresyl Violet, the results were analyzed using grain counting over individual cells within high-power microscopic fields under brightfield illumination with an MCID image analysis system (Imaging Research Inc., St. Catherines, Ontario). For each individual cellfield, grains over every identifiable cell were counted, with 40 to 60 cells per area per section, with three sections per animal. Brain regions were identified using the rat brain atlas of Paxinos and Watson (1986). For the sake of the hippocampus, we focused on the pyramidal cell layers (CA1 and CA3) and the granule cell layers of the dentate gyrus. After subtraction of background (grains/neuropil), mean values were obtained for each animal. Background was less than 10% for all brain regions. Grain counts are presented as a function of the cell area

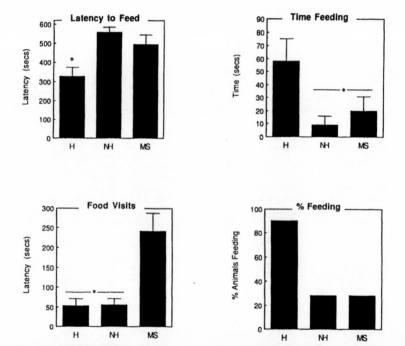

Figure 1.   The results of the neophagia test for handled (H), nonhandled (NH), and maternal separation (MS) animals ($n = 7$–10 per group). The mean ± SEM for the latency to begin feeding (upper left), the amount of time spent feeding (upper right), the latency to first visit to the food (lower left), and the percentage of animals within each group feeding at anytime during the test. *$p < .01$ from other groups; in cases where groups fall under a common line, the asterisks indicate a significant difference from the remaining group.

to account for any morphological differences (see Mc-Cabe et al. 1989).

Statistical Analysis

All data were analyzed using a one-way (group) or two-way (group × sample) analysis of variance (ANOVA) with Tukey post hoc tests, where appropriate.

RESULTS

Behavioral Testing

The results of the behavioral testing revealed consistent evidence for decreased fearfulness in the presence of novelty in adult animals exposed to handling during the first weeks of life, as compared with either NH or MS animals. In the neophagia test, food-deprived, handled (H) animals provided food in a novel setting ate significantly faster (i.e., a significantly shorter latency to feed, see Figure 1) and for a longer period of time (i.e., time eating, Figure 1) than did either NH or MS rats. NH and MS animals did not differ on these measures; however, the MS rats took significantly longer then either H or NH animals to approach the food source first (food visit latency; see Figure 1) than did either the H or the NH rats (see Figure 1). Overall, the percentage of either NH or MS rats that actually fed in the novel setting (see % feeding, Figure 1) was considerably lower in the NH and MS groups as compared with the H group. Note, there were no differences among the groups on any of these measures when food was provided animals in the home cage. Under these conditions, animals ate readily throughout the test period (the means for all groups were < 10 s; data not shown). The differences in the latency to begin feeding were apparent only in the novel environment, suggesting that the relevant variable was the animals' reaction to novelty, and not differences in hunger. To examine the responses to novelty further, animals were evaluated in an open-field test. In this test, H animals spent significantly more time exploring the center area (see Figure 2A), a measure that is thought to reflect the reduced fear in these animals. There were no differences between NH and MS rats.

Differences in fearfulness as a function of early rearing environment were also apparent in the results of the startle response test. H animals showed reduced startle responses, as compared with both NH and MS rats (see Figure 2B). At the higher decibel tones, there was also evidence for an increased startle response in the MS rats, as compared with the NH animals.

GABA$_A$/CBZ Receptor Levels

There were no differences in [^{3}H]GABA binding (GABA$_A$ receptor levels) in any corticolimbic area ex-

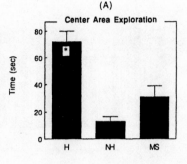

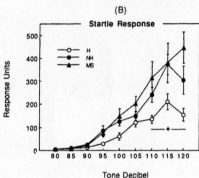

Figure 2. (A) The amount of time (mean ± SEM) exploring the center area of a novel open field arena in handled (H), nonhandled (NH), and maternal separation (MS) animals (*n* = 8–10 per group, * *p* < .01 from other groups). (B) The startle response (mean ± SEM) in handled (H), nonhandled (NH), and maternal separation (MS) animals (*n* = 8–11 per group) in response to 80–120 decibel tones (* indicates significant difference at *p* < .05 between H and NH or MS rats for each datapoint indicated by the solid line).

amined in this study, except for the medial prefrontal cortex region (see Figure 3A). In the medial prefrontal cortex, [^{3}H]GABA binding was significantly higher in H as compared to MS rats. In the midbrain, there were significant differences in [^{3}H]GABA binding in the locus coeruleus and the nucleus tractus solitarius (see Figure 3B). In these regions, [^{3}H]GABA binding was two to threefold higher in the H animals, as compared with both NH and MS rats. In the nucleus tractus solitarius, [^{3}H]GABA binding in the MS rats was especially low, significantly lower than in either H or NH animals.

A similar, but more extensive, pattern of differences emerged for [^{3}H]flunitrazepam binding. In corticolimbic

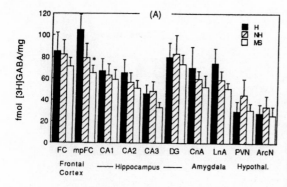

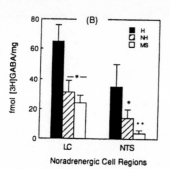

Figure 3. GABA$_A$ receptor binding (fmol [^{3}H]GABA binding per mg protein; mean ± SEM) in corticolimbic (upper panel) and noradrenergic cell body regions (lower panel) in handled (H), nonhandled (NH), and maternal separation (MS) animals (n = 5–6 per group). Abbreviations: frontal cortex (FC), medial prefrontal cortex (mpFC), hippocampal regions of the Ammon's Horn (CA1-4), and dentate gyrus (DG), the central (CnA) and lateral (LnA) n. of the amygdala, the periventricular (PVN) and arcuate regions (ArcN) of the hypothalamus, the locus coeruleus (LC) and the n. tractus solitarius (NTS). (A) *p < .05 for comparison of H versus MS rats; (B) *p < .05 or **p < .01 for comparison of H versus NH/MS rats.

structures, there were significant differences in [^{3}H]flunitrazepam binding in the lateral and central nuclei of the amygdala (see Figure 4A). Within both regions, [^{3}H]flunitrazepam binding was significantly higher in H as compared with NH or MS animals. There were also significant differences in [^{3}H]flunitrazepam binding in the locus coeruleus, the C1 catecholamine cell body regions, and the nucleus tractus solitarius (see Figure 4B). Again, in the nucleus tractus solitarius, the [^{3}H]flunitrazepam binding in the MS rats was greatly reduced.

[^{3}H]flunitrazepam binding reflects both type I and II CBZ receptor types. To examine the relevant receptor subtype, we examined CBZ binding using [^{3}H]zolpidem, which selectively labels the type I receptor subtype (Ruano et al. 1993). The differences in [^{3}H]zolpidem binding paralleled those for [^{3}H]flunitrazepam. Thus, H animals showed increased [^{3}H]zolpidem binding in the central and lateral n. of the amygdala, as well as in the locus coeruleus and n. tractus solitarius (see Figure 5). In addition, using the more specific type I

CBZ receptor ligand, we found decreased [^{3}H]zolpidem binding in the medial prefrontal cortex of the MS rats.

γ_2 In Situ Hybridization

The results of the γ_2 in situ hybridization study paralleled those of the CBZ receptor autoradiography. Thus, there was significantly higher levels of γ_2 mRNA expression in the lateral, basolateral, and central nuclei of the amygdala as well as in the locus coeruleus and the nucleus tractus solitarius in handled, as compared with either nonhandled or maternal separation rats (see Figure 6). There were no group differences in the CA1 region of the hippocampus; these findings again parallel the result of the receptor binding studies. Note, two forms of the γ_2 subunit are generated by alternative RNA splicing, resulting in the short (γ_{2s}) and long (γ_{2L}) variants (Whiting et al. 1990). Our probe was not selective; thus, we are unable to determine whether differences reflect greater levels of one variant or another.

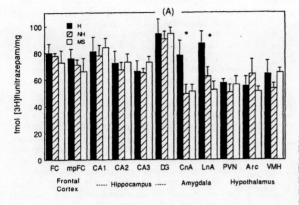

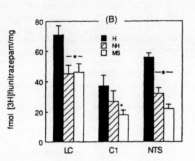

Figure 4. Central benzodiazepine receptor binding (fmol [³H]flunitrazepam binding per mg protein; mean ± SEM) in corticolimbic (upper panel) and noradrenergic cell body regions (lower panel) in handled (H), nonhandled (NH), and maternal separation (MS) animals (*n* = 5–6 per group). See Figure 3 legend for abbreviations. **(A)** * *p* < .01 for comparison of H versus NH/MS rats; **(B)** *p* < .01 for comparison with H rats.

DISCUSSION

The results of these studies confirm and extend previous research on the effects of early rearing conditions on behavioral responses to stress. The classical studies of Denenberg, Levine, and colleagues showed that postnatal handling decreased the expression of fear-related behaviors under stressful conditions (see Denenberg 1964; Levine 1975). More recent studies have shown that these effects are particularly notable under conditions of novelty (e.g., Bodnoff et al. 1987; Nunez et al. 1996; Escorihuela et al. 1992). In the present studies, differences in the expression of both appetitive and exploratory behaviors between H and NH or MS rats were apparent in response to novelty.

The results of a recent study (Plotsky et al. 1999) show that, in terms of HPA responses to stress, H rats are actually comparable to laboratory rats reared under standard conditions. Most breeding colonies perform cage cleaning repeatedly during the first 2 weeks of life, and this involves briefly removing the mother and the

pups from the maternity cage. This procedure represents a variant of the handling procedure. Thus, the NH rats represent an interesting group, the absence of this manipulation results in increased fearfulness.

In recent studies, we have found evidence for the idea that the effects of handling on either endocrine (Liu et al. 1997) or behavioral/emotional (Caldji et al. 1998) responses to stress are mediated by handling-induced changes in maternal behavior (Smotherman and Bell 1980; Hennessy et al. 1982). Mothers of handled pups exhibit increased licking/grooming and arched-back nursing (Lee and Williams 1975; Liu et al. 1997; Caldji et al. 1998). Thus, handling seemss to exert its effects on the development of fear-related behaviors by ensuring a consistently high level of licking/grooming and arched-back nursing during early life. The importance of maternal care is also reflected in the effects of repeated periods of prolonged maternal separation, which produce increased fearfulness in response to novelty, as compared to the handling manipulation. Such effects are apparent in rhesus monkeys, where re-

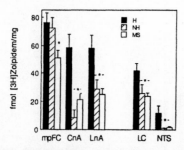

Figure 5. Type I central benzodiazepine receptor binding (fmol [³H]zolpidem binding per mg protein; mean ± SEM) in corticolimbic (upper panel) and noradrenergic cell body regions (lower panel) in handled (H), nonhandled (NH), and maternal separation (MS) animals (*n* = 5–6 per group). See Figure 4 legend for abbreviations. *$p < .01$ for comparison of H versus NH/MS rats.

peated periods of maternal separation resulted in increased fearfulness (e.g., Sackett 1969). Maternal separation in the rat, unlike handling, does not produce an increase in maternal licking/grooming or arched-back nursing; in fact, the opposite occurs. The offspring in the maternal separation condition experience long periods during which maternal care is absent. Moreover, even when the dam is present, the frequency of licking/grooming and arched-back nursing is reduced to levels typical of those observed in the mothers of NH litters. Taken together, these findings underscore the impor-

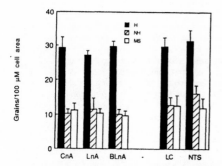

Figure 6. Mean ± SEM levels of expression of the mRNA for the γ₂ subunit of the GABA_A receptor complex (number of grains per cell area) amygdaloid, and noradrenergic cell body regions in handled (H), nonhandled (NH), and maternal separation (MS) animals (*n* = 5–6 per group). Levels are significantly higher in H animals cas ompared with either NH or MS animals for each region shown, $p < .0001$. See Figure 3 legend for abbreviations.

tance of maternal care in the development of fearfulness and provide an explanation for the comparable performance of the MS and NH animals.

These behavioral differences were associated with substantial effects of early experience on both GABA_A and CBZ receptor levels. The CBZ site is a component of the GABA_A receptor complex, and agonist binding to the CBZ site is associated with increased affinity of the GABA_A receptor for GABA. CBZ activation is thought to enhance GABAergic inhibition of fear and anxiety. It is interesting that the differences observed in GABA_A and CBZ receptor binding in corticolimbic structures were anatomically distinguishable. Thus, differences in GABA_A, but not CBZ binding were apparent in the frontal cortex; whereas, the opposite was true for differences in the lateral and central nuclei of the amygdala (see Figures 3 and 4). In contrast, in the locus coeruleus and the nucleus tractus solitarius MS and NH rats showed greatly reduced levels of both GABA_A and CBZ receptors. In addition, levels of the mRNA encoding for the γ2 GABA_A receptor subunit were significantly elevated in the amygdala, locus coeruleus, and nucleus tractus solitarius of H animals. The γ2 subunit seems to be essential for high affinity CBZ binding to the GABA_A receptor complex (e.g., Pritchett et al. 1989). Interestingly, Caldji et al. (1998) found that the adult offspring of High Licking/Grooming and Arched-Back Nursing (High LG-ABN) mothers showed significantly increased GABA_A and CBZ receptor binding in the amygdala as well as in the LC and NTS in comparison to the offspring of Low Licking/Grooming and Arched-Back Nursing (Low LG-ABN) mothers.

Although these data are correlational, there is evidence for the idea that differences in fearful responses to novelty could be associated with differences in GABA_A/CBZ receptor levels. Of particular interest are the results of human clinical studies. Glue et al. (1995) found that subjects that were high on measures of neuroticism showed reduced sensitivity to the benzodiazepine midazolam. In a series of studies, Roy-Byrne and colleagues (see Roy-Byrne et al. 1990, 1996) found reduced sensitivity to diazepam in patients with panic disorders and obsessive compulsive disorders and proposed that the reduced CBZ sensitivity was related to the phenomenon of anxiety. Although these studies have directly not shown decreased CBZ receptor levels, the findings are certainly consistent with the idea that decreased receptor levels in humans could be related to increased vulnerability to anxiety disorders. The hypothesis here is that there exists an endogenous anxiolytic ligand for the CBZ receptor and that decreased CBZ binding sites would, thus, result in enhanced fearfulness in the face of threat. The results of at least one study directly relate the effects of rearing condition on CBZ receptor levels with those on behavior. Escorihuela et al. (1992) found that postnatal handling improved performance in a test of two-way avoidance task. The effect of handling was significantly reversed in animals treated acutely with the CBZ receptor antagonist, RO 15-1788.

We observed differences in GABA$_A$/CBZ receptor binding as a function of early rearing condition at a number of sites, including the lateral and central n. of the amygdala, the medial prefrontal cortex, as well as directly in the regions containing noradrenergic cell bodies. BZ agonists have been thought to exert anxiolytic effects via their actions at a number of limbic areas (e.g., Thomas et al. 1985; Gray 1987; Persold and Treit 1995; Gonzalez et al. 1996). To date, the evidence is perhaps strongest for BZ effects at the level of the lateral and central n. of the amygdala. Thus, the direct administration of drugs that enhance GABAergic activity via actions at BZ receptor sites into the amygdala yields an anxiolytic effect (Hodges et al. 1987). There is evidence for BZ action directly at the level of both the lateral and the central n. of the amygdala. The results of recent studies have indicated that the corticotropin-releasing factor (CRF) neurons within the amygdala might serve as a specific target for BZ effects. The BZ receptor agonist, alprazolam, has been shown to reduce CRF content in the locus coeruleus (Owens et al. 1991). The amygdala is a significant source of the CRF in the region of the locus coeruleus (Gray et al. 1989; Valentino 1990; Koegler-Muly et al. 1993; van Bockstaele et al. 1996). de Boer et al. (1992) have shown that BZ administration attenuates the effects of intracerebroventricular (ICV) CRF treatment, suggesting that the CRF system is a target for the anxiolytic effects of the BZs (also see Swerdlow et al. 1986). We have recently reported significantly elevated CRF mRNA in amygdala of MS and, to a lesser extent, NH rats as compared with H rats (Plotsky et al. 1999, submitted). The same pattern was observed for Corticotropin-Releasing Factor Immunoreactivity (CRFir) in the locus coeruleus (also see Ladd et al. 1996). Considering the importance of this amygdaloid CRF system in mediating behavioral responses to novelty (Hitchcock and Davis 1986; Liang et al. 1992; Krahn et al. 1988), we propose that BZ–CRF interactions within the amygdala serve as a critical neural substrate for the behavioral differences in response to novelty observed among H, NH, and MS rats.

In addition to the amygdala, there is also evidence for the importance of BZ action at the level of the frontal cortex (Lippa et al. 1979) for anxiolytic effects. It seems likely that a variety of structures are involved in mediating the anxiolytic effects of BZs, depending upon the nature of the stressor (see Gonzalez et al. 1996). In this respect, because we have found alterations at several sites, the differences in GABA$_A$/CBZ receptor binding as function of early rearing condition could serve to influence a wide range of behavioral and endocrine responses.

These findings are also of interest in light of the substantial differences in HPA responses to stress in H versus NH or MS rats (Plotsky and Meaney 1993). HPA responses to stress are mediated by the release of CRF from the paraventricular n. of the hypothalamus. Interestingly, we found no differences in GABA$_A$/CBZ receptor binding in the Paraventricular-Releasing Factor Immuno-reactivity (PVNh). However, there were highly significant differences in the noradrenergic cell body regions, including C1, the locus coeruleus, and the NTS. Noradrenergic input to the PVNh provides the major known source of activation for CRF synthesis and release (see Plotsky et al. 1995; Pacak et al. 1995). Thus, the increased GABA$_A$/CBZ receptor binding observed in these regions in the H rats may also serve to dampen HPA responses to stress by decreasing the magnitude of the noradrenergic signal.

Our findings are also interesting to consider in light of the known effects of BZs on responses to different forms of stress (see Malizia et al. 1995; O'Boyle et al. 1986; Goldstein et al. 1982). BZs are known to decrease autonomic, endocrine, and emotional responses to anticipatory forms of stress, where the threat is implied. In contrast, BZs do not affect responses to forms of stress that involve actual pain or tissue damage. A comparable distinction has emerged in studies of HPA responses to stress in H and NH rats. H rats show reduced plasma ACTH and corticosterone responses to novelty, air-puff startle, restraint, and human handling, but not to cold or to endotoxin injection (see Bhatnagar et al. 1995; Meaney et al. 1996). These findings lend further support for the idea that differences in CBZ receptor levels may contribute to the differences in behavioral and endocrine responses to stress observed among H, NH, and MS rats.

ACKNOWLEDGMENTS

This research was supported by NIMH Grant MH50113 to PMP and MJM and by a grant from the Medical Research Council of Canada to MJM. MJM is supported by a MRCC Senior Scientist career award from the Medical Research Council of Canada. CC is supported by a graduate fellowship from the Fonds de la Recherche en Santé du Québec (FRSQ).

REFERENCES

Bhatnagar S, Shank N, Meaney MJ (1995): Hypothalamic-pituitary-adrenal function in handled and nonhandled rats in response to chronic stress. J Neuroendocrinol 7:107–119

Bodnoff SR, Suranyi-Cadotte BE, Quirion R, Meaney MJ (1987): Postnatal handling reduces novelty-induced fear and increases [3H] flunitrazepam binding in rat brain. Eur J Pharmacol 144:105–108

Bodnoff SR, Suranyi-Cadotte BE, Quirion R, Meaney MJ (1989): Role of the central benzodiazepine receptor system in behavioral habituation to novelty. Behav Neurosci 103:209–212

Britton DR, Thatcher-Britton R (1981): A sensitive open-field measure of anxiolytic drug action. Pharmacol Biochem Behav 15:577–580

Bureau MH, Olsen RW (1993): GABA_A receptor subtypes: Ligand binding heterogeneity demonstrated by photoaffinity labeling and autoradiography. J Neurochem 61:1479–1491

Caldji C, Francis F, Tannenbaum B, Sharma S, Meaney MJ (1998): Maternal care in infancy influences the development of neural systems mediating fearfulness in the rat. Proceedings of the National Academy of Sciences 95: 5335–5340

Chrousos GP, Gold PW (1992): The concepts of stress and stress system disorders. JAMA 267:1244–1252

Chu DMC, Albin RL, Young AB, Penney JB (1990): Distribution and kinetics of GABA_B binding sites in rat central nervous system: A quantitative autoradiographic study. Neuroscience 34:341–357

de Boer SF, Katz JL, Valentino RJ (1992): Common mechanism underlying the proconflict effects of corticotropin-releasing factor, a benzodiazepine inverse agonist and electric footshock. J Pharmacol Expt Therapeu 262:335–342

Denenberg, VH (1964): Critical periods, stimulus input, and emotional reactivity: A theory of infantile stimulation. Psychol Rev 71:335–351

Escorihuela RM, Fernandez-Teruel A, Nunez FJ, Zapata A, Tobena A (1992): Infantile stimulation and the role of the benzodiazepine receptor system in adult acquisition of two-avoidance behavior. Psychopharmacol 106:282–284

File SE (1995): Animal models of different anxiety states. In Biggio G, Costa E (eds), GABA_A Receptors and Anxiety: From Neurobiology to Treatment. New York, Raven Press, pp 93–113

Glue P, Wilson S, Coupland N, Ball D, Nutt D (1995): The relationship between benzodiazepine receptor sensitivity and neuroticism. J Anx Disord 9:33–45

Goldstein DS, Dionne R, Sweet J (1982): Circulatory, plasma catecholamine, cortisol, lipid and psychological responses to a real-life stress (third molar extraction): Effects of diazepam sedation and of inclusion of epinephrine with local anesthetic. Psychosom Med 44:259–272

Gonzalez LE, Andrews N, File SE (1996): 5-HT1A and benzodiazepine receptors in the basolateral amygdala modulate anxiety in the social interaction test, but not in the elevated plus-maze. Brain Res 732:145–153

Gray JA (1987): The Psychology of Fear and Stress. Cambridge, UK, Cambridge University Press, pp 16–21

Gray TS, Carney ME, Magnuson DJ (1989): Direct projections from the central amygdaloid nucleus to the hypothalamic paraventricular nucleus: Possible role in stress-induced adrenocorticotropin release. Neuroendocrinology 50:433–446

Hennessy MB, Vogt J, Levine S (1982): Strain of foster mother determines long-term effects of early handling: Evidence for maternal mediation. Physiol Psychol 10:153–157

Higley JD, Haser MF, Suomi SJ, Linnoila M (1991): Nonhuman primate model of alcohol abuse: Effects of early

experience, personality, and stress on alcohol consumption. Proc Nat Acad Sci USA 88:7261–7265

Hitchcock JM, Davis M (1986): Lesions of the amygdala, but not of the cerebellum or red nucleus, block conditioned fear as measured with the potentiated startle paradigm. Behav Neurosci 100:11–22

Hodges H, Green S, Glenn B (1987): Evidence that the amygdala is involved in benzodiazepine and serotonergic effects on punished responding, but not discrimination. Psychopharmacology 92:491–504

Jans J, Woodside BC (1990): Nest temperature: Effects on maternal behavior, pup development, and interactions with handling. Develop Psychobiol 23:51–534

Koegler-Muly SM, Owens MJ, Kilts GNED, Nemeroff CB (1993): Potential corticotropin-releasing factor pathways in the rat brain as determined by bilateral electrolytic lesions of the central amygdaloid nucleus and the paraventricular nucleus of the hypothalamus. J Neuroendocrinol 5:95–98

Krahn DD, Gosnell BA, Levine AS, Morley JE (1988): Behavioral effects of corticotropin-releasing factor: Localization and characterization of central effects. Brain Res 443:63–69

Ladd CO, Owens MJ, Nemeroff CB (1996): Persistent changes in corticotropin-releasing factor neuronal systems induced by maternal deprivation. Endocrinology 137:1212–1218

Lee MHS, Williams DI (1975): Long term changes in nest condition and pup grooming following handling of rat litters. Developmental Psychobiology 8:91–95

Leon M, Croskerry PG, Smith GK (1978): Thermal control of mother–infant contact in rats. Physiol Behav 21:793–811

Levine S (1957): Infantile experience and resistence to physiological stress. Science 126:405–406

Levine S (1962): Plasma-free corticosteroid response to electric shock in rats stimulated in infancy. Science 135:795–796

Levine S (1975): Psychosocial factors in growth and development. In Levi L (ed), Society, Stress, and Disease. London, Oxford University Press, pp 43–50

Liang KC, Melia KR, Campeau S, Falls WA, Miserendino MJD, Davis M (1992): Lesions of the central nucleus of the amygdala, but not the paraventricular nucleus of the hypothalamus, block the excitatory effects of corticotropin-releasing factor on the acoustic startle reflex. J Neurosci 12:2313–2320

Lippa AS, Critchett D, Sano MC, Klepner CA, Greenblat EN, Coupet J, Beer B (1979): Benzodiazepine receptors: Cellular and behavioral characteristics. Pharmacol Biochem Behav 10:831–843

Liu D, Tannenbaum B, Caldji C, Francis D, Freedman A, Sharma S, Pearson D, Plotsky PM, Meaney MJ (1997): Maternal care, hippocampal glucocorticoid receptor gene expression and hypothalamic-pituitary-adrenal responses to stress. Science 277:1659–1662

Malizia AL, Coupland NJ, Nutt DJ (1995): Benzodiazepine receptor function in anxiety disorders. In Biggio E, Sanna F, Costa, E (eds), GABAA Receptors and Anxiety: From Neurobiology to Treatment. New York, Raven Press, pp 115–133

McCabe JT, Desharnais RA, Pfaff DW (1989): Graphical and

statistical approaches to data analysis for in situ hybridization. Meth Enz 168:822–845

McEwen BS, Steller E (1993): Stress and the individual: Mechanisms leading to disease. Arch Intern Med 153:2093–2101

Meaney MJ, Diorio J, Widdowson J, LaPlante P, Caldji C, Seckl JR, Plotsky PM (1996): Early environmental regulation of forebrain glucocorticoid receptor gene expression: Implications for adrenocortical responses to stress. Develop Neurosci 18:49–72

Medina JH, Novas ML, Wolfman CNV, Levi de Stein M, De Robertis E (1983): Benzodiazepine receptors in the rat cerebral cortex and hippocampus undergo rapid and reversible changes following actue stress. Neuroscience 9:33–335

Niehoff DL, Kuhar MJ (1983): Benzodiazepine receptors: Localization in rat amygdala. J Neurosci 3:2091–2097

Nunez JF, Ferre P, Escorihuela RM, Tobena A, Fernandez-Teruel A (1996): Effects of postnatal handling of rats on emotional, HPA-axis, and prolactin reactivity to novelty and conflict. Physiology and Behavior 60:1355–1359

O'Boyle CA, Harris D, Barry H, Cullen JH (1986): Differential effect of benzodiazepine sedation in high and low anxious patients in a "real life" setting. Psychopharmacology 88:226–229

Owens MJ, Vargas MA, Knight DL, Nemeroff CB (1991): The effects of alprazolam on corticotropin-releasing factor neurons in the rat brain: Acute time course, chronic treatment, and abrupt withdrawal. J Pharmacol Experiml Therap 258:349–356

Pacak K, Palkovits M, Kopin I, Goldstein DS (1995): Stress-induced norepinepherine release in hypothalamic paraventricular nucleus and pituitary-adrenorcortical and sympathoadrenal activity: In vivo microdialysis studies. Front Neuroendocrinol 16:89–150

Paxinos G, Watson C (1986): The Rat Brain in Stereotaxic Coordinates. San Diegp, CA: Academic Press

Persold C, Treit D (1995): The central and basolateral amygdala differentially mediate the anxiolytic effects of benzodiazepines. Brain Res 671: 213–221

Plotsky PM, Meaney MJ (1993): Early, postnatal experience alters hypothalamic corticotropin-releasing factor (CRF) mRNA, median eminence CRF content, and stress-induced release in adult rats. Mol Brain Res 18:195–200

Plotsky PM, Caldji C, Sharma S, Meaney MJ (1999): The effects of early rearing environment on CRF gene expression and CRF receptor levels in rat brain. Proceedings of the National Academy of Sciences

Plotsky PM, Cunningham ET, Widmaier EP (1989): Catecholaminergic modulation of corticotropin-releasing factor and adrenocorticotropin secretion. Endocr Rev 10:437–458

Pritchett DB, Sontheimer H, Shivers BO, Ymer S, Kettenmann H, Schofield PR, Seeburg PH (1989): Importance of a novel GABAA receptor subunit for benzodiazepine pharmacology. Nature 338:582–585

Roy-Byrne P, Cowley DS, Greenblatt DJ, Shader RI, Hommer D (1990): Reduced benzodiazepine sensitivity in panic disorder. Arch Gen Psychiat 47:534–538

Roy-Byrne P, Wingerson DK, Radant A, Greenblatt DJ, Cowley DS (1996): Reduced benzodiazepine sensitivity in patients with panic disorder: Comparison with patients with obsessive-compulsive disorder and normal subjects. Am J Psychiat 153:1444–1449

Ruano D, Benavides J, Machlo A, Vitorica J (1993): Regional differences in the enhancement by GABA of [^{3}H]zolpidem binding to ω1 sites in rat membranes and sections. Brain Res 600:134–400

Sackett GP (1969): The persistence of abnormal behaviour in monkeys following isolation rearing. International Psychiatric Clinics 6:3–37

Seckl JR, Meaney MJ (1994): Early life events and later development of ischaemic heart disease. Lancet 342:1236

Shivers BD, Killisch I, Sprengel R, Sontheimer H, Kohler M, Schofield PR, Seeburg PH (1989): Two novel GABA$_A$ receptor subunits exist in distinct neuronal populations. Neuron 3:327–337

Smotherman WP, Bell RW (1980): Maternal mediation of early experience. In Bell RW, Smotherman WP (eds), Maternal Influences and Early Behavior. New York, SP Medical and Scientific Books, pp 201–210

Swerdlow NR, Geyer MA, Vale WW, Koog GF (1986): Corticotropin-releasing factor potentiates acoustic startle in rats: Blockade by chlordiazepoxide. Psychopharmacology 88:147–162

Thomas SR, Lewis ME, Iversen SD (1985): Correlation of [3H]diazepam binding density with anxiolytic locus in the amygdala complex of the rat. Brain Res 342:85–90

Valentino RJ (1990): Effects of CRF on spontaneous and sensory-evoked activity of locus coeruleus neurons. In Nemeroff CB (ed), Corticotropin-releasing Factor: Basic and Clinical Studies of a Neuropeptide. Boca Raton, FL, CRC Press, pp 218–231

van Bockstaele EJ, Colago EEO, Valentino RJ (1996): Corticotropin-releasing factor containing axon terminals synapse onto catecholamine dendrites and may presynaptically modulate other afferents in the rostral pole of the nucleus locus coeruleus in the rat brain. J Comp Neurol 364:523–534

Whiting P, McKernan PM, Iversen LL (1990): Another mechanism for creating diversity in γ-aminobutyric type A rceptors: RNA splicing directs expression of two forms of γ2 subunit, one of which contains a protein kinase C phosphorylation site. Proc Nat Acad Sci USA 87:9966–9970

PERGAMON

Neuroscience and Biobehavioral Reviews 23 (1999) 743–760

NEUROSCIENCE AND
BIOBEHAVIORAL
REVIEWS

www.elsevier.com/locate/neubiorev

The neuroanatomical and neurochemical basis of conditioned fear

M. Fendt[a,*], M.S. Fanselow[b]

[a]*Tierphysiologie, Universität Tübingen, Auf der Morgenstelle 28, D-72076 Tübingen, Germany*
[b]*Department of Psychology and Brain Research Institute, University of California, Los Angeles, CA 90095, USA*

Received 16 August 1998; received in revised form 1 March 1999; accepted 14 March 1999

Abstract

After a few pairings of a threatening stimulus with a formerly neutral cue, animals and humans will experience a state of conditioned fear when only the cue is present. Conditioned fear provides a critical survival-related function in the face of threat by activating a range of protective behaviors. The present review summarizes and compares the results of different laboratories investigating the neuroanatomical and neurochemical basis of conditioned fear, focusing primarily on the behavioral models of freezing and fear-potentiated startle in rats. On the basis of these studies, we describe the pathways mediating and modulating fear. We identify several key unanswered questions and discuss possible implications for the understanding of human anxiety disorders. © 1999 Elsevier Science Ltd. All rights reserved.

Keywords: Conditioned fear; Fear-potentiated startle; Conditioned stimulus; Unconditioned stimulus; Periaqueductal gray; Amygdala; Freezing

1. Introduction

Acute fear can be one of the most potent emotional experiences of our lifetime. The strength of this subjective experience may be because fear serves a function that is critical to the survival of higher vertebrates. It can be thought of as activation of a defensive behavioral system [1] that protects animals or humans against potentially dangerous environmental threats. For a small vertebrate such as a rat, an example of such an environmental threat would be predation. These threats may be innately recognized or learned [2,3]. For example, in the presence of a cat or a stimulus that predicts potential injury, a rat will become completely motionless and freeze, no movements except those associated with respiration are observable [4–6]. Furthermore, the rat shows a fear-potentiated startle response [7–9], analgesia [10], a host of autonomic changes [11,12] and increased release of several hormones [13]. In humans, these responses are correlated with a subjective state of fear [14–17]. The brain and body are dedicated to fast and effective defense to increase the chances of survival. Therefore, we use the term "fear" to refer to the activation of the defensive behavioral system that gives rise to this constellation of reactions to threatening stimuli.

There are three major reasons why scientists investigate the neuronal basis of fear. First, they use fear-modulated behaviors as models to understand how emotions influence behavior. Second, the investigation of the neuroanatomical and neurochemical basis of fear and anxiety is a prerequisite to develop strategies to treat and cure anxiety disorders. Anxiety disorders, such as specific phobias (agoraphobia, social phobia, etc.), panic disorder, post-traumatic stress disorder and generalized anxiety disorder are among the most common psychopathologies in the industrial states. Third, fearful experiences are rapidly learned about and long remembered. Hence, fear-conditioning has become an excellent model for trying to unravel the processes and mechanisms underlying learning and memory.

The development of several reliable behavioral tasks for investigating fear has led to major developments in our understanding of the neuronal basis of fear and anxiety in just the last decade. These behavioral tasks fall into two general classes: learned and unlearned. Tests of unlearned fear rely on stimuli that naturally provoke fear even when the animal has had no prior experience with the stimulus. The most frequently used stimuli in these tasks are natural predators (e.g. [18]) and exposure to a novel place (especially one that is brightly lighted [19] or elevated [20]). Approaches using learned fear examine conditioned behaviors provoked by stimuli that have become associated with something aversive, usually an electric footshock. These Pavlovian fear stimuli provoke many of the same behaviors that innate fear stimuli do. For example, rats freeze to both cats and conditioned stimuli associated with shock. To

* Corresponding author. Tel.: + 49-7071-297-5347; fax: + 49-7071-292-618.
E-mail address: markus.fendt@uni-tuebingen.de (M. Fendt)

measure the conditioned fear, a number of specific responses can be easily quantified such as fear-potentiated startle [7,8], freezing [3,21], tachycardia [22], conditioned defensive burying [23] and ultrasonic vocalization [24–26]. Alternatively, conditioned fear can be measured as a disruption of ongoing behaviors (e.g. conditioned suppression [27,28] and conflict tests [29,30]).

Validity for this approach to fear is obtained when a variety of stimuli that present clear threats to the subject generate a consistent set of behaviors that are tailored to protect against the threat. Additionally, these perceptual-motor organizations should have a common neuronal basis that overlaps considerably with the neural systems that mediate human fear and anxiety. Furthermore, the potency of drugs that modulate human fear and anxiety should correlate with their effectiveness in altering the behavior in these animal models.

The present review will primarily compare two specific responses to learned fear, freezing and fear-potentiated startle because these are most clearly identified with specific neural mechanisms that mediate between environmental stimulus and behavioral response. We go on to describe a hypothetical neuronal circuit which characterizes conditioned fear and helps organize existing knowledge about several conditioned defensive behaviors. Finally, we indicate what we feel to be some of the most critical open questions remaining for the analysis of fear.

2. The fear-conditioning procedure

Fear-conditioning is a form of Pavlovian conditioning where a subject is trained to associate a neutral stimulus (e.g. a 10 s presentation of light) with an aversive, unconditioned stimulus (US), such as an electric footshock. After such pairings, the light alone predicts the occurrence of the shock and acts as a conditioned stimulus (CS), eliciting a state of fear. Tones, lights, odors and tactile stimuli have been used as CS in fear-conditioning experiments. These stimuli range from a few seconds to a few minutes in duration and because of this brevity are called discrete CS. However, the subject also has fear responses conditioned to the setting in which the discrete CS and shock US was presented. Such stimuli, which are less temporally restricted and are made up of many separate features, are referred to as contextual stimuli. The fear of contextual and discrete CS can be acquired as rapidly as a single trial.

When examining the neural circuitry mediating fear learning, there are three different time-points at which experimental manipulations can be made. Manipulations during the training procedure affect the acquisition of conditioned fear, while manipulations during the testing procedure affect the expression of conditioned fear. If consolidation of a fear memory is to be targeted, the manipulation is made after acquisition, but before testing. If a brain structure were lesioned, the time-point when the lesion

was carried out can help us to make a statement about the influence of this lesion on the acquisition or on the expression of conditioned fear. If this brain structure were only involved in the acquisition of conditioned fear, only pre-training, and not post-training lesions would affect the measure of fear. On the contrary, if this brain structure was only involved in the expression of conditioned fear, both the pre- and post-training lesions should affect conditioned fear. Manipulations that affect consolidation are usually temporally graded such that the greatest effect occurs when the manipulation is carried out immediately after training. Obviously, reversible treatments provide the most powerful tools for separating acquisition, consolidation and expression processes.

2.1. Fear-potentiated startle

A startle response is elicited by a sudden acoustic, visual or tactile stimuli and is found in every mammal studied so far [31]. A typical startle response is composed of a fast, sequential muscle contraction, with the most prominent reaction around the face, neck and shoulders [15,31]. Possible functions of the startle response are to reduce the latency of a flight reaction [32] and/or a protection from a predator's attacks from behind by contraction of the dorsal muscles [33]. The electromyographically measured latency of the startle response in rats is only 5–10 ms [34,35], indicating a relatively short neuronal startle pathway with only a few central synapses. The elementary startle pathway was initially described by Davis and co-workers [36], and further detailed by Lingenhöhl and Friauf [37,38] and Lee and co-workers [39]. It includes the cochlear root neurons, the giant neurons of the caudal pontine nucleus of the reticular formation (PnC) and spinal motorneurons. Yeomans and Frankland [33] suggested a further parallel pathway additionally including the ventrolateral pons and spinal interneurons. In the last decade, the startle response became a valuable model for investigating behavioral modulations such as habituation [40,41], sensitization [42,43], pre-pulse inhibition [44,45] and Pavlovian conditioning [7,8]. Furthermore, appetitive emotions weaken the startle response [17,46,47], while aversive emotions such as fear or anxiety enhance the startle response [7,8,13,17,41].

The fear-potentiated startle paradigm was initially described by Brown, Kalish and Farber [7]. Rats are given several pairings of a light CS and footshock. After this procedure, the mean amplitude of the acoustic startle response to a loud noise is usually 50–100% higher in the presence of the light CS than to the noise alone [8]. The difference between these two trial types (light-noise and noise alone) represents the fear-potentiation of the startle response and acts as a measure of fear. Fear-potentiated startle is very sensitive to drugs that are known to modulate the state of fear: norepinephrine antagonists [49], benzodiazepine agonists [50], dopamine antagonists [8], opioid agonists [51], $5\text{-}HT_{1A}$ agonists [52], $5\text{-}HT_3$ antagonists

[53], corticotropin-releasing factor antagonists [54], cholecystokinin antagonists [55], neuropeptide Y agonists [56], NMDA-associated glycine receptor antagonists [57], NMDA antagonists [57] and ethanol [58,59] block or reduce the fear-potentiation of the startle response after systemic injections (reviewed in Refs. [8,60]). Most of these drugs were also tested in humans and had an anxiolytic effect [61–65].

Sensitization of the acoustic startle response is another approach used to investigate the effects of aversive stimuli on reflexes. Sensitization of the startle response is the immediate enhancement of startle amplitude after shock [42]. Initially this excitatory effect of footshock on startle was thought to be an unconditioned response to footshock [42]. Recent work indicates that sensitization reflects a rapid conditioning to the test environment [66,67]. Therefore, it is suggested that the mechanisms underlying the sensitization of the startle are largely identical to those that mediate fear-potentiated startle [68].

2.2. Freezing

Over a century ago, Darwin recognized that fear produces a profound suppression of activity in several species (see [69, p. 260]). Small [21] reported freezing as a characteristic fear response of rats and Griffith [5] reported that rats would show pronounced freezing in the presence of a cat. While freezing was reported to occur in aversive conditioning experiments using shock, it was initially considered a nuisance variable (e.g. [70]). Earlier studies of Pavlovian conditioned fear used measures such as bar press suppression that relied on what the rat was not doing (i.e. it had stopped eating [71,72]). Investigation of direct observational measures of freezing (e.g. [4,73]) and crouching [74] to shock associated cues began in earnest in the early 1970s, but these typically looked at reactions to contextual cues. Direct measures of freezing to discrete CS such as tones and lights began in Robert Bolles' laboratory in the late 1970s (e.g. [75,76]). Bouton and Bolles [77] showed that direct visual observation of freezing to tones paired with shock provided a measure that correlated highly with, but tended to be more sensitive than, other measures such as conditioned suppression. There tends to be no baseline freezing in control rats that have not received shock. There is reliable freezing with even a single brief (0.75 s) mild (0.5 mA) shock conditioning trial, and more robust training parameters can easily result in freezing levels near 100% (e.g. [78]). For rats, freezing is a highly selected response because movement makes the rat more detectable to predators and because predators are much more likely to attack moving than still prey. In other words, movement acts as a releasing stimulus for predatory attacks. This is probably why freezing is observed even in situations that afford the opportunity for other behaviors such as escape (see [79] for a review).

2.3. Other behavioral indices

There are certainly other behavioral manifestations of fear in aversive Pavlovian conditioning situations. Obviously, there are profound changes in autonomic function. Defecation covaries with other measures of fear [80] and blood pressure shows a reliable increase (e.g. [81–84]). While fear CS influence heart rate as well, these changes are much less consistent than the hypertensive effects of fear stimuli [84]. Both tachycardia (e.g. [22]) and bradycardia (e.g. [85,86]) have been reported. What determines the direction of the heart rate change is not clear at this time, but whether or not the rat is restrained [86,87], the type of conditioning control one uses [88] and the baseline heart rate (e.g. [85]) appear to contribute and possibly interact.

There are, of course, other responses that characterize the fear response. For example, rats show ultrasonic vocalizations (e.g. [24–26]) and a loss in pain sensitivity [89,90]. Such responses add to the validity that the fear state is related to a species typical survival function (e.g. [10,91,92]).

3. The role of the amygdala

It is now well established that the amygdala plays a pivotal role in fear. The initial hints of this were provided by Brown and Schaffer [93] who reported that large lesions of the temporal lobe tamed previously ferocious monkeys. Kluver and Bucy [94] characterized the rather widespread emotional disturbance caused by such brain damage and this psychopathology became known as the Kluver–Bucy syndrome. Weiskrantz [95] reported that many aspects of the Kluver–Bucy syndrome could be produced by damage restricted to the amygdala. Fuster and Uyeda [96] were the first to show that there were cells within the amygdala that selectively respond to a CS paired with shock. Subsequently, it has been confirmed that cells in both the central [97] and lateral nuclei [98] of the amygdala show short latency CS specific activity. The fact that these neurons in the amygdala will show increased responsiveness to stimuli after they were paired with shock indicates that the structure is sensitive to the convergence of the CS and US information. The dorsal subdivision of the lateral amygdala may be important for the processing of this convergence as it has cells that respond to both tones and footshock [99].

Stimulation of afferent pathways to the amygdala can lead to an enhanced responsiveness of cells in the amygdala; in other words, the amygdala shows long-term potentiation (LTP [100–103]). Using lateral amygdala slices, Huang and Kandel [102] showed that LTP depends on post-synaptic depolarization and calcium influx into the post-synaptic cell. As this LTP accludes paired-pulse facilitation, Maren and Fanselow suggested that the potentiation was expressed through a pre-synaptic mechanism [103]. Huang and Kandel [102] have subsequently confirmed this observation.

225

Glutamate receptors, particularly NMDA receptors, play a critical role in these responses [102–104]. Indeed, fear-conditioning itself can potentiate amygdala responses [105,106]. Together these electrophysiological data indicate that the amygdala has the potential to be a point where the CS and US converge to produce fear-conditioning. Therefore, in the next sections we examine the amygdala's contribution to two specific behavioral indices of conditioned fear, freezing and fear-potentiated startle.

3.1. The amygdala and fear-potentiated startle

The first studies investigating the neuroanatomical basis of fear-potentiated startle were carried out in the mid 1980s. A series of studies by Davis and colleagues showed that the pathway from the amygdala to the PnC is essential for the potentiation of the startle response by conditioned fear. First, they showed that fear-conditioning potentiates the startle response at the level of the PnC [107,108]. Second, lesions of the amygdala blocked fear-potentiated startle using a visual CS [109] or an auditory CS [110], while lesions of other nuclei (e.g. the cerebellum or the red nucleus, which are both known to be involved in Pavlovian conditioning of reflexive responses [111,112]) had no effect. Third, destruction of the direct pathway from the central nucleus of the amygdala to the PnC—the ventral amygdalofugal pathway [113]—blocked fear-potentiation of the startle response [114]. Thus, the amygdala is necessary to observe fear-potentiation of startle.

Activity in the amygdala is sufficient for potentiation of startle as electrical stimulation there increases the amplitude of the startle response [115–117]. Koch and colleagues showed a strong short-latency potentiation of the startle amplitude after injections of glutamate into the central nucleus of the amygdala [118], confirming that it was the activity of neurons intrinsic to the amygdala that potentiated the response. A longer latency increase of startle amplitude could be produced when selective metabotropic glutamate receptor agonists were applied to the amygdala [119].

3.1.1. Acquisition of fear-potentiated startle

To test the hypothesis that NMDA receptor-dependent LTP in the amygdala mediates fear-conditioning, Davis and colleagues microinjected NMDA receptor antagonists (AP-5 and AP-7) and pertussis toxin into the basolateral nucleus of the amygdala. These LTP-impairing treatments blocked acquisition, consistent with the suggestion that NMDA receptors in the basolateral nucleus of the amygdala are involved in the plasticity underlying fear-conditioning [120–122]. Interestingly, the elimination of fear-potentiated startle during extinction is an NMDA-dependent process, as well. Injections of AP-5, but not of the non-NMDA receptor antagonist CNQX into the basolateral amygdala blocked extinction of fear-potentiated startle [123].

Gewirtz and Davis [124] extended these results to second-order conditioning. This occurs when a previously conditioned CS (first-order CS) is paired with another CS (second-order CS). The first-order CS functions like a US, giving the second-order CS the ability to produce a conditioned response. Injections of AP-5 into the basolateral nucleus of the amygdala during the acquisition of second-order fear-conditioning blocks the acquisition of fear-potentiation to the second-order CS. Interestingly, the expression of fear-potentiation by the first-order CS was slightly increased during testing. One explanation of this finding is that AP-5 blocked the extinction of the first-order CS that normally occurs during second-order training.

A lesion study by Tischler and Davis [125] led to the initial hypothesis that the amygdala receives information about a visual CS via a pathway from the retina to the dorsal lateral geniculate nucleus to the visual cortex to the deep layers of the superior colliculus and down to the elementary startle pathway. Further extensive lesion studies by the Davis group [126–129] suggested that the basolateral and/or the lateral nucleus of the amygdala receives CS information from the perirhinal cortex. Auditory CS are mediated from the cochlea via different subnuclei of the auditory thalamus to the perirhinal cortex, while visual CS are mediated from the retina via the lateral geniculate body to the perirhinal cortex.

There are several routes by which information about shock can reach the amygdala, but it seems unlikely that any single one of these pathways is necessary and sufficient as a US pathway for conditioning. Fendt and colleagues [130] suggested that US information for fear-potentiated startle is carried from the spinal cord, through the nucleus paragigantocellularis and the locus coeruleus to the amygdala. This was based on the finding that the locus coeruleus is activated by footshock via the nucleus paragigantocellularis [131–133], which in turn projects to the amygdala. The locus coeruleus-amygdala pathway uses noradrenaline as a transmitter [134] and a reduction of noradrenaline release in the amygdala blocks the enhanced startle seen immediately after footshock [130]. However, the hypothesis that noradrenaline release in the amygdala mediates the reinforcing aspects of the US was contradicted by the finding that a blockade of amygdaloid β-adrenergic receptors has no effect on the acquisition of fear-potentiated startle [122].

The central nucleus of the amygdala also receives nociceptive information via a projection from the nucleus parabrachialis [135,136]. The transmitters of this projection are mainly neuropeptides but also noradrenaline [137]. While this pathway may make a contribution to conditioning the fact that, at least in rat, there do not appear to be projections from the central nucleus to the lateral nucleus suggests that this pathway cannot support the CS–US convergence found in the lateral nucleus [138].

Based on anatomical tracing and electrolytic lesions experiments, Shi and Davis [139,140] recently suggested that two parallel pathways can provide the amygdala with nociceptive input. Footshocks information is conveyed from the spinal cord to the basolateral nucleus of the amygdala

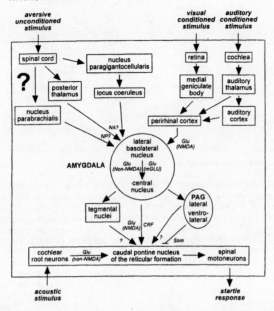

Fig. 1. Hypothetical circuit mediating fear-potentiated startle. Abbreviations: CRF, corticotropin-releasing factor; Glu, glutamate; NA, noradrenaline; NP, neuropeptides; Som, somatostatin.

via a direct pathway that synapses in the posterior intralaminar nucleus. An additional indirect pathway includes synapses in the ventral posteriolateral thalamic nucleus, the posterior thalamic nucleus, the posterior intralaminar nucleus, the areas S1 and S2 and the caudal insular cortex. Acquisition of fear-potentiated startle was only blocked when both the direct and indirect pathways were lesioned, thus either one is sufficient to support conditioning. As combined lesions in these pathways affected acquisition but not expression of fear-potentiated startle they may indeed function as parallel US pathways. However, the pattern of data also leaves open the possibility that these pathways modulate memory storage within the amygdala.

3.1.2. Expression of fear-potentiated startle

Injections of the non-NMDA receptor antagonist CNQX [141] or NBQX [142] but not of the NMDA receptor antagonist AP-5 [120] into the central or the basolateral nucleus of the amygdala blocked the expression of fear-potentiated startle. This suggests that fear-potentiation is mediated by a projection from the lateral and/or basolateral nucleus of the amygdala to the central nucleus of the amygdala activating non-NMDA receptors. As intra-amygdaloid injections of the CCK_B receptor agonist pentagastrin [143,144] increased the baseline startle amplitude and

systemic injections of CCK_B antagonists blocked the fear-potentiated startle [55], amygdaloid CCK_B receptors seem to be involved in the expression of fear-potentiated startle, as well.

The central nucleus of the amygdala is the origin of a direct pathway to the elementary startle pathway [113,118,145], mediating the expression of fear-potentiated startle [114]. Koch and Ebert [146] showed that the effect of amygdaloid stimulation on the activity of PnC neurons can be blocked by microiontophoretic applications of the NMDA receptor antagonist AP-5 into the PnC. These results and the fact that AP-5 microinjections into the PnC block fear-potentiated startle [147] suggested that the direct pathway from the central nucleus of the amygdala to the PnC mediates fear-potentiated startle, uses glutamate as a transmitter and acts via NMDA receptors. This hypothesis is supported by previous studies, showing that NMDA receptors in the PnC are involved in the up-modulation of the startle response, while the non-NMDA receptors are involved in the direct mediation of the startle response [148–150]. Anatomical experiments showed that the direct pathway from the central nucleus of the amygdala to the PnC uses the neuropeptide corticotropin-releasing factor (CRF) as a transmitter [145]. Microinjections of CRF receptor antagonists into the PnC block the expression of

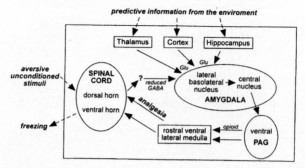

Fig. 2. Hypothetical circuit mediating conditional fear-induced freezing and opioid analgesia. Abbreviations: Glu, glutamate; GABA, γ-amino butyric acid.

fear-potentiated startle [145], while injections of CRF into the PnC increased the baseline startle response [151].

Conditioned inhibition of fear-potentiation of startle occurs when a second stimulus (e.g. a tone) signals that the CS (e.g. a light) will not be followed by the usual foot-shock during training [152]. Conditioned inhibition was not blocked by amygdaloid lesions suggesting that conditioned inhibitors acts through another brain structure [153].

3.1.3. Summary

The amygdala is a critical structure for the acquisition of fear-potentiated startle. Information about the CS and the US converge in the lateral, and perhaps basolateral amygdala (Fig. 1). A direct pathway from the central nucleus of the amygdala to the PnC uses CRF and glutamate as a transmitter and modulates the primary startle circuit to produce fear-potentiation.

3.2. The amygdala and freezing

The involvement of the amygdala in freezing to shock associated cues was first demonstrated by Blanchard and Blanchard [2], who found that large lesions of the amygdala abolished freezing to a context associated with shock. LeDoux and colleagues extended this earlier findings by showing that selective destruction of cells within the lateral amygdala block freezing to auditory CS [154]. This critical role of the amygdala has been confirmed for virtually all CRs to fear stimuli as blood pressure [154], heart rate [155], analgesia [156,157] and ultrasonic vocalizations [158] are blocked by amygdala lesions. Fig. 2 indicates a circuit responsible for the mediation of two of these fear CRs, freezing and opioid analgesia.

3.2.1. Acquisition of freezing

The basolateral complex of the amygdala, particularly the lateral and basolateral nuclei, appears to be critical for acquisition of freezing. Blockade of NMDA receptor activity [159–161] or enhanced GABAergic inhibition

[162–164] within the amygdala during acquisition blocks the expression of freezing in the undrugged state. Consistent with the electrophysiological and fear-potentiated startle data reviewed before, the lateral and/or basolateral nuclei seem to be the important site of CS–US convergence and neural plasticity as AP-5 prevented acquisition when given to the basolateral complex but not when injected into the central nucleus [159]. Extinction of fear-induced freezing to both the discrete and contextual CS is also prevented by administering AP-5 to the basolateral complex [160].

Although fear-potentiated startle studies have typically used a light as a discrete CS, freezing experiments have typically used tone. Information about the discrete CS, provoking freezing, appears to arrive at the amygdala via direct thalamo-amygdala and also thalamo-cortico-amygdala projections [154]; either pathway appears to be suffi-cient for mediating a conditioned freezing response to tone. The primary pathway mediating freezing to a discrete CS appears to be the direct thalamo-amygdala pathway. The cortico-amygdala pathway may serve more complex fear-related information-processing, and also provide a redun-dant pathway capable of supporting simple conditioning as well [165–167]. The properties of freezing make it ideal for analyzing fear of more static, or contextual cues [78,168]. The hippocampal formation appears to play a criti-cal role in providing the amygdala with information about contextual CS [86,103,169].

As with fear-potentiated startle, the nature of the pathway carrying US information is not clear, even though footshock is known to evoke responses in the lateral amygdala [99]. Currently, the best candidate is the spinothalamic tract, which carries somatosensory information about the shock US to the posterior intralaminar nucleus (PIN) of the thala-mus. The PIN is immediately ventromedial to the areas of the medial geniculate that carry auditory CS information [170,171]. Tone footshock pairings result in altered tuning curves of cells in the medial geniculate [172] and electrical stimulation of the PIN can serve as an US for conditioned bradycardia in rabbits to auditory stimuli [170]. It is not known if this specific pathway or some analogue supports conditioning in other CS modalities. Additionally, because lesions that damaged the PIN did not prevent acquisition of freezing to a tone paired with footshock, other US pathways must be sufficient. As was shown with fear-potentiated startle, the insular cortex may be the redundant pathway [140], but that has yet to be tested for freezing.

In a more general sense, GABA antagonism has been found to function as an US for Pavlovian fear-conditioning [173] and as mentioned before, GABAergic agonists block acquisition of conditioned fear. Transgenic mice with the B_3 subunit of the $GABA_A$ receptor deleted show an impairment in the acquisition of conditioned freezing [174]. Therefore, it seems possible that a reduction in tonic GABAergic inhibition at the amygdala acts as the ultimate effect of the US to promote conditioning.

There is a serious conceptual problem with any potential US pathway for fear-conditioning if fear-conditioning is to be linked to a mechanism of cellular plasticity like LTP. The LTP analogy suggests that a CS cannot initially activate cells that can produce fear, but it acquires the ability to do so because it is paired with a US that can effectively depolarize these cells. This would suggest that the US should be capable of generating the constellation of fear responses that the LTP is presumed to support. However, while CS paired with shock readily produce freezing as a conditioned response, the shock US itself has no ability to provoke freezing [80,168]. Future research will need to reconcile this discrepancy between behavior and cellular mechanism, but the neural basis of how the US fosters learning currently stands as the most open question in the acquisition of Pavlovian fear.

3.2.2. Expression of freezing

As with fear-potentiated startle, the amygdala is important for expression of conditioned fear-induced freezing. If a rat is trained with an intact amygdala, excitotoxic lesions of the structure abolish expression of freezing to both tone and contextual CS even when a substantial consolidation period is given between training and testing [175]. Amygdala application of lidocaine, muscimol and diazepam all block expression of freezing [156,162,163]. AP-5 blocks expression of freezing to both discrete [160] contextual stimuli [161], and this contrasts with the lack of effect of AP-5 on the expression of fear-potentiated startle to a fear-inducing tone [120] or light [122]. However, these effects of AP-5 are consistent with the finding that AP-5 also blocks evoked potentials in the lateral and basolateral nuclei in response to electrical stimulation of the pathways carrying information about contextual [103] and discrete CS to the amygdala [104].

As with fear-potentiated startle, the central nucleus acts as an output pathway to brain structures that generate freezing. However, for freezing these projections from the central nucleus terminate in the midbrain rather than the brain stem.

3.3. Other models

The involvement of the amygdala in several other indices of Pavlovian fear appears to be consistent with the data from freezing and fear-potentiated startle. Kapp and colleagues [155] were the first to show that amygdala lesions blocked autonomic responses to Pavlovian fear stimuli—in this case it was conditioned bradycardia in rabbits. Iwata et al. extended this finding to arterial hypertension in the rat [154]. Conditioned fear-induced analgesia is also blocked by amygdala lesions [176].

In humans, damage to the amygdala precludes fear-conditioning as assessed by changes in skin conductance [177,178]. While the emotional component fear of conditioning was blocked in these patients, as long as the hippocampus was intact they remembered the events that happened during training. This indicates that the amygdala is specifically involved in learning the emotional aspects of the fear-conditioning experience. Other, non-emotional information is encoded in parallel by other brain systems.

The data reviewed above indicate four important points: (1) a large number of very different indices of conditioned fear are abolished by amygdala lesions; (2) this structure receives convergence of CS and US information; (3) pharmacological manipulations targeted at neural plasticity in this structure also abolish learning; and (4) evoked activity in this structure shows changes following Pavlovian fear-conditioning. When these are taken together, the inescapable conclusion is that the amygdala is a crucial structure for the learning of fear.

The central nucleus may be the end of the common pathway mediating fear as "fear state" and it appears that different efferents from the central nucleus mediate different fear responses. Central nucleus projections to the PnC mediate the fear-potentiation of startle. However, efferents to the lateral hypothalamus [179] and medulla, e.g. [180], mediate autonomic responses. Finally, projections to the periaqueductal gray (PAG) are critical for freezing and analgesia [81,179,181], but may be important for the expression of fear-potentiated startle, as well [48,181–183]. Indeed, second to the amygdala, the PAG may be the most critical area in the brain for fear and defensive behaviors [184,185].

4. The role of the periaqueductal gray

4.1. The periaqueductal gray and fear-potentiated startle

Cassella and Davis [186] first showed that the PAG is involved in the modulation of startle responding. They reported that electrolytic lesions of the dorsal PAG enhanced baseline amplitude, habituation and sensitization of the startle response. Although these lesions increased the sensitization of the startle response, no influences on the potentiation of startle by conditioned fear could be observed [186]. Some of Cassella's and Davis' data were supported later by Borszcz et al. [187], showing that electrolytic lesions of the ventrolateral PAG enhance both short-term and long-term habituation. Chemical PAG lesions by Fendt and co-workers [184] totally blocked the sensitization of the startle response without affecting the baseline startle amplitude. Furthermore, anatomical data of this study showed a possible indirect pathway from the central nucleus of the amygdala via the lateral PAG to the PnC mediating the effects of aversive stimuli on the startle response. A follow-up study showed that PAG lesions prevent fear-potentiated startle [48], suggesting that the PAG is involved in the mediation of fear-potentiated startle too. In both lesion studies, mainly the lateral and the dorsal part of the PAG was lesioned.

Walker and Davis [188] chemically lesioned the dorsolateral PAG more rostrally than the lesions of Fendt and colleagues, and found that these lesions did not block fear-potentiated startle if the rats were trained with moderate footshock (0.6 mA). If strong footshocks (1.6 mA) were used, fear-potentiated startle was reliable only in lesioned rats but not in control rats. Furthermore, chemical stimulation of the dorsolateral PAG reduced fear-potentiated startle without affecting baseline startle amplitudes. The authors suggested that the dorsolateral PAG is activated by particularly aversive events and this activation may interfere with the expression of fear-potentiated startle.

These data suggest that different regions of the PAG differentially influence fear-potentiated startle. For example, weak chemical stimulation of the lateral PAG enhances fear-potentiated startle [182] and electrical stimulation of the same area increases the startle baseline amplitude [189], while chemical stimulation of the ventrolateral PAG attenuates the expression of fear-potentiated startle [182].

4.1.1. Expression of fear-potentiated startle

Fendt and colleagues [48] lesioned the PAG before and after the fear-conditioning training procedure. Both the pre- and post-training lesions prevented fear-potentiated startle, indicating that the PAG is certainly involved in the expression of fear-potentiated startle. However, these experiments do not rule out a potential role of the PAG in the acquisition of fear-potentiated startle. Further experiments are necessary to resolve this question.

4.1.2. Inhibition of fear-potentiated startle

Anatomical and electrophysiological experiments revealed a somatostatinergic projection from the ventrolateral PAG to the PnC, which may act to reduce the excitatory effects of glutamate on tone-evoked activity of the PnC [190]. Weak chemical stimulation of the ventrolateral PAG led to a decrease of fear-potentiated startle [181,182] and injections of somatostatin into the PnC dose-dependently reduced fear-potentiation of the startle response [190]. These results suggested that this somatostatinergic

projection from the ventrolateral PAG to the PnC is involved in the inhibition of fear-potentiated startle.

Recent results suggest that inhibition of fear-potentiated startle by the ventrolateral PAG is not involved in conditioned inhibition of fear-potentiation of startle as chemical stimulation of the ventrolateral PAG decreased the fear-potentiated startle, but did not affect the conditioned inhibition of fear-potentiated startle [182]. In contrast, there are indications that the dorsal PAG is involved in the mediation of conditioned inhibition, as chemical stimulation of the dorsal PAG reduces conditioned inhibition of fear-potentiated startle [182].

4.1.3. Summary

A pathway from the central nucleus of the amygdala to the PnC via the lateral PAG is involved in the mediation of the effects of conditioned fear on the elementary startle circuit. Additionally, the ventrolateral PAG has a somatostatinergic projection to the elementary startle circuit, which is involved in the inhibition of fear-potentiated startle.

4.2. The periaqueductal gray and freezing

As stated earlier, the PAG is absolutely critical for freezing. Liebmann et al. [191] discovered the PAG's involvement in this response when they found that rats with large lesions of the PAG did not freeze following an extended series of strong shocks. Lesions of the PAG eliminate freezing of rats not only to conditioned fear stimuli but to cats as well [92]. These lesions attenuate conditioned freezing when made either before or after training [192]. The ventrolateral PAG seems to be the region critical for freezing. First, lesions of the PAG that completely spare the tissue ventral and ventrolateral to the aqueduct do not reduce freezing [193]. Furthermore, lesions of the dorsal raphe that spare the surrounding ventral PAG also fail to reduce freezing [194]. Carrive and colleagues [185] examined Fos immunoreactivity in rats following exposure to a context previously paired with shock. They found that these rats both froze and showed the greatest number of Fos stained nuclei in the ventrolateral column of the PAG compared to the control.

As with fear-potentiated startle, dorsolateral PAG lesions have a modulatory effect on freezing. Dorsolateral PAG lesions made before, but not after training, will enhance the level of freezing observed on testing [192,193]. However, this enhancing effect is confined to training parameters that show paradoxically reduced freezing because of very dense shock schedules.

Within the PAG, expression of the unconditioned response and the conditioned response to shock can be doubly dissociated [181]. Lesions of the dorsolateral PAG reduce the unconditioned burst of activity produced by the shock, but do not reduce the conditioned freezing. Ventrolateral regions have the opposite effect; they reduce conditioned freezing but do not affect the unconditioned activity burst. This dissociation further illustrates the profound separation of the CR and the UR in Pavlovian fear-conditioning.

4.3. Other models

While direct stimulation of the PAG can have pronounced autonomic effects [195], it has been repeatedly demonstrated that the autonomic reactions to conditioned fear stimuli do not depénd on the PAG [81,179]. However, like freezing, fear-induced analgesia depends on the PAG as lesions of this structure block the reduction in pain sensitivity produced by conditional fear [81]. Within the PAG, freezing and analgesia are dissociable as injections of the opioid antagonist naltrexone into the ventral PAG block analgesia but not freezing [196]. This conditioned fear-induced analgesia is realized from projections from the PAG to the rostral ventromedial medulla [81]. Fig. 2 summarizes this information.

5. Other brain regions

Although the amygdala and PAG play a central role in the acquisition and expression of fear-related behavior, certainly several other brain regions play an important role as well. In the ensuing paragraphs, we will discuss the two brain regions that have been shown to play a role in fear-potentiated startle and freezing, the tegmental area and the hippocampal formation, respectively.

5.1. Tegmental nuclei

The tegmental nucei play a role in fear-potentiated startle, but this area is yet to be examined for freezing response. Sensitization of the startle response after application of footshock is blocked by microinjections of substance P antagonists into the PnC [197]. This indicates that the laterodorsal tegmental nucleus is involved in the potentiation of the startle response by fear, as the laterodorsal tegmental nucleus is the only brain structure providing substance P-ergic input to the PnC [198]. Electrolytic lesions of the midbrain tegmental area (including the lateral tegmental nucleus) blocked fear-potentiation of the startle response [114].

Frankland and Yeomans [199] made chemical lesion of the rostrolateral midbrain, a brain area including the lateral tegmental nucleus, and showed that these lesions also block fear-potentiated startle. They suggested that a further parallel pathway from the amygdala via the rostrolateral midbrain (the lateral tegmental nucleus?) to the brainstem is involved in the mediation of fear-potentiated startle. Anatomical tracing studies showed that the amygdalofugal pathway (including the direct pathway from the amygdala to the PnC) cross the midbrain tegmental nuclei but there is also a projection from the central nucleus of the amygdala terminating in this area [113,183].

The ventral tegmental area (VTA) plays a role in fear-potentiated startle [189]. Chemical lesions of the VTA blocked the expression of fear-potentiated startle. Electrical stimulation of the VTA enhanced the baseline startle amplitude and increased the fear-potentiation of the startle response, while microinjections of the $D_{2/3}$ receptor antagonist quinpirole into the VTA totally blocked the fear-potentiated startle [190].

Injections of CCK-8S, a CCK receptor agonist, into the PnC increase the baseline startle amplitude [200], suggesting that an excitatory CCK-ergic projection to the PnC is involved in the expression of fear-potentiated startle. The VTA, the central nucleus of the amygdala and the PAG show a high density of CCK containing neurons [201] and project to the PnC, so any or all of these projections may use CCK as a transmitter.

5.2. Hippocampus

As might be expected from its role in spatial [202] and/or configural [203] learning, the hippocampus plays a disproportionate role in the fear acquired in the situation where fear-conditioning occurred. When tones were paired with shock, lesions of the hippocampus blocked freezing to the contextual cues associated with shock, but the same rats froze normally to the tone [204,205]. Lesions of the hippocampus made shortly after training produce a severe retrograde amnesia for contextual fear [169,206]. If the lesions are made prior to conditioning, anterograde amnesia is also observed, although it seems to be less pronounced than retrograde amnesia [206–208]. Retrograde amnesia for conditioned freezing to contextual cues is time-limited, as the interval between training and lesion increases the retrograde amnesia decreases [169,206,208]. The effects of hippocampal lesions on freezing to contextual cues are remarkably selective, in a way that accords well with the human amnesic syndrome [209]. Some forms of memory are drastically impaired (context conditioning), while others are spared (conditioned freezing to auditory cues) and the type of memory that is lost shows a temporal gradient for retrograde amnesia [210].

McNish et al. [211] reported that while lesions of the hippocampus disrupt freezing to contextual cues, they do not affect the fear-potentiated startle to the same contextual cues. Unfortunately, a flaw in this study makes it premature to conclude that the hippocampus plays a different role in these two measures of contextual fear. McNish et al. did not include an assessment of the effects of hippocampal lesions on baseline startle magnitude. As the hippocampal lesions have been reported to increase the baseline startle response [212], the effects of hippocampal lesions on fear-potentiated startle would be masked by any increases in baseline startle response. It should be noted that the specificity of the deficit in the contextual freezing described before, indicates that hippocampal lesions do not affect the rat's ability to freeze [207,209]. Given the very selective effects of hippocampal

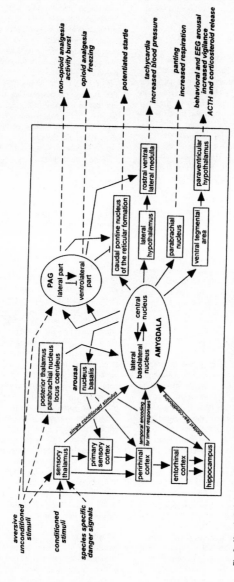

Fig. 3. Hypothetical circuit mediating the different aspects of conditioned fear. Abbreviations: ACTH, adrenocorticotrophic hormone; EEG, electro-encephalogram; PAG, periaqueductal gray.

lesions on fear and its more general role in memory, it seems likely that its function is to convey a configural or spatial memory of context to the amygdala, where it can be associated with shock [103]. This places the hippocampus on the input side of fear-conditioning.

6. Summary, a neural circuitry and open questions

The studies reviewed here suggest a certain neural circuitry and this is shown in Fig. 3. This circuit goes a long way in integrating and summarizing the extensive data on Pavlovian fear-conditioning.

As shown in the figure, the amygdala plays the central role in the acquisition and expression of fear to the conditioned stimulus [136,213–216]. The amygdala is the interface between the sensory system that carry information about the CS and US, and the different motor and autonomic systems that control the conditioned reactions. If any one structure is to be associated with the acquisition of conditioned fear, it is the lateral and/or basolateral amygdala. It seems likely that the cellular mechanism underlying this learning is NMDA-receptor dependent long-term potentiation (LTP) [106,217–219].

The amygdala receives information about the US from several sources that act in parallel. How they act to foster association formation is unknown. The problem arises because in fear-conditioning the conditioned and the unconditioned response are different; the US conditions responses it does not normally activate.

The CS pathway to the amygdala seems well characterized. As is shown in Figs. 2 and 3, the lateral and basolateral amygdala receive direct input from the thalamus as well as cortically processed input via the perirhinal cortex and hippocampal formation. What function do each of these pathways serve? As has been described earlier, for the hippocampus the case seems clear; information processed by the hippocampus normally functions to provide contextual information to the amygdala [169,205]. However, the available data does not provide any clear picture for a differential role of cortico- and thalamo-amygdala projections in excitatory fear-conditioning to discrete CS. The pathways seem to function somewhat redundantly as either route seems sufficient to support fear-conditioning on its own [126,167,220]. The sorts of discriminations, such as sound localization, considered to depend on the auditory cortex have yet to be tested with fear-conditioning [221–223]. After sufficient overtraining, fear-potentiated startle seems to peak at the point when the US is normally delivered [224]. Such temporal encoding is likely to require processing in cortical regions such as the perirhinal cortex [225].

There also seem to be pharmacological differences in the pathways that carry CS information to the amygdala. Projections from the hippocampal formation [103] and medial geniculate body [104,226] use both the NMDA and the AMPA receptors for normal synaptic transmission,

as NMDA antagonists reduce evoked potentials in the amygdala produced by stimulation of these structures. On the contrary, AMPA and not NMDA antagonists [104,226] reduce amygdala responses to activity in auditory cortex. Expression of freezing to conditioned tone and contextual stimuli is reduced by NMDA antagonists applied to the amygdala of rats trained in the absence of drug [160,161], but expression of fear-potentiated startle to a tone CS is not affected by NMDA antagonists [120]. The most straightforward explanation of this pattern is that fear-potentiated startle depends on a cortico-amygdala glutamatergic pathway that requires only AMPA activity to drive action potentials. However, thalamo- and hippocampo-amygdala glutamatergic pathways that require both the NMDA and the AMPA currents for the generation of action potentials may drive freezing. Note that the Campeau et al. [120] study used a relatively large number of training trials and examined a response that is well timed [224]. The freezing study used few trials and a response that is not particularly well-timed [161]. Thus, the pattern of data is consistent with the idea that cortico-amygdala projections are particularly important for temporal encoding that is revealed when very discrete fear responses are observed in overtrained animals. Certainly, this hypothesis is in need of further analysis.

Given the schema presented here and the generally devastating effects of amygdala lesions on Pavlovian conditioned fear, one might expect that rats with amygdala lesions might never express fear-related behavior. While this seems to be the case under normal training conditions, recent data suggests that fear may be present when extensive overtraining is given. Kim and Davis [227] found that while rats given extensive overtraining completely lost fear (as measured by fear-potentiated startle) following amygdala lesions, fear could be reacquired by these overtrained rats. Reacquisition of fear-potentiated startle progressed to near normal levels. Using the freezing preparation, Maren [228] found a similar pattern. However, reacquisition was only complete in animals that had partial lesions of the basolateral nucleus. Animals with total basolateral lesions still showed a large, albeit incomplete, deficit despite pre-lesion overtraining. Maren went on to show that this same pattern was obtained when the lesions were made before training. Including the central nucleus in the lesion did not alter the pattern of behavior. Thus, pre-training while intact does not appear to be the critical variable in the survival of fear following amygdala lesions. Rather the two crucial factors are the amount of spared amygdala tissue and the amount of training. With the freezing measure there is significant acquisition in a single trial and freezing is asymptotic at about six trials. In animals with complete basolateral lesions, freezing was abolished even with 25 training trials and was still significantly impaired at 35 trials. Killcross and co-workers [229] gave far more extensive training in a complex discrimination task and found that while some components of the fear response reached near normal levels, others were still dramatically impaired. Thus, without an

233

amygdala fear responses never appear completely normal, although very extensive overtraining allows some expression of the standard fear measures (fear-potentiated startle and freezing). It remains to be demonstrated what brain structures allow this residual fear-related behavior.

Within the present framework, the amygdala is playing the role of sensory-motor interface for fear. The simplest translation of this theory would suggest that when the amygdala is functional, all the fear responses it is essential for should occur in concert. Data on the ontogeny of fear calls this most parsimonious version into question [85,229,231]. Fear to tones, lights and contexts first develops at different ages with tone appearing first and context appearing last [85,231]. This is true for at least three measures of fear (freezing, fear-potentiated startle and heart rate changes). However, these different measures of fear also appear at different ages; with freezing appearing first and fear-potentiated startle appearing last [85,230]. Thus, a 23-day old rat can freeze and show fear-potentiated startle to a tone associated with a shock, but only freezing and not fear-potentiated startle, is observed in a light associated with shock [85]. This ontological pattern suggests that the sensory-motor organization within the amygdala and its afferent structures is quite complex. Note that this pattern cannot be due simply to maturation of structures afferent to the amygdala (i.e. sensory information) as there is an age at which rats will respond with freezing to a light CS, but not show fear-potentiated startle to the same stimulus. However, the pattern cannot be simply maturation of response pathways either. Rats will show fear-potentiated startle to a tone before they can show it to a light.

Obviously, there are different pathways mediating the expression of conditioned fear. The PAG seems to be involved in the expression of several measures of conditioned fear (e.g. analgesia, freezing and fear-potentiated startle). Whether the different fear responses have common or separated processing in the several regions of the PAG, should be a question of further study. Another important aim of future investigation should be elucidation of neurochemical differences in the different pathways from the amygdala to the other brain structures mediating different fear responses. For example, the parabrachial nucleus mediates changes in respiration, the lateral hypothalamus and parts of the medulla oblongata mediate cardiovascular responses. The bed nucleus of the stria terminalis mediates stress reactions and the ventral tegmental area and the paraventricular hypothalamus seem to be involved in the modulation of arousal and vigilance by conditioned fear (reviewed in Refs. [136,213–216]). Once the amygdala recognizes that the situation predicts danger, it generates the constellation of fear responses through multiple parallel and sometimes redundant channels. These pathways may mediate slightly different aspects of fear, allowing fine-tuning of the ultimate behavioral response to fear-provoking stimuli under a variety of external and internal conditions. This implies that different parallel pathways make the "fear system" more plastic, and thus more responsive to variable external demands. A ripe area for future research is in the coordination of these various response components of fear into integrated and functional defensive behavior [92,181]. Additionally, the neurochemical separation of these various pathways may allow the development of new drugs capable of differentiating between the several behavioral and autonomic problems that humans with anxiety disorders suffer.

In humans suffering from anxiety disorders, this system is functioning so effectively that fear is disproportionate to the actual threat predicted by the situation. Therefore, the investigation of the neuroanatomy and the neurochemistry of extinction and inhibition of conditioned fear could be a key to new strategies in the treatment of anxiety disorders. As would be expected, analysis of the neural mechanisms that inhibit fear lags far behind that of the mechanisms that produce fear. Specific drugs could enhance the extinction of the associations that produce fear or increase the inhibition of fear-related behavior and autonomic changes of patients at critical moments.

Acknowledgements

This work was supported by the Deutsche Forschungsgemeinschaft (SFB 307/C2 and Fe 483/1-1) to M.F. and National Science Foundation (US) grant # IBN-9723295 to M.S.F. M.F. specially thanks Dr. Michael Koch for helpful discussions during the work on the manuscript.

References

[1] Fanselow MS. The midbrain periaqueductal gray as a coordinator of action in response to fear and anxiety. In: Depaulis A, Bandler R, editors. The midbrain periaqueductal gray matter, New York: Plenum Press, 1991. pp. 151.

[2] Blanchard DC, Blanchard RJ. Innate and conditioned reactions to threat in rats with amygdaloid lesions. J Comp Physiol Psychol 1972;81:281–290.

[3] Blanchard RJ, Blanchard DC. Defensive reactions in the albino rat. Learn Motiv 1971;2:351–362.

[4] Bolles RC, Collier AC. Effect of predictive cues on freezing in rats. Anim Learn Behav 1976;4:6–8.

[5] Griffith CR. The behavior of white rats in the presence of cats. Psychobiology 1920;2:19–28.

[6] Morris BJ. Neuronal localisation of neuropeptide Y gene expression in the rat brain. J Comp Neurol 1989;290:358–368.

[7] Brown JS, Kalish HI, Farber IE. Conditioned fear as revealed by magnitude of startle response to an auditory stimulus. J Exp Psychol 1951;41:317–328.

[8] Davis M, Falls WA, Campeau S, Kim M. Fear-potentiated startle: a neural and pharmacological analysis. Behav Brain Res 1993;58:175–198.

[9] Leaton RN, Borszcz GS. Potentiated startle: its relation to freezing and shock intensity in rats. J Exp Psychol: Animal Behav Proc 1985;11:421–428.

[10] Bolles RC, Fanselow MS. A perceptual-defensive-recuperative model of fear and pain. Behav Brain Sci 1980;3:291–301.

[11] Black AH, de Toledo L. The relationship among classically conditioned responses: heart rate and skeletal behavior. In: Black AH,

Prokasy WF, editors. Classical conditioning. II. Current theory and research, New York: Appleton (Century/Crofts), 1972 pp. 290–311.

[12] LeDoux JE. Brain mechanisms of emotion and emotional learning. Curr Op Neurobiol 1992;2:191–197.

[13] Davis M, Hitchcock JM, Rosen JB. Neural mechanism of fear conditioning measured with the acoustic startle reflex. In: Madden IV J, editor. Neurobiology of learning, emotion and affect, New York: Raven Press, 1991 pp. 67–95.

[14] Bradley MM, Lang PJ, Cuthbert BN. Emotion novelty and the startle reflex: habituation in humans. Behav Neurosci 1993; 107:970–980.

[15] Brown P. Physiology of startle phenomena. In: Fahn S, Hallett M, Lüders HO, Marsden CD, editors. Negative motor phenomena, Philadelphia: Lippincott-Raven Publishers, 1995 pp. 273–287.

[16] Howard R, Ford R. From the jumping Frenchmen of Maine to post-traumatic stress disorder: the startle response in neuropsychiatry. Psychol Med 1992;22:695–707.

[17] Lang PJ, Bradley MM, Cuthbert BN. Emotion attention and the startle reflex. Psychol Rev 1990;97:377–395.

[18] Blanchard RJ, Blanchard DC, Agullana R, Weiss SM. Twenty-two kHz alarm cries to presentation of a predator by laboratory rats living in a visible burrow system. Physiol Behav 1991;50:967–972.

[19] Montgomery KC, Monkman JA. The relation between fear and exploratory behavior. J Comp Physiol Psychol 1955;48:132–136.

[20] Graeff FG, Viana MB, Tomaz C. The elevated T maze a new experimental model of anxiety and memory: effect of diazepam. Brazilian J Med Biol Res 1993;26:67–70.

[21] Small W. Notes on the psychic development of the white rat. Am J Psychol 1899;11:80–100.

[22] LeDoux JE, Sakaguchi A, Reis DJ. Subcortical efferent projections of the geniculate nucleus mediate emotional responses conditioned to acoustic stimuli. J Neurosci 1984;4:683–698.

[23] Treit D, Pinel JP, Fibiger HC. Conditioned defensive burying: a new paradigm for the study of anxiolytic agents. Pharmacol Biochem Behav 1981;15:619–626.

[24] Borszcz GS. Pavlovian conditional vocalizations of the rat: A model system for analyzing the fear of pain. Behav Neurosci 1995;109:648–662.

[25] Kaltwasser MT. Acoustic startle induced ultrasonic vocalization in the rat: a novel animal model of anxiety. Behav Brain Res 1991;43:133–137.

[26] Miczek KA, Weerts EM, Vivian JA, Barros HM. Aggression anxiety and vocalizations in animals: GABA_A and 5-HT anxiolytics. Psychopharmacology 1995;121:38–56.

[27] English HB. Three cases of the "conditioned fear responses". J Abn Social Psychol 1929;24:221–225.

[28] Millenson JR, Leslie J. The conditioned emotional response (CER) as a baseline for the study of anti-anxiety drugs. Neuropharmacology 1974;13:1–9.

[29] Dooley DJ, Klamt I. Differential profile of the CCK_B receptor antagonist CI-988 and diazepam in the four-plate test. Psychopharmacology 1993;112:452–454.

[30] Geller I, Seifter J. The effects of memprobamate barbiturates d-amphetamine and promazine on experimentally induced conflict in the rat. Psychopharmacologia 1960;1:482–492.

[31] Landis C, Hunt WA. The startle pattern. New York: Farrar and Rinehart, 1939.

[32] Pilz PKD, Schnitzler HU. Habituation and sensitization of the acoustic startle response in rats: amplitude threshold and latency measures. Neurobiol Learn Memory 1996;66:67–79.

[33] Yeomans JS, Frankland PW. The acoustic startle reflex: neurons and connections. Brain Res Rev 1996;21:301–314.

[34] Caeser M, Ostwald J, Pilz PKD. Startle response measured in muscles innervated by facial and trigeminal nerves show common modulation. Behav Neurosci 1989;103:1075–1081.

[35] Cassella JV, Harty TP, Davis M. Fear conditioning prepulse inhibition and drug modulation of a short latency startle response

measured electromyographically from neck muscles in the rat. Physiol Behav 1986;36:1187–1191.

[36] Davis M, Gendelman DS, Tischler MD, Gendelman PM. A primary acoustic startle circuit: lesion and stimulation studies. J Neurosci 1982;2:791–805.

[37] Lingenhöhl K, Friauf E. Giant neurons in the caudal pontine reticular formation receive short latency acoustic input: an intracellular recording and HRP-study in the rat. J Comp Neurol 1992;325:473–492.

[38] Lingenhöhl K, Friauf E. Giant neurons in the rat reticular formation: a sensorimotor interface in the elementary acoustic startle circuit. J Neurosci 1994;14:1176–1194.

[39] Lee Y, Lopez DE, Meloni EG, Davis M. A primary acoustic startle pathway: obligatory role of cochlear root neurons and the nucleus reticularis pontis caudalis. J Neurosci 1996;16:3775–3789.

[40] Moyer KE. Startle response: habituation over trials and days and sex and strain differences. J Comp Physiol Psychol 1963;56:863–865.

[41] Plappert CF, Pilz PKD, Schnitzler HU. Acoustic startle response and habituation in freezing and nonfreezing rats. Behav Neurosci 1993;107:981–987.

[42] Davis M. Sensitization of the acoustic startle reflex by footshock. Behav Neurosci 1989;103:495–503.

[43] Davis M, Cedarbaum JM, Aghajanian GK, Gendelman DS. Effects of clonidine on habituation and sensitization of acoustic startle in normal decerebrate and locus coeruleus lesioned rats. Psychopharmacology 1977;51:243–253.

[44] Hoffman HS, Searle JL. Acoustic variables in the modification of startle reaction in the rat. J Comp Physiol Psychol 1965;60:53–58.

[45] Swerdlow NR, Caine SB, Braff DL, Geyer MA. The neural substrates of sensorimotor gating of the startle reflex: a review of recent findings and their implications. J Psychopharmacol 1992;6:176–190.

[46] Koch M, Schmid A, Schnitzler HU. Pleasure-attenuation of startle is disrupted by lesions of the nucleus accumbens. NeuroReport 1996;7:1442–1446.

[47] Schmid A, Koch M, Schnitzler HU. Conditioned pleasure attenuates the startle response in rats. Neurobiol Learn Memory 1995;64:1–3.

[48] Fendt M, Koch M, Schnitzler HU. Lesions of the central gray block conditioned fear as measured with the potentiated startle paradigm. Behav Brain Res 1996;74:127–134.

[49] Davis M, Redmond DE, Baraban JM. Noradrenergic agonists and antagonists: effects on conditioned fear as measured by the potentiated startle paradigm. Psychopharmacology 1979;65:111–118.

[50] Davis M. Diazepam and flurazepam: effects on conditioned fear as measured with the potentiated startle paradigm. Psychopharmacology 1979;62:1–7.

[51] Davis M. Morphine and naloxone: effects on conditioned fear as measured with the potentiated startle paradigm. Eur J Pharmacol 1979;54:341–347.

[52] Kehne JH, Cassella JV, Davis M. Anxiolytic effects of buspirone and gepirone in the fear-potentiated startle paradigm. Psychopharmacology 1988;94:8–13.

[53] Nevins ME, Anthony EW. Antagonists at the serotonin-3 receptor can reduce the fear-potentiated startle response in the rat: Evidence for different types of anxiolytic activity. J Pharmacol Exp Ther 1994;268:248–268.

[54] Swerdlow NR, Britton KT, Koob GF. Potentiation of acoustic startle by corticotropin-releasing factor (CRF) and by fear are both reversed by α-helical CRF (9-41). Neuropsychopharmacology 1989;2:285–292.

[55] Josselyn SA, Frankland PW, Petrisano S, Bush DEA, Yeomans JS, Vaccarino FJ. The CCK_B antagonist L-365, 260 attenuates fear-potentiated startle. Peptides 1995;16:1313–1315.

[56] Broqua P, Wettstein JG, Rocher MN, Gauthier-Martin B, Junien JL. Behavioral effects of neuropeptide Y receptor agonists in the elevated plus-maze and fear-potentiated startle procedure. Behav Pharmacol 1995;6:215–222.

[57] Anthony EW, Nevins ME. Anxiolytic-like effects of N-methyl-D-aspartate-associated glycine receptor ligands in the rat potentiated startle test. Eur J Pharmacol 1993;250:317–324.

[58] Miller NE, Barry III H. Motivational effects of drugs: methods which illustrate some general problems in psychopharmacology. Psychopharmacologia 1960;1:169–199.

[59] Pohorecky LA, Cagan M, Brick J, Jaffe LS. The startle response in rats: effects of ethanol. Pharmacol Biochem Behav 1976;4: 311–316.

[60] Hijzen TH, Houtzager SWJ, Joordens RJE, Olivier B, Slangen JL. Predictive validity of the potentiated startle response as a behavioral model for anxiolytic drugs. Psychopharmacology 1995;118:150–154.

[61] Handley S. Future prospects for the pharmacological treatment of anxiety. CNS Drugs 1994;2:397–414.

[62] Harro J, Vasar E, Bradwejn J. CCK in animal and human research on anxiety. Trends Pharmacol Sci 1993;14:244–249.

[63] Olivier B, Molewijk E, van Oorschot R, van der Poel G, Zethof T, van der Heyden J, Mos J. New animal models of anxiety. Eur Neuropsychopharmacol 1994;4:93–102.

[64] Price LH, Goddard AW, Barr LC, Goodman WK. Pharmacological challenges in anxiety disorders. In: Bloom FE, Kupfer DJ, editors. Psychopharmacology: the fourth generation of progress, New York: Raven Press, 1995 pp. 1311–1323.

[65] Rasmussen K. CCK schizophrenia and anxiety. Ann New York Acad Sci 1994;713:300–311.

[66] Pilz PKD. Sensitization of the acoustic startle response in rats is sensitive to a change of the environment. In: Elsner N, Schnitzler H-U, editors. Brain and evolution, Stuttgart: Georg Thieme, 1996. pp. 223.

[67] Richardson R, Elsayed H. Shock sensitization of startle in rats: the role of contextual conditioning. Behav Neurosci 1998;112:1136–1141.

[68] Koch M, Schnitzler HU. The acoustic startle response in rats - circuits mediating evocation inhibition and potentiation. Behav Brain Res 1997;89:35–49.

[69] Darwin C. The expression of the emotions an man and animals. Chicago: University of Chicago Press, 1960.

[70] Miller NE. An experimental study of acquired drives. Psychol Bull 1941;38:534–535.

[71] Annau Z, Kamin LJ. The conditioned emotional response as a function of intensity of the US. J Comp Physiol Psychol 1961;54:428–432.

[72] Estes WK, Skinner BF. Some quantitative properties of anxiety. J Exp Psychol 1941;29:390–400.

[73] Bolles RC, Riley AL. Freezing as an avoidance response: another look at the operant-respondent distinction. Learn Mem 1973;4:268–275.

[74] Blanchard RJ, Blanchard DC. Passive and active reactions to fear-eliciting stimuli. J Comp Physiol Psychol 1969;68:129–135.

[75] Collier AC. Preference for shock signals as a function of the temporal accuracy of the signals. Learn Mem 1977;8:159–170.

[76] Fanselow MS, Bolles RC. Naloxone and shock-eliciting freezing in the rat. J Comp Physiol Psychol 1979;93:736–744.

[77] Bouton ME, Bolles RC. Conditioned fear assessed by freezing and by the suppression of three different baselines. Anim Learn Behav 1980;8:429–434.

[78] Fanselow MS. Conditioned and unconditioned components of post-shock freezing. Pav J Biol Sci 1980;15:177–182.

[79] Fanselow MS, Lester LS. A functional behavioristic approach to aversively motivated behavior: predatory imminence as a determinant of the topography of defensive behavior. In: Bolles RC, Beecher MD, editors. Evolution and learning, New York: Hillsdale, 1988. pp. 185.

[80] Fanselow MS. Conditioned fear-induced opiate analgesia: a competing motivational state theory of stress analgesia. Ann New York Acad Sci 1986;467:40–54.

[81] Helmstetter FJ, Tershner SA. Lesions of the periaqueductal gray and rostral ventromedial medulla disrupt antinociceptive but not cardiovascular aversive conditional responses. J Neurosci 1994;14:7099–7108.

[82] LeDoux JE, Sakaguchi A, Reis DJ. Alpha-methyl-DOPA dissociates hypertension cardiovascular reactivity and emotional behavior in spontaneously hypertensive rats. Brain Res 1983;259:69–76.

[83] LeDoux JE, Sakaguchi A, Reis DJ. Strain differences in fear between spontaneously hypertensive and normotensive rats. Brain Res 1983;277:137–143.

[84] Pappas BA, DiCara LV, Miller NE. Acute sympathectomy by 6-hydroxydopamine in the adult rat: effects on cardiovascular conditioning and fear retention. J Comp Physiol Psychol 1972;79:230–236.

[85] Hunt PS, Campbell BA. Developmental dissociation of the components of conditioned fear. In: Bouton ME, Fanselow MS, editors. Learning, motivation, and cognition: the functional behaviorism of Robert C Bolles, Washington, DC: American Psychological Association, 1997. pp. 53.

[86] Richardson R, Wang P, Campbell BA. Delayed development of conditioned heart rate responses to auditory stimuli in the rat. Dev Psychobiol 1995;28:221–238.

[87] Supple Jr WF, Leaton RN. Cerebellar vermis: essential for classically conditioned bradycardia in the rat. Brain Res 1990;509:17–23.

[88] Iwata J, LeDoux JE. Dissociation of associative and nonassociative concomitants of classical fear conditioning in the freely behaving rat. Behav Neurosci 1988;102:66–76.

[89] Chance WT, Krynock GM, Rosecrans JA. Antinociception following lesion-induced hyperemotionality and conditioned fear. Pain 1978;4:243–252.

[90] Fanselow MS, Baackes MP. Conditioned fear-induced opiate analgesia on the formalin test: evidence for two aversive motivational systems. Learn Motiv 1982;13:200–221.

[91] Bolles RC. Species-specific defensive reactions and avoidance learning. Psychol Rev 1970;71:32–48.

[92] Fanselow MS. Neural organization of the defensive behavior system responsible for fear. Psychol Bull Rev 1994;1:429–438.

[93] Brown S, Schaffer A. An investigation into the functions of the occipital and temporal lobes of the monkey's brain. Trans R Soc London 1886;179:303–327.

[94] Kluver H, Bucy PC. Preliminary analysis of the temporal lobes in monkeys. Biol Psychiatry 1939;42:461–471.

[95] Weiskrantz L. Behavioral changes associated with ablations of the amygdaloid complex in monkeys. J Comp Physiol Psychol 1956;49:381–391.

[96] Fuster JM, Uyeda AA. Reactivity of limbic neurons of the monkey to appetitive and aversive signals. Electroencephalogr Clin Neurophysiol 1971;30:281–293.

[97] Applegate CD, Frysinger RC, Kapp BS, Gallagher M. Multiple unit activity recorded from amygdala central nucleus during Pavlovian heart conditioning in rabbit. Brain Res 1982;238:457–462.

[98] Quirk GJ, Repa JC, LeDoux JE. Fear conditioning enhances short-latency auditory responses of lateral amygdala neurons: parallel recordings in the freely behaving rat. Neuron 1995;15:1029–1039.

[99] Romanski LM, Clugnet MC, Bordi F, LeDoux JE. Somatosensory and auditory convergence in the lateral nucleus of the amygdala. Behav Neurosci 1993;107:444–450.

[100] Chapman PF, Kairiss EW, Keenan CL, Brown TH. Long-term synaptic potentiation in the amygdala. Synapse 1990;6:271–278.

[101] Clugnet MC, LeDoux JE. Synaptic plasticity in fear conditioning circuits: induction of LTP in the lateral nucleus of the amygdala by stimulation of the medial geniculate body. J Neurosci 1990;10:2818–2824.

[102] Huang YY, Kandel ER. Postsynaptic induction and PKA-dependent expression of LTP in the lateral amygdala. Neuron 1998;21:169–178.

[103] Maren S, Fanselow MS. Synaptic plasticity in the basolateral

236

amygdala induced by hippocampal formation stimulation in vivo. J Neurosci 1995;15:7548–7564.

[104] Li XF, Phillips RG, LeDoux JE. NMDA and non-NMDA receptors contribute to synaptic transmission between the medial geniculate body and the lateral nucleus of the amygdala. Exp Brain Res 1995;105:87–100.

[105] McKernan MG, Shinnick-Gallagher P. Fear conditioning induces a lasting potentiation of synaptic currents in vivo. Nature 1997;390:607–611.

[106] Rogan MT, Stäubli UV, LeDoux JE. Fear conditioning induces associative long-term potentiation in the amygdala. Nature 1997;390:604–607.

[107] Berg WK, Davis M. Associative Learning modifies startle reflexes at the lateral lemniscus. Behav Neurosci 1985;99:191–199.

[108] Davis M. Pharmacological and anatomical analysis of fear conditioning using the fear-potentiated startle paradigm. Behav Neurosci 1986;100:814–824.

[109] Hitchcock JM, Davis M. Lesions of the amygdala but not of the cerebellum or red nucleus block conditioned fear as measured with the potentiated startle paradigm. Behav Neurosci 1986;100:11–22.

[110] Hitchcock JM, Davis M. Fear-potentiated startle using an auditory conditioned stimulus: effect of lesions of the amygdala. Physiol Behav 1987;39:403–408.

[111] Gallagher M, Kapp BS, Pascoe JP, Rapp PR. A neuropharmacology of amygdala systems which contribute to learning and memory. In: Ben-Ari Y, editor. The amygdaloid complex, Amsterdam: Elsevier, 1981. pp. 343.

[112] Thompson RF. The neurobiology of learning and memory. Science 1986;233:941–947.

[113] Rosen JB, Hitchcock JM, Sananes CB, Miserendino MJD, Davis M. A direct projection from the central nucleus of the amygdala to the acoustic startle pathway: anterograde and retrograde tracing studies. Behav Neurosci 1991;105:817–825.

[114] Hitchcock JM, Davis M. The efferent pathway of the amygdala involved in conditioned fear as measured with the fear-potentiated startle paradigm. Behav Neurosci 1991;105:826–842.

[115] Rosen JB, Davis M. Enhancement of acoustic startle by electrical stimulation of the amygdala. Behav Neurosci 1988;102:195–202.

[116] Rosen JB, Davis M. Temporal characteristics of enhancement of startle by stimulation of the amygdala. Physiol Behav 1988;44:117–123.

[117] Rosen JB, Davis M. Enhancement of electrically elicited startle by amygdaloid stimulation. Physiol Behav 1990;48:343–349.

[118] Koch M, Ebert U. Enhancement of the acoustic startle response by stimulation of an excitatory pathway from the central amygdala/basal nucleus of Meynert to the pontine reticular formation. Exp Brain Res 1993;93:231–241.

[119] Koch M. Microinjections of the metabotropic glutamate receptor agonist, trans-(+/−)-1-amino-cyclopentane-1,3-dicarboxylate (trans-ACPD) into the amygdala increase the acoustic startle response of rats. Brain Res 1993;629:176–179.

[120] Campeau S, Miserendino MJD, Davis M. Intra-amygdaloid infusion of the N-methyl-D-aspartate receptor antagonist AP5 blocks acquisition but not expression of fear-potentiated startle to an auditory conditioned stimulus. Behav Neurosci 1992;106:569–574.

[121] Melia KR, Falls WA, Davis M. Involvement of pertussis toxin sensitive G-proteins in conditioned fear-potentiated startle: possible involvement of the amygdala. Brain Res 1992;584:141–148.

[122] Miserendino MJD, Sananes CB, Melia KR, Davis M. Blocking of acquisition but not expression of conditioned fear-potentiated startle by NMDA antagonists in the amygdala. Nature 1990;345:716–718.

[123] Falls WA, Miserendino MJD, Davis M. Extinction of fear-potentiated startle: blockade by infusion of an NMDA antagonist into the amygdala. J Neurosci 1992;12:854–863.

[124] Gewirtz JC, Davis M. Second-order fear conditioning prevented by blocking NMDA receptors in amygdala. Nature 1997;388:471–474.

[125] Tischler MD, Davis M. A visual pathway that mediates fear-conditioned enhancement of acoustic startle. Brain Res 1983;276:55–71.

[126] Campeau S, Davis M. Involvement of subcortical and cortical afferents to the lateral nucleus of the amygdala in fear conditioning measured with fear-potentiated startle in rats trained concurrently with auditory and visual conditioned stimuli. J Neurosci 1995;15:2312–2327.

[127] Campeau S, Davis M. Involvement of the central nucleus and basolateral complex of the amygdala in fear conditioning measured with fear-potentiated startle in rats trained concurrently with auditory and visual conditioned stimuli. J Neurosci 1995;15:2301–2311.

[128] Falls WA, Davis M. Visual cortex ablations do not prevent extinction of fear-potentiated startle using a visual conditioned stimulus. Behav Neural Biol 1993;60:259–270.

[129] Rosen JB, Hitchcock JM, Miserendino MJD, Falls WA, Campeau S, Davis M. Lesions of the perirhinal cortex but not of the frontal medial pre-frontal visual or insular cortex block fear-potentiated startle using a visual conditioned stimulus. J Neurosci 1992;12:4624–4633.

[130] Fendt M, Koch M, Schnitzler HU. Amygdaloid noradrenaline is involved in the sensitization of the acoustic startle response in rats. Pharmacol Biochem Behav 1994;48:307–314.

[131] Chiang C, Aston-Jones G. Response of locus coeruleus neurons to footshock stimulation is mediated by neurons in the rostral ventral medulla. Neuroscience 1993;53:705–715.

[132] Galvez R, Mesches MH, McGaugh JL. Norepinephrine release in the amygdala in response to footshock stimulation. Neurobiol Learn Mem 1996;66:253–257.

[133] Quirarte GL, Galvez R, Roozendaal B, McGaugh JL. Norepinephrine release in the amygdala in response to footshock and opioid peptidergic drugs. Brain Res 1998;808:134–140.

[134] Fallon JH. Histochemical characterization of dopaminergic, noradrenergic and serotonergic projections to the amygdala. In: Ben-Ari Y, editor. The amygdaloid complex, Amsterdam: Elsevier, 1981. pp. 175.

[135] Bernard JF, Besson JM. The spino(trigemino)pontoamygdaloid pathway: electrophysiological evidence for an involvement in pain processes. J Neurophysiol 1990;63:473–490.

[136] Davis M, Rainnie D, Cassell M. Neurotransmission in the rat amygdala related to fear and anxiety. Trends Neurosci 1994;17:208–214.

[137] Roberts GW. Neuropeptides: cellular morphology, major pathways, and functional considerations. In: Aggleton JP, editor. The amygdala: neurobiological aspects of emotion, memory, and mental dysfunction, New York: Wiley-Liss, 1992. pp. 115.

[138] McDonald AJ. Cell types and intrinsic connections of the amygdala. In: Aggleton JP, editor. The amygdala: neurobiological aspects of emotion, memory, and mental dysfunction, New York: Wiley-Liss, 1992. pp. 67.

[139] Shi C, Davis M. Anatomical tracing and lesion studies of pain pathways involved in fear conditioning measured with fear potentiated startle. Soc Neurosci Abstr 1997;23:627.12.

[140] Shi C, Davis M. Pain pathways involved in fear conditioning measured with fear-potentiated startle: lesion studies. J Neurosci 1999;19:420–430.

[141] Kim M, Campeau S, Falls WA, Davis M. Infusion of the non-NMDA receptor antagonist CNQX into the amygdala blocks the expression of fear-potentiated startle. Behav Neural Biol 1993;59:5–8.

[142] Walker DL, Davis M. Double dissociation between the involvement of the bed nucleus of the stria terminalis and the central nucleus of the amygdala in startle increases produced by conditioned versus unconditioned fear. J Neurosci 1997;17:000.

[143] Frankland PW, Josselyn SA, Bradwejn J, Vaccarino FJ, Yeomans JS. Activation of amygdala cholecystokinin$_B$ receptors potentiates the acoustic startle response in the rat. J Neurosci 1997;17:1838–1847.

[144] Frankland PW, Josselyn SA, Vaccarino FJ, Yeomans JS, Bradwejn J. Intracerebroventricular infusion of the CCK$_B$ receptor agonist

237

pentagastrin potentiates acoustic startle. Brain Res 1996;733:129–132.

[145] Fendt M, Koch M, Schnitzler HU. Corticotropin-releasing factor is involved in the expression of fear-potentiated startle: an anatomical electrophysiological and behavioral study. Eur J Neurosci 1997;9:299–305.

[146] Koch M, Ebert U. Enhancement of auditory responses of pontine reticular brainstem neurons by glutamate and stimulation of the amygdaloid complex. Eur J Neurosci 1992;5:142.

[147] Fendt M, Koch M, Schnitzler HU. NMDA receptors in the pontine brainstem are necessary for fear-potentiation of the startle response. Eur J Pharmacol 1996;318:1–6.

[148] Ebert U, Koch M. Glutamate receptors mediate acoustic input to the reticular brain stem. NeuroReport 1992;3:429–432.

[149] Krase W, Koch M, Schnitzler HU. Glutamate antagonists in the reticular formation reduce the acoustic startle response. NeuroReport 1993;4:13–16.

[150] Miserendino MJD, Davis M. NMDA and non-NMDA antagonists infused into the nucleus reticularis pontis caudalis depress the acoustic startle reflex. Brain Res 1993;623:215–222.

[151] Birnbaum SG, Davis M. Modulation of the acoustic startle reflex by infusion of corticotropin-releasing hormone into the nucleus reticularis pontis caudalis. Brain Res 1998;782:318–323.

[152] Falls WA, Davis M. Inhibition of fear-potentiated startle can be detected after the offset of a feature trained in a serial feature-negative discrimination. J Exp Psychol: Animal Behav Proc 1997;23:3–14.

[153] Falls WA, Davis M. Lesions of the central nucleus of the amygdala block conditioned excitation but not conditioned inhibition of fear as measured with the fear-potentiated startle effect. Behav Neurosci 1995;109:379–387.

[154] Iwata J, LeDoux JE, Meeley MP, Americ S, Reis DJ. Intrinsic neurons in the amygdaloid field projected to by the medial geniculate body mediate emotional responses conditioned to acoustic stimuli. Brain Res 1986;383:195–214.

[155] Kapp BS, Frysinger RC, Gallagher M, Haselton JR. Amygdala central nucleus lesions: effect on heart rate conditioning in the rabbit. Physiol Behav 1979;23:1109–1117.

[156] Helmstetter FJ. Contribution of the amygdala to learning and performance of conditional fear. Physiol Behav 1992;51:1271–1276.

[157] Watkins LR, Wiertelak EP, Maier SF. The amygdala is necessary for the expression of conditioned but not unconditioned analgesia. Behav Neurosci 1993;107:402–405.

[158] Goldstein LE, Rasmusson AM, Bunney BS, Roth RH. Role of the amygdala in the coordination of behavioral neuroendocrine and prefrontal cortical monoamine responses to psychological stress in the rat. J Neurosci 1996;16:4787–4798.

[159] Fanselow MS, Kim JJ. Acquisition of contextual Pavlovian fear conditioning is blocked by application of an NMDA receptor antagonist D,L-2-amino-5-phoshonovaleric acid to the basolateral amygdala. Behav Neurosci 1994;108:210–212.

[160] Lee H, Kim JJ. Amygdalar NMDA receptors are critical for new fear learning in previously fear-conditioned rats. J Neurosci 1998;18:8444–8454.

[161] Maren S, Aharanov G, Stote DL, Fanselow MS. N-Methyl-D-aspartate receptors in the basolateral amygdala are required for both acquisition and expression and expression of conditioned fear in rats. Behav Neurosci 1996;110:1365–1375.

[162] Helmstetter FJ. Stress-induced hypoalgesia and defensive freezing are attenuated by application of diazepam to the amygdala. Pharmacol Biochem Behav 1993;44:433–438.

[163] Helmstetter FJ, Bellgowan PS. Effects of muscimol applied to the basolateral amygdala on acquisition and expression of contextual fear conditioning in rats. Behav Neurosci 1994;108:1005–1009.

[164] Muller J, Corodimas KP, Fridel Z, LeDoux JE. Functional inactivation of the lateral and basal nuclei of the amygdala by muscimol

infusion prevents fear conditioning to an explicit conditioned stimulus and to contextual stimuli. Behav Neurosci 1997;111:683–691.

[165] Armony JL, Quirk GJ, LeDoux JE. Differential effects of amygdala lesions on early and late plastic components of auditory cortex spike trains during fear conditioning. J Neurosci 1998;18:2592–2601.

[166] Quirk GJ, Armony JL, LeDoux JE. Fear conditioning enhances different temporal components of tone-evoked spike trains in auditory cortex and lateral amygdala. Neuron 1997;19:613–624.

[167] Romanski LB, LeDoux JE. Equipotentially of thalamo-amygdala and thalamo-cortico-amygdala circuits in auditory fear conditioning. J Neurosci 1992;12:4501–4509.

[168] Fanselow MS. Associative vs. topographical accounts of the immediate shock freezing deficit in rats: implications for the response selection rules governing species specific defensive reactions . Learn Motiv 1986;17:16–39.

[169] Kim JJ, Fanselow MS. Modality-specific retrograde amnesia of fear. Science 1992;256:675–677.

[170] Cruikshank SJ, Edeline JM, Weinberger NM. Stimulation at a site of auditory-somatosensory convergence in the medial geniculate nucleus is an effective unconditioned stimulus for fear conditioning. Behav Neurosci 1992;106:471–483.

[171] LeDoux JE, Ruggiero DA, Forest R, Stornetta R, Reis DJ. Topographic organization of convergent projections to the thalamus from the inferior colliculus and spinal cord in the rat. J Comp Neurol 1987;264:123–146.

[172] Edeline JM, Weinberger NM. Associative retuning in the thalamic source of input to the amygdala and auditory cortex: receptive field plasticity in the medial division of the medial geniculate body. Behav Neurosci 1992;106:81–105.

[173] Fanselow MS, Kim JJ. The benzodiazepine inverse agonist DMCM as an unconditioned stimulus for fear-induced analgesia: Implications for the role of GABAA receptors in fear-related behavior. Behav Neurosci 1992;106:336–344.

[174] DeLorey TM, Handforth A, Anagnostaras SG, Homanics GE, Minassian BA, Asatourian A, Fanselow MS, Delgado-Escueta A, Ellison GD, Olsen RW. Mice lacking the β_3 subunit of the GABAA receptor have the epilepsy phenotype and many of the behavioral characteristics of Angelman syndrome. J Neurosci 1998;18:8505–8514.

[175] Maren S, Aharanov G, Fanselow MS. Retrograde abolition of conditioned fear after excitotoxic lesions in the basolateral amygdala of rats: absence of a temporal gradient. Behav Neurosci 1996;110:718–726.

[176] Helmstetter FJ. The amygdala is essential for the expression of conditioned hypoalgesia. Behav Neurosci 1992;106:518–528.

[177] Bechara A, Tranel D, Damasio H, Adolphs R, Rockland C, Damasio AR. Double dissociation of conditioning and declarative knowledge relative to the amygdala and hippocampus in humans. Science 1995;269:1115–1118.

[178] LaBar KS, LeDoux JE, Spencer DD, Phelps EA. Impaired fear conditioning following unilateral temporal lobectomy in humans. J Neurosci 1995;10:6846–6855.

[179] LeDoux JE, Iwata J, Cicchetti P, Reis DJ. Different projections of the central amygdaloid nucleus mediate autonomic and behavioral correlates of conditioned fear. J. Neurosci. 1988;8:2517–2529.

[180] Kapp BS, Gallagher M, Underwood MD, McNall CL, Whitehorn D. Cardiovascular responses elicited by electrical stimulation of the amygdala central nucleus in the rabbit. Brain Res 1982;234:251–262.

[181] Fendt M. Stimulation of startle modulating midbrain areas has different effects on the acoustic startle response. Soc Neurosci Abstr 1997;23:627.14.

[182] Fendt M. Different regions of the periaqueductal grey are involved differently in the expression and conditioned inhibition of fear-potentiated startle. Eur J Neurosci 1998;10:3876–3884.

[183] Fendt M, Koch M, Schnitzler HU. Lesions of the central gray block

the sensitization of the acoustic startle response in rats. Brain Res 1994;661:163–173.

[184] Bandler R, Shipley MT. Columnar organization in the midbrain periaqueductal gray: modules for emotional expression. Trends Neurosci 1994;17:379–389.

[185] Carrive P, Leung P, Harris JA, Paxinos G. Conditioned fear to context is associated with increased fos expression in the caudal ventrolateral region of the midbrain periaqueductal gray. Neuroscience 1997;78:165–177.

[186] Cassella JV, Davis M. Sensitization fear conditioning and pharmacological modulation of acoustic startle following lesions of the dorsal periaqueductal gray. Soc Neurosci Abstr 1984;10:1067.

[187] Borszcz GS, Cranney J, Leaton RN. Influence of long-term sensitization on long-term habituation of the acoustic startle response in rats: Central gray lesions preexposure and extinction. J Exp Psychol: Animal Behav Proc 1989;15:54–64.

[188] Walker DL, Davis M. Involvement of the dorsal periaqueductal gray in the loss of fear-potentiated startle accompanying high footshock training. Behav Neurosci 1997;111:692–702.

[189] Borowski TB, Kokkinidis L. Contribution of ventral tegmental area dopamine neurons to expression of conditional fear: effects of electrical stimulation excitotoxin lesions and quinpirole infusion on potentiated startle in rats. Behav Neurosci 1996;110:1349–1364.

[190] Fendt M, Koch M, Schnitzler HU. Somatostatin in the pontine reticular formation modulates fear- potentiation of the acoustic startle response: an anatomical electrophysiological and behavioral study . J Neurosci 1996;16:3097–3103.

[191] Liebman JM, Mayer DJ, Liebeskind JC. Mesencephalic central gray lesions and fear-motivated behavior in rats. Brain Res 1970;23:353–370.

[192] De Oca BM, DeCola JP, Maren S, Fanselow MS. Distinct regions of the periaqueductal gray are involved in the acquisition and expression of defensive responses. J Neurosci 1998;18:3426–3432.

[193] Fanselow MS, DeCola JP, De Oca B, Landeira-Fernandez J. Ventral and dorsolateral regions of the midbrain periaqueductal gray (PAG) control different stages of defensive behavior: dorsolateral PAG lesions enhance the defensive freezing produced by massed and immediate shock. Aggress Behav 1995;21:61–77.

[194] Maier SF, Grahn RE, Kalman BA, Sutton LC, Wiertelak EP, Watkins LR. The role of the amygdala and dorsal raphe nucleus in mediating the behavioral consequences of inescapable shock. Behav Neurosci 1993;107:377–388.

[195] Bandler R, Depaulis A. Midbrain periaqueductal gray control of defensive behavior in the cat and the rat. In: Depaulis A, Bandler R, editors. The midbrain periaqueductal gray, New York: Plenum Press, 1991 pp. 175–198.

[196] Helmstetter FJ, Landeira-Fernandez J. Conditioned hypoalgesia is attenuated by naltrexone applied to the periaqueductal gray. Brain Res 1990;537:88–92.

[197] Krase W, Koch M, Schnitzler HU. Substance P is involved in the sensitization of the acoustic startle response by footshocks in rats. Behav Brain Res 1994;63:81–88.

[198] Kungel M, Ebert U, Herbert H, Ostwald J. Substance P and other putative transmitters modulate the activity of reticular pontine neurons: an electrophysiological and immunohistochemical study. Brain Res 1994;643:29–39.

[199] Frankland PW, Yeomans JS. Fear-potentiated startle and electrically evoked startle mediated by synapses in rostrolateral midbrain. Behav Neurosci 1995;109:669–680.

[200] Fendt M, Koch M, Kungel M, Schnitzler HU. Cholecystokinin enhances the acoustic startle response in rats. NeuroReport 1995;6:2081–2084.

[201] Vanderhaeghen JJ. Neuronal cholecystokinin. In: Björklund A, Hökfelt T, editors. Handbook of chemical neuroanatomy. Vol. 4: GABA and Neuropeptides in the CNS, Amsterdam: Elsevier, 1985. pp. 406 Part I.

[202] O'Keefe J, Nadel L. The hippocampus as a cognitive map. New York: Oxford University Press, 1978.

[203] Sutherland RJ, Rudy JW. Configural association theory: the role of the hippocampal formation in learning memory and amnesia. Psychobiology 1989;17:129–144.

[204] Kim JJ, Rison RA, Fanselow MS. Effects of amygdala hippocampus and periaqueductal gray lesions on short- and long-term contextual fear. Behav Neurosci 1994;107:1088–1092.

[205] Phillips RG, LeDoux JE. Differential contribution of amygdala and hippocampus to cued and contextual fear conditioning. Behav Neurosci 1992;106:274–285.

[206] Maren S, Aharanov G, Fanselow MS. Neurotoxic lesions of the dorsal hippocampus and Pavlovian fear conditioning in rats. Behav Brain Res 1997;88:261–274.

[207] Maren S, Anagnostaras SG, Fanselow MS. The startled seahorse: Is the hippocampus necessary for contextual fear conditioning. Psychol Rev 1998;2:195–231.

[208] Maren S, Fanselow MS. Electrolytic lesions of the fimbria/fornix dorsal hippocampus or entorhinal cortex produce anterograde deficits in contextual fear conditioning in rats. Neurobiol Learn Memory 1997;67:142–149.

[209] Squire LR. Memory and the hippocampus: A synthesis from findings with rats monkeys and humans. Psychol Rev 1992;2:195–231.

[210] Anagnostaras SG, Maren S, Fanselow MS. Temporally graded retrograde amnesia of contextual fear after hippocampal damage in rats: within-examination. J Neurosci 1999;19:1106–1114.

[211] McNish KA, Gewirtz JC, Davis M. Evidence of contextual fear after lesions of the hippocampus; a disruption of freezing but not fear-potentiated startle. J Neurosci 1997;17:9353–9360.

[212] Coover GD, Levine ES. Auditory startle response of hippocampectomized rats. Physiol Behav 1972;9:75–77.

[213] Graeff FG. Neuroanatomy and neurotransmitter regulation of defensive behaviors and related emotions in mammals. Brazilian J Med Biol Res 1994;27:811–829.

[214] Lavond DG, Kim JJ, Thompson RF. Mammalian brain substrates of aversive classical conditioning. Annu Rev Psychol 1993;44:317–342.

[215] LeDoux JE. Emotion: clues from the brain. Annu Rev Psychol 1995;46:209–235.

[216] Maren S, Fanselow MS. The amygdala and fear conditioning: has the nut been cracked. Neuron 1996;16:237–240.

[217] Collingridge GL, Bliss TVP. NMDA receptors—their role in long-term potentiation. Trends Neurosci 1987;10:288–293.

[218] Rison RA, Stanton PK. Long-term potentiation and N-methyl-D-aspartate receptors: foundations of memory and neurological disease. Neurosci Biobehav Rev 1995;19:533–552.

[219] Rogan MT, LeDoux JE. LTP is accompanied by commensurate enhancement of auditory-evoked responses in a fear conditioning circuit. Neuron 1995;15:127–136.

[220] Teich AH, McCabe PM, Gentile CG, Jarrell TW, Winters RW, Liskowsky DR, Schneiderman N. Role of the auditory cortex in the acquisition of differential heart rate conditioning. Physiol Behav 1988;44:405–412.

[221] Neff WD, Diamond IT. The neural basis of auditory discrimination. In: Harlow HF, Woolsey CN, editors. Biological and biochemical bases of behavior, Madison: University of Wisconsin Press, 1958. pp. 101.

[222] Thompson RF. Function of the auditory cortex of cat in frequency discrimination. J Neurophysiol 1960;23:321–334.

[223] Whitfield IC, Cranford J, Ravizza R, Diamond IT. Effects of unilateral ablation of auditory cortex in cat on complex sound localization. J Neurophysiol 1972;35:718–731.

[224] Davis M, Schlesinger LS, Sorenson CA. Temporal specificity of fear conditioning: effects of different conditioned stimulus - unconditioned stimulus intervals on the fear-potentiated startle effect. J Exp Psychol: Animal Behav Proc 1989;15:295–310.

[225] Faulkner B, Tieu KH, Brown TH. Mechanism for temporal encoding

in fear conditioning: delay lines in perirhinal cortex and lateral amygdala. In: Bower G, editor. Computational neuroscience, New York: Plenum Press, 1997. pp. 641.

[226] Li XF, Stutzmann GE, LeDoux JE. Convergent but temporally separated inputs to lateral amygdala neurons from the auditory thalamus and auditory cortex use different postsynaptic receptors: in vivo intracellular and extracellular recordings in fear conditioning pathways. Learn Mem 1996;3:229–242.

[227] Kim M, Davis M. Electrolytic lesions of the amygdala block acquisition and expression of fear-potentiated startle even with extensive training but do not prevent reacquisition. Behav Neurosci 1993;107:580–595.

[228] Maren S. Overtraining does not mitigate contextual fear conditioning deficits produced by neurotoxic lesions of the basolateral amygdala. J Neurosci 1998;18:3088–3097.

[229] Killcross SS, Robbins TW, Everitt BJ. Different types of fear-conditioned behavior mediated by separate nuclei within the amygdala. Nature 1997;388:77–380.

[230] Moye TB, Rudy JW. Ontogenesis of learning. VI. Learned and unlearned responses to visual stimulation in the infant hooded rat . Dev Psychobiol 1985;18:887–891.

[231] Rudy JW. Contextual and auditory cue conditioning dissociate during development. Behav Neurosci 1993;107:887–891.

The amygdala modulates prefrontal cortex activity relative to conditioned fear

René Garcia*, Rose-Marie Voulmba†, Michel Baudry†
& Richard F. Thompson†

* Laboratoire de Neurosciences Cognitives, CNRS UMR 5807,
Université de Bordeaux I, Avenue des Facultés, 33405 Talence, France
† Neuroscience Program, University of Southern California, Los Angeles,
California 90089-2520, USA

Animals learn that a tone can predict the occurrence of an electric shock through classical conditioning. Mice or rats trained in this manner display fear responses, such as freezing behaviour, when they hear the conditioned tone. Studies using amygdalectomized rats have shown that the amygdala is required for both the acquisition and expression of learned fear responses[1-3]. Freezing to a conditioned tone is enhanced following damage to the dorsal part of the medial prefrontal cortex[4], indicating that this area may be involved in fear reduction. Here we show that prefrontal neurons reduce their spontaneous activity in the presence of a conditioned aversive tone as a function of the degree of fear. The depression in prefrontal spontaneous activity is related to amygdala activity but not to the freezing response itself. These data indicate that, in the presence of threatening stimuli, the amygdala controls both fear expression and prefrontal neuronal activity. They suggest that abnormal amygdala-induced modulation of prefrontal neuronal activity may be involved in the pathophysiology of certain forms of anxiety disorder.

To test whether neurons in the medial prefrontal cortex are involved in mechanisms of fear modulation, mice were implanted with two recording electrodes in the dorsal part of this cortical area. The whole experiment comprised four phases, each separated by a 3-day period: habituation phase (5 days), first training phase (2 days), second training phase (5 days) and test phase (1 day). The habituation and test phases took place in a recording chamber with behavioural and electrophysiological equipment for assessing freezing and recording multi-unit activity, respectively. The training phase took place in a different chamber. We used two conditioned stimuli: conditioned fear excitation (CS: 20-s tone) and conditioned

fear inhibition (CI: 20-s light). An electric shock was the unconditioned stimulus (US). In the first phase of training, five CS–US pairings were presented with a variable intertrial interval (60–180 s) on each of two consecutive days. Following this fear-conditioning phase, animals were divided into two groups (CI–CS paired and CI–CS unpaired groups). All animals underwent a second training phase in which five CS–US pairings were randomly mixed with five additional trials, where either the CS was preceded immediately by the CI and the US was withheld (CI–CS paired group) or the CI was presented alone (CI–CS unpaired group). The intertrial interval ranged from 60–180 s. Animals in the CI–CS paired group were then trained according to a Pavlovian conditioned inhibition procedure[5] that reduces behavioural changes normally attributed to fear excitation. For example, it has been reported that, following conditioning (light–shock and tone–light compounds), rats displayed less fear-potentiated startle to the light CS when it was preceded by the tone CI[6]. We hypothesized that animals in the CI–CS paired group would display less freezing than animals in the CI–CS unpaired group, which is considered to be a good control group for conditioned inhibition[7].

To test the effects of both CI and CS on spontaneous neuronal activity in the medial prefrontal cortex, multi-unit recordings were performed in the recording chamber on the last day of the experiment

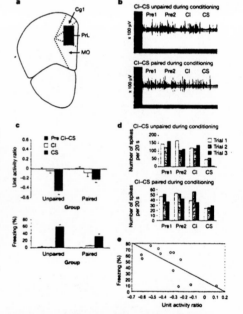

Figure 1 Conditioned inhibition: electrophysiology and behaviour. a, Electrode placements in the prefrontal cortex (grey area) Cg1: cingulate area 1; PrL and MO: prefrontal and medial orbital cortices, respectively[30]. b, d, Representative changes in activity before (Pre 1 and 2) and during CI–CS presentation. c, Top, mean unit activity ratios. CS presentation caused a greater decrease in prefrontal activity in unpaired animals than in paired animals ($F_{1,10} = 5.9$; $P < 0.05$). Bottom, mean percentage freezing. Unpaired mice displayed more freezing than paired mice ($F_{1,10} = 7.77$; $P < 0.02$). e, Relationship between behavioural and electrophysiological data from all 12 animals ($r = 0.73$; $P = 0.0063$).

242

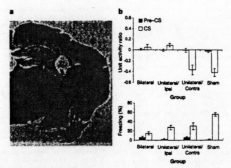

Figure 2 Effect of amygdala lesion. **a**, Representative photomicrograph of a coronal section showing lesion (circle) through the basolateral amygdala. **b**, Top, mean unit activity ratios. During CS presentation, unilateral/contra animals displayed a significant decrease in prefrontal activity compared to both bilateral and unilateral/ipsi animals (both $P < 0.05$), but did not differ from sham animals. Bottom, mean percentage freezing. In the bilateral group, CS presentation did not induce any significant freezing. In the presence of the CS, animals with unilateral lesions displayed significantly more freezing than the bilateral animals ($P < 0.05$), but less freezing than the sham animals ($P < 0.05$).

(test phase). Prefrontal electrical activity was accepted for recordings only if the signal-to-noise ratio was at least 4:1 for the largest spikes. Under these conditions, the activities of at least two units were discriminable by amplitude window. Three CI–CS pairings were presented with an intertrial interval of 60–180 s. Multi-unit analysis was performed as described[8], and changes in firing were quantified according to the formula $(B - A)/(B + A)$, where B is the total number of spikes during the CS or CI presentation and A is the total number of spikes during the pre-CI–CS period. The same formula was used to determine the stability of the response during the pre-CI–CS period.

Examination of counterstained brain sections revealed that electrode tips were all located in the prelimbic cortex (Fig. 1a). The spontaneous firing rates of neurons in these areas ranged from 1 to 8 Hz and were stable during the pre-CI–CS period (Fig. 1d). In response to CS, neuronal activity was exclusively inhibited (Fig. 1b, d). A similar decrease in excitability in the presence of a conditioned stimulator of fear occurs in the lateral septum[8]. However, in contrast to septal neurons, which display an opposite pattern of spontaneous activity in the presence of a conditioned inhibitor of fear (an increase in activity[9]), prefrontal neurons did not present any significant change in response to CI presentation. Nevertheless, the decrease in activity observed with conditioned fear excitation was significantly reduced in animals submitted to conditioned inhibition (CI–CS paired group, Fig. 1b, c).

The amount of freezing time was measured during the 20 s immediately before the CI onset (pre-CI–CS period) and during both the 20-s CI and 20-s CS presentations. After conditioning, mice in the CI–CS unpaired group displayed a marked freezing response as compared to freezing level during the pre CI–CS period. Mice in the CI–CS paired group displayed less freezing than mice in the CI–CS unpaired group, indicating the acquisition of conditioned inhibition (Fig. 1c).

These electrophysiological and behavioural data indicate that the level of CS-induced depression in prefrontal spontaneous activity is related to the level of CS-evoked freezing behaviour (Fig. 1e). If this were true, a strong reduction in conditioned freezing produced by postconditioning amygdalectomy should abolish CS-induced changes in prefrontal neuronal activity. In addition, as the amygdala from one side of the brain projects poorly to the contralateral prefrontal cortex[9] and as unilateral amygdalectomy reduces but does not abolish conditioned freezing[10], such a lesion should block CS-induced depression in the ipsilateral prefrontal cortex while leaving intact CS-induced depression in the contralateral prefrontal

cortex. To test this, mice were implanted with recording electrodes in medial prefrontal cortex and lesioning electrodes in the basolateral complex. Animals were submitted only to the first training phase (tone–shock association) because it was assumed that, if amygdalectomy were to suppress CS-induced depression in prefrontal spontaneous activity in the presence of the CS alone, it would also do so following conditioned inhibition of fear (when the CS is preceded by the CI). Thus, animals received, 30 min after the tone–shock association, either a bilateral lesion (bilateral lesion group), a unilateral lesion (unilateral/ipsi group, with recording electrodes in the ipsilateral prefrontal cortex; unilateral/contra group, with recording electrodes in the contralateral prefrontal cortex), or no lesion of the basolateral complex (sham lesion group). The auditory test was performed 3 days later.

Figure 2a shows a representative photomicrograph of the amygdala lesion. Only animals with large electrolytic lesions including the basolateral nucleus of the amygdala were considered for data analyses ($n = 18$). Electrophysiological data show that, in the presence of the conditioned tone, animals in the sham lesioned group ($n = 6$) displayed a strong decrease in prefrontal multi-unit activity (Fig. 2b). This effect was completely suppressed in animals from the bilateral lesion group ($n = 6$). However, in the unilateral lesion groups ($n = 12$), prefrontal recordings from the contralateral side to the lesion (unilateral/contra; $n = 6$) were characterized by a CS-induced decrease in prefrontal activity similar to that observed in sham lesioned animals. Recordings performed on the side ipsilateral to the lesion (unilateral/ipsi; $n = 6$) indicated a lack of CS-induced depression in prefrontal activity. No animals exhibited freezing behaviour in the pre-CS period. However, during the CS presentation, animals with bilateral amygdala lesions froze less than animals with unilateral lesions, which in turn displayed less freezing behaviour than animals from the sham lesioned group (Fig. 2b). Thus, postconditioning amygdalectomy led to behavioural results similar to those reported[10] for preconditioning amygdalectomy.

Our findings provide direct evidence for the control by the basolateral amygdala of learned auditory fear-induced changes in neuronal activity in the medial prefrontal cortex. These data fit well with and account for numerous pieces of information. First, anatomical and electrophysiological studies provide evidence for auditory connections in the basolateral complex of the amygdala[11–13]. Second, both unconditioned and conditioned stimuli induce long-term potentiation of auditory-evoked synaptic transmission in the basolateral complex of the amygdala[14–16]. Third, stimulation of the basolateral nucleus predominantly induces inhibitory responses in the medial prefrontal cortex[17]. Collectively, these observations indicate that detection of a conditioned aversive auditory stimulus may activate neurons in the basolateral complex of the amygdala, which may in turn control both the expression of learned fear and electrical activity in the medial prefrontal cortex (characterized by an inhibitory effect). As the direct projection from the basolateral nucleus of the amygdala to the medial prefrontal cortex involves pyramidal neurons which contain excitatory neurotransmitters[18], the indirect brain circuit by which the amygdala exerts its inhibitory effect on prefrontal neuronal activity remains to be determined. One of the putative inhibitory pathways may be the amygdale–brainstem–prefrontal cortex connection. Indeed, the amygdala sends fibres to the brainstem dopaminergic ventral tegmental area[19] which, in turn, projects to prefrontal cortex[20,21]. Moreover, (i) threatening stimuli activate the dopaminergic system in the medial prefrontal cortex[22], (ii) amygdala lesions suppress this activation[22,23] and (iii) activation of the dopaminergic system decreases prefrontal spontaneous activity[24,25]. Thus, the amygdala may exert its influence (inhibitory effect on prefrontal spontaneous activity) through activation of the mesocortical dopaminergic system. Alternatively, the amygdala may also exert its influence through other extracortical pathways and systems or directly through intracortical networks[26].

The functional role of amygdala activity-induced inhibition of prefrontal cortex activity also remains to be determined. However, it is known both in humans[27] and in animals[4], that, unlike the amygdala, the medial prefrontal cortex is not necessary to represent the affective attributes of an explicit CS. Taking into account the role of the prefrontal cortex in cognitive functions and the fact that lesion of the prefrontal cortex retards fear extinction[4], we suggest that CS-induced prefrontal neuronal plasticity may be related to representation of how well the CS predicts danger. More precisely, when danger is well predicted by the CS, prefrontal neuronal activity is strongly depressed (which may encode the strong certainty of the occurrence of danger). However, when the predictive ability of the CS for danger is weakened, for instance by a conditioned inhibition procedure (as here) or an extinction procedure (repeated presentations of the CS alone)[28], there is weak depression (as here) and even potentiation[28] of prefrontal neuronal activity (which may encode the low certainty of the occurrence of danger). Therefore, as shown for decision-making[27] or for expected outcomes[29], the integrity of the amygdala appears to be necessary for the formation of a representation of the degree of predictability of an aversive event in the prefrontal cortex. At a more clinical level, we suggest that abnormal amygdala-induced modulation of prefrontal neuronal activity may be involved in the pathophysiology of certain forms of anxiety disorder. □

Methods

Electrode implantation, electrophysiology and lesion

We used 36 male mice (C57BL/6 JI Co; 4–6 months; 28–32 g) with electrodes implanted under anaesthetic (a mixture of ketamine at 80 mg kg^{-1} and xylazine at 20 mg kg^{-1}). Electrodes were made of platinum–iridium wires (50 μm in diameter) and were positioned in the dorsal part of the medial prefrontal cortex for multi-unit activity recording and in the basolateral complex for postconditioning lesioning. Three days after surgery, animals were handled for 1 min and placed in a Plexiglas recording chamber (17 × 17 × 20 cm high with a plastic floor) for 10 min on five consecutive days. The recording chamber was washed with 1% acetic acid before and after each session. The behaviour of the mice was observed using a video camera monitor system. Spontaneous multi-unit activity was recorded through JFET operational amplifiers connected to the mouse's head to minimize artefacts due to head movement. Microcables from the JFET were relayed at the top of the recording chamber by a multichannel rotating connector. This system allowed the animal free movement within the recording chamber. Prefrontal neuronal activity was sent to a differential band-pass amplifier (0.3–10 kHz; gain × 10,000) and a discriminator set to count only the larger spikes (Axoscope, Axon Instruments). For lesioning, an anodal current (1 mA) was passed through the basolateral electrode for 20 s with the mice anaesthetized. Unlesioned mice were also anaesthetized but no current was passed through the amygdala electrode. The exact placement of both the recording and lesioning electrodes was verified at the end of the experiments by standard histological methods.

Conditioning

Computerized training (Forth software, USC) took place in a semi-opaque box (20 × 20 × 25 cm high) with a shock grid made of stainless steel rods (0.45 cm in diameter, spaced 1.9 cm apart) and a removable 12 W light bulb at the top of the box. A speaker providing a 1 kHz, 80 dB tone was located 15 cm in front of the box. The shock grid was connected to a shock generator and scrambler to provide a 0.5 s, 0.5 mA footshock. The conditioning box and the floor were cleaned with 70% ethanol before and after each session. A background noise of 55 dB was provided throughout all experiments.

Received 21 July; accepted 8 September 1999.

1. Davis, M. in *The Amygdala: Neurobiological Aspects of Emotion, Memory, and Mental Dysfunction* (ed. Aggleton, J. P.) 255–305 (Wiley-Liss, New York, 1992).
2. LeDoux, J. E. Emotion: clues from brain. *Annu. Rev. Psychol.* 46, 209–235 (1995).
3. Maren, S. & Fanselow, M. S. The amygdala and fear conditioning: has the nut been cracked? *Neuron* 16, 237–240 (1996).
4. Morgan, M. A. & LeDoux, J. E. Differential contribution of dorsal and ventral medial prefrontal cortex to acquisition and extinction of conditioned fear in rats. *Behav. Neurosci.* 109, 681–688 (1995).
5. Rescorla, R. A. Pavlovian conditioned inhibition. *Psychol. Bull.* 72, 77–94 (1969).
6. Campeau, S. *et al.* Elicitation and reduction of fear: behavioural and neuroendocrine indices and brain induction of the immediate-early gene c-fos. *Neuroscience* 78, 1087–1104 (1997).
7. Papini, M. R. & Bitterman, M. E. The two-test strategy in the study of inhibitory conditioning. *J. Exp. Psychol. Anim. Behav. Process.* 19, 342–352 (1993).
8. Thomas, E. & Yadin, E. Multiple unit activity in the septum during Pavlovian aversive conditioning: evidence for an inhibitory role for the septum. *Exp. Neurol.* 69, 50–60 (1980).
9. McDonald, A. J. Organization of amygdaloid projections to the prefrontal cortex and associated striatum in the rat. *Neuroscience* 44, 1–14 (1991).
10. LaBar, K. S. & LeDoux, J. E. Partial disruption of fear conditioning in rats with unilateral amygdala damage: correspondence with unilateral temporal lobectomy in humans. *Behav. Neurosci.* 110, 991–997 (1996).
11. Farb, C. R. & LeDoux, J. E. NMDA and AMPA receptors in the lateral nucleus of the amygdala are postsynaptic to auditory thalamic afferents. *Synapse* 27, 106–121 (1997).
12. LeDoux, J. E., Farb, C. & Ruggiero, D. A. Topographic organization of neurons in the acoustic thalamus that project to the amygdala. *J. Neurosci.* 10, 1043–1054 (1990).
13. Turner, B. H. & Herkenham, M. Thalamo-amygdaloid projections in the rat: a test of the amygdala's role in sensory processing. *J. Comp. Neurol.* 313, 295–325 (1991).
14. Garcia, R., Paquereau, J., Vouimba, R. M. & Jaffard, R. Conditioned fear stress enhances auditory-evoked potentials in the basolateral amygdala of the awake rat. *Eur. J. Neurosci.* (Suppl.) 9, 194 (1996).
15. Garcia, R., Paquereau, J., Vouimba, R. M. & Jaffard, R. Footshock stress but not contextual fear conditioning induces long-term enhancement of auditory-evoked potentials in the basolateral amygdala of the freely behaving rat. *Eur. J. Neurosci.* 10, 457–463 (1998).
16. Rogan, M. T., Stäubli, U. V. & LeDoux, J. E. Fear conditioning induces associative long-term potentiation in the amygdala. *Nature* 390, 604–607 (1997).
17. Pérez-Jaranay, J. M. & Vives, F. Electrophysiological study of the response of medial prefrontal cortex neurons to stimulation of the basolateral nucleus of the amygdala in the rat. *Brain Res.* 564, 97–101 (1991).
18. McDonald, A. J. Organization of amygdaloid projections to the mediodorsal thalamus and prefrontal cortex: a fluorescence retrograde transport study in the rat. *J. Comp. Neurol.* 262, 46–58 (1987).
19. Gonzales, C. & Chesselet, M. F. Amygdalo-nigral pathways: an anterograde study in the rat with phaseolus vulgaris leucoagglutinin (PHAL-L). *J. Comp. Neurol.* 297, 182–200 (1990).
20. Lindvall, O., Björklund, A., Moore, R. Y. & Stenevi, U. Mesencephalic dopamine neurons projecting to neocortex. *Brain Res.* 81, 325–331 (1974).
21. Fuxe, K., Hokfelt, T., Johansson, O., Lidbrink, P. & Ljungdahl, A. The origin of the dopamine nerve terminals in limbic and frontal cortex. Evidence for meso-cortico dopamine neurons. *Brain Res.* 82, 349–355 (1974).
22. Davis, M. *et al.* Stress-induced activation of prefrontal cortex dopamine turnover: blockade by lesions of the amygdala. *Brain Res.* 664, 207–210 (1994).
23. Goldstein, L. E., Rasmusson, A. M., Bunney, B. S. & Roth, R. H. Role of the amygdala in the coordination of behavioral, neuroendocrine, and prefrontal cortical monoamine responses to psychological stress in the rat. *J. Neurosci.* 16, 4787–4798 (1996).
24. Ferron, A., Thierry, A. M., Le Douarin, C. & Glowinski, J. Inhibitory influence of the mesocortical dopaminergic system on spontaneous activity or excitatory response induced from the thalamic mediodorsal nucleus in the rat medial prefrontal cortex. *Brain Res.* 302, 257–265 (1984).
25. Mantz, J., Milla, C., Glowinsky, J. & Thierry, A. M. Differential effects of ascending neurons containing dopamine and noradrenaline in the control of spontaneous activity and of evoked responses in the rat prefrontal cortex. *Neuroscience* 27, 517–526 (1988).
26. Schoenbaum, G., Chiba, A. A. & Gallagher, M. Neural encoding in orbitofrontal cortex and basolateral amygdala during olfactory discrimination learning. *J. Neurosci.* 19, 1876–1884 (1999).
27. Bechara, A., Damasio, H., Damasio, A. R. & Lee, G. P. Different contributions of the human amygdala and ventromedial prefrontal cortex to decision-making. *J. Neurosci.* 19, 5473–5481 (1999).
28. Herry, C., Vouimba, R. M. & Garcia, R. Plasticity in the thalamo-prefrontal cortical transmission in behaving mice. *J. Neurophysiol.* (in the press).
29. Schoenbaum, G., Chiba, A. A. & Gallagher, M. Orbitofrontal cortex and basolateral amygdala encode expected outcomes during learning. *Nature Neurosci.* 1, 155–159 (1998).
30. Franklin, K. B. J. & Paxinos, G. *The Mouse Brain in Stereotaxic Coordinates* (Academic, San Diego, 1997).

Acknowledgements

This work was supported by grants from the Fondation Fyssen (R.M.V.) and from NATO (R.G.).

Correspondence and requests for materials should be addressed to R.G. (e-mail: garcia@neurocog.u-bordeaux.fr).

296

244

Special Article

Neuroanatomical Hypothesis of Panic Disorder, Revised

Jack M. Gorman, M.D., Justine M. Kent, M.D.,
Gregory M. Sullivan, M.D., and Jeremy D. Coplan, M.D.

Objective: In a 1989 article, the authors provided a hypothesis for the neuroanatomical basis of panic disorder that attempted to explain why both medication and cognitive behavioral psychotherapy are effective treatments. Here they revise that hypothesis to consider developments in the preclinical understanding of the neurobiology of fear and avoidance. **Method:** The authors review recent literature on the phenomenology, neurobiology, and treatment of panic disorder and impressive developments in documenting the neuroanatomy of conditioned fear in animals. **Results:** There appears to be a remarkable similarity between the physiological and behavioral consequences of response to a conditioned fear stimulus and a panic attack. In animals, these responses are mediated by a "fear network" in the brain that is centered in the amygdala and involves its interaction with the hippocampus and medial prefrontal cortex. Projections from the amygdala to hypothalamic and brainstem sites explain many of the observed signs of conditioned fear responses. It is speculated that a similar network is involved in panic disorder. A convergence of evidence suggests that both heritable factors and stressful life events, particularly in early childhood, are responsible for the onset of panic disorder. **Conclusions:** Medications, particularly those that influence the serotonin system, are hypothesized to desensitize the fear network from the level of the amygdala through its projects to the hypothalamus and the brainstem. Effective psychosocial treatments may also reduce contextual fear and cognitive misattributions at the level of the prefrontal cortex and hippocampus. Neuroimaging studies should help clarify whether these hypotheses are correct.

(Am J Psychiatry 2000; 157:493–505)

In 1989, we (1) articulated a neuroanatomical hypothesis of panic disorder that was essentially an attempt to understand how two seemingly diverse treatments—medication and cognitive behavioral therapy—could both be effective interventions. This theory posited that a panic attack itself stems from loci in the brainstem that involve serotonergic and noradrenergic transmission and respiratory control, that anticipatory anxiety arises after the kindling of limbic area structures, and, finally, that phobic avoidance is a function of precortical activation. The hypothesis then asserted that medication exerts its therapeutic effect by normalizing brainstem activity in patients with panic disorder, whereas cognitive behavioral therapy works at the cortical level.

In succeeding years, studies have continued to accumulate demonstrating that medications, particularly those that affect serotonergic neurotransmission (2), and cognitive behavioral therapy (3) are indeed robustly effective for patients with panic disorder. Further, the notion that respiratory (4) and cardiovascular

Received Feb. 25, 1999; revision received Aug. 3, 1999; accepted Aug. 4, 1999. From the Department of Psychiatry, College of Physicians and Surgeons, Columbia University; and the Department of Clinical Psychobiology, New York State Psychiatric Institute, New York. Address reprint requests to Dr. Gorman, Department of Psychiatry, College of Physicians and Surgeons, Columbia University, 1051 Riverside Dr., New York, NY 10032; jmg9@columbia.edu (e-mail).

Supported in part by an NIMH grant to Drs. Kent and Sullivan (MH-15144), a Senior Scientist Award to Dr. Gorman (MH-00416), and a Research Scientist Development Award to Dr. Coplan (MH-01039).

The authors thank Barbara Barnett, Christopher Tulysewski, David Ruggiero, and Jose Martinez for their help in the preparation of this manuscript.

reactivity (5) is abnormal in panic disorder, pointing to brainstem involvement, has also been strengthened. However, our original hypothesis is now seen as clearly deficient because it is almost completely divorced from exciting preclinical and basic research that has elegantly mapped out the neuroanatomical basis for fear. We now wish to revisit our neuroanatomical hypothesis of panic disorder and address these critical novel elements. The result will propose that panic disorder may involve the same pathways that subserve conditioned fear in animals, including the central nucleus of the amygdala and its afferent and efferent projections.

ANATOMY OF CONDITIONED FEAR

One of the greatest challenges in modern psychiatry is to make use of advanced preclinical information from basic and behavioral neuroscience. Strides have been made in developing animal models of emotional and behavioral states, a task seen as critical in developing a coherent understanding of any human disease state. However, it has been difficult to understand how any animal, lacking the capacity to express in words its emotional state, could meaningfully reflect human psychopathology. It is problematic to conceive of an animal model for depression or psychosis, for example, because these illnesses seemingly depend on the ability of the human patient to inform us verbally about symptoms that are necessary for diagnosis. Although even in these instances cogent animal models are now available, two human psychiatric syndromes seem best suited for analogy with animal states: anxiety and substance abuse. In the latter case, it is possible to addict animals to a variety of substances and then study the neural pathways that subserve the continued acquisition of these substances. This has led to remarkable insights into brain pathways necessary to sustain the abuse of substances like cocaine (6), some of which can be confirmed in humans with neuroimaging techniques (7).

In the case of anxiety, it is well understood that fear, escape, or avoidance behavior and panic-like responses are ubiquitous throughout animal phylogeny. It takes relatively little intuition to recognize that a rodent that avoids entering a cage in which an adverse stimulus has been presented in the past appears similar to a phobic patient refusing to drive across a bridge on which panic attacks previously occurred. Similarly, an animal manifesting increases in heart rate, blood pressure, respiration, and glucocorticoid release after the presentation of a tone that had previously been paired with a mild electric shock demonstrates many of the autonomic features characteristic of a panic attack.

The analogy of panic attacks to animal fear and avoidance responses is, to be sure, imperfect. Most animal models of anxiety states involve conditioning, and it is not at all clear that panic disorder or any other anxiety disorder except posttraumatic stress disorder (PTSD) involves prior exposure to any aversive stimulus. Further, because animals cannot tell us about the experience of anxiety and fear, we miss a rich source of information that is readily obtained from humans with anxiety disorders. In addition, animal models of fear may not truly reflect anxiety status. Klein (8) has written persuasively that there may be major biological differences in humans between fear and the manifestations of anxiety disorders.

Nevertheless, as we will detail, there are many aspects of conditioned fear in animals that make the analogy with panic attacks irresistible. Most important, it would be a mistake, in our view, to miss the opportunity to study pathways in humans that have been carefully elucidated in animals during anxious responses. We take, then, as a starting point that a consideration of the neuroanatomy of conditioned fear in rodents and other animals may give us important insights that can then be studied in patients with panic disorder.

The conditioned-fear paradigm used in neurobiological studies is well known to the most elementary students of behavior. In a typical study, a rat is presented with a stimulus—usually a tone or flash of light—at the same time it receives a mild electric shock. The former is called the conditioned stimulus, and the latter, the unconditioned stimulus. After several pairings, the rat learns to respond to the conditioned stimulus with the same autonomic and behavioral array even when no unconditioned stimulus is presented. The paradigm originates from the work of Pavlov (9) and has occupied the time of countless psychology students for generations.

What is new is an understanding of the brain pathways and neurotransmitters that are required for the acquisition of conditioned fear. The critical pathways are shown in figure 1. The sensory input for the conditioned stimulus runs through the anterior thalamus to the lateral nucleus of the amygdala and is then transferred to the central nucleus of the amygdala (10). The central nucleus of the amygdala stands as the central point for dissemination of information that then coordinates autonomic and behavioral responses (11, 12). In preclinical work, amygdalar projections have been established that may carry out these responses. Efferents of the central nucleus of the amygdala have many targets: the parabrachial nucleus, producing an increase in respiratory rate (13); the lateral nucleus of the hypothalamus, activating the sympathetic nervous system and causing autonomic arousal and sympathetic discharge (14); the locus ceruleus, resulting in an increase in norepinephrine release and contributing to increases in blood pressure, heart rate, and the behavioral fear response (15); and the paraventricular nucleus of the hypothalamus, causing an increase in the release of adrenocorticoids (16). A projection from the central nucleus of the amygdala to the periaqueductal gray region is responsible for additional behavioral responses, including defensive behaviors and postural freezing, that may be the animal equivalent of phobic avoidance (17). In fact, it can readily be seen from

246

FIGURE 1. Neuroanatomical Pathways of Viscerosensory Information in the Brain[a]

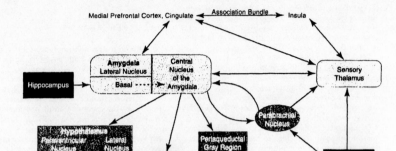

[a] Viscerosensory information is conveyed to the amygdala by two major pathways: downstream, from the nucleus of the solitary tract via the parabrachial nucleus or the sensory thalamus; and upstream, from the primary viscerosensory cortices and via corticothalamic relays allowing for higher-level neurocognitive processing and modulation of sensory information. Contextual information is stored in memory in the hippocampus and conveyed directly to the amygdala. Major efferent pathways of the amygdala relevant to anxiety include the following: the locus ceruleus (increases norepinephrine release, which contributes to physiologic and behavioral arousal), the periaqueductal gray region (results in defensive behaviors and postural freezing), the hypothalamic paraventricular nucleus (activates the hypothalamic-pituitary-adrenal axis, releasing adrenocorticoids), the hypothalamic lateral nucleus (activates the sympathetic nervous system), and the parabrachial nucleus (influences respiratory rate and timing).

figure 1, which is based mainly on the work of Joseph LeDoux et al. (11) and Michael Davis (12), that the autonomic, neuroendocrine, and behavioral responses that occur during panic attacks are remarkably similar to the symptoms occurring in animals as a result of activity in these brain regions during fearful response to conditioned stimuli. This striking overlap between the consequences of stimulation by the central nucleus of the amygdala of brainstem sites and the biological events that occur in humans during panic attacks is compelling. However, this is not the complete story. It is clear that there are important reciprocal connections between the amygdala and the sensory thalamus, prefrontal cortex, insula, and primary somatosensory cortex (18). So although the amygdala receives direct sensory input from brainstem structures and the sensory thalamus, enabling a rapid response to potentially threatening stimuli, it also receives afferents from cortical regions involved in the processing and evaluation of sensory information. Potentially, a neurocognitive deficit in these cortical processing pathways could result in the misinterpretation of sensory information (bodily cues) known to be a hallmark of panic disorder, leading to an inappropriate activation of the "fear network" via misguided excitatory input to the amygdala. Although much remains to be elucidated regarding the amygdala's role in panic, it seems reasonable to speculate that there may be a deficit in the relay and coordi-

nation of "upstream" (cortical) and "downstream" (brainstem) sensory information, which results in heightened amygdalar activity with resultant behavioral, autonomic, and neuroendocrine activation.

One must pause at this point, however, to consider how often patients with panic disorder actually demonstrate autonomic and neuroendocrine activation during attacks. Studies here are incomplete and somewhat inconsistent. For example, some, but not all, ambulatory monitoring studies have shown an increase in heart rate (19) and respiration (20) during panic attacks recorded outside of the laboratory. Although patients with panic disorder respond to CO_2 inhalation with more anxiety, panic, and increase in respiratory rate than do normal volunteers or patients with other psychiatric illnesses (21), studies of the most sensitive measure of physiological response to CO_2 inhalation—the ratio of change in minute ventilation to change in end tidal CO_2 concentration—have yielded conflicting results (22). Although some investigators have found evidence for CO_2 hypersensitivity, others have found that patients with panic fall within the normal range on this measure. Cortisol elevation in patients with panic disorder is reliably observed only during the anticipation of panic attacks (23), not during the attacks themselves (24). Taken together, the evidence suggests that some, but not all, panic attacks are accompanied by autonomic and neuroendocrine activation.

247

This last point serves to highlight what we think is an important error in our original neuroanatomic hypothesis of panic disorder. If, as argued there, panic attacks are the direct result of abnormal autonomic control at the level of the brainstem, we would expect to find autonomic and neuroendocrine activation a common property of all panic attacks. The fact that this is not the case suggests that brainstem activation is probably an epiphenomenon of activity in another area of the brain. The finding in preclinical research that activity in the central nucleus of the amygdala initiates stimulation of all of the relevant brainstem centers and that disrupting specific projections from the central nucleus of the amygdala to brainstem neurons selectively interferes with autonomic responses is consonant with this idea. Thus, for example, if the projection from the central nucleus of the amygdala to the central gray region is lesioned, all autonomic responses are seen, but the animal does not posturally freeze or attempt to flee (17).

Another finding that continues to contradict the idea that there is a specific abnormality in autonomic brainstem control in panic disorder is that a variety of agents with dissimilar biological properties all produce panic attacks in patients with panic disorder but not in healthy comparison subjects or patients with other psychiatric illnesses. The list of such agents is long, seems to grow annually, and includes sodium lactate (25), CO_2 (26), yohimbine (27), fenfluramine (28), m-CPP (29), noradrenaline (30), adrenaline (31), hypertonic sodium chloride (32), and analogues of cholecystokinin (33). It remains difficult to understand what abnormal brainstem nucleus could be specifically triggered by such a diverse group of agents.

An alternative explanation that takes into account the inconsistency of autonomic responses and the heterogeneity of agents capable of producing panic attacks in susceptible patients is that panic originates in an abnormally sensitive fear network, which includes the prefrontal cortex, insula, thalamus, amygdala, and amygdalar projections to the brainstem and hypothalamus. When administering an agent that causes panic attacks, sometimes called a panicogen, we are not interacting with a specific brainstem autonomic area but, rather, activating the entire fear network. Patients with panic disorder experience unsettling somatic sensations on a regular basis. The administration of a panicogenic substance represents nonspecific activation; because each of the panicogens produces acutely uncomfortable physical sensations, we suppose that they act to provoke a sensitized brain network that has been conditioned to respond to noxious stimuli. Over time, various projections from the central nucleus of the amygdala to brainstem sites such as the locus ceruleus, periaqueductal gray region, and hypothalamus may become stronger or weaker. There may be interindividual differences in the strength of these afferent projections as well. Hence, the actual pattern of autonomic and neuroendocrine responses during panic may vary within any given patient with panic over time and even

widely across patients with panic. These observations are clearly in line with what both researchers and clinicians observe.

ROLE OF MEDICATION

It is useful to consider how medications might act at the level of the central nucleus of the amygdala and its projections to reduce the severity and frequency of panic attacks. Although many classes of medication have been shown to be more effective than placebo in treating panic disorder, we select only one class for this discussion—the selective serotonin reuptake inhibitors (SSRIs). We do this because SSRIs are rapidly becoming the first-line medication treatment for panic disorder (34), their acute mechanism of action in the central nervous system is fairly well understood (35), and they may be more effective than other classes of medication for panic disorder (36).

SSRIs have in common the property of inhibiting the protein responsible for transporting serotonin (5-HT) back into the presynaptic neuron. This effectively increases the amount of 5-HT available in the synapse to bind to both pre- and postsynaptic receptors. There are at least 13 subtypes of 5-HT receptors established in humans (37), although the function and anatomical distribution of all of them have not been fully characterized. Nevertheless, functional studies demonstrate that over time, treatment with SSRIs leads to an increase in overall serotonergic neurotransmission in the central nervous system (38).

When attempting to understand the mechanism of action of SSRIs in panic disorder, a paradox arises as soon as animal models are considered. Acutely increasing 5-HT levels either globally or regionally in the brain of an experimental animal has been shown by many—although not all studies—to increase fear and avoidance (39). Although long-term studies are not available, and there are contradictory data, even some longer-term administrations of 5-HT precursors or agonists appear to maintain this increase in fear. By contrast, although some patients initially complain of increased anxiety and agitation when given treatment with SSRIs, these adverse events are generally mild and subside over subsequent weeks. By 4 weeks, most patients with panic report feeling less anxious and are having fewer panic attacks (and of diminished intensity) than before medication was initiated.

The solution to this paradox may come from a more refined understanding of the pathways involved in serotonergic neurotransmission. Serotonergic neurons originate in the brainstem raphe region and project widely throughout the entire central nervous system (40). Three of these projections are of particular relevance to an understanding of the SSRI antipanic effect.

First, the projection of 5-HT neurons to the locus ceruleus is generally inhibitory (41), such that the greater the activity of the serotonergic neurons in the raphe, the smaller the activity of the noradrenergic neurons in the locus ceruleus. Indeed, Coplan et al. (42) showed that after 12 weeks of fluoxetine treatment, patients with panic who responded to treatment showed a decrease in plasma levels of 3-methoxy-4-hydroxyphenylglycol, the main metabolite of noradrenaline. This suggests that SSRIs, by increasing serotonergic activity in the brain, have a secondary effect of decreasing noradrenergic activity. This would lead to a decrease in many of the cardiovascular symptoms associated with panic attacks, including tachycardia and increased diastolic blood pressure.

Second, the projection of the raphe neurons to the periaqueductal gray region appears to modify defense/escape behaviors. Viana and colleagues (43) have shown that stimulation of the dorsal raphe nucleus dramatically increases 5-HT release acutely in the dorsal periaqueductal gray region, resulting in diminished periaqueductal gray region activity. This finding supports the original suggestion of Deakin and Graeff (44) that serotonergic projections from the dorsal raphe nuclei play a role in modifying defense/escape responses by means of their inhibitory influence on the periaqueductal gray region.

Third, evidence now suggests that long-term treatment with an SSRI may reduce hypothalamic release of corticotropin-releasing factor (CRF) (45). CRF, which initiates the cascade of events that leads to adrenal cortical production of cortisol, is also a neurotransmitter in the central nervous system and has been shown on numerous occasions to increase fear in preclinical models (46). When administered directly into the brain, CRF also increases the firing rate of the locus ceruleus (47). CRF antagonists decrease both physiological (48) and behavioral consequences of CRF stimulation (49). Indeed, CRF antagonists are now being examined for their potential as anxiolytics in both animals and humans.

Hence, by looking at the specific pathways that originate from serotonergic neurons in the raphe, one can find at least three mechanisms by which increased serotonergic activity produced by long-term SSRI administration might produce an antipanic effect. By diminishing arousal, defense/escape behavior, and levels of the anxiogenic substance CRF, SSRIs are likely to block many of the downstream manifestations of panic.

Equally intriguing as the three examples given above is the possibility that SSRIs, by increasing serotonergic activity, have an effect on the central nucleus of the amygdala itself. Studies here are in the early stages, but it is already known that serotonergic neurons originating in the dorsal and medial raphe nuclei project directly to the amygdala via the medial forebrain bundle (40). At the level of the amygdala, Stutzmann and LeDoux (50) have demonstrated that 5-HT modulates sensory input at the lateral nucleus of the amygdala, inhibiting excitatory inputs from glutamatergic thalamic and cortical pathways. Because the amygdala is known to receive dense serotonergic input from the raphe nuclei, this may be a prime site for the anxiolytic action of the SSRIs, whereby an increase in 5-HT in-

hibits excitatory cortical and thalamic inputs from activating the amygdala.

We propose, then, that it is most likely that medications known to be effective in treating panic disorder diminish the activity of brainstem centers that receive input from the central nucleus of the amygdala and control autonomic and neuroendocrine responses during attacks. In addition to their psychic effects, drugs such as SSRIs may eliminate most of the troubling physical effects that occur during panic by affecting heart rate, blood pressure, breathing rate, and glucocorticoid release. This would then lead to a secondary decrease in anticipatory anxiety as a patient recognizes that the seemingly life-threatening physical manifestations of panic have been blocked. It is not uncommon, particularly in the early stages of medication treatment of a patient with panic disorder, to hear "I sometimes feel as if the attack is coming on, especially when I am in a situation in which attacks have occurred in the past. I get afraid, but then nothing happens. No palpitations, no dizziness, no difficulty breathing. My thoughts don't seem to be able to cause a panic attack anymore." We interpret this to suggest that the projections from the central nucleus of the amygdala to the brainstem and hypothalamus have been inhibited by medication treatment.

NEUROIMAGING AND PANIC DISORDER

If the amygdala, thalamus, periaqueductal gray region, parabrachial nucleus, locus ceruleus, and hypothalamus are so important in coordinating the manifestations of panic, it would be a logical next step to attempt to image these brain regions during attacks and determine if they are particularly active compared to other brain regions. This has proven to be a daunting task. First, although the amygdala occupies a significant portion of the anterior part of the temporal lobe, it is a small structure in the human brain and is therefore difficult to distinguish with all but the most sensitive positron emission tomography (PET) cameras. Separating the amygdala from adjoining brain structures and the cortex is not a trivial task. Further, it is not yet possible with PET to distinguish among smaller brainstem nuclei. Functional magnetic resonance imaging (fMRI) potentially has the resolution to make this possible, but the technology is still in development to clearly image deeper subcortical and brainstem structures.

Sensitive PET cameras can now resolve the amygdala and other structures in the fear network like the thalamus as distinct neuroanatomical loci, but at least two other problems exist in learning whether they play a special role in panic. The first is in trying to capture the attack itself. Because panic attacks occur at seemingly random intervals, it is obviously impossible to place a patient in a scanner and wait for a spontaneous panic attack to occur. This means that some panicogenic agent must be administered that will reliably produce

FIGURE 2. Change In Global CBF, Corrected for Degree of Hypocapnia, During Voluntary Hyperventilation in Three Patients With Panic Disorder and Three Normal Comparison Subjects[a]

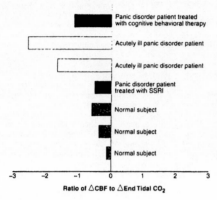

Panic disorder patient treated with cognitive behavioral therapy

Acutely ill panic disorder patient

Acutely ill panic disorder patient

Panic disorder patient treated with SSRI

Normal subject

Normal subject

Normal subject

Ratio of $\triangle$CBF to $\triangle$End Tidal CO_2

[a] Significant difference between groups, with the patient taking an SSRI excluded (t=3.26, df=4, p=0.03, N=6).

an attack. Several are available, as discussed above, but the attacks that occur when they are administered are, like naturally occurring panic attacks, brief. Radiotracers like [18F]fluorodeoxyglucose (FDG) that enable quantification of regional brain metabolism cannot capture events that occur over periods of time as short as a few minutes. Hence, PET scanning using FDG may not be able to tell us definitively if a change in metabolism has occurred acutely during the actual panic attack itself. Radiotracers such as [15O]water do provide temporal resolution compatible with capturing a panic attack, but they only allow us to measure regional cerebral blood flow (rCBF), not metabolism. The majority of studies have shown that there is a high correlation between brain metabolism and blood flow in healthy subjects (51, 52), such that increased neuronal activity in a given region is accompanied by increased blood flow to that region. However, other studies have suggested that this relationship may not hold consistently during physiologic activation (53). The possibility always exists that the uncoupling of CBF and metabolism may occur under circumstances of heightened stress, such as a panic attack. However, this uncoupling would be expected to be global, and, therefore, specific regional differences in CBF would be expected to still reflect changes in local neuronal metabolic activity.

A second problem for brain imaging studies is that patients with panic hyperventilate when they are anxious, and the resultant hypocapnia-induced vasoconstriction may obscure results, especially by counteracting expected increases in blood flow, reflecting neuronal activation and increased metabolism in cer-

tain structures. Most of the neuroimaging studies in populations with panic disorder have reported regional reductions in CBF or metabolism. Because the degree of hypocapnia (end tidal CO_2) has not generally been controlled in these studies, it is difficult to interpret the results knowing that patients with panic disorder have a greater tendency to hyperventilate in stressful situations than normal comparison subjects (22). In support of this idea is a study by Stewart and colleagues (54), in which rCBF was measured during rest and immediately after a lactate infusion with xenon-133 single photon emission computed tomography ([133Xe]-SPECT). Normal comparison subjects and nonpanicking patients with panic disorder showed an increase in CBF after lactate infusion, whereas patients with panic disorder who panicked after lactate infusion demonstrated a smaller increase or an actual decrease in CBF. This finding may be accounted for by the vasoconstrictive effect of hyperventilation in overcoming the expected lactate-induced increase in CBF in the panicking patients. We suspect this is likely because we have previously shown that patients who panic during lactate infusion do hyperventilate more than those who do not panic (55).

In addition, there is growing evidence that patients with panic disorder are more sensitive to the vasoconstrictive effects of hyperventilation-induced hypocapnia than are comparison subjects. Ball and Shekhar (56) have reported a differentially greater hyperventilation-induced decrease in basilar arterial blood flow in patients with panic attacks than in comparison subjects by means of transcranial Doppler ultrasonography. Dager et al. (57) measured brain lactate levels by using magnetic resonance spectroscopy during voluntary hyperventilation in a group of patients with panic disorder and a group of normal comparison subjects. Although they controlled for differing degrees of hyperventilation by monitoring Pco_2 with capnometry, hyperventilating subjects with panic disorder increased their brain lactate levels disproportionately, suggesting that they may have an exaggerated hypersensitivity to the vasoconstrictive effect of hypocapnia.

Our group has recently generated pilot data consistent with this notion (figure 2). A small number of patients with panic disorder, one of whom had been treated with cognitive behavioral therapy and was entirely asymptomatic at the time of the study, one of whom had been successfully treated with fluoxetine, and healthy comparison subjects, were asked to hyperventilate during [133Xe]-SPECT scanning. When corrected for level of hypocapnia, as measured by the end tidal CO_2 level, the patients showed significantly greater decreases in CBF than the healthy comparison subjects. The only exception was the remitted patient who was taking fluoxetine at the time and who appeared by inspection to have the same level of vasoconstriction as the healthy comparison subjects.

Conclusions from so preliminary a study are obviously perilous, but the results are consistent with those of many other neuroimaging observations with patients with panic disorder. The greater vasoconstriction found in the patients with panic disorder cannot be secondary to more hyperventilation or greater hypocapnia because these were carefully controlled, and observed levels were equivalent to those found in the healthy comparison subjects. Some additive mechanism must be involved. Two possibilities arise. First, as discussed earlier, it is well known from the work of Goddard et al. (58) and others that the noradrenergic system is more active and more sensitive in patients with panic than in healthy comparison subjects. Matthews (59) has argued convincingly that this, plus the fact that noradrenergic fibers innervate cerebral blood vessels and cause vasoconstriction (60), explains the heightened vasoconstriction in patients with panic during hyperventilation. Patients with panic may respond with more fear during hyperventilation than do healthy comparison subjects, thus activating the locus ceruleus and causing noradrenergic-mediated vasoconstriction that adds to the effects of hyperventilation.

A second possibility arises from the preclinical studies of Marovitch and colleagues (61), showing that stimulation of the parabrachial nucleus, which is adjacent to the locus ceruleus in the brainstem, also causes cerebral vasoconstriction. The widespread reduction in CBF seen with stimulation of the parabrachial nucleus may be mediated by yet another subcortical site, since projections of the parabrachial nucleus do not reach the entire cortex. Marovitch and colleagues have suggested that the rostral raphe nuclei, which are capable of modulating cortical vasoconstriction through serotonergic projections, may be such a site. In this role, the raphe nuclei might relay information from the parabrachial nucleus to the cerebral cortex, resulting in a more global vasoconstrictive effect. In either event, we postulate once again that activation of the amygdala during a fearful episode—in this case, hyperventilating in the enclosed space of a PET or SPECT scanner—may produce by its projections an increase in activity in either the locus ceruleus, the parabrachial nucleus, or both. This would increase the amount of vasoconstriction in patients with panic relative to healthy comparison subjects, leading to the exaggerated decreases in CBF observed in several neuroimaging studies.

The observation that one patient with panic treated with an SSRI did not show exaggerated vasoconstriction during hyperventilation is consonant with our theory. If, indeed, SSRIs produce inhibition of the locus ceruleus or parabrachial nucleus, either directly or through an effect on the amygdala, one would expect to see a normalization of the vasoconstrictive effect of hyperventilation. This speculation obviously calls for further studies because it could be a marker for the success of SSRI therapy in the treatment of panic disorder.

Although neuroimaging studies to date in patients with panic disorder have not implicated fear network structures established in preclinical models (perhaps because of methodological and technical limitations), neuroimaging studies in human fear conditioning have demonstrated the importance of these structures. Early

PET studies attempting to look at changes in the brains of healthy subjects during aversive classical (fear) conditioning (62) demonstrated significant increases in rCBF in several subcortical structures implicated in the fear network, including the thalamus, hypothalamus, and periaqueductal gray region, in addition to somatosensory and associative cortices and the cingulate. However, most PET studies have not found activation of the amygdala during fear conditioning paradigms using subtractive PET methods (62–65). Although these studies did not find an outright increase in amygdalar rCBF in fear conditioning, a positive correlation between nonspecific electrodermal fluctuations (reflecting degree of conditioning) and rCBF in the right amygdala was reported (64).

Recently, fMRI has been used to overcome some of the difficulties evident in PET approaches, such as temporal sequencing and nonassociative effects, and one group has successfully demonstrated activation of the amygdala and periamygdaloid cortical areas during conditioned fear acquisition and extinction (66). In addition, several investigators have shown specific activation of the amygdala in response to presentations of affectively negative or fearful visual stimuli using fMRI techniques (67). fMRI permits far better anatomical and temporal resolution than PET or SPECT; however, its ability to delineate deeper subcortical and brainstem structures has been limited in the past by field inhomogeneity. With the advent of cardiac gating and other advances in fMRI technology, this problem is being overcome. fMRI is therefore a logical technology to extend to the study of patients with panic disorder, since its superior anatomical and temporal resolution should allow the investigation of fear network structures during a real-time panic attack.

What is specifically needed for the study of panic disorder is a method that can provoke anxiety or panic without causing hyperventilation-induced hypocapnia. One possibility is to ask subjects to inhale small amounts of CO_2 during brain imaging studies. Concentrations as low as 5% in room air have been shown to increase anxiety levels in most subjects, with patients with panic disorder showing significantly more anxiety and higher rates of frank panic (21). Inhalation of CO_2 does produce increases in both tidal volume and respiratory rate (68), but because CO_2 is continuously supplied, there is no opportunity for hypocapnia to develop. The difficulty with this technique, however, is that CO_2 inhalation produces a global increase in CBF, making it unclear whether regional activation of a network responsible for panic would once again be obscured by blood flow changes, albeit in the opposite direction as those caused by hyperventilation. Corfield and colleagues (69) recently showed that there are regional differences in response to CO_2 inhalation, with the amygdala showing particularly strong effects. Such preliminary findings suggest that CO_2 inhalation may provide a method of overcoming the problems associated with hyperventilation-induced hypocapnia that attend most neuroimaging studies in panic disorder reported so far.

GENETICS OF FEAR AND PANIC DISORDER

If we accept the hypothesis that patients with panic disorder suffer from an abnormally sensitive fear network that includes the central nucleus of the amygdala, hippocampus, periaqueductal gray region, and other brainstem areas, the next issue to address is why this is the case. One possibility is that there is an inherited tendency for fearfulness, perhaps manifested as a neurocognitive deficit resulting in an abnormal response to or modulation of the fear network. Once again, an appeal to preclinical work is helpful.

A number of studies have now indicated that quantitative trait loci on specific chromosomes are associated with heightened emotionality and with fear-conditioning in rodents. For example, Flint et al. (70) showed that three loci on mouse chromosomes 1, 12, and 15 were associated with decreased activity and increased defecation in a novel environment. They concluded that these loci were responsible for heightened "emotionality" and speculated that "there are cogent reasons for expecting that the genetic basis of emotionality is similar in other species and that it may underlie the psychological trait of *susceptibility* [emphasis added] to anxiety in humans. The pattern of behavioral effects of anxiolytic drugs in rodents together with the results of electrophysiological and lesion experiments suggest conservation between species of a common neural substrate, probably determined by homologous genes" (p. 1434). Both Wehner et al. (71) and Caldarone et al. (72) found quantitative trait loci associated with contextual fear conditioning in rodents on several chromosomes, with both groups implicating chromosome 1. In an editorial accompanying the Wehner et al. and Calderone et al. studies, Flint (73) commented that "the locus on chromosome 1 that was identified by both groups has in fact already been shown to influence fearfulness in two independent studies...the fact that four studies working on such different measures of the same trait have succeeded in identifying the same chromosomal region is very encouraging" (p. 251).

Is there evidence that panic disorder is genetic? There is no question that it is highly familial. A number of studies have now shown that the chance of having panic disorder is substantially elevated over the base rate in the population if one has a first-degree relative with panic disorder (74). But this is hardly evidence of a genetic cause; one can easily imagine that growing up with anxious relatives could condition an individual to develop heightened levels of fear, anxiety, or even panic attacks. The next best data come from studies comparing the concordance rate for panic disorder between monozygotic (identical) and between dizygotic (fraternal) twins. For most medical illnesses, finding a higher rate of concordance between monozy-

gotic than between dizygotic twins for a disease implies a genetic basis. For psychiatric illness we must make the additional assumption that parents maintain as similar an environment for dizygotic twins as they do for monozygotic twins. At least three studies (75–77) have examined the concordance rates for panic disorder among twins, and all find a higher concordance for monozygotic than for dizygotic twins, with one (75) specifically showing a higher concordance rate for panic attacks than for the syndromal disorder itself. The conclusion at first glance seems clear: panic disorder must have a genetic component.

A closer examination of the twin studies, however, suggests a retreat from such a broad statement. In none of the studies was the concordance rate for panic between monozygotic twins even close to 50% (range= 14%–31%). This means that although genetically identical twins are more likely to both have panic disorder than are twins who are no more genetically identical than ordinary brothers and sisters, there are many cases in which one identical twin has panic disorder and the other does not. The conclusion seems clear. If genes are involved in causing panic disorder, they cannot be the whole story.

Taking the preclinical studies and the twin studies together, the most logical assumption is that what is inherited is a susceptibility to panic, not panic disorder itself. It is well known that children exhibit varying levels of anxiety and fear. Some children are extremely anxious and have been called "behaviorally inhibited to the unfamiliar" by Kagan and colleagues (78). The presence of an anxiety disorder in childhood or adolescence confers a substantially increased risk for having a recurrent anxiety disorder in young adulthood (79). Nevertheless, many anxious children do not develop anxiety disorders as adults, and many people with first-degree relatives, even identical twins, with panic disorder never have a panic attack themselves.

The elegant behavioral genetic work of Flint and others suggests that it is possible to inherit a vulnerability to fearfulness and anxiety. Further, this may be traced to relatively few genes and may involve areas of the brain such as the amygdala and its projection sites or the cortical areas involved in modulating amygdalar activity. We conclude, then, that patients with panic disorder very likely inherit a susceptibility to panic that has its basis in an unusually sensitive fear network, with the central nucleus of the amygdala playing a significant role.

ENVIRONMENTAL BASIS FOR PANIC DISORDER

The most likely candidate for the part of panic disorder etiology not likely to be explained by genetics is an environmental insult. In our original neuroanatomical hypothesis, we made a similar claim, but since then the evidence that this is plausible has increased both from animal and human studies.

Am J Psychiatry 157:4, April 2000

Several studies have now suggested that disruptions of early attachment to parents may be associated with the later development of panic disorder. For example, using data from the Epidemiological Catchment Area study, Tweed et al. (80) reported that adults whose mothers died before they were age 10 were almost seven times more likely than those without a history of early maternal death to be diagnosed with agoraphobia with panic attacks. Those adults whose parents separated or divorced before age 10 also had a greater likelihood of being diagnosed with agoraphobia with panic attacks—almost four times the rate of those without a history of early parental separation. Stein et al. (81) found that patients with panic disorder reported more instances of childhood sexual and physical abuse than did healthy comparison subjects. The idea that disrupted emotional attachments with significant caregivers during childhood may be a risk factor for panic disorder is consonant with the clinical observation that patients with panic disorder are unusually sensitive to perceived, threatened, or actual separations. Indeed, patients with panic are less likely to experience a panic attack when surrounded by trusted companions. One study showed that having a companion present reduced the likelihood of a panic attack during CO_2 inhalation (82). This is striking because our attempts to reduce the rate of panic during CO_2 inhalation by cognitive manipulation have not proven successful (83).

The preclinical literature now strongly indicates that early disruptions of the attachment between infants and mothers (in animals fathers rarely play a substantial role in rearing offspring) produce long-lived behavioral and biological changes. For example, Michael Meaney, Paul Plotsky, and others (84–87; Plotsky et al., unpublished 1996 presentation) have shown that in rodents, alterations in mother-offspring interactions produce changes in the infant's subsequent hormonal and physiological responses to stress that endure throughout the lifetime. These altered responses appear to be mediated at least in part by changes in central CRF function. Furthermore, these changes vary across different genetic strains of rodent so that "in relatively hardy animals the early-life manipulations may have less obvious effects" (85).

Andrews, Rosenblum, Coplan, and colleagues (88–90; Coplan et al., unpublished 1997 presentation) have pursued an interesting behavioral paradigm in nonhuman primates. Infant bonnet macaques are exposed to either a low foraging demand condition, in which mothers are given immediate direct access to food, or a variable foraging demand condition, in which, at randomly selected intervals, the mother is forced to search for food, thus interfering with her attention to the infant. Both infant and mother receive adequate nutrition in both conditions. It is of interest that infants exposed to the variable foraging demand condition do not seem particularly distressed while the mother searches for food, but the mothers appear stressed, and some begin to neglect the emotional needs of the infant

over time. The infants raised under the variable foraging demand condition appear normal in most respects, but they exhibit more fearfulness and less social gregariousness throughout their lives when compared to animals raised under low foraging demand conditions (88). As adults, the animals raised under the variable foraging demand condition also exhibit increased CRF levels in CSF (89), exaggerated behavioral response to noradrenergic stimulation, blunted behavioral response to serotonergic agonists (90), and blunted growth hormone response to a clonidine treatment condition (Coplan et al., unpublished 1997 presentation). Thus, even years after a relatively subtle disruption of maternal-infant interaction, animals whose mothers underwent an uncertain variable foraging demand condition are fearful and shy and show evidence of enduring biological disruption.

There is evidence that experiencing traumatic events during childhood and adulthood is associated with the development of panic disorder (91–94). Nevertheless, our model asserts that patients with panic disorder, by virtue of a genetically imposed abnormality in the intrinsic brain fear network, are more susceptible to the effects of trauma, particularly those involving separation and disrupted attachment, than are individuals without panic disorder. That recent traumatic stress may also play a role in stimulating the onset of panic is clearly compatible with this model. This abnormality could take a number of forms, including tonic autonomic hyperactivity or a neurocognitive defect that would prevent the appropriate interpretation of fear network signals and/or the appropriate cortical feedback to limit anxiety and panic responses. Hence, we propose an interaction between life stress and genetic susceptibility as the root cause of panic disorder in adults.

The invocation of adverse life events may help us understand why anxious children may grow up to be depressed, have one or more of a number of different anxiety disorders, or exhibit no psychopathology at all. It is possible that a similar genetic vulnerability is common to several of these conditions and whether, or which, one of them is actually expressed in adult life depends on the kind of environmental influences to which a child is exposed. The same fear network that we have posited to be abnormal in panic disorder may also function abnormally in social phobia, PTSD, generalized anxiety disorder, or depression. The relationships among the different parts of the network may differ, however, among these disorders. Such a theory would explain the commonly observed high levels of comorbidity among anxiety disorders and between anxiety and depression. It would also explain why the same medications are effective for all of these conditions—presumably because all involve some hyperactivity of the amygdala and its projections—but cognitive behavioral therapies differ, perhaps because of different degrees of abnormality in the hippocampus and prefrontal cortex.

253

This hypothesis imposes learned reactions and unconscious emotional states onto genetic vulnerability. It predicts in at least two ways that psychotherapy of several types should be useful in treating panic disorder. First, we will argue that phobic avoidance represents a type of contextual learning analogous to that seen in fear-conditioned animals. This learned phenomenon has its neural basis in the memory systems of the hippocampus. Second, we will argue that sensitivity to separation, fear of impending doom and death, and overreaction to somatic cues are mediated by higher cortical centers. In both cases, behavioral, cognitive, and possibly psychodynamic therapies play a role in modifying these systems.

CONTEXTUAL LEARNING IN PANIC DISORDER

As we noted in our introduction, one of the puzzles in understanding panic disorder is the frequent observation that even when patients report few or no panic attacks, they still exhibit avoidant behavior. This has led to the widespread recommendation that clinical trials examining antipanic treatments should measure the effect of the putative treatment on more domains than just the reduction in frequency or severity of panic attacks (95). A patient who has stopped having attacks but will not leave the house is probably not appropriately considered a responder to treatment.

It is well known that animals who have undergone a fear-conditioning experience also become conditioned to the context in which the experience occurred (96). For example, a rat conditioned to have the same behavioral and autonomic reaction to a tone as was elicited by mild electrical shock will also demonstrate these reactions when simply placed in the cage in which the conditioning experiment took place, even without presentation of the tone. This contextual conditioning is known to require intact hippocampal neurons (97). If after conditioning to the tone has occurred the amygdala is lesioned, the animal will no longer exhibit a fearful response to the tone but will respond fearfully when placed back in the cage. If on the other hand, the hippocampus is lesioned, the animal maintains the response to the tone but no longer responds to placement in the cage.

The analogy with patients with panic disorder appears obvious. Phobic avoidance arises, in part, from an association of panic attacks with the context in which they occurred. Patients who have had, for example, a panic attack in a car while driving over a bridge in rush hour traffic remain fearful of cars, traffic, and bridges. This can generalize to any situation in which egress is not immediately possible and help not automatically available. It is of interest that clinicians observe that some patients treated with medication no longer panic but still maintain some level of phobic avoidance. This may improve over time as deconditioning occurs, but in many patients it becomes a lifelong problem despite adequate pharmacological treat-

ment. Such patients often require and do well when offered behavioral therapy aimed at desensitizing them to feared contexts.

Perhaps the reaction of the patient with panic to minor physical discomfort also represents a kind of contextual fear conditioning. Many patients with panic disorder are unbearably sensitive to relatively trivial somatic sensations such as mild dizziness, increase in heart rate, or slight tingling in a limb. Although it is difficult to make analogies with animal models of fear conditioning, it is plausible that somatic sensation is a kind of context that becomes capable of triggering panic over time.

Cognitive behavioral therapy for panic disorder focuses, in part, on eliminating contextual fear by desensitizing the patient to both physical and somatic cues for panic (98). This may represent an effect on memory mediated by the hippocampus. Imaging studies should be very helpful in determining if this is indeed the case.

ROLE OF HIGHER CORTICAL CENTERS IN PANIC DISORDER

Beyond contextual learning, patients with panic disorder frequently exhibit widespread catastrophic thinking (99) and an increased risk for the development of major depression (100). They can become tied to "phobic partners," sometimes maintaining attachments that are not in their best interest because of an exaggerated fear that separation will cause life-threatening consequences. The toll on the patient and significant others can be substantial, and marital discord among patients with panic disorder is frequently observed (101).

There are many neuroanatomical sites that likely subserve the cognitive and relationship difficulties that ultimately may be the worst part of panic disorder. We have suggested that cortical sites, particularly those that process higher-order sensory information such as the medial prefrontal cortex, are important in modulating anxiety responses. As LeDoux has suggested (102), psychotherapy may work, in part, by strengthening the ability of these cortical projections to assert reason over automatic behavioral and physical responses. Medications, in our opinion, are only partially helpful in reversing the incessantly gloomy predictions of patients with panic disorder or in helping them rearrange relationships that are based on safety and dependency. Depending on the severity of these problems, which often correlates with how long a patient has had panic disorder, psychotherapy becomes invaluable.

We propose then that psychotherapies that are effective for panic disorder, including cognitive behavioral therapy and possibly psychodynamic treatment, operate upstream from the amygdala and exert powerful inhibitory effects on a variety of learned responses. At least in the case of cognitive behavioral therapy, for which most evidence now exists, these

254

treatments are capable of reducing the frequency of panic attacks themselves and also of decreasing phobic avoidance and catastrophic thinking (103). Dynamic therapy may be most helpful for dealing with the effects of early disruptions in parental/child attachments that appear important for some patients in the development of panic disorder, but this requires empirical validation.

CONCLUSIONS

We are left with a model for panic disorder that asserts, exactly as did our original neuroanatomical hypothesis, that medication and psychotherapy can both be effective treatments for panic disorder and that they operate at different levels of the brain. Beyond this, the revised hypothesis presented here is substantially altered from the original. Using information from preclinical science, we now hypothesize that patients with panic disorder inherit an especially sensitive central nervous system fear mechanism that has at its center the central nucleus of the amygdala and includes the hippocampus, thalamus, and hypothalamus, as well as the periaqueductal gray region, locus ceruleus, and other brainstem sites. Medications such as SSRIs may reduce panic attacks by decreasing the activity of the amygdala and interfering with its ability to stimulate projection sites in the hypothalamus and brainstem. Once the physiologic/somatic symptoms of anxiety are lessened, there is a secondary reduction in anticipatory anxiety and phobic avoidance. Cognitive behavioral and other effective psychotherapies most likely operate upstream from the amygdala, reducing phobic avoidance by deconditioning contextual fear learned at the level of the hippocampus and decreasing cognitive misattributions and abnormal emotional reactions by strengthening the ability of the medial prefrontal cortex to inhibit the amygdala.

This model suggests many experimental tests. We have already outlined the promise of neuroimaging studies in detailing the exact neuroanatomical substrates for panic and phobic avoidance and also the sites of action of effective therapies. Genetic research should be targeted at uncovering susceptibility genes, rather than attempting to find genes for panic disorder itself. The continued development of animal models will help elucidate the exact neural mechanisms that translate early rearing stress into permanent disorders of behavior and neurobiology.

Although many aspects of our revised neuroanatomical hypothesis are likely to prove incorrect, it is our profound hope that it will stimulate a renewed interest in basic and clinical research of anxiety disorders such as panic. In our opinion, anxiety disorders are among the most likely psychiatric disturbances to yield to modern scientific inquiry. The results should be better treatment for our patients.

REFERENCES

1. Gorman JM, Liebowitz MR, Fyer AJ, Stein J: A neuroanatomical hypothesis for panic disorder. Am J Psychiatry 1989; 146: 148–161
2. Kent JM, Coplan JD, Gorman JM: Clinical utility of the selective serotonin reuptake inhibitors in the spectrum of anxiety. Biol Psychiatry 1998; 44:812–824
3. Welkowitz LA, Papp LA, Cloitre M, Liebowitz MR, Martin LY, Gorman JM: Cognitive-behavior therapy for panic disorder delivered by psychopharmacologically oriented clinicians. J Nerv Ment Dis 1991; 179:473–477
4. Papp LA, Martinez JM, Klein DF, Coplan JD, Norman RG, Cole R, de Jesus MJ, Ross D, Goetz R, Gorman JM: Respiratory psychophysiology of panic disorder: three respiratory challenges in 98 subjects. Am J Psychiatry 1997; 154:1557–1565
5. Yeragani VK, Pohl R, Berger R, Balon R, Ramesh C, Glitz D, Srinivasan K, Weinberg P: Decreased heart rate variability in panic disorder patients: a study of power-spectral analysis of heart rate. Psychiatry Res 1993; 46:89–103
6. Callahan PM, de la Garza R II, Cunningham KA: Mediation of the discriminative stimulus properties of cocaine by mesocorticolimbic dopamine systems. Pharmacol Biochem Behav 1997; 57:601–607
7. Breiter HC, Gollub RL, Weisskoff RM, Kennedy DN, Makris N, Berke JD, Goodman JM, Kantor HL, Gastfriend DR, Riorden JP, Mathew RT, Rosen BR, Hyman SE: Acute effects of cocaine on human brain activity and emotion. Neuron 1997; 19: 591–611
8. Klein DF: False suffocation alarms, spontaneous panics, and related conditions: an integrative hypothesis. Arch Gen Psychiatry 1993; 50:306–317
9. Pavlov IP: Conditioned Reflexes: An Investigation of the Physiological Activity of the Cerebral Cortex (1927). Edited by Anrep GV. New York, Boyer, 1960
10. LeDoux JE, Cicchetti P, Xagoraris A, Romanski LM: The lateral amygdaloid nucleus: sensory interface of the amygdala in fear conditioning. J Neurosci 1990; 10:1062–1069
11. LeDoux JE, Iwata J, Cicchetti P, Reis DJ: Different projections of the central amygdaloid nucleus mediate autonomic and behavioral correlates of conditioned fear. J Neurosci 1988; 8: 2517–2519
12. Davis M: The role of the amygdala in fear and anxiety. Annu Rev Neurosci 1992; 15:353–375
13. Takeuchi Y, McLean JH, Hopkins DA: Reciprocal connections between the amygdala and parabrachial nuclei: ultrastructural demonstration by degeneration and axonal transport of horseradish peroxidase in the cat. Brain Res 1982; 239:583–588
14. Price JL, Amaral DG: An autoradiographic study of the projections of the central nucleus of the monkey amygdala. J Neurosci 1981; 1:1242–1259
15. Cedarbaum JM, Aghajanian GK: Afferent projections to the rat locus coeruleus as determined by a retrograde tracing technique. J Comp Neurol 1978; 178:1–16
16. Dunn JD, Whitener J: Plasma corticosterone responses to electrical stimulation of the amygdaloid complex: cytoarchitectural specificity. Neuroendocrinology 1986; 42:211–217
17. De Oca BM, DeCola JP, Maren S, Fanselow MS: Distinct regions of the periaqueductal gray are involved in the acquisition and expression of defensive responses. J Neurosci 1998; 18:3426–3432
18. de Olmos J: Amygdaloid nuclear gray complex, in The Human Nervous System. Edited by Paxinos G. San Diego, Academic Press, 1990, pp 583–710
19. Freedman RR, Ianni P, Ettedgui E, Puthezhath N: Ambulatory monitoring of panic disorder. Arch Gen Psychiatry 1985; 42: 244–248
20. Martinez JM, Papp LA, Coplan JD, Anderson DE, Mueller CM, Klein DF, Gorman JM: Ambulatory monitoring of respiration in anxiety. Anxiety 1996; 2:296–302
21. Gorman JM, Papp LA, Coplan JD, Martinez JM, Lennon S, Goetz RR, Ross D, Klein DF: Anxiogenic effects of CO_2 and

255

hyperventilation in patients with panic disorder. Am J Psychiatry 1994; 151:547–553

22. Papp LA, Klein DF, Gorman JM: Carbon dioxide hypersensitivity, hyperventilation. and panic disorder. Am J Psychiatry 1993; 150:1149–1157

23. Coplan JD. Goetz R, Klein DF. Papp LA, Fyer AJ. Liebowitz MR, Davies SO, Gorman JM: Plasma cortisol concentrations preceding lactate-induced panic: psychological. biochemical. and physiological correlates. Arch Gen Psychiatry 1998; 55: 130–136

24. Woods SW, Charney DS, McPherson CA. Gradman AH, Heninger GR: Situational panic attacks: behavioral. physiologic, and biochemical characterization. Arch Gen Psychiatry 1987; 44:365–375

25. Liebowitz MR, Gorman JM, Fyer AJ. Levitt M. Dillon D, Levy G, Appleby IL, Anderson S, Palij M, Davies SO. Klein DF: Lactate provocation of panic attacks, II: biochemical and physiological findings. Arch Gen Psychiatry 1985; 42:709–719

26. Gorman JM, Fyer MR. Goetz R, Askanazi J. Liebowitz MR, Fyer AJ, Kinney J, Klein DF: Ventilatory physiology of patients with panic disorder. Arch Gen Psychiatry 1988; 45:31–39

27. Charney DS, Heninger GR, Breier A: Noradrenergic function in panic anxiety: effects of yohimbine in healthy subjects and patients with agoraphobia and panic disorder. Arch Gen Psychiatry 1984; 41:751–763

28. Targum SD, Marshall LE: Fenfluramine provocation of anxiety in patients with panic disorder. Psychiatry Res 1989; 28:295–306

29. Klein E, Zohar J, Geraci MF, Murphy DL, Uhde TW: Anxiogenic effects of m-CPP in patients with panic disorder: comparison to caffeine's anxiogenic effects. Biol Psychiatry 1991; 30:973–984

30. Pyke RE, Greenberg HS: Norepinephrine challenges in panic patients. J Clin Psychopharmacol 1986; 6:279–285

31. Veltman DJ, van Zijderveld GA, van Dyck R: Epinephrine infusions in panic disorder: a double-blind placebo-controlled study. J Affect Disord 1996; 39:133–140

32. Jensen CF, Peskind ER, Veith RC, Hughes J, Cowley DS, Roy-Byrne P, Raskind MA: Hypertonic saline infusion induces panic in patients with panic disorder. Biol Psychiatry 1991; 30: 628–630

33. Bradwejn J, Koszycki D: The cholecystokinin hypothesis of anxiety and panic disorder. Ann NY Acad Sci 1994: 713:273–282

34. American Psychiatric Association: Practice Guideline for the Treatment of Patients With Panic Disorder. Am J Psychiatry 1998; 155(May suppl)

35. Kreiss DS, Lucki I: Effects of acute and repeated administration of antidepressant drugs on extracellular levels of 5-hydroxytryptamine measured in vivo. J Pharmacol Exp Ther 1995; 274:866–875

36. Boyer W: Serotonin uptake inhibitors are superior to imipramine and alprazolam in alleviating panic attacks: a meta-analysis. Int Clin Psychopharmacol 1995; 10:45–49

37. Hoyer D, Martin G: 5-HT receptor classification and nomenclature: toward a harmonization with the human genome. Neuropharmacology 1997; 36:419–428

38. Blier P, DeMontigny C, Chaput Y: Modifications of the serotonin system by antidepressant treatments: implications for the therapeutic response in major depression. J Clin Psychopharmacol 1987: 7:24S–35S

39. Handley SL: 5-Hydroxytryptamine pathways in anxiety and its treatment. Pharmacol Ther 1995; 66:103–148

40. Tork I, Hornung J-P: Raphe nuclei and the serotonergic system, in The Human Nervous System. Edited by Paxinos G. San Diego. Academic Press, 1990, pp 1001–1022

41. Aston-Jones G, Akaoka H, Charlety P, Chouvet G: Serotonin selectively attenuates glutamate-evoked activation of noradrenergic locus coeruleus neurons. J Neurosci 1991; 11:760–769

42. Coplan JD, Papp LA, Pine DS, Martinez JM, Cooper TB, Rosenblum L. Klein DF, Gorman JM: Clinical improvement

with fluoxetine therapy and noradrenergic function in patients with panic disorder. Arch Gen Psychiatry 1997; 54:643–648

43. Viana MB, Graeff FG, Loschmann PA: Kainate microinjection into the dorsal raphe nucleus induces 5-HT release in the amygdala and periaqueductal gray. Pharmacol Biochem Behav 1997: 58:167–172

44. Deakin JFW, Graeff F: 5-HT and mechanisms of defence. J Psychopharmacol 1991; 5:305–315

45. Brady LS, Gold PW. Herkenham M. Lynn AB, Whitfield HJ Jr: The antidepressants fluoxetine. idazoxan and phenelzine alter corticotropin-releasing hormone and tyrosine hydroxylase mRNA levels in rat brain: therapeutic implications. Brain Res 1992: 572:117–125

46. Elkabir DR, Wyatt ME. Vellucci SV. Herbert J: The effects of separate or combined infusions of corticotrophin-releasing factor and vasopressin either intraventricularly or into the amygdala on aggressive and investigative behaviour in the rat. Regul Pept 1990; 28:199–214

47. Butler PD, Weiss JM, Stout JC, Nemeroff CB: Corticotropin-releasing factor produces fear-enhancing and behavioral activating effects following infusion into the locus coeruleus. J Neurosci 1990; 10:176–183

48. Baram TZ, Mitchell WG, Haden E: Inhibition of pituitary-adrenal secretion by a corticotropin releasing hormone antagonist in humans. Mol Psychiatry 1996; 1:320–324

49. Griebel G, Perrault G, Sanger DJ: Characterization of the behavioral profile of the non-peptide CRF receptor antagonist CP-154,526 in anxiety models in rodents: comparison with diazepam and buspirone. Psychopharmacology (Berl) 1988; 138:55–66

50. Stutzmann GE. LeDoux JE: GABAergic antagonists block the inhibitory effects of serotonin in the lateral amygdala: a mechanism for modulation of sensory inputs related to fear conditioning. J Neurosci 1999; 19:RC8

51. Sokoloff L: Relationships among local functional activity, energy metabolism, and blood flow in the central nervous system. Fed Proc 1981; 40:2311–2316

52. Raichle ME. Grubb RL Jr, Gado MH. Eichling JO, Ter-Pogossian MM: Correlation between regional cerebral blood flow and oxidative metabolism. Arch Neurol 1976; 33:523–526

53. Fox PT, Raichle ME: Cerebral blood flow and oxidative metabolism are focally uncoupled by physiological activation: a positron-emission tomographic study. in Cerebrovascular Diseases. Edited by Raichle ME, Powers WJ. New York, Raven Press, 1987, pp 129–138

54. Stewart RS, Devous MD Sr. Rush AJ. Lane L, Bonte FJ: Cerebral blood flow changes during sodium-lactate-induced panic attacks. Am J Psychiatry 1988: 145:442–449

55. Gorman JM, Goetz R. Uy J, Ross D. Martinez J, Fyer AJ, Liebowitz MR, Klein DF: Hyperventilation occurs during lactate-induced panic. J Anxiety Disorders 1988; 2:193–202

56. Ball S, Shekhar A: Basilar artery response to hyperventilation in panic disorder. Am J Psychiatry 1997; 154:1603–1604

57. Dager SR. Strauss WL. Marro KI. Richards TL. Metzger GD. Artru AA: Proton magnetic resonance spectroscopy investigation of hyperventilation in subjects with panic disorder and comparison subjects. Am J Psychiatry 1995; 152:666–672

58. Goddard AW. Gorman JM, Charney DS: Neurobiology of panic disorder, in Panic Disorder and Its Treatment. Edited by Rosenbaum JF, Pollack MH. New York. Marcel Dekker, 1998, pp 57–92

59. Matthews RJ: Sympathetic control of cerebral circulation: relevance to psychiatry. Biol Psychiatry 1995; 37:283–285

60. Kalaria RN, Stockmeier CA, Harik SI: Brain microvessels are innervated by locus ceruleus noradrenergic neurons. Neurosci Lett 1989; 97:203–208

61. Marovitch S. Iadecola C. Ruggiero DA. Reis DJ: Widespread reductions in cerebral blood flow and metabolism elicited by electrical stimulation of the parabrachial nucleus in the rat. Brain Res 1985; 314:283–296

62. Fredrikson M, Wik G, Fischer H. Andersson J: Affective and attentive neural networks in humans: a PET study of Pavlovian conditioning. Neuroreport 1995: 7:97–101

256

63. Morris J, Frith C, Perret D, Rowland D, Young A, Calder A, Dolan R: A differential neural response in the human amygdala to fearful and happy facial expressions. Nature 1996; 383:812–815

64. Furmark T, Fischer H, Wik G, Larsson M, Fredrikson M: The amygdala and individual differences in human fear conditioning. Neuroreport 1997; 8:3957–3960

65. Hugdahl K, Beraki A, Thompson W, Kosslyn S, Macy R, Baker D, Alpert N, LeDoux JE: Brain mechanisms in human classical conditioning: a PET blood flow study. Neuroreport 1995; 6: 1723–1728

66. LaBar KS, Gatenby JC, Gore JC, LeDoux JE, Phelps EA: Human amygdala activation during conditioned fear acquisition and extinction: a mixed-trial fMRI study. Neuron 1998; 20: 937–945

67. Grodd W, Schneider F, Klose U, Nagele T: [Functional magnetic resonance tomography of psychological functions exemplified by experimentally induced emotions]. Radiologe 1995; 35:283–289 (German)

68. Papp LA, Martinez J, Coplan JD, Gorman JM: Rebreathing tests in panic disorder. Biol Psychiatry 1995; 38:240–245

69. Corfield DR, Fink GR, Ramsay SC, Murphy K, Harty HR, Watson JDG, Adams L, Frackowiak RSJ, Guz A: Activation of limbic structures during C02-stimulated breathing in awake man, in Modeling and Control of Ventilation. Edited by Semple SJG, Adams L, Whipp BJ. New York, Plenum, 1995, pp 331–334

70. Flint J, Corley R, DeFries JC, Fulker DW, Gray JA, Miller S, Collins AC: A simple genetic basis for a complex psychological trait in laboratory mice. Science 1995; 269:1432–1435

71. Wehner JM, Radcliffe RA, Rosmann ST, Christensen SC, Rasmussen DL, Fulker DW, Wiles M: Quantitative trait locus analysis of contextual fear conditioning in mice. Nat Genet 1997; 17:331–334

72. Caldarone B, Saavedra C, Tartaglia K, Wehner JM, Dudek BC, Flaherty L: Quantitative trait loci analysis affecting contextual conditioning in mice. Nat Genet 1997; 17:335–337

73. Flint J: Freeze! Nat Genet 1997; 17:250–251

74. Weissman MM, Wickramaratne P, Adams PB, Lish JD, Horwath E, Charney D, Woods SW, Leeman E, Frosch E: The relationship between panic disorder and major depression: a new family study. Arch Gen Psychiatry 1993; 50:767–780

75. Togersen S: Genetic factors in anxiety disorders. Arch Gen Psychiatry 1983; 40:1085–1089

76. Kendler KS, Neale MC, Kessler RC, Heath AC, Eaves LJ: Panic disorder in women: a population-based twin study. Psychol Med 1993; 23:397–406

77. Skre I, Onstad S, Togersen S, Lygren S, Kringlen E: A twin study of DSM-III-R anxiety disorders. Acta Psychiatr Scand 1993; 88:85–92

78. Kagan J, Reznick JS, Snidman N: The physiology and psychology of behavioral inhibition. Child Dev 1987; 58:1459–1473

79. Pine DS, Cohen P, Gurley D, Brook J, Ma Y: The risk for early-adulthood anxiety and depressive disorders in adolescents with anxiety and depressive disorders. Arch Gen Psychiatry 1998; 55:56–64

80. Tweed JL, Schoenbach VJ, George LK, Blazer DG: The effects of childhood parental death and divorce on six-month history of anxiety disorders. Br J Psychiatry 1989; 154:823–828

81. Stein MB, Walker JR, Anderson G, Hazen AL, Ross CA, Eldridge G, Forde DR: Childhood physical and sexual abuse in patients with anxiety disorders and in a community sample. Am J Psychiatry 1996; 153:275–277

82. Carter MM, Hollon SD, Carson R, Shelton RC: Effects of a safe person on induced distress following a biological challenge in panic disorder with agoraphobia. J Abnorm Psychol 1995; 104:156–163

83. Papp LA, Welkowitz LA, Martinez JM, Klein DF, Browne S, Gorman JM: Instructional set does not alter outcome of respiratory challenges in panic disorder. Biol Psychiatry 1995; 38: 826–830

84. Francis DD, Meaney MJ: Maternal care and the development of stress responses. Curr Opin Neurobiol 1999; 9:128–134

85. Anisman H, Zaharia MD, Meaney MJ, Merali Z: Do early-life events permanently alter behavioral and hormonal responses to stressors? Int J Dev Neurosci 1998; 16:149–164

86. Caldji C, Tannenbaum B, Sharma S, Francis D, Plotsky PM, Meaney JM: Maternal care during infancy regulates the development of neural systems mediating the expression of fearfulness in the rat. Proc Natl Acad Sci USA 1998; 95:5335–5340

87. Liu D, Diorio J, Tannenbaum B, Caldji C, Francis D, Freedman A, Sharma S, Pearson D, Plotsky PM, Meaney JM: Maternal care, hippocampal glucocorticoid receptors, and hypothalamic-pituitary-adrenal responses to stress. Science 1997; 277:1659–1662

88. Andrews MW, Rosenblum LA: The development of affiliative and agonistic social patterns in differentially reared monkeys. Child Dev 1994; 65:1398–1404

89. Coplan JD, Andrews MW, Rosenblum LA, Owens MJ, Gorman JM, Nemeroff CB: Increased cerebrospinal fluid CRF concentration in adult non-human primates previously exposed to adverse experiences as infants. Proc Natl Acad Sci USA 1996; 93:1619–1623

90. Rosenblum LA, Coplan JD, Friedman S, Bassoff TB, Gorman JM: Adverse early experiences affect noradrenergic and serotonergic functioning in adult primates. Biol Psychiatry 1994; 35:221–227

91. Tweed JL, Schoenbach VJ, George LK, Blazer DG: The effects of childhood parental death and divorce on six-month history of anxiety disorders. Br J Psychiatry 1989; 154:823–828

92. Faravelli C, Webb T, Ambonetti A, Fonnesu F, Sessarego A: Prevalence of traumatic early life events in 31 agoraphobic patients with panic attacks. Am J Psychiatry 1985; 142:1493–1494

93. Faravelli C, Pallanti S: Recent life events and panic disorder. Am J Psychiatry 1989; 146:622–626

94. Horesh N, Amir M, Kedem P, Goldberger Y, Kotler M: Life events in childhood, adolescence and adulthood and the relationship to panic disorder. Acta Psychiatr Scand 1997; 96: 373–378

95. Shear MK, Masur JD: Standardized assessment for panic disorder research: a conference report. Arch Gen Psychiatry 1994; 51:346–354

96. Phillips RG, LeDoux JE: Differential contribution of amygdala and hippocampus to cued and contextual fear conditioning. Behav Neurosci 1992; 106:274–285

97. Kim JJ, Fanselow MS: Modality-specific retrograde amnesia of fear. Science 1992; 256:675–677

98. Barlow DH: Cognitive-behavioral therapy for panic disorder: current status. J Clin Psychiatry 1997; 58(suppl 2):32–36

99. Hibbert GA: Ideational components of anxiety: their origin and content. Br J Psychiatry 1984; 144:618–624

100. Klerman GL: Depression and panic anxiety: the effect of depressive comorbidity on response to drug treatment of patients with panic disorder and agoraphobia. J Psychiatr Res 1990; 24(suppl 2):27–41

101. Markowitz JS, Weissman MM, Ouellette R, Lish JD, Klerman GL: Quality of life in panic disorder. Arch Gen Psychiatry 1989; 46:984–992

102. LeDoux JE: The Emotional Brain: The Mysterious Underpinnings of Emotional Life. New York, Simon & Schuster, 1996

103. Otto MW, Whittal ML: Cognitive-behavior therapy and the longitudinal course of panic disorder. Psychiatr Clin North Am 1995; 18:803–820

257

Annu. Rev. Neurosci. 2000. 23:155–184

EMOTION CIRCUITS IN THE BRAIN

Joseph E. LeDoux

Center for Neural Science, New York University, New York, New York 10003; e-mail: ledoux@cns.nyu.edu

Key Words   fear, memory, learning, conditioning, amygdala, limbic system

■ **Abstract**   The field of neuroscience has, after a long period of looking the other way, again embraced emotion as an important research area. Much of the progress has come from studies of fear, and especially fear conditioning. This work has pinpointed the amygdala as an important component of the system involved in the acquisition, storage, and expression of fear memory and has elucidated in detail how stimuli enter, travel through, and exit the amygdala. Some progress has also been made in understanding the cellular and molecular mechanisms that underlie fear conditioning, and recent studies have also shown that the findings from experimental animals apply to the human brain. It is important to remember why this work on emotion succeeded where past efforts failed. It focused on a psychologically well-defined aspect of emotion, avoided vague and poorly defined concepts such as "affect," "hedonic tone," or "emotional feelings," and used a simple and straightforward experimental approach. With so much research being done in this area today, it is important that the mistakes of the past not be made again. It is also time to expand from this foundation into broader aspects of mind and behavior

INTRODUCTION

After decades of neglect, neuroscience has again embraced emotion as a research topic. This new wave of interest raises the question of why emotion was overlooked for so long. It is instructive to consider this question before examining what has been learned about emotional circuits, as some of the factors that led brain researchers to turn away from this topic may again hamper progress unless they can be grappled with.

Why Did Interest in Emotion Wane?

During the first half of the twentieth century, brain researchers were immensely interested in the brain mechanisms of emotional behavior. Some of the early pioneers in neuroscience worked in this area, including Sherrington, Cannon, Papez, and Hebb. Responses that occur when we defend against danger, interact with sexual partners, fight with an enemy, or have a tasty bite to eat promote the survival of individuals and their species. Emotional responses are thus inherently

0147–006X/00/0301–0155$12.00   **155** interesting and important. So what happened? Why did research on the brain mechanisms of emotion come to a halt after midcentury?

For one thing, emotion research was a victim of the cognitive revolution. The emergence of cognitive science shifted the interest of those concerned with the relation between psychological functions and neural mechanisms toward processes (perception and memory, for example) that were readily thought of in terms of computer-like operations. From the start, cognitive scientists claimed that their field was not about emotion and other such topics (see Neisser 1967, Gardner 1987). The cognitive approach came to be the dominant approach in psychology and brain science, and research interest in emotion dwindled.

Another factor that hindered work on emotions in neuroscience was that the problem of how the brain makes emotions seemed to have been solved in the early 1950s by the limbic system concept (MacLean 1949, 1952). This appealing and convincing theory was the culmination of research on the brain mechanisms of emotion by many researchers, extending back to the late nineteenth century (see LeDoux 1987, 1991). Studies of how the brain mediates cognitive processes seemingly had a long way to go to catch up with the deep understanding that had been achieved about emotions, and researchers flocked to the new and exciting topic of cognition and the brain to begin filling the gap.

Cognitive questions also seemed more tractable than emotional ones, due in part to the dark cloud of subjectivity that hung over the topic of emotion. Although subjective experience and its relation to neural mechanisms is a potential difficulty for any area of psychology, cognitive scientists figured out how to study mental processes without having to solve the mind-body problem. They showed, for example, that it is possible to study how the brain processes (computes and represents) external stimuli without first resolving how the conscious perceptual experiences come about. In fact, it is widely recognized that most cognitive processes occur unconsciously, with only the end products reaching awareness, and then only sometimes (see Kihlstrom 1987). Emotion researchers, though, did not make this conceptual leap. They remained focused on subjective emotional experience. In spite of the fact that most research on emotions and the brain was, and still is, conducted with experimental animals, creatures in which subjective states are difficult if not impossible to prove, theoretical discussions of emotions and the brain typically reverted back to the age-old question of feelings. This approach puts the mind-body problem right smack in the middle of the path of progress.

The main lesson to be learned from this brief excursion into history is that emotion researchers need to figure out how to escape from the shackles of subjectivity if emotion research is to thrive. It is ironic that cognitive science, which led to the neglect of emotion research, may also be able to help in its resurrection by providing a strategy that allows the study of emotion independent of subjective emotional experiences. It is possible, for example, to ask how the brain processes emotional information (i.e. detects and responds to danger) without necessarily first solving the question of where conscious feelings come from. Contrary to popular belief, conscious feelings are not required to produce emotional responses, which, like cognitive processes, involve unconscious processing mechanisms (see Öhman 1992, LeDoux 1996). If we want to understand feelings, it is likely going to be necessary to figure out how the more basic systems work. Failure to come to terms theoretically with the importance of processing systems that operate essentially unconsciously has been a major impediment to progress in understanding the neural basis of emotion. To overcome this, brain researchers need to be more savvy about the nature of emotions, rather than simply relying on common sense beliefs about emotions as subjective feeling states.

Research on emotion can also help cognitive science. A pure cognitive approach, one that omits consideration of emotions, motivations, and the like, paints an artificial, highly unrealistic view of real minds. Minds are not either cognitive or emotional, they are both, and more. Inclusion of work on emotion within the cognitive framework can help rescue this field from its sterile approach to the mind as an information-processing device that lacks goals, strivings, desires, fears, and hopes.

Once a processing approach to emotion is taken, emotion and cognition can be studied similarly: as unconscious processes that can, but do not necessarily, lead to conscious experiences. This would open the door for the integration of emotion and cognition, and such integration should be a major goal for the immediate future.

Should We Integrate the Cognitive Brain with the Limbic System?

The rise of cognitive science led to important advances in understanding the brain mechanisms of perception, attention, memory, and other cognitive processes. One might be tempted to say that the way to foster the synthesis of cognition and emotion into a new science of mind would be to put all this new information about the cognitive brain together with the definitive view of the emotional brain provided long ago by the limbic system concept. However, this would be a mistake. In spite of the fact that the limbic system concept remains the predominant view about how the brain makes emotions, it is a flawed and inadequate theory of the emotional brain.

The limbic system concept was put forth in the context of an evolutionary explanation of mind and behavior (MacLean 1949, 1952, 1970; Isaacson 1982). It built upon the view, promoted by comparative anatomists earlier in the century, that the neocortex is a mammalian specialization—other vertebrates have primordial cortex but only mammals were believed to have neocortex. And because thinking, reasoning, memory, and problem solving are especially well developed in mammals, particularly in humans and other primates that have relatively more neocortical tissue, these cognitive processes must be mediated by the neocortex and not by the old cortex or other brain areas. In contrast, the old cortex and related subcortical ganglia form the limbic system, which was said to mediate the evolutionarily older aspects of mental life and behavior, our emotions. In this way, cognition came to be thought of as the business of the neocortex and emotions of the limbic system.

The limbic system theory began to run into trouble almost immediately when it was discovered, in the mid-1950s, that damage to the hippocampus, the centerpiece of the limbic system, led to severe deficits in a distinctly cognitive function, long-term memory (Scoville & Milner 1957). This was incompatible with the original idea that the primitive architecture of the limbic system, and especially of the hippocampus, was poorly suited to participate in cognitive functions (MacLean 1949, 1952). Subsequently, in the late 1960s, it was discovered that the equivalent of mammalian neocortex is present, though rudimentary, in non-mammallian vertebrates (see Nauta & Karten 1970). As a result, the old/new cortex distinction broke down, challenging the evolutionary basis of the assignment of emotion to the limbic system and cognition to the neocortex (Swanson 1983).

The limbic system itself has been a moving target. Within a few years after inception, it expanded from the original notion of "old cortex" and related subcortical forebrain nuclei to include some areas of the midbrain (Nauta 1979), and even some regions of neocortex (Kaada 1960). Several attempts have been made to salvage the limbic system by defining it more precisely (see Isaacson 1982, Swanson 1983, Livingston & Escobar 1971). Nevertheless, after half a century of debate and discussion, there are still no agreed upon criteria that can be used to decide which areas of the brain belong to the limbic system. Some have suggested that the concept be abandoned (Brodal 1982; LeDoux 1987, 1991; Kotter & Meyer 1992).

In spite of these difficulties, the limbic system continues to survive, both as an anatomical concept and as an explanation of emotions, in textbooks, research articles, and scientific lectures. This is in part attributable to the fact that both the anatomical concept and the emotional function it was supposed to mediate were defined so vaguely as to be irrefutable. For example, in most discussions of how the limbic system mediates emotion, the meaning of the term emotion is presumed to be something akin to the common English language use of the term (because no other definition is given). However, the common English use of the term emotion is at best a poor theoretical notion, for emotion is a rich and complex theoretical concept with many subtle aspects, some of which are nonintuitive and thus inconsistent with the common use of the term (for discussions see Lewis & Haviland 1992, Ekman & Davidson 1994, LeDoux 1996). On the neural side, the criteria for inclusion of brain areas in the limbic system remain undefined, and evidence that any limbic area, however defined, contributes to any aspect of any emotion has tended to validate the whole concept. Mountains of data on the role of limbic areas in emotion exist, but there is still little understanding of how our emotions might be the product of the limbic system.

Particularly troubling is the fact that one cannot predict, on the basis of the original limbic theory of emotion or any of its descendants, how specific aspects of emotion work in the brain. The explanations are all post hoc. Nowhere is this more apparent than in recent work using functional imaging to study emotions in the human brain. Whenever a so-called emotional task is used, and a limbic area is activated, the activation is explained by reference to the fact that limbic areas mediate emotion. And when a limbic area is activated in a cognitive task, it is often assumed that there must have been some emotional undertone to the task. We are, in other words, at a point where the limbic theory has become an off-the-shelf explanation of how the brain works. However, this explanation is grounded in tradition rather than data. Deference to the concept is inhibiting creative thought about how mental life is mediated by the brain.

Although the limbic system theory is inadequate as an explanation of the specific brain circuits of emotion, MacLean's (1949, 1952, 1970) original ideas are very interesting in the context of a general evolutionary explanation of emotion and the brain. In particular, the notion that emotions involve relatively primitive circuits that are conserved throughout mammalian evolution seems right on target. Furthermore, the idea that cognitive processes might involve other circuits, and might function relatively independent of emotional circuits, at least in some circumstances, also seems correct. These functional ideas are worth holding on to, even if we abandon the limbic system as a structural theory of the emotional brain.

ESCAPING THE LIMBIC SYSTEM LEGACY: FEAR CIRCUITS

One of the main exceptions to the bleak state of affairs regarding the brain mechanisms of emotion is the body of research concerned with neural system underlying fear, especially in the context of the behavioral paradigm called fear conditioning. It has, in fact, been research on fear conditioning, and the progress that has been made on this topic, that has been largely responsible for the renaissance of interest of emotion within neuroscience. In this work, the fear system has been treated as a set of processing circuits that detect and respond to danger, rather than as a mechanism through which subjective states of fear are experienced. Through this approach, fear is operationalized, or made experimentally tractable. Some limbic areas turn out to be involved in the fear system, but the exact brain areas and the nature of their involvement would never have been predicted by the limbic system theory.

Before describing research on fear, several other approaches to the study of emotion and the brain that are not discussed further should be mentioned. One involves stimulus-reward association learning (Aggleton & Mishkin 1986, Gaffan 1992, Everitt & Robbins 1992, Ono & Nishijo 1992, Rolls 1999, Gallagher & Holland 1994, Holland & Gallagher 1999). Another involves the role of septo-hippocampal circuits in anxiety (Gray 1982), and still another involves distinct hypothalamic and brainstem circuits for several different emotions (Panksepp 1998, Siegel & Edinger 1981, Siegel et al 1999).

What is Fear Conditioning

Since Pavlov (1927), it has been known that an initially neutral stimulus [a conditioned stimulus (CS)] can acquire affective properties on repeated temporal pairings with a biologically significant event [the unconditioned stimulus (US)]. As the CS-US relation is learned, innate physiological and behavioral responses come under the control of the CS (Figure 1). For example, if a rat is given a tone CS followed by an electric shock US, after a few tone-shock pairings (one is often sufficient), defensive responses (responses that typically occur in the presence of danger) will be elicited by the tone. Examples of species-typical defensive responses that are brought under the control of the CS include defensive behaviors (such as freezing) and autonomic (e.g. heart rate, blood pressure) and endocrine (hormone release) responses, as well as alterations in pain sensitivity (analgesia) and reflex expression (fear-potentiated startle and eyeblink responses). This form of conditioning works throughout the phyla, having been observed in flies, worms, snails, fish, pigeons, rabbits, rats, cats, dogs, monkeys, and humans.

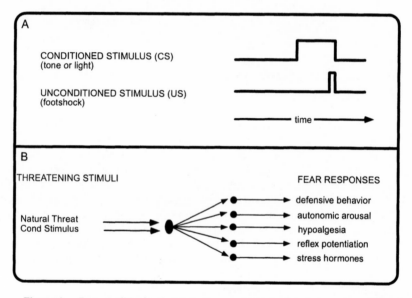

Figure 1   Fear conditioning involves the presentation of a noxious unconditioned stimulus, typically footshock, at the end of the occurrence of a relatively neutral conditioned stimulus (CS), such as a light or tone (*top*). After conditioning, the CS elicits a wide range of behavioral and physiological responses that characteristically occur when an animal encounters a threatening or fear-arousing stimulus (*bottom*). Thus, a rat that has been fear conditioned will express the same responses to a CS as to a natural threat (i.e. a cat).

Neuroanatomy of Fear Conditioning

Research from several laboratories combined in the 1980s to paint a relatively simple and remarkably clear picture of the neuroanatomy of conditioned fear (see Kapp et al 1992, LeDoux 1992, Davis 1992, Fanselow 1994). In short, conditioned fear is mediated by the transmission of information about the CS and US to the amygdala, and the control of fear reactions by way of output projections from the amygdala to the behavioral, autonomic, and endocrine response control systems located in the brainstem. Below, the input and output pathways, as well as the connections within the amygdala that link inputs and outputs, are described. The focus is on findings from rodents and other small mammals, as most of the work on fear conditioning has involved these species (for the contribution of the primate amygdala to fear and other emotions see Pribram et al 1979, Pribram & Melges 1969, Aggleton & Mishkin 1986, Ono & Nishijo 1992, Gaffan 1992, Rolls 1992, 1999).

Amygdala Terminology and Connections   The amygdala consists of approximately 12 different regions, each of which can be further divided into several subregions (Figure 2). Although a number of different schemes have been used to label amygdala areas (see Krettek & Price 1978, de Olmos et al 1985, Amaral et al 1992), the scheme adopted by Amaral et al (1992) for the primate brain and applied to the rat brain by Pitkänen et al (1997) is followed here. The areas of most relevance to fear conditioning are the lateral (LA), basal (B), accessory basal (AB), and central (CE) nuclei and the connections between these (Figure 2). In other classification schemes, B is known as the basolateral nucleus and AB as the basomedial nucleus. The term basolateral complex is sometimes used to refer to LA and B (and sometimes AB) together. Studies in several species, including rats, cats, and primates, are in close agreement about the connections of LA, B, AB, and CE (see Pitkänen et al 1997, Paré et al 1995, Amaral et al 1992, Cassell et al 1999). In brief, LA projects to B, AB, and CE, and both B and AB also project to CE. However, it is important to recognize that the connections of these areas are organzied at the level of subnuclei within each region rather than at the level of the nuclei themselves (see Pitkänen et al 1997). For simplicity, though, for the most part we focus below on nuclei rather than subnuclei.

CS Pathways   The pathways through which CS inputs reach the amygdala have been studied extensively in recent years. Much of the work has involved the auditory modality, which is focused on here.

Auditory and other sensory inputs to the amygdala terminate mainly in LA (see LeDoux et al 1990b, Romanski & LeDoux 1993, Mascagni et al 1993, Amaral et al 1992, McDonald 1998), and damage to LA interferes with fear conditioning to an acoustic CS (LeDoux et al 1990a, Campeau & Davis 1995).

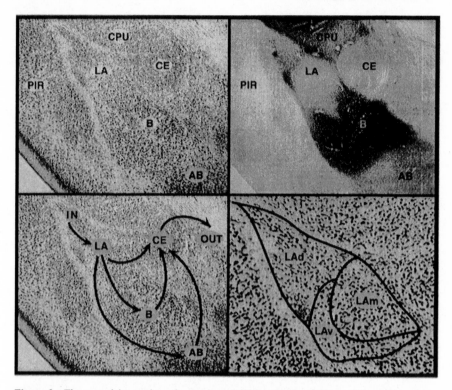

Figure 2 The amygdala consists of a number of different regions. Those of most relevance to the pathways of fear conditioning are the lateral (LA), basal (B), accessory basal (AB), and central (CE) nuclei. The piriform cortex (PIR) lies lateral to the amygdala, and the caudate-putamen (CPU) is just dorsal to it. Comparison of the Nissl-stained section (*upper left*) and an adjacent section stained for acetylcholinesterase (*upper right*) helps identify the different nuclei. The major pathways connecting LA, B, AB, and CE are shown (*lower left panel*). (*Lower right*) A blowup of the LA, emphasizing the fact that each nucleus can be divided into subnuclei. Although anatomical studies have shown that the pathways are organized at the level of the subnuclei, rather than the nuclei (see Pitkänen et al 1997), the nuclear connections (*lower left panel*) provide a sufficiently detailed approximation of the connections for the purposes of considering how the fear conditioning system is, in general, organized.

Auditory inputs to LA come from both the auditory thalamus and the auditory cortex (see LeDoux et al 1990b, Romanski & LeDoux 1993, Mascagni et al 1993), and fear conditioning to a simple auditory CS can be mediated by either of these pathways (Romanski & LeDoux 1992) (Figure 3). It appears that the projection to LA from the auditory cortex is involved with a more complex auditory stimulus pattern (Jarrell et al 1987), but the exact conditions that require the cortex are poorly understood (Armony et al 1997). Although some lesion studies have ques-

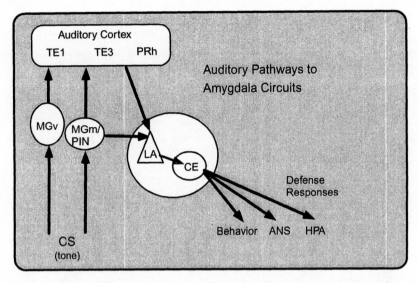

Figure 3   The neural pathways involved in fear conditioning are well characterized. When the CS is an acoustic stimulus, the pathways involve transmission to the lateral nucleus of the lateral amygdala (LA) from auditory processing areas in the thalamus [medial division of the medial geniculate body (MGm/PIN)] and cortex [auditory association cortex (TE3)]. LA, in turn, projects to the central amygdala (CE), which controls the expression of fear responses by way of projections to brainstem areas. ANS, Autonomic nervous system; CS, conditioned stimulus; HPA, hypothalamic-pituitary axis; MGv, ventral division of the medial geniculate body; PRh, perirhinal cortex; TE1, primary auditory cortex.

tioned the ability of the thalamic pathway to mediate conditioning (Campeau & Davis 1995, Shi & Davis 1998), single-unit recordings show that the cortical pathway learns more slowly over trials than does the thalamic pathway (Quirk et al 1995, 1997), thus indicating that plasticity in the amygdala occurs initially through the thalamic pathway. Recent functional magnetic resonance imaging studies in humans have found that the human amygdala shows activity changes during conditioning that correlate with activity in the thalamus but not the cortex (Morris et al 1999), further emphasizing the importance of the direct thalamo-amygdala pathway.

In addition to expressing fear responses to the CS, rats also exhibit these when returned to the chamber in which the tone and shock were paired, or a chamber in which shocks occur alone. This is called contextual fear conditioning and requires both the amygdala and the hippocampus (see Blanchard et al 1970, Phillips & LeDoux 1992, Maren et al 1997, Kim & Fanselow 1992, Frankland et al 1998). Areas of the ventral hippocampus (CA1 and subiculum) project to the B and AB nuclei of the amygdala (Canteras & Swanson 1992), and damage to these areas interferes with contextual conditioning (Maren & Fanselow 1995, Majidi-shad et al 1996). Hippocampal projection to B and AB thus seem to be involved in contextual conditioning (for a comparison of the amygdala pathways involved in conditioning to a tone CS and to a context, see Figure 4).

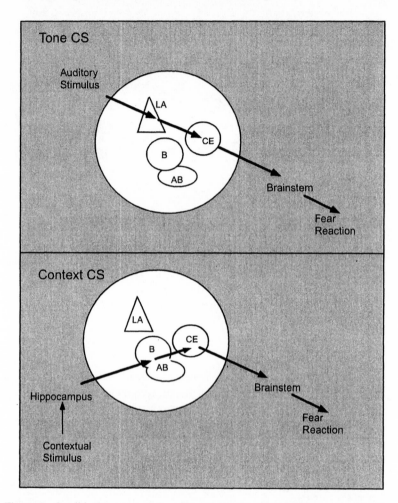

Figure 4   Conditioning to a tone [conditioned stimulus (CS)] involves projections from the auditory system to the lateral nucleus of the amygdala (LA) and from LA to the central nucleus of the amygdala (CE). In contrast, conditioning to the apparatus and other contextual cues present when the CS and unconditioned stimulus are paired involves the representation of the context by the hippocampus and the communication between the hippocampus and the basal (B) and accessory basal (B) nuclei of the amygdala, which in turn project to CE. As for tone conditioning, CE controls the expression of the responses.

US Pathways   For conditioning to occur, pathways transmitting the CS and US have to converge in the brain. It is widely believed that the amygdala is a site of plasticity during conditioning, and thus of CS-US convergence. Although the US pathways have received less attention than CS pathways, some progress has nevertheless been made.

Given that LA is the site of termination within the amygdala of pathways carrying acoustic CS inputs, it is important to ask whether US inputs might also reach this area and potentially lead to plasticity in this region. Thalamic areas that receive afferents from the spino-thalamic tract (LeDoux et al 1987) project to LA (LeDoux et al 1990a) (Figure 3). Furthermore, cells in LA are responsive to nociceptive stimulation, and some of the same cells respond to auditory inputs as well (Romanski et al 1993). Thus, the substrate for conditioning (convergence of CS and US information) exists in LA, and as shown below, conditioning induces plasticity in CS-elicited responses in this area.

Cortical areas that process somatosensory stimuli, including nociceptive stimuli, project to LA and some other amygdala nuclei (see Turner & Zimmer 1984, McDonald 1998). Recent behavioral studies show that conditioning can be mediated by US inputs to the amygdala from either thalamic or cortical areas (Shi & Davis 1998), a finding that parallels the conclusions above concerning CS inputs.

The accessory basal amygdala (AB) receives inputs from the posterior thalamus (PO) (LeDoux et al 1990a), which is a terminal region of the spinothalamic tract (LeDoux et al 1987). Although AB does not receive CS inputs from auditory systems, it does receive inputs from the hippocampus (Canteras & Swanson 1992). The hippocampus, as described above, is necessary for forming a representation of the context, and these contextual representations, transmitted from the hippocampus to AB, may be modified by the US inputs to the AB.

CE receives nociceptive inputs from the parabrachial area (Bernard & Besson 1990) and directly from the spinal cord (Burstein & Potrebic 1993). Although the CE does not receive inputs from sensory areas processing acoustic CSs, it is a direct recipient of inputs from LA, and from B and AB. US inputs to CE could be involved in higher-order integration. For example, representations created by CS-US convergence in LA or context-US convergence in AB, after transfer to CE, might converge with and be further modified by nociceptive inputs to CE.

Output Pathways   CE projects to brainstem areas that control the expression of fear responses (see LeDoux et al 1988, Kapp et al 1992, Davis 1992). It is thus not surprising that damage to CE interferes with the expression of conditioned fear responses (Kapp et al 1979, Hitchcock & Davis 1986, Iwata et al 1986, van der Kar et al 1991, Gentile et al 1986). In contrast, damage to areas to which CE projects selectively interrupts the expression of individual responses. For example, damage to the lateral hypothalamus affects blood pressure but not freezing responses, and damage to the peraqueductal gray interferes with freezing but not blood pressure responses (LeDoux et al 1988). Similarly, damage to the bed nucleus of the stria terminalis has no effect on either blood pressure or freezing responses (LeDoux et al 1988), but it disrupts the conditioned release of pituitary-adrenal stress hormones (van der Kar et al 1991). Because CE receives inputs from LA, B, and AB (Pitkänen et al 1997), it is in a position to mediate the expression of conditioned fear responses elicited by both acoustic and contextual CSs (Figure 4).

Intraamygdala Pathways   From the findings described above, it would appear that information about a simple CS (such as a tone paired with shock) is directed toward CE (where response execution is initiated) by way of pathways that origi-nate in LA. Although LA projects to CE directly, and by way of B and AB, the direct projection from LA to CE seems to be sufficient because lesions of B and AB have no effect on simple fear conditioning to a tone (Majidishad et al 1996). An alternative was recently proposed by Killcross et al (1997). They argued that a direct projection to CE that bypasses LA can mediate conditioning. However, fibers from auditory areas terminate mainly in LA (see above). Moreover, auditory response latencies in LA are shorter than in CE (both before and after condition-ing) (see next section below), which suggests that CE depends on LA for its inputs. These facts aside, though, it is important to point out that the task used to rule out LA as a way station to CE involved hundreds of training trials, whereas the tasks used to implicate LA have involved tens of trials (see Nader & LeDoux 1997). It is possible that the additional training trials used in the Killcross study allowed the brain to learn in a way that is not normally used when fewer trials are given. At most, a direct pathway to CE would be an alternative rather than the main route of transmission through the amygdala.

Physiological Plasticity in the Amygdala Related to Fear Conditioning

With the basic elements of the circuitry understood from lesion studies, research-ers have turned to questions about the nature of the plasticity within the amygdala that might underlie fear learning. Fear plasticity in the amygdala has been studied in three closely intertwined ways. First, single-unit recordings have been made in areas of the amygdala implicated in fear conditioning by lesion studies. Second, long-term potentiation (LTP), an experimentally advantageous but artificial form of plasticity, has been studied in these same areas. Third, drugs that block LTP have been infused into amygdala areas where LTP is believed to occur, and effects on the acquisition of conditioned fear behavior assessed. These approaches are summarized below. In addition, evidence regarding the molecular basis of fear learning is described.

Unit Recordings   Pathway tracing and lesion studies suggest that LA is the sensory gateway to the amygdala, and thus the first possible site in the amygdala where cells processing the CS might be modified by association with the US in fear conditioning. As already noted, some cells in LA are responsive to both CS and US inputs. Further, CS-elicited responses in LA cells are modified after pairing with the US (Quirk et al 1995, 1997) (Figure 5). Conditioned plasticity also occurs in the auditory cortex (Weinberger 1995, 1998; Quirk et al 1997). However, the response latencies in LA within trials (<20 ms) and the rate of acquisition (one to three trials) are best explained in terms of direct auditory thalamo-amygdala transmission, rather than cortico-amygdala transmission, because conditioned responses in the auditory cortex occur later both within and across trials (Quirk et al 1997). Plasticity in the auditory thalamus (Weinberger 1995, 1998) could contribute to LA plasticity. Plasticity has also been observed in B (Maren et al 1991, Uwano et al 1995) and CE (Pascoe & Kapp 1985) during aversive conditioning, but the acoustic responses latencies both before and after conditioning are longer than in LA. LA thus seems to be both the initial point of sensory processing and the initial site of plasticity in the amygdala.

Long-Term Potentiation   LTP is a physiological procedure pioneered in studies of the hippocampus (Bliss & Lomo 1973) and is believed to engage the cellular mechanisms similar to those that underlie natural learning (see Lynch 1986, Bliss & Collingridge 1993). The most extensively studied form of LTP occurs in the CA1 region of the hippocampus and involves the interaction between presynaptic glutamate and two classes of postsynaptic receptors (Nicoll & Malenka 1995). First, glutamate binds to AMPA receptors and depolarizes the postsynaptic cell. The depolarization allows glutamate to bind to the N-methyl-D-aspartate (NMDA) class of receptors. Calcium then flows into the cell through the NMDA channel and triggers a host of intracellular events that ultimately result in gene induction and synthesis of new proteins (Dudai 1989, Huang et al 1996, Kandel 1997). These then help stabilize the changes over long periods of time.

There have been a number of studies of LTP in the amygdala, mostly involving in vitro brain slices and pathways carrying information from the cortex to LA and B (Chapman et al 1990, Chapman & Bellevance 1992, Gean et al 1993, Huang & Kandel 1998). These studies have led to mixed results regarding the possible role of NMDA receptors in cortico-amygdala LTP, with some studies finding effects (Huang & Kandel 1998) and some not (Chapman & Bellevance 1992). Recent in vitro studies indicate that LTP in the thalamo-amygdala pathway requires postsynaptic calcium but the calcium does not enter through NMDA receptors (Weisskopf et al 1999). Instead, calcium entry appears through L-type voltage-gated calcium channels. These channels have also been implicated in a form of LTP that occurs in the hippocampus (Cavus & Teyler 1996). It has also been shown that prior fear conditioning leads to an enhancement in synaptic responses recorded subsequently in vitro from amygdala slices (McKernan & Schinnick-Gallagher 1997). The receptor mechansims underlying this form of plasticity have not been elucidated.

LTP has also been studied in vivo in the thalamo-amygdala pathway using recordings of extracellular field potentials (Clugnet & LeDoux 1990, Rogan & LeDoux 1995, Rogan et al 1997). These studies show that LTP occurs in fear

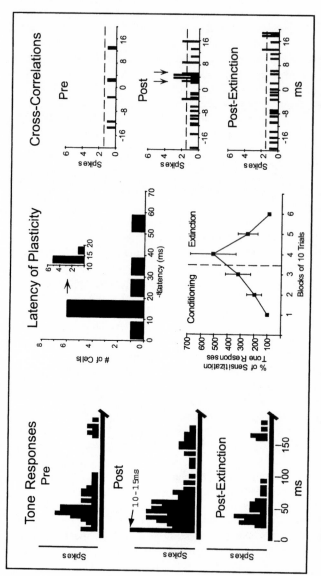

Figure 5 During fear conditioning, cells in the lateral amygdala (LA) of rats show plasticity (increased firing rates) during exposure to a conditioned stimulus tone. (*Left*) Some cells are responsive to tones prior to conditioning (Pre), but their rate of firing increases after conditioning, esepcially the earliest latency response (10–15 ms after tone onset). This early plasticity goes away after extinction. From simultaneously recorded cells, it can be seen that conditioning also leads to an increase in the synchrony of firing, such that cells that were not correlated before conditioning become so afterward (*right panel*). In some cases (not shown), the synchrony remained even after extinction, which suggests that long-term memory may be in part encoded by connections between cells rather than just in the rate of firing. Based on Quirk et al (1995).

processing pathways, that the processing of natural stimuli similar to those used as a CS in conditioning studies is facilitated following LTP induction, and that fear conditioning and LTP induction produce similar changes in the processing of CS-like stimuli (Figure 6). Although exploration of mechanisms are difficult in these in vivo studies, they nevertheless provide some of the strongest evidence to date in any brain system of a relation between natural learning and LTP (Barnes 1995, Eichenbaum 1995, Stevens 1998). LTP has been found in vivo in the hippocampal-amygdala pathway, which is believed to be involved in context conditioning (Maren & Fanselow 1995).

Infusion of Drugs that Block LTP   The fact that blockade of NMDA receptors with the drug D,L-2-amino-5-phosphonovaerate (APV) prevents LTP from occurring in the CA1 region of the hippocampus inspired researchers to attempt to prevent fear conditioning by infusion of APV into the amygdala. Initial studies were promising (Miserendino et al 1990). Infusion of APV prior to learning blocked fear conditioning, but infusion proior to testing had no effect. NMDA receptors thus seemed to be involved in the plasticity underlying learning and not in the transmission of signals through the amygdala. However, subsequently both in vivo (Li et al 1995, 1996; Maren & Fanselow 1996) and in vitro (Weisskopf & LeDoux 1999) studies have suggested that NMDA receptors make significant contributions to synaptic transmission in pathways that provide inputs to the amygdala. Furthermore, several studies have found that blockade of NMDA receptors affects both the acquisition and the expression of fear learning (Maren et al 1996, Lee & Kim 1998), which is more consistent with the transmission rather than the plasticity hypothesis, but others have confirmed that acquisition could be affected independently from expression (Gewirtz & Davis 1997).

The contribution of NMDA receptors to fear conditioning and its underlying plasticity, as opposed to synaptic transmission in amygdala circuits, remains unresolved. Given the relatively weak contribution of NMDA receptors to transmission in the cortical input, perhaps the disruption of fear learning is explained by a combination of different effects on the two pathways: blockade of transmission and plasticity in the thalamic pathway, and blockade of plasticity in the cortical pathway. It is also possible that behaviorally significant plasticity occurs downstream from LA input synapses in the amygdala, and that the effects of APV infusions is on this plasticity rather than on the plasticity at input synapses. Additional work is needed.

Intracellular Signaling Mechanisms   Some progress has been made in elucidating intracellular signals that underlie long-term memory. These mechanisms are best worked out in invertebrates, but many of the details also seem to apply to hippocampal LTP and spatial learning (Kandel 1997, Huang et al 1996). The general view is that the molecular cascade starts with the influx of calcium during action potentials. The rise in calcium then triggers several kinases and transcription factors, including calmodium-activiated kinase II, mitogen-activated protein

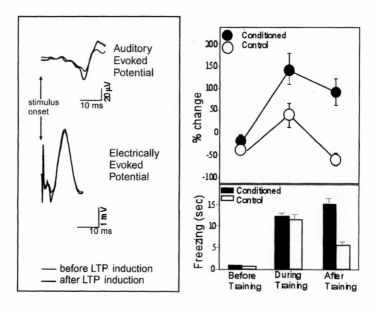

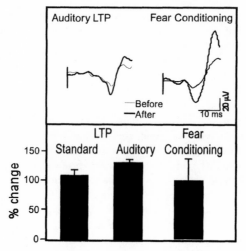

Figure 6   Following high-frequency electrical stimulation of the thalamo-amygdala pathway, low-frequency electrical stimulation of the same pathway or external auditory stimulation elicits a larger evoked potential with a sharper slope than before (*upper left*). This pathway thus shows long-term potentiation (LTP), which can be measured by electrical stimulation or natural stimulation of the inputs to the amygdala. Similar changes in auditory-evoked potentials are elicited following fear conditioning (*bottom*). The enhancement of the evoked response by fear conditioning is further illustrated (*upper right panel*).
(*Caption continues at bottom of next page.*)

(MAP) kinase, cAMP-dependent kinase, protein kinase C, and cAMP response element binding protein (CREB). These act, possibly in concert, to induce genes and initiate synthesis of new proteins. Many of these same intracellular signals have been implicated in fear conditioning through studies of genetically altered mice (Bourtchouladze et al 1994, Mayford et al 1996, Abel et al 1997). However, recent studies have also turned to the use of specific blockers of various signaling pathways in the brain (Bourtchouladze et al 1998, Atkins et al 1998, Josselyn et al 1998, Schafe et al 1999). For example, Schafe et al (1999) recently found that interference with MAP kinase, protein kinase A, and protein synthesis disrupted long-term (but not short-term) memory of both tone and contextual fear conditioning (Figure 7).

But Is the Amygdala Necessary?

In spite of a wealth of data implicating the amygdala in fear conditioning, some authors have recently suggested that the amygdala is not a site of plasticity or storage during fear conditioning (e.g. Cahill & McGaugh 1998, Vazdarjanova & McGaugh 1998). They argue instead that the amygdala modulates memories that are formed elsewhere. It is clear that multiple memory systems exist in the brain (see Squire et al 1993, Eichenbaum 1994, McDonald & White 1993), and that the amygdala does indeed modulate memories formed in other systems, such as declarative or explicit memories formed through hippocampal circuits or habit memories formed through striatal circuits (Packard et al 1994). However, evidence for a role of the amygdala in modulation should not be confused with evidence against a role in plasticity (Fanselow & LeDoux 1999). That the amygdala is indeed important for Pavlovian fear conditioning is suggested by studies showing that inactivation of the amygdala during learning prevents learning from taking place (e.g. Muller et al 1997, Helmstetter & Bellgowan 1994). Furthermore, if the inactivation occurs immediately after training, then there is no effect on subsequent memory, showing that the effects of pretraining treatment is on

---

Before conditioning, the auditory-evoked potential elicted by the conditioned stimulus (CS) in the lateral amygdala did not differ in groups that were to be given paired conditioning trials or unpaired presentations of the CS and the unconditioned stimulus. The responses separated during conditioning and remained different after training. (*Bottom*) Behavioral conditioned fear learning in the same animals. The groups do not differ before conditioning. During training both groups "freeze." Freezing in the control group during training was not due to the formation of a conditioned fear memory because as soon as training was terminated the response decreased. Only the paired group showed training-induced enhancement of the auditory-evoked response and of fear behavior. The similarity of the behavioral responses during training, a time when the neural responses differed, indicates that the response after training is unlikely to be due to nonspecific factors related to the expression of the behavior. Based on Rogan & LeDoux (1995) and Rogan et al (1997).

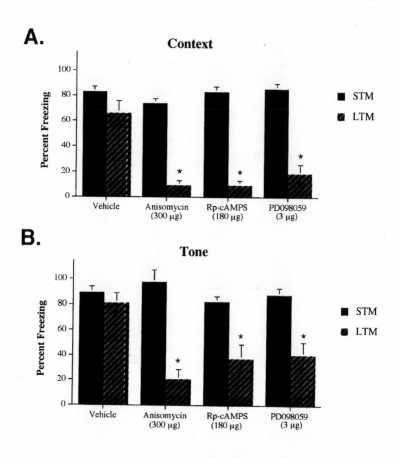

Figure 7   Blockade of protein synthesis (with anisomycin), protein kinase A (with Rp-cAMPS), or mitogen-activated protein kinase (with PD098059) interferes with the expression of long-term memory (LTM), but not short-term memory (STM), for fear conditioning in rats. Drugs were administered intraventricularly immediately after conditioning, and fear respones were tested 24 h later while the rats were drug free. Based on Schafe et al (1999).

learning and not on processes that occur after learning (Wilensky et al 1999). The amygdala thus seems to be essential for Pavlovian fear conditioning and does not modulate its own learning.

Two additional points should be noted. First, although plasticity in the amygdala appears to be required for Pavlovian fear conditioning to occur, the site of long-term memory storage is not known. It is possible that the storage is in the amygdala itself or, alternatively, that the storage is distributed and involves interactions between the amygdala and cortical or other areas. Second, plasticity within the amygdala is probably not required for learning cognitive aspects of fear, as suggest by Cahill & McGaugh (1998). This would explain why humans with amygdala damage are able to lead fairly normal lives in spite of the fact that they have certain deficits in processing danger signals (see below).

THE HUMAN AMYGDALA

Over the past several years, there has been an explosion of interest in the role of the human amygdala in fear. Deficits in the perception of the emotional meaning of faces, especially fearful faces, have been found in patients with amygdala damage (Adolphs et al 1995, Calder et al 1996). Similar results were reported for detection of the emotional tone of voices (Scott et al 1997). Furthermore, damge to the amygdala (Bechara et al 1995) or areas of temporal lobe including the amygdala (LaBar et al 1995) produced deficits in fear conditioning in humans. Functional imaging studies have shown that the amygdala is activated more strongly in the presence of fearful and angry faces than of happy ones (Breiter et al 1996) and that subliminal presentations of such stimuli lead to stronger acti-vations than do freely seen ones (Whalen et al 1998). Fear conditioning also leads to increases in amygdala activity, as measured by functional magnetic resonance imaging (LaBar et al 1998, Buchel et al 1998), and these effects also occur to subliminal stimuli (Morris et al 1998). Additionally, when the activity of the amygdala during fear conditioning is cross correlated with the activity in other regions of the brain, the strongest relations are seen with subcortical (thalamic and collicular) rather than cortical areas, further emphasizing the importance of the direct thalamao-amygdala pathway in the human brain (Morris et al 1999). Other aspects of emotion and the human brain area are reviewed by Davidson & Irwin (1999), Phelps & Anderson (1997), Cahill & McGaugh (1998).

CLINICAL IMPLICATIONS

Although it is clear that studies of acute fear responses elicited by conditioned fear stimuli cannot account for all aspects of fear and fear disorders, there is growing enthusiasm for the notion that fear learning processes similar to those occurring in fear conditioning experiments might indeed be an important factor in certain anxiety disorders. For example, fear conditioning models of posttrau-matic stress disorder and panic disorder (Pitman & Orr 1999, Goddard et al 1998) have been proposed recently by researchers in these fields.

Earlier in this century, the notion that conditioned fear contributes to phobias and related fear disorders was fairly popular. However, this idea fell out of favor because laboratory fear conditioning seemed to produce easily extinguishable fear, whereas clinical fear is difficult to treat. The notion arose that fear disorders involve a special kind of learning, called prepared learning, where the CS is biologically significant rather than neutral (Seligman 1971, Marks 1987, Öhman 1992). Although preparedness may indeed contribute, there is another factor to consider. In studies of rats, Morgan et al (1993; but see Gewirtz & Davis 1997) found that easily extinguished fear could be converted into difficult-to-extinguish fear in rats with damage to the medial prefrontal cortex. This suggested that alterations in the organization of the medial prefrontal regions might predispose certain people in some circumstances (such as stressful situations) to learn fear in a way that is difficult to extinguish (treat) under normal circumstances. These changes could come about because of genetic or experiential factors, or some combination.

COGNITIVE-EMOTIONAL INTERACTIONS IN THE BRAIN FROM THE PERSPECTIVE OF FEAR CONDITIONING

One of the key issues for the coming years is to integrate research on emotion and cognition. As already noted, this will not be achieved by simply linking research on the limbic system with research on the cortex. An approach that offers more anatomical precision on the emotion side is needed. Studies of fear conditioning provide a framework for beginning such an endeavor. Although this bottom up approach focused on fear may seem needlessly tedious, it is possible that once other emotions are understood in sufficient anatomical detail, some general principles that apply to other emotions will emerge. For the time being, it is best to restrict the discussion to fear circuits and their interactions with cognitive systems. Thus, in this section we consider how fear processing by the amygdala is influenced by and can influence perceptual, attentional, and memory functions of the cortex.

The amygdala receives inputs from cortical sensory processing regions of each sensory modality and projects back to these as well (Amaral et al 1992, Turner et al 1980, McDonald 1998). As shown above, these projections allow the amygdala to determine whether danger is present in the sensory world. But in addition to processing the significance of external stimuli, the amygdala can also influence sensory processing occurring in cortical areas. The amygdala only receives inputs from the late stages of cortical sensory processing, but it projects back to the earliest stages (Turner et al 1980, Amaral et al 1992). Thus, once the amygdala is activated by a sensory event from the thalamus or cortex, it can begin to regulate the cortical areas that project to it, controlling the kinds of inputs it receives from the cortex. The amygdala also influences cortical sensory processes indirectly, by way of projections to various "arousal" networks, including the basal forebrain cholinergic system, the brainstem cholinergic system, and the locus ceruleus noradrenergic system, each of which innervates widespread areas of the cortex (e.g. Aston-Jones et al 1996, Gallagher & Holland 1994, Holland & Gallagher

1999, Kapp et al 1992, Weinberger 1995). Thus, once the amygdala detects danger, it can activate these arousal systems, which can then influence sensory processing. The bodily responses initiated by the amygdala can also influence cortical areas, by way of feedback either from proprioceptive or visceral signals or hormones (e.g. McGaugh et al 1995, Damasio 1994). Amygdala regulation of the cortex by either direct or indirect routes could facilitate the processing of stimuli that signal danger even if such stimuli occur outside the attention field (Armony et al 1996, 1998; Armony & LeDoux 1999).

In humans, damage to the amygdala interferes with implicit emotional memories but not explicit memories about emotions, whereas damage to the medial temporal lobe memory system interferes with explicit memories about emotions but not with implicit emotional memories (Bechara et al 1995, LaBar et al 1995). Although explicit memories with and without emotional content are formed by way of the medial temporal lobe system, those with emotional content differ from those without such content. The former tend to be longer lasting and more vivid (see Christianson 1989, Cahill & McGaugh 1998). Lesions of the amygdala or systemic administration of a beta-adrenergic antagonist prevent this amplifying effect of emotion on declarative memory (Cahill & McGaugh 1998), which suggests that the amygdala can modulate the storage of explicit memories in cortical areas. At the same time, the medial temporal lobe memory system projects to the amygdala (Amaral et al 1992). Retrieval of long-term memories of traumatic events may trigger fear reactions by way of these projections to the amygdala.

Although there has been relatively little work on the role of the amygdala in cognitive-emotional interactions, the importance of the amygdala as a bridge between emotion and attention was pointed out over thirty years ago (e.g. Pribram & Melges 1969). Given the extensive connections between the amygdala and cortical areas, this topic is begging for research.

WHAT ABOUT FEELINGS?

Consciousness is an important part of the study of emotion and other mental processes. Although we are far from understanding what consciousness is, a number of theorists have proposed that it may be related to working memory, a serially organized mental workspace where things can be compared and contrasted and mentally manipulated (Baddeley 1992). A variety of studies of humans and nonhuman primates point to the prefrontal cortex, especially the dorsolateral prefrontal areas—as well as the anterior cingulate and orbital cortical regions—as being involved in working memory (Fuster 1998, Goldman-Rakic 1996, Braver et al 1997, Carter et al 1998). Immediately present stimuli and stored representations are integrated in working memory by way of interactions between prefrontal areas, sensory processing systems (which serve as short-term memory buffers, as well as perceptual processors), and the long-term explicit (declarative) memory system involving the hippocampus and related areas of the temporal lobe.

In the case of an affectively charged stimulus, such as a trigger of fear, the same sorts of processes will be called upon as for stimuli without emotional implications, but in addition, working memory will become aware of the fact that the fear system of the brain has been activated (Figure 8). This additional information, when added to perceptual and mnemonic information about the object or event, could be the condition for the subjective experience of an emotional state of fear (LeDoux 1996).

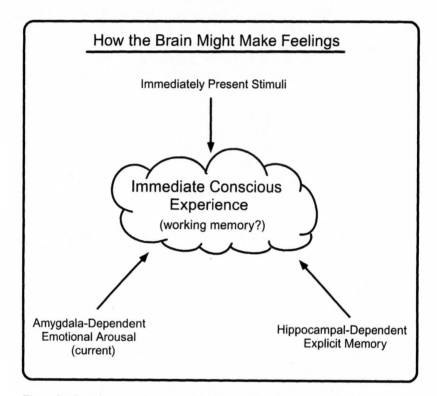

Figure 8   Conscious experiences are often said to reflect the contents of working memory. In this sense, a conscious emotional experience may not be that different from any other kind of conscious experience. The difference would be more in the systems that are providing inputs to working memory rather than in the mechanisms of consciousness itself. In the case of fearful experiences, or fearful feelings, the conscious emotion may be the result of some immediately present stimulus triggering long-term explict memories and amygdala activation. The simultaneous representation in working memory of the outputs of these three, and perhaps other, systems may be the stuff that fearful feelings are made of. Other feelings would come about similarly but would not necessarily involve the amygdala.

By way of projections to cortical areas, the amygdala can influence the operation of perceptual and short-term memory processes, as well as processes in higher-order areas. Although the amygdala does not have extensive connections with the dorsolateral prefrontal cortex, it does communicate with the anterior cingulate and orbital cortex, two other components of the working memory network. But in addition, the amygdala projects to nonspecific systems involved in the regulation of cortical arousal and it controls bodily responses (behavioral, autonomic, endocrine), which then provide feedback that can influence cortical processing indirectly. Thus, working memory receives a greater number of inputs, and receives inputs of a greater variety, in the presence of an emotional stimulus than in the presence of other stimuli. These extra inputs may just be what is required to add affective charge to working memory representations, and thus to turn subjective experiences into emotional experiences.

CONCLUSION

Research on the emotional brain has progressed significantly in recent years, largely as a result of a highly focused approach centered on the study of fear mechanisms, and especially the mechanisms underlying fear conditioning. This work has mapped out pathways involved in fear learning in both experimental animals and humans, and it has begun to shed light on interactions between emotional and cognitive processes in the brain. Although the focus on fear conditioning has its limits, it has proven valuable as a research strategy and provides a foundation upon which to build a broader understanding of mind and brain.

At the same time, there is a disturbing rush to embrace the amygdala as the new center of the emotional brain. It seems unlikely that the amygdala is the answer to how all emotions work, and it may not even explain how all aspects of fear work. There is some evidence that the amygdala participates in postitive emotional behaviors, but that role is still poorly understood. If an amygdala theory of emotion is on the horizon, let it get there by data rather than by faith.

Neuroscience meetings these days have numerous papers on the role of the brain in emotion, affect, hedonic tone, and the like. Unless these vague concepts can be operationalized, as was done in the work on fear, they are likely to impede, if not recede, the progress. The future of emotion research can be bright if we keep in mind the way that emotion became respectable again: by focusing on a psychologically well-defined aspect of emotion, by using an experimental approach that simplified the problem in such a way as to make it tractable, by circumventing vague and poorly defined aspects of emotion, and by removing subjective experience as a roadblock to experimentation. This is not to suggest that the hard problems should not be worked on but instead that they should be worked on in a way that advances the field.

Visit the Annual Reviews home page at www.AnnualReviews.org.

LITERATURE CITED

Abel T, Nguyen PV, Barad M, Deuel TAS, Kandel ER, Bourtchuladze R. 1997. Genetic demonstration of a role for PKA in the phase of LTP and in hippocampus-based long-term memory. *Cell* 88:615–26

Adolphs R, Tranel D, Damasio H, Damasio AR. 1995. Fear and the human amygdala. *J. Neurosci.* 15:5879–91

Aggleton JP, ed. 1992. *The Amygdala: Neurobiological Aspects of Emotion, Memory, and Mental Dysfunction.* New York: Wiley-Liss

Aggleton JP, Mishkin M. 1986. The amygdala: sensory gateway to the emotions. In *Emotion: Theory, Research and Experience,* ed. R Plutchik, H Kellerman, 3:281–99. Orlando, FL: Academic

Amaral DG, Price JL, Pitkänen A, Carmichael ST. 1992. Anatomical organization of the primate amygdaloid complex. See Aggleton 1992, pp. 1–66

Armony JL, LeDoux JE. 1999. How danger is encoded: towards a systems, cellular, and computational understanding of cognitive-emotional interactions in fear circuits. See Gazzaniga 1999. In press

Armony JL, Quirk GJ, LeDoux JE. 1998. Differential effects of amygdala lesions on early and late plastic components of auditory cortex spiketrains during fear conditioning. *J. Neurosci.* 18:2592–601

Armony JL, Servan-Schreiber D, Cohen JC, LeDoux JE. 1996. Emotion and cognition interactions in the thalalmo-cortico-amygdala network: theory and model. *Cogn. Neurosci. Soc. Abstr.* 3:76

Armony JL, Servan-Schreiber D, Romanski LM, Cohen JD, LeDoux JE. 1997. Stimulus generalization of fear responses: effects of auditory cortex lesions in a computational model and in rats. *Cereb. Cortex* 7:157–65

Aston-Jones G, Rajkowski J, Kubiak P, Valentino RJ, Shipley MT. 1996. Role of the locus coeruleus in emotional activation. *Prog. Brain. Res.* 107:379–402

Atkins CM, Selcher JC, Petraitis JJ, Trzaskos JM, Sweatt JD. 1998. The MAPK cascade is required for mammalian associative learning. *Nat. Neurosci.* 1:602–9

Baddeley A. 1992. Working memory. *Science.* 255:556–59

Barnes CA. 1995. Involvement of LTP in memory: Are we searching under the streetlight? *Neuron* 15:751–54

Bechara A, Tranel D, Damasio H, Adolphs R, Rockland C, Damasio AR. 1995. Double dissociation of conditioning and declarative knowledge relative to the amygdala and hippocampus in humans. *Science* 269:1115–18

Bernard JF, Besson JM. 1990. The spino(trigemino)pontoamygdaloid pathway: electrophysiological evidence for an involvement in pain processes. *J. Neurophysiol.* 63:473–89

Blanchard RJ, Blanchard DC, Fial RA. 1970. Hippocampal lesions in rats and their effect on activity, avoidance, and aggression. *J. Comp. Physiol. Psychol.* 71(1):92–102

Bliss TVP, Collingridge GL. 1993. A synaptic model of memory: long-term potentiation in the hippocampus. *Nature* 361:31–39

Bliss TVP, Lomo T. 1973. Long-lasting potentiation of synaptic transmission in the dentate area of the anaesthetized rabbit following stimulation of the perforant path. *J. Physiol.* 232:331–56

Bourtchouladze R, Abel T, Berman N, Gordon R, Lapidus K, Kandel ER. 1998. Different training procedures recruit either one or two criticial periods for contextual memory consolidation, each of which requires protein synthesis and PKA. *Learn. Mem.* 5:365–74

Bourtchouladze R, Frenguelli B, Blendy J, Cioffi D, Schutz G, Silva AJ. 1994. Deficient long-term memory in mice with a targeted mutation of the cAMP-responsive element-binding protein. *Cell* 79:59–68

Braver TS, Cohen JD, Jonides J, Smith EE, Noll DC. 1997. A parametric study of prefrontal cortex involvement in human working memory. *NeuroImage* 5(1):49–62

Breiter HC, Etcoff NL, Whalen PJ, Kennedy WA, Rauch SL, et al. 1996. Response and habituation of the human amygdala during visual processing of facial expression. *Neuron* 17:875–87

Brodal A, ed. 1982. *Neurological Anatomy.* New York: Oxford Univ. Press

Buchel C, Morris J, Dolan RJ, Friston KJ. 1998. Brain systems mediating aversive conditioning: an event-related fMRI study. *Neuron* 20:947–57

Burstein R, Potrebic S. 1993. Retrograde labeling of neurons in the spinal cord that project directly to the amygdala or the orbital cortex in the rat. *J. Comp. Neurol.* 335:469

Cahill L, McGaugh JL. 1998. Mechanisms of emotional arousal and lasting declarative memory. *Trends Neurosci.* 21:294–99

Calder AJ, Young AW, Rowland D, Perrett D, Hodges JR, Etcoff NL. 1996. Facial emotion recognition after bilateral amygdala damage: differentially severe impairment of fear. *Cogn. Neuropsychol.* 13:699–745

Campeau S, Davis M. 1995. Involvement of the central nucleus and basolateral complex of the amygdala in fear conditioning measured with fear-potentiated startle in rats trained concurrently with auditory and visual conditioned stimuli. *J. Neurosci.* 15:2301–11

Canteras NS, Swanson LW. 1992. Projections of the ventral subiculum to the amygdala, septum, and hypothalamus: a PHAL anterograde tract-tracing study in the rat. *J. Comp. Neurol.* 324:180–94

Cassell MD, Freedman LL, Shi C. 1999. The intrinsic organization of the central extended amygdala. *Ann. NY Acad. Sci.* 877:217–41

Carter CS, Braver TS, Barch DM, Botvinick MM, Noll D, Cohen JD. 1998. Anterior cingulate cortex, error detection, and the online monitoring of performance. *Science* 280:747–49

Cavus I, Teyler T. 1996. Two forms of long-term potentiation in area CA1 activate different signal transduction cascades. *J. Neurophysiol.* 76:3038–47

Chapman PF, Bellavance LL. 1992. NMDA receptor-independent LTP in the amygdala. *Synapse* 11:310–18

Chapman PF, Kairiss EW, Keenan CL, Brown TH. 1990. Long-term synaptic potentiation in the amygdala. *Synapse* 6:271–78

Christianson SA. 1989. Flashbulb memories: special, but not so special. *Mem. Cogn.* 17:435–43

Clugnet MC, LeDoux JE. 1990. Synaptic plasticity in fear conditioning circuits: induction of LTP in the lateral nucleus of the amygdala by stimulation of the medial geniculate body. *J. Neurosci.* 10:2818–24

Damasio A, 1994. *Descarte's Error: Emotion, Reason, and the Human Brain.* New York: Gosset/Putnam

Davidson RJ, Irwin W. 1999. The functional neuroanatomy of emotion and affective style. *Trends Cogn. Sci.* 3:211–21

Davis M. 1992. The Role of the Amygdala in Conditioned Fear. See Aggleton 1992, pp. 255–306

de Olmos J, Alheid G, Beltramino C. 1985. Amygdala. In *The Rat Nervous System,* ed. G Paxinos, pp. 223–334. Orlando, FL: Academic

Dudai Y. 1989. *The Neurobiology of Memory.* New York: Oxford Univ. Press

Eichenbaum H. 1994. The hippocampal system and declarative memory in humans and animals: experimental analysis and historical origins. In *Memory Systems,* ed. DL Schacter, E Tulving, pp. 147–201. Cambridge, MA: MIT Press

Eichenbaum H. 1995. The LTP-memory connection. *Nature* 378:131–32

Ekman P, Davidson R. 1994. *The Nature of Emotion: Fundamental Questions.* New York: Oxford Univ. Press

Everitt BJ, Robbins TW. 1992. Amygdala-ventral striatal interactions and reward-related processes. See Aggleton 1992, pp. 401–29

Fanselow MS. 1994. Neural organization of the defensive behavior system responsible for fear. *Psychon. Bull. Rev.* 1:429–38

Fanselow MS, LeDoux JE. 1999. Why we think plasticity underlying Pavlovian fear conditioning occurs in the basolateral amygdala. *Neuron* 23:229–32

Frankland PW, Cestari V, Filipkowski RK, McDonald RJ, Silva A. 1998. The dorsal hippocampus is essential for context discrimination, but not for contextual conditioning. *Behav. Neurosci.* 112:863–74

Fuster JM. 1998. Distributed memory for both short and long term. *Neurobiol. Learn. Mem.* 70:268–74

Gaffan D. 1992. Amygdala and the memory of reward. See Aggleton 1992, pp. 471–83

Gallagher M, Holland PC. 1994. The amygdala complex: multiple roles in associative learning and attention. *Proc. Natl. Acad. Sci. USA* 91:11771–76

Gardner H. 1987. *The Mind's New Science: A History of the Cognitive Revolution.* New York: Basic Books

Gazzaniza MS, ed. 1999. *The Cognitive Neurosciences.* Cambridge, MA: MIT Press. In press

Gean P-W, Chang F-C, Hung C-R. 1993. Use-dependent modification of a slow NMDA receptor-mediated synaptic potential in rat amygdalar slices. *J. Neurosci. Res.* 34:635–41

Gentile CG, Jarrell TW, Teich A, McCabe PM, Schneiderman N. 1986. The role of amygdaloid central nucleus in the retention of differential Pavlovian conditioning of bradycardia in rabbits. *Behav. Brain Res.* 20:263–73

Gewirtz JC, Davis M. 1997. Second-order fear conditioning prevented by blocking NMDA receptors in amygdala. *Nature* 388:471–74

Goddard AW, Gorman JM, Charney DS. 1998. Neurobiology of panic disorder. In *Panic Disorder and its Treatment,* ed. JF Rosenblaum, MH Pollack, pp. 57–92. New York: Dekker

Goldman-Rakic PS. 1996. Regional and cellular fractionation of working memory. *Proc. Natl. Acad. Sci. USA* 93:13473–80

Gray JA. 1982. *The Neuropsychology of Anxiety.* New York: Oxford Univ. Press

Helmstetter FJ, Bellgowan PS. 1994. Effects of muscimol applied to the basolateral amygdala on acquisition and expression of contextual fear conditioning in rats. *Behav. Neurosci.* 108:1005–9

Hitchcock J, Davis M. 1986. Lesions of the amygdala but not of the cerebellum or red nucleus block conditioned fear as measured with the potentiated startle paradigm. *Behav. Neurosci.* 100:11–22

Holland PC, Gallagher M. 1999. Amygdala circuitry in attentional and representational processes. *Trends Cogn. Sci.* 3:65–73

Huang YY, Kandel ER. 1998. Postsynaptic induction and PKA-dependent expression of LTP in the lateral amygdala. *Neuron* 21:169–78

Huang YY, Nguyen PV, Abel T, Kandel ER. 1996. Long-lasting forms of synaptic potentiation in the mamalian hippocampus. *Learn. Mem.* 3:74–85

Isaacson RL. 1982. *The Limbic System.* New York: Plenum

Iwata J, LeDoux JE, Meeley MP, Arneric S, Reis DJ. 1986. Intrinsic neurons in the amygdaloid field projected to by the medial geniculate body mediate emotional responses conditioned to acoustic stimuli. *Brain Res.* 383:195–214

Jarrell TW, Gentile CG, Romanski LM, McCabe PM, Schneiderman N. 1987. Involvement of cortical and thalamic auditory regions in retention of differential bradycardia conditioning to acoustic conditioned stimulii in rabbits. *Brain Res.* 412:285–94

Josselyn SA, Carlezon, WA, Shi C, Neve RL, Nestler EJ, Davis M. 1998. Overexpression of CREB in the amygdala of rats facilitates long term memory formation. *Soc. Neurosci. Abs.*

Kaada BR. 1960. Cingulate, posterior orbital, anterior insular and temporal pole cortex. In

Handbook of Physiology: Neurophysiology II, ed. J Field, HJ Magoun, VE Hall, pp. 1345–72. Washington, DC: Am. Physiol. Soc.

Kandel ER. 1997. Genes, synapses, and long-term memory. *J. Cell Physiol.* 173:124–25

Kapp BS, Frysinger RC, Gallagher M, Haselton J. 1979. Amygdala central nucleus lesions: effect on heart rate conditioning in the rabbit. *Physiol. Behav.* 23:1109–17

Kapp BS, Whalen PJ, Supple WF, Pascoe JP. 1992. Amygdaloid contributions to conditioned arousal and sensory information processing. See Aggleton 1992, pp. 229–54

Kihlstrom JF. 1987. The cognitive unconscious. *Science* 237:1445–52

Killcross S, Robbins TW, Everitt BJ. 1997. Different types of fear-conditioned behavior mediated by separate nuclei within amygdala. *Nature* 388:377–80

Kim JJ, Fanselow MS. 1992. Modality-specific retrograde amnesia of fear. *Science* 256:675–77

Kotter R, Meyer N. 1992. The limbic system: a review of its empirical foundation. *Behav. Brain Res.* 52:105–27

Krettek JE, Price JL. 1978. A description of the amygdaloid complex in the rat and cat with observations on intra-amygdaloid axonal connections. *J. Comp. Neurol.* 178:255–80

LaBar KS, Gatenby JC, Gore JC, LeDoux JE, Phelps EA. 1998. Human amygdala activation during conditioned fear acquisition and extinction: a mixed-trial fMRI study. *Neuron* 20:937–45

LaBar KS, LeDoux JE, Spencer DD, Phelps EA. 1995. Impaired fear conditioning following unilateral temporal lobectomy in humans. *J. Neurosci.* 15:6846–55

LeDoux JE. 1987. Emotion. In *Handbook of Physiology. 1: The Nervous System,* ed. F Plum, pp. 419–60. Bethesda, MD: Am. Physiol. Soc.

LeDoux JE. 1991. Emotion and the limbic system concept. *Concepts Neurosci.* 2:169–99

LeDoux JE. 1992. Emotion and the Amygdala. See Aggleton 1992, pp. 339–51

LeDoux JE, ed. 1996. *The Emotional Brain.* New York: Simon & Schuster

LeDoux JE, Cicchetti P, Xagoraris A, Romanski L-M. 1990a. The lateral amygdaloid nucleus: Sensory interface of the amygdala in fear conditioning. *J. Neurosci.* 10:1062–69

LeDoux JE, Farb CF, Ruggiero DA. 1990b. Topographic organization of neurons in the acoustic thalamus that project to the amygdala. *J. Neurosci.* 10:1043–54

LeDoux JE, Iwata J, Cicchetti P, Reis DJ. 1988. Different projections of the central amygdaloid nucleus mediate autonomic and behavioral correlates of conditioned fear. *J. Neurosci.* 8:2517–29

LeDoux JE, Ruggiero DA, Forest R, Stornetta R, Reis DJ. 1987. Topographic organization of convergent projections to the thalamus from the inferior colliculus and spinal cord in the rat. *J. Comp. Neurol.* 264:123–46

Lee H, Kim JJ. 1998. Amygdalar NMDA receptors are critical for new fear learning in previously fear-conditioned rats. *J. Neurosci.* 18:8444–54

Lewis M, Haviland J, eds. 1992. *Handbook of Emotions.* New York: Guilford

Li X, Phillips RG, LeDoux JE. 1995. NMDA and non-NMDA receptors contribute to synaptic transmission between the medial geniculate body and the lateral nucleus of the amygdala. *Exp. Brain Res.* 105:87–100

Li XF, Stutzmann GE, LeDoux JL. 1996. Convergent but temporally separated inputs to lateral amygdala neurons from the auditory thalamus and auditory cortex use different postsynaptic receptors: *in vivo* intracellular and extracellular recordings in fear conditioning pathways. *Learn. Mem.* 3:229–42

Livingston KE, Escobar A. 1971. Anatomical bias of the limbic system concept. *Arch. Neurol.* 24:17–21

Lynch G, ed. 1986. *Synapses, Circuits, and the Beginnings of Memory.* Cambridge, MA: MIT Press

MacLean PD. 1949. Psychosomatic disease and the "visceral brain": recent developments bearing on the Papez theory of emotion. *Psychosom. Med.* 11:338–53

MacLean PD. 1952. Some psychiatric implications of physiological studies on frontotemporal portion of limbic system (visceral brain). *Electroencephalogr. Clin. Neurophysiol.* 4:407–18

MacLean PD. 1970. The triune brain, emotion and scientific bias. See Schmitt 1970, pp. 336–49

Majidishad P, Pelli DG, LeDoux JE. 1996. Disruption of fear conditioning to contextual stimuli but not to a tone by lesions of the accessory basal nucleus of the amygdala. *Soc. Neurosci. Abstr.* 22:1116

Maren S, Aharonov G, Fanselow MS. 1997. Neurotoxic lesions of the dorsal hippocampus and Pavlovian fear conditioning in rats. *Behav. Brain Res.* 88:261–74

Maren S, Aharonov G, Stote DL, Fanselow MS. 1996. N-methyl-d-aspartate receptors in the basolateral amygdala are required for both acquisition and expression of the conditional fear in rats. *Behav. Neurosci.* 110:1365–74

Maren S, Fanselow MS. 1995. Synaptic plasticity in the basolateral amygdala induced by hippocampal formation stimulation *in vivo. J. Neurosci.* 15:7548–64

Maren S, Poremba A, Gabriel M. 1991. Basolateral amygdaloid multi-unit neuronal correlates of discriminative avoidance learning in rabbits. *Brain. Res.* 549:311–16

Marks I, ed. 1987. *Fears, Phobias, and Rituals: Panic, Anxiety and Their Disorders.* New York: Oxford Univ. Press

Mascagni F, McDonald AJ, Coleman JR. 1993. Corticoamygdaloid and corticocortical projections of the rat temporal cortex: a phaseolus vulgaris leucoagglutinin study. *Neuroscience* 57:697–715

Mayford M, Bach ME, Huang Y-Y, Wang L, Hawkins RD, Kandel ER. 1996. Control of memory formation through regulated expression of a CaMKII transgene. *Science* 274:1678–83

McDonald AJ. 1998. Cortical pathways to the mammalian amygdala. *Prog. Neurobiol.* 55:257–332

McDonald RJ, White NM. 1993. A triple dissociation of memory systems: hippocampus, amygdala, and dorsal striatum. *Behav. Neurosci.* 107:3–22

McGaugh JL, Mesches MH, Cahill L, Parent MB, Coleman-Mesches K, Salinas JA. 1995. Involvement of the amygdala in the regulation of memory storage. In *Plasticity in the Central Nervous System,* ed. JL McGaugh, F Bermudez-Rattoni, RA Prado-Alcala, pp. 18–39. Mahwah, NJ: Erlbaum

McKernan MG, Shinnick-Gallagher P. 1997. Fear conditioning induces a lasting potentiation of synaptic currents in vitro. *Nature* 390:607–11

Miserendino MJD, Sananes CB, Melia KR, Davis M. 1990. Blocking of acquisition but not expression of conditioned fear-potentiated startle by NMDA antagonists in the amygdala. *Nature* 345:716–18

Morgan MA, Romanski LM, LeDoux JE. 1993. Extinction of emotional learning: contribution of medial prefrontal cortex. *Neurosci. Lett.* 163:109–13

Morris JS, Ohman A, Dolan RJ. 1998. Conscious and unconscious emotional learning in the human amygdala. *Nature* 393:467–70

Morris JS, Ohman A, Dolan RJ. 1999. A subcortical pathway to the right amygdala mediating "unseen" fear. *Proc. Natl. Acad. Sci. USA* 96:1680–85

Muller J, Corodimas KP, Fridel Z, LeDoux JE. 1997. Functional inactivation of the lateral and basal nuclei of the amygdala by muscimol infusion prevents fear conditioning to an explicit CS and to contextual stimuli. *Behav. Neurosci.* 111:683–91

Nader K, LeDoux JE. 1997. Is it time in invoke multiple fear learning system? *Trends Cogn. Sci.* 1:241–44

Nauta WJH. 1979. Expanding borders of the limbic system concept. In *Functional Neurosurgery,* ed. T Rasmussen, R Marino, pp. 7–23. New York: Raven

Nauta WJH, Karten HJ. 1970. A general profile of the vertebrate brain, with sidelights on the ancestry of cerebral cortex. See Schmitt 1970, pp. 7–26

Neisser U. 1967. *Cognitive Psychology*. Englewood Cliffs, NJ: Prentice Hall

Nicoll RA, Malenka RC. 1995. Contrasting properties of two forms of long-term potentiation in the hippocampus. *Nature* 377:115–18

Öhman A. 1992. Fear and anxiety as emotional phenomena: clinical, phenomenological, evolutionary perspectives, and information-processing mechanisms. See Lewis & Haviland, pp. 511–36

Ono T, Nishijo H. 1992. Neurophysiological basis of the Kluver-Bucy syndrome: responses of monkey amygdaloid neurons to biologically significant objects. See Aggleton 1992, pp. 167–90

Packard MG, Cahill L, McGaugh JL. 1994. Amygdala modulation of hippocampal-dependent and caudate nucleus-dependent memory processes. *Proc. Natl. Acad. Sci. USA* 91:8477–81

Panksepp J. 1998. *Affective Neuroscience: The Foundations of Human and Animal Emotions*. New York: Oxford Univ. Press

Paré D, Smith Y, Paré JF. 1995. Intra-amygdaloid projections of the basolateral and basomedial nuclei in the cat: *Phaseolus vulgaris*–leucoagglutinin anterograde tracing at the light and electron microscopic level. *Neuroscience* 69:567–83

Pascoe JP, Kapp BS. 1985. Electrophysiological characteristics of amygdaloid central nucleus neurons during Pavlovian fear conditioning in the rabbit. *Behav. Brain. Res.* 16:117–33

Pavlov IP. 1927. *Conditioned Reflexes*. New York: Dover

Phelps EA, Anderson AK. 1997. Emotional memory: What does the amygdala do? *Curr. Biol.* 7:311–14

Phillips RG, LeDoux JE. 1992. Differential contribution of amygdala and hippocampus to cued and contextual fear conditioning. *Behav. Neurosci.* 106:274–85

Pitkänen A, Savander V, LeDoux JL. 1997. Organization of intra-amygdaloid circuitries: an emerging framework for understanding functions of the amygdala. *Trends Neurosci.* 20:517–23

Pitman RK, Orr SP. 1999. Post-traumatic stress disorder: emotion, conditioning, and memory. See Gazzaniga 1999. In press

Pribram KH, Melges FT. 1969. Psychophysiological basis of emotion. In *Handbook of Clinical Neurology*, ed. PJ Vinken, GW Bruyn, pp. 316–42. Amsterdam: North-Holland Publ.

Pribram KH, Reitz S, McNeil M, Spevack AA. 1979. The effect of amygdalectomy on orienting and classical conditioning in monkeys. *Pavlov. J. Biol. Sci.* 14:203–17

Quirk GJ, Armony JL, LeDoux JE. 1997. Fear conditioning enhances different temporal components of toned-evoked spike trains in auditory cortex and lateral amygdala. *Neuron* 19:613–24

Quirk GJ, Repa JC, LeDoux JE. 1995. Fear conditioning enhances short-latency auditory responses of lateral amygdala neurons: parallel recordings in the freely behaving rat. *Neuron* 15:1029–39

Rogan M, Staubli U, LeDoux J. 1997. Fear conditioning induces associative long-term potentiation in the amygdala. *Nature* 390:604–7

Rogan MT, LeDoux JE. 1995. LTP is accompanied by commensurate enhancement of auditory—evoked responses in a fear conditioning circuit. *Neuron* 15:127–36

Rolls ET. 1992. Neurophysiology and functions of the primate amygdala. See Aggleton 1992, pp. 143–65

Rolls ET. 1999. *The Brain and Emotion*. New York: Oxford Univ. Press

Romanski LM, LeDoux JE. 1992. Equipotentiality of thalamo-amygdala and thalamo-cortico-amygdala projections as auditory conditioned stimulus pathways. *J. Neurosci.* 12:4501–9

Romanski LM, LeDoux JE. 1993. Information cascade from primary auditory cortex to the amygdala: corticocortical and corticoamygdaloid projections of temporal cortex in the rat. *Cereb. Cortex.* 3:515–32

Romanski LM, LeDoux JE, Clugnet MC, Bordi F. 1993. Somatosensory and auditory convergence in the lateral nucleus of the amygdala. *Behav. Neurosci.* 107:444–50

Schafe GE, Nadel NV, Sullivan GM, Harris A, LeDoux JE. 1999. Memory consolidation for contextual and auditory fear conditioning is dependent on protein synthesis, PKA, and MAP kinase. *Learn. Mem.* 6:97–110

Schmitt FO, ed. 1970. *Neurosciences: Second Study Program.* New York: Rockefeller Univ. Press

Scott SK, Young AW, Calder AJ, Hellawell DJ, Aggleton JP, Johnson M. 1997. Impaired auditory recognition of fear and anger following bilateral amygdala lesions. *Nature* 385:254–57

Scoville WB, Milner B. 1957. Loss of recent memory after bilateral hippocampal lesions. *J. Neurol. Psychol.* 20:11–21

Seligman MEP. 1971. Phobias and preparedness. *Behav. Ther.* 2:307–20

Shi C, Davis M. 1998. Pain pathways involved in fear conditioning measured with fear potentiated startle: lesion studies. *J. Neurosci.* 19:420–30

Siegel A, Edinger H. 1981. Neural control of aggression and rage behavior. In *Handbook of the Hypothalamus.* Vol. 3. *Behavioral Studies of the Hyphothalamus,* ed. PJ Morgane, J Panksepp, pp. 203–40. New York: Dekker

Siegel A, Roeling TA, Gregg TR, Kruk MR. 1999. Neuropharmacology of brain-stimulation-evoked aggression. *Neurosci. Biobehav. Rev.* 23:359–89

Squire LR, Knowlton B, Musen G. 1993. The structure and organization of memory. *Annu. Rev. Psychol.* 44:453–95

Stevens CF. 1998. A million dollar question: Does LTP = memory? *Neuron* 20:1–2

Swanson LW. 1983. The hippocampus and the concept of the limbic system. In *Neurobiology of the Hippocampus,* ed. W Seifert, pp. 3–19. London: Academic

Turner BH, Mishkin M, Knapp M. 1980. Organization of the amygdalopetal projections from modality-specific cortical association areas in the monkey. *J. Comp. Neurol.* 191:515–43

Turner BH, Zimmer J. 1984. The architecture and some interconnections of the rat amygdala and lateral periallocortex. *J. Comp. Neurol.* 227:540–57

Uwano T, Nishijo H, Ono T, Tamura R. 1995. Neuronal responsiveness to various sensory stimuli, and associative learning in the rat amygdala. *Neuroscience* 68:339–61

van de Kar LD, Piechowski RA, Rittenhouse PA, Gray TS. 1991. Amygdaloid lesions: differential effect on conditioned stress and immobilization-induced increases in corticosterone and renin secretion. *Neuroendocrinology* 54:89–95

Vazdarjanova A, McGaugh JL. 1998. Basolateral amygdala is not critical for cognitive memory of contextual fear conditioning. *Proc. Nat. Acad. Sci. USA* 95:15003–7

Weinberger NM. 1995. Retuning the brain by fear conditioning. In *The Cognitive Neurosciences,* ed. MS Gazzaniga, pp. 1071–90. Cambridge, MA: MIT Press

Weinberger NM. 1998. Physiological memory in primary auditory cortex: characteristics and mechanisms. *Neurobiol. Learn. Mem.* 70:226–51

Weisskopf MG, Bauer E, LeDoux JE. 1999. L-type voltage gated calcium channels mediate NMDA-independent associative long-term potentiation at thalamic input synapses to the amygdala. *J. Neurosci.* 10512–19

Weisskopf MG, LeDoux JE. 1999. Distinct populations of NMDA receptors at subcortical and cortical inputs to principal cells of the lateral amygdala. *J. Neurophysiol.* 81:930–34

Whalen PJ, Rauch SL, Etcoff NL, McInerney SC, Lee MB, Jenike MA. 1998. Masked presentations of emotional facial expressions modulate amygdala activity without explicit knowledge. *J. Neurosci.* 18:411–18

Wilensky AE, Schafe GE, LeDoux JE. 1999. Functional inactivation of the amygdala before but not after auditory fear conditioning prevents memory formation. *J. Neurosci.* 19 RC48 1–5

Activation of the left amygdala to a cognitive representation of fear

Elizabeth A. Phelps[1], Kevin J. O'Connor[2], J. Christopher Gatenby[3], John C. Gore[3], Christian Grillon[4] and Michael Davis[5]

[1] Department of Psychology, New York University, 6 Washington Place, 8th Floor, New York, New York 10003, USA

[2] Department of Brain and Cognitive Sciences, NE20-439, 77 Massachussetts Avenue, Cambridge, Massachussetts 02139, USA

[3] Department of Radiology, Yale School of Medicine, PO Box 208042, New Haven, Connecticut 06520-8042, USA

[4] National Institue of Mental Health, 9000 Rockville Drive, Room 3N212, Bethesda, Maryland 20892, USA

[5] Department of Psychiatry and Behavioral Sciences, Emory University School of Medicine, 1639 Pierce Drive, Atlanta, Georgia 30322, USA

Correspondence should be addressed to E.A.P. (liz.phelps@nyu.edu)

We examined the neural substrates involved when subjects encountered an event linked verbally, but not experientially, to an aversive outcome. This instructed fear task models a primary way humans learn about the emotional nature of events. Subjects were told that one stimulus (threat) represents an aversive event (a shock may be given), whereas another (safe) represents safety (no shock will be given). Using functional magnetic resonance imaging (fMRI), activation of the left amygdala was observed in response to threat versus safe conditions, which correlated with the expression of the fear response as measured by skin conductance. Additional activation observed in the insular cortex is proposed to be involved in conveying a cortical representation of fear to the amygdala. These results suggest that the neural substrates that support conditioned fear across species have a similar but somewhat different role in more abstract representations of fear in humans.

A primary adaptive function of emotion is to influence future interactions with stimuli associated with emotional reactions. To discover the neuroscientific principles underlying this emotional learning, fear conditioning has traditionally been used as the behavioral task. The amygdala is critical for learning the aversive properties of events, across species and stimulus types[1,2,3]. However, fear conditioning may not be the primary means by which humans learn about the aversive nature of events. Although there are situations in which people learn about the emotional properties of a neutral event by its co-occurrence with an aversive event, we often learn about potentially dangerous situations through language. An analogy to traditional fear conditioning would be learning to fear a neighborhood dog because it once bit you unexpectedly. You develop a fear from direct experience with the dog in conjunction with the aversive experience of a painful bite. However, a similar fear reaction could be elicited not because the dog bit you, but because you heard that it bit someone else. In this case, there is no direct experience with the dog or with an aversive event. Instead, the dog is associated with an imagined and anticipated aversive event, resulting in a cognitive representation of the aversive properties of the dog.

This awareness of the aversive nature of events or stimuli is sufficient to guide our actions. We avoid dangerous neighborhoods or shark-infested waters, not necessarily because we have been crime victims or attacked by sharks in those locations, but rather because we have been told about their aversive properties. Previous research in humans using fear conditioning has found that the amygdala is not necessary for the acquisition of an explicit, cognitive representation of the aversive properties of a stimulus. This cognitive representation depends on the hippocampal memory system, which is important for the acquisition of explicit or declar-

ative memories[4]. However, the amygdala is necessary for the expression of a conditioned fear response to that same stimulus[4,5]. But what if the cognitive representation of the aversive properties of a stimulus is acquired without direct experience, as in the examples above? Based on previous results, we do not expect the acquisition of this representation to depend on amygdala function[4]. In the present study, we ask if the amygdala is involved in non-experiential fear-evoking situations.

We addressed this question by examining activity in the human amygdala using fMRI with a task called instructed fear. During instructed fear, subjects do not actually receive an aversive stimulus, but they are told that an event might occur in conjunction with a neutral stimulus. Previous research on normal adults has shown that this type of task, which has also been called anticipatory anxiety, results in fear responses similar to those observed in traditional fear conditioning, as measured by startle potentiation and skin conductance response[6,7,8]. Here we explore whether the same neural system underlies these similar response patterns, focusing on the involvement of the amygdala.

During image acquisition, subjects had an electrode attached to their wrists that they were told would be used to deliver an uncomfortable, but not painful, mild electric shock. They were told to expect no more than three shocks and no less than one shock during the experiment. Three types of stimuli representing the three trial types were presented: a blue square, a yellow square, and the word 'rest.' Subjects were told that they might receive a shock when one of the colored squares were presented (the threat condition), but not when the other colored square was presented (the safe condition) or the word rest (the rest condition) were presented. There were five 18-second trials of each type. Skin conductance responses (SCR) were recorded. No

Fig. 1. Threat versus safe activation. (a) Contrast composite map of activation for first-half threat versus safe (*n* = 12). Comparison is averaged BOLD signal across all 5 blocks for the first 6 (of 12) images during threat versus safe trials. Across subjects, significantly active pixels were observed in the left dorsal amygdala (Talairach coordinates, –13, –5, –26), extending into the basal forebrain (–8, –5, –18), the left insula (1.5, –5, –44) and right premotor cortex (37, –5, 32). All coordinates listed are for the largest area of activation within a region,

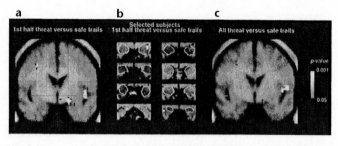

although additional areas of activation were observed within some regions. The slice represented in this composite is the slice (of three acquired) that covered the largest portion of the amygdala. (b) Representative individual subjects for the first-half threat versus safe comparison. The slice shown for each subject was chosen from among the three slices acquired that covered portions of the amygdala (outlined in green). Individual subjects showed regions of activation consistent with the group composite. However, most subjects also showed regions of activation in the anterior cingulate, the right insula and the striatum. (c) Contrast composite map for the total threat versus safe comparison, including responses in the second-half of the trials. Activation in amygdala is diminished when these later responses are included, suggesting an attenuation of amygdala activation within the 18-s trial. Other regions of activation do not show a similar pattern of attenuation.

shocks were administered in this study. The experimental design was chosen to obtain maximal behavioral effects based on previous research with similar tasks[7,8] and pilot studies.

RESULTS

To assess if the instructed fear task was successful in eliciting an arousal response consistent with a fear reaction, SCR was compared across the three trial types. There was a significant increase in SCR during the threat trials compared to rest. There was no difference in SCR between safe and rest (mean change in square-root-transformed SCR compared to rest baseline, threat, 0.098 µS; safe, 0.0069 µS; $F_{1,11}$ = 13.94, p > 0.01). In addition, subjective emotional responses were assessed after the imaging session. All subjects indicated that they thought they would receive a shock at some point during the threat stimulus, and all subjects reported feeling more anxious during the threat condition.

We then assessed if the amygdala showed greater activation during the threat trials than the safe trials. Two types of analyses were done. We averaged across all trials for each condition and compared activation patterns across conditions. We also conducted an analysis comparing the activation patterns across conditions for the average of the first half of each trial. This second analysis was done because we expected an attenuation of the amygdala response. Previous studies of both human neuroimaging[9,10,11] and electrophysiological recording from the amygdala in rats[12,13,14] have shown that the amygdala response attenuates over time. Two types of attenuation have been observed. Human and animal studies have shown across-trial attenuation in studies with a relatively large number of trials. Specifically, the amygdala response seems to attenuate after four to five presentations of a single conditioned stimulus in fear conditioning[10,12], or a few blocks of stimulus presentation in studies that display a series of similar but different stimuli, such as fearful faces[9]. In addition, studies with animals have shown within-trial attenuation of the amygdala response to a longer conditioned stimulus or stimulus presentation, with the maximal amygdala response occurring to the onset of an aversive stimulus[12,13,14]. In the present study, we had a single-threat stimulus with only five trials of this stimulus. Given the small number of trials, we did not expect significant across-trial attenuation of the amygdala response. However, the duration of the stimulus presentation in each trial was relatively long (18 seconds). Therefore,

we expected there might be some within-trial attenuation of the amygdala response. For this reason, we chose to examine the early amygdala response across all five of the trials for each condition.

There was significant activity in the left amygdala that extended to the basal forebrain when the first half of the threat trials was compared with the first half of safe trials (Fig. 1). It is sometimes hard to determine precise anatomy on composite activation and anatomical maps because of subject averaging, so we conducted an region-of-interest (ROI) analysis confined to the amygdala. This revealed that 11 of 12 subjects showed significant activity in the left amygdala (Fig. 1b). Only some of these subjects showed additional activation in the basal forebrain, suggesting the activation observed on the composite map may be primarily due to the amygdala. Although the group composite revealed left amygdala activity, the pattern of amygdala response varied somewhat across individuals, and 7 of 12 individuals showed less extensive but significant right amygdala activation. The separate analysis that included the total activation responses, not just those early in each trial, indicated that there was an attenuation of amygdala activation. There was relatively little amygdala/basal forebrain activation on the composite activation map when the analysis was extended to include the entire length of each trial. Additional analyses comparing the other conditions were also conducted. Although most subjects revealed less extensive amygdala activation when comparing first half of threat versus first half of rest trials, this was not significant on the composite analysis. A similar pattern was seen in the first half of threat versus first half of rest comparison for other brain regions in which activation was observed. There was no consistent pattern of activation in the amygdala or other regions when safe was compared to rest.

Although we were primarily interested in the response of the amygdala during instructed fear, and restricted our image acquisition to coronal slices covering the amygdala, there were additional regions of activation. We observed scattered activation in the striatum and prefrontal cortex, primarily premotor cortex, in 10 of 12 subjects. Activation was also observed in the anterior cingulate in 8 of 12 subjects. In all subjects, we observed robust activation of the insular cortex, extensive and strong in the left insula and somewhat more limited in the right insula. The activation in these regions did not show the same pattern of attenuation observed in the amygdala (Fig. 1a and c).

Fig. 2. Time course of amygdala activation. Functional time-course analysis by image number within each trial averaged across all 5 blocks. Average standardized scores of activation for significantly active pixels in early threat versus early safe comparison ($p < 0.05$) within the amygdala ($n = 11$), as defined by ROI analysis. The first image of the time course corresponds to the image acquired 3 s following stimulus onset, to control for the delay in hemodynamic response. Individual subjects' standardized activation levels are calculated relative to their overall average magnitude of BOLD signal throughout image acquisition. These averaged z-scores were submitted to a two-factor (condition × image number) ANOVA. A significant effect for condition was found ($F_{2,20} = 9.41$, $p < 0.01$) and a significant interaction between condition and trial was found ($F_{22,220} = 2.01$, $p = 0.001$). To investigate the effects of attenuation across image number (over trials), time-course data were collapsed into first half (images 1–6) and second half (images 7–12). Pairwise t-tests between first-half threat and first-half safe trials revealed a significant difference ($t = 10.16$, $p < 0.01$), whereas second-half threat trials were found to be indistinguishable from second-half safe trials ($t = 0.213$, $p > 0.85$). A comparison between first-half safe and first-half rest trials also revealed a significant difference ($t = -4.30$, $p < 0.01$), whereas second half-safe trials were not found to differ from second-half rest trials ($t = 0.183$, $p > 0.85$).

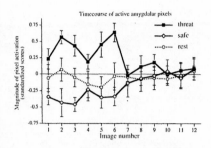

Timecourse of active amygdalar pixels

Legend: ■ threat, ○ safe, ○ rest

y-axis: Magnitude of pixel activation (standardized z scores)
x-axis: Image number

To examine the pattern and attenuation of the amygdala response across each trial type, a time-course analysis was conducted on the significantly active pixels within the amygdala (**Fig. 2**). The response during threat trials was greater than during safe and rest trials, but only early in the first nine seconds of the block. This result is consistent with other findings showing attenuation of the amygdala response across time, suggesting this response may be primarily linked to signaling the emotional properties of a stimulus[10,12–14]. In addition, there was a tendency for a reduction in amygdala activation during the safe condition compared to rest early in the block. The mean percent signal change between early rest and early safe conditions was 0.26%, compared to a 1.1% signal change between early threat and early safe. This slight decrease in amygdala activation during the safe trials is consistent with animal studies showing a decrease in amygdala response to stimuli that are thought to represent safety[15].

To evaluate the relationship between the strength of the arousal response as measured by SCR and activation when the aversive event is only anticipated, we correlated the difference in the SCR response to threat trials compared to safe trials across subjects with the magnitude of activation within the amygdala, insular cortex and anterior cingulate, as defined by ROI analysis. There was a strong and significant correlation between the SCR response across the entire block and left amygdala activation ($r = 0.59$, **Fig. 3a**); the right amygdala showed a non-significant correlation ($r = 0.14$). Unlike amygdala activation that was greater in the first half of each block and attenuated over time, the SCR response was maintained over the entire block. This decoupling of the temporal pattern of the amygdala activation and correlated SCR response has been reported previously[10] and suggests that the amygdala activation is related to this arousal response, but not critical for the response. In addition, there was a significant correlation between the magnitude of activation in the insula and SCR (**Fig. 3b**). This correlation was stronger than that between amygdala activation and SCR, suggesting that the insula may also be important in the expression of the fear response in this task. Unlike the lateralized response of the amygdala, this correlation was significant for both the right ($r = 0.58$) and left insula ($r = 0.86$), even though the left insula showed greater activation overall, as well as higher correlation with SCR. There was no significant correlation between activation of the anterior cingulate and SCR.

Discussion

In the instructed fear protocol, subjects showed an arousal response, consistent with fear, to a stimulus that they were told might be linked to an aversive event. The presentation of this stimulus led to activation of the amygdala. Across subjects, the magnitude of the amygdala response was correlated with SCR, suggesting that this amygdala activation is related to the expression of the fear response. Unlike previous studies that showed activation of the amygdala in response to stimuli that were linked to aversive events either presented or imagined[9–11,16], subjects in the present study had no direct experience with the aversive event. These results suggest that the amygdala is involved in the expression of the fear response in the instructed fear task, which models a common way humans learn about the emotional properties of stimuli.

When we compare the present results using the instructed fear protocol to our previous study with fear conditioning[10], there are several similarities, but also several important differences. In both studies, we found activation of the amygdala that attenuates across time and is correlated with the strength of the fear response. In fear conditioning, this correlation was carried by the right amygdala; in the present study, activation of the left amygdala was predominant and more strongly correlated with the fear response.

What might account for these differences in laterality in conditioned versus instructed fear? In the instructed fear task, subjects are aware of the aversive nature of the stimulus before scanning. A previous study has suggested that the left amygdala responds when subjects are aware of the aversive nature of the stimulus, whereas the right amygdala responds when subjects are unaware of this contingency[17]. Although subjects in the fear conditioning study were aware of the conditioned stimulus from the beginning of the study, they were unaware that it predicted an aversive event for the first few trails. However, after a few trials of fear conditioning, subjects acquired an awareness of the aversive properties of the conditioned stimulus. However, in spite of this awareness, the activation did not switch to the left amygdala in the later trials of fear conditioning.

A second possibility for the difference in laterality of the amygdala response across these two protocols is the nature of learned material and the type of representation that is evoked. Studies with brain-injured patients have shown that the right amygdala may modulate the fear response when the aversive properties of the

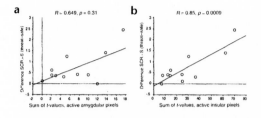

a $R = 0.649, p = 0.31$ **b** $R = 0.85, p = 0.0009$

Sum of t-values, active amygdalar pixels

Sum of t-values, active insular pixels

Fig. 3. Correlation between SCR and activation strength for amygdala and insular cortex. Correlation between measures of autonomic arousal (difference SCR) and (a) magnitude of amygdalar functional activation and (b) magnitude of insular functional activation. Difference SCR is expressed as mean threat SCR minus mean safe SCR. Regional magnitude of functional activation was obtained by summing the t-values of all significantly active pixels within an ROI for each brain structure for early threat versus early safe trial comparison ($p < 0.05$).

stimulus are visual in nature[18], whereas the left amygdala may modulate the fear response when the aversive nature of the stimulus is learned through verbal communication, as in the instructed fear protocol[19]. Visually aversive stimuli elicit an immediate, negative representation that is not dependent on elaboration by the subjects. When the aversive nature of the stimulus is learned verbally, the subjects must generate a mental representation of the aversive event because it does not exist in the immediate environment. The difference in laterality of amygdala activation may reflect the extent to which the representation elicited by the fearful stimulus depends on elaboration and interpretation by the subjects.

The insular cortex is another region that was active in both the fear conditioning and the instructed fear protocols. There are numerous, reciprocal connections between the amygdala and insular cortex[20]. However, the properties of the insula response across these two protocols differed. In instructed fear, we observed extensive and strong activation of the left insula and additional activation in the right insula. This insular cortex activation was present from the early trials and was strongly correlated with the strength of the arousal response. In fear conditioning, the insula activation was less robust and appeared only after the initial pairings of the neutral and aversive events, when subjects had become aware of the conditioned stimulus–unconditioned stimulus contingency. At that point, the subjects may have been consciously anticipating the aversive shock, consistent with a previous study suggesting the insular cortex is involved in the anticipation of pain[21].

The present results, when compared to fear conditioning, suggest that the insular cortex may be more integral in the instructed fear task in which the representation of the aversive properties of the event is purely cognitive in nature. It has been suggested that there are two parallel cortical and subcortical pathways for conveying information about the aversive nature of a stimulus to the amygdala[22]. A previous study[23] suggested that the insula is involved in conveying cortical somatosensory information to the amygdala. In the present study, the aversive stimulus was the imagined discomfort of receiving a shock that was never experienced. We suggest that this imagined and anticipated discomfort results in a cortical representation of fear, which may be relayed to the amygdala via the insula.

Finally, in both fear conditioning and instructed fear, we observed similar patterns of activation in the premotor cortex, striatum and anterior cingulate. The observed activation in premotor cortex and striatum may be related to subtle tensing that occurs when shock is anticipated[10,11]. Activation in the anterior cingulate has been linked to attentional processes, as well as evaluation of emotional stimuli[24,25].

In the present study, we examined the neural substrates involved when subjects encountered an event that was linked to an aversive outcome through verbal communication, in the absence of aversive experience. Fears that are imagined and

anticipated but never experienced can have a profound influence on everyday behavior. In spite of the known involvement of the amygdala in emotional learning, the acquisition of this cognitive representation of the aversive nature of an event does not seem to depend on the amygdala[4]. However, the present study suggests that the left amygdala may be involved in the expression of the fear response when this type of fearful event is encountered. The insular cortex may be involved in conveying this cortical representation of fear to the amygdala.

METHODS

Subjects. Twelve subjects (six female, six male) were submitted to final analysis. A total of 22 subjects were run. Five subjects were excluded because center-of-mass motion during scan exceeded our criterion of 0.33 pixels in any direction. One subject's functional data exhibited severe artifactual activations outside the head, and was also excluded. Two subjects were excluded from analysis as being SCR 'non-responders.' This is characterized in this case by a lack of discernible variability in the subject's SCR output waveform, which can be due to a number of factors. Two additional subjects were also excluded because of SCR recording equipment failure and functional data recording media failure, respectively. All subjects gave informed consent.

Behavioral task. Subjects were asked to lie in an MRI scanner, and electrodes were attached to their left wrist and the second and fourth fingers of the left hand. They were told that the electrodes attached to their fingers would be used to record their SCR during the experiment, but they would not feel any sensation from the electrodes on their fingers. They were told that the electrode attached to their wrist would be used to deliver a mild electric shock during the threat condition and that there would be between one and three shocks delivered throughout the study. The colors representing threat and safe were counterbalanced across subjects. Each trial lasted 18 seconds. The blue and yellow squares had digits presented in the middle of the square that counted down the seconds in the trial from 18 to 1. Each trial type was presented five times. Each block of three trials began with a rest trial. This was followed by a threat and a safe trial, the order of which was counterbalanced across subjects, but did not vary across blocks for an individual subject. After five trials of each type, the experiment ended. The subjects were unaware that the shock electrode on the wrist was not attached to any stimulating device. They were told at the end of the experiment that they were in a non-shock condition. They were asked to indicate whether they thought they would receive a shock in the experiment. All subjects indicated that they believed a shock would be delivered. The subjects were then debriefed.

SCR acquisition and analysis. SCR telemetry was acquired through constant voltage (0.5 V) excitation method with Ag-AgCl electrodes attached to the middle phalanges of the second and fourth digits of the left hand (BIOPAC Systems, Santa Barbara, California). Lafayette Instruments electrode gel was used as an electrolyte (Lafayette, Indiana). Electrode leads were tightly twisted, to minimize electromagnetic interference, and were connected to shielded leads. Lead shield was grounded through an RF filter at an MRI room to control room junction. The SCR signal was amplified and recorded with a BIOPAC Systems skin conductance module connected to an Apple Powerbook 3400c running AcqKnowledge software (BIOPAC Systems). Data were recorded continuously at a rate of 200 samples per second. Off-line analysis of SCR waveforms was done using AcqKnowledge software. Specifically, waveforms were low-pass filtered (Blackman –61 dB, 7 Hz cutoff) to reduce high frequency noise induced by electromagnetic interference. SCR waveforms were smoothed with a smoothing factor of 30 points. Average, tonic means of SCR levels were then calculated for each 18-s block.

fMRI acquisition. Before image acquisition, the anterior and posterior commisures were localized for slice orientation. Whole-brain sagittal T1-weighted anatomical images were acquired using a spin echo-pulse sequence (5-mm contiguous slices; TE, 12 ms; TR, –600 ms; matrix size, 256 × 192; in-plane resolution, 1.56 × 1.56 mm; FOV, 40 × 40 cm). Five 6-mm coronal slices (slice skip, 2 mm) were then prescribed perpendicular to the AC-PC line, with the middle slice centered on the amygdala. Amygdala localization was accomplished by placing the middle (third) slice 4–5 mm posterior to the anterior commisure in the midsagittal view, and assessing the position of the amygdala in the subsequent coronal sections using anatomical landmarks and a standardized atlas[26]. During the study, echoplanar functional images were acquired using an asymmetric spin echo pulse sequence (TE, 30 ms; echo offset, 30 ms; TR, 1.5 s; in-plane resolution, 3.125 × 3.125 mm; matrix size, 128 × 64; FOV, 40 × 20 cm). These scanning parameters yielded a total of 192 functional images per slice for each experimental condition.

fMRI analysis. The experimental task was a standard block design consisting of five intermixed trials of each stimulus condition, rest, safe and threat, resulting in 15 trials. During each trial, 12 images were acquired over 18 s (TR, 1.5 s). There were two types of analyses that differed only in the portion of the trial that was included. In the first-half analysis, subjects' functional activation was averaged across the first six images of each trial of each condition (allowing 3 s for the delay in the hemodynamic response). In the total analysis, all 12 images in each trial were included. Resultant t-maps were generated by subtraction to reveal differential activation between conditions. Pixels showing significant differential activation ($p < 0.05$) were used in subsequent ROI and time-course analysis. The SPMs and the anatomic images were transformed by in-plane transformation into a proportional three-dimensional grid[26]. To obtain p-values for significantly active pixels across subjects, a contrast composite map was generated using a randomization test to create a distribution of task-related t-values[27]. The p-value for each pixel was overlaid upon a mean anatomic image. Only significantly active pixels are displayed.

fMRI ROI and correlation analysis. For each subject, ROI analyses were conducted on the amygdala, insular cortex and anterior cingulate. All ROI analyses were done on data obtained from the first-half threat versus safe trial comparison. The specified regions were first outlined on the three anatomical images acquired per subject that covered portions of the of the amygdala. The functional maps of threat-safe were then superimposed on the anatomical images to identify active pixels within these regions. To calculate the correlation between arousal response and activation, the two subject variables submitted to the regression, sum of t-values and difference SCR were obtained as follows. The magnitude of t-values for significantly active pixels (t-value; $p < 0.05$; cluster value, 0) occurring within each ROI was summed[28]. Tonic SCR means of threat and safe for each epoch were obtained from subjects' low-pass-filtered and smoothed SCR waveforms, and averaged across epochs. Subtracting these two values yielded threat-safe SCR. Eleven of twelve subjects were submitted to the regression analysis. One subject was excluded because of a highly uncharacteristic SCR waveform that occurred in the latter half of image acquisition, which may have been the result of equipment malfunction or electrode movement. An additional regression analysis was done identically to the one described above except the strength of amygdala activation was assessed by summing the number of active pixels within a region (as opposed to summing the t-values of these pixels). Similar results were obtained with both methods, so only the results of the first analyses are reported.

ACKNOWLEDGEMENTS

The authors acknowledge the inspiration of Charles Oakley. We also thank M. Nordan and K. LaBar for work on a pilot study. This research was supported by McDonnell-Pew Program in Cognitive Neuroscience 97-26 and National Institutes of Health grants MH50812 to E.A.P. and NS33332 to J.C.G.

RECEIVED 2 AUGUST 2000; ACCEPTED 16 JANUARY 2001

1. Davis, M. Neurobiology of fear responses: the role of the amygdala. *J. Neuropsychiatry Clin. Neurosci.* 9, 382–402 (1997).
2. Kapp, B. S., Pascoe, J. P., & Bixler, M. A. in *The Neuropsychology of Memory* (eds. Butters, N. & Squire, L. S.) 473–488 (Guilford, New York, 1984).
3. LeDoux, J. E. *The Emotional Brain* (Simon & Schuster, New York, 1996)
4. Bechara, A. *et al.* Double dissociation of conditioning and declarative knowledge relative to the amygdala and hippocampus in humans. *Science* 269, 1115–1118 (1995)
5. LaBar, K. S., LeDoux, J. E., Spencer, D. D. & Phelps, E. A. Impaired fear conditioning following unilateral temporal lobectomy in humans. *J. Neurosci.* 15, 6846–6855 (1995).
6. Deane, G. E. Human heart rate responses during experimentally induced anxiety. *J. Exp. Psychol.* 61, 489–493 (1961).
7. Grillon, C., Ameli, R., Woods, S. W., Merikangas, K. & Davis, M. Fear potentiated startle in humans: effects of anticipatory anxiety on the acoustic blink reflex. *Psychophysiology* 28, 588–595 (1991).
8. Grillon, C. & Davis, M. Effects of stress and shock anticipation on prepulse inhibition of the startle reflex. *Psychophysiology* 34, 511–517 (1997).
9. Breiter, H. C. *et al.* Response and habituation of the human amygdala during visual processing of facial expression. *Neuron* 17, 875–887 (1996).
10. LaBar, K. S., Gatenby, J. C., Gore, J. C., LeDoux, J. E. & Phelps, E. A. Human amygdala activation during conditioned fear acquisition and extinction: a mixed trial fMRI study. *Neuron* 20, 937–945 (1998).
11. Buchel, C., Morris, J., Dolan, R. J. & Friston, K. J. Brain systems mediating aversive conditioning: an event-related fMRI study. *Neuron* 20, 947–957 (1998).
12. Quirk G. J., Armony, J. L. & LeDoux, J. E. Fear conditioning enhances different temporal components of tone-evoked spike trains in auditory cortex and lateral amygdala. *Neuron* 19, 613–624 (1997).
13. Pascoe, J. P. & Kapp, B. S. Electrophysiological characteristics of amygdaloid central nucleus neurons in the awake rabbit. *Brain Res. Bull.* 14, 331–338 (1985).
14. Maeda, H. Morimoto, H. & Yanagimoto, K. Response characteristics of amygdaloid neurons provoked by emotionally significant environmental stimuli in cats, with special reference to response durations. *Can. J. Physiol. Pharmacol.* 71, 374–378 (1993).
15. Collins, D. R. & Pare, D. Reciprocal changes in the firing probability of lateral and central medial amygdala neurons. *J. Neurosci.* 19, 836–844 (1999).
16. Rauch, S. L., van der Kolk, B. A., Fisler, R. E. & Alpert N. M. A symptom provocation study of posttraumatic stress disorder using positron emission tomography and script-driven imagery. *Arch. Gen. Psychiatry* 53, 380–387 (1996).
17. Morris, J. S., Ohmann, A. & Dolan, R. J. Conscious and unconscious emotional learning in the human amygdala. *Nature* 393, 467–470 (1998).
18. Angrilli A. *et al.* Startle reflex and emotion modulation impairment after a right amygdala lesion. *Brain* 119, 1991–2000 (1997).
19. Funayama, E. S., Grillon, C. G., Davis, M. & Phelps, E. A. A double dissociation in the affective modulation of startle in humans: effects of unilateral temporal lobectomy. *J. Cogn. Neurosci.* (in press).
20. Shi, C. J. & Cassell, M. D. Cascade projections from somatosensory cortex to the rat basolateral amygdala via the parietal insular cortex. *J. Comp. Neurol.* 399, 469–491 (1998).
21. Ploghaus, A. *et al.* Dissociating pain from its anticipation in the human brain. *Science* 284, 1979–1981 (1999).
22. Romanski, L. M. & LeDoux, J. E. Equipotentiality of thalamo-amygdala and thalamo-cortico-amygdala circuits in auditory fear conditioning. *J. Neurosci.* 12, 4501–4509 (1992).
23. Shi, C.-J. & Davis, M. Pain pathways involved in fear conditioning measured with fear-potentiated startle: lesion studies. *J. Neurosci.* 19, 420–430 (1999).
24. Bush, G. *et al.* The counting Stroop: an interference task specialized for functional neuroimaging: validation study with functional MRI. *Hum. Brain Mapp.* 6, 270–282 (1998)
25. Lane, R. D., Fink G. R., Gereon, R., Chau, P. M. & Dolan R. J. Neural activation during selective attention to subjective emotional responses. *Neuroreport* 8, 3969–3972 (1997).
26. Talairach, J. & Tournoux, P. *Co-Planar Stereotaxic Atlas of the Human Brain* (Thieme, New York, 1988).
27. Bullmore, E. *et al.* Statistical methods of estimation and interference for functional MR image analysis. *Magn. Reson. Med.* 35, 261–277 (1996).
28. Constable, R. T. *et al.* Quantifying and comparing region-of-interest activation patterns in functional brain imaging: methodology considerations. *Mag. Reson. Imaging* 16, 289–300 (1998).

441

Neurobiological Perspectives on Social Phobia: From Affiliation to Zoology

Murray B. Stein

Social phobia (or "social anxiety disorder") is a prevalent condition that has been the subject of increased scrutiny in recent years. The purpose of this paper is to review the neurobiology of social phobia. It is apparent from the extant literature that this disorder is poorly understood from a neurobiological perspective. There are nonetheless a number of clinical and preclinical observations which, at times, converge to illuminate areas worthy of further study. Included in this category are suggestive findings of central serotonergic dysregulation in social phobia, response to serotonin reuptake inhibitors in social phobia, and the role of serotonergic function in septohippocampal models of anxiety. Abnormalities in central dopaminergic function are also posited, supported to some extent by recent neuroimaging findings. There are in addition a number of animal and human behavioral models in existence that may be relevant to the study of social phobia. Included in this category are models of social dominance in wild baboons, social affiliation in the prairie vole, and behavioral inhibition to the unfamiliar in childhood. Newer technologies that are likely to play a major role in the delineation of the neural circuitry (e.g., functional magnetic resonance imaging and heritability (e.g., molecular genetics) of social phobia are discussed. Finally, an interactive role for biology and experience in the expression of social phobia is considered. Biol Psychiatry 1998;44:1277–1285 © 1998 Society of Biological Psychiatry

Key Words: Serotonin, dopamine, neuropeptide, shyness, social anxiety

What Is Social Phobia?

S ocial phobia (also known as "social anxiety disorder") is characterized by a fear of situations where the individual may be exposed to the scrutiny of others (American Psychiatric Association 1994). The hallmark of this disorder is a fear of negative evaluation. Specifically,

From the Department of Psychiatry, University of California San Diego, La Jolla, California.
Address reprint requests to Murray B. Stein, MD, Department of Psychiatry (0985), University of California San Diego, 9500 Gilman Drive, La Jolla, CA 92093-0985.
Received April 23, 1998; revised July 15, 1998; accepted July 24, 1998.

the person fears that he or she will say or do something humiliating or that they may show signs of anxiety or embarrassment in front of others. As a result, social situations are either avoided, or endured with distress. In its severe forms, social phobia may therefore become a disabling disorder, limiting achievement in education or employment and eroding self-esteem and confidence (Schneier et al 1994; den Boer 1997). Patients may also become socially isolated, depressed, and demoralized, and some may turn to alcohol in an attempt to self-medicate (Schneier et al 1989; Merikangas and Angst 1995; Schneier et al 1992).

Although experiencing some degree of anxiety in social situations is neither atypical nor pathological, social phobia is distinguished by the intensity of the anxiety that is experienced and by the accompanying distress or interference in functioning. Similarly, whereas shyness is neither uncommon nor necessarily pathological, the shyness exhibited by many social phobics is quantitatively (and some would argue, qualitatively, though this is debatable) distinct. Thus, although the study of biologic mechanisms involved in the mediation of these individual differences (i.e., social anxiety; shyness) may be informative with regard to the understanding of social phobia, this is not necessarily the case. This is discussed further below.

Subtypes of Social Phobia

Most authorities now agree upon the existence of at least two subtypes of social phobia. The first type, alternatively referred to as "discrete," "specific," or "nongeneralized" social phobia, is the stereotypical version of social phobia. It is usually confined to a fear of one or a few performance situations, of which the most common is speaking in front of an audience (Schneier et al 1992; Stein et al 1996). The second type, referred to in DSM-IV as "generalized" social phobia, involves fear of a broad array of social situations, typically including both social interactional (e.g., speaking to peers over lunch; going to parties; asking a teacher for help) and performance situations (e.g., speaking in public; performing in front of an audience). It is the generalized type of social phobia that overlaps conceptually and definitionally with avoidant personality

0006-3223/98/$19.00
PII S0006-3223(98)00265-0

disorder (Brown et al 1995; Herbert et al 1992; Hofmann et al 1995). Although there is a paucity of research comparing the generalized and discrete subtypes along any biological parameters, the available evidence (e.g., comparison of cardiovascular responses to public speaking, see discussion below) suggests that these two subtypes of social phobia are sufficiently distinct that it would be prudent to study them independently. In this paper, the focus is on the best-studied of the two subtypes, generalized social phobia, unless otherwise indicated.

Neurobiology of Social Phobia

Only in the last decade have investigators begun to study the neurobiology of social phobia. As a consequence, relatively little is known at this time about the biology of this disorder. I will review what is known about the neurobiology of social phobia and use the clues provided by these data as a basis from which to speculate more broadly about which neural systems and circuits may be important to study further, and why.

Autonomic Nervous System Functioning in Social Phobia

Levin et al (1993) reported on heart rate and catecholamine responses to a public speaking challenge in patients with social phobia and healthy comparison subjects. They found that patients with nongeneralized social phobia had excessive heart rate responses to this task compared to generalized social phobic and healthy control subjects. Heimberg et al (1990) also used a behavioral challenge paradigm and similarly found that patients with generalized social phobia had less of a heart rate response than did public-speaking (nongeneralized) social phobics. We performed an orthostatic challenge in patients with social phobia, panic disorder, and healthy control subjects wherein we found that patients with social phobia had higher plasma norepinephrine levels before and after the orthostatic challenge compared to the panic disorder or healthy control groups (Stein et al 1992). This finding was not, however, replicated in a subsequent study where subtle evidence of parasympathetic—but not sympathetic—dysfunction was observed in generalized social phobic patients (Stein et al 1994).

At the present time, one may conclude that there is at best suggestive evidence to support the presence of autonomic nervous system dysfunction in some forms of social phobia, but further research is needed. Unfortunately, none of the aforementioned studies point to particular brain circuits that may be dysfunctional in social phobia. In panic disorder and posttraumatic stress disorder investigators have begun to use fear-potentiated startle as a means

to study brain functioning within well-defined neural systems (Davis et al 1993; Grillon et al 1994; Morgan et al 1995a). In some such investigations, the effects of noradrenergic "amplifiers" such as yohimbine have been used to help define a role for noradrenergic functioning in these disorders (Morgan et al 1995b). Surprisingly, the noradrenergic system has been little studied in social phobia, despite the fact that "anxiety attacks" in social situations are commonly a feature of the disorder, and despite the fact that social phobia is not infrequently comorbid with panic disorder (Kessler et al 1998). The application of these techniques (e.g., yohimbine challenge; fear-potentiated startle) to the study of social phobia should be undertaken in an effort to illuminate potential differences between the anxiety disorders in these response dimensions.

Respiratory Function and Carbon Dioxide Sensitivity in Social Phobia

A well-established finding is that patients with panic disorder are sensitive to the panic-provoking effects of CO_2 inhalation (Woods et al 1986; Papp et al 1993a; Gorman et al 1994; Perna et al 1994). This observation is central to many of the biological theories of panic disorder pathophysiology (Klein 1993; see article by Coplan and Lydiard in this issue). In fact, this characteristic has been so well replicated that CO_2 responsivity has been examined as a potential biologic risk factor for the disorder. Perna and colleagues have shown that first-degree family members of patients with panic disorder are more likely than first-degree relatives of control subjects to experience panic attacks during 35% CO_2 inhalation (Perna et al 1995). They also found that panic disorder patients who panic in response to 35% CO_2 inhalation are more likely to have a positive family history of panic disorder than patients who are 35% CO_2-nonresponsive (Perna et al 1996). These intriguing observations have led to suppositions about CO_2-responsiveness as a key biological characteristic that might be inherited in panic disorder.

Patients with generalized anxiety disorder, obsessive–compulsive disorder, and animal-specific phobias have sensitivity similar to healthy control subjects (Perna et al 1995; Verburg et al 1995; Papp et al 1993b). Given the plethora of data in panic disorder, a disorder with which social phobia is frequently comorbid, it is surprising that CO_2 sensitivity has been so little studied in social phobia. Three studies have examined 35% CO_2 sensitivity in social phobic patients, with varying results. The first two studies reported rates of CO_2-induced panic in social phobic patients higher than those in healthy control subjects, but lower than those in patients with panic disorder (Gorman et al 1990; Papp et al 1993b). In the latest study, investigators examined 35% CO_2 sensitivity in five groups of subjects: 16 patients with panic disorder, 16 patients with social phobia, 13 patients with both social phobia and panic disorder, 7 patients with social phobia and sporadic unexpected panic attacks, and healthy control subjects (Caldirola et al 1997). The subtype of social phobia was not specified in this report. All subjects were tested in a double-blind, randomized, crossover design in which a 35% $CO_2/65\%$ O_2 and room air were alternately inhaled through a self-administration mask. The investigators found that all four patients groups had stronger anxiogenic reactions (whether measured as an increase in state anxiety or as the proportion of subjects who experienced panic attacks) than the healthy control subjects to 35% CO_2. If replicated in still larger samples, including patients with generalized social phobia, then CO_2 hypersensitivity might be considered part of the pathophysiology of a spectrum of disorders that links panic disorder and social phobia. This deserves further consideration and further study that may usefully extend to the investigation of first-degree relatives of patients with social phobia.

Neuroimaging in Social Phobia

Two studies using magnetic resonance spectroscopy (MRS) have found abnormal choline metabolite levels in patients with social phobia (Davidson et al 1993; Tupler et al 1997). This may represent an abnormality in cell membrane composition or function in the disorder, though this remains to be replicated and further explained. A brain single photon emission computerized tomography (SPECT) study in generalized social phobia failed to reveal evidence of a focal abnormality in cerebral blood flow (Stein and Leslie 1996); however, a recent SPECT study using a specific ligand for the dopamine transporter site found markedly reduced binding to the basal ganglia of patients with generalized social phobia (Tiihonen et al 1997). Given the high rates of social phobia seen in a condition known to be associated with abnormal brain dopaminergic function—Parkinson's disease (Stein et al 1990)—this finding is particularly intriguing. If replicated, it may point to the importance of regionally altered dopaminergic function in the etiopathology of generalized social phobia.

To date, there have been no published positron-emission tomographic (PET) or functional magnetic resonance imaging (fMRI) studies in social phobia, although these are ongoing at several laboratories around the world. It is anticipated that these studies will add to our understanding of the role of particular neural systems in the mediation of self-consciousness, social anxiety, and ultimately, social phobia.

Neuroendocrine Function in Social Phobia

As a stress hormone, it has been posited that cortisol levels would be elevated in patients with social phobia. In fact, the two studies that have examined urinary or plasma cortisol levels and/or responses to dexamethasone have found these aspects of the hypothalamic–pituitary–adrenal (HPA) axis to be normal in patients with social phobia (Potts et al 1992; Uhde et al 1994). These findings suggest that shyness in children and social phobia in adulthood are discontinuous (see below for more extensive discussion of this topic) in that shy children tend to have higher salivary cortisol levels than their nonshy peers (Flinn and England 1997; Schmidt et al 1997). The complicated neural regulation of the HPA axis renders a finding of hypercortisolism (or, more correctly, the lack thereof) in social phobia completely nonspecific with regard to implicating particular neural systems or substrates. Still, the possible relevance of social dominance theory to social phobia deserves further consideration, in part because it attempts to explain the interactive effects between milieu, "stress" system (e.g., HPA axis) responsiveness, and social interactional behavior.

Hypercortisolemia, Social Dominance in Primates, and Social Phobia

Sapolsky and colleagues have shown that social status and degree of social affiliation are associated with altered HPA axis functioning among free-ranging wild baboons (Sapolsky et al 1997; Virgin and Sapolsky 1997). In those studies, socially subordinate baboons exhibited basal hypercortisolism as well as resistance to feedback inhibition with dexamethasone. Socially isolated animals also manifested basal hypercortisolism. As the authors indicate, "These studies cannot reveal whether there is any causality in this link (i.e., if hypercortisolism makes animals less socially affiliated or if social isolation stimulates adrenocortical secretion)" (Sapolsky et al 1997, p 1141). Still, as the authors point out, the extant stress literature would strongly support a causal interpretation of these data (Dimsdale et al 1999).

One might question whether social dominance in wild baboons can tell us anything about social phobia in humans. This is a reasonable question. Sapolsky doubts that HPA axis abnormalities cause the alterations in social behavior; rather, he posits that the physical and psychological demands of social submissiveness and social isolation cause the hypercortisolism (Sapolsky et al 1997). If this is the case, then primate social dominance cannot model the etiology of social phobia; individual differences that might predispose to being socially submissive do not enter the equation. Rather, these data may be able to model some of the consequences of being social phobic, i.e., What happens to an individual who experiences prolonged and repeated social anxiety and avoidance? The establishment of social submissiveness—which may be akin to what social phobics experience when exposed to or in anticipation of social situations—could result in sustained or episodic hypercortisolism, which could theoretically perpetuate or exacerbate the individual's propensity for social anxiety. There are animal data to support the notion that hypercortisolism can result in perpetuation of the fear-related behaviors through amygdala kindling (Rosen et al 1996) or through other biological mechanisms (Takahashi and Rubin 1993). To the extent that these animal data can be applied to humans, they support a mutually reinforcing link between "experience" and "biology" that deserves further scrutiny in the study of social phobia. These data, once better understood, may illuminate a neurobiological basis for the behavioral finding that social fear and avoidance form part of a vicious circle that rules the lives of socially phobic individuals.

Interestingly, socially subordinate male baboons have also been noted to have lower insulinlike growth factor I (IGF-I) levels than their socially dominant peers (Sapolsky and Spencer 1997). This finding may help explain the association between short stature and social phobia that has been observed in some studies (Stabler et al 1996).

The Neurobiology of Social Affiliation

While on the topic of animal models of social affiliation and social attachment, it should be noted that other models may be of some relevance to the study of social phobia. As reviewed by Insel (1997), oxytocin and vasopressin are believed to be involved in the central mediation of attachment behaviors. Most of these studies have been conducted in the prairie vole, an animal that seems to thrive on social contact (Insel 1992; Winslow et al 1993). At present, the relevance of these neuropeptides to human attachment behaviors remains to be determined. Insel states that "there is not a single circuit, but there are specific neural pathways that repeatedly emerge as critical for reproductive behaviors as well as attachment" (Insel 1997, p 733). Given the anatomic specificity of these circuits, it is doubtful that the study of basal or stimulated plasma or cerebrospinal fluid oxytocin or vasopressin in patients with social phobia would be informative.

Insel suggests that "Pathways from the rostral hypothalamus to the ventral tegmental area may be critical for integrating social information with reward pathways, especially in highly affiliative species that respond to social stimuli as reinforcers" (Insel 1997, p 733). These pathways, in theory, might provide a conceptual link between the hypothetical "dopaminergic" dysfunction in social

phobia (see below) and the models of affiliative dysfunction posited here. To speculate further, one might develop a model of social phobia as an illness characterized by dysfunction within the system(s) that evaluate the risks and benefits of social affiliation. In other words, social phobia might be characterized by exaggerated appraisal of the "risks" involved in social interaction, in conjunction with dysfunction in systems that register the "reward" of such interactions.

It may indeed be worthwhile to consider further the relationship between social affiliation and social phobia, from both a phenomenological and a biological perspective. Most clinicians would rightly point out that social phobics do not suffer from a deficit in the ability to form attachments, nor in a reduced desire or capacity for social affiliation. On the contrary, social phobics seem to crave social affiliation and social approval, but their fear of rejection inhibits them from seeking out and sustaining such relationships. Thus, social phobia may not be related to disorders such as autism that are characterized by an inability to form normal social attachments. On the other hand, a recent study finding an increase in social phobia among first-degree relatives of autistic children throws this conclusion into question (Smalley et al 1995). If an autism–social phobia link is found in future studies, then it would be prudent to consider the emerging genetic findings in autism—and, more broadly, disorders of social attachment—as worthy candidates for study in social phobia. Included here would be the search for "functional variations in oxytocin or vasopressin receptor genes" (Insel 1997, p 734).

Brain Monaminergic Systems and Social Phobia

Serotonergic Function in Social Phobia

In the only study to employ a neuroendocrine challenge of multiple neurotransmitter systems in patients with social phobia, Tancer and colleagues (Tancer et al 1994/1995) administered levodopa (a dopamine precursor), clonidine (an alpha-2-adrenergic agonist), fenfluramine (a nonspecific serotonin-releasing agent), and placebo on four separate days. Social phobics displayed neuroendocrine responses that were indistinguishable from those of normal control subjects, with the exception of the cortisol response to fenfluramine. Social phobics displayed augmented cortisol responses to fenfluramine, an effect that is thought to predominantly reflect stimulation of central serotonin $(5\text{-HT})_{2C}$ receptors. This finding raises the possibility that social phobia may be characterized by abnormal functioning of brain serotonin receptors, though it is obviously impossible from this one study to identify precisely which systems or circuits may be involved.

Still, the idea that serotonergic function may be aberrant in anxiety disorder is not a new one, based in part on the known role of the predominantly serotonergically innervated septohippocampal system in the mediation of anxietylike behaviors in certain animal models (Gray 1992). Some primate social dominance models, discussed in greater detail above, also demonstrate an important contribution of serotonergic mechanisms to these social behaviors. In adult male vervet monkeys, drugs that enhance brain serotonergic activity (e.g., tryptophan or fluoxetine) promote the acquisition of social dominance (Raleigh et al 1991). Many of the anxiety disorders, including social phobia, are now known to be responsive to drugs that inhibit serotonin reuptake (SSRIs) in the brain (Katzelnick et al 1995; Bouwer and Stein 1998; Stein et al in press). Furthermore, a fascinating new study has suggested that SSRIs may increase sociability even in normal volunteers (Knutson et al 1998). Taken together, this wide-ranging set of studies hints strongly at an important role for serotonergic functioning in the pathophysiology of social phobia, but much further research is needed to delineate the nature of the serotonergic "lesion" in social phobia.

Dopaminergic Function in Social Phobia

I have already alluded above to several clinical phenomenologic (e.g, Stein et al 1990) and neuroimaging (Tiihonen et al 1997) studies that implicate a possible role for central dopaminergic functioning in social phobia. But there are additional data that support this hypothesis. Liebowitz et al (1987) were the first to postulate the existence of dopaminergic dysregulation in social phobia. They based their hypothesis on several lines of evidence, including findings of abnormal homovanillic acid (HVA) levels in spinal fluids of extraverted but not introverted depressives, as well as the observation that monoamine oxidase inhibitors (MAOIs) were effective in treating social phobia, but tricyclic antipressants (TCAs) were not (Liebowitz et al 1987). More recently, in addition to the SPECT study of Tiihonen et al (1997), there are PET data that may bear upon this discussion. If social dominance in primates can serve as a model for social phobia (and this is questionnable, as discussed above), then the finding that social status in monkeys is reflected in differences in dopamine D2 striatal density is of considerable interest (Grant et al 1998). This study supports the notion that differences in brain dopaminergic functioning may influence (or be influenced by—this remains to be determined) some very complex social behaviors that impinge upon what, in humans, we might refer to as "personality."

Along these lines, Farde et al (1997) recently demonstrated in a PET study that dopamine D2-receptor binding to the putamen (as measured with the radioligand [11C]

raclopride) was significantly associated with particular personality traits that may be relevant to social phobia. Specifically, they found that D2-receptor density strongly correlated with the Karolinska Scales of Personality "detachment" scale (one of 15 personality scales measured by this instrument) with $r = -.68, p < .001$, a correlation that remained significant even after Bonferroni correction for the 15 comparisons. The authors point out that the "detachment" scale includes the tendency to avoid giving and taking confidences and to avoid involvement with other people, and that individuals who scored high on this scale describe themselves as "cold, socially aloof and vindictive in their relationships." This study raises numerous questions, not the least of which is whether or not these D2-receptor findings in the putamen are generalizable to other behaviorally relevant brain regions (e.g., neocortex). For our purposes, we must also question whether or not "detachment" is actually a characteristic of individuals with generalized social phobia [or its "alter ego" on the Axis II dimension, avoidant personality disorder (Stein et al 1998)], or whether it is a personality trait that is more characteristic of individuals with various schizoid styles of relating. Fortunately, this is a question that further research will readily answer. Given the available evidence, one must say that a role for dysfunction within dopaminergic circuits in social phobia seems probable, and that efforts to further delineate the nature of this dysfunction are likely to be fruitful.

Familial Nature and Heritability in Social Phobia

Mancini et al (1996) found that children of social phobics are at increased risk for the development of social phobia and other anxiety disorders. Fyer et al (1993) found that social phobia was familial, and went on to note that this was limited to families of probands with generalized social phobia (Mannuzza et al 1995). We replicated and extended these findings by demonstrating that only the generalized type of social phobia (and its presumed Axis II counterpart, avoidant personality disorder) was elevated in frequency among the first-degree relatives of generalized social phobic probands (Stein et al 1998). The morbid risk for generalized social phobia in first-degree relatives was elevated to such a degree (approximately 10 times compared to relatives of not socially phobic comparison subjects), that a genetic contribution is almost irrefutable (Stein et al 1998). Several groups of investigators are currently conducting genetic studies in social phobia, but findings have yet to be published.

If, as suspected, there is a genetic risk for social phobia, then one must ask the question "What, precisely, is inherited?" Is it likely that the answer is "social phobia," a full-blown disorder? Probably not. A better candidate would be some sort of trait that predisposes to the development of anxiety disorders in general, or social phobia in particular. Involvement of amygdaloid circuitry is one strong possibility (see the paper by Davis in this issue), supported further by the findings of abnormal startle modulation among children of anxiety-disordered parents (Grillon et al 1997). Another strong possibility is that a predisposition to excessive shyness—a trait whose heritability is well-established (Rowe and Plomin 1977) — or an even broader tendency toward fearfulness, may be inherited. One excellent candidate in this regard is the behavioral construct known as "behavioral inhibition" (BI).

Kagan and colleagues define BI as a tendency in certain children to display fear and wariness in response to novel stimuli (Kagan et al 1987, 1988). BI children display long latencies to approach novel stimuli and stay in close contact with their mothers when exposed to such stimuli. BI is relatively stable over time and, moreover, seems to have a heritable component (Kagan et al 1987; Robinson et al 1992). There is evidence that BI may be a risk factor for (or an early manifestation of) the development of anxiety disorders in later life. In one study, children who remained inhibited throughout early childhood (i.e., those with so-called "stable" BI) were at risk for anxiety disorders in later childhood (Hirshfeld et al 1992). In another study, BI children of agoraphobic parents had high rates of anxiety disorders (Biederman et al 1990) and, in a related study, parents of BI children had high rates of anxiety disorders including panic disorder, agoraphobia, and social phobia (Rosenbaum et al 1993).

Taken together, these data provide a compelling rationale for positing BI (or a definitional variant thereof) as a precursor to the development of social phobia, and perhaps other anxiety disorders characterized by excessive levels of fear and/or avoidance (i.e., panic disorder, agoraphobia). Presumably, BI might be a temperamental foundation upon which particular life experiences mount to result in the expression of social phobia. Recent findings suggest that particular kinds of parent–child interactions [e.g., maternal criticism (Hirshfeld et al 1997)] may be among the kinds of experiences that play an important role in this regard. Additional studies will need to be conducted to confirm these hypotheses and to map out the pathways from which BI as a trait may develop into social phobia as a disorder. An admittedly speculative model for such a pathway is illustrated in Figure 1.

Conclusions

It is clear that we have a long way to go before we can speak with any authority about the "neurobiology of social

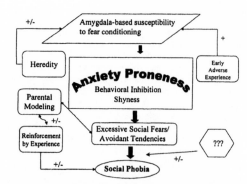

Figure 1. This is a hypothetical model for critical pathways involved in the development of social phobia. It is speculated that a hereditary propensity for "anxiety-proneness" exists, but that early adverse experiences may also play a role. It is posited that this "anxiety-proneness" may manifest as a tendency toward general fearfulness or toward excessive conditionability to fear-related stimuli, and that this propensity may be neuranatomically based within circuitry involving component(s) of the amygdala. This "anxiety-proneness" may be expressed behaviorally by the constructs of shyness or behavioral inhibition, and may be accentuated [+] (or mitigated [−]) on the basis of contributions from the environment (e.g., parental modeling; negative reinforcement provided by the anxiety-reducing effects of avoidance, or positive reinforcement provided by successful or pleasurable social experiences), which result in a greater or lesser tendency to exhibit social fears and social avoidance. Some individuals, for unknown reasons, go beyond the level of social fears and social avoidance to develop social phobia, which by definition is a pathologic condition.

phobia." In this review, several animal (e.g., social dominance in primates; social affiliation and neuropeptides) and human (e.g., behavioral inhibition) models were discussed that offer potential as a means to further explore and better understand the pathophysiology of social phobia. Shortly, the use of receptor-specific PET and SPECT ligands will offer the opportunity to study brain dopamine and serotonin functioning with great neuroanatomic precision. The use of functional neuroimaging techniques (fMRI) during the performance of disorder-relevant neuropsychologic tasks [e.g., visual processing of facial expression (Morris et al 1996)] promises to elucidate the neural circuitry of social anxiety and "self-consciousness." Further on the horizon, it is anticipated that behavioral genetic and molecular genetic approaches will clarify some of the risk factors for the development of social phobia. It is likely that these risk factors will characterize the "genotype" for the disorder, and that they will ultimately be found to operate in conjunction with particular classes of experience to result in the expression of the "phenotype," social phobia.

BIOL PSYCHIATRY 1283
1998;44:1277-1285

The author is grateful to the anonymous reviewers of an early draft of the manuscript for their thoughtful recommendations. Many of their insights have found their way into the current version of this paper.

This work was presented at the Research Symposium on "Brain Neurocircuitry of Anxiety and Fear: Implications for Clinical Research and Practice" in Boston, Massachusetts, on March 26, 1998. The symposium was jointly sponsored by the Anxiety Disorders Association of America and the National Institute of Mental Health through an unrestricted educational grant provided by Wyeth-Ayerst Laboratories.

References

American Psychiatric Association (1994): *Diagnostic and Statistical Manual for Mental Disorders*, 4th ed. Washington, DC: American Psychiatric Press.

Biederman J, Rosenbaum JF, Hirshfeld DR, et al (1990): Psychiatric correlates of behavioral inhibition in young children of parents with and without psychiatric disorders. *Arch Gen Psychiatry* 47:21-26.

Bouwer C, Stein DJ (1998): Use of the selective serotonin reuptake inhibitor citalopram in the treatment of generalized social phobia. *J Affect Disord* 49:79-82.

Brown EJ, Heimberg RG, Juster HR (1995): Social phobia subtype and avoidant personality disorder: Effect on severity of social phobia, impairment, and outcome of cognitive-behavioral treatment. *Behav Ther* 26:467-480.

Caldirola D, Perna G, Arancio C, Bertani A, Bellodi L (1997): The 35% CO2 challenge test in patients with social phobia. *Psychiatry Res* 71:41-48.

Davidson JR, Krishnan KR, Charles HC, et al (1993): Magnetic resonance spectroscopy in social phobia: Preliminary findings. *J Clin Psychiatry* 54(suppl):19-25.

Davis M, Falls WM, Campeau S, Kim M (1993): Fear-potentiated startle: A neural and pharmacological analysis. *Behav Brain Res* 58:175-198.

den Boer JA (1997): Social phobia: Epidemiology, recognition, and treatment. *Br Med J* 315:796-800.

Dimsdale JE, Keefe F, Stein MB (in press): Stress and psychiatry. In: Kaplan HI, Sadock BJ, editors. *Kaplan & Sadock Comprehensive Textbook of Psychiatry*, 7th ed. Baltimore, MD: Williams & Wilkins.

Farde L, Gustavsson JP, Jönsson E (1997): D2 dopamine receptors and personality traits. *Nature* 385:590.

Flinn M, England BG (1997): Social economics of childhood glucocorticoid stress response and health. *Am J Phys Anthropol* 102:33-53.

Fyer AJ, Mannuzza S, Chapman TF, Liebowitz M, Klein DF (1993): A direct-interview family study of social phobia. *Arch Gen Psychiatry* 50:286-293.

Gorman JM, Papp LA, Goetz RR, Martinez JM, Hollander E, Jordan F (1990): High dose carbon dioxide challenge test in anxiety disorder patients. *Biol Psychiatry* 28:743-757.

Gorman JM, Papp LA, Coplan JD, et al (1994): Anxiogenic effects of CO2 and hyperventilation in patients with panic disorder. *Am J Psychiatry* 151:547-553.

Grant KA, Shively CA, Nader MA, et al (1998): Effect of social status on striatal dopamine D2 receptor binding characteristics in cynmolgus monkeys assessed with positron emission tomography. *Synapse* 29:80-83.

Gray JA (1992): Precis of the neuropsychology of anxiety: An enquiry into the function of the septohippocampal system. *Brain Sci* 5:469-534.

Grillon C, Ameli R, Goddard A, Woods SW, Davis M (1994): Baseline and fear-potentiated startle in panic disorder patients. *Biol Psychiatry* 35:431-439.

Grillon C, Dierker L, Merikangas KR (1997): Startle modulation in children at risk for anxiety disorders and/or alcoholism. *J Am Acad Child Adolesc Psychiatry* 36:925-932.

Heimberg RG, Hope DA, Dodge CS, et al (1990): DSM-III-R subtypes of social phobia: Comparison of generalized social phobics and public speaking phobics. *J Nerv Ment Dis* 173:172-179.

Herbert JD, Hope DA, Bellack AS (1992): Validity of the distinction between generalized social phobia and avoidant personality disorder. *J Abnorm Psychol* 101:332-339.

Hirshfeld DR, Rosenbaum JF, Biederman J, et al (1992): Stable behavioral inhibition and its association with anxiety disorder. *J Am Acad Child Adolesc Psychiatry* 31:103-111.

Hirshfeld DR, Biederman J, Brody D, Faraone SV, Rosenbaum JF (1997): Expressed emotion toward children with behavioral inhibition: Associations with maternal anxiety disorder. *J Am Acad Child Adolesc Psychiatry* 36:910-917.

Hofmann SG, Newman MG, Becker E, Taylor CB, Roth WT (1995): Social phobia with and without avoidant personality disorder: Preliminary behavior therapy outcome findings. *J Anxiety Disord* 2:427-438.

Insel TR (1992): Oxytocin: A neuropeptide for affiliation—Evidence from behavioral, receptor autoradiographic, and comparative studies. *Psychoneuroendocrinology* 17:3-33.

Insel TR (1997): A neurobiological basis of social attachment. *Am J Psychiatry* 154:726-735.

Kagan J, Reznick JS, Snidman N (1987): The physiology and psychology of behavioral inhibition in children. *Child Dev* 58:1459-1473.

Kagan J, Reznick JS, Snidman N (1988): Biological basis of childhood shyness. *Science* 240:167-171.

Katzelnick DJ, Kobak KA, Greist JH, Jefferson JW, Mantle JM, Serlin RC (1995): Sertraline for social phobia: A double-blind, placebo-controlled crossover study. *Am J Psychiatry* 152:1368-1371.

Kessler RC, Stein MB, Berglund P (1998): Social phobia subtypes in the National Comorbidity Survey. *Am J Psychiatry* 155:613-619.

Klein DF (1993): False suffocation alarms, spontaneous panics and related conditions: An integrative hypothesis. *Arch Gen Psychiatry* 50:306-317.

Knutson B, Wolkowitz OM, Cole SW, et al (1998): Selective alteration of personality and social behavior by serotonergic intervention. *Am J Psychiatry* 155:373-379.

Levin AP, Saoud JB, Gorman JM, Fyer AJ, Crawford R, Liebowitz MR (1993): Responses of generalized and discrete social phobias during public speaking challenge. *J Anxiety Disord* 7:207-221.

Liebowitz MR (1987): Social phobia. *Modern Problems in Pharmacopsychiatry* 33:141-173.

Mancini C, Van Ameringen M, Szatmari M, Fugere P, Boyle M (1996): A high-risk pilot study of the children of adults with social phobia. *J Am Acad Child Adolesc Psychiatry* 35:1511–1517.

Mannuzza S, Schneier FR, Chapman TF, Liebowitz MR, Klein DF, Fyer AJ (1995): Generalized social phobia. Reliability and validity. *Arch Gen Psychiatry* 52:230–237.

Merikangas KR, Angst J (1995): Comorbidity and social phobia: Evidence from clinical, epidemiologic, and genetic studies. *Eur Arch Psychiatry Clin Neurosci* 244:297–303.

Morgan CA III, Grillon C, Southwick SM, Davis M, Charney DS (1995a): Fear-potentiated startle in posttraumatic stress disorder. *Biol Psychiatry* 38:378–385.

Morgan CA III, Grillon C, Southwick SM, et al (1995b): Yohimbine facilitated acoustic startle in combat veterans with post-traumatic stress disorder. *Psychopharmacology (Berl)* 117:466–471.

Morris JS, Frith CD, Perrett DI, et al (1996): A differential neural response in the human amygdala to fearful and happy facial expressions. *Nature* 383:812–815.

Papp LA, Klein DF, Gorman JM (1993a): Carbon dioxide hypersensitivity, hyperventilation, and panic disorder. *Am J Psychiatry* 150:1149–1157.

Papp LA, Klein DF, Martinez JM, et al (1993b): Diagnostic and substance specificity of carbon dioxide-induced panic. *Am J Psychiatry* 150:250–257.

Perna G, Battaglia M, Garberi A, Arancio C, Bertani A, Bellodi L (1994): Carbon dioxide/oxygen challenge test in panic disorder. *Psychiatry Res* 52:159–171.

Perna G, Cocchi S, Bertani A, Arancio C, Bellodi L (1995): Sensitivity to 35% CO2 in healthy first-degree relatives of patients with panic disorder. *Am J Psychiatry* 152:623–625.

Perna G, Bertani A, Caldirola D, Bellodi L (1996): Family history of panic disorder and hypersensitivity to CO2 in patients with panic disorder. *Am J Psychiatry* 153:1060–1064.

Potts NL, Davidson JRT, Krishnan KR, Doriswamy PM, Ritchie JC (1992): Levels of urinary free cortisol in social phobia. *J Clin Psychiatry* 52:41–42.

Raleigh MJ, McGuire MT, Brammer GL, Pollack DB, Yuwiler A (1991): Serotonergic mechanisms promote dominance acquisition in adult male vervet monkeys. *Brain Res* 559:181–190.

Robinson JL, Kagan J, Reznick JS, Corley RP (1992): The heritability of inhibited and uninhibited behavior: A twin study. *Dev Psychol* 28:1030–1037.

Rosen JB, Hammerman E, Sitcoske M, Glowa JR, Schulkin J (1996): Hyperexcitability and exaggerated fear-potentiated startle produced by partial amygdala kindling. *Behav Neurosci* 110:43–50.

Rosenbaum JF, Biederman J, Bolduc-Murphy EA, et al (1993): Behavioral inhibition in childhood: A risk factor for anxiety disorders. *Harvard Rev Psychiatry* 1:2–16.

Rowe DC, Plomin R (1977): Temperament in early childhood. *J Pers Assess* 41:150–156.

Sapolsky RM, Spencer EM (1997): Insulin-like growth factor I is suppressed in socially subordinate male baboons. *Am J Physiol* 273:R1346–R1351.

Sapolsky RM, Alberts SC, Altmann J (1997): Hypercortisolism

associated with social subordinance or social isolation among wild baboons. *Arch Gen Psychiatry* 54:1137–1143.

Schmidt LA, Fox NA, Rubin KH, et al (1997): Behavioral and neuroendocrine responses in shy children. *Dev Psychobiol* 30:127–140.

Schneier FR, Martin LY, Liebowitz MR, Gorman JM, Fyer AJ (1989): Alcohol abuse in social phobia. *J Anxiety Disord* 3:15–23.

Schneier FR, Johnson J, Hornig CD, Liebowitz MR, Weissman MM (1992): Social phobia: Comorbidity and morbidity in an epidemiological sample. *Arch Gen Psychiatry* 49:282–288.

Schneier FR, Heckelman LR, Garfinkel R, et al (1994): Functional impairment in social phobia. *J Clin Psychiatry* 55:322–331.

Smalley SL, McCracken J, Tanguay P (1995): Autism, affective disorders, and social phobia. *Am J Med Genet* 60:19–26.

Stabler B, Clopper RR, Siegel PT, et al (1996): Links between growth hormone deficiency, adaptation and social phobia. *Horm Res* 45:30–33.

Stein MB, Leslie WD (1996): A brain single photon-emission computed tomography (SPECT) study of generalized social phobia. *Biol Psychiatry* 39:825–828.

Stein MB, Heuser IJ, Juncos JL, Uhde TW (1990): Anxiety disorders in patients with Parkinson's disease. *Am J Psychiatry* 147:217–220.

Stein MB, Tancer ME, Uhde TW (1992): Physiologic and plasma norepinephrine responses to orthostasis in patients with panic disorder and social phobia. *Arch Gen Psychiatry* 49:311–317.

Stein MB, Asmundson GJG, Chartier M (1994): Autonomic responsivity in generalized social phobia. *J Affect Disord* 31:211–221.

Stein MB, Walker JR, Forde DR (1996): Public-speaking fears in a community sample: Prevalence, impact on functioning, and diagnostic classification. *Arch Gen Psychiatry* 53:169–174.

Stein MB, Chartier MJ, Hazen AL, et al (1998): A direct-interview family study of generalized social phobia. *Am J Psychiatry* 155:90–97.

Stein MB, Liebowitz MR, Lydiard RB, Pitts CD, Bushnell W, Gergel I (1998): Paroxetine treatment of generalized social phobia (social anxiety disorder): A randomized controlled trial. *JAMA* 280:708–713.

Takahashi LK, Rubin WW (1993): Corticosteroid induction of threat-induced behavioral inhibition in preweanling rats. *Behav Neurosci* 107:860–868.

Tancer ME, Mailman RB, Stein MB, Mason GA, Carson SW, Golden RN (1994/1995): Neuroendocrine responsivity to monoaminergic system probes in generalized social phobia. *Anxiety* 1:216–223.

Tiihonen J, Kuikka J, Bergstrom K, Lepola U, Koponen H, Leinonen E (1997): Dopamine reuptake site densities in patients with social phobia. *Am J Psychiatry* 154:239–242.

Tupler LA, Davidson JRT, Smith RD, Lazeyras F, Charles HC, Krishnan KR (1997): A repeat proton magnetic resonance spectroscopy study in social phobia. *Biol Psychiatry* 42:419–424.

Uhde TW, Tancer ME, Gelernter CS, Vittone BJ (1994): Normal urinary free cortisol and postdexamethasone cortisol in social phobia: Comparison to normal volunteers. *J Affect Disord* 30:155–161.

Verburg K, Griez E, Meijer J, Pols H (1995): Discrimination between panic disorder and generalized anxiety disorder by 35% carbon dioxide challenge. *Am J Psychiatry* 152:1081–1083.

Virgin CEJ, Sapolsky RM (1997): Styles of male social behavior and their endocrine correlates among low-ranking baboons. *Am J Primatol* 42:25–39.

Winslow JT, Hastings N, Carter CS, Harbaugh CR, Insel TR (1993): A role for central vasopressin in pair bonding in monogamous prairie voles. *Nature* 365:545–548.

Woods SW, Charney D, Loke J, Goodman W, Redmond E Jr, Heninger GR (1986): Carbon dioxide sensitivity in panic anxiety: Ventilatory and anxiogenic responses to carbon dioxide in healthy subjects and patients with panic anxiety before and after alprazolam treatment. *Arch Gen Psychiatry* 43:900–909.

Molecular and Neuronal Substrate for the Selective Attenuation of Anxiety

Karin Löw,[1*†] Florence Crestani,[1*] Ruth Keist,[1*]
Dietmar Benke,[1] Ina Brünig,[1] Jack A. Benson,[1]
Jean-Marc Fritschy,[1] Thomas Rülicke,[2] Horst Bluethmann,[3]
Hanns Möhler,[1] Uwe Rudolph[1†‡]

Benzodiazepine tranquilizers are used in the treatment of anxiety disorders. To identify the molecular and neuronal target mediating the anxiolytic action of benzodiazepines, we generated and analyzed two mouse lines in which the α2 or α3 GABA$_A$ (γ-aminobutyric acid type A) receptors, respectively, were rendered insensitive to diazepam by a knock-in point mutation. The anxiolytic action of diazepam was absent in mice with the α2(H101R) point mutation but present in mice with the α3(H126R) point mutation. These findings indicate that the anxiolytic effect of benzodiazepine drugs is mediated by α2 GABA$_A$ receptors, which are largely expressed in the limbic system, but not by α3 GABA$_A$ receptors, which predominate in the reticular activating system.

Excessive or inappropriate anxiety can be controlled by enhancing inhibitory synaptic neurotransmission mediated by GABA (GABAergic

[1]Institute of Pharmacology and Toxicology, University of Zürich, and Swiss Federal Institute of Technology Zürich (ETH), Winterthurerstrasse 190, CH-8057 Zürich, Switzerland. [2]Biological Central Laboratory, University Hospital, Sternwartstrasse 6, CH-8091 Zürich, Switzerland. [3]Department Pharma Research Gene Technology, F. Hoffmann–La Roche Ltd., CH-4002 Basel, Switzerland.

*These authors contributed equally to this report.
†Present address: Department of Neurosciences, University of California, San Diego, 9500 Gilman Drive, La Jolla, CA 92093, USA.
‡To whom correspondence should be addressed. E-mail: rudolph@pharma.unizh.ch

inhibitory neurotransmission) using clinically effective benzodiazepine drugs (1). However, to date it has not been possible to identify the one or more GABA$_A$ receptor subtypes that mediate the attenuation of anxiety. Four types of diazepam-sensitive GABA$_A$ receptors can be distinguished on the basis of the presence of α1, α2, α3, or α5 subunits. These receptors can be rendered insensitive to diazepam in vitro by replacing a conserved histidine residue by arginine in the drug binding site (2, 3). Introduction of the respective point mutation into mouse lines enables the pharmacological profile of benzodiazepine drugs to be attributed to defined receptor subtypes. Using this approach, we have attributed the sedative and amnesic prop-

305

erties of diazepam, but not its anxiolytic action, to α1 GABA_A receptors (4, 5). We hypothesized that the anxiolytic action of benzodiazepine drugs might be mediated by α2 or α3 GABA_A receptors on the basis of their distinct neuroanatomical expression patterns. Whereas α2 GABA_A receptors are preponderant in areas of the limbic system as well as in the cerebral cortex and striatum, α3 GABA_A receptors are selectively expressed in noradrenergic and serotonergic neurons of the brainstem reticular formation, the basal forebrain cholinergic neurons, and GABAergic neurons in the reticular nucleus of the thalamus (6).

To distinguish the pharmacology of the α2 receptor subtype from that of the α3 subtype, we generated two mouse lines in which a point mutation was introduced into homologous positions of the α2 subunit gene (Fig. 1) and the α3 subunit gene (7), rendering the respective receptors insensitive to diazepam. [The point mutations were His^{101} → Arg and His^{126} → Arg, respectively, hence the mouse lines are denoted α2(H101R) and α3(H126R).] The mutants did not display an overt distinctive phenotype, bred normally, and expressed all subunits tested (α1, α2, α3, β2/3, and γ2) at normal levels (Fig. 2A)

and with unaltered distribution. Ro15-4513 is an inverse agonist at the benzodiazepine binding site and binds to both diazepam-sensitive and diazepam-insensitive GABA_A receptors. The proportion of diazepam-insensitive [^{3}H]Ro15-4513 binding sites was increased from 5% in wild-type mice to 17% in α2(H101R) mice and to 11% in α3(H126R) mice [α2 wild-type controls: maximum number of binding sites B_{max} = 0.08 ± 0.02 pmol/mg protein, dissociation constant K_d = 4.3 ± 0.8 nM (n = 3); α2(H101R) mice: B_{max} = 0.26 ± 0.01 pmol/mg protein, K_d = 8.0 ± 1.3 nM (n = 3); α3 wild-type controls: B_{max} = 0.06 ± 0.01 pmol/mg protein, K_d = 4.9 ± 2.1 nM (n = 3); and α3(H126R) mice: B_{max} = 0.11 ± 0.02 pmol/mg protein, K_d = 6.5 ± 1.6 nM (n = 3)]. In line with the known distribution of the α2 subunit (6), novel diazepam-insensitive sites in α2(H101R) mice were visualized in all regions expressing α2 GABA_A receptors, as shown autoradiographically in parasagittal brain sections using 10 nM [^{3}H]Ro15-4513 in the presence of 100 μM diazepam (Fig. 2B). Similarly, in α3(H126R) mice, the novel diazepam-insensitive [^{3}H]Ro15-4513 binding sites displayed a distribution corresponding to that of the α3 subunit (Fig. 2B)

(6). After immunoprecipitation with α2 or α3 subunit–specific antisera, [^{3}H]Ro15-4513 binding revealed a decrease of more than three orders of magnitude in the affinity of diazepam to the α2 and α3 subunits from the respective mutant mice.

In cultured hippocampal pyramidal cells (8), the electrophysiological response to GABA (3 μM) was indistinguishable between cells from wild-type and α2(H101R) mice (Fig. 2C). However, the potentiation by diazepam (1 μM) was reduced in cells from α2(H101R) mice relative to cells from wild-type mice [17.6 ± 4.5% (n = 29) versus 48.1 ± 7.9% (n = 18), P = 0.001] (Fig. 2C); the remaining potentiation presumably can be attributed to GABA_A receptors other than α2. The inverse agonistic action of Ro15-4513 (1 μM) in wild-type cells was converted into an agonistic response in cells derived from α2(H101R) mice [–39 ± 5.2% (n = 13) versus 11.7 ± 7.5% (n = 23), P = 0.003] (Fig. 2C). This is consistent with the switch in efficacy of Ro15-4513 from inverse agonism to agonism, as shown for recombinant α2(H101R)β3γ2 receptors expressed in HEK-293 cells (3).

The pharmacological importance of the

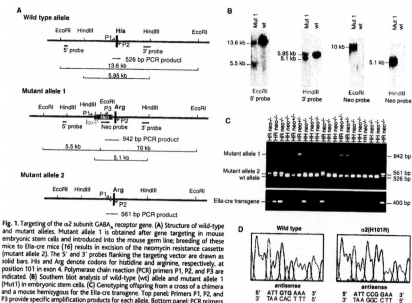

Fig. 1. Targeting of the α2 subunit GABA_A receptor gene. (A) Structure of wild-type and mutant alleles. Mutant allele 1 is obtained after gene targeting in mouse embryonic stem cells and introduced into the mouse germ line; breeding of these mice to Ella-cre mice (16) results in excision of the neomycin resistance cassette (mutant allele 2). The 5' and 3' probes flanking the targeting vector are drawn as solid bars. His and Arg denote codons for histidine and arginine, respectively, at position 101 in exon 4. Polymerase chain reaction (PCR) primers P1, P2, and P3 are indicated. (B) Southern blot analysis of wild-type (wt) allele and mutant allele 1 (Mut1) in embryonic stem cells. (C) Genotyping offspring from a cross of a chimera and a mouse hemizygous for the Ella-cre transgene. Top panel: Primers P1, P2, and P3 provide specific amplification products for each allele. Bottom panel: PCR primers UR26 and UR36 amplify the cre transgene. (D) Verification of the α2(H101R) point mutation by automated DNA sequencing.

306

mutated α2 and α3 GABA$_A$ receptors was assessed by comparing the diazepam-induced behavior of α2(H101R) and α3(H126R) mice

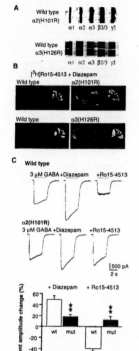

Fig. 2. Molecular characteristics of GABA$_A$ receptors in α2(H101R) and α3(H126R) mice. (**A**) Western blots of whole brain membranes from wild-type, α2(H101R), and α3(H126R) mice using antisera recognizing the α1, α2, α3, β2/3, and γ2 subunits. (**B**) Receptor autoradiography of diazepam-insensitive sites in wild-type, α2(H101R), and α3(H126R) brains. Parasagittal sections were incubated with 10 nM [³H]Ro15-4513 in the presence of 100 μM diazepam to reveal the diazepam-insensitive [³H]Ro15-4513 binding sites. In wild-type mice, diazepam-insensitive [³H]Ro15-4513 binding is due to α4 and α6 GABA$_A$ receptors. (**C**) GABA responses in cultured hippocampal pyramidal cells from α2(H101R) mice. The holding potential in the patch-clamp analysis was −60 mV; the chloride concentration was symmetrical. GABA was applied for 5 s. Hippocampal neurons from embryonic day 16.5 embryos were cultured for 10 to 14 days. **, $P < 0.001$ (Student's t test).

with that of wild-type mice (9). When tested in a dose-dependent manner, the sedative, motor-impairing, and anticonvulsant actions of diazepam (10) were not impaired in either α2(H101R) mice or α3(H126R) mice relative to wild-type mice (Fig. 3).

The anxiolytic-like action of diazepam in α2(H101R) and α3(H126R) mice was investigated in the light-dark choice test (11) and the elevated plus-maze test (12). In the light-dark choice test, the α2(H101R) mice did not show the behavioral disinhibition by diazepam that was apparent in wild-type mice. Diazepam up to 2 mg/kg body weight did not increase the time spent in the lit area in α2(H101R) mice relative to wild-type mice ($P < 0.05$ versus vehicle) (Fig. 4A). This effect was not due to a motor deficit in α2(H101R) mice, because no behavioral differences in the dark area were observed between wild-type and α2(H101R) mice under either vehicle or diazepam treatment. Furthermore, α2(H101R) mice retained the ability to display an anxiolytic-like response to ligands acting at GABA$_A$ receptor sites other than the benzodiazepine site. Sodium phenobarbital (15 mg/kg subcutaneously) induced a

behavioral disinhibition in the light/dark choice test in α2(H101R) mice similar to that seen in wild-type mice [time in lit area, wild-type: vehicle, 70.5 ± 10.5 s, phenobarbital, 111.75 ± 10.0 s; α2(H101R): vehicle, 75.3 ± 11.5 s, phenobarbital, 110.9 ± 9.6 s; $F(1,24) = 13.44$, $P < 0.01$, $n = 6$ to 8].

The absence of an anxiolytic-like effect of diazepam in α2(H101R) mice was confirmed in the elevated plus-maze test. In wild-type mice, diazepam facilitated the exploratory behavior by increasing both the amount of time spent ($P < 0.01$ versus vehicle) and the number of entries in the open arms ($P < 0.05$). In contrast, in α2(H101R) mice, diazepam failed to increase both parameters of exploratory behavior (Fig. 4, B and C). Again the failure was not due to motor impairment, because the motor activity in the enclosed arms was similar in α2(H101R) and wild-type mice irrespective of the treatment.

The potential contribution of α3 GABA$_A$ receptors to the anxiolytic-like activity of diazepam was examined in α3(H126R) mice. Both α3(H126R) and wild-type mice displayed similar dose-dependent anxiolytic-like

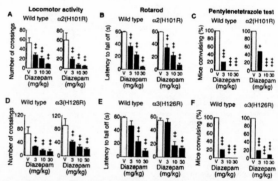

Fig. 3. Behavioral assessment of the sedative, motor-impairing, and anticonvulsant properties of diazepam in α2(H101R) and α3(H126R) mice relative to wild-type mice. (**A**) Dose-dependent inhibition of locomotor activity in wild-type and α2(H101R) mice [$F(3,71) = 19.31$, $P < 0.001$, $n = 9$ or 10 mice per group]. (**B**) Dose-dependent decrease in the latency to fall off the rotating rod (fixed 2 rpm) in wild-type and α2(H101R) mice [$F(3,153) = 71.01$, $P < 0.001$, $n = 20$ or 21 mice per group]. (**C**) Dose-dependent decrease of the percentage of mice developing tonic convulsions in wild-type ($\chi^2 = 32.38$, $P < 0.001$, $n = 10$ mice per group) and α2(H101R) mice ($\chi^2 = 28.13$, $P < 0.001$, $n = 10$ mice per group). (**D**) Dose-dependent inhibition of locomotor activity in wild-type and α3(H126R) mice [$F(3,64) = 14.70$, $P < 0.001$, $n = 8$ to 10 mice per group]. (**E**) Dose-dependent decrease in the latency to fall off the rotating rod (fixed 2 rpm) in wild-type and α3(H126R) mice [$F(3,64) = 36.78$, $P < 0.001$, $n = 8$ to 10 mice per group]. (**F**) Dose-dependent decrease of the percentage of mice developing tonic convulsions in wild-type ($\chi^2 = 32.38$, $P < 0.001$, $n = 10$ mice per group) and α3(H126R) mice ($\chi^2 = 28.60$, $P < 0.001$, $n = 10$ mice per group). Results are given as means ± SEM. +, $P < 0.05$; ++, $P < 0.01$; +++, $P < 0.001$ (Dunnett's post hoc comparisons or Fisher's exact tests). V, vehicle. The rotarod and pentylenetetrazole convulsion tests were performed according to Bonetti et al. (10). Locomotor activity was automatically recorded for 30 min. Mice were treated with either vehicle or diazepam (3, 10, and 30 mg/kg orally) 30 min before testing.

307

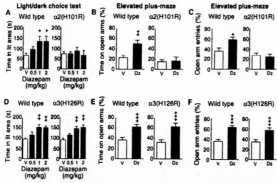

Fig. 4. Behavioral assessment of anxiolytic-like action of diazepam in α2(H101R) and α3(H126R) mice relative to wild-type mice. (**A**) Light/dark choice test. Diazepam dose-dependently increased the time spent in the lit area in wild-type mice [$F(3,36) = 3.14$, $P < 0.05$] but not in α2(H101R) mice [$F(3,36) = 0.32$, not significant] ($n = 10$ mice per group). (**B** and **C**) Elevated plus-maze. Diazepam (2 mg/kg) increased the percentage of time spent on the open arms and the number of entries on the open arms in wild-type mice ($P < 0.01$ and $P < 0.05$ versus vehicle) but not in α2(H101R) mice [$F(1,32) = 4.31$ and $F(1,32) = 4.76$, $P < 0.05$, respectively] ($n = 8$ to 10 mice per group). (**D**) Light/dark choice test. Both wild-type and α3(H126R) mice displayed a dose-dependent increase in the time spent in the lit area [$F(1,70) = 14.74$, $P < 0.001$, $n = 9$ or 10 mice per group]. (**E** and **F**) Elevated plus-maze. Diazepam (2 mg/kg) increased the percentage of time spent on the open arms and the number of entries on the open arms to the same extent in wild-type and α3(H126R) mice [$F(1,36) = 26.52$ and $F(1,36) = 37.31$, $P < 0.001$, respectively] ($n = 10$ mice per group). Results are given as means ± SEM. +, $P < 0.05$; ++, $P < 0.01$; +++, $P < 0.001$ (Dunnett's or Fisher's pairwise post hoc comparisons or Fisher's exact tests). V, vehicle; Dz, diazepam. The light-dark choice test was carried out as described (11) with an illumination of 500 lux. Mice were given vehicle or increasing doses of diazepam (0.5, 1, and 2 mg/kg orally). The elevated plus-maze was performed according to Lister (12) under an indirect dim-light illumination (< 10 lux). Vehicle or diazepam were administered 30 min before testing.

3. J. A. Benson, K. Löw, R. Keist, H. Möhler, U. Rudolph, *FEBS Lett.* **431**, 400 (1998).
4. U. Rudolph et al., *Nature* **401**, 796 (1999).
5. The α1(H101R) point mutation in mice described in (4) was also developed by R. M. McKernan et al. [*Nature Neurosci.* **3**, 587 (2000)].
6. J.-M. Fritschy and H. Möhler, *J. Comp. Neurol.* **359**, 154 (1995).
7. Details of the generation of the α2(H101R) and α3(H126R) mouse lines are available at Science Online (www.sciencemag.org/feature/data/1052988.shl). The mice that were used in this report were backcrossed for five or six generations to the 129/SvJ background.
8. Cultured hippocampal pyramidal cells were chosen as a model system to confirm that the pharmacological properties of recombinant mutant α2 GABA$_A$ receptors can also be demonstrated for GABA$_A$ receptors in mutant mice.
9. Experimental details are available at *Science* Online (www.sciencemag.org/feature/data/1052988.shl).
10. E. P. Bonetti et al., *Pharmacol. Biochem. Behav.* **31**, 733 (1988).
11. R. Misslin, C. Belzung, E. Vogel, *Behav. Proc.* **18**, 119 (1989).
12. R. G. Lister, *Psychopharmacology* **92**, 180 (1987).
13. R. Marksitzer et al., *J. Recept. Res.* **13**, 467 (1993).
14. Z. Nusser, W. Sieghart, D. Benke, J.-M. Fritschy, P. Somogyi, *Proc. Natl. Acad. Sci. U.S.A.* **93**, 11939 (1996).
15. J.-M. Fritschy, O. Weinmann, A. Wenzel, D. Benke, *J. Comp. Neurol.* **390**, 194 (1998).
16. M. Lakso et al., *Proc. Natl. Acad. Sci. U.S.A.* **93**, 5860 (1996).
17. We thank Y. Lang for blastocyst injection; P. Fakitsas and C. Michel for performing immunoblot, autoradiography, and ligand binding experiments; C. Sidler for hippocampal cell culture; D. Blaser, H. Pochetti, and G. Schmid for animal care; H. Westphal for Ella-cre mice; H. Hengartner for E14 embryonic stem cells; and E. M. Simpson for mEMS32 embryonic stem cells. Supported by a grant from the Swiss National Science Foundation.

9 June 2000; accepted 10 August 2000

responses to diazepam in the light/dark choice test ($P < 0.01$ versus vehicle) (Fig. 4D) and in the elevated plus-maze ($P < 0.001$ versus vehicle) (Fig. 4, E and F). These results indicate that the anxiolytic action of diazepam in wild-type mice does not involve interaction with α3 GABA$_A$ receptors.

The anxiolytic-like action of diazepam is selectively mediated by the enhancement of GABAergic transmission in a population of neurons expressing the α2 GABA$_A$ receptors, which represent only 15% of all diazepam-sensitive GABA$_A$ receptors (13). The α2 GABA$_A$ receptor–expressing cells in the cerebral cortex and hippocampus include pyramidal cells that display very high densities of α2 GABA$_A$ receptors on the axon initial segment, presumably controlling the output of these principal neurons (14, 15). Our findings indicate that the α2 GABA$_A$ receptors are highly specific targets for the development of future selective anxiolytic drugs.

References and Notes
1. R. I. Shader and D. J. Greenblatt, *N. Engl. J. Med.* **328**, 1398 (1993).
2. H. A. Wieland, H. Lüddens, P. H. Seeburg, *J. Biol. Chem.* **267**, 1426 (1992).

308

FLUVOXAMINE FOR THE TREATMENT OF ANXIETY DISORDERS IN CHILDREN AND ADOLESCENTS

THE RESEARCH UNIT ON PEDIATRIC PSYCHOPHARMACOLOGY ANXIETY STUDY GROUP*

ABSTRACT

Background Drugs that selectively inhibit serotonin reuptake are effective treatments for adults with mood and anxiety disorders, but limited data are available on the safety and efficacy of serotonin-reuptake inhibitors in children with anxiety disorders.

Methods We studied 128 children who were 6 to 17 years of age; who met the criteria for social phobia, separation anxiety disorder, or generalized anxiety disorder; and who had received psychological treatment for three weeks without improvement. The children were randomly assigned to receive fluvoxamine (at a maximum of 300 mg per day) or placebo for eight weeks and were evaluated with rating scales designed to assess the degree of anxiety and impairment.

Results Children in the fluvoxamine group had a mean ($\pm$SD) decrease of 9.7 ± 6.9 points in symptoms of anxiety on the Pediatric Anxiety Rating Scale (range of possible scores, 0 to 25, with higher scores indicating greater anxiety), as compared with a decrease of 3.1 ± 4.8 points among children in the placebo group (P<0.001). On the Clinical Global Impressions–Improvement scale, 48 of 63 children in the fluvoxamine group (76 percent) had a response to the treatment, as indicated by a score of less than 4, as compared with 19 of 65 children in the placebo group (29 percent, P<0.001). Five children in the fluvoxamine group (8 percent) discontinued treatment because of adverse events, as compared with one child in the placebo group (2 percent).

Conclusions Fluvoxamine is an effective treatment for children and adolescents with social phobia, separation anxiety disorder, or generalized anxiety disorder. (N Engl J Med 2001;344:1279-85.)

Copyright © 2001 Massachusetts Medical Society.

A NXIETY disorders are the most common psychiatric illnesses in children,[1-3] but most children with anxiety disorders do not receive treatment.[4,5] Several studies have documented the safety and efficacy of drug therapy for children with obsessive–compulsive disorder, but there have been few studies of drug therapy for children with more prevalent anxiety disorders.[6,7]

Social phobia, separation anxiety disorder, and generalized anxiety disorder in children cause substantial distress and interfere with academic as well as social functioning.[1,2,8,9] Childhood anxiety disorders also foreshadow psychiatric illness later in life. Specifically, these disorders predict an increase by a factor of two to five in the risk of later anxiety disorders, major depression, suicide attempts, and hospitalization for psychiatric illness.[1,2,10,11]

Selective serotonin-reuptake inhibitors are well-established treatments for virtually all anxiety disorders in adults.[12-15] These drugs also appear to be effective in children with obsessive–compulsive disorder and major depression.[6,7,16,17] Open trials suggest that selective serotonin-reuptake inhibitors may be effective in children with various anxiety disorders.[18,19] On the basis of these reports, we carried out a randomized, double-blind trial of fluvoxamine and a placebo in children with social phobia, separation anxiety disorder, or generalized anxiety disorder. We recruited children with any of these disorders rather than one specific anxiety disorder because these conditions typically occur together.[1-3,10,11] Therefore, a trial focusing on only one of these anxiety disorders would inevitably include children with the other two disorders. Fluvoxamine was selected since it was the only selective serotonin-reuptake inhibitor approved by the Food and Drug Administration for use in children at the time the study was designed in 1996.

METHODS

Patients

This study was conducted between July 1997 and September 1999 at five medical centers — Johns Hopkins University, New York State Psychiatric Institute–Columbia University, New York University, Duke University, and the University of California at Los Angeles — under the auspices of the Research Unit on Pediatric Psychopharmacology (RUPP) network. The protocol was approved by the institutional review board at each center and by the data and safety monitoring board of the National Institute of Mental Health. Written informed consent was obtained from all parents, and assent was obtained from all children.

We studied 128 children 6 to 17 years of age who met the diagnostic criteria of the *Diagnostic and Statistical Manual of Mental Disorders* (fourth edition)[20] for social phobia, separation anxiety disorder, or generalized anxiety disorder on the basis of comprehensive, semistructured psychiatric interviews. There were three other criteria for inclusion. First, the child had to have clinically important symptoms of anxiety according to the Pediatric Anxiety Rating Scale.[21,22] With this scale, the clinician assesses the child's degree of suffering and limitation in functioning associated with

Address reprint requests to Dr. Daniel S. Pine at the Program on Mood and Anxiety Disorders, National Institute of Mental Health–Intramural Research Program, Bldg. 10, Rm. 4N-222 (MSC-1381), Bethesda, MD 20892-1381, or at daniel.pine@nih.gov.

Dr. Pine accepts responsibility for the overall content and integrity of the manuscript.

*The authors of the study are John T. Walkup, M.D., Michael J. Labellarte, M.D., and Mark A. Riddle, M.D., Johns Hopkins University; Daniel S. Pine, M.D., Laurence Greenhill, M.D., Rachel Klein, Ph.D., Mark Davies, M.P.H., and Michael Sweeney, Ph.D., Columbia University and New York State Psychiatric Institute; Howard Abikoff, Ph.D., Sabine Hack, M.D., and Brian Klee, M.D., New York University; James McCracken, M.D., Lindsey Bergman, Ph.D., and John Piacentini, Ph.D., University of California at Los Angeles; John March, M.D., M.P.H., and Scott Compton, Ph.D., Duke University; James Robinson, M.Ed., Thomas O'Hara, M.B.A., and Sherryl Baker, Ph.D., Nathan Kline Institute; and Benedetto Vitiello, M.D., Louise Ritz, M.B.A., and Margaret Roper, M.P.H., National Institute of Mental Health.

anxiety during the previous week. Second, the child had to have clinically important impairment according to the Children's Global Assessment Scale (a score of less than 60).[23] This scale assesses the degree to which psychiatric symptoms impede functioning. Third, both the child and a parent had to agree to attend the clinic weekly. Criteria for exclusion included current therapy with any psychoactive substance; a current diagnosis of major depression, Tourette's syndrome, obsessive–compulsive disorder, post-traumatic stress disorder, conduct disorder, or panic disorder; a history of or a current diagnosis of mania, psychosis, or pervasive developmental disorder; current suicidal ideation; mental retardation (an IQ of less than 70) as assessed with the Kaufman Brief Intelligence Test[24]; previous treatment with a selective serotonin-reuptake inhibitor; or a current diagnosis of attention-deficit–hyperactivity disorder of sufficient severity to require drug therapy.

We initially evaluated 153 children who presented, with their families, for treatment of anxiety at a participating center (Fig. 1). The children and their families underwent three weeks of open treatment with supportive, psychoeducational therapy. As described previously,[25,26] psychoeducational therapy is designed to teach families about the origins and typical course of mental illness while emphasizing the good outcome in many cases. During this three-week phase, we identified five children whose conditions improved with brief psychotherapeutic interventions and who therefore did not require drug therapy. Another 20 children were excluded because they could not attend weekly sessions. The remaining 128 children were randomly assigned to receive fluvoxamine or placebo for eight weeks, during which time supportive psychotherapy

continued. The dose of fluvoxamine was increased by approximately 50 mg per week to a maximum of 300 mg per day in adolescents and 250 mg per day in children less than 12 years of age. The capsules of placebo and fluvoxamine were identical in appearance, so that the clinicians who were treating the children and who adjusted the doses of the study drug were unaware of the treatment-group assignments. Dose escalation was delayed in children who had adverse effects or a remission of their anxiety disorder.

The treating clinicians saw the children and parents weekly during weeks 1 through 6 and at the end of week 8. During each visit, the clinician administered supportive psychotherapy, assessed the severity of symptoms using the Pediatric Anxiety Rating Scale, and monitored the patient for adverse effects. Clinical indications for removal from the trial were determined before the study began; decisions to remove children were based on the consensus of a group of expert clinicians, including both clinicians who treated the children and clinicians who did not, all of whom remained unaware of the treatment-group assignments.

Diagnosis and Outcome Measures

The criteria for inclusion and exclusion according to diagnosis were assessed by experienced clinicians in semistructured interviews using the Schedule for Affective Disorders and Schizophrenia for School-Age Children.[27]

The two primary outcome measures were the change in the score on the Pediatric Anxiety Rating Scale, which was assessed each week, and the score on the Clinical Global Impressions–Improvement scale at the end of the study.

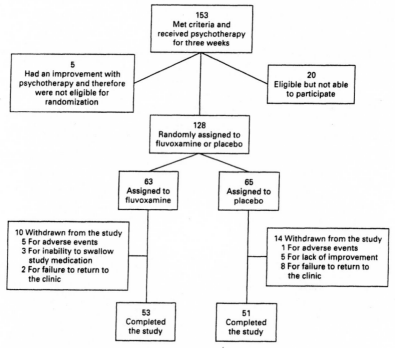

Figure 1. Numbers of Children with Anxiety Disorders during Each Phase of the Study.

310

Symptoms of Anxiety

Before the trial, a clinician-rated scale was not available for assessing the symptoms of the targeted disorders.[21] To meet this need, the Pediatric Anxiety Rating Scale was developed and validated in children with clinically significant anxiety disorders, who were identified through standardized interviews with clinicians.[22] With this scale, the clinician uses a checklist of questions regarding the symptoms of anxiety during the past week to elicit responses from parents and children. After completing this checklist, the clinician rates five general items: the severity of the child's distress due to anxiety, the frequency of anxiety, the degree to which the child avoided anxiety-provoking situations, and the degree to which the anxiety limited the child's participation in typical daily activities both at home and in other environments, such as school. The sum of the scores on these five items, which can range from 0 to 25, served as the primary continuous outcome measure. A rating of 10 indicates mild but clinically meaningful levels of anxiety, whereas a rating of 20 indicates extremely high levels of anxiety.

Global Improvement

During each visit, global improvement was rated by the treating clinician on the Clinical Global Impressions–Improvement scale with the use of data from all other measures in the study. An eight-point scale was used, as in prior studies of children.[28,29] Children who received scores of 3 (improved), 2 (much improved), or 1 (free of symptoms) were defined as having had a clinically meaningful response to the treatment. This meant that the clinician would recommend continuing the medication rather than changing to an alternative treatment.

Other Measures

At base line and at weeks 4 and 8, each child completed the Multidimensional Anxiety Scale for Children,[30] and both the child and a parent rated the condition of the child with the Screen for Child Anxiety Related Emotional Disorders.[31] These scales record the answers of the child and parent to written questions concerning the child's level of anxiety; the reliability of these scales has been established.[30,31] At the same times, clinicians also assigned a score for global functional impairment[23] and physiologic symptoms of anxiety.[32] To assess the interrater reliability of the ratings made by the clinicians participating in the trial, each clinician rated 16 children using all scales. Acceptable interrater reliability (an intraclass correlation of more than 0.80) was obtained for all scales.

At each visit, the frequency, severity, and effect on treatment of adverse events were rated, in order to screen for possible adverse effects of the drug.

Statistical Analysis

The total score on the Pediatric Anxiety Rating Scale was the primary continuous outcome measure, and the proportion with a score of less than 4 on the Clinical Global Impressions–Improvement scale was the primary categorical outcome measure. For the Pediatric Anxiety Rating Scale, the effect of treatment was analyzed with the use of a mixed model, with treatment group and center as fixed effects and the time of treatment as a random effect.[33] Efficacy was evaluated by tests of the interaction of treatment with time; all interactions were included (treatment with center, time with center, and treatment with time with center). Estimates of regression slopes and intercepts for individual subjects were generated in the mixed model with the use of all available data. Although the results for children with missing data were weighted less heavily than the results for those with complete data, having missing data did not exclude a child from the analysis.[33] However, the results from four children were excluded from this analysis because of scoring errors. For the Clinical Global Impressions–Improvement scale, we used logistic-regression analysis for all 128 children to assess the effect of treatment on the ratings at week 8, carrying forward the last available rating and including the center as an independent variable. Analyses were performed according to the intention-to-treat principle and included all children, with the exception of the four children who were excluded from the Pediatric Anxiety Rating Scale analysis. All statistical tests were two-tailed.

RESULTS

The base-line characteristics of children in the fluvoxamine and placebo groups were similar (Table 1). The scores on the Pediatric Anxiety Rating Scale indicated that the children in both groups had high levels of anxiety. The children in the fluvoxamine group

TABLE 1. BASE-LINE CHARACTERISTICS OF THE 128 CHILDREN IN THE FLUVOXAMINE AND PLACEBO GROUPS.*

CHARACTERISTIC	FLUVOXAMINE (N=63)	PLACEBO (N=65)
Demographic characteristics		
Age of 6–12 yr — no. (%)	48 (76)	47 (72)
Male sex — no. (%)	32 (51)	33 (51)
Race or ethnic group — no. (%)		
White	41 (65)	40 (62)
Black	6 (10)	3 (5)
Hispanic	12 (19)	12 (18)
Other	4 (6)	10 (15)
Total annual family income — no. (%)		
<$25,000	9 (14)	10 (15)
$25,000–$39,999	10 (16)	10 (15)
$40,000–$59,999	9 (14)	9 (14)
≥$60,000	28 (44)	27 (42)
Unknown	7 (11)	9 (14)
Two parents in home — no. (%)	47 (75)	45 (69)
Mean age — yr	10.4±2.8	10.3±3.1
Psychiatric profile		
Current separation anxiety disorder — no. (%)	40 (63)	36 (55)
Current generalized anxiety disorder — no. (%)	32 (51)	41 (63)
Current social phobia — no. (%)	39 (62)	45 (69)
Past or current attention-deficit–hyperactivity disorder — no. (%)	11 (17)	9 (14)
Past or current oppositional defiant disorder — no. (%)	4 (6)	3 (5)
Past conduct disorder — no. (%)	0	2 (3)
Past obsessive–compulsive disorder — no. (%)	3 (5)	3 (5)
Past major depressive disorder — no. (%)	3 (5)	3 (5)
Past enuresis — no. (%)	3 (5)	5 (8)
Past encopresis — no. (%)	3 (5)	0
Past tics — no. (%)	1 (2)	0
Past post-traumatic stress disorder — no. (%)	1 (2)	2 (3)
MASC total score	54.8±18.5	53.6±19.0
SCARED-P total score	35.9±14.4	37.3±12.4
SCARED-Y total score	31.0±12.9	32.1±14.8
Dose of medication or placebo and participation in study		
Average dose — mg/kg of body weight†	2.9±1.3	3.8±1.7
Last dose — mg/kg‡	4.0±2.2	5.9±2.8
No. of visits during trial	7.7±2.0	7.8±1.7

*Plus–minus values are means ±SD. MASC denotes the Multidimensional Anxiety Scale for Children (range of scores, 0 to 117), and SCARED the Screen for Child Anxiety Related Emotional Disorders, parent rated (P) or child rated (Y) (range of scores, 0 to 82). Higher scores indicate more anxiety. Except as noted, P>0.05.

†P=0.001.

‡P<0.001.

were prescribed lower doses of drug than the children in the placebo group. Given that dose escalation continued only in children with symptoms of anxiety, this difference in doses is consistent with the superior efficacy of fluvoxamine as compared with placebo.

Efficacy

The children in the fluvoxamine group had greater reductions in symptoms of anxiety and higher rates of clinical response than the children in the placebo group (Table 2 and Fig. 2 and 3). On the Pediatric Anxiety Rating Scale, significant differences between the treatment groups were detectable by week 3 and increased through week 6, with little change during the final two weeks of the trial. At the end of the trial, the average rating on the Pediatric Anxiety Rating Scale in the fluvoxamine group was below 10 — a score that indicates no more than mild anxiety — whereas the rating in the placebo group remained high (above 14). On the Clinical Global Impressions–Improvement scale, 48 of 63 children in the fluvoxamine group (76 percent) had scores of less than 4, as compared with 19 of 65 children in the placebo group (29 percent). For both measures, these effects of treatment with fluvoxamine are considered large, given the results of other treatment studies of mood and anxiety disorders in children.[6,7,16,17,34] Neither analysis revealed interactions of the center with treatment.

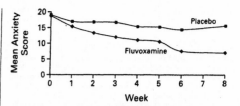

Figure 2. Mean Total Score on the Pediatric Anxiety Rating Scale in the Fluvoxamine and Placebo Groups during the Eight-Week Trial.

Curves were estimated with the use of random regression for 61 children in the fluvoxamine group and 63 children in the placebo group ($P<0.001$ for the interaction of treatment with time). The score on the Pediatric Anxiety Rating Scale can range from 0 to 25, with a score of 10 indicating mild but clinically meaningful levels of anxiety and a score of 20 indicating severe anxiety.

Adverse Events

Adverse events that were recorded at any time during the trial are listed in descending order of prevalence in Table 3. Abdominal discomfort was significantly more prevalent in the fluvoxamine group than in the placebo group ($P=0.02$); there was also a trend toward a greater frequency of increased motor activity in the fluvoxamine group ($P=0.06$).

TABLE 2. CHANGE IN SCORES ON THE PEDIATRIC ANXIETY RATING SCALE AND CLINICAL GLOBAL IMPRESSIONS–IMPROVEMENT SCALE IN THE FLUVOXAMINE AND PLACEBO GROUPS.*

VARIABLE	WEEK OF STUDY									P VALUE FOR INTERACTION OF TREATMENT WITH TIME
	0	1	2	3	4	5	6	8	END OF STUDY†	
Weeks from base line	0.0±0.0	1.1±0.3	2.1±0.3	3.1±0.4	4.2±0.4	5.2±0.5	6.2±0.5	8.3±0.7	7.5±2.0	
Fluvoxamine										
No. tested	61	55	53	56	52	49	47	50	61	
Pediatric Anxiety Rating Scale score	18.7±2.9	15.4±5.4	13.4±5.7	12.0±5.4	11.1±6.0	10.6±6.1	7.6±5.6	7.1±6.1	9.0±7.0	<0.001
Placebo										
No. tested	63	60	55	54	56	55	54	49	63	
Pediatric Anxiety Rating Scale score	19.0±3.0	17.0±3.6	16.8±4.3	16.7±4.0	15.4±4.6	15.3±4.4	14.5±5.0	15.7±5.4	15.9±5.3	
Fluvoxamine										
No. tested		58	56	58	54	51	49	52	63	
Clinical Global Impressions–Improvement scores <4 (% of patients)		19	38	59	59	69	84	86	76	<0.001
Placebo										
No. tested		64	58	56	59	57	54	50	65	
Clinical Global Impressions–Improvement scores <4 (% of patients)		5	17	12	29	25	30	32	29	

*Plus–minus values are means ±SD. The possible range of Pediatric Anxiety Rating Scale scores was 0 to 25, with higher scores indicating greater anxiety. The possible range of Clinical Global Impressions–Improvement scores was 1 to 8, with a score less than 4 indicating a response to treatment.

†These are the last values obtained for each subject.

312

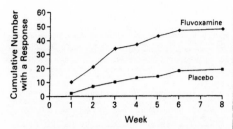

Figure 3. Cumulative Response Rates on the Clinical Global Impressions–Improvement Scale during the Eight-Week Trial in the Fluvoxamine and Placebo Groups.

Data are from 63 patients in the fluvoxamine group, 48 of whom had a response (76 percent), and 65 patients in the placebo group, 19 of whom had a response (29 percent, P<0.001 for the difference in response rates between the two treatments). On the eight-point Clinical Global Impressions–Improvement scale, a score of less than 4 was defined as a response to treatment (symptoms of anxiety had improved or ceased).

TABLE 3. ADVERSE EVENTS THAT OCCURRED AT ANY TIME DURING THE TRIAL IN THE FLUVOXAMINE AND PLACEBO GROUPS.

ADVERSE EVENT	FLUVOXAMINE (N=63)	PLACEBO (N=65)	TOTAL	P VALUE*
	no. (%)		%	
Headache	27 (43)	24 (37)	40	NS
Abdominal discomfort	31 (49)	18 (28)	38	0.02
Increased motor activity	17 (27)	8 (12)	20	0.06
Difficulty falling asleep	12 (19)	13 (20)	20	NS
Nasal congestion	11 (17)	12 (18)	18	NS
Drowsiness or sedation	13 (21)	10 (15)	18	NS
Nausea	12 (19)	9 (14)	16	NS
Diarrhea	9 (14)	10 (15)	15	NS
Influenza or upper respiratory symptoms	12 (19)	7 (11)	15	NS
Vomiting	12 (19)	6 (9)	14	NS
Sore throat	10 (16)	6 (9)	12	NS
Tiredness or fatigue	11 (17)	5 (8)	12	NS
Muscle or joint pain	11 (17)	5 (8)	12	NS
Coughing	6 (10)	9 (14)	12	NS
Skin irritation	6 (10)	9 (14)	12	NS
Decreased appetite	10 (16)	4 (6)	11	NS

*Values were determined by means of a chi-square statistic with Yates' correction. NS denotes not significant.

Premature Discontinuation of Treatment and Worsening of Anxiety

A total of 10 of the 63 children in the fluvoxamine group (16 percent) withdrew from the trial, as compared with 14 of the 65 children in the placebo group (22 percent). The reasons for withdrawal from the fluvoxamine group were failure to return to the clinic (two children), inability to swallow medication (three children), and adverse events (sedation, somatic discomfort, or hyperactivity; five children). The reasons for withdrawal from the placebo group were irritability and insomnia (one child), failure to return (eight children), and lack of efficacy (five children). The Clinical Global Impressions–Improvement ratings indicated that anxiety did not increase after the initiation of treatment with fluvoxamine, as has been reported in some trials of selective serotonin-reuptake inhibitors in adults.[12-15] Specifically, in the first three weeks of the trial, the condition of 3 of 63 children in the fluvoxamine group (5 percent) was rated worse than at base line on the Clinical Global Impressions–Improvement scale, as compared with 6 of 65 children in the placebo group (9 percent).

DISCUSSION

Our report demonstrates the efficacy of fluvoxamine in the treatment of children with social phobia, separation anxiety disorder, or generalized anxiety disorder. Fluvoxamine treatment was generally well tolerated but was associated with significantly more gastrointestinal symptoms, as found in other trials,[6,7,13-17] and with greater increases in children's levels of activity than was placebo. Effects on activity have been found in previous trials of selective serotonin-reuptake inhibitors in children, particularly in children younger

than 13 years of age,[7] but such effects typically have not been found in adults.[12-14] This increase in activity in children may relate to subjective effects in adults taking these drugs, who sometimes report increases in energy. Regardless of the mechanism, the side effects in the fluvoxamine group were usually mild. Only 5 of the 63 children in the fluvoxamine group discontinued treatment as a result of adverse events, as compared with 1 of the 65 children in the placebo group.

The efficacy of treatment with selective serotonin-reuptake inhibitors for anxiety in children in our trial is consistent with data obtained in studies of adults. Panic disorder, social phobia, and obsessive–compulsive disorder are the three specific anxiety disorders in adults whose treatment with these drugs has been studied most intensively.[12-15] In general, approximately 50 to 70 percent of patients with these disorders respond to therapy with selective serotonin-reuptake inhibitors; response rates in patients with panic disorder are usually higher than in patients with the other disorders. The results of our trial in children with social phobia, separation anxiety disorder, and generalized anxiety disorder are also consistent with the results of trials of these drugs in children with obsessive–compulsive disorder and major depression.[6,7,16,17,26]

Trials of cognitive–behavioral psychotherapy for children with anxiety disorders have found response rates in the range of 70 to 80 percent.[35,36] The response rates in trials of supportive therapies that pro-

313

vide encouragement and education to patients and their families about symptoms are similar to those for cognitive–behavioral therapy, although supportive therapies may include techniques of cognitive–behavioral therapy.[36] Without direct systematic comparisons between selective serotonin-reuptake inhibitors and psychotherapy, the relative merits of each treatment remain unknown. There is a particular need for studies of the comparative efficacy of treatment methods in children with anxiety, since such children have a more robust response to psychotherapy than children with other psychiatric disorders, such as attention-deficit–hyperactivity disorder.[37]

Treatment recommendations might follow from the current finding of a clinically meaningful effect of fluvoxamine on the symptoms of anxiety in children, for three main reasons. The study design satisfies standard criteria of evidence-based medicine for the generalizability of results.[38] The treatment had a large effect on symptoms.[39] Finally, fluvoxamine was generally well tolerated. Given these results, treatment with a selective serotonin-reuptake inhibitor becomes an important option for the treatment of children with anxiety disorders.

Our study had at least three limitations. First, the children were recruited if they met the criteria for any one of three anxiety disorders but not if they had several other disorders that often coexist with anxiety disorders. Second, the study lasted only eight weeks. Long-term trials and follow-up studies are needed, given the evidence from studies in animals of developmental plasticity in serotonergic neurons.[40] For example, treatment with selective serotonin-reuptake inhibitors in immature rodents may alter cortical and hippocampal synapses.[41,42] It is important to note that basic-science research has also established the long-term effects of stress, which is an integral aspect of anxiety in children, on the developing nervous system.[43] Stress has been shown to have long-term effects on behavior, neurochemistry, autonomic control, and hormonal regulation in developing rodents and primates.[43-45] Therefore, untreated anxiety in children may also have neurodevelopmental effects. Since there is a range of outcomes in children with anxiety disorders, from remission to chronic illness,[1,2,10,11] a study of maintenance treatment with selective serotonin-reuptake inhibitors is needed to assess the benefits and risks of long-term use. Moreover, given the evidence of neurodevelopmental effects of these drugs in animals, it will be important to study the effects of anxiety, stress, and selective serotonin-reuptake inhibitors on brain structure and function in children. Finally, despite a large therapeutic effect, the results of this trial must be interpreted cautiously, since the treating clinicians — rather than independent evaluators — rated both clinical outcome and adverse events, a design that may have created opportunities for bias in favor of active treatments.[46]

Supported by contracts from the National Institute of Mental Health to Johns Hopkins University (N01MH60016; principal investigator, Dr. Riddle) and the Research Foundation for Mental Hygiene (N01MH60005; principal investigator, Dr. Greenhill); by a contract from the National Institute of Mental Health to the University of California at Los Angeles (N01MH70010; principal investigator, Dr. McCracken); by Solvay Pharmaceuticals; by grants from the National Institute of Mental Health to Dr. Pine (MH57503 and MH01391); and by a grant from the National Center for Research Resources–National Institutes of Health General Clinical Research Center to Johns Hopkins University School of Medicine (M01 RR00052).

The opinions and assertions contained herein are the private views of the authors and are not to be construed as official or as reflecting the views of the National Institute of Mental Health or the Department of Health and Human Services.

We are indebted to the following members of the RUPP Network: Dana Raab, R.N., Hyung Koo, R.N., and Margaret Schlossberg, Ph.D., Johns Hopkins University; Anne Skrobala, Adriana Notarfrancesco, M.D., and Alice Park, New York State Psychiatric Institute; Thomas Cooper, M.S., Nathan Kline Institute; Peter Jensen and Joanne Severe, National Institute of Mental Health; Melvin Otis, M.D., New York University; and Deborah Lynn, M.D., and Jolie Kretchman, University of California at Los Angeles. We are also indebted to the following members of the RUPP Scientific Advisory Board: Joseph De Veaugh-Geiss, M.D., Glaxo–Wellcome; Robert Gibbons, Ph.D., University of Illinois; Henrietta Leonard, M.D., Brown University; and Susan Swedo, M.D., National Institute of Mental Health; and the members of the National Institute of Mental Health data and safety monitoring board.

REFERENCES

1. Klein RG, Pine DS. Anxiety disorders. In: Rutter M, Taylor E, Hersov L, eds. Child and adolescent psychiatry: modern approaches. 4th ed. London: Blackwell Scientific (in press).
2. Pine DS. Childhood anxiety disorders. Curr Opin Pediatr 1997;9:329-38.
3. Shaffer D, Fisher P, Dulcan MK, et al. The NIMH Diagnostic Interview Schedule for Children version 2.3 (DISC-2.3): description, acceptability, prevalence rates, and performance in the MECA Study: Methods for the Epidemiology of Child and Adolescent Mental Disorders Study. J Am Acad Child Adolesc Psychiatry 1996;35:865-77.
4. Costello EJ, Janiszewski S. Who gets treated? Factors associated with referral in children with psychiatric disorders. Acta Psychiatr Scand 1990;81:523-9.
5. Meredith LS, Sherbourne CDE, Jackson CA, Camp P, Wells KB. Treatment typically provided for comorbid anxiety disorders. Arch Fam Med 1997;6:231-7.
6. March JS, Biederman J, Wolkow R, et al. Sertraline in children and adolescents with obsessive-compulsive disorder: a multicenter randomized controlled trial. JAMA 1998;280:1752-6. [Erratum, JAMA 2000;283:1293.]
7. Labellarte MJ, Ginsburg GS, Walkup JT, Riddle MA. The treatment of anxiety disorders in children and adolescents. Biol Psychiatry 1999;46:1567-78.
8. Ialongo N, Edelsohn G, Werthamer-Larsson L, Crockett L, Kellam S. The significance of self-reported anxious symptoms in first grade children: prediction to anxious symptoms and adaptive functioning in fifth grade. J Child Psychol Psychiatry 1995;36:427-37.
9. Hansen C, Sanders SL, Massaro S, Last CG. Predictors of severity of absenteeism in children with anxiety-based school refusal. J Clin Child Psychol 1998;27:246-54.
10. Pine DS, Cohen P, Gurley D, Brook JS, Ma Y. The risk for early-adulthood anxiety and depressive disorders in adolescents with anxiety and depressive disorders. Arch Gen Psychiatry 1998;55:56-64.
11. Costello EJ, Angold A, Keeler GP. Adolescent outcomes of childhood disorders: the consequences of severity and impairment. J Am Acad Child Adolesc Psychiatry 1999;38:121-8.
12. Greist JH, Jefferson JW, Kobak KA, Katzelnick DJ, Serlin RC. Efficacy and tolerability of serotonin transport inhibitors in obsessive-compulsive disorder: a meta-analysis. Arch Gen Psychiatry 1995;52:53-60.
13. Liebowitz MR. Update on the diagnosis and treatment of social anxiety disorder. J Clin Psychiatry 1999;60:Suppl 18:22-6.
14. Stein MB. Medication treatments for panic disorder and social phobia. Depress Anxiety 1998;7:134-8.
15. Brady K, Pearstein T, Asnis GM, et al. Efficacy and safety of sertraline

314

treatment of posttraumatic stress disorder: a randomized controlled trial. JAMA 2000;283:1837-44.

16. Emslie GJ, Walkup JT, Pliszka SR, Ernst M. Nontricyclic antidepressants: current trends in children and adolescents. J Am Acad Child Adolesc Psychiatry 1999;38:517-28.

17. Emslie GJ, Rush AJ, Weinberg WA, et al. A double-blind, randomized, placebo-controlled trial of fluoxetine in children and adolescents with depression. Arch Gen Psychiatry 1997;54:1031-7.

18. Birmaher B, Waterman GS, Ryan N, et al. Open fluoxetine treatment of mixed anxiety disorders in children and adolescents. J Child Adolesc Psychopharmacol 1997;7:17-29.

19. Birmaher B, Waterman GS, Ryan N, et al. Fluoxetine for childhood anxiety disorders. J Am Acad Child Adolesc Psychiatry 1994;33:993-9.

20. Diagnostic and statistical manual of mental disorders, 4th ed.: DSM-IV. Washington, D.C.: American Psychiatric Association, 1994.

21. Greenhill LL, Pine D, March J, Birmaher B, Riddle M. Assessment issues in treatment research of pediatric anxiety disorders: what is working, what is not working, what is missing, and what needs improvement. Psychopharmacol Bull 1998;34:155-64.

22. Walkup J, Davies M. The Pediatric Anxiety Rating Scale (PARS): a reliability study. In: Scientific proceedings of the 46th Annual Meeting of the American Academy of Child and Adolescent Psychiatry, Chicago, October 19–24, 1999:NR78. abstract.

23. Shaffer D, Gould MS, Brasic J, et al. A children's global assessment scale (CGAS). Arch Gen Psychiatry 1983;40:1228-31.

24. Kaufman AS, Kaufman NL. Kaufman Brief Intelligence Test (K-BIT). Odessa, Fla.: Psychological Assessment Resources, 1987.

25. Graae F, Milner J, Rizzotto L, Klein RG. Clonazepam in childhood anxiety disorders. J Am Acad Child Adolesc Psychiatry 1994;33:372-6.

26. Wagner KD, Birmaher B, Carlson G, et al. Multi-center trial of paroxetine and imipramine in the treatment of adolescent depression. In: Scientific proceedings of the 45th Annual Meeting of the American Academy of Child and Adolescent Psychiatry, Anaheim, Calif., October 27–November 1, 1998:S12D. abstract.

27. Kaufman J, Birmaher B, Brent D, et al. Schedule for Affective Disorders and Schizophrenia for School-Age Children-Present and Lifetime Version (K-SADS-PL): initial reliability and validity data. J Am Acad Child Adolesc Psychiatry 1997;36:980-8.

28. Abikoff H, Gittelman R. Hyperactive children treated with stimulants: is cognitive training a useful adjunct? Arch Gen Psychiatry 1985;42:953-61.

29. Klein RG, Koplewicz HS, Kanner A. Imipramine treatment of children with separation anxiety disorder. J Am Acad Child Adolesc Psychiatry 1992;31:21-8.

30. March JS, Parker JD, Sullivan K, Stallings P, Conners CK. The Multidimensional Anxiety Scale for Children (MASC): factor structure, reliability, and validity. J Am Acad Child Adolesc Psychiatry 1997;36:554-65.

31. Birmaher B, Khetarpal S, Brent D, et al. The Screen for Child Anxiety Related Emotional Disorders (SCARED): scale construction and psychometric characteristics. J Am Acad Child Adolesc Psychiatry 1997;36:545-53.

32. Jolly JB, Wiesner DC, Wherry JN, Jolly JM, Dykman RA. Gender and the comparison of self and observer ratings of anxiety and depression in adolescents. J Am Acad Child Adolesc Psychiatry 1994;33:1284-8.

33. Gibbons RD, Hedeker D, Elkin I, et al. Some conceptual and statistical issues in analysis of longitudinal psychiatric data: application to the NIMH Treatment of Depression Collaborative Research Program dataset. Arch Gen Psychiatry 1993;50:739-50.

34. Cohen J. Statistical power analysis for the behavioral sciences. 2nd ed. Rev. Hillsdale, N.J.: Lawrence Erlbaum, 1988.

35. Kendall PC. Empirically supported psychological therapies. J Consult Clin Psychol 1998;66:3-6.

36. Last CG, Hansen C, Franco N. Cognitive-behavioral treatment of school phobia. J Am Acad Child Adolesc Psychiatry 1998;37:404-11.

37. The MTA Cooperative Group. A 14-month randomized clinical trial of treatment strategies for attention-deficit/hyperactivity disorder. Arch Gen Psychiatry 1999;56:1073-86.

38. Guyatt GH, Sackett DL, Cook DJ. Users' guides to the medical literature. II. How to use an article about therapy or prevention. A. Are the results of the study valid? JAMA 1993;270:2598-601.

39. Idem. Users' guides to the medical literature. II. How to use an article about therapy or prevention. B. What were the results and will they help me in caring for my patients? JAMA 1994;271:59-63.

40. Azmitia EC. Serotonin neurons, neuroplasticity, and homeostasis of neural tissue. Neuropsychopharmacology 1999;21:Suppl:33S-45S.

41. Wegerer V, Moll GH, Bagli M, Rothenberger A, Ruther E, Huether G. Persistently increased density of serotonin transporters in the frontal cortex of rats treated with fluoxetine during early juvenile life. J Child Adolesc Psychopharmacol 1999;9:13-24.

42. Norrholm SD, Ouimet CC. Chronic fluoxetine administration to juvenile rats prevents age-associated dendritic spine proliferation in hippocampus. Brain Res 2000;883:205-15.

43. Francis DD, Caldji C, Champagne F, Plotsky PM, Meaney MJ. The role of corticotropin-releasing factor–norepinephrine systems in mediating the effects of early experience on the development of behavioral and endocrine responses to stress. Biol Psychiatry 1999;46:1153-66.

44. Ladd CO, Huot RL, Thrivikraman KV, Nemeroff CB, Meaney MJ, Plotsky PM. Long-term behavioral and neuroendocrine adaptations to adverse early experience. Prog Brain Res 2000;122:81-103.

45. Coplan JD, Trost RC, Owens MJ, et al. Cerebrospinal fluid concentrations of somatostatin and biogenic amines in grown primates reared by mothers exposed to manipulated foraging conditions. Arch Gen Psychiatry 1998;55:473-7.

46. Quitkin FM, Rabkin JG, Gerald J, Davis JM, Klein DF. Validity of clinical trials of antidepressants. Am J Psychiatry 2000;157:327-37.

315

PSYCHIATRIC REACTION PATTERNS TO IMIPRAMINE [1]

DONALD F. KLEIN, M.D.,[2] AND MAX FINK, M.D.[3]

Clinical psychiatric experience demonstrates a wide range of variation in behavioral responses to physiological therapies. Present techniques of evaluating therapies by global improvement scores, imprecise diagnostic classification, and target symptoms abstracted from their context were felt to be methodologically inadequate. Following our experience in describing the behavioral reaction patterns to convulsive (4) and phenothiazine(6) therapies, a similar analysis of the data derived from imipramine (Tofrånil) therapy was undertaken.

In this report various patterns of behavioral response to imipramine are described ; and the relationship to such factors as age, sex, pretreatment behavioral pattern, hospital diagnosis, and hospital discharge evaluation are assessed.

METHOD

Hillside Hospital is a 196-bed, open ward, voluntary psychiatric facility for the treatment of patients with early and acute mental disorders whose stay is independent of their ability to pay. All patients are seen in individual psychotherapy, with the expectation that psychotherapy should be given a trial prior to other measures. Somatic therapies are employed by joint decision of the resident therapist and supervising psychiatrist, with the management of medication restricted to the research staff.

Before starting medication each patient is interviewed by a research psychiatrist. During drug therapy the patient's response is assessed in weekly interviews with both the patient and ward personnel, reviewing changes in mental status and hospital ad-

justment. In biweekly conferences with the psychiatric resident and his supervisor the patient's progress in psychotherapy, affective and symtomatic state, utilization of hospital facilities, and social and familial relationships are discussed.

When it was evident that the standard diagnostic nomenclature was of little use in categorizing behavioral reactions to drugs, and that psychodynamic formulations lacked predictive clarity, it was decided to derive a descriptive behavioral typology for each agent studied. The detailed longitudinal research records were reviewed and a summary statement concerning the patient's behavioral reaction during treatment was made. The patients were categorized on the basis of changes in symptoms, affect, patterns of communication and participation in psychotherapy and social activity. In each category the drug reaction was the determining feature. While no attention was paid at this point to the patient's pretreatment behavioral patterns, except as relevant to the perceived changes, inspection of these groups showed that not only did the patients share similar behavioral changes with drug therapy, but that they also showed similar behavioral pretreatment characteristics.

For certain patients no discernible change in behavior was observed. It was possible to characterize these subjects by their pretreatment behavioral patterns alone, and these patterns did not occur among those groups showing an imipramine effect.

Treatment was begun orally at 75 mg. daily and usually increased each week in 75 mg. steps, to a modal maximum of 300 mg. day in 80% of the patients.

Between October 1958 and July 1961, 215 patients received imipramine. During the early use of the drug it had not been firmly established that an adequate trial of medication required at least three to four weeks. Therefore, 13 patients who had not responded within two weeks had the medi-

[1] Aided, in part, by grants MY-2715 and MY-4798, National Institute of Mental Health, U.S. P.H.S. The cooperation and assistance of Geigy Pharmaceuticals is gratefully acknowledged.

[2] Mental Health Career Investigator, U.S.P.H.S.

[3] Dept. Experimental Psychiatry, Hillside Hospital, Glen Oaks, L. I., N. Y.

432

 cation discontinued. In retrospect, these patients had not received an adequate course of imipramine. Records were incomplete in 3 patients and at the time of writing 19 patients had not yet been discharged. These 35 patients are not included in the data analysis.

Of the 180 remaining patients, 67 were diagnosed as psychoneurotic depressive reactions, involutional melancholia, manic-depressive reaction, or psychotic depressive reaction. Schizophrenia in various subtypes was diagnosed in 102 patients. Ten patients received diagnoses of psychoneurosis or personality disorder, and one patient was diagnosed as chronic brain syndrome. Since the use of specific affective or schizophrenic subtypes was not discriminating in our analyses, the subgroups were combined.

There were 58 men and 122 women reflecting the sex distribution of the hospital. In this population schizophrenia was diagnosed most commonly in patients below 30 years of age, and affective disorders in patients above 40. However, there was no association of diagnosis or age, with sex.

Two methods of evaluating behavioral change were used—a medication management index and a discharge evaluation. The medication management index was based on the various patterns of medication use, reflecting the decision of the therapist as to the value of the medication to the patient —actions proverbially speaking louder than words. Eight patterns were observed, three implying a favorable and five an unfavorable evaluation. Favorable medication management evaluations by the therapist were seen in 115 subjects (68%) and included patients discharged to the community with the recommendation to continue on imipramine therapy (68 patients); patients discharged to the community after imipramine was discontinued with a clinical note that it had accomplished its therapeutic goals and without other somatic therapy prior to discharge (28 patients); and patients discharged to the community to continue imipramine with concurrent phenothiazine medication (19 patients).

Patterns reflecting a therapist's negative evaluation of the behavioral response were seen in 65 patients (32%). These included imipramine discontinued and subsequent treatment with phenothiazines or convulsive therapy prior to discharge (38 patients); imipramine discontinued with the clinical note that it was ineffective and the patients discharged without further somatic treatment (19 patients); and the abrupt ending of imipramine treatment by discharge to another inpatient facility (5 patients), suicide (1 patient), or leaving the hospital against medical advice (2 patients). In this report, the first three patterns of medication use will be referred to as "favorable medication management" and the latter five as "unfavorable medication management."

In addition, at discharge each patient is given a summary rating as "recovered," "much improved," "improved," or "unimproved" by the staff. This discharge rating is a guide to the effect of hospitalization. It is not the same as the medication management index since other treatment measures may have been interposed after the imipramine treatment. However, this measure will aid in placing the imipramine effects within the context of the general hospital psychiatric treatment. In view of the small number of patients considered "recovered," this category was combined with "much improved."

The chi square method of statistical analysis was used and all stated findings are at the .05 level of confidence or better.

RESULTS

General Medication Response. The behavioral effect of imipramine required two to three weeks to become evident for the majority of cases. An occasional case responded within a few days, and one case responded after 5 weeks of medication.

Complaints of sweating, tremulousness, dry mouth, and constipation were frequent, but interfered little with the treatment course. Two patients developed grand mal epileptic attacks (at 300 mg./day and 450 mg./day) which ceased with medication reduction or termination. There was one instance of pseudo-tumor cerebri(2) and one instance of agranulocytosis. Both occurred during the concomitant administration of phenothiazines, and may have been unrelated to imipramine.

In 22 of 26 patients receiving imipramine in 300 mg. daily doses for periods of two months or more, and rapidly withdrawn from the drug, the occurrence of a physiological withdrawal syndrome of nausea, vomiting, headache, giddiness, coryza, chills, weakness, fatigue and musculoskeletal pain was documented(7). These symptoms were related to the length of treatment and the abruptness of the withdrawal. It was also observed that these symptoms could be minimized by gradual withdrawal over one to two weeks.

Patterns of Behavioral Response. The relation of the behavioral response patterns to medication management, hospital discharge evaluation, age, sex and diagnosis are presented in Tables 1 and 2.

1. Mood Elevation Response.

Before Treatment : These patients were depressed, self-depreciatory and hopeless. Many patients exhibited a rigid, perfectionistic and obsessional personality, although tendencies to minimize and deny difficulty were not conspicuous. They related to the examiner in an apathetic and passive fashion, although a few patients were agitated, fearful and demanding. On inquiry, they complained of anorexia, insomnia, unhappiness, loss of interest in their activities, and inability to cope with their responsibilities, to concentrate, or to make decisions. They had difficulty in staying asleep rather than falling asleep. Somatic complaints other than insomnia, anorexia and constipation would only occasionally be in evidence. However, when present they formed a major preoccupation. Suicidal ideation and frank delusional states were infrequent. These patients did not spontaneously participate in ward activities and if activity was not stimulated and guided they lapsed into apathetic indifference.

With Treatment : There was a marked decrease in expressions of disinterest in the environment, apathy, depression, suicidal rumination, retardation, agitation, insomnia and anorexia. Participation in hospital activities and

TABLE 1
Behavioral Response Patterns, Medication Management, and Hospital Evaluations

BEHAVIORAL RESPONSE	N	% FAVORABLE MEDICATION MANAGEMENT	HOSPITAL DISCHARGE RATING		
			% UNIMPROVED	% IMPROVED	% MUCH IMPROVED & RECOVERED
Mood elevation	67	96%	0%	63%	37%
Explicit verbal denial	22	95	0	59	41
Manic	10	40	10	60	30
Reduction episodic anxiety	14	100	0	79	21
Agitated disorganization	19	5	58	42	0
Anhedonic socialization	8	63	25	50	25
Non-response	40	15	38	55	7
Total	180	62%	16%	59%	25%

TABLE 2
Behavioral Response Patterns, Sex, Age and Diagnosis

BEHAVIORAL RESPONSE	N	% MALE	% AGE <=30	DIAGNOSIS		
				% SCHIZOPHRENIA	% AFFECTIVE DISORDER	% OTHER
Mood elevation	67	31%	43%	49%	46%	5%
Explicit verbal denial	22	32	9	14	86	0
Manic	10	20	40	60	40	0
Reduction episodic anxiety	14	43	43	43	14	43
Agitated disorganization	19	63	95	100	0	0
Anhedonic socialization	8	25	88	100	0	0
Non-response	40	18	50	68	28	4
Total	180	32%	48%	57%	37%	6%

social relationships increased. Complaints of tension and apprehension relating to difficulties in discharge planning and returning to the community remained, however, with anxious procrastinating attempts to evolve a foolproof plan. Symptoms frequently increased prior to discharge.

Mood elevation was a response frequently associated with favorable medication management and hospital discharge evaluation. Special relationships to age, sex or diagnosis were not evident.

2. Explicit Verbal Denial Response.

Before Treatment : These patients closely resembled those described under mood elevation, although there was more denial and minimization of their difficulties which were usually referred to external events or bodily states rather than emotional distress.

With Treatment : As with mood elevation, depressive symptoms decreased and goal-directed action increased. In contrast to mood elevation, all complaints and difficulties were denied, the patients stating that they were entirely well and should be discharged forthwith, disregarding realistic familial and economic difficulties.

The explicit verbal denial response was generally associated with favorable medication management, an older age group, and a diagnosis of affective disorder. This group received the most favorable hospital discharge evaluations, probably as a consequence of their gross denial of residual difficulties.

Comment : These patients possessed many of the premorbid personality attributes described by Kahn and Fink(5) as characteristic of patients who responded well to convulsive therapy. Specifically, they were minimizing, denying of difficulty, non-empathic, non-introspective, communicating non-verbally, highly conventional and stereotyped.

3. Manic Response.

Before Treatment : These patients resembled closely the patients described under mood elevation response.

With Treatment : They first exhibited explicit verbal denial, but then became vociferous with a great display made of their logic as opposed to others illogic. There were periods of psychomotor acceleration accompanied by flights of ideas, loss of frustration tolerance, and lack of self-criticism. In psychotherapy, aggressive verbal attacks upon significant life

figures, most frequently spouses and mothers, became common with much talk of divorce or moving away from home. Long standing resentments, previously dealt with by submissive denial, became the focus of therapy with prominent attempts to gain the therapist as an ally against relatives. If this alliance was denied, the patient became hostile and accusatory towards the therapist. Their demanding hostility frequently led them into dictatorial, manipulative, and derogatory attitudes towards both staff and patients. They energetically participated in numerous hospital activities with great self-confidence, occasionally becoming the nucleus for a clique of hostile and negativistic patients. Delusions and bizarre activity did not occur.

Cessation of imipramine medication did not result in a reversion to their previous state, and interruption of this response by large doses of phenothiazine was usually necessary, and helpful.

Manic response was associated with a moderately unfavorable medication management. No special relationships to age, sex, or diagnosis were observed, although the 4 cases of affective disorder showing this response were diagnosed as manic-depressive disorder. There were, however, 15 other subjects with the same diagnosis who did not show a manic response to imipramine.

These patients' medication management classification as unfavorable was determined by their imipramine being replaced by phenothiazines ; however, their subsequent improvement resulted in an average discharge evaluation.

4. Reduction of Episodic Anxiety Response.

Before Treatment : Typically, subjects noted the sudden onset of inexplicable "panic" attacks, accompanied by rapid breathing, palpitations, weakness, and a feeling of impending death. Their activities became progressively constricted, until they were no longer able to travel alone for fear of being suddenly rendered helpless while isolated from help. Depressive complaints were infrequent and associated with feelings of futility. Although fear of open spaces was not the hallmark of this condition but rather expectant fear of lack of support when overwhelmed, their condition was often referred to as agoraphobia. They engaged in prolonged outpatient psychotherapy, usually devoted to the exploration of unconscious sexual and aggressive impulses, with the interpretation of the phobically barred areas as situations of forbidden symbolic temptation. Hospitalization occurred after the family could no longer tolerate the restrictions placed upon them.

With Treatment : Under imipramine treatment the "panic" attacks ceased, although both phenothiazines and sedatives had been previously ineffective. However, the patients were reluctant to change their phobic behavior pattern and required much persuasion, direction and support. Their social interaction increased markedly with a surprising rise in aggressive self-assertion and rejection of domination.

The reduction of episodic anxiety response was usually associated with a favorable medication management. This was the only group with a large proportion of psychoneurosis and personality disorder diagnoses. There was no special relationship to age or sex.

Comment : The reaction to imipramine is of considerable interest since the "anxiety" of the panic attack is sharply diminished while expectant "anxiety" related to the "phobic" patterns remains. The use of the common term "anxiety" may thus obscure an underlying difference in these processes.

Bowlby(3) has emphasized that separation anxiety does not have to be learned via noxious experiences of separation. In this view, separation anxiety has the biological function of evoking the retrieving and mothering response in a parent and is an innate mechanism of social control. One may speculate that imipramine, in these patients, has some specific reparative effects upon this disordered mechanism.

5. Agitated Disorganization Response.

Before Treatment : These patients were withdrawn, preoccupied, defensive, suspicious, minimizing and denying. After specific questioning they admitted to ego-alien thoughts but conveyed the impression that their hospitalization was a mistake. Their affect was flat, frequently inappropriate, and apathetic, they appeared to consciously suppress delusional material.

A history of poor social, education and vocational attainment was uniformly present, with many indications of childhood disorder.

They spoke little and by confining themselves to stereotyped utterances preserved a façade of being rational and relevant. However, any extended speech revealed peculiar and bizarre language patterns with neologisms and autistic word usage. Formal thought disorder was evident, with over-concreteness,

over-abstraction and loose associations. Psychotherapy was a barren experience as the patients made no effort to relate to their therapists and avoided any discussion of their feelings.

Social contact was actively rejected, the patients remaining isolated on the wards or roaming aimlessly about the grounds. At times they were prankish, eccentric and unpredictable and at best cooperated passively with ward routines and activities.

With Treatment : They first developed an inappropriate euphoria, which was often misinterpreted as the onset of improvement. This was soon followed by bizarre, disorganized, aggressive hyperactivity associated with intolerable tension, fragmentation of thought and marked somatic and paranoid delusions. This response uniformly required the interruption of imipramine treatment and the immediate use of convulsive or phenothiazine therapy.

Agitated disorganization was associated with a negative medication management evaluation and occurred mostly in young, schizophrenic males. This behavioral reaction was a grave prognostic sign as 58% of these patients were discharged "unimproved" and none considered "much improved" or "recovered," despite subsequent treatment.

Comment : Of interest is the marked similarity of this group of patients to those described as having the reaction pattern of autistic compliance to phenothiazines(6). The predominance of males is similar to the sex ratio of childhood schizophrenia.

6. Anhedonic Socialization.

Before Treatment : These patients related to the examiner in a discouraged and dependent fashion with manipulative tendencies. They spontaneously grumbled of an anxious depression, also the observed affective display was less than the extensiveness of their complaints. These complaints concerned fluctuating feelings of withdrawal, anxiety, tension, depression, depersonalization, phobic compulsions, ruminative thoughts, and inertia. A lack of feelings of pleasure and competence was prominent.

They were rational, relevant and coherent, and described their complaints in abstract psychiatric terms. It was difficult to obtain a specific connected story concerning their symptomatology. If the psychotherapist indicated certain strengths, this was immediately met by a burst of self-derogatory expressions. Many of these patients had previously received prolonged outpatient psychotherapy.

They associated with similar patients in tight cliques, preserving a friendly relationship. While few of the hospital activities were interesting to them they stayed active rather than withdrawn. They frequently had a history of good social and educational achievement marred by a pervasive anhedonia.

With Treatment : This group manifested an increase in alertness, definiteness and precision. Dependent demands were diminished. Their verbal affective complaints were modified only slightly, although they appeared to be less anxious and depressed. Symptoms of apathy and inability to function were alleviated, while feelings of depersonalization, phobic compulsive and ruminative thoughts were maintained. The effects of the medication were minimized by the patients, yet their symptoms exacerbated on medication withdrawal.

In psychotherapy a degree of overt self-assertion became apparent, associated with some guilt and apprehension over aggressiveness. They became more active, dressed more attractively and associated with more people, achieving responsible positions in their ward or peer group organizations. Hospital activities were utilized more fully and in a more interested fashion.

This response was associated with a favorable management evaluation. This group consisted of young schizophrenic patients without relationship to sex distribution or hospital outcome. The only suicide in this study occurred in this group.

7. Non-Responding Patients.

No significant behavioral changes were observed in 40 patients. In pretreatment characteristics, these subjects were classified into a few subgroups.

A group of 13 patients showed histrionic labile affect, with depressive, fearful, paranoid and agitated displays rapidly alternating with affable friendly periods. Their lability made evaluations of drug effect very difficult, requiring long observation periods before an evaluation could be made. The histrionic manipulative character of these patients gave the impression that their affective displays were goal-oriented and ludic devices for manipulation of the environment rather than direct expressions of internal distress. Phenothiazine medications were also ineffective in modifying their behavior.

Other patients had a variety of syndromes with the common thread of marked fixity of symptomatology over a period of years prior to hospitalization. These syndromes were so-matic preoccupation (10 patients), obsessional rumination (6 patients), fearful paranoid referential states (4 patients), and a variety of schizoid and psychopathic character disorders (7 patients). Phenothiazine medications were also ineffective in modifying their symptoms.

The "non-responders" were preponderantly female without a special relationship to age or diagnosis. Hospital outcome was poor.

Relation of Age and Diagnosis to Medication Evaluation. By grouping the subjects according to medication management, age and diagnosis, we observed that the percentage of favorable medication management is approximately 51% for schizophrenia, and 79% for affective disorder, at all age levels. We would conclude that diagnosis is more closely related than age to clinical evaluations of imipramine therapy.

CONCLUSIONS

Imipramine appears to be a safe and valuable medication in the treatment of a variety of psychiatric conditions. It produces various behavioral change patterns that are related to both the personality of the patient and the symptom pattern of the illness. While these response patterns cut across the usual nosologic categories, there is a significant statistical relationship to the distinction between schizophrenic and affective disorders. These patterns of behavioral response are highly associated with pretreatment behavioral patterns, and further study may serve to define subgroups whose response to imipramine can be predicted with high probability.

Similar observations are reported by Ayd (1) in a review of the current status of the "major antidepressants." Allowing for differences in terminology, his findings closely parallel our own. For example, Ayd notes :

Dramatic therapeutic results were seen in those patients often diagnosed anxiety hysteria because their depression was overshadowed by severe anxiety with hysterical features. [They] . . . had good pre-illness personalities despite an anxious, phobic temperament. In contrast to the classical endogenous depressive, these patients had a normal sleep pattern or insomnia, which readily responded to barbiturate hypnotics, rather than an early morning awakening. Usually they complained of feeling worse as the day wore on. They had little appetite disturbance and no great weight loss. They had many somatic complaints. Seldom were they self-depreciatory. They detested being alone, were voluble, anxious, and tremulous and exhibited psychomotor stimulation instead of inhibition . . . Tranquilizers invariably made them feel worse, ECT enhanced their anxiety . . . When treated with an antidepressant they reacted promptly . . .

The personality organization and behavioral response of these patients are strikingly similar to those described as showing a reduction of episodic anxiety response to imipramine.

This response was seen by Ayd as indicating that in these patients "depression was overshadowed by severe anxiety." In similar fashion, others have referred to "underlying" or "masked" depressions. The basis for these formulations appears to be the positive behavioral response to "antidepressants," as the classical signs and symptoms of depression are not clinically manifest. Yet, these patients are refractory to convulsive therapy, which should lead to the inference that they do not have an "underlying" depression.

Such terms represent *ad hoc* formulations that obscure common characteristics distinctive in these patients. In an earlier study (6) we indicated that the behavioral patterns after phenothiazine medication are related to the antecedent behavior, as seen in characteristic adaptive mechanisms, communication patterns, affect, symptoms, psychotherapy participation and social activity. The responses to medication may be used as dissecting tools to uncover various subpopulations and to permit the discovery of specific developmental, physiological, psychological and social similarities within each subpopulation. These common characteristics may also clarify questions of etiology and pathogenesis of psychiatric disorders, and provide rational indications and contraindications for drug therapy. The observations with imipramine reported here suggest that these generalizations may be true for a wide variety of psychotropic agents.

SUMMARY

1. One hundred and eighty voluntary inpatients (102 schizophrenic subjects, 67 subjects with affective disorders, and 11 "other" diagnoses) were studied during treatment with imipramine.

2. Seven imipramine induced behavioral reaction patterns and their relationships to diagnosis, age, sex, patterns of medication use, and hospital discharge evaluation are presented. These include mood elevation, explicit verbal denial, manic, reduction of episodic anxiety, agitated disorganization, anhedonic socialization, and non-response.

3. Imipramine was favorably evaluated in 79% of subjects with affective disorders and 51% of schizophrenic patients.

4. The use of psychiatric reaction patterns to psychotropic drugs for categorizing patients and providing a basis for a more rational pharmacotherapy are emphasized.

BIBLIOGRAPHY

1. Ayd, F. J., Jr.: APA Psychiatric Research Reports, Detroit, 213, 1959.

2. Blumberg, A. G., and Klein, D. F.: Am. J. Psychiat., 118 : 168, 1961.

3. Bowlby, J.: Int. J. Psychoanal., 51 : 89, 1960.

4. Fink, M., and Kahn, R. L.: A.M.A. Arch. Gen. Psychiat., 5 : 30, 1961.

5. Kahn, R. L., and Fink, M.: J. Neuropsychiat., 1 : 1, 1959.

6. Klein, D. F., and Fink, M.: A.M.A. Arch. Gen. Psychiat. In Press.

7. Kramer, J. C., Klein, D. F., and Fink, M.: Am. J. Psychiat., 118 : 549, 1961.

Cognitive-Behavioral Therapy, Imipramine, or Their Combination for Panic Disorder
A Randomized Controlled Trial

David H. Barlow, PhD

Jack M. Gorman, MD

M. Katherine Shear, MD

Scott W. Woods, MD

PANIC DISORDER (PD) IS A chronic condition associated with substantial reduction in quality of life,[1] and lifetime prevalence rates are approximately 3%.[2,3] Role functioning is substantially lower in patients with PD than in patients with diabetes, heart disease, or arthritis.[4] Individuals with PD frequently use both emergency department and general medical services,[5] presenting with high rates of unexplained cardiac symptoms,[6,7] dizziness, and bowel distress.[6,8] These patterns continue indefinitely.[9,10] The social and economic costs of PD are considerable.[11-13] Successfully treating PD can produce medical cost offsets as high as 94%.[12] Thus, efforts to ascertain effective treatments or a combination of treatments for PD are important.

Earlier psychosocial treatments were directed specifically at unexpected panic attacks and associated anxiety.[14,15] A growing number of studies support the effectiveness of these psychosocial approaches for PD compared with no treatment or credible psychosocial placebos.[16] By the 1980s, the efficacy of pharmacological treatment with imipramine in patients with PD had been well

For editorial comment see p 2573.

established.[17-21] Imipramine was regarded as the pharmacological criterion standard for the treatment of PD for more than 20 years,[22-24] until the emer-

Context Panic disorder (PD) may be treated with drugs, psychosocial intervention, or both, but the relative and combined efficacies have not been evaluated in an unbiased fashion.

Objective To evaluate whether drug and psychosocial therapies for PD are each more effective than placebo, whether one treatment is more effective than the other, and whether combined therapy is more effective than either therapy alone.

Design and Setting Randomized, double-blind, placebo-controlled clinical trial conducted in 4 anxiety research clinics from May 1991 to April 1998.

Patients A total of 312 patients with PD were included in the analysis.

Interventions Patients were randomly assigned to receive imipramine, up to 300 mg/d, only (n=83); cognitive-behavioral therapy (CBT) only (n=77); placebo only (n=24); CBT plus imipramine (n=65); or CBT plus placebo (n=63). Patients were treated weekly for 3 months (acute phase); responders were then seen monthly for 6 months (maintenance phase) and then followed up for 6 months after treatment discontinuation.

Main Outcome Measures Treatment response based on the Panic Disorder Severity Scale (PDSS) and the Clinical Global Impression Scale (CGI) by treatment group.

Results Both imipramine and CBT were significantly superior to placebo for the acute treatment phase as assessed by the PDSS (response rates for the intent-to-treat [ITT] analysis, 45.8%, 48.7%, and 21.7%; P=.05 and P=.03, respectively), but were not significantly different for the CGI (48.2%, 53.9%, and 37.5%, respectively). After 6 months of maintenance, imipramine and CBT were significantly more effective than placebo for both the PDSS (response rates, 37.8%, 39.5%, and 13.0%, respectively; P=.02 for both) and the CGI (37.8%, 42.1%, and 13.0%, respectively). Among responders, imipramine produced a response of higher quality. The acute response rate for the combined treatment was 60.3% for the PDSS and 64.1% for the CGI; neither was significantly different from the other groups. The 6-month maintenance response rate for combined therapy was 57.1% for the PDSS (P=.04 vs CBT alone and P=.03 vs imipramine alone) and 56.3% for the CGI (P=.03 vs imipramine alone), but was not significantly better than CBT plus placebo in either analysis. Six months after treatment discontinuation, in the ITT analysis CGI response rates were 41.0% for CBT plus placebo, 31.9% for CBT alone, 19.7% for imipramine alone, 13% for placebo, and 26.3% for CBT combined with imipramine.

Conclusions Combining imipramine and CBT appeared to confer limited advantage acutely but more substantial advantage by the end of maintenance. Each treatment worked well immediately following treatment and during maintenance; CBT appeared durable in follow-up.

JAMA. 2000;283:2529-2536   www.jama.com

Author Affiliations and Financial Disclosures are listed at the end of this article.

Corresponding Author and Reprints: David H. Barlow, PhD, Center for Anxiety and Related Disorders, Boston University, 648 Beacon St, Sixth Floor, Boston, MA 02215.

323

gence of the selective serotonin reuptake inhibitors (SSRIs).

Despite the proven efficacy of both drug and psychosocial treatments for PD and some emerging evidence on the possible synergistic effects of these approaches, particularly on phobic behavior,[25] studies of medication and psychosocial approaches have, until recently, run on parallel and sometimes hostile tracks.[15,26-29] We assembled a team of 4 investigators, 2 committed to each approach, to undertake a comparative study that would determine optimal treatment for PD.

METHODS
Study Design
We conducted a randomized controlled trial comparing cognitive-behavioral therapy (CBT), imipramine plus medical management, the combination of CBT and imipramine (CBT+imipramine), pill placebo plus medical management, and CBT+placebo for PD (FIGURE). Randomization was stratified by site and presence of *Diagnostic and Statistical Manual of Mental Disorders, Revised Third Edition*–defined current major depression and was blocked within stratum. To improve trial efficiency,[30] unequal numbers of patients were randomized to the treatments (6 CBT, 6 imipramine, 5 CBT+ imipramine, 25 CBT+placebo, and 2 placebo per block of 24) based on expected pairwise comparison effect sizes. The acute treatment phase consisted of 11 sessions during 12 weeks. Each CBT session lasted approximately 50 minutes

and each drug treatment session approximately 30 minutes. Patients in combined treatment saw 2 therapists for a total of about 75 minutes per week. Responders to acute treatment entered a 6-month maintenance phase without breaking the study blind. Maintenance-phase treatment consisted of 6 monthly appointments in which treatment similar to the acute treatment was continued. After 9 months of treatment (3 months acute and 6 months maintenance), patients were assessed again. Responders to maintenance treatment were then assigned to discontinuation of treatment, except for 17 patients who were randomized to an extended maintenance pilot project. Remaining patients were assessed again after 6 months of follow-up (15 months after

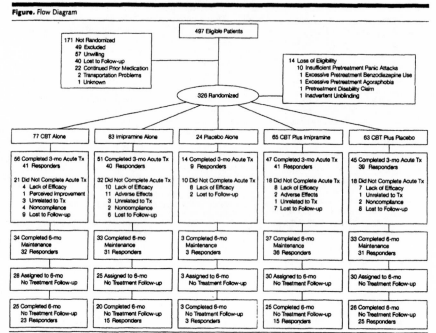

Figure. Flow Diagram

CBT indicates cognitive-behavioral therapy; Tx, treatment. Responders are defined in the "Assessment" section.

324

treatment was initiated). The trial was conducted between May 1991 and April 1998 and was approved by institutional review boards at each site.

Subjects

All patients passing diagnostic screening for a principal diagnosis of PD with or without mild agoraphobia (N = 497) were entered in the pretreatment phase after signing written, informed consent. Pretreatment included drug washout for patients taking anxiolytic or antidepressant medication. Patients were permitted up to 10 doses of benzodiazepine (0.5 mg of alprazolam-equivalent) in the 2 weeks before the first treatment visit and up to 20 doses during baseline and acute treatment combined. During the 2 weeks prior to the first treatment visit, patients underwent physical and laboratory examinations, and diagnosis was confirmed using the Anxiety Disorders Interview Schedule-Revised (ADIS-R).[31,32] Mild agoraphobia was operationally defined as a score less than or equal to 18 on the ADIS-R avoidance scale. In addition, inclusion required at least 1 full or limited panic attack in the 2 weeks before the first treatment visit.

Exclusion criteria were psychotic, bipolar, or significant medical illnesses, suicidality, significant substance abuse, contraindications to either treatment, prior nonresponse to similar treatments, and concurrent competing treatment or pending disability claims. More details are available on request from the authors. Patients with comorbid unipolar depression were not excluded unless suicidal. A detailed analysis of reasons for pretreatment attrition is provided elsewhere.[33]

Therapists

Therapists providing CBT were doctoral-level clinicians who underwent extensive training and certification supervised by the Boston site prior to treating study patients. Clinicians were not required to have prior training in cognitive-behavioral procedures. Pharmacotherapists were experienced psychiatrists who underwent additional training and certification in the study protocol

under the direction of the Columbia/Hillside site. All CBT therapists and pharmacotherapists received ongoing supervision of their cases from the responsible site during biweekly telephone calls, and adherence and competence ratings were routinely collected after listening to a sample of audiotaped sessions.

Treatment Conditions

Cognitive-behavioral therapy for PD, developed at the Boston site, combines interoceptive exposure, cognitive restructuring, and breathing retraining. This treatment was described in a manual containing detailed instructions for the conduct of each session.[34]

The imipramine and placebo interventions were administered in a double-blind, fixed flexible-dose design, according to a manual developed for this study. Both the imipramine and placebo arms included a medical management component, specified in the manual. The purpose of medical management was to monitor adverse effects, clinical state, and the patient's physical/mental condition; maximize compliance with the pharmacological treatment protocol; and proscribe specific interventions included in CBT (eg, cognitive restructuring of anxiety and panic symptoms). Patients who experienced clinical deterioration were removed from the study and offered alternative treatment for 3 months free of charge.

Starting dosages of imipramine were 10 mg/d (or pill placebo equivalent), increased every other day by 10 mg until 50 mg/d was reached. The dosage was then increased more rapidly, with an effort made to reach 100 mg/d by the end of week 3 and 200 mg/d by week 5, even if the patient became symptom-free earlier, unless adverse effects became intolerable. If the patient was not symptom-free, the dosage could be increased up to 300 mg/d by week 5. Blood levels of imipramine were assessed at 6 and 12 weeks and benzodiazepine screening of urine samples performed by local commercial laboratories.

The combined treatment conditions were administered according to

a manual essentially consisting of the CBT and the imipramine manuals.

Assessment

Prior to beginning the study, independent evaluators participated in training and certification on the rating instruments, supervised by the Pittsburgh site. Bimonthly conference calls were held for evaluators to discuss any questions and/or discrepancies among sites, and regular, random interviews were monitored for continued reliability of diagnosis and ratings. Reliability on main measures remained above 90%. Evaluator assessments occurred at baseline and after acute, maintenance, and follow-up phases, and evaluators were blind to treatment assignment.

The primary continuous outcome measure was the average item score for the Panic Disorder Severity Scale (PDSS), a clinician-rated scale of PD severity.[35] We also present results for a 40% reduction from baseline on PDSS. The primary categorical outcome measure involved determination of a responder based on the Clinical Global Impression Scale (CGI),[36] consisting of 7-point scales rating overall improvement and severity. We added specific PD-based anchor points for rating the CGI in this study. To be a responder, a patient needed to achieve a score of 2 (much improved) or better while being rated as 3 (mild) or less on CGI severity. Receipt of nonstudy treatment was evaluated at each assessment point. Patients who received nonstudy treatment for anxiety or panic were determined to be nonresponders, both for PDSS and CGI responder definitions.

Statistical Analyses

The study was designed to address if both CBT alone and imipramine alone performed better than placebo; if either CBT or imipramine performed better relative to each other; and if there was an advantage to combining CBT and imipramine as evidenced by superiority of CBT+imipramine to CBT+placebo, imipramine alone, and CBT alone. These questions were addressed at each of 3 assessment points: postacute, postmain-

325

tenance, and follow-up. At each point, we performed an intent-to-treat (ITT) analysis, using an early-termination assessment. The baseline was carried forward as an assumption of nonresponse or return to baseline if the early-termination assessment was missing or contaminated by nonstudy treatment. Similarly, the baseline was also carried forward in follow-up analyses for the same reasons. Intent-to-treat analyses included all randomized patients except those discovered to be ineligible after randomization (Figure). At postmaintenance and follow-up assessments, we also conducted intent-to-continue (ITC) analyses, restricted to patients completing the preceding phase as responders. At postacute assessment, we present results for completers only.

Data were subjected first to omnibus testing of all 5 treatments and then to pairwise post hoc testing when the omnibus test indicated statistical significance. The Freeman-Halton and Fisher exact tests were used for categorical measure analyses, analysis of variance for PDSS baseline analysis, and analysis of covariance for subsequent analyses using baseline as the covariate. When analyses indicated a significant baseline-by-treatment interaction on the dependent measure, analysis of covariance was replaced by repeated-measures analysis of variance, with treatment assignment as the independent (between groups) variable and time as the dependent (within groups) variable. Significance was defined as $P \le .05$ with a 2-tailed test.

RESULTS

Of the 326 patients randomized, 312 are included in the analysis. Thirteen were excluded following uniform screening for loss of eligibility, and 1 was removed because of inadvertent unblinding. Proportions of excluded patients were not significantly different among treatment assignments.

Baseline, Site, and Stratum Analyses

There were no significant differences on demographic measures or on baseline PDSS score among the 5 randomized groups (TABLE 1). The mean PDSS scores indicate a moderate-to-average severity. No significant site effect, depression stratum effect, site-by-treatment interaction, or stratum-by-treatment interaction was observed in the acute ITT analyses for any of the 3 measures; thus, all data were aggregated across sites and across strata. Similarly, there were no significant interactions between treatment and other baseline variables (Table 1) in multivariate acute ITT analyses for any of the 3 measures. No important differences at baseline were observed between treatment groups entering vs not entering maintenance or follow-up. It has been suggested that when $P < .10$ level heterogeneity of the slope is present across treatments, treatment effects that apply to an important portion of the baseline severity spectrum may be obscured in analyses of covariance.[37] For slope heterogeneity, $P > .25$ for 8 of 9 omnibus

PDSS analyses of covariance, suggesting little heterogeneity.

Subject Disposition, Dosing, and Laboratory Analyses

Acute completion rates did not differ significantly across treatment groups. Among the 8 noncompliant patients was 1 patient receiving imipramine alone who violated protocol by using benzodiazepines at rates exceeding those allowed, and 1 patient receiving CBT who began nonprotocol antidepressant treatment during acute treatment. The Figure also shows that 82% to 90% of maintenance-eligible patients completed maintenance across active treatments, compared with 33% of placebo patients. The omnibus test for this analysis was significant. Pairwise comparisons were significant for all active treatments vs placebo, including CBT alone ($P = .006$), imipramine alone ($P = .007$), CBT+imipramine ($P = .001$), and CBT+placebo ($P = .004$).

Patients receiving medication reported taking doses of 175 to 180 mg/d across treatments by week 6 and 214 to 239 mg/d by week 12. Mean (SD) imipramine+desipramine plasma levels at week 6 were 219 (186) ng/dL and 223 (127) ng/dL for CBT+imipramine and imipramine alone, respectively, and 225 (148) ng/dL and 263 (156) ng/dL at week 12.

Rates of urine samples that tested positive for benzodiazepines were low. At week 6, 3 (1.5%) of 197 samples tested positive (1 CBT+imipramine, 1 CBT, 1

Table 1. Baseline Analyses*

Variable	CBT Alone	Imipramine Alone	Placebo Alone	CBT Plus Imipramine	CBT Plus Placebo	Total†	P Value‡
No. of subjects	77	83	24	65	63	312	
Female sex, %	63.2	60.2	75.0	64.1	58.1	62.5	.67
Age, mean (SD), y	37.5 (10.9)	35.5 (9.7)	34.2 (9.7)	34.1 (11.4)	37.8 (11.3)	36.1 (10.7)	.23
White race, %	89.0	89.0	91.3	95.3	90.3	90.8	.71
Currently married, %	52.1	45.1	39.1	48.4	58.1	49.7	.45
Duration of illness, mean (SD), y	6.61 (8.55)	6.38 (7.54)	6.64 (10.4)	6.60 (8.99)	5.50 (8.17)	6.33 (8.43)	.96
PDSS average item score, mean (SD)§	1.82 (0.55)	1.88 (0.56)	1.86 (0.52)	1.86 (0.57)	1.74 (0.51)	1.83 (0.54)	.58
Current major depression, %	23.7	30.1	29.2	26.6	27.0	27.1	.92

*CBT indicates cognitive-behavioral therapy; placebo, pill placebo plus medical management; and PDSS, Panic Disorder Severity Scale. No. of subjects for each cell may vary slightly from the number of subjects in each treatment arm due to occasional missing data (exact numbers available on request).
†Total of all 5 treatments combined.
‡P value for omnibus analysis of variance (for continuous measures) or 5 × 2 Freeman-Halton exact test (for categorical measures).
§A higher PDSS score indicates greater severity.

326

imipramine), and at week 12, 3 (1.8%) of 164 (1 CBT+imipramine, 1 CBT, 1 imipramine) tested positive. Rates of missing urine samples were not significantly different across treatments.

CBT Alone and Imipramine Alone vs Placebo. In the acute ITT analysis, both CBT alone and imipramine alone were superior to placebo for the PDSS continuous measure (TABLE 2). Both treatments had significantly fewer dropouts for lack of efficacy than did placebo (4/18 for CBT and 10/30 for imipramine vs 8/10 for placebo [Figure]), and the imipramine group had significantly more dropouts for adverse effects than did the placebo group. Maintenance ITT analysis (Table 2) confirms the superiority of both CBT alone and imipramine alone to placebo.

CBT vs Imipramine. We found no significant difference between CBT alone and imipramine alone in the acute ITT or completer analyses or in the maintenance ITT or ITC analyses (Table 2). As expected, significantly more patients in the imipramine group than in the CBT group dropped out because of adverse effects (Figure). The follow-up analyses (Table 2) show trends favoring CBT over imipramine.

Combined CBT+Imipramine vs Single Treatment. We hypothesized that CBT+imipramine would be better than all 3 of the relevant comparison groups. Table 2 shows that CBT+imipramine was superior to CBT alone on 1 of 3 ITT analyses and 1 of 3 completer analyses but was not superior to CBT+placebo. In the maintenance ITT analysis (Table 2), combined treatment was better in the PDSS average analysis than in all 3 comparison treatments (thereby meeting our criteria for superiority) and better than CBT and CBT+placebo on ITC analyses.

Intent-to-continue analyses showed that responders to imipramine, with or without CBT, fared significantly worse in the no-treatment follow-up period than those who received either CBT alone or CBT+placebo (Table 2). After treatment discontinuation in the follow-up ITT analyses, the treatments that continued to show evidence of superiority to placebo were CBT alone (Table 2) and

CBT+placebo (statistically significant for all 3 measures).

Quality of Response
In a secondary analysis restricted to responders based on the CGI definition (TABLE 3), acute imipramine responders had significantly lower PDSS average scores than acute CBT responders, indicating a higher quality of response. Maintenance responders showed the same pattern at the trend level. Responders to combined CBT+imipramine had higher-quality responses than CBT responders at acute and maintenance points, as well as a higher quality of response than patients taking CBT+placebo at maintenance.

Timing of Loss of Response
Timing of loss of response could be determined in 4 of 5 imipramine follow-up completers, losing response during months 3, 4, 5, and 6 (1 case each) and in 1 of 2 CBT follow-up completers, losing response during month 3. Among 9 CBT+imipramine follow-up completers losing response, relapse occurred during months 2, 4, and 5 (2 cases each), months 1, 3, and 6 (1 case each), and in the CBT+placebo relapser during month 1.

COMMENT
Our results demonstrate that both imipramine and CBT are better than pill placebo for treatment of PD. Imipramine produced a superior quality of response, but CBT had more durability and was somewhat better tolerated.

In our study, ITT placebo response did not differ from active treatment on acute-phase assessment when CGI was used to determine responder status. By contrast, the 7-item PDSS successfully discriminated between conditions. Moreover, the placebo response in the ITT analysis of 37.5% based on CGI criteria after 3 months drops to 13% after 9 months of treatment. Several studies have made similar observations in the treatment of depression and PD.[38-41] While attrition in the placebo group may have compromised comparisons at the end of maintenance, placebo re-

sponse is weak in magnitude and transient in duration.[1,24]

There are several differences between active treatments. Although no differences emerged on a priori planned completer or ITT analyses, patients treated with imipramine and designated responders based on CGI criteria following the acute phase showed significantly more improvement on the PDSS than patients who responded to CBT. A trend level of significance remained at the end of maintenance. Thus, among those who did well with either treatment, patients receiving imipramine responded more completely. However, at follow-up, patients who had received CBT alone maintained their improvement significantly better (4% relapse) than those treated with imipramine (25% relapse) based on PDSS responder criteria. We discontinued imipramine by tapering during a 1- to 2-week period, following standard practice at the time. Relapses in medication-treated patients appeared to be evenly distributed across follow-up, suggesting that withdrawal played little role in the results. We did not aim to determine optimal tapering strategy or to ascertain the duration of medication maintenance that produces the best long-term outcome. Our results indicate the need for such work.

Findings of high acceptability and durability of CBT are consistent with previous reports,[16] although attrition in the CBT-alone group was higher than reported previously.[6,14,15,42] Adverse effects with imipramine and relapse following discontinuation are also consistent with previous reports.[38-40] However, our results that show a superior quality of response with imipramine among responders to both treatments in the acute phase underscore the need to reduce attrition and develop optimal maintenance and discontinuation procedures for those receiving medication.

Acute coadministration of imipramine and CBT resulted in limited benefit over monotherapy. Adding medication to CBT achieved significantly better results than CBT alone at postacute assessment on some measures, but this

JAMA, May 17, 2000—Vol 283, No. 19 **2533**

327

combination was never better than CBT+placebo. By the end of maintenance, CBT+imipramine was superior to both CBT alone and CBT+placebo (as well as imipramine alone) on the PDSS average measure. However, this robust combination treatment produced the highest relapse rate at follow-up assessment. Surprisingly, the addition of CBT

Table 2. Treatment and Follow-up Analyses*

Analysis	Measure	CBT Alone	Imipramine Alone	Placebo Alone	CBT Plus Imipramine	CBT Plus Placebo	Total	P Value	Pairwise Comparisons†					
									I vs P	C vs P	I vs C	C + I vs C + P‡	C + I vs C‡	C + I vs I‡
					Acute Treatment Analyses									
Acute completers	No. of subjects	56	51	14	47	45	213							
	PDSS average item score, mean (SD)	0.95 (0.65)	0.75 (0.65)	1.15 (0.86)	0.60 (0.61)	0.72 (0.62)	0.79 (0.66)	.003	.03	.17	.13	.22	.002	.23
	PDSS response rate, %	67.3	74.5	38.5	84.4	80.0	73.7	.01	.02	.08	.52	.78	.06	.32
	CGI response rate, %	74.5	78.4	64.3	89.1	86.7	80.6	.13	NA	NA	NA	NA	NA	NA
Acute intention-to-treat	No. of subjects	77	83	24	65	63	312							
	PDSS average item score, mean (SD)§	1.14 (0.74)	1.05 (0.77)	1.52 (0.90)	0.88 (0.74)	0.99 (0.70)	1.06 (0.76)	.003	.009	.02	.41	.34	.02	.15
	PDSS response rate, %	48.7	45.8	21.7	60.3	57.1	50.0	.02	.05	.03	.75	.86	.18	.10
	CGI response rate, %	53.9	48.2	37.5	64.1	61.9	54.8	.10	NA	NA	NA	NA	NA	NA
					Maintenance Treatment Analyses									
Intention-to-continue in maintenance	No. of subjects	41	40	9	41	39	170							
	PDSS average item score, mean (SD)§	0.76 (0.77)	0.54 (0.72)	1.03 (0.84)	0.29 (0.60)	0.67 (0.67)	0.60 (0.71)	.005	.12	.32	.16	.006	.001	.07
	PDSS response rate, %	73.2	79.5	37.5	90.0	76.3	77.7	.03	.03	.09	.60	.13	.08	.22
	CGI response rate, %	78.0	79.5	37.5	87.8	82.1	79.6	.06	NA	NA	NA	NA	NA	NA
Maintenance intention-to-treat	No. of subjects	77	83	24	65	63	312							
	PDSS average item score, mean (SD)§	1.18 (0.86)	1.14 (0.87)	1.54 (0.83)	0.78 (0.86)	1.08 (0.79)	1.09 (0.86)	.001	.04	.05	.72	.04	.004	.01
	PDSS response rate, %	39.5	37.8	13.0	57.1	46.8	42.2	.003	.02	.02	.87	.28	.04	.03
	CGI response rate, %	42.1	37.8	13.0	56.3	50.0	43.3	.003	.02	.01	.63	.59	.13	.03
					Follow-up Analyses									
Intention-to-continue in follow-up	No. of subjects	28	25	3	30	30	116							
	PDSS average item score, mean (SD)§	0.56 (0.72)	0.81 (0.90)	-0.11 (0)	1.11 (1.02)	0.53 (0.70)	0.71 (0.87)	.02	.20	.10	.23	[.007]	[.01]	.30
	PDSS response rate, %	85.2	60.0	100	50.0	83.3	70.5	.01	.52	1.00	[.06]	[.01]	[.009]	.58
	CGI response rate, %	82.1	60.0	100	51.7	83.3	70.4	.02	.53	1.00	.12	[.01]	[.02]	.59
Follow-up intention-to-treat	No. of subjects	73	77	24	59	62	295							
	PDSS average item score, mean (SD)§	1.33 (0.93)	1.45 (0.83)	1.62 (0.77)	1.45 (0.90)	1.18 (0.92)	1.37 (0.89)	.12	NA	NA	NA	NA	NA	NA
	PDSS response rate, %	32.4	19.7	9.1	25.0	41.0	27.6	.01	.34	.05	[.09]	[.08]	.43	.41
	CGI response rate, %	31.9	19.7	13.0	26.3	41.0	28.0	.03	.55	.11	[.09]	.12	.56	.41

*See first 3 footnotes to Table 1. P value for omnibus analysis of the continuous measure used analysis of covariance with baseline as covariate or repeated-measures analysis of variance when analysis of covariance assumptions were not met. CGI indicates Clinical Global Impression Scale; I, imipramine; P, placebo; C, CBT; C + I, CBT + imipramine; and C + P, CBT + placebo.

†Pairwise comparisons are for 2-tailed Fisher exact tests; analyses were for continuous data, as per first footnote. Boldface indicates P values significant at ≤.05; gray tint indicates therapy listed on top is better than therapy listed below (consistent with hypotheses); boxed values indicate bottom therapy is better than top therapy (counter to hypotheses) at significant or trend levels. Exact P values are shown, rounded to 2 significant digits when P≥.01, otherwise to 3 significant digits when P≥.01. NA indicates post hoc pairwise comparisons not applicable because of nonsignificant omnibus test results.

‡All 3 comparisons of C + I>C + P, C + I>C, and C + I>I were required to indicate superiority of combined treatment.

§Baseline adjusted means.

328

Table 3. Analysis of PDSS Average Item Score for Responders*

	CBT Alone	Imipramine Alone	Placebo Alone	CBT Plus Imipramine	CBT Plus Placebo	Total	P Value	I vs P	C vs P	I vs C	C+I vs C+P	C+I vs C	C+I vs I
	Mean (SD)							Pairwise Comparisons					
No. of subjects	41	40	9	41	39	170							
Acute	0.69 (0.41)	0.47 (0.45)	0.77 (0.58)	0.48 (0.50)	0.56 (0.43)	0.58 (0.45)	.03	.08	.66	.01	.34	.01	.83
No. of subjects	32	31	3	36	31	133							
Maintenance	0.49 (0.43)	0.32 (0.42)	0.26 (0.50)	0.19 (0.33)	0.45 (0.42)	0.35 (0.41)	.02	.81	.37	.09	.006	.001	.11
No. of subjects	23	15	3	15	25	81							
Follow-up	0.26 (0.30)	0.15 (0.21)	−0.05 (0.0)	0.20 (0.26)	0.20 (0.24)	0.19 (0.25)	.39	NA	NA	NA	NA	NA	NA

*First 4 footnotes to Table 2 apply.

to imipramine did not mitigate relapse following medication discontinuation; addition of imipramine appeared to reduce the long-term durability of CBT. More work is needed to elucidate this result. A selection effect may account for the relatively poor outcome of combined treatment after discontinuation. Combined treatment could conceivably select patients who had been in particular need of long-term treatment from the beginning. We have not been able to detect important differences at baseline on variables in Table 1 between patients who did and did not enter the follow-up phase, but these analyses do not exclude the possibility of selection on an unmeasured prognostic factor.

There are several limitations of this study. First, to avoid the complications and possible confounding factors of adding exposure-based interventions to each condition, we enrolled patients with only limited degrees of phobic avoidance, and results are generalizable only to this group. Second, it could be argued that we underestimate the benefits of medication by using a tricyclic antidepressant instead of an SSRI. Current recommendations[43] (not yet in place when this study began) consider SSRIs to be the first-line medication. While there is little question that SSRIs are more convenient and have a more limited adverse-effect profile, studies examining differences from tricyclic antidepressants do not consistently find higher efficacy for SSRIs. In fact, of 4 randomized studies, none found significant differences in the end-of-study acute ITT analyses.[44-47] One study found evidence for a more rapid response for the SSRI,[44] and another

found that the tricyclic antidepressant but not the SSRI was more effective than placebo.[46] Moreover, there have also been refinements in CBT since we began our study. Thus, we believe it likely that results of a similar comparative study using an SSRI would not differ substantially from ours. Third, at the time we designed this study, a consensus existed that an adequate dose of imipramine should be at least 200 mg/d. A recent study, however, suggests that imipramine/desipramine plasma levels of about 150 mg/mL may be optimal in treating PD.[48] Hence, it is conceivable that we underestimate the therapeutic potential of imipramine in this study. Finally, the use of nonstudy medication is a possible confounding factor to any anxiety study. We made the decision to permit limited use of benzodiazepines, because we sought to simulate clinical practice. Rates of urine samples that tested positive for benzodiazepine use among the 5 treatments were equivalent and low. Only 1 subject's data were censored because of excessive benzodiazepine use. Thus, we believe benzodiazepine use did not play a significant role in our results.

This study represents, to our knowledge, the first multicenter trial comparing medication and psychosocial therapies and their combination for PD. Prior studies contrasting the 2 approaches have been criticized because of possible investigator-allegiance bias in study design, implementation, and/or analysis. Our study sites included 2 with psychotherapy and 2 with pharmacotherapy expertise. In this context, the absence of site differences in ITT outcome supports the important implica-

tion that both types of treatment should be transportable to most clinical settings and confirms the generalizability of the results.

Author Affiliations: Center for Anxiety and Related Disorders and Department of Psychology, Boston University, Boston, Mass (Dr Barlow); Department of Psychiatry, Columbia University, New York, and Long Island Jewish/Hillside Medical Center, Glen Oaks, NY (Dr Gorman); Department of Psychiatry, University of Pittsburgh School of Medicine, Pittsburgh, Pa (Dr Shear); and Department of Psychiatry, Yale University School of Medicine, New Haven, Conn (Dr Woods).
Financial Disclosure: Dr Barlow has received research support from Pfizer and the National Institute of Mental Health and has served as a consultant for or received honoraria or royalties from Guilford Press, The Psychological Corporation, and Wyeth-Ayerst Pharmaceuticals. Dr Gorman has received research support from Pfizer, Eli Lilly, and the National Alliance for Research on Schizophrenia and Depression and has served as a consultant for or received honoraria or royalties from Pfizer, Eli Lilly, Bristol-Myers Squibb, Wyeth Ayerst, SmithKline Beecham, AstraZeneca, Janssen, Organon, Forest, Parke Davis, Lundbeck, Solvay, and Merck. Dr Shear has received research support from Eli Lilly, Pfizer, the National Institute of Mental Health, and SmithKline Beecham and has served as a consultant for or received honoraria or royalties from Pfizer, Glaxo, Hoffmann-LaRoche, SmithKline Beecham, and Upjohn. Dr Woods has received research support from the National Institute of Mental Health and has served as a consultant for or received honoraria or royalties from Eli Lilly, Janssen, and Wyeth Ayerst.
Funding/Support: This work was supported by National Institute of Mental Health grant MH45964 (University of Pittsburgh School of Medicine); MH45965 (Boston University); MH45966 (Yale University School of Medicine); MH45963 and MH00416 (Senior Scientist Award) (Columbia University). Drs Barlow, Gorman, Shear, and Woods have received research support from the National Institute of Mental Health. Imipramine and matching placebo were provided by Teva Pharmaceuticals USA.
Acknowledgment: We are deeply indebted to the following collaborators on this study:
Investigators: Laszlo A. Papp, MD, Columbia/Hillside; Duncan Clark, MD, PhD, Marylene Cloitre, PhD, Western Psychiatric Institute and Clinic and/or Cornell University; Roy Money, MS, Diane E. Sholomskas, PhD, Yale University.
Project Directors: Susan E. Ray, MS, Columbia/Hillside; Karla Moras, PhD, Jennifer C. Jones, PhD, Guylaine Côté, PhD, Stefan G. Hofmann, PhD, State University of New York at Albany and/or Boston University; Jane Levitan, RN, MA, CS, NPP, Carol Heape, RN, MSN, Mark Jones, LSW, Mary McShea, MS, West-

329

ern Psychiatric Institute and Clinic and/or Cornell University; Gale Banks, RN, MS, Yale University.
Pharmacotherapists: Jeremy D. Coplan, MD, Columbia/Hillside; Deborah Cross, MD, Russell Denea, MD, Robert M. Hertz, MD, David A. Spiegel, MD, State University of New York at Albany and/or Boston University; Lynn Schackman, MD, Western Psychiatric Institute and Clinic and/or Cornell University; Andrew W. Goddard, MD, Yale University.
CBT Therapists: Scott B. Schnee, PhD, Joyce E. Tanzer, PhD, Columbia/Hillside; Michele M. Carter, PhD, Anne Chosak, BA, State University of New York at Albany and/or Boston University; Leora Heckleman, PhD, Western Psychiatric Institute and Clinic and/or Cornell University; Kevin Smith, PhD, Michael Greenwald, PhD, Pamela Stimac, LSW; Carlos M. Grilo, PhD, Stuart J. Sokol, PhD, Christina J. Taylor, PhD, Yale University.

CBT Therapists' Supervisors: Timothy A. Brown, PsyD, Michelle G. Craske, PhD, State University of New York at Albany.
Nurse: Ann Conklin, RN, State University of New York at Albany and/or Boston University.
CBT Adherence Rating Coordinators: Deborah J. Dowdall, MA, Jonathan A. Lerner, BA, State University of New York at Albany and/or Boston University.
Independent Evaluators: David L. Roll, PhD, Jayne L. Rygh, PhD, Columbia/Hillside; Tracy Sbrocco, PhD, Lenna Knox, BA, Janene L. Esler, BA, State University of New York at Albany and/or Boston University; Janet Klosko, PhD, Ellen Franty, RN, Carolyn Hughes, MSW, Susan Barbour, EdD, Western Psychiatric Institute and Clinic and/or Cornell University; Lynn H. Collins, PhD, Kim R. Owen, MD, Jaak Rakfeldt, PhD, Yale University.

Research Technicians or Assistants/Data Managers: Evelyn Abeshouse, BA, Vincent Passarelli, BS, Linda Soterakis, BA, Mirsonia Tricarico, Columbia/Hillside; Gillian Malken, BA, Jillian Shipherd, BA, Michael Detweiler, BA, David Hershberger, BA, State University of New York at Albany and/or Boston University; Karen Trager, MA, Annette Wood, Joel Wood, BS, Barbara Kumer, MSIS, Gloria Klima, MA, Miyako Hamekamp, BS; Western Psychiatric Institute and Clinic and/or Cornell University; Botonya Barnes-Harris, Sarah Saiano, Yale University.
Administrative Support: Mary Ann Beals, Irene Farrugio, Bonnie Conklin, RN, Bette Selwyn, BA, State University of New York at Albany and/or Boston University; Sandy Barbieri, Jane Borowski, Western Psychiatric Institute and/or Cornell University; Nancy T. Ryan, AS, Yale University.

REFERENCES

1. Keller MB, Yonkers KA, Warshaw, MG, et al. Remission and relapse in subjects with panic disorder and panic with agoraphobia. *J Nerv Ment Dis.* 1994;182:290-290.
2. Robins LN, Regier DA, eds. *Psychiatric Disorders in America: The Epidemiologic Catchment Area Study.* New York, NY: The Free Press; 1991.
3. Kessler RC, McGonagle KA, Zhao S, et al. Lifetime and 12-month prevalence of DSM-III-R psychiatric disorders in the United States. *Arch Gen Psychiatry.* 1994;51:8-19.
4. Sherbourne CD, Wells KB, Judd LL. Functioning and well-being of patients with panic disorder. *Am J Psychiatry.* 1996;153:213-218.
5. Klerman GL, Weissman MM, Ouellette R, et al. Panic attacks in the community. *JAMA.* 1991;265:742-746.
6. Katon W. Primary care-psychiatry panic disorder management module. In: Wolfe BE, Maser JD, eds. *Treatment of Panic Disorder: A Consensus Development Conference.* Washington, DC: American Psychiatric Press Inc; 1994:4-56.
7. Beitman BD, Thomas AM, Kushner MG. Panic disorder in the families of patients with normal coronary arteries and non-fear panic disorder. *Behav Res Ther.* 1992;30:403-406.
8. Walker EA, Roy-Byrne PP, Katon WJ, et al. Psychiatric illness in irritable bowel syndrome. *Am J Psychiatry.* 1990;147:1656-1661.
9. Katerndahl DA, Realini JP. Where do panic attack sufferers seek care? *J Fam Pract.* 1995;40:237-243.
10. Swinson RP, Cox BJ, Woszczyna CB. Use of medical services and treatment for panic disorder with agoraphobia and for social phobia. *CMAJ.* 1992;147:878.
11. Leon AC, Portera L, Weissman MM. The social costs of anxiety disorders. *Br J Psychiatry Suppl.* 1995;166:19-22.
12. Salvador-Carulla L, Segui J, Fernandez-Cano P, Canet J. Costs and offset effect in panic disorders. *Br J Psychiatry Suppl.* 1995;166:23-28.
13. Hofmann S, Barlow DH. The costs of anxiety disorders. In: Miller NE, Magruder, KM eds. *Cost-Effectiveness of Psychotherapy: A Guide for Practitioners, Researchers and Policymakers.* New York, NY: Oxford University Press Inc; 1999:224-234.
14. Barlow DH, Craske MG, Cerny JA, Klosko JS. Behavioral treatment of panic disorder. *Behav Ther.* 1989;20:261-282.
15. Clark DM, Salkovskis PM, Hackmann A, et al. A comparison of cognitive therapy, applied relaxation and imipramine in the treatment of panic disorder. *Br J Psychiatry.* 1994;164:759-769.
16. Barlow DH, Lehman CL. Advances in the psychosocial treatment of anxiety disorders. *Arch Gen Psychiatry.* 1996;53:727-735.
17. Zitrin CM, Klein DF, Woerner MG. Treatment of agoraphobia with group exposure in vivo and imipramine. *Arch Gen Psychiatry.* 1980;37:63-72.

18. Zitrin CM, Klein DF, Woerner MG, Ross DC. Treatment of phobias, I: comparison of imipramine hydrochloride and placebo. *Arch Gen Psychiatry.* 1983;40:125-138.
19. Mavissakalian M, Michelson L. Two-year follow-up of exposure and imipramine treatment of agoraphobia. *Am J Psychiatry.* 1986;143:1106-1112.
20. Marks IM, Gray S, Cohen D, et al. Imipramine and brief therapist-aided exposure in agoraphobics having self-exposure homework. *Arch Gen Psychiatry.* 1983;40:153-162.
21. Mavissakalian MR, Perel JM. Imipramine treatment of panic disorder with agoraphobia. *Am J Psychiatry.* 1995;152:673-682.
22. Lydiard RB, Brawman-Mintzer O, Ballenger JC. Recent developments in the psychopharmacology of panic disorder. *J Consult Clin Psychol.* 1996;64:660-668.
23. Liebowitz MR, Barlow DH. Panic disorder: the latest on diagnosis and treatment. *J Pract Psychiatry Behav Health.* 1995;1:10-19.
24. Wolfe BE, Maser JD. Origins and overview of the consensus development conference on the treatment of panic disorder. In: Wolfe BE, Maser JD, eds. *Treatment of Panic Disorder: A Consensus Development Conference.* Washington, DC: American Psychiatric Press Inc; 1994:3-16.
25. Mavissakalian MR. Antidepressant medications for panic disorder. In: Mavissakalian MR, Prien RF, eds. *Long-term Treatment of Anxiety Disorders.* Washington, DC: American Psychiatric Press Inc; 1996:265.
26. Black DW, Wesner R, Bowers W, Gabel J. A comparison of fluvoxamine, cognitive therapy, and placebo in the treatment of panic disorder. *Arch Gen Psychiatry.* 1993;50:44-50.
27. Marks IM, Swinson RP, Basoglu M, et al. Alprazolam and exposure alone and combined in panic disorder with agoraphobia. *Br J Psychiatry.* 1993;162:776-787.
28. Oehrburg S, Christiansen PE, Behnke K, et al. Paroxetine in the treatment of panic disorder. *Br J Psychiatry.* 1995;167:374-379.
29. Sharp DM, Power KG, Simpson RJ. Fluvoxamine, placebo, and cognitive behaviour therapy used alone and in combination in the treatment of panic disorder and agoraphobia. *J Anxiety Disord.* 1996;10:219-242.
30. Woods SW, Sholomskas DE, Shear MK, et al. Efficient allocation of patients to treatment cells in clinical trials with more than two treatment conditions. *Am J Psychiatry.* 1998;155:1446-1448.
31. Di Nardo PA, Barlow DH. *Anxiety Disorders Interview Schedule–Revised: (ADIS-R).* San Antonio, Tex: Graywind Publications Inc/The Psychological Corp; 1988.
32. Di Nardo PA, Moras K, Barlow DH, et al. Reliability of DSM-III-R anxiety disorder categories. *Arch Gen Psychiatry.* 1993;50:251-256.

33. Hofmann SG, Barlow DH, Papp LA, et al. Pretreatment attrition in a comparative treatment outcome study on panic disorder. *Am J Psychiatry.* 1998;155:43-47.
34. Barlow DH, Craske MG. *Mastery of Your Anxiety and Panic, II.* San Antonio, Tex: Graywind Publications Inc/The Psychological Corp; 1994.
35. Shear MK, Brown TA, Barlow DH, et al. Multicenter collaborative Panic Disorder Severity Scale. *Am J Psychiatry.* 1997;154:1571-1575.
36. Guy W. *ECDEU Assessment Manual for Psychopharmacology, Revised.* Washington, DC: US Government Printing Office; 1976. DHEW publication ADM 76-338.
37. Klein DF, Ross DC. Reanalysis of the National Institute of Mental Health Treatment of Depression Collaborative Research Program General Effectiveness Report. *Neuropsychopharmacology.* 1993;8:241-251.
38. Quitkin FM, Rabkin JG, Ross D, Stewart JW. Identification of true drug response to antidepressants. *Arch Gen Psychiatry.* 1984;41:782-786.
39. Quitkin FM, Rabkin JD, Markowitz JM, et al. Use of pattern analysis to identify true drug response. *Arch Gen Psychiatry.* 1987;44:259-264.
40. Stewart JW, Quitkin FM, McGrath PJ, et al. Use of pattern analysis to predict differential relapse of remitted patients with major depression during 1 year of treatment with fluoxetine or placebo. *Arch Gen Psychiatry.* 1998;55:334-343.
41. Lepola UM, Wade AG, Leinonen EV, et al. A controlled, prospective, 1-year trial of citalopram in the treatment of panic disorder. *J Clin Psychiatry.* 1998;59:528-534.
42. Telch MJ, Lucas JA, Schmidt NB, et al. Group cognitive-behavioral treatment of panic disorder. *Behav Res Ther.* 1993;31:279-287.
43. American Psychiatric Association, for the Work Group on Panic Disorder. Practice guideline for the treatment of patients with panic disorder. *Am J Psychiatry.* 1998;155(suppl 5):1-34.
44. Lecrubier V, Bakker A, Dunbar G, Judge R, for The Collaborative Paroxetine Panic Study Investigators. A comparison of paroxetine, clomipramine and placebo in the treatment of panic disorder. *Acta Psychiatr Scand.* 1997;95:145-152.
45. Bystritsky A, Rosen RM, Murphy KJ, et al. Double-blind pilot trial of desipramine versus fluoxetine in panic patients. *Anxiety.* 1994-1995;1:287-290.
46. Nair NP, Bakish D, Saxena B, et al. Comparison of fluvoxamine, imipramine, and placebo in the treatment of outpatients with panic disorder. *Anxiety.* 1996;2:192-198.
47. Wade AG, Lepola U, Koponen HJ, et al. The effect of citalopram in panic disorder. *Br J Psychiatry.* 1997;170:549-553.
48. Uhlenhuth EH, Matuzas W, Warner TD, Thompson PM. Growing placebo response rate. *Psychopharmacol Bull.* 1997;33:31-39.

330

Multicenter, Double-blind Comparison of Sertraline and Placebo in the Treatment of Posttraumatic Stress Disorder

Jonathan R. T. Davidson, MD; Barbara O. Rothbaum, PhD; Bessel A. van der Kolk, MD; Carolyn R. Sikes, PhD; Gail M. Farfel, PhD

Background: Posttraumatic stress disorder (PTSD) is a common illness associated with significant disability. Few large, placebo-controlled trials have been reported.

Methods: Outpatients with a *DSM-III-R* diagnosis of moderate-to-severe PTSD were randomized to 12 weeks of double-blind treatment with either sertraline (N=100) in flexible daily doses in the range of 50 to 200 mg or placebo (N=108). Primary outcome measures consisted of the Clinician-Administered PTSD Scale (CAPS-2) total severity score, the patient-rated Impact of Event Scale (IES), and the Clinical Global Impression-Severity (CGI-S) and -Improvement (CGI-I) ratings.

Results: Mixed-effects analyses found significantly steeper improvement slopes for sertraline compared with placebo on the CAPS-2 ($t=2.96$, $P=.003$), the IES ($t=2.26$,

$P=.02$), the CGI-I score ($t=3.62$, $P<.001$), and the CGI-S score ($t=4.40$, $P<.001$). An intent-to-treat end-point analysis found a 60% responder rate for sertraline and a 38% responder rate for placebo ($\chi^2_1=8.48$, $P=.004$). Sertraline treatment was well tolerated, with a 9% discontinuation rate because of adverse events, compared with 5% for placebo. Adverse events that were significantly more common in subjects given sertraline compared with placebo consisted of insomnia (35% vs 22%), diarrhea (28% vs 11%), nausea (23% vs 11%), fatigue (13% vs 5%), and decreased appetite (12% vs 1%).

Conclusion: The results of the current study suggest that sertraline is a safe, well-tolerated, and significantly effective treatment for PTSD.

Arch Gen Psychiatry. 2001;58:485-492

From the Anxiety and Traumatic Stress Program, Department of Psychiatry and Behavioral Sciences, Duke University Medical Center, Durham, NC (Dr Davidson); the Emory Clinic and Department of Psychiatry and Behavioral Sciences, Atlanta, Ga (Dr Rothbaum); the Human Resource Institute, Brookline, Mass (Dr van der Kolk); and Pfizer Inc, New York, NY (Drs Sikes and Farfel).

S INCE ITS original diagnostic formulation in 1980, considerable research has been conducted on posttraumatic stress disorder (PTSD). This research has established that PTSD is common, with a lifetime prevalence in the range of 7% to 12% and a 2:1 female-to-male ratio[1-3]; chronic, with a median time-to-recovery in the range of 3 to 5 years[1,4]; and has high comorbidity, with a 6-fold increased risk, compared with community norms, of major depression, a 3-fold increased risk of alcoholism or substance abuse, an approximately 4-fold increased risk of panic disorder or agoraphobia, and an estimated suicide attempt rate of approximately 20%.[1,5,6] Posttraumatic stress disorder is also associated with significant functional and psychosocial disability[7,8] and notable increases in physical symptoms and health care utilization.[5,9-11]

Currently, it is estimated that the most widely used treatments for PTSD in the community consist of counseling,[12] symptomatic treatment of associated in-

somnia and anxiety with benzodiazepines or low-dose antidepressants, or self-medication with alcohol.[13]

An increasing number of studies have been conducted in an attempt to establish effective treatments for PTSD. Initial studies have reported promising results for cognitive and behavioral treatments,[13-16] but confirmation of the efficacy of cognitive or behavior therapies for PTSD awaits the results of additional well-designed clinical trials, with blinded and parallel control groups, and with larger sample sizes.

Controlled trials testing the efficacy of drug therapy for PTSD are sparse. A comprehensive review published in 1992[17] found few placebo-controlled clinical trials, and limited efficacy for the few that were reported, although phenelzine and, to a lesser extent, imipramine and amitriptyline, were more effective than placebo in combat veterans with PTSD.[18,19] Since that time, 2 equivocal or negative double-blind, placebo-controlled clinical trials have been published of brofaromine (since discontinued).[20,21] Re-

331

SUBJECTS AND METHODS

SUBJECTS

The subjects were male and female outpatients 18 years and older who met *DSM-III-R*[36] criteria for a primary diagnosis of PTSD as determined by part 1 of the Clinician-Administered PTSD Scale (CAPS-1). A minimum 6-month duration of PTSD illness was required (exceeding the 1-month minimum required by *DSM-III-R*), as well as a total score of 50 or higher on part 2 of the Clinician-Administered PTSD Scale (CAPS-2) at the end of a 1-week placebo run-in period. All subjects were required to be free of psychotropic medication for at least 2 weeks before beginning treatment, or 5 weeks for fluoxetine. Female participation was contingent on a negative β-human chorionic gonadotropin pregnancy test and stable use of a medically accepted form of contraception. Exclusion criteria included (1) current or past history of bipolar, schizophrenic, or other psychotic disorder; (2) current organic mental disorder, factitious disorder, or malingering, or primary diagnosis of major depression; (3) alcohol or substance abuse or dependence in the past 6 months; (4) evidence of clinically significant hepatic or renal disease, or any other acute or unstable medical condition that might interfere with the safe conduct of the study; (5) intolerance or hypersensitivity to sertraline, or nonresponse to a previous adequate trial; and (6) current use of any medication (except occasional use of chloral hydrate) with clinically significant psychotropic properties. Subjects were not permitted to participate in cognitive-behavioral therapy during the trial, but were permitted to attend ongoing psychotherapy or counseling that was initiated at least 3 months before randomization.

Subjects were recruited from current clinical populations and through the use of flyers, newspaper advertisements, and radio advertisements. The study was approved by the institutional review board, or by a national institutional review board, at each of the 12 collaborating centers. The benefits and risks of study participation were fully explained to each subject, and written informed consent was obtained.

STUDY DESIGN

The study was a double-blind, randomized, flexible-dose comparison of sertraline and placebo for the treatment of PTSD in outpatients. After a 1-week, single-blind, placebo run-in period, subjects were randomized, using computer-generated random numbers, to 12 weeks of double-blind, parallel treatment with either matched placebo or sertraline. Sertraline treatment was initiated at 25 mg per day for 1 week, with flexible daily dosing thereafter in the range of 50 to 200 mg, based on clinical response and tolerability.

Study visits took place at baseline and at the end of study treatment weeks 1, 2, 3, 4, 6, 8, 10, and 12, or at the time of discontinuation if before week 12.

ASSESSMENTS

Baseline

Subjects were evaluated for study entry by a research clinician (physician, psychologist, or psychiatric nurse) with experience in conducting psychopharmacology research. The current severity of PTSD symptoms was determined by a psychiatric history and by the CAPS-1, a structured interview that includes the *DSM-III-R* PTSD diagnostic criteria.[37,38] A structured clinical interview based on *DSM-III-R*[39] was performed to evaluate the presence of comorbid psychiatric illness. A medical history, physical examination, and routine laboratory tests were performed. Baseline PTSD symptoms was rated by the investigators using CAPS-2 and the Clinical Global Impression-Severity Scale (CGI-S).

Efficacy and Safety

The primary outcome measures for the study consisted of the 17-item total severity score of the CAPS-2,[37,38] which is an investigator-completed assessment instrument that rates the frequency and intensity of PTSD symptoms on separate 5-point severity scales; the Impact of Event Scale (IES),[40,41] a 15-item subject-rated instrument that assesses intrusion

---

sults of 2 placebo-controlled studies have also been published, each with approximately 50 outpatients, suggesting efficacy for fluoxetine in PTSD in civilians, but not in combat veterans.[22,23]

A potential therapy for PTSD must effectively treat the core symptoms of the disorder,[24] consisting of reexperiencing (intrusive thoughts, nightmares, flashbacks, images, or memories); phobic avoidance of trauma-related situation; emotional numbing (flattened affect or detachment and/or loss of interest and motivation); and hyperarousal (startle reactions, poor concentration, irritability and jumpiness, insomnia, and hypervigilance). Optimally, a candidate therapy should also be effective in restoring normal functioning and improving symptoms associated with common psychiatric comorbidity. Sertraline would seem to be such a drug, with demonstrated efficacy in the treatment of depression[25-28] and panic disorder,[29-31] and preliminary evidence of efficacy in alcoholism,[32,33] as well as uncontrolled pilot studies suggesting efficacy in PTSD.[34,35] We report here results of a large, multisite, placebo-controlled, double-blind trial

designed to test the efficacy and tolerability of sertraline in the treatment of PTSD.

RESULTS

SUBJECT CHARACTERISTICS

Two hundred eight subjects were randomly assigned to sertraline or placebo, of whom 98 sertraline-treated subjects and 104 placebo-treated subjects were available for at least 1 postbaseline efficacy assessment, and so constituted the intent-to-treat sample.

Demographic and clinical characteristics for the subject sample are shown in **Table 1**. The only significant difference between the 2 treatment groups in any of the baseline variables was the smaller percentage of males in the sertraline group. Women constituted the majority of the sample. The age of subjects ranged from 18 to 69 years, with 75% younger than 45 years. An analysis by sex revealed no significant differences in any of the baseline variables. The difference observed in Table 1 be-

and avoidance symptoms on a 4-point severity scale; and the CGI-S and CGI-Improvement (CGI-I) scales.[42] Assessment of primary outcome measures was performed at baseline (except CGI-I) and at every study visit.

Secondary outcome measures consisted of (1) the 17-item Davidson Trauma Scale (DTS),[43,44] which rates frequency and severity of DSM-III-R–defined PTSD symptoms on separate 5-point scales; (2) the 24-item Hamilton Depression Rating Scale (HAM-D)[45]; (3) the Hamilton Anxiety Rating Scale (HAM-A)[46]; (4) DSM-III-R–defined clusters of the CAPS-2, IES, and the DTS: reexperiencing/intrusion, avoidance/numbing, and arousal; (5) individual global ratings (social functioning, occupational functioning, overall improvement, and severity of illness) from the CAPS-2, rated from 0 to 4; (6) CAPS-2 items that rate associated features of PTSD in terms of frequency and intensity, including guilt and hopelessness; and (7) the Pittsburgh Sleep Quality Index.[47] The CAPS-2 and DTS were administered at every study visit, while the HAM-D, HAM-A, and Pittsburgh Sleep Quality Index were administered at baseline and study end point only.

Safety assessments included evaluation at each study visit of weight, sitting blood pressure, and heart rate. Adverse effects that were spontaneously reported or observed were recorded with regard to their time of onset, duration, severity, action taken, and outcome. Use of concomitant medications was recorded in terms of daily dose, stop and start dates, and reason for use. Laboratory assessments (eg, clinical chemistry, hematology, urinalysis) were performed initially at screen, and repeated at weeks 6 and 12 (or at the time of study discontinuation). A physical examination and electrocardiogram were performed at screen and at week 12 (or at the time of discontinuation if before week 12).

Compliance was monitored by pill counts of returned medication; subjects were counseled if found to be noncompliant.

DATA ANALYSIS

Baseline characteristics were compared between the treatment groups using analysis of variance or χ^2 (for sex). The

main efficacy analyses were preformed using change from baseline to end point during the 12-week treatment period. The efficacy variables were analyzed via analysis of covariance, with the effects of site and treatment in the model and baseline scores as the covariate. For the CGI-I scale, there is no baseline value and therefore an analysis of variance was performed on the end-point score with site and treatment in the model. Treatment×site interactions were examined in all analyses, but none were significant and therefore interaction terms were deleted from all further analyses. Statistical analyses were performed on SAS, version 6.12. All statistical tests were 2-sided and performed at the .05 level of significance.

Clinical response to treatment was defined in 2 ways: (1) a 30% or greater decrease in the CAPS-2 scores and (2) a CGI-I rating of 1 (very much improved) or 2 (much improved). The post hoc decision to add the CAPS-2 criteria was based on the recommendation of an expert consensus panel (unpublished data, Pfizer Inc, New York, NY, March 4, 1998), which suggested that a symptomatic improvement criterion was a necessary component of determining response status. Analysis of responder rates employed a Mantel-Haenszel χ^2 statistic stratifying by site.

The incidence of adverse events, the percentage of subjects who discontinued because of adverse events, and the incidence of clinically significant laboratory abnormalities were compared between treatment groups using Fisher exact test. Changes in vital signs (blood pressure, heart rate, and body weight) were compared for the 2 treatment groups using the Wilcoxon rank-sum test.

Finally, the temporal course of response to treatment was examined using a mixed-effects model for longitudinal data.[48] For the CAPS-2 total severity score, IES, and DTS, the change from baseline to each treatment week was fit to linear and quadratic terms of duration of treatment. The CGI-I score at each treatment visit was fit directly to linear and quadratic terms of duration of treatment. We examined the response curves for each treatment group and compared the difference in curves between the 2 treatment groups.

tween the duration of illness, and the time since the traumatic event seems to be attributable to several factors, including presence in an individual of more than 1 trauma and delayed onset of the full diagnosis. Consistent with many other PTSD treatment studies in civilian populations, the most common trauma category was physical/sexual assault (**Table 2**).

EFFICACY

At baseline there were no significant between-treatment group differences on any of the efficacy variables. Treatment with sertraline resulted in significantly greater improvement compared with placebo in all 4 primary efficacy measures that had been defined a priori (**Table 3**). The benefit of sertraline on the 2 PTSD severity scales (the CAPS-2 and the IES) was confirmed both by global (CGI) measures of severity and improvement, as well as by the subject-rated scale, the DTS. An analysis of completers showed similar trends in favor of the sertraline-treated group, but failure to reach significance was prob-

ably attributable to the reduced statistical power caused by the 22% dropout rate.

Figure 1 shows the results of a Kaplan-Meier analysis of time to response using the post hoc consensus criteria CGI-I score of 2 or less and 30% or more reduction from baseline in the CAPS-2 total score. As can be seen, significantly ($\chi^2_1 = 8.48$, $P = .004$) more sertraline-treated subjects were classified as responders at end point compared with placebo subjects.

Figure 2 shows the change scores on both the clinician-rated CAPS-2 total severity measure (A), and on the subject-rated DTS (B) estimated from mixed-effects analyses plotted over the 12-week course of study treatment. As can be seen, a significantly steeper improvement slope was observed with sertraline compared with placebo on both measures ($t_{1379} = -2.96$, $P = .003$ for CAPS-2, and $t_{1377} = -3.45$, $P < .001$ for DTS). Additional mixed-effects analyses also found significantly steeper improvement slopes in favor of sertraline for the IES ($t_{1375} = -2.26$, $P = .02$), for the CGI-I score ($t_{1178} = -3.62$, $P < 0.001$), and for CGI-S ($t_{1380} = -4.40$, $P < .001$).

333

Table 1. Demographic and Clinical Characteristic of Study Subjects Diagnosed as Having Posttraumatic Stress Disorder (PTSD)

Patient Variable	Sertraline (N = 100)	Placebo (N = 108)	Test Statistic	P
Subjects Diagnosed as Having PTSD				
Female, %	84	72	$\chi^2 = 4.18$	.04
Age, y, mean ± SD	37.6 ± 11.1	36.6 ± 10.1	$t = 0.58$	.56
Race, %			$\chi^2 = 0.06$	
Black	13	11		
White	83	84		
Other	4	5		.81
Duration of illness, y, mean ± SD	11.7 ± 11.1	12.8 ± 12.4	$t = 0.06$	.51
Time from traumatic event, y, mean ± SD	18.3 ± 12.8	18.5 ± 15.5	$t = 0.04$	.97
Current major depression, %	40	40	$\chi^2 < 0.01$	.98
Current anxiety disorder, %	23	18	$\chi^2 = 0.94$	.33
History of alcohol dependence/ abuse, %	24	27	$\chi^2 = 0.02$	.64
History of substance dependence/ abuse, %	14	18	$\chi^2 = 0.50$	.46
Frequency of Index Traumatic Event by Category, %				
Physical or sexual assault	64	60		
Seeing someone hurt or die	11	12		
Serious accident/fire/ injury	8	15	$\chi^2_3 = 2.83$	.42
Being in a war or combat*	5	5		
Natural disaster*	0	1		
Other event*	12	7		

*Because of the small sample sizes, the bottom 3 categories are grouped for the purpose of the analysis.

Analysis of the core PTSD symptom cluster subscales showed a similar, although less consistently significant, advantage for sertraline at study end point on both clinician- and subject-rated measures (Table 3). The mean percentage of reduction from baseline in the reexperiencing/intrusion symptom cluster was 50% and 53%, respectively, on the CAPS-2 and IES, a 47% reduction in the avoidance/numbing symptom cluster on both the CAPS-2 and IES, and a 40% reduction on the arousal symptom cluster of the CAPS-2.

A treatment×sex analysis was performed on the CAPS-2 change score and was not found to be significant. The number of males in the study (46 males [22%]) was too small to perform meaningful analyses, especially since there were other sex-related confounding factors (eg, differential trauma type) that would have to be accounted for.

Among the secondary efficacy measures (Table 3), moderate improvement was observed on the HAM-D and HAM-A, but there was no significant difference from placebo. Similarly, sertraline improved sleep quality as measured by the Pittsburgh Sleep Quality Index, but not significantly more than placebo.

EFFECT OF STUDY TREATMENT ON FUNCTIONAL AND PSYCHOSOCIAL MEASURES

Social functioning, as measured by the global rating on the CAPS-2, showed significantly greater improvement on sertraline (2.6 ± 0.8 to 1.2 ± 1.1) compared with placebo (2.7 ± 0.9 to 1.7 ± 1.1; $t = 2.48$; P = .01). Similarly, the CAPS-2 rating of occupational functioning also showed significantly greater improvement for sertraline compared with placebo, with an adjusted mean change score, respectively, of 0.9 vs 0.6 ($t = 2.24$; P = .02). These results should be interpreted with caution because the social and occupational ratings on CAPS-2 have been less well validated than the symptom severity ratings.

TREATMENT AND TOLERABILITY

The mean ± SD daily dose of sertraline at study end point for completers was 146.3 ± 49.3 mg. Sertraline was generally well tolerated. Subjects reported the following rates of adverse events for sertraline and placebo, respectively: insomnia (35% vs 22%, P = .04); headache (33% vs 24%, P = .17); diarrhea (28% vs 11%, P = .003); nausea (23% vs 11%, P = .03); drowsiness (17% vs 11%, P = .24); nervousness (14% vs 8%, P = .27); fatigue (13% vs 5%; P = .05); decreased appetite (12% vs 1%, P = .001); dry mouth (10% vs 7%, P = .45); and vivid dreams (10% vs 4%, P = .10).

Thirty-two subjects discontinued sertraline treatment (30%) compared with 35 subjects who discontinued placebo treatment (27%). The primary reason cited for discontinuation of sertraline and placebo, respectively, was as follows: adverse events (9.1% vs 4.7%); withdrawal of consent (6.1% vs 3.8%); lost to follow-up (5.1% vs 10.4%); protocol violation (2.0% vs 4.7%); laboratory abnormality (2.0% vs 0%); insufficient therapeutic response (0% vs 4.7%); and miscellaneous other reasons (2.0% vs 1.9%). Two sertraline subjects discontinued prematurely because of mild elevations in aspartate aminotransferase and alanine aminotransferase values. There were no serious electrocardiographic or laboratory abnormalities during the course of the study, nor were there any significant differences between the 2 treatment groups in the incidence of electrocardiographic or laboratory abnormalities.

There were no significant differences between the sertraline group and the placebo group in terms of changes in vital signs, with the exception of sitting heart rate. Sertraline-treated subjects showed a decrease from baseline to end point, while placebo-treated subjects showed an increase (−2.7 and 1.71 beats/min, respectively; $t = 2.68$; P = .007). However, no subjects in either group showed a clinically significant change in heart rate or blood pressure.

COMMENT

The results of the present study indicate that sertraline is an effective acute treatment for PTSD. This investigation, together with a companion study[49] that was also positive on all primary outcome measures, represent

334

Table 2. Effect of Study Treatment on Primary and Secondary Efficacy Measures In Subjects Diagnosed as Having Posttraumatic Stress Disorder (PTSD), Change From Baseline to End Point*

Efficacy Variables	Sertraline (N = 98)	Placebo (N = 104)	t Test Statistic	P
Primary Outcome Measures				
CAPS-2 total score, mean ± SD				
Baseline	73.9 ± 16.2	73.5 ± 16.1	2.02	.04
Change	−33.0 ± 2.4	−26.2 ± 2.3		
IES total score, mean ± SD				
Baseline	38.5 ± 15.6	40.0 ± 14.5	2.36	.02
Change	−19.2 ± 1.5	−14.1 ± 1.5		
CGI-Severity, mean ± SD				
Baseline	4.6 ± 1.0	4.6 ± 0.9	2.09	.04
Change	−1.3 ± 0.1	−1.0 ± 0.1		
CGI-Improvement, mean ± SD	2.3 ± 0.1	2.8 ± 0.1	2.46	.01
Secondary Outcome Measures				
Davidson PTSD Scale total score, mean ± SD				
Baseline	74.5 ± 26.9	73.8 ± 26.2	3.08	.002
Change	−32.3 ± 2.8	−20.0 ± 2.7		
HAM-D, 21-item total score, mean ± SD				
Baseline	21.7 ± 8.2	21.2 ± 8.3	0.97	.33
Change	−7.7 ± 1.0	−6.3 ± 1.0		
HAM-A total score, mean ± SD				
Baseline	20.0 ± 7.9	19.3 ± 7.4	1.12	.26
Change	−7.8 ± 0.8	−6.4 ± 0.9		
Pittsburgh Sleep Quality Scale, mean ± SD				
Baseline	11.7 ± 3.7	12.1 ± 3.8	0.75	.45
Change	−3.0 ± 0.5	−2.5 ± 0.5		

*CAPS-2 indicates Clinician-Administered PTSD Scale, Part 2; IES, Impact of Event Scale; CGI, Clinical Global Impression Scale; HAM-D, Hamilton Rating Scale for Depression; and HAM-A, Hamilton Rating Scale for Anxiety.

the largest randomized placebo-controlled trials published to date on the treatment of PTSD.

Acute treatment with sertraline in the present study resulted in a clinically significant mean reduction from baseline in the range of 45% to 50% on the 2 primary measures of overall PTSD symptom severity, the CAPS-2 and the IES (Table 3). On both the CAPS-2 and the IES, approximately 70% of the improvement in PTSD symptoms occurred during the first 4 weeks of treatment. The mixed-effects analysis confirmed that the improvement observed over the 12 weeks of sertraline treatment was consistently greater than placebo across both of these primary outcome measures (Figure 2).

The severity of the 3 PTSD core symptom clusters also improved with sertraline treatment (Table 4), but the improvement was less consistently significant on the clinician-rated CAPS-2 when compared with placebo. In contrast, the subject-rated DTS and IES consistently detected significantly greater efficacy advantage for sertraline over placebo on all 3 PTSD symptom clusters, suggesting that subject self-rating scales may be more sensitive measures for evaluating treatment effects in PTSD than clinician ratings.

Paralleling improvement in PTSD symptoms, global measures of social functioning and occupational functioning also showed rapid and significant improvement. In a similar 12-week, double-blind study of sertraline and placebo using the Quality of Life, Enjoyment, and Satisfaction Questionnaire,[49,50] sertraline-treated subjects were improved on measures of social relationships, leisure activities, ability to function daily, living situation, ability to get around physically, and ability to work after 12 weeks of treatment. The results from the CAPS-2 function items in this study indicate similar improvements. Posttraumatic stress disorder has been characterized as one of the most functionally debilitating disorders, and small symptom improvements leading to resumed daily activities, such as driving or taking elevators, can have a profound impact on family and work life.

Although sertraline, relative to placebo, improved the symptoms of PTSD and its associated features, no significant differences between sertraline and placebo were found on either the HAM-A or HAM-D change scores at end point. Subjects with primary diagnoses of major depression or most anxiety disorders were excluded from the current trial. However, mild-to-moderate levels of both anxiety and depression were reported by most subjects at baseline, as evidenced by mean HAM-A and HAM-D scores near 20. The lack of differential improvement in anxiety and depressive symptoms, therefore, was unlikely to be a function of limited room for change on these scales because of low baseline scores. It is possible that chronic, subsyndromic anxious and depressive symptoms associated with PTSD may require a longer course of therapy. However, this is speculation, and arguing against this hypothesis is the larger, and earlier-onset, treatment effect found for sertraline treatment of subjects with dysthymic disorder and double depression.[27,28] The relative lack of acute antidepressant effect in the current subject sample makes it unlikely that an antidepressant response is a necessary precondition for the efficacy of sertraline in the treatment of PTSD.

335

Table 3. Effect of Study Treatment on Posttraumatic Stress Disorder (PTSD) Symptom Cluster Subscales in Subjects Diagnosed as Having PTSD, Change From Baseline to End Point

PTSD Symptom Clusters, Subscales of Primary Measures	Sertraline (N = 98)	Placebo (N = 104)	t Test Statistic	P
Reexperiencing/Intrusion				
CAPS-2, mean ± SD				
Baseline	15.1 ± 5.6	15.3 ± 6.3	1.05	.29
Change	–7.5 ± 0.7	–6.5 ± 0.7		
IES, mean ± SD				
Baseline	18.0 ± 8.6	19.6 ± 8.1	2.21	.03
Change	–9.6 ± 0.8	–6.9 ± 0.8		
DTS, mean ± SD				
Baseline	14.8 ± 7.5	15.1 ± 7.6	2.18	.03
Change	–6.7 ± 0.8	–4.4 ± 0.8		
Avoidance/Numbing				
CAPS-2, mean ± SD				
Baseline	31.4 ± 9.0	31.2 ± 8.9	2.41	.02
Change	–14.7 ± 1.2	–10.6 ± 1.2		
IES, mean ± SD				
Baseline	20.5 ± 9.8	20.5 ± 9.2	1.98	.05
Change	–9.6 ± 0.9	–7.1 ± 0.9		
DTS, mean ± SD				
Baseline	30.3 ± 13.2	30.4 ± 12.4	2.96	.003
Change	–12.8 ± 1.3	–7.2 ± 1.3		
Arousal/Hyperarousal				
CAPS-2, mean ± SD				
Baseline	27.3 ± 6.6	27.0 ± 6.3	1.55	.12
Change	–10.8 ± 0.9	–8.9 ± 0.9		
DTS, mean ± SD				
Baseline	28.2 ± 10.3	26.3 ± 10.2	2.69	.007
Change	–11.6 ± 1.1	–7.8 ± 1.0		
Associated Features				
CAPS-2, mean ± SD				
Baseline	25.1 ± 10.0	23.8 ± 10.3	2.56	.01
Change	–10.5 ± 1.0	–6.8 ± 1.0		

*CAPS-2 indicates Clinician-Administered PTSD Scale, Part 2; IES, Impact of Event Scale; and DTS, Davidson Trauma Scale.

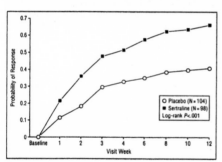

Figure 1. Kaplan-Meier time-to-response analysis. The responder is defined by scoring 1 or 2 on the Clinical Global Impression-Improvement Scale, and a decrease of 30% or more in the total score from baseline on part 2 of the Clinician-Administered Posttraumatic Stress Disorder Scale.

Sertraline was well tolerated, with 9% of sertraline-treated subjects, compared with 5% of placebo-treated subjects, discontinuing treatment during the 12-week study period because of adverse events. There were no differences between the sertraline group and the placebo group in the incidence of laboratory abnormali-ties, and no clinically significant changes in vital signs or electrocardiogram were found for any subjects.

The study as conducted has several limitations. First, study entry criteria excluded patients with a current history of alcohol or substance abuse. Other study entry criteria required a moderate-or-higher level of current symptom severity. The generalizability of our study results to patients in the community suffering from PTSD must be made with an awareness of potential differences between the 2 populations. Another limitation is that the study was not powered to evaluate the influence of potentially important clinical variables, such as sex, type of trauma, duration of illness, or presence of comorbidity on treatment response. We plan to pool the data from the current study with data from a study of very similar design[49] to undertake exploratory analyses of some of these issues. Another limitation of the current study is that it provides no information on the longer-term effects of sertraline in consolidating the improvement in PTSD symptoms obtained during acute therapy and in sustaining this level of improvement (ie, in preventing relapse). The results of a recently completed 12-month treatment study should provide data on this topic (J.R.T.D., P. Londberg, MD, T. Pearlstein, MD, K. T. Brady, MD, PhD, B.O.R., J. Bell, MD, R. Mad-

336

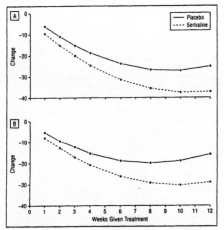

Figure 2. *Results of random regression analyses comparing the effects of a 12-week treatment with sertraline and placebo. A, Mean change score estimate from a random regression analysis on part 2 of the Clinician-Administered Posttraumatic Stress Disorder Scale ($t_{1379} = -2.96$, $P = .003$). B, Mean change scores from a random regression analysis on the Impact of Event Scale ($t_{1377} = -3.45$, $P = .0006$).*

dock, MD, M. T. Hegel, PhD, and G.M.F., unpublished data, 2000).

How do the results of the current study compare with previously conducted PTSD treatment research? First, in terms of indexing the results obtained here against previous results, it should be noted that the placebo response rate in the current study (38%) was comparable with rates reported in previously published placebo-controlled drug therapy studies.[20-23] Placebo response rates in these studies range as high as 62% (in the study reported by Connor et al[23]) when no symptom severity reduction criteria were applied. The current study joins a growing number of well-designed studies of drug therapy[20-23] and cognitive or behavioral therapy[13-16] that have reported efficacy in the treatment of PTSD, but there are still relatively few placebo-controlled studies with larger sample sizes available. For example, among psychosocial treatments, cognitive-behavior therapy is the most well established as a treatment, but the largest and most positive recent study testing its efficacy[13] had only 20 subjects at end point in the exposure-alone treatment group and 19 subjects at end point in the exposure-plus-cognitive-therapy treatment group. Confidence in the positive results of this study were further complicated by the fact that subjects in each group were concurrently being treated with antidepressants (17% in the former and 42% in the latter treatment group), as well as by other significant between-treatment group differences, most notably a duration of illness that ranged from 23 to 61 months.

The importance of the current study is increased by the relative dearth of large-scale controlled treatment studies, which is surprising given the high prevalence,[1-3] chronicity,[1,4] comorbidity,[1,5,6] and disability[7,8] associated with

PTSD. The similarly positive results of a second study[49] provide further evidence suggesting that sertraline is a safe, well-tolerated, and, compared with placebo, significantly effective treatment for this long-neglected public health problem.

Accepted for publication December 21, 2000.

Financial support for this study was provided by Pfizer Inc, New York, NY.

Presented at the American College of Neuropharmacology, Kamuela, Hawaii, December 1997; and at the International Society for Traumatic Stress Studies, Washington, DC, November 1998.

The investigators in this study and the corresponding sites at which the study was conducted were Jessy Colah, MD, and Renuka Tank, MD, Adult and Geriatric Outpatient Services, Brooklyn, NY; Kathleen Brady, PhD, MD, Institute of Psychiatry, Charleston, SC; Paul Newhouse, MD, Fletcher Allen Healthcare, Burlington, Vt; Barbara O. Rothbaum, PhD, The Emory Clinic, and the Department of Psychiatry and Behavioral Sciences, Atlanta, Ga; Hisham Hafez, MD, and Phillip Santora, MD, Charter Brookside Hospital and Research Department, C. Brookside Hospital, Nashua, NH; Peter Londborg, MD, Seattle Clinical Research Center, Seattle, Wash; Teri Pearlstein, MD, Butler Hospital, Providence, RI; Bessel van der Kolk, MD, PhD, Human Resource Institute, Brookline, Mass; Wayne Phillips, MD, PhD, Boulder PTSD Center, Boulder, Colo; Katherine Shear, MD, University of Pittsburgh School of Medicine, Pittsburgh, Pa; Richard Weisler, MD, Raleigh, NC; William Patterson, MD, Birmingham Research Group Inc, Birmingham, Ala; Phebe Tucker, MD, University of Oklahoma Health Sciences Center, Oklahoma City.

Corresponding author and reprints: Jonathan R.T. Davidson, MD, Department of Psychiatry and Behavioral Sciences, Anxiety and Traumatic Stress Program, Duke University Medical Center, Box 3812, Durham, NC 27710.

REFERENCES

1. Kessler RC, Sonnega A, Bromet E, Hughes M, Nelson CB. Posttraumatic stress disorder in the National Comorbidity Survey. *Arch Gen Psychiatry.* 1995;52: 1048-1060.
2. Breslau N, Davis GC, Andreski P, Peterson E. Traumatic events and posttraumatic stress disorder in an urban population of young adults. *Arch Gen Psychiatry.* 1991;48:216-222.
3. Resnick HS, Kilpatrick DG, Dansky BS, Saunders BE, Best CL. Prevalence of civilian trauma and posttraumatic stress disorder in a representative national sample of women. *J Consult Clin Psychol.* 1993;61:984-991.
4. Breslau N, Davis GC. Posttraumatic stress disorder in an urban population of young adults: risk factors for chronicity. *Am J Psychiatry.* 1992;149:671-675.
5. Davidson JR, Hughes D, Blazer DG, George LK. Post-traumatic stress disorder in the community: an epidemiological study. *Psychol Med.* 1991;21:713-721.
6. Breslau N, Davis GC, Peterson EL, Schultz L. Psychiatric sequelae of posttraumatic stress disorder in women. *Arch Gen Psychiatry.* 1997;54:81-87.
7. Solomon SD, Davidson JR. Trauma: prevalence, impairment, service use, and cost. *J Clin Psychiatry.* 1997;58:5-11.
8. Zatzick DF, Marmar CR, Weiss DS, Browner WS, Metzler TJ, Golding JM, Stewart A, Schlenger WE, Wells KB. Posttraumatic stress disorder and functioning and quality of life outcomes in a nationally representative sample of male Vietnam veterans. *Am J Psychiatry.* 1997;154:1690-1695.
9. Friedman MJ, Schnurr PP. The relationship between trauma, posttraumatic stress disorder, and physical health. In: Friedman MJ, Charney DS, Deutch AY, eds. *Neurobiological and Clinical Consequences of Stress: From Normal Adaptation to PTSD.* Philadelphia, Pa: Lippincott-Raven Publishers; 1995:507-524.
10. Kimerling R, Calhoun KS. Somatic symptoms, social support, and treatment-

337

seeking among sexual assault victims. *J Consult Clin Psychol.* 1994;62:333-340.

11. Golding JM, Stein J, Siegel J. Sexual assault history and use of health and mental health services. *Am J Community Psychol.* 1988;16:625-640.

12. Cohen MA, Miller TR. *Mental Health Care for Crime Victims.* Nashville, Tenn: Vanderbilt University; 1994.

13. Foa EB, Rothbaum BO, Riggs DS, Murdock TB. Treatment of posttraumatic stress disorder in rape victims: a comparison between cognitive-behavioral procedures and counseling. *J Consult Clin Psychol.* 1991;59:715-723.

14. Boudewyns PA, Hyer L. Physiological response of combat memories and preliminary treatment outcome in Vietnam veteran PTSD patients treated with direct therapeutic exposure. *Behav Ther.* 1990;21:63-87.

15. Brom D, Kleber RJ, Defares PB. Brief psychotherapy for posttraumatic stress disorders. *J Consult Clin Psychol.* 1989;57:607-612.

16. Marks I, Lovell K, Noshirvani H, Livanou M, Thrasher S. Treatment of posttraumatic stress disorder by exposure and/or cognitive restructuring: a controlled study. *Arch Gen Psychiatry.* 1998;55:317-325.

17. Solomon SD, Gerrity ET, Muff AM. Efficacy of treatments for posttraumatic stress disorder: an empirical review. *JAMA.* 1992;268:633-638.

18. Kosten TR, Frank JB, Dan E, McDouble CJ, Giller EL. Pharmacotherapy of posttraumatic stress disorder using phenelzine or imipramine. *J Nerv Ment Dis.* 1991; 179:366-370.

19. Davidson J, Kudler H, Smith R, Mahorney SL, Lipper S, Hammett E, Saunders WB, Cavenar JO Jr. Treatment of posttraumatic stress disorder with amitriptyline and placebo. *Arch Gen Psychiatry.* 1990;47:259-266.

20. Katz RJ, Lott MH, Arbus P, Crocq L, Herlobsen P, Lingjaerde O, Lopez G, Loughrey GC, MacFarlane DJ, McIvor R. Pharmacotherapy of post-traumatic stress disorder with a novel psychotropic. *Anxiety.* 1994-1995;1:169-174.

21. Baker DG, Diamond BI, Gillette G, Hamner M, Katzelnick D, Keller T, Mellman TA, Pontius E, Rosenthal M, Tucker P, van der Kolk BA, Katz RJ, Lott MH. A double-blind, randomized, placebo-controlled, multi-center study of brofaromine in the treatment of post-traumatic stress disorder. *Psychopharmacology (Berl).* 1995; 122:386-389.

22. van der Kolk BA, Dreyfuss D, Michaels M, Shera D, Berkowitz R, Fisler R, Saxe G. Fluoxetine in posttraumatic stress disorder. *J Clin Psychiatry.* 1994;55:517-522.

23. Connor KM, Sutherland SM, Tupler LA, Malik ML, Davidson JR. Fluoxetine in post-traumatic stress disorder: randomised, double-blind study. *Br J Psychiatry.* 1999;175:17-22.

24. American Psychiatric Association. *Diagnostic and Statistical Manual of Mental Disorders, Fourth Edition.* Washington, DC: American Psychiatric Association; 1994.

25. Fabre LF, Abuzzahab FS, Amin M, Claghorn JL, Mendels J, Petrie WM, Dube S, Small JG. Sertraline safety and efficacy in major depression: a double-blind fixed-dose comparison with placebo. *Biol Psychiatry.* 1995;38:592-602.

26. Reimherr FW, Chouinard G, Cohn CK, Cole JO, Itil TM, LaPierre YD, Masco HL, Mendels J. Antidepressant efficacy of sertraline: a double-blind, placebo- and amitriptyline-controlled, multicenter comparison study in outpatients with major depression. *J Clin Psychiatry.* 1990;51(suppl B):18-27.

27. Keller MB, Gelenberg AJ, Hirschfeld RM, Rush AJ, Thase ME, Kocsis JH, Markowitz JC, Fawcett JA, Koran LM, Klein DN, Russell JM, Kornstein SG, McCollough JP, Davis SM, Harrison WM. The treatment of chronic depression, part 2: a double-blind, randomized trial of sertraline and imipramine. *J Clin Psychiatry.* 1998;59:598-607.

28. Thase ME, Fava M, Halbreich U, Kocsis JH, Koran L, Davidson J, Rosenbaum J, Harrison W. A placebo-controlled, randomized clinical trial comparing sertraline and imipramine for the treatment of dysthymia. *Arch Gen Psychiatry.* 1996;53: 777-784.

29. Londborg PD, Wolkow R, Smith WT, DuBoff E, England D, Ferguson J, Rosenthal M, Weise C. Sertraline in the treatment of panic disorder: a multisite, double-

blind, placebo-controlled fixed dose investigation. *Br J Psychiatry.* 1998;173: 54-60.

30. Pollack MH, Otto MW, Worthington JJ, Manfro GG, Wolkow R. Sertraline in the treatment of panic disorder: a flexible-dose multicenter trial. *Arch Gen Psychiatry.* 1998;55:1010-1016.

31. Pohl RB, Wolkow RM, Clary CM. Sertraline in the treatment of panic disorder: a double-blind multicenter trial. *Am J Psychiatry.* 1998;155:1189-1195.

32. Roy A. Placebo-controlled study of sertraline in depressed recently abstinent alcoholics. *Biol Psychiatry.* 1998;44:633-637.

33. Pettinati HM, Volpicelli JR, Cnaan A, Luck GJ. Placebo-controlled trial of sertraline (Zoloft) for primary alcoholism. Presented as a poster at: the annual meeting of the American College of Neuropsychopharmacology; December 14-17, 1999; Acapuco, Mexico.

34. Brady KT, Sonne SC, Roberts JM. Sertraline treatment of comorbid posttraumatic stress disorder and alcohol dependence. *J Clin Psychiatry.* 1995;56:502-505.

35. Rothbaum BO, Ninan PT, Thomas L. Sertraline in the treatment of rape victims with posttraumatic stress disorder. *J Trauma Stress.* 1996;9:865-871.

36. American Psychiatric Association. *Diagnostic and Statistical Manual of Mental Disorders, Revised Third Edition.* Washington, DC: American Psychiatric Association; 1987.

37. Weathers FW, Litz BT. Psychometric properties of the Clinician-Administered PTSD Scale, CAPS-1. *PTSD Res Q.* 1994;5: 2-6.

38. Blake DD, Weathers FW, Nagy LM, Kaloupek DG, Klauminzer G, Charney DS, Keane TM. A clinician rating scale for assessing current and lifetime PTSD: the CAPS-1. *Behav Ther.* 1990;13:187-188.

39. Spitzer RL, Williams JB, Gibbons M, First MB. The Structured Clinical Interview for *DSM-III-R* (SCID), I: history, rationale, and description. *Arch Gen Psychiatry.* 1992;49:624-629.

40. Horowitz M, Wilner N, Alvarez W. Impact of Event Scale: a measure of subjective stress. *Psychosom Med.* 1979;41:209-218.

41. Zilberg N, Weiss D, Horowitz M. Impact of Event Scale: a cross-validation study. *J Consult Clin Psychol.* 1982;50:407-414.

42. Guy W. *ECDEU Assessment Manual for Psychopharmacology.* Washington, DC: National Institute of Mental Health; 1976. Dept of Health, Education, and Welfare publication 76-338.

43. Davidson JR, Book SW, Colket JT, Tupler LA, Roth S, David D, Hertzberg M, Mellman T, Beckham JC, Smith RD, Davison RM, Katz R, Feldman ME. Assessment of a new self-rating scale for post-traumatic stress disorder. *Psychol Med.* 1997; 27:153-160.

44. Zlotnick C, Davidson J, Shea MT, Pearlstein T. Validation of the Davidson Trauma Scale in a sample of survivors of childhood sexual abuse. *J Nerv Ment Dis.* 1996; 184:255-257.

45. Hamilton MA. A rating scale for depression. *J Neurol Neurosurg Psychiatry.* 1960; 23:56-62.

46. Hamilton M. The assessment of anxiety states by rating. *Br J Med Psychol.* 1959; 32:50-55.

47. Buysse DJ, Reynolds CF III, Monk TH, Berman SR, Kupfer DJ. The Pittsburgh Sleep Quality Index: a new instrument for psychiatric practice and research. *Psychiatry Res.* 1989;28:193-213.

48. Laird NM, Ware JH. Random-effects models for longitudinal data. *Biometrics.* 1982;38:963-974.

49. Brady K, Pearlstein T, Asnis GM, Baker D, Rothbaum B, Sikes CR, Farfel GM. Efficacy and safety of sertraline treatment of posttraumatic stress disorder: a randomized controlled trial. *JAMA.* 2000;283:1837-1844.

50. Endicott J, Nee J, Harrison W, Blumenthal R. Quality of Life, Enjoyment, and Satisfaction Questionnaire: a new measure. *Psychopharmacol Bull.* 1993;29:321-326.

338

Paroxetine Treatment of Generalized Social Phobia (Social Anxiety Disorder)

A Randomized Controlled Trial

Murray B. Stein, MD; Michael R. Liebowitz, MD; R. Bruce Lydiard, PhD, MD; Cornelius D. Pitts, RPh; William Bushnell, MS; Ivan Gergel, MD

Context.—The generalized type of social phobia (social anxiety disorder) is a severe and often disabling form of social anxiety that affects approximately 5% of the general population. Earlier research has shown monoamine oxidase inhibitors or benzodiazepines to be effective in treating this condition, but neither has achieved widespread use.

Objective.—To compare the efficacy of paroxetine, a selective serotonin reuptake inhibitor, with placebo in adults with generalized social phobia.

Design.—Twelve-week, multicenter, randomized, double-blind trial.

Setting.—Thirteen centers across the United States and 1 in Canada.

Participants.—Between April 13, 1995, and February 28, 1996, 187 persons meeting *Diagnostic and Statistical Manual of Mental Disorders, Fourth Edition* criteria for generalized social phobia were randomized (and 183 returned for at least 1 efficacy assessment) to treatment.

Intervention.—After a 1-week, single-blind, placebo, run-in period, patients received a double-blind, 11-week course of either paroxetine or matching-image placebo. The initial daily dosage of paroxetine (or placebo) was 20 mg with increases of 10 mg/d weekly (flexible dosing to a maximum of 50 mg/d) permitted after the second week of treatment.

Main Outcome Measures.—Number of responders based on the Clinical Global Impression Global Improvement Item ("much improved" or "very much improved"); mean change from baseline on the Liebowitz Social Anxiety Scale total score.

Results.—Fifty (55.0%) of 91 persons taking paroxetine and 22 (23.9%) of 92 persons taking placebo were much improved or very much improved at the end of treatment (odds ratio [OR], 3.88; 95% confidence interval [CI], 2.81-5.36). Mean Liebowitz Social Anxiety Scale total scores were reduced by 39.1% (the mean baseline score of 78.0 declined by a mean of 30.5 points at follow-up) in the paroxetine group compared with 17.4% (the mean baseline score of 83.5 declined 14.5 points at follow-up) in the placebo group, a difference of 21.7% (95% CI, 8.7%-34.7%) favoring paroxetine.

Conclusions.—Paroxetine is an effective treatment for patients with generalized social phobia. Short-term (ie, 11-week) treatment results in substantial and clinically meaningful reductions in symptoms and disability. Future research should test whether these may be further reduced by extended treatment or supplementation with specific educational-cognitive-behavioral techniques.

JAMA. 1998;280:708-713

From the Department of Psychiatry, University of California at San Diego, La Jolla (Dr Stein); Department of Psychiatry, College of Physicians and Surgeons, Columbia University, New York, NY (Dr Liebowitz); Department of Psychiatry, Medical University of South Carolina, Charleston (Dr Lydiard); and Clinical Research, Development, and Medical Affairs, North America, SmithKline Beecham Pharmaceuticals, Collegeville, Pa (Messrs Pitts and Bushnell and Dr Gergel).

Reprints: Murray B. Stein, MD, Department of Psychiatry (0985), University of California, San Diego, 9500 Gilman Dr, La Jolla, CA 92093-0985 (e-mail: mstein@ucsd.edu).

SOCIAL PHOBIA, also known as social anxiety disorder, is characterized by the fear of being observed or evaluated by others.[1] In such situations, individuals with social phobia fear that they will say or do something to embarrass or humiliate themselves or that others will notice that they are anxious. Consequently, people with social phobia often avoid situations where such scrutiny might take place or they endure them with intense distress. Not surprisingly, this can result in impaired functioning and reduced quality of life.[2-6] Patients with social phobia may have few friendships, experience trouble dating, drop out of school, reject promotions at work, become demoralized and depressed, abuse alcohol, and develop other psychiatric comorbidities.[2-7]

Most clinicians associate the term *social phobia* with a fear of public speaking. Indeed, social phobia often involves public speaking and, in some cases, does so exclusively.[8] However, it has recently been recognized that there is a subgroup of social phobic people whose social anxiety is far more pervasive and usually far more disabling. Persons with this variant of the disorder, known as generalized social phobia (GSP), typically fear and avoid a broad array of situations that most people take for granted.[4,5,7] Examples might include speaking in small groups (eg, at work or school), attending social gatherings, talking to people in authority (eg, teachers, employers), or interacting with peers in informal settings (eg, talking to colleagues over lunch).

Previously believed to be a rare disorder based on prevalence estimates from psychiatric clinics, recent epidemiologic surveys have demonstrated that social phobia is highly prevalent.[9-12] After major depression and alcohol dependence, social phobia is the third most common psychiatric disorder in the general population with lifetime, 12-month, and 30-day prevalence rates of 13.3%, 7.9%, and 4.5%, respectively.[9-10] Although precise rates of GSP are lacking, it is estimated that approximately two thirds of people with social phobia in the community would fall into this category.[13] It is this 4% to 5% of persons in the community who warrant our attention as suffering from a public health problem of considerable importance.[5,13]

Social phobia, like many other anxiety disorders,[14,15] is highly prevalent in the primary care setting but goes largely undiagnosed and untreated.[16-18] In a recent primary care study, social phobia was noted to be associated with meaningfully reduced role functioning and sense of well-being.[17] In the only in-depth study to date of social phobia in the general medical health care system, investigators found a 1-month prevalence of 4.9% in a French primary care clinic but poor recognition of the disorder on the part of general practitioners.[18] Unfortunately, the low rate of recognition and appropriate treatment reflect the fact that social phobia remains a largely neglected anxiety disorder.[19]

This neglect also extends into the area of treatment. Whereas most physicians equate treating social phobia with the prescription of as-needed β-blockers or benzodiazepines (which can be useful in treating social phobia limited to public speaking or other kinds of performance anxiety), these are not useful in the treatment of GSP.[20-24] Because patients with GSP find so many situations frightening, and because they encounter these situations on a daily, often unpredictable basis, the use of occasional "as needed" medications for GSP is not an option. Treatment options for generalized social phobia include monoamine oxidase inhibitors (MAOIs), reversible inhibitors of monoamine oxidase A (RIMAs), and benzodiazepines.[21-27] However, these treatment choices are associated with dietary restrictions (MAOIs), potential difficulties with withdrawal and dependence (benzodiazepines), and questionable efficacy in some studies (RIMAs[27]). Specific psychotherapies focused on changing maladaptive thoughts and behaviors (ie, cognitive and behavioral therapies) have also shown considerable promise in the treatment of social phobia.[28-30] Access to these psychotherapies is often limited, however, by an inadequate supply of trained therapists, insurance barriers, and other cost factors.

Based on their success in the treatment of many mood and other anxiety disorders,[31] the selective serotonin reuptake inhibitors (SSRIs) have been investigated in the treatment of social phobia. Case reports and open-label trials had suggested considerable potential for

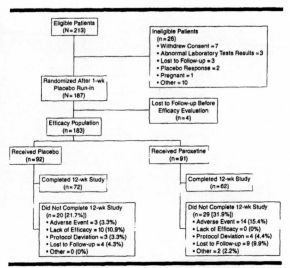

Figure 1.—Study profile of 213 patients who were first screened for eligibility. After screening and 1-week placebo run-in, 93 patients were randomized to placebo and 94 to paroxetine groups. Of the 187 randomized patients, 72% completed the study.

the treatment of this condition.[32-38] In the 2 double-blind, comparative, single-site studies published to date, sertraline hydrochloride[39] and fluvoxamine maleate[40] were more effective than placebo with relatively small sample sizes of 12 patients[39] and 30 patients,[40] respectively.

Based on these encouraging preliminary reports, the first double-blind, randomized, multicentered trial of paroxetine in patients with social phobia was undertaken. The trial was limited to patients with the generalized subtype of social phobia (GSP) because of its greater severity and more specific response (ie, lower placebo-response rate) compared with nongeneralized social phobia in prior treatment trials.[41]

METHODS
Study Design

This was a double-blind, placebo-controlled trial in patients diagnosed as having GSP under the guidelines of the *Diagnostic and Statistical Manual of Mental Disorders, Fourth Edition (DSM-IV)*.[1] Investigators at 13 centers in the United States and Canada (see acknowledgement) participated in this 12-week study. The protocol was approved by the institutional review boards at all centers. After a complete description of the study to the patients, written, informed consent was obtained prior to enrollment. A total

of 213 patients entered the screening phase of this study (although additional subjects were excluded at the prescreening phase based on obvious ineligibility for the protocol). A Structured Clinical Interview for the *DSM-IV* (SCID)[42] (modified by M.B.S. and Andrea L. Hazen, PhD), which has been shown to reliably distinguish between generalized vs nongeneralized subtypes (κ = 0.84; M.B.S. and Andrea L. Hazen, PhD, unpublished observations, July 1996), was used to confirm that GSP was the predominant diagnosis. In addition to meeting *DSM-IV* criteria for social phobia, patients were required to exhibit fear and/or avoidance of at least 4 social situations. At least 2 of these were required to involve interpersonal interactions.

Patient Eligibility

Eligible patients were 18 years of age or older; adults older than 65 years were permitted if they were able to tolerate a starting paroxetine dose of at least 20 mg/d. Patients who required concurrent psychoactive medication (except chloral hydrate for insomnia), narcotic analgesics, warfarin sodium, digitalis glycosides, phenytoin, cimetidine, or sulfonylurea derivatives were excluded. Patients who had taken any psychotropic agent or β-blockers within 14 days prior to the study were ineligible, as were those who

341

Table 1.—Demographic Characteristics and Mean Baseline Rating Scale Scores of Randomized Patients*

Variable	Paroxetine (n = 94)	Placebo (n = 93)
Age, mean (range), y	35.9 (18-59)	36.7 (18-76)
Sex, No.		
Male	44	37
Female	50	56
Race, No.		
African American	15	8
Asian	3	1
White	71	80
Other	5	4
Current major depression, No. (%)	6 (6.4)	3 (3.2)
Current panic disorder, No. (%)	1 (1.1)	2 (2.2)
No prior SSRI treatment, No. (%)	90 (97)	90 (97)
Duration of social anxiety symptoms, mean (SD), y†	21.9 (12.0)	23.3 (14.4)
Age of onset of social anxiety symptoms, mean (SD), y†	14.7 (8.8)	14.3 (6.3)
LSAS total (±SE)	78.0 (2.3)	83.5 (2.3)
LSAS fear (±SE)	41.2 (1.1)	43.3 (1.1)
LSAS avoidance (±SE)	36.9 (1.3)	40.2 (1.3)
SADS total (±SE)	22.5 (0.5)	22.3 (0.5)
SDI work (±SE)	4.8 (0.3)	5.1 (0.3)
SDI social life (±SE)	6.9 (0.2)	6.9 (0.2)
SDI family life (±SE)	3.2 (0.3)	3.1 (0.3)

*SSRI indicates selective serotonin reuptake inhibitor; LSAS, Liebowitz Social Anxiety Scale; SADS, Social Avoidance and Distress Scale; and SDI, Sheehan Disability Inventory.
†These data were available for 73 patients in the paroxetine group and 75 in the placebo group.

Table 2.—Reasons for Early Study Discontinuation Among 187 Randomized Patients

	No. (%) Patients Taking	
Reason	Paroxetine (n = 94)	Placebo (n = 93)
Adverse event	14 (14.9)	3 (3.2)
Lost to follow-up	12 (12.8)	5 (5.4)
Protocol deviation	4 (4.3)	3 (3.2)
Lack of efficacy	0	10 (10.8)
Other	2 (2.1)	0
Total Discontinuations	32 (34.0)	21 (22.6)
Completed study	62 (66.0)	72 (77.4)

had received depot neuroleptics within the previous 12 weeks. Also excluded were patients with any other Axis I diagnosis that was considered to be clinically predominant within the previous 6 months. Patients who met *DSM-IV* criteria for substance abuse or dependence within 3 or 6 months prior to this study, respectively, were excluded, as were those judged to be serious suicidal or homicidal risks. Additional reasons for exclusion were body dysmorphic disorder, history of seizure disorder, schizophrenia or bipolar affective disorder, any serious or uncontrolled medical illness or condition that precluded paroxetine use, electroconvulsive therapy within the previous 3 months, investigational drug use or participation in a clinical trial within the previous 12 months, and previous intolerance of or lack of response to paroxetine (no subject was excluded on this basis). Women who were pregnant, lactating, or not using a clinically acceptable method of birth control also were ineligible. Finally, patients with clinically significant abnormal laboratory or electrocardiographic findings that could not be resolved prior to baseline evaluations were not included.

Blinding, Randomization, and Treatment

Following initial screening procedures, potential subjects entered a 1-week, single-blind, placebo run-in period, after which a baseline Clinical Global Impression (CGI) Global Improvement rating was performed. Patients who were rated no more than minimally improved (CGI Global Improvement rating >2) and who continued to meet all inclusion criteria were randomized to receive paroxetine or placebo (identical in appearance). Patients were randomly assigned in a balanced fashion to the 2 treatment groups

(in blocks of 4) using a computer-generated randomization code for up to 300 patients. For the purposes of blinding, dosage was referred to as level 1 (20 mg), level 2 (30 mg), level 3 (40 mg), or level 4 (50 mg). Patients received an initial dose of level 1 medication once daily. After 2 weeks, the dosage could be increased to the next level (ie, in 10-mg increments) up to level 4 (ie, 50 mg/d) based on clinical response as determined by the treating physician. Dosage could be reduced to a minimum of level 1 (ie, 20 mg/d) at any time if the physician felt that adverse effects warranted this adjustment.

Efficacy and Safety Evaluation

Patients were evaluated for safety and efficacy at weeks 1, 2, 3, 4, 6, 8, and 12. Adverse events were also assessed by telephone at week 10. The primary efficacy variables were (1) the percentage of responders at end point, defined as those rated on the CGI Global Improvement Item as 1 (very much improved) or 2 (much improved) and (2) the mean change from baseline at end point on the Liebowitz Social Anxiety Scale[63] total score, which is a 24-question assessment of fear and avoidance of public and social situations. Secondary efficacy variables included mean changes from baseline at end point in the Social Avoidance and Distress Scale (a measure of social avoidance and discomfort[44]); the Sheehan Disability Inventory for work, social life, and family life (a measure of quality of life[45]); and the fear/anxiety and avoidance subscales of the Liebowitz Social Anxiety Scale. Safety analyses included routine adverse-event monitoring and vital-sign assessment.

Statistical Methods

The proportion of patients achieving a dichotomous response (CGI Global

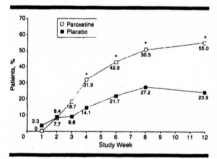

Figure 2.—Percentage of paroxetine-treated and placebo-treated patients from the efficacy population (with last observation carried forward) considered therapeutic responders using the Clinical Global Impression Global Improvement Item over time (P = .001 vs placebo).

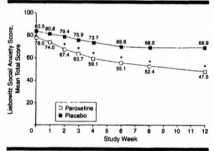

Figure 3.—Mean total Liebowitz Social Anxiety Score for paroxetine-treated and placebo-treated patients from the efficacy population (with last observation carried forward) at baseline and by weekly visits through week 12 (P<.001 vs placebo).

342

Improvement score of 1 or 2) was analyzed by logistic analysis using the categorical modeling procedure of the SAS system (SAS Statistical Software, Cary, NC); this model included treatment and investigator effects. Changes from baseline scores of the various efficacy scales were analyzed using parametric analysis of variance. The general linear model of the SAS system, including treatment and investigator effects, was used. Type III sums of squares were used. The treatment-by-investigator interaction was not significant for any variable and subsequently was removed from the models.

All statistical tests comparing paroxetine with placebo were 2-tailed and performed at an α of .05. Using a power $(1-\beta)$ of 0.90 to detect a difference between paroxetine and placebo responders on the CGI Global Improvement Item, the target recruitment for the study was set at (180 patients with 90 per group). Efficacy analyses were carried out on the sample of patients with at least 1 postbaseline efficacy evaluation and those who had received at least 1 dose of double-blind medication (N = 183, referred to herein as the *efficacy population*). For patients who did not complete the entire study, the last evaluation during treatment was used as an estimate of the missing data (ie, last observation carried forward). Data are reported as mean values (SE), and 95% confidence intervals (CIs) are reported where appropriate.

RESULTS

Of the 213 patients who were screened, 187 patients were enrolled and randomized to either paroxetine (n = 94) or placebo (n = 93) treatment arms (Figure 1). The typical patient was relatively young (mean age, approximately 36 years) and white. No statistically significant differences between groups were detected with regard to demographic characteristics or mean baseline rating scale scores (Table 1). Though not excluded by the protocol, few subjects had current comorbid major depressive or panic disorder (Table 1).

Of the 187 patients randomized in this study, 4 patients received the drug but were lost to follow-up prior to the first efficacy evaluation. Therefore, the efficacy data for the remaining 183 patients (ie, the efficacy population) are reported. Safety assessments were obtained for all 187 patients who were randomized.

Premature Discontinuation

In the paroxetine group, 62 (66%) of 94 patients completed the 12-week trial. The most common reasons for patient withdrawal were adverse events (15% [14/94]) or lost to follow-up (13% [12/94]). In the placebo group, 72 (77%) of 93 patients (*P* = .03 vs paroxetine) completed the trial. The most common reason for discontinuation was lack of efficacy (11% [10/93]) (Table 2).

Efficacy Results

Fifty (55.0%) of 91 persons who received to paroxetine and 22 (23.9%) of 92 persons who received placebo were much or very much improved at the end of treatment (odds ratio [OR], 3.88; 95% CI, 2.81-5.36). The proportion of paroxetine responders (ie, CGI Global Improvement score of 1 or 2) was significantly greater than placebo beginning at week 4 and continuing through week 12 (Figure 2). No interactions were found between sex and response (either on the CGI or on the measures listed below).

The mean change from baseline on the Liebowitz Social Anxiety Scale total score was more than twice as large in the paroxetine group (−30.5 ± 2.66; 39.1% decrease from mean baseline total score of 78.0) than in the placebo group (−14.5 ± 2.63; 17.4% decrease from mean baseline total score of 83.5), a difference of 21.7% (95% CI, 8.7%-34.7%) favoring paroxetine. Significant differences that were apparent by week 2 continued through the end of the study (Figure 3). Paroxetine was significantly superior to placebo on 5 of 6 secondary efficacy measures (Liebowitz Social Anxiety Scale, avoidance and fear/anxiety subscales; Social Avoidance and Distress Scale; and Sheehan Disability Inventory, work and social life) (Table 3). Although the improvement from baseline at end point for the Sheehan Disability

Table 3.—Summary of Secondary Efficacy Variables at Baseline and Study End Point in Patients Treated With Paroxetine or Placebo for Social Phobia*

Measure	Mean (SE) of Patients Taking		P Value	95% Confidence Interval
	Paroxetine (n = 90)	Placebo (n = 92)		
LSAS avoidance				
Baseline	36.9 (1.3)	40.2 (1.3)	.07	
Week 12 end point	22.1 (1.4)	32.6 (1.4)	<.001	−11.1 to −3.3
LSAS fear/anxiety				
Baseline	41.2 (1.1)	43.3 (1.1)	.17	
Week 12 end point	25.4 (1.4)	36.3 (1.3)	<.001	−12.5 to −5.0
SADS total				
Baseline	22.5 (0.5)	22.3 (0.5)	.75	
Week 12 end point	14.7 (0.8)	19.5 (0.8)	<.001	−7.2 to −2.8
SDI social life†				
Baseline	6.9 (0.2)	6.9 (0.2)	.85	
Week 12 end point	4.2 (0.3)	5.5 (0.3)	<.001	−2.1 to −0.6
SDI work†				
Baseline	4.8 (0.3)	5.1 (0.3)	.53	
Week 12 end point	3.4 (0.3)	4.4 (0.3)	.03	−1.5 to −0.1
SDI family life†				
Baseline	3.2 (0.3)	3.1 (0.3)	.73	
Week 12 end point	2.2 (0.2)	2.5 (0.2)	.17	−1.1 to 0.1

*The last evaluation during treatment for patients who did not complete the entire study (ie, the last observation carried forward) is reported. LSAS indicates Liebowitz Social Anxiety Scale; SADS, Social Avoidance and Distress Scale; and SDI, Sheehan Disability Inventory.
†Sample size was 89 in the paroxetine group.

Table 4.—Most Frequent Adverse Experiences (>5%) That Are at Least 2 Times Greater Than in Placebo Group*

Experience	Paroxetine (n = 94)	Placebo (n = 93)
Abnormal ejaculation†	18 (36.0)	0
Somnolence	25 (26.6)	9 (9.7)
Nausea	24 (25.5)	11 (11.8)
Sweating	9 (9.6)	3 (3.2)
Female sexual dysfunction†	4 (9.1)	0
Yawn	8 (8.5)	1 (1.1)
Tremor	8 (8.5)	2 (2.2)
Decreased appetite	8 (8.5)	2 (2.2)
Constipation	7 (7.4)	2 (2.2)
Dry mouth	7 (7.4)	2 (2.2)
Pharyngitis	7 (7.4)	2 (2.2)
Decreased libido	6 (6.4)	0

*Values are expressed as number (percentage) of patients.
†Percentage corrected for sex.

Inventory family life item was numerically greater with paroxetine (−1.0) than with placebo (−0.6), this difference was not statistically significant.

Medication Dosages

The mean dose of paroxetine at study end point was 36.6 mg (SD, 12.1 mg); mean dose of placebo at study end point was dose level 3.5 (SD, 0.90) (equivalent to 45 mg [SD, 18 mg]).

Adverse Experiences

The reported incidence and severity of adverse experiences in paroxetine-treated patients were as expected, and no unusual experiences were reported (Table 4). The most frequently occurring adverse experiences in paroxetine-treated patients were headache (37.2%), delayed ejaculation (36% of males), somnolence (26.6%), and nausea (25.5%). In

343

placebo-treated patients, these events occurred at the rates of 32.3%, 0%, 9.7%, and 11.8%, respectively. Most adverse experiences were of mild to moderate intensity.

COMMENT

This is the first multicenter, double-blind, randomized study of an SSRI in social phobia (social anxiety disorder). The results clearly demonstrate that paroxetine treatment effectively reduces the symptoms and avoidance associated with generalized social phobia. Paroxetine was statistically superior to placebo on both primary efficacy criteria and on 5 of 6 secondary efficacy variables. Among the latter, it is noteworthy that disability associated with generalized social phobia improved significantly as demonstrated by significantly greater reductions in the Sheehan Disability Inventory work and social life subscales compared with placebo. Given the early age at onset and chronicity of this disorder, detecting a reduction in disability after a 12-week trial is noteworthy. It is hoped, but remains to be shown in future studies, that longer duration of treatment might result in even further consolidation of gains and reduction of functional impairment.

Paroxetine was well tolerated in this study as evidenced by the relatively low incidence of withdrawal because of adverse experiences (15%) and the lack of serious adverse experiences. The adverse-event profile is in concordance with the findings of other efficacy and safety studies of paroxetine and other SSRIs.[44-47]

As reported in this study, paroxetine was clearly effective for generalized social phobia. The response to paroxetine therapy among patients with this most serious and recalcitrant form of social phobia is a rigorous demonstration of efficacy. Unfortunately, the lack of direct, comparative studies precludes between-treatment efficacy comparisons. To the extent that indirect comparisons are valid, the response rate to paroxetine in this generalized social phobia study (55% in the efficacy population) compares favorably with double-blind, placebo-controlled study response rates of 52% for moclobemide (severely ill subset)[35]; 68% for phenelzine sulfate (GSP subset)[41]; and 78% for clonazepam.[23] The response rate to paroxetine in this study is particularly notable when the fact that this was a 13-center study is taken into account. In such studies, drug-placebo differences often tend to be less robust than those in the hands of highly expert investigators at single-center sites.

Although the benzodiazepines, MAOIs, and other pharmacological treatments have been shown to be effective for generalized social phobia,[21-35,41] there are some relative disadvantages as well. High-potency benzodiazepines have limited antidepressant effects, which is an important consideration in a disorder for which major depression is commonly comorbid.[2,10,13] The benzodiazepines have the potential for abuse or misuse and can also cause physical dependence with long-term use. Nonselective MAOIs sometimes cause unpleasant activation or a hypomanialike effect, postural hypotension, and other adverse effects and require dietary restriction to avoid hypertensive reactions; all of these can limit clinical acceptance by physicians and patients. In this study, paroxetine had a side effect profile consistent with its use in other mood and anxiety disorders. In general, these side effects tend to be benign, leading to good patient tolerance (with the possible exception of the relatively high rate of abnormal ejaculation in men; although only 2 of 16 men with this side effect elected to discontinue treatment prematurely as a result). Based on its efficacy, safety, and relatively good tolerability, paroxetine can be considered among the first-line treatments for social phobia. Given the experience that all SSRIs tend to be effective for those conditions in which any have demonstrated efficacy, we would surmise that efficacy for the treatment of generalized social phobia will eventually be shown to extend to other SSRIs as well.

There are a number of limitations to this study. Social phobia is a chronic, potentially disabling disease that may require long-term therapy. By design, this study did not assess treatment effects beyond the acute, 12-week treatment period. It is possible, albeit not yet proven, that a longer course of therapy could result in continued and even greater reductions in impairment and in improvement in quality of life. A previous study suggested that relapse rates may be very high when treatment with paroxetine is discontinued after only 12 weeks of treatment.[38] Further studies of long-term treatment with paroxetine are warranted to determine optimal duration of therapy, efficacy in sustaining remission, and the role of concomitant psychotherapy (eg, cognitive behavioral therapy), which can be effective for many patients with this condition.[28-30,48]

Another limitation of this study is its inability to definitively demonstrate that reductions in social phobic symptoms were not merely a secondary manifestation of an antidepressant effect. Although few patients (4.8%) in this study had comorbid major depressive disorder at the time of entry into the study, it is possible that other patients may have had subsyndromal symptoms that could be antide-

pressant responsive. The next study with an SSRI for social phobia should measure depressive symptoms throughout the trial to determine whether or not these appear to drive the reduction in social anxiety symptoms.

In conclusion, this controlled clinical trial confirmed the suggestions from earlier reports and demonstrated that paroxetine is an effective and well-tolerated treatment for patients with generalized social phobia. Future research should address questions of optimal dose and duration of treatment, as well as the potential utility of educational and psychotherapeutic strategies to augment response and/or reduce relapse.

Financial support for this study was provided by SmithKline Beecham Pharmaceuticals, Collegeville, Pa.

The authors are grateful to the following investigators at the 13 sites who participated in this study: Bijan Bastani, MD (Comprehensive Psychiatric Services, Beachwood, Ohio), Catheryn Clary, MD (Clary Research Associates, New Castle, Del), Larry Davis, MD (The Davis Clinic, Indianapolis, Ind), Eugene DuBoff, MD (Center for Behavioral Medicine, Denver, Colo), Robert DuPont, MD (Institute for Behavior and Health, Rockville, Md), James Ferguson, MD (Pharmacology Research Corporation, Salt Lake City, Utah), James Jefferson, MD (The Dean Foundation for Health Research and Education, Madison, Wis), Richard Kavoussi, MD (Eastern Pennsylvania Psychiatric Institute, Philadelphia), Michael Liebowitz, MD (New York State Psychiatric Institute, New York), R. Bruce Lydiard, PhD, MD (Medical University of South Carolina, Charleston), Robin Reesal, MD (Western Canada Behavioural Research Centre, Calgary, Alberta), Edward Schweizer, MD (University of Pennsylvania, Philadelphia), and Murray Stein, MD (University of California-San Diego, La Jolla).

References

1. American Psychiatric Association. *Diagnostic and Statistical Manual of Mental Disorders.* 4th ed. Washington, DC: American Psychiatric Association Inc; 1994.
2. Schneier FR, Johnson J, Hornig CD, Liebowitz MR, Weissman MM. Social phobia: comorbidity and morbidity in an epidemiological sample. *Arch Gen Psychiatry.* 1992;49:282-288.
3. Schneier FR, Heckelman LR, Garfinkel R, et al. Functional impairment in social phobia. *J Clin Psychiatry.* 1994;55:322-331.
4. Stein MB. How shy is too shy? *Lancet.* 1996;347: 1131-1132.
5. den Boer JA. Social phobia: epidemiology, recognition, and treatment. *BMJ.* 1997;315:796-800.
6. Safren SA, Heimberg RG, Brown EJ, Holle C. Quality of life in social phobia. *Anxiety.* 1997;4:126-133.
7. Hazen AL, Stein MB. Clinical phenomenology and comorbidity. In: Stein MB, ed. *Social Phobia: Clinical and Research Perspectives.* Washington, DC: American Psychiatric Press Inc; 1995:3-41.
8. Stein MB, Walker JR, Forde DR. Public speaking fears in a community sample: prevalence, impact on functioning, and diagnostic classification. *Arch Gen Psychiatry.* 1996;53:169-174.
9. Kessler RC, McGonagle KA, Zhao S, et al. Lifetime and 12-month prevalence of *DSM-III-R* psychiatric disorders in the United States: results from the National Comorbidity Survey. *Arch Gen Psychiatry.* 1994;51:8-19.
10. Magee WJ, Eaton WW, Wittchen HU, McGonagle KA, Kessler RC. Agoraphobia, simple phobia, and social phobia in the National Comorbidity Survey. *Arch Gen Psychiatry.* 1996;53:159-168.

344

11. Stein MB, Walker JR, Forde DR. Setting diagnostic thresholds for social phobia: considerations from a community survey of social anxiety. *Am J Psychiatry.* 1994;11:408-412.

12. Offord DR, Boyle MH, Campbell D, et al. One year prevalence of psychiatric disorder in Ontarians 15 to 64 years of age. *Can J Psychiatry.* 1996;41:559-563.

13. Kessler RC, Stein MB, Berglund PA. Social phobia subtypes in the National Comorbidity Survey. *Am J Psychiatry.* 1998;155:613-619.

14. Spitzer RL, Williams JB, Kroenke K, et al. Utility of a new procedure for diagnosing mental disorders in primary care: the PRIME-MD 1000 Study. *JAMA.* 1994;272:1749-1756.

15. Spitzer RL, Kroenke K, Linzer M, et al. Health-related quality of life in primary care patients with mental disorders: results from the PRIME-MD 1000 Study. *JAMA.* 1995;274:1511-1517.

16. Fifer SK, Mathias SD, Patrick DL, Mazonson PD, Lubeck DP, Buesching DP. Untreated anxiety among adult primary care patients in a health maintenance organization. *Arch Gen Psychiatry.* 1994; 51:740-750.

17. Schonfeld WH, Verboncoeur CJ, Fifer SK, Lipschutz RC, Lubeck DP, Buesching DP. The functioning and well-being of patients with unrecognized anxiety disorders and major depressive disorder. *J Affect Disord.* 1997;43:105-119.

18. Weiller E, Bisserbe JC, Boyer P, Lepine JP, Lecrubier Y. Social phobia in general health care: an unrecognised undertreated disabling disorder. *Br J Psychiatry.* 1996;168:169-174.

19. Liebowitz MR, Gorman JM, Fyer AJ, et al. Social phobia: a review of a neglected anxiety disorder. *Arch Gen Psychiatry.* 1985;42:729-736.

20. Antony MM, Barlow DH. Social and specific phobias. In: Tasman A, Kay J, Lieberman JA, eds. *Psychiatry.* Philadelphia, Pa: WB Saunders; 1997: 1037-1059.

21. Liebowitz MR. Pharmacotherapy of social phobia. *J Clin Psychiatry.* 1993;54(suppl 12):31-35.

22. Marshall RD, Schneier FR, Fallon BA, Feerick J, Liebowitz MR. Medication therapy for social phobia. *J Clin Psychiatry.* 1994;44(suppl 6):33-37.

23. Jefferson JW. Social phobia: a pharmacologic treatment overview. *J Clin Psychiatry.* 1995;56 (suppl 5):18-24.

24. Lydiard RB, Brawman-Mintzer O, Ballenger JC. Recent developments in the psychopharmacology of anxiety disorders. *J Consult Clin Psychol.* 1996;64:660-668.

25. Davidson JRT, Potts N, Richichi E, et al. Treatment of social phobia with clonazepam and placebo. *J Clin Psychopharmacol.* 1993;13:423-428.

26. Katschnig H, Stein M, Buller R, on behalf of the International Multicenter Clinical Trial Group on Moclobemide in Social Phobia. Moclobemide in social phobia: a double-blind, placebo-controlled clinical study. *Eur Arch Psychiatry Clin Neurosci.* 1997; 247:71-80.

27. Noyes R, Moroz G, Davidson JRT, et al. Moclobemide in social phobia: a controlled dose-response trial. *J Clin Psychopharmacol.* 1997;17:247-254.

28. Heimberg RG, Juster HR. Cognitive-behavioral treatments: literature review. In: Heimberg RG, Liebowitz MR, Hope DA, Schneier FR, eds. *Social Phobia: Diagnosis, Assessment, and Treatment.* New York, NY: Guilford; 1995:261-301.

29. Scholing A, Emmelkamp PMG. Treatment of generalized social phobia: results at long-term follow-up. *Behav Res Ther.* 1996;34:447-452.

30. Taylor S. Meta-analysis of cognitive-behavioral treatments for social phobia. *J Behav Ther Exp Psychiatry.* 1996;27:1-9.

31. Andrews JM, Nemeroff CB. Contemporary management of depression. *Am J Med.* 1994;97 (suppl 6A):24S-32S.

32. Berk M. Fluoxetine and social phobia [letter]. *J Clin Psychiatry.* 1995;56:36-37.

33. Black B, Uhde TW, Tancer ME. Fluoxetine for the treatment of social phobia [letter]. *J Clin Psychopharmacol.* 1992;12:293-295.

34. Ringold AL. Paroxetine efficacy in social phobia [letter]. *J Clin Psychiatry.* 1994;55:363-364.

35. Schneier FR, Chin SJ, Hollander E, Liebowitz MR. Fluoxetine in social phobia [letter]. *J Clin Psychopharmacol.* 1992;12:62-64.

36. Sternbach H. Fluoxetine treatment of social phobia [letter]. *J Clin Psychopharmacol.* 1990;10: 230-231.

37. van Ameringen M, Mancini C, Streiner DL. Fluoxetine efficacy in social phobia. *J Clin Psychiatry.* 1993;54:27-32.

38. Stein MB, Chartier MJ, Hazen AL, et al. Paroxetine in the treatment of generalized social phobia: open-label treatment and double-blind, placebo-controlled discontinuation. *J Clin Psychopharmacol.* 1996;16:218-222.

39. Katzelnick DJ, Kobak KA, Greist JH, Jefferson JW, Mantle JM, Serlin RC. Sertraline for social phobia: a double-blind, placebo-controlled, crossover study. *Am J Psychiatry.* 1995;152:1368-1371.

40. van Vliet IM, den Boer JA, Westenberg HGM. Psychopharmacological treatment of social phobia: a double-blind, placebo-controlled study with fluvoxamine. *Psychopharmacology.* 1994;115:128-134.

41. Liebowitz MR, Schneier F, Campeas R, et al. Phenelzine vs atenolol in social phobia: a placebo-controlled comparison. *Arch Gen Psychiatry.* 1992; 49:290-300.

42. First M, Spitzer RL, Williams JBW, Gibbon M. *Structured Clinical Interview for DSM-IV—Patient Edition.* Washington, DC: American Psychiatric Press; 1995.

43. Liebowitz MR. Social phobia. In: Ban TA, Pichot P, Poldinger W, eds. *Modern Problems of Pharmacopsychiatry.* New York, NY: Karger; 1987;22:152.

44. Watson P, Friend R. Measurement of social-evaluative anxiety. *J Consult Clin Psychol.* 1969; 33:448-457.

45. Leon AC, Shear MK, Portera L, Klerman GL. Assessing impairment in patients with panic disorder: the Sheehan Disability Scale. *Soc Psychiatry Psychiatr Epidemiol.* 1992;27:78-82.

46. Cohn CK, Shrivastava R, Mendels J, et al. Double-blind, multicenter comparison of sertraline and amitriptyline in elderly depressed patients. *J Clin Psychiatry.* 1990;51(suppl 12B):28-33.

47. De Wilde J, Spiers R, Mertens C, Bartholomé F, Schotte G, Leyman S. A double-blind, comparative, multicentre study comparing paroxetine with fluoxetine in depressed patients. *Acta Psychiatr Scand.* 1993;87:141-145.

48. Mattick RP, Page A, Lampe L. Cognitive and behavioral aspects. In: Stein MB, ed. *Social Phobia: Clinical and Research Perspectives.* Washington, DC: American Psychiatric Association; 1996:189-228.

345

Acknowledgments

Yonkers, K.A., Warshaw, M.G., Massion, A.O., and Keller, M.D. "Phenomenology and Course of Generalized Anxiety Disorder." *Brit J Psychiatry* 168 (1996): 308–313. Reprinted with the permission of the British Journal of Psychiatry.

Liebowitz, M.R., Gorman, J.M., Fyer, A.J., and Klein, D.F. "Social Phobia: Review of a Neglected Anxiety Disorder." *Arch Gen Psychiatry* 42 (1985): 729–736. Reprinted with the permission of American Medical Association.

Weissman, M.M., Bland, R.C., Canino, G.J., Faravelli, C., Greenwald, S., Hwu, H.G., Joyce, P.R., Karam, E.G., Lee, C.K., Lellouch, J., Lepine, J.P., Newman, S.C., Oakley-Browne, M.A., Rubio-Stipec, M., Wells, J.E., Wickramaratne, P.J., Wittchen, H.U., and Yeh, E.K. "The Cross-National Epidemiology of Panic Disorder." *Arch Gen Psychiatry* 54 (1997): 305–309. Reprinted with the permission of American Medical Association.

Kessler, R.C., DuPont, R.L., Berglund, P., and Wittchen, H.U. "Impairment in Pure and Comorbid Generalized Anxiety Disorder and Major Depression at 12 Months in Two National Surveys." *Am J Psychiatry* 156 (1999): 1915–1923. Copyright 1999, the American Psychiatric Association. Reprinted by permission.

Kessler, R.C., Stein, M.B., and Berglund, P.A. "Social Phobia Subtypes in the National Comorbidity Survey." *Am J Psychiatry* 155 (1998): 613–619. Copyright 1999, the American Psychiatric Association. Reprinted by permission.

Biederman, J., Faraone, S.V., Hirshfeld-Becker, D.R., Friedman, D., Robin, J.A., and Rosenbaum, J.F. "Patterns of Psychopathology and Dysfunction in High-Risk Children of Parents with Panic Disorder and Major Depression." *Am J Psychiatry* 158 (2001): 49–57. Copyright 2001, the American Psychiatric Association. Reprinted by permission.

Merikangas, K.R., Avenevoli, S., Dierker, L., and Grillon, C. "Vulnerability Factors among Children at Risk for Anxiety Disorders." *Biol Psychiatry* 46, 11 (1999): 1523–1535. Reprinted with the permission of Elsevier Science. Copyright 1999 by the Society of Biological Psychiatry.

Kagan, J., and Snidman, N. "Early Childhood Predictors of Adult Anxiety Disorders." *Biol Psychiatry* 46 (1999): 1536–1541. Reprinted with the permission of Elsevier Science. Copyright 1999 by the Society of Biological Psychiatry.

Katsching, H., and Amering, M. "The Long-Term Course of Panic Disorder and Its Predictors." *J Clin Psychopharmacol* 18, supp. (1998): 6–11. Reprinted with the permission of Williams & Wilkins.

Shalev, A.Y., Freedman, S., Peri, T., Brandes, D., Sahar, T., Orr, S.P., and Pitman, R.K. "Prospective Study of Posttraumatic Stress Disorder and Depression following Trauma." *Am J Psychiatry* 155 (1998): 630–637. Copyright 1998, the American Psychiatric Association. Reprinted by permission.

Merikangas, K.R., Stevens, D.E., Fenton, B., Stolar, M., O'Malley, S., Woods, S.W., and Risch, N. "Co-morbidity and Familial Aggregation of Alcoholism and Anxiety Disorders." *Psychological Medicine* 28 (1998): 773–788. Reprinted with the permission of Cambridge University Press.

Mineka, S., Watson, D., and Clark, L.A. "Comorbidity of Anxiety and Unipolar Mood Disorders." *Annu Rev Psychology* 49 (1998): 377–412. Reprinted with permission from the Annual Review of Psychology, Volume 49,©1998, by Annual Reviews www.AnnualReviews.org.

Regier, D.A., Rae, D.S., Narrow, W.E., Kaelber, C.R., and Schatzberg, A.F. "Prevalence of Anxiety Disorders and Their Comorbidity with Mood and Addictive Disorders." *Brit J Psychiatry* 173, supp. 34 (1998): 24–28. Reprinted with the permission of the British Journal of Psychiatry.

Marks, I.M., and Nesse, R.M. "Fear and Fitness: An Evolutionary Analysis of Anxiety Disorders." *Ethology and Sociobiology* 15 (1994): 247–261.

Bouton, M.E., Mineka, S., and Barlow, D.H. "A Modern Learning Theory Perspective on the Etiology of Panic Disorder." *Psychol Rev* 108, 1 (2001): 4–32. Copyright © 2001 by the American Psychological Association. Reprinted with permission.

Buchel, C., Morris, J., Dolan, R.J., and Friston, K.J. "Brain Systems Mediating Aversive Conditioning: An Event-Related fMRI Study." *Neuron* 20 (1998): 947–957. Copyright 1998, with permission from Elsevier Science.

Caldji, C., Francis, D., Sharma, S., Plotsky, P.M., and Meaney, M.J. "The Effects of Early Rearing Environment on the Development of GABAA and Central Benzodiazepine Receptor Levels and Novelty-Induced Fearfulness in the Rat." *Neuropsychopharmacology* 22 (2000): 219–229. Reprinted by permission of Elsevier Science. Copyright 2000 by American College of Neuropsychopharmacology.

Fendt, M., and Fanselow, M.S. "The Neuroanatomical and Neurochemical Basis of Conditioned Fear." *Neuroscience and Biobehavioral Reviews* 23 (1999): 743–760.

Garcia, R., Vouimba, R.-M., Baudry, M., and Thompson, R.F. "The Amygdala Modulates Prefrontal Cortex Activity Relative to Conditioned Fear." *Nature* 402 (1999): 294–296. Reprinted by permission from Nature Vol. 402 pp. 294–296. Copyright © 1999 Macmillan Magazines Ltd.

Gorman, J.M., Kent, J.M., Sullivan, G.M., and Coplan, J.D. "Neuroanatomical Hypotheses of Panic Disorder, Revised." *Am J Psychiatry* 157 (2000): 493–505. Copyright 1998, the American Psychiatric Association. Reprinted by permission.

LeDoux, J.E. "Emotion Circuits in the Brain." *Annu Rev Neurosci* 23 (2000): 155–184.

Phelps, E.A., O'Connor, K.J., Gatenby, J.C., Gore, J.C., Grillon C., and Davis, M. "Activation of the Left Amygdala to a Cognitive Representation of Fear." *Nat Neurosci* 4, 4 (2001): 437–441. Reprinted with the permission of Nature America, Inc.

Stein, M.D. "Neurobiological Perspectives on Social Phobia from Affiliation to Zoology." *Biol Psychiatry* 44 (1998): 1277–1285. Reprinted with the permission of Elsevier Science. Copyright 1998 by the Society of Biological Psychiatry.

Low, K., Crestani, F., Keist, R., Benke, D., Brunig, I., Benson, J.A., Fritschy, J.M., Rulicke, T., Bluethmann, H., Mohler, H., and Rudolph, U. "Molecular and Neuronal Substrate for the Selective Attenuation of Anxiety." *Science* 6, 290, 5489 (2000): 131–134. Reprinted from *Science* 6; 290, 5489 (2000): 131–134. Copyright (2000) American Association for the Advancement of Science.

The Research Unit on Pediatric Psychopharmacology Anxiety Study Group. "Fluvoxamine for the Treatment of Anxiety Disorders in Children and Adolescents." *N Engl J Med* 344 (2001): 1279–1285. Copyright © 2001 Massachusetts Medical Society. All rights reserved.

Klein, D., and Fink, M. "Psychiatric Reaction Patterns to Imipramine." *Am J Psychiatry* 119 (1962): 432–438.

Barlow, D.H., Gorman, J.M., Shear, M.K., and Woods, S.W. "Cognitive Behavioral Therapy, Imipramine, or Their Combination for Panic Disorder: A Randomized Controlled Trial." *JAMA* 283 (2000): 2529–2536. Copyright 2000. The American Medical Association.

Davidson, J.R.T., Rothbaum, B.O., van der Kolk, B.A., Sikes, C.R., and Farfel, G.M. "Multicenter, Double-Blind Comparison of Sertraline and Placebo in the Treatment of Posttraumatic Stress Disorder." *Arch Gen Psychiatry* 58 (2001): 485–492. Reprinted with the permission of American Medical Association.

Foa, E.B., and Meadows, E.A. "Psychosocial Treatments for Posttraumatic Stress Disorder: A Review." *Annu Rev Psychol* 48 (1997): 449–480. Reprinted with permission from the Annual Review of Psychology, Volume 48, ©1997, by Annual Reviews www.AnnualReviews.org.

Stein, M.B., Liebowitz, M.R., Lydiard, R.B., et al. "Paroxetine Treatment of Generalized Social Phobia: A Randomized, Double, Blind, Placebo-Controlled Study." *JAMA* 280 (1998): 387–402. Copyright 1998, The American Medical Association.